The Works of William James

Editors
Frederick H. Burkhardt, General Editor
Fredson Bowers, Textual Editor
Ignas K. Skrupskelis, Associate Editor

Advisory Board

Max H. Fisch
John J. McDermott
Maurice Mandelbaum

Eugene T. Long
Edward H. Madden
H. S. Thayer

*This edition of the Works of William James
is sponsored by the American Council of
Learned Societies*

Introduction to this volume by
Robert A. McDermott

William James in 1894–95?

Essays in Psychical Research

William James

HARVARD UNIVERSITY PRESS
Cambridge, Massachusetts
and London, England
1986

CENTER FOR
SCHOLARLY EDITIONS
AN APPROVED EDITION
MODERN LANGUAGE
ASSOCIATION OF AMERICA

Library of Congress Cataloging in Publication Data

√ James, William, 1842–1910.
Essays in psychical research.
(The Works of William James)
Includes bibliographical references and index.
1. Psychical research—Collected works. I. Title.
II. Series: James, William, 1842–1910. Works. 1975.
BF1031.J225 1986   133.8   85–7595
ISBN 0–674–26708–7 (alk. paper)

Foreword

Essays in Psychical Research is the fourteenth title and sixteenth volume to be published in THE WORKS OF WILLIAM JAMES. It contains every writing known to have been published by James on the subject. An article and an address that James used as the basis for an essay in his *Will to Believe*, which has been published as the sixth title of this edition, have been included in *Essays in Psychical Research*; the other writings, except for a brief passage on automatic writing in *The Principles of Psychology*, Chapter X, are a collection of reviews, circulars, reports, public letters, and essays that appeared in various journals, mostly between 1884 and 1909, the period of James's active work on the subject. The essays reprinted in *William James on Psychical Research*, compiled and edited by Gardner Murphy and Robert O. Ballou, now out of print, have been edited in conformance with the editorial policy of this edition. In the case of the most extensive and best-known essay in that volume, "Report on Mrs. Piper's Hodgson-Control," the availability of the original manuscript has made it possible to use as copy-text the version submitted to the English Society for Psychical Research instead of the version submitted to the American Society, which is reprinted in the Murphy-Ballou volume. The manuscript provides new information about the names of sources and many alterations made by James in preparing the published version.

The text of the essays has been established by the Textual Edi-

v

tor of the WORKS, Fredson Bowers, Linden Kent Professor of English, Emeritus, at the University of Virginia. The Note on the Editorial Method sets forth the principles and techniques involved in the preparation of an authoritative text, which represents so far as the evidence will permit James's final intentions. Professor Bowers has also provided a discussion of the texts and the apparatus with which the documents used in the editing can be reconstructed. The reference notes to the text and the index have been prepared by the Associate Editor, Professor Ignas K. Skrupskelis, of the Department of Philosophy, University of South Carolina.

Professor Robert A. McDermott, of the Philosophy Department of Baruch College, City University of New York, has provided the Introduction, which, as in all volumes of the WORKS, discusses the relationship of the essays to James's other work in philosophy, psychology, and religion. He makes clear that James's work in psychical research was not an eccentric hobby but a serious and sympathetic concern. The writings in this volume are the record of a sustained interest in phenomena of a highly controverted nature, over a period of more than two decades. James was open-minded in his approach but was also tough-minded in his demands that investigations be conducted in rigorous, scientific terms. His observations and insights on psychic phenomena not only are consistent with the views expounded in his philosophical and psychological writings, but enable us to understand those works better. It is clear that James hoped his investigations would strengthen the philosophy of an open-ended, pluralistic universe which he was formulating during the same period, and that he looked forward to the new horizons for human experience and the human condition that a successful outcome of his research would bring about.

It remains for the editors to acknowledge their indebtedness to the institutions and individuals who have helped to make this volume possible.

The Advisory Board of scholars listed in the front matter was appointed by the American Council of Learned Societies, which sponsors the WORKS. From the members the editors have had the benefit of general policy guidance and suggestions on matters of substance and interpretation.

The National Endowment for the Humanities has generously continued its support of this edition by providing funds for the editorial work and for the typesetting of the apparatus and other end matter. The staff members of the Division of Research Grants, and especially Kathy Fuller and George F. Farr, Jr., have been a steady source of advice and guidance for the entire project.

The editors are also grateful to the Barra Foundation and to its President, Robert L. McNeil, Jr., for generous and timely matching grants in support of the edition.

Alexander James and Dr. William Bond of the Houghton Library have granted permission to use and reproduce both printed and manuscript texts and illustrations in the James Collection at Harvard University. The Houghton Library staff members have given generous and patient help to the editors in their work with the James Papers.

The Reference Room staff of the Alderman Library of the University of Virginia have furnished expert assistance in locating references and source material pertinent to the editorial work.

The University of South Carolina has provided the Associate Editor with research assistance and working space.

The editors also wish to acknowledge their indebtedness to the following:

The Society for Psychical Research in London provided access to their archives. Mr. D. N. Clark-Lowes, Librarian, was most generous with his time. He and his staff provided not only manuscripts of articles and sittings but also correspondence between James and various members of the Society: letters and postcards from James to Richard Hodgson; letters and a postcard to Sir Oliver Lodge; a letter to Mrs. Henry Sidgwick; and a letter from Alfred Lehmann to James.

The Boston Public Library made available a letter from James to Hugo Münsterberg.

The William L. Clements Library, University of Michigan, furnished and gave permission to quote from a letter from James to Mrs. Elizabeth Cass Goddard.

Princeton University Library, Special Collections, provided access to the Henry Holt archives.

The Department of Manuscripts and University Archives at Cornell University furnished letters from James to E. B. Titchener.

The Library of Congress furnished letters from James to J. McKeen Cattell and a letter from James to Sarah Whitman.

Stanford University Libraries provided a letter from James to F. C. S. Schiller.

Colby College Library provided a letter from James to Mary Hillard.

Hartford Seminary Foundation made available a letter from James to Duncan Macdonald.

The Society for Psychical Research, New York, furnished a letter from James to James H. Hyslop and gave access to their archives.

Ruthe R. Battestin, Charlottesville, Virginia, did research on behalf of the edition at the Society for Psychical Research in London.

Richard Hocking, Madison, New Hampshire, gave the Textual Editor permission to copy James's letters to Henry W. Rankin, now on loan to the Houghton Library.

Professor Louise DeSalvo of Hunter College, City University of New York, reviewed the volume for the seal of the Center for Scholarly Editions.

Audrone Skrupskelis assisted the Associate Editor in the preparation of the reference notes and index.

Charlotte Bowman contributed her services as Administrative Assistant to the General Editor.

Anne McCoy, before her resignation from the editorial staff, supervised preparatory work for this volume. Elizabeth Berkeley, her successor as Editorial Coordinator of the WORKS, and her staff, Judith Nelson, Mary Mikalson, Bernice Grohskopf, and Claudia Garthwait, prepared the manuscript for publication with their usual skill and meticulous attention to detail.

Frederick H. Burkhardt

Contents

Contents

Contents

Contents

Introduction
by
Robert A. McDermott

Plato's statement that reflection arises when perception yields contradictory impressions finds dramatic application in the field of
psychical research.[1] Unfortunately, however, the impressions generated by psychic phenomena so radically contradict those which
appear to follow scientific order that such impressions tend to be
ignored or denied, and reflection concerning them seldom takes
place. William James was exceptional among philosophers and
psychologists in that he sustained the conflict between psychic phenomena and scientific thinking, and in the process reaped the rich
rewards of careful, imaginative reflection on such conflict. For
James, as for his collaborators in the Society for Psychical Research
during the last two decades of the nineteenth century, the positive
and negative attitudes toward psychic phenomena sprang from the
deeper conflict of scientific and religious views of the world. As this
volume shows repeatedly, James's reflection was intellectually re-
warding because he sought to preserve the most valuable features
of both the scientific and religious perspectives. This attempt to
reconcile science and religion may characterize much of James's
work, but with respect to psychical research it is the primary motivation and goal of his labors; it is also the tension that renders his
work in this area original and enduring.

[1] *Republic*, 7.523.

The present volume, with offerings from nearly every year of James's life from 1885 until just prior to his death in 1910, clearly shows that psychical research represented a continuing intellectual concern throughout his career. Ralph Barton Perry, in his indispensable *Thought and Character of William James*, notes that "James's interest in 'psychical research' was not one of his vagaries, but was central and typical."[2] We can extend Perry's observation by suggesting that for James psychical research was central in that it put to the test religious and scientific claims which were at the core of his philosophy, and typical in its sympathetic curiosity concerning the varieties of experience. Despite its being at once the most controverted and neglected area of his thought, it is also one that presents James's philosophical method and goals in sharp outline and detail. Fidelity to fact, avoidance of abstract categories, patient attention to ultimate questions, and preference for complexities over the dogmatism of either the skeptic or the believer are all evident in James's work of nearly three decades as a psychical researcher.

In James's psychical research as in his philosophy generally, the religious question, or claims for and against a spiritual basis of reality, seems to provide the motivation, while science, or a true empiricism, provides the method and criteria. By holding out for the possibility of a religious interpretation of human experience, James was able to resist the negative and limiting effects of the scientific mentality dominant at the end of the nineteenth century; insisting on a scientific or empirical approach to the study of psychic phenomena, he avoided the ill-founded claims of spiritualist advocates. Thus, James dismisses as dogmatic both scientific skepticism and religious belief. Weaving his way between these competing dogmatisms, James provided a model approach to psychical research as well as some significant insights into the continuing struggle between scientific and religious modes of perception. In reflecting on this struggle, not only in his own experience but also with respect to the findings of his colleagues in the Society for Psychical Research, James advanced psychical research and enriched his own psychological and philosophical thought.

[2] Ralph Barton Perry, *The Thought and Character of William James* (Boston: Little, Brown, 1935), vol. 2, p. 155.

Introduction

Psychical research is necessarily a collaborative effort, involving a network of subjects, investigators, editors, publishers, and an enormous amount of financial support. James's career as a psychical researcher, from his meeting with the founders of the Society for Psychical Research in 1882 until his death in 1910, coincided with a remarkable convergence of intellectually gifted, totally dedicated, wealthy individuals whose work was synonymous with psychical research in the English-speaking world during these years. These personalities—Henry Sidgwick (1838–1900) and his wife Eleanor (1845–1936), Frederic W. H. Myers (1843–1901), Edmund Gurney (1847–1888), and Richard Hodgson (1855–1905)—so dominated the field that it would be difficult and misleading to consider James's work as a psychical researcher apart from theirs. As evidenced by his enormous and far-flung correspondence, James collaborated with colleagues in all areas of his work, but particularly in psychical research his thought and writings were conceived and executed within the framework of these personal and professional associations.

As the present volume attests, James's writings on psychical research consist of addresses, reports of experiments (or sittings), book reviews, and letters. The fragmentary character of these writings is due partly to the collaborative nature of the work, but even more to James's perception of the state of the field. From the results of his own sittings and those of other psychical researchers, the persistent conflict of perception concerning psychic phenomena did not permit elaborate or systematic interpretations. Although James admired Myers' *Human Personality and Its Survival of Bodily Death* (1903), he also was convinced that its speculation was somewhat premature and overdrawn. Consistent with his repeated plea for facts over speculation, James restricted his writings to summaries and interpretations of cases and commentaries on the work of the Society.

Fortunately for progress in this inherently controversial area of inquiry, James was not the only cautious researcher: Henry and Eleanor Sidgwick maintained the highest possible standards of scientific and philosophical rigor, and both Gurney and Hodgson, until their untimely deaths, had well-deserved reputations for exposing frauds, inconsistencies, and complexities of all kinds. His colleagues wondered whether Hodgson found it more frustrating than satisfying that he was unable to find a flaw in the character or lapse in the powers of Mrs. Piper, the remarkable medium whom he observed for more than a decade. As with James's speculative reticence in this field, the methodological and interpretive caution of his colleagues in the Society for Psychical Research worked against their own predisposition to accept a spiritual or psychic reality behind observable phenomena. The individual combinations of predisposition and caution, affirmation and resistance, vary in each of these powerful personalities, and each combination influenced the psychical research movement and James's work on its behalf.

From the first discussion concerning the founding of the Society for Psychical Research, it was clear that the ideal president would be Henry Sidgwick, Professor of Moral Philosophy at Cambridge and brother-in-law to both Arthur James Balfour, a future prime minister of Great Britain (1902–1905), and Edward White Benson, Archbishop of Canterbury (1883–1896). Myers and Gurney wisely made Sidgwick's acceptance of the presidency a condition of their joining the Society.[3] With Sidgwick as president, it was difficult for the Society to be perceived as anything less than scholarly, scientific, and in all ways respectable. The ideals for which Sidgwick was esteemed coincided perfectly with the aims of the Society, which were summarized as follows: "To investigate that large body of debatable phenomena designated by such terms as mesmeric, psychical and spiritualistic, (and to do so) without prejudice or prepossession of any kind, and in the same spirit of exact and unimpassioned enquiry which has enabled science to solve so many problems, once not less obscure nor less hotly debated."[4]

Eleanor Balfour Sidgwick was no less exacting than her husband in her commitment to scientific criteria. More than ample proof of Mrs. Sidgwick's eminence as a researcher is to be found in the summaries and analyses of cases which were published in the *Proceedings* of the Society for Psychical Research (1923) and which she edited in *Phantasms of the Living*.[5] In his introduction to that

---

[3] Alan Gauld, *The Founders of Psychical Research* (London: Routledge & Kegan Paul, 1968), p. 138.

[4] Ibid.

[5] The full title of this volume is *Phantasms of the Living: Cases of Telepathy Printed in the Journal of the Society for Psychical Research During Thirty-five Years* [1886–1921], bound in one volume with *Phantasms of the Living*, by Edmund Gurney,

double volume, Gardner Murphy refers to Mrs. Sidgwick as "the finest mind so far in the history of psychical research" (p. vi). Concerning the publication itself, he writes: "It is not arrogant to claim that this combination of the two studies is the best collection of spontaneous cases of telepathy yet published" (p. x). The Society for Psychical Research and the larger cause of psychical research, both dear to James, were doubly blessed by the Sidgwicks—by Henry for his high-minded guidance during the first eighteen years of the Society's existence (during which he served nine years as president) and by Eleanor for her sober, scholarly leadership throughout the subsequent four decades.

The only other individual who exercised an influence comparable to that of the Sidgwicks on the Society and on William James was Frederic W. H. Myers, whose *Human Personality and Its Survival of Bodily Death* (1903) was the first and remains the most systematic full-length treatise in psychology based on psychical research. Although accused of being mystical—or at least too spiritual—in his approach to psychic phenomena and in his theory of the subliminal self, Myers was intensely committed to scientific experimentation and criteria, particularly as a means of exposing the uncritical claims of religious believers. In his presidential address, Myers stated his position succinctly: "Our duty is not the founding of a new sect, nor even the establishment of a new science, but is rather the expansion of Science herself until she can satisfy those questions which the human heart will rightly ask. . . ."[6] James repeatedly lauded Myers' attempt to introduce scientific methods into psychology and philosophy—or, in more Jamesian terms, to approach telepathy with a truly empirical method. In "The Confidences of a 'Psychical Researcher'" (1909), James continued to recommend the direction charted by Myers' theory of the subliminal self:

Not only psychic research, but metaphysical philosophy and speculative biology are led in their own ways to look with favor on some such 'panpsychic' view of the universe as this. Assuming this common reservoir of consciousness to exist, this bank upon which we all draw, and

---

Frederic W. H. Myers, and Frank Podmore, as abridged and edited by Eleanor Mildred Sidgwick (New Hyde Park, N.Y.: University Books, 1962).

[6] "Presidential Address of F. W. H. Myers to the Society for Psychical Research," May 18, 1900, *Presidential Addresses to the SPR*, p. 119.

in which so many of earth's memories must in some way be stored, or mediums would not get at them as they do, the question is, What is its own structure? What is its inner typography? This question, first squarely formulated by Myers, deserves to be called 'Myers's problem' by scientific men hereafter. What are the conditions of individuation or insulation in this mother-sea? (*Essays in Psychical Research,* hereafter *EPR*, p. 374).

With typical generosity, James here credits Myers with an original formulation even though his own theory of "The Hidden Self" had anticipated Myers' theory of the subliminal self by two years.[7] James is equally generous in describing Myers as the leader of the new "romantic" movement in psychology (*EPR*, p. 195).[8] In fact, it was James who complemented his own psychical research by original psychological and philosophical speculation. But there is no doubt that Myers confirmed and extended James's attempt to bring the concerns and results of psychical research to bear on orthodox psychology and philosophy. In addition to his contributions to psychical research as a case-by-case researcher and as a theoretician, Myers also served as the "despot" who pressured James into ever-greater commitments to psychical research,[9] including two years as president of the Society.

In "What Psychical Research Has Accomplished," James described Edmund Gurney, who died in 1888 at the age of 41, as "the *worker* of the Society . . . a man of the rarest sympathies and gifts" (*EPR*, p. 92). He summarized two of Gurney's contributions that had significantly influenced psychical research—first, his experiments on the automatic writing of subjects who had received post-hypnotic suggestions:

Experiments like this, which were repeated in great variety, prove that below the upper consciousness the hypnotic consciousness persists, engrossed with the suggestion and able to express itself through the involuntarily moving hand.

Gurney shares, therefore, with Janet and Binet, . . . the credit of demonstrating the simultaneous existence of two different strata of consciousness, ignorant of each other, in the same person. . . . This discovery

[7] See Jacques Barzun, *A Stroll with William James* (New York: Harper & Row, 1983), p. 230n*.
[8] See also Perry, *Thought and Character*, vol. 2, p. 168.
[9] Ibid., p. 163.

marks a new era in experimental psychology; it is impossible to overrate its importance.

Gurney's second contribution resulted from his study of more than 700 cases of apparitions described and analyzed in *Phantasms of the Living*: "A large number of these were 'veridical,' in the sense of coinciding with some calamity happening to the person who appeared. Gurney's explanation is that the mind of the person undergoing the calamity was at that moment able to impress the mind of the percipient with an hallucination" (*EPR*, p. 95).

Richard Hodgson, an Australian student of Henry Sidgwick at Cambridge, joined the Society as an undergraduate. Two years later he was sent by Professor Sidgwick to investigate the claims by and about Madame Blavatsky, who had moved the Theosophical Society to Adhyar, India, in 1879. Hodgson's report was extremely critical of Mrs. Blavatsky's claims to physical mediumship.[10] Hodgson quickly developed an exceptional ability to detect sleights of hand and other means of fraud, and wrote a revealing report exposing the credulity of even the most attentive witnesses to purported psychic phenomena. James refers to this report, written by Hodgson in collaboration with S. J. Davey, as "the most damaging document concerning eye-witnesses' evidence which has ever been produced" (*EPR*, p. 96). Hodgson's work is further discussed in the section following, where he appears as a central figure in the discussion of James's research based on the medium Mrs. Leonora Piper.

With all the founders of the Society for Psychical Research, James shared a double commitment: first, to investigate psychic phenomena according to the methods and criteria of science; and second, to enlarge the scope of science to include the study of phenomena that are random, nonrepeatable, and dependent on unusual personal capacities and dispositions. James's summary of Sidgwick's first presidential address expresses his own view of science: "Professor Sidgwick, in his introductory address, insisted that the divided state of public opinion on all these matters was a scandal to science, absolute disdain on *a priori* grounds characterizing what may be called professional opinion, whilst completely uncritical and indiscriminate credulity was too often found amongst those who pretended to have a first-hand acquaintance with the

10 *Proceedings of the Society for Psychical Research*, 3 (1885).

facts" (*EPR*, p. 90). James's position is no less pointed: "The writer of these pages . . . now believes that he who will pay attention to facts of the sort dear to mystics, while reflecting upon them in academic-scientific ways, will be in the best possible position to help philosophy."[11] In short, James is at one with Sidgwick and Myers in advocating the scientific method provided that it be an enlightened and tolerant science, one responsive to the essential nature of the subject matter. Throughout their careers in psychical research, Sidgwick, Myers, and James remained convinced that by fidelity to fact and to a truly empirical method, psychical research, along with other areas disallowed by the materialistic presuppositions of science, would be restored as a proper subject of scientific and philosophical inquiry.

As early as 1869, when James was in his last year of medical school, he used the occasion of a book review to call for the presentation of verifiable psychic facts accompanied by appropriate commentary (*EPR*, p. 2). More than two decades later, in a letter to Myers in which he refused to write a historical and expository paper for an international congress to be held in Chicago, James again called for fidelity to fact: "What we want is *facts*, not popular papers, it seems to me; and until the facts thicken, papers may do more harm than good."[12] In the same year, James again credited the *Proceedings* of the Society for Psychical Research for meeting the critical need for empirical fact: "Outside of these *Proceedings*, I know of no systematic attempt to *weigh* the evidence for the supernatural. This makes the value of the seven volumes already published unique, and I firmly believe that as the years go on and the ground covered grows still wider, the Society's *Proceedings* will more and more tend to supersede all other sources of empirical information concerning phenomena traditionally deemed occult" (*EPR*, p. 91). It is easier to proclaim than to realize such testimonials on behalf of experimentation and empirical fact. Not the least of the problems is that most purported psychical phenomena are random and unexpected. Planned experiments are possible, of course, but the rewards seldom justify the considerable expenditure of resources.

For a person with James's varied interests and his many oppor-

11 William James, *The Will to Believe*, WORKS, p. 224.
12 Quoted in Perry, *Thought and Character*, vol. 2, p. 171.

tunities for productive research and writing, time spent in fruitless labors must have tried his patience. He persisted because he wanted to believe that positive results would be forthcoming—eventually. As Jacques Barzun notes: "James did not enjoy this kind of inquiry. He pursued it in part to maintain a critical pressure on what he called Scientific Sectarianism—the people who were sure beforehand. But the work itself James found tedious, undignified, often disgusting—'a human rathole life.' He reflected that there was no reason why spirit messages—or 'counterfeits' either—should be entertaining or dramatic, anymore than ordinary backyard conversation."[13]

One reading of a verbatim report from a sitting with a medium should be more than ample evidence that spirit messages—whether authentic or fraudulent (and the fraudulent seem frequently to be more compelling than the authentic)—may be less entertaining and dramatic, as well as less revealing and intelligible, than the average conversation. Typically, experiments in physical phenomena such as automatic speaking and writing, psychokinesis, and levitation were (and are) even more frustrating than mental phenomena such as clairvoyance, telepathy, and spirit apparition (*EPR*, p. 368). We can be grateful to James for having spared us the thousands of verbatim stenographic records of the countless sittings that he endured. Even the sittings with the celebrated Mrs. Piper, the medium with whom James worked for twenty-five years and whom he believed to possess "supernormal knowledge," must have tested his determination to the limits. While referring to Mrs. Piper as his "white-crow" (*EPR*, p. 131)—that is, the one phenomenon that stood on its own as a verifiable exception to scientific accounts of knowledge and communication—James admitted to uninterest in the trivia of the subject and to fatigue from the dead ends.

From the time she was discovered by James's mother-in-law, Mrs. Elizabeth Gibbens, in 1885, Mrs. Piper was the favorite medium of the Society, and particularly of James himself. James and Hodgson reported on Mrs. Piper from 1886 to 1892, and summarized this period in "A Record of Observations of Certain Phenomena of Trance" (*EPR*, pp. 79–88). From 1892 to 1897, while "G.P." was her control, Hodgson and W. R. Newbold reported on her work. James Hervey Hyslop reported from 1897–1905, while the

---

13 Barzun, *A Stroll with William James*, p. 240.

"Imperator Band" served as Mrs. Piper's control. James's "Report on Mrs. Piper's Hodgson-Control" (*EPR*, pp. 253–360) covers the period immediately following Hodgson's death in 1905 until January 1908. James concluded, against the precautions to which he was committed in theory and practice, that Mrs. Piper's psychic powers represented the particular instance which negates the a priori proposition that all purported psychic phenomena are physical events. In response to such a position, James retorted, largely on the strength of the Piper phenomena: "But I believe there is no source of deception in the investigation of nature which can compare with a fixed belief that certain kinds of phenomenon are *impossible*." [14]

In response to the skeptic, James offered a rather minimal claim—namely, that psychic phenomena are not impossible. In effect he contends that if one were to sit in the presence of a medium (or, more accurately, a psychic), particularly in the presence of Mrs. Piper on a good day, the burden of proof (or disproof) would seem to fall on the side of the skeptic. But as he repeatedly noted, the scientific community is as capable of negative superstition as it is of demolishing the superstition of the believer. Partly to overcome the hold of scientific arrogance (or perhaps the scientist's anxiety concerning possible implications of psychical research for the scientific world view) and partly out of his own need for answers, James continued to observe, summarize, and interpret countless cases of physical and mental phenomena, most of which were unedifying in the process and unproductive of results. On her bad days, even Mrs. Piper would generate hours of uninteresting trivia—and in the process embarrass the arrangers (often William James himself) and reinforce the observers who opposed psychical research.

To deserve her status as James's "white-crow," Mrs. Piper had to be the instrument, agency, or medium of verifiable knowledge which she could not have known from a natural (or normal) channel.[15] Short of this combination, according to James and others

[14] Letter to Carl Stumpf, January 1, 1886, quoted in Gardner Murphy and Robert O. Ballou, eds., *William James on Psychical Research* (New York: Viking Press, 1960), p. 65; also in *The Letters of William James*, ed. Henry James (Boston: Atlantic Monthly Press, 1920), vol. 1, p. 248.

[15] The term *medium* is less preferable than *sensitive* or *psychic* because *medium* implies a "between" of two entities, one of which would be the discarnate personality, the reality of which is in dispute; *medium* is used in this Introduction, however, be-

working in his circle, a medium's disclosures may be revealing and convincing for the sitter, but not evidential. James explains that when one is sitting as an observer, there is a definite tendency to fill in the gaps, giving the words and actions their most veridical interpretation, and to ignore information that is either mistaken or trivial (*EPR*, p. 281). At several points in his report James indicates that he is not particularly impressed by the results of the Hodgson-Control sittings (*EPR*, p. 277), but at other places he acknowledges that the messages and other disclosures sent to, or through, Mrs. Piper fit the character of the recently deceased psychical researcher Richard Hodgson. This resemblance includes the use of Hodgson's vocabulary and phrasing, as well as specific references to persons and events that Mrs. Piper could not have known independently, which manifested themselves through her scribbling hand while she was in trance. Several times James admitted that these signs were indeed accurate, and that he was definitely convinced that Mrs. Piper was the agency of significant bodies of fact to which she could not have had access in any other way (*EPR*, pp. 322–323, 359).

There are at least four instances of Mrs. Piper's knowledge that James regarded as convincing—that is, he felt that only Richard Hodgson could have been the source of these disclosures. These four are as follows: the disclosures concerning Huldah, a woman with whom Hodgson had enjoyed a secret relationship (*EPR*, pp. 270–273); the "pecuniary messages" (*EPR*, pp. 276–277); the Old-farm Series (*EPR*, pp. 287–294); and the case of James's Harvard colleague and friend, F. J. Child (*EPR*, pp. 352–353). Why, then, does James resist the claim that the reality of a discarnate Hodgson spirit is established by these four examples or by any number of other cases drawn from seventy-five sittings with Mrs. Piper? James several times repeats his reservations and reveals his continuing struggle with the "ever-not-quite" character of the evidence for an independent Hodgson-spirit. In reflecting on "The Pecuniary Messages," James writes: "Few persons will ascribe the affair to chance-coincidence, but with both thought-transference and trance-memory as possible explanations, the incident cannot be deemed to furnish certain proof of Hodgson's personal survival" (*EPR*,

cause it is the term that James used consistently. For a useful glossary, see Robert H. Ashby, *The Guidebook for the Study of Psychical Research* (London: Rider & Company, 1972), pp. 144–157.

p. 277). At the end of his lengthy report (by far the longest single writing on psychical research that he produced), James offers the following general conclusion:

I myself feel as if an external will to communicate were probably there, that is, I find myself doubting, in consequence of my whole acquaintance with that sphere of phenomena, that Mrs. Piper's dream-life, even equipped with 'telepathic' powers, accounts for all the results found. But if asked whether the will to communicate be Hodgson's, or be some mere spirit-counterfeit of Hodgson, I remain uncertain and await more facts, facts which may not point clearly to a conclusion for fifty or a hundred years (*EPR*, p. 359) .

In addition to passages such as the two just quoted in which James judges the evidence for spirit survival to be just short of proof, he also acknowledges that the fault may be his own "deaf ears" (*EPR*, p. 278)—perhaps a kind of compensatory resistance to his wish (if not his will) to believe that the control is a Hodgson-spirit. James dared not give full sway to his belief—or in the language of his *Varieties of Religious Experience*, his "overbelief"—if he was to meet the scientific criteria he imposed on himself as a way of winning the respect, and eventually the cooperation and agreement, of the scientific community.

As was so often the case, James's most succinct statement is to be found in a letter. Writing to Charles Lewis Slattery, April 21, 1907, James offered the following summary:

Mrs. Piper has supernormal knowledge in her trances; but whether it comes from "tapping the minds" of living people, or from some common cosmic reservoir of memories, or from surviving "spirits" of the departed, is a question impossible for *me* to answer just now to my own satisfaction. The spirit-theory is undoubtedly not only the most natural, but the simplest, and I have great respect for Hodgson's and Hyslop's arguments when they adopt it. At the same time the electric current called *belief* has not yet closed in my mind.

Whatever the explanation be, trance-mediumship is an excessively complex phenomenon, in which many concurrent factors are engaged. That is why interpretation is so hard.[16]

---

[16] Murphy and Ballou, *James on Psychical Research*, pp. 112–113; also in *The Letters of William James*, ed. Henry James, vol. 2, p. 287.

Although it seems not to have made the communications from the Hodgson-control any more telling than the messages of other controls, Hodgson during his lifetime had an awesome familiarity with the workings of mediums and their controls. James seems to have taken some comfort in Hodgson's comparison of the working "of spirit-communication to those of two distant persons on this earth who should carry on their social intercourse by employing each of them a dead-drunk messenger" (*EPR*, pp. 277–278). Yet James was one with the other principals of the psychical research movement in working toward a new science of human nature that would include the results of psychical research. It was with such a hope for the future science to which they were both major contributors that Myers, who died in 1900, and Hodgson, who died in 1905, made arrangements while living to communicate with James after death. We know that James was disappointed in the results of their "efforts." We do not know any better than James whether there was a Myers or a Hodgson to be disappointed.[17]

James was not only disappointed in the failure of his deceased colleagues to provide incontestable proof of personal survival, but

[17] A rather unconvincing case for spirit messages from William James after his death can be found in Jane Revere Burke, *Let Us In* (New York: E. P. Dutton, 1931), *The Bundle of Life* (New York: E. P. Dutton, 1934), and *Messages on Healing* (New York: E. P. Dutton, 1936). James seems to have been unaware of the cross-correspondences which reportedly began to appear in 1907. James's judgment of this phenomenon would have been especially interesting because, if valid, it would seem to meet his argument that messages could be explained by thought-transference. Cross-correspondence phenomena consist in the revelation of extremely arcane information, and specifically fragments of classical scholarship, such as would be known to Myers and Sidgwick, and quite obviously inaccessible to a medium of limited education such as Mrs. Piper. The pieces of the puzzle, which were described by J. G. Piddington as "links in a concatenation, or cubes in a mosaic of ideas," were revealed to several mediums working in isolation from one another. In his excellent treatment of cross-correspondences, G. N. M. Tyrrell explains that to the extent that the pieces could be made to show an intelligent design, it would be correspondingly difficult to favor telepathy over spirit-survival as an interpretation of mediumship. Tyrrell also acknowledges that "nearly all the actual cases are imperfect and, in one way or another, fall short of the ideal" (*Science and Psychical Phenomena & Apparitions*, in one volume [New Hyde Park, N.Y.: University Books, 1961], pp. 234–235). It seems probable that the reason for James's neglect of cross-correspondences was not the imperfection of the examples, particularly since some are remarkable and collectively represent a significant case, but rather that it was not until after his death that some pieces of the puzzle were put together.

was also generally disappointed with the results of his own and his colleagues' labors. And if he was disappointed in mental phenomena, specifically messages from the dead to a medium in trance, he was even less satisfied with, and increasingly uninterested in, psychical phenomena such as table raising and slate writing (*EPR*, p. 132), phenomena that not only invited fraud and errant nonsense but lacked the potentially profound implications of the telepathic medium. It must also be admitted, however, that James believed his research would be more valuable for future generations than for his contemporaries. With Henry Sidgwick, whose devotion to psychical research was likewise motivated by "the religious question," James concluded his career as a psychical researcher with a library of data that he personally found convincing, but with little or no proof with which to convince the previously unconvinced. In "The Confidences of a 'Psychical Researcher,'" written the year before his death, James offers this sober report:

Like all founders, Sidgwick hoped for a certain promptitude of result; and I heard him say, the year before his death, that if anyone had told him at the outset that after twenty years he would be in the same identical state of doubt and balance that he started with, he would have deemed the prophecy incredible. It appeared impossible that that amount of handling evidence should bring so little finality of decision.

My own experience has been similar to Sidgwick's. For twenty-five years I have been in touch with the literature of psychical research, and have had acquaintance with numerous 'researchers.' I have also spent a good many hours (though far fewer than I ought to have spent) in witnessing (or trying to witness) phenomena. Yet I am theoretically no 'further' than I was at the beginning . . . .

The peculiarity of the case is just that there are so many sources of possible deception in most of the observations, that the whole lot of them *may* be worthless, and yet that in comparatively few cases can aught more fatal than this vague general possibility of error be pleaded against the record. Science meanwhile needs something more than bare possibilities to build upon; so your genuinely scientific inquirer—I don't mean your ignoramus 'scientist'—has to remain unsatisfied. It is hard to believe, however, that the creator has really put any big array of phenomena into the world merely to defy and mock our scientific tendencies; so my deeper belief is that we psychical researchers have been too precipitate with our hopes, and that we must expect to mark progress not by quarter-centuries but by half-centuries or whole centuries (*EPR*, pp. 361–362).

Characteristically, James locates himself between two competing positions: he is willing to persevere in the belief that further research will turn up an explanation for the "white-crow," and confidently recommends that subsequent generations take up this important if frustrating work; at the same time he readily admits that merely a close look at a "white-crow" does not offer sufficient proof to the rest of the inquiring world of the existence, or more pressingly, the source and modus operandi, of this phenomenon.

As does every great teacher, James labored for the removal of those ideas, beliefs, and habits of mind that block insight and imagination, whether of his students, audiences, or readers. Perhaps the prejudice that James opposed most emphatically is the separation of thought or experience into discrete areas. James himself was a master weaver of intellectual and experiential threads. The year 1896 is instructive in this regard. In January, James delivered a major address marking the conclusion of his two-year term as president of the Society for Psychical Research. In October and November, he delivered the 1896 Lowell Lectures on exceptional mental states.[18] In December, he delivered a brief lecture in honor of Louis Agassiz in which he advocated a commitment to concrete, diverse, empirical facts: "We cannot all escape from being abstractionists. I myself, for instance, have never been able to escape; but the hours I spent with Agassiz so taught me the difference between all possible abstractionists and all livers in the light of the world's concrete fulness, that I have never been able to forget it."[19] In James's view, psychical research and psychopathology ought to be among the most obvious sources of "the world's concrete fulness."

Thirty-five years earlier, in a letter to his father describing his first months of study at the Lawrence Scientific School of Harvard University, James had written of his recently acquired insight that "a naturalist could feel about his trade in the same way that an artist does about his. For instance, Agassiz would rather take wholly uninstructed people, 'for he has to unteach them all that they have learnt.' He does not let them *look* into a book for a long while, what they learn they must learn for themselves, and be

18 Eugene Taylor, *William James on Exceptional Mental States: The 1896 Lowell Lectures* (New York: Charles Scribner's Sons, 1982). Taylor's brilliant reconstruction of James's lecture notes is an important contribution to the study of James's research on psychopathology and its relation to other areas of his thought.

19 *Memories and Studies*, ed. Henry James (New York: Longmans, Green, 1911), p. 14. James accompanied Agassiz on an expedition to Brazil, 1865–1866.

masters of it all."[20] The words of James the undergraduate presage the attention to lived experience that characterized his work as psychical researcher and psychopathologist: in his presidential address before the Society for Psychical Research James chronicled a decade of careful observations of psychic phenomena, and in the Lowell Lectures he summarized his equally careful study of exceptional mental states such as hysteria, multiple personality, demoniacal possession, witchcraft, degeneration, and genius, as well as phenomena associated with hypnotism and automatism.

As Eugene Taylor effectively argues, James's 1896 lectures on psychopathology are important not only in their own right but also for the light they shed on James's development during the period from the publication of his *Principles of Psychology* in 1890 to *The Varieties of Religious Experience* a decade later.[21] A similar case needs to be made for the place of psychical research throughout James's career—not only between *Principles* and *Varieties,* but also before *Principles* and after *Varieties.* Through both psychical research and psychopathology James was teaching himself and others to attend to the margins and unusual modes of consciousness, but by far the greater commitment was to psychic phenomena, since it involved research and reporting for more than twenty-five years. Although this claim for the importance of psychical research in James's thought does not imply that this area of interest transformed other areas, or that other areas cannot be properly understood apart from his psychical research, it does suggest that psychical research provides clear evidence of James's sustained efforts to unlearn orthodox approaches to psychology, religion, and philosophy. Psychical research served as a constant reminder that "there is a continuum of cosmic consciousness, against which our individuality builds but accidental fences, and into which our several minds plunge as into a mother-sea or reservoir" (*EPR*, p. 374). One of the essential aims of James's thought was to remove the "accidental fences" between psychology, religious thought, and philosophy; and for all three of these areas, psychical research served as a stimulus for integration and a check against artificial separations.

James's research on psychical phenomena and psychopathology

---

20 Perry, *Thought and Character,* vol. 1, p. 211; also in Henry James, *Notes of a Son and Brother* (New York: Charles Scribner's Sons, 1914), pp. 131–134.

21 Taylor, *Exceptional Mental States,* p. 11.

did not generate the kind of revolutionary or "knock-down" proofs that he sought, but together these areas enabled him to fill in the terrain on several sides of so-called normal consciousness. What he wrote concerning psychopathology had long been, and continues to be, true of psychical research: "In law courts no *tertium quid* is recognized between insanity and sanity. If sane, a man is punished; if insane, acquitted; and it is seldom hard to find two experts who will take opposite views of his case. All the while nature is more subtle than our doctors."[22] James's research concerning psychical phenomena may be understood as his effort to generate a *tertium quid*, or third position, between the equally unacceptable extremes of skepticism and uncritical acceptance. In his attempt to link so-called normal to abnormal states of consciousness, James extended the theory of the subliminal self which he developed concurrently with Myers. He was convinced that the subliminal region, which each individual can develop, operates according to laws unknown to waking consciousness.[23] James accepted Myers' theory that genius may best be understood as "an 'uprush' of contents from the subliminal."[24]

The theory of the subliminal self occupies an important place in James's religious thought, particularly in his Gifford Lectures, published as *The Varieties of Religious Experience*. Alternately using the terms *subliminal* and *subconscious*, James refers to the discovery of this psychic region as "the most important step forward that has occurred in psychology" since he became a student of that science, and one which "casts light on many phenomena of religious biography."[25] In addition to its importance in the context of James's religious thought, the theory of the subliminal (or subconscious) is significant here because it exemplifies the way in which James's psychical research contributed first to his study of exceptional mental states, and subsequently to his study of religious experience.

Nor is the theory of the subliminal self the only such link: the affirmation of the personal and subjective, so important in psychical research, is the essential feature of James's *Varieties of Religious Experience*, where he again criticizes science for its neglect

[22] Ibid., p. 131.
[23] Ibid., pp. 43, 52–53.
[24] Ibid., p. 149.
[25] William James, *The Varieties of Religious Experience*, WORKS, p. 190.

of private experience. James admits that an individual's religion may be egotistic and narrow, "but at any rate it always remains infinitely less hollow and abstract, as far as it goes, than a Science which prides itself on taking no account of anything private at all."[26] James was fully confident that as psychical research had begun to make certain phenomena respectable, and as psychopathology had begun to exert a similar effect on certain previously taboo exceptional mental states,[27] the empirical study of religious experience would eventually legitimize prophecy, levitation, and other occult spiritual phenomena.[28]

James's religious thinking, particularly evident in his *Varieties of Religious Experience,* is in accord with his methods in psychical research both in its pursuit of concrete facts concerning the widest range of experience and in its willingness to leave problems short of resolution. This tension or polarity between skepticism and belief, between empiricism and a religious sensibility, is evident in James's approach to the question of the self and its relation to a larger reality. Neither his psychical research nor his study of religious experience led James to affirm a personal immortality, but neither did he dismiss the possibility. He concluded his research on Mrs. Piper's "mediumistic phenomena" with the cautiously optimistic announcement, "there is 'something in' these never ending reports of physical phenomena" (*EPR,* p. 371); he concluded his *Varieties* with the assertion that "*the conscious person is continuous with a wider self through which saving experiences come.*"[29] Both of these studies reveal James's belief as well as his lack of certitude: at the end of "The Confidences of a 'Psychical Researcher,' " James admits that he is baffled, but has the hope that each limited, tentative, clearly perceived fact will help to point in a definite direction and will add up to the beginning of a solid science of the psychic (*EPR,* p. 371). Similarly, he concludes his *Varieties* by neither affirming nor denying salvation, but holding to the chance of it.[30]

26 Ibid., p. 394.

27 "Demon possession of old has now been transformed into an optimistic mediumship, related not to devil worship and psychopathology but to personal growth, healing, especially of functional disorders, and to religious or philosophical concerns" (Taylor, *Exceptional Mental States,* pp. 108–109).

28 James, *Varieties,* WORKS, p. 394.

29 Ibid., p. 405.

30 Ibid., pp. 396–397.

The passion for the empirical observation of personal experience which James carried forward from psychical research to his study of religious experience is also evident in his last major works, *A Pluralistic Universe* and *Essays in Radical Empiricism*. In the conclusion of *A Pluralistic Universe* James reveals the same commitment and hope that he had previously expressed concerning empiricism and psychical research: "Let empiricism once become associated with religion, as hitherto, through some strange misunderstanding, it has been associated with irreligion, and I believe that a new era of religion as well as of philosophy will be ready to begin."[31] Although James's philosophy does not include extended treatments of ideas derived from psychical research, nor does it exhibit the influence of such research, there are several ways in which his enormous labors in the psychical vineyard seem to have affected the formation and articulation of his philosophy. That James neither wrote a philosophy of psychical phenomena nor conducted his psychical research with an explicit concern for philosophical implications should not minimize the strong complementarity of these parallel modes of inquiry. The interpenetration between James's psychical research and his philosophy is so general and pervasive that it can easily be missed, but it seems clear that there is a positive relationship between these two early and enduring intellectual passions which includes several shared attitudes and positions.

First, James's philosophy and his psychical research are equally committed to the reconciliation of science and religion. James tried to show that if they were true to the complexities of experience, both psychical research and philosophy would preserve the positive features of science and religion, both of which have tended to offer one-sided versions of reality. Despite their differences in problems and terminology, both of these disciplines ought to show, by argument and example, that religious experience could be illuminated by a sympathetic science, and that science could be rendered a more powerful servant of truth by recognizing the reality of religious experience.

Second, both studies attest to James's essential commitment to a radical empirical approach. James could not be more consistent in his commitment to the facts of human experience—whether to the

---

31 James, *A Pluralistic Universe*, WORKS, p. 142.

average person, the psychotic, the medium, the saint, or the philosopher—and his corresponding rejection of any a priori positions. Observation of psychical phenomena, which is the substance of psychical research, is more limited and specific than the broad range of observation required for a full-blown philosophy, but these two activities should be seen as similar and complementary: similar in that in both contexts human experiences, from commonplace to bizarre, should generate and revise theories, not the reverse; complementary in that philosophy, as the older and more developed enterprise, needs enthusiasm for the novel and the marginal, whereas psychical research, which is more on the cutting edge, needs the intellectual scope and patience of philosophy.

Third, both philosophy and psychical research admit to provisional conclusions on ultimate questions. In addressing such questions as the nature of the self and the world, the source and reliability of knowledge, James's philosophy and psychical research reach conclusions that cannot help but be tentative and incomplete. Since facts keep coming, each conclusion must await further observation and revision. James may be alone among psychical researchers in the degree to which he maintained a creative tension between a philosopher's commitment to the largest interpretive framework and an enthusiasm for the rush of diverse, if not contradictory, individual experiences. Similarly, James strove to keep his philosophical thought within the bounds of the observed facts of experience—including the complicating facts generated by psychical research and other controverted disciplines.

Fourth, both studies emphasize the personal and subjective character of knowledge. James repeatedly criticized the resistance to the personal and subjective dimension of human experience that too often characterizes the scientific ideal. Psychic phenomena, of course, are intrinsically subjective and consequently tend to be regarded by scientists as inaccessible and unintelligible. Both in his psychical research and in his philosophy James sought to show that by this self-imposed restriction, science risks losing the truth it jealously seeks to seize and control.

Finally, James sought to blur the modern Western dualism between the mental and the physical. He concluded from his psychical research that the beginning and end, and the varied modes of interaction, of the mental and the physical are rendered more rather than less complicated by such study. A similar respect for this complexity runs through James's philosophy, influenced at least in part by his having so effectively unlearned the prevailing philosophical solutions while studying psychic phenomena.

The following review of the critical reception accorded the publication of James's writings on psychical research, and the influence they exercised on the field, is necessarily less positive than the foregoing discussion of James's original research. The reasons for this disparity are revealing with respect to both James and psychical research. First, James himself enjoyed more prestige than did his work on behalf of psychical research. Like the parent society in London, founded in 1882, the American Society for Psychical Research, founded in 1885, gained respectability by the eminence of its founders, the most outstanding of whom was William James. In 1884 James wrote: "We are founding here a 'Society for Psychical Research,' under which innocent sounding name ghosts, second sight, spiritualism and all sorts of hobgoblins are going to be 'investigated' by the most high-toned and 'cultured' members of the community."[32] Despite the jocular tone, James's reference to the cultured members of the community is entirely to the point. The prospects for psychical research were tied to the prominence of the Society's founders and guiding personalities. During the two decades before and after the turn of the century, which were also the years when psychical research in England was in the control of the remarkable Sidgwick group, James continued to bask in the international acclaim accorded his *Principles of Psychology*, which in 1890 "burst upon the world like a volcanic eruption."[33] Not that criticism was wanting—Hugo Münsterberg, James's colleague at Harvard, was one of many psychologists who criticized his alleged involvement in mysticism and the occult[34]—but his writings, even those on psychical research, were received with a high level of anticipation and respect.

James's writings on psychical research were not published as a

[32] Perry, *Thought and Character*, vol. 2, p. 160.

[33] Gardner Murphy, *Historical Introduction to Modern Psychology* (New York: Harcourt Brace and World, 1949), p. 195.

[34] Perry, *Thought and Character*, vol. 2, p. 153. James's rejoinder to Münsterberg and other colleagues critical of his involvement in psychical research is discussed in Daniel W. Bjork, *The Compromised Scientist: William James in the Development of American Psychology* (New York: Columbia University Press, 1983).

book until 1960. During his lifetime and for fifty years after his death, "What Psychical Research Has Accomplished," a twenty-page essay written from 1890 to 1896 and published in *The Will to Believe* (1897), was the only publication by James on psychical research that a student of philosophy or psychology would have encountered. Most of James's other writings on psychical research were published within the semiprivate world of the Society, and consequently the controversial contents of these writings were little known even to the scholarly community.

The writings in *Essays in Psychical Research* were obviously not conceived by James as constituting a volume, and, despite the book's title, they do not include essays in the usual sense of the term. Rather, most of the selections are summaries and explanations of cases, as well as responses to developments in the collaborative work of the Society for Psychical Research. The scattered quality of these writings—in addition, obviously, to their controversial content—helps to account for the fact that so little notice has been taken of James's psychical research by scholars and students well versed in *Pragmatism, The Varieties of Religious Experience,* and *Essays in Radical Empiricism.* Whereas James's writings in psychology and philosophy were received by a large and active community of mainstream scholars, his writings on psychical research, to the extent that they were read at all, were taken up by two extreme groups—those in almost total agreement with these writings, such as the members of the Society for Psychical Research, and those equally opposed not only to their conclusions but to the research itself.

By the time the bulk of James's writing on psychical research was made available through the publication of *William James on Psychical Research,* edited by Gardner Murphy and Robert O. Ballou, neither James's thought in general nor his approach to psychical research was at center stage. James's great contributions in psychology had been pushed to the side by psychoanalysis (of several Freudian and neo-Freudian varieties) and behaviorism (as espoused by B. F. Skinner, who was ironically, James's successor twice removed at Harvard). Thus, far from bursting on the intellectual scene like a "volcanic eruption," the publication in 1960 of *William James on Psychical Research* was then regarded and has been regarded since, by psychical researchers as well as by psychologists and philosophers, as being merely of historical interest. The following brief review of psychical research during recent decades, however, will suggest that the neglect of James's work in this area continues to be a loss to psychology, philosophy, and religion, as well as to psychical research itself.

Since James's death, and increasingly in recent decades, psychical research has been fragmented and internally at odds. The ostensible heir to the Jamesian mantle in psychical research was the distinguished psychologist William McDougall, who in 1927 was appointed head of the newly created department of psychology at Duke University. Joseph B. Rhine and Louisa Rhine joined McDougall soon after, and in 1935, after a storm of controversy concerning charges of fraudulent evidence, founded the Parapsychology Laboratory as an autonomous unit of the Duke University campus. Within a theoretical framework for which they coined the term *extrasensory perception* (ESP), the Rhines tested for evidence of clairvoyance (ESP concerning a physical object or event), telepathy (ESP concerning another person's thoughts) and precognition (noninferential awareness of a future event); they also tested for psychokinesis (ability of the human mind to move a physical object).[35] James would have been interested in the tasks which the Rhines set for their dedicated group of collaborators, but he would have opposed the sacrifice of spontaneous phenomena and complex situations on the altar of quantitative measurement. In this respect, James's legacy is perhaps more faithfully represented by Gardner Murphy, coeditor of *William James on Psychical Research* and author of the most reliable introduction to the field of psychical research, *Challenge of Psychical Research: A Primer of Parapsychology.*[36]

Among the English-language philosophers writing in the past thirty years, there are at least four for whom psychical research is an important concern,[37] though none of them (with the possible

[35] For discussions of the research conducted by the Rhines, see J. B. Rhine, *Extrasensory Perception*, rev. ed. (Boston: Bruce Humphries, 1964), and *The Reach of the Mind*, rev. ed. (New York: William Sloan Associates [Apollo Editions], 1960) and two volumes by Louisa E. Rhine: *Hidden Channels of the Mind* (New York: William Sloan Associates, 1961) and *ESP in Life and Lab: Tracing Hidden Channels* (New York: Macmillan, 1967).

[36] Written in collaboration with Laura A. Dale (New York: Harper and Row, 1961). See also Gardner Murphy, *Three Papers on the Survival Problem* (New York: American Society for Psychical Research, 1970).

[37] C. D. Broad: *The Mind and Its Place in Nature* (New York: Harcourt Brace,

exception of C. D. Broad) has developed a philosophy based primarily on psychical research, and none can be counted in the Jamesian philosophical tradition. Outside of academic philosophy, James probably would have felt a kinship with the work of Ian Stevenson, a psychiatrist who has researched, mostly in Asia, hundreds of contemporary cases suggestive of reincarnation.[38] He would most assuredly have agreed with Stevenson's preference for on-the-scene empirical observation of available cases, and his accompanying lack of interest in Rhine's statistical computations. Overall, James would surely have been disappointed that psychical research has experienced grave difficulty in gaining academic acceptance, and that no significant advances have been made in the mutually beneficial cooperation between psychical research and psychology, philosophy, and religious studies.

As is evident in the dozen or more anthologies on psychical research published since 1965, psychical researchers are continuing to work on the problems that occupied James throughout the last twenty-five years of his life, but few of them address more than a narrow range of his topics, and fewer still offer even a modicum of his sympathy for personal nuances and complexities, or his imaginative grasp of subtlety and significance. Readers of J. B. Rhine or C. D. Broad (to choose two representatives of their respective approaches—parapsychology and philosophy of psychical phenomena) will be treated to quantitative and philosophical analysis, but they will miss the experience of reading one who believes "there is 'something in' [it]," and who on every page compels the reader to join in the ever-widening search.

1949); *Religion, Psychical Research: Selected Essays* (New York: Harcourt Brace, 1953); *Lectures on Psychical Research* (New York: Humanities Press, 1962); C. J. Ducasse: *Nature, Mind and Death* (LaSalle, Illinois: Open Court Publishing Company, 1951); *A Critical Examination of the Belief in Life after Death* (Springfield, Ill.: Charles C. Thomas, 1961); *Paranormal Phenomena, Science, and Life after Death*, Parapsychological Monograph No. 8 (New York: Parapsychological Foundation, 1969); Anthony Flew: *A New Approach to Psychical Research* (London: Watts, 1953); H. H. Price: "Psychical Research and Human Personality," *Hibbert Journal* (January 1949), vol. 47; "Presidential Address to the Society for Psychical Research" (*Proceedings*, SPR), vol. 50.

38 For a brief annotated bibliography for psychical research, see Robert H. Ashby, *The Guidebook for the Study of Psychical Research* (London: Rider & Company, 1972); C. J. Ducasse, Foreword, in Ian Stevenson, *Twenty Cases Suggestive of Reincarnation* (New York: American Society for Psychical Research, 1966).

Essays in Psychical Research

Review of *Planchette*, by Epes Sargent (1869)

The pretty little book whose title we give below,[1] and of which Mr. Epes Sargent is known as the author, is a brief general history or treatise of so-called spiritualistic phenomena, the particular instrument, Planchette, which gives the name to the whole, being disposed of in very few lines.

The work is entertaining, and characterized by a perfect freedom from extravagance of manner or opinion, its contents mainly consisting of quotations from other writers—either reports of "manifestations," or discussions polemical and speculative as to their cause. The author himself, to be sure, appears at intervals, corroborating "things seen and heard," or applauding and reënforcing, sometimes with a good deal of epigrammatic force, the theoretic arguments of the authorities on whose shoulders he seems to have preferred to rest the burden of his cause; but his mind is not felt through the book, as if it had grasped the subject as a whole with any degree of energy. This feebleness of handling, although in a literary point of view a defect, is nevertheless probably fitted to render the book all the more popular. A reader of scientific habits of thought would have been more interested by a very few cases described by the author over his own signature, and with every pos-

---

[1] *Planchette: or the Despair of Science*, being a full account of modern Spiritualism, its phenomena and the various theories regarding it; with a survey of French Spiritism. Boston: Roberts Brothers, 1869.

sible detail given, in which pedantically minute precautions had been taken against illusion of the senses or deceit. Of course it is quite natural that people who are comfortably in possession of a season-ticket over the Stygian ferry, and daily enjoying the privileges it confers of correspondence with the "summer-land," should grow out of all sympathy with the critical vigilance and suspicion about details which characterize the intellectual condition of the "Sadducees," as our author loves to call the earth-bound portion of the community. From his snug home in an atmosphere in which pianos float, "soft warm hands" bud forth from vacant space, and lead pencils write alone, the spiritualist has a right to feel a personal disdain for the "scientific man" who stands inertly aloof in his pretentious enlightenment. Scientific men seem to demand that spiritualists should *come* and demonstrate to them the truth of their doctrine, by something little short of a surgical operation upon their intellects. But the spiritualist, from his point of view, is quite justified in leaving them forever on their "laws of nature," unconverted, since he no way needs their countenance.

But an author writing avowedly for purposes of propagandism should have recognized more fully the attitude of this class, and recollected that one narrative personally vouched for and *minutely* controlled, would be more apt to fix their attention, than a hundred of the striking but comparatively vaguely reported second-hand descriptions which fill many of the pages of this book. The present attitude of society on this whole question is as extraordinary and anomalous as it is discreditable to the pretensions of an age which prides itself on enlightenment and the diffusion of knowledge. We see tens of thousands of respectable people on the one hand admitting as facts of every day certainty, what tens of thousands of others equally respectable claim to be abject and contemptible delusion; while other tens of thousands are content to stand passively in the dark between these two hosts and in doubt, the matter meanwhile being—rightfully considered—one of really transcendent interest. In this state of things recrimination is merely lost time. Those people who have the interests of truth at heart should remember that personal dignity is of very little comparative consequence. If our author, in concert with some good mediums, had instituted some experiments in which everything should be protected from the possibility of deceit, remembering that the morality of no one in such a case is to be taken for granted, and that

2

such personal precautions cannot be offensively construed, he would probably have made a better contribution to clearing up the subject than he has now done.

Perhaps after all, though, even such evidence would be ineffectual. The attitude of the average carnal mind towards the "manifestations" seems to be pretty well expressed by the words quoted from a Mr. Bell, who described some of Home's wonders in the *Cornhill Magazine*:—"I refuse to believe such things upon the evidence of other people's eyes; and I may possibly go so far as to protest that I would not believe them even on the evidence of my own. *When I have seen them,* however, I am compelled to regard the subject from an entirely different point of view." Our author probably considers that if what has already been published is not sufficient to convince, no possible addition to it could help it, ocular evidence being alone adequate. It is pretty certain that a mere admission of the facts in dispute on the testimony of others, would bear little scientific fruit. If true they should be actively embraced in one conception with the other facts of the universe, and no one can at present conceive of them in this vivid natural way without much personal familiarity. As the book before us is written from a much less esoteric point of view than most other publications dealing with the same subject, it will doubtless awaken the curiosity of many outsiders, the very looseness of the treatment forming a part of its attractiveness.

To the *"cui bono"* objection to spiritualism the author in many places replies, and often with much sarcastic point. "What is the use"—he quotes from Franklin—"of a new-born baby?" Certainly, *from the scientific point of view,* few things can be imagined more idiotic than Faraday's demand, in a letter fixing the preliminary conditions of an interview which some persons tried to bring about between him and the medium Home:—"If the effects are miracles, or the work of spirits, does he (Home) admit the utterly contemptible character both of them and their results, up to the present time, in respect either of yielding information or instruction, or supplying any force or action of the least value to mankind?" But, *from the point of view of ordinary human interest,* and as opposed to the jubilation which the spiritualist circles themselves keep up, we must confess to a certain sympathy with the dictum of the *Saturday Review*:—"If this is the spirit-world,—it is much better to be a respectable pig and accept annihilation, than to be cursed with

3

such an immortality." The existence of the phenomena as a class once being granted we fail to discover among all the facts given in *Planchette* a single one possessing either esthetic beauty, intellectual originality, or material usefulness.

The latter half of the book is occupied by quotations from various authors, concerning the philosophy of spiritualism, much of it being that serene, optimistic musing "into the blue," in which the sect seems chiefly to delight, and which the reader may obtain by the bucketful, if he wish, in the *Banner of Light*. It remains quite detached from the other scientific and philosophical problems of the day, except perhaps in the case of a single extract from Mr. S. J. Finney, "one of the most eloquent of American mediums"; but we are not told whether the words quoted from him were delivered in the trance state or not.

To sum up, we hope sincerely that this little book will succeed in waking up a few capable and critical people, whose authority will help along a reconciliation. The phenomena seem in their present state to pertain more to the sphere of the disinterested student of nature, than to that of the ordinary layman. It is certain that, if once admitted, they must make a great revolution in our conception of the physical universe; but that being done, they would seem to have no more claim on the attention of each particular individual, than any of the special problems of organic chemistry, for instance, or of pathological anatomy.

Circulars of the American Society for Psychical Research (1884–1906)

a. Organization (1884)

Circular No. 1, Issued by the Council

At a meeting held in Boston, Sept. 23 [1884], for the purpose of considering the advisability of forming a Society for Psychical Research in America, a committee with full powers was appointed; and under its auspices The American Society for Psychical Research has been organized, and is now in a position to invite the adhesion of members. The aims of the English society of similar name can be best understood from the following extracts from its printed proceedings:—

"The Society for Psychical Research was formed in the beginning of 1882, for the purpose of making an organized and systematic attempt to investigate that large group of debatable phenomena designated by such terms as 'mesmeric,' 'psychical,' and 'spiritualistic.' From the recorded testimony of many competent witnesses, past and present, including observations recently made by scientific men of eminence in various countries, there appears to be, amidst much illusion and deception, an important body of remarkable phenomena, which are *primâ facie* inexplicable on any generally recognized hypothesis, and which, if incontestably established, would be of the highest possible value. The task of examining such residual phenomena has often been undertaken by individual effort, but never hitherto by a scientific society organized on a sufficiently broad basis.

"The aim of the Society is to approach these various problems without prejudice or prepossession of any kind, and in the same spirit of exact and unimpassioned inquiry which has enabled science to solve so many problems, once not less obscure nor less hotly debated. The founders of this Society fully recognize the exceptional difficulties which surround this branch of research; but they nevertheless hope that, by patient and systematic effort, some results of permanent value may be attained."

The following are among the subjects which have been intrusted to special committees:—

"1. An examination of the nature and extent of any influence which may be exerted by one mind upon another, apart from any generally recognized mode of perception.

"2. The study of hypnotism, and the forms of so-called mesmeric trance (with its alleged insensibility to pain); clairvoyance and other allied phenomena.

"3. A critical revision of Reichenbach's researches with certain organizations called 'sensitive,' and an inquiry whether such organizations possess any power of perception beyond a highly exalted sensibility of the recognized sensory organs."

The following are the officers of the English society: President, Professor Henry Sidgwick; Vice-Presidents, Arthur J. Balfour, M.P., Professor W. F. Barrett, Rt. Rev. the Bishop of Carlisle, John R. Hollond, M.P., Richard H. Hutton, the Rev. W. Stainton Moses, the Hon. Roden Noel, Professor Lord Rayleigh, Professor Balfour Stewart, and Hensleigh Wedgwood.

Professor Barrett, who was present at the preliminary meeting in Boston, after reading the brief outline of the objects of the English society, as given above, made the following statement of the results already obtained:—

"Once the Society's work begun, a stream of testimony set in, and offers of evidence were many. Every possibility of error suggested by experience and ingenuity was eliminated. The experiments made in the last two years by members of the Society will carry conviction, I think, to every candid mind. Many tests were made in which the subject reproduced a diagram or drawing of which some other person thought. . . .

6

The other committees of the Society have studied the subjects assigned to them with great assiduity, and have obtained a vast amount of information and data. . . . The work of sifting out of the mass of errors, misconceptions, and ignorance, which usually surround such stories, the data which may serve for scientific purposes, is an intensely interesting one. Of course persons who take up the matter must expect no little ridicule, and perhaps some abuse. But out of alchemy came chemistry; and out of astrology, astronomy. There may be much in these extraordinary accounts of second-sight, thought-reading, apparitions, and so forth, fit only to ridicule; but if there are any facts at the bottom, we want to find them."

The Council of the American society feel that the evidence published by the English society is of a nature not to be ignored by scientific men, especially where the alleged facts would, if real, permit verification, and the conditions allow control.

In other branches of human experience, the publication of observations, made with as much apparent care, and under such distinguished auspices, immediately invites many careful students to the work of corroboration or disproof. The personal ability and character of the English investigators, and the accuracy of their methods, if they do not compel the doubter forthwith to believe their conclusions, seem at least to make it impossible for him dogmatically to deny them, without support from something more solid than general presumptions about the order of nature, and the fallibility of human testimony.

The Council of the American society therefore feels that the duty can be no longer postponed of systematically repeating observations similar to those made in England, with a view to confirming them if true, to definitely pointing out the sources of error in them if false. If true, they are of value, and the tracing of their limits becomes a scientific duty. If false, no time should be lost in publishing their refutation; for, if allowed long to stand uncontradicted, their only effect will be to re-enforce powerfully the popular drift toward superstition.

The Council therefore begs all persons to whom this circular is sent, who agree with these practical conclusions, and who believe that the exact study of this border-land of human experience is an urgent scientific need, to send in their names to the secretary of the society.

COUNCIL OF THE SOCIETY.

To hold office till October, 1885.

Prof. G. F. BARKER, Philadelphia.
Rev. C. C. EVERETT, Cambridge.
Mr. SAMUEL H. SCUDDER,
 Cambridge.
Mr. COLEMAN SELLERS,
 Philadelphia.

Mr. MOORFIELD STOREY, Boston.
Prof. JOHN TROWBRIDGE,
 Cambridge. (Resigned.)
Prof. WILLIAM WATSON, Boston.

To hold office till October, 1886.

Dr. HENRY P. BOWDITCH, Boston.
Mr. C. C. JACKSON, Boston.
Col. T. W. HIGGINSON,
 Cambridge.
Mr. N. D. C. HODGES, Cambridge.

Dr. CHARLES S. MINOT, Boston.
Prof. SIMON NEWCOMB,
 Washington.
Mr. W. H. PICKERING, Boston.

To hold office till October, 1887.

Prof. G. S. FULLERTON,
 Philadelphia.
Prof. WILLIAM JAMES, Cambridge.
Prof. G. STANLEY HALL,
 Baltimore.
Prof. JAMES M. PEIRCE,
 Cambridge.

Prof. E. C. PICKERING, Cambridge.
Mr. R. PEARSALL SMITH,
 Philadelphia.
Major A. A. WOODHULL,
 New York.

b. REQUEST FOR INFORMATION (1884)

Circular No. 2, Issued by the Committee on Work

CAMBRIDGE, MASS., Dec. 19, 1884.

DEAR SIR,—The first stated meeting of the AMERICAN SOCIETY FOR PSYCHICAL RESEARCH was held yesterday, and a Council partly elected. This practically completes the formal part of the organization of the Society. The Council, anxious to proceed without loss of time to the accomplishment of material results, desires to gain such information from members and associates as will assist it in deciding what lines of investigation had better immediately be entered upon, and of what persons the respective committees may most advantageously be composed. This circular is therefore addressed to you as one of the Society, with the request that you fill out the appended sheet of questions as fully as lies in your power, and mail it promptly to the address given.

The English society has established permanent committees, as follows:—

Committee on Thought-Transference.

      "   " Hypnotism (Mesmerism).

      "   " Apparitions and Haunted Houses.

      "   " Physical Phenomena (Spiritualism).

      "   " Reichenbach's Experiments.

Literary Committee.

Temporary committees have also been formed to report on special subjects, such as the divining-rod. Under these titles, those of our Society who desire to share in the labor of research may conveniently express their preference for one direction of inquiry rather than another; but if any member or associate have inclination or opportunity for work in a direction not embraced under any of these heads, or if he care particularly to study some one phenomenon of one of the classes, it is hoped he will make as definite a statement as possible to that effect.

It is earnestly hoped that volunteers enough will be forthcoming to form committees whose personal composition will be a guaranty of the character of the investigation performed by them. Without such volunteers, it is to be feared that the American Society for Psychical Research may fail to justify its foundation.

We remain very respectfully yours,

WILLIAM JAMES,

HENRY P. BOWDITCH,

Committee on Work.

1. Are you personally able to devote any time to investigation, alone or with others? If so, please state roughly how many hours a week you might possibly give.
2. What subject or subjects should you prefer to study?
3. Will you furnish us with the names and addresses of any other competent persons who might be willing to engage in such labor?
4. Will you give us the names and addresses of any remarkable mediums, mind-readers, clairvoyants, mesmeric subjects, etc., of whom you may have knowledge, and who would be willing to have their powers subjected to examination? Private (that is,

unpaid) subjects are preferred, but references to professionals are also desired.

The American Society for Psychical Research, having been organized to make investigations similar to those which for two years have been carried on by the English society of the same name, we, the undersigned, have been appointed by the council a committee to study mediumistic phenomena.

We therefore invite coöperation from those disposed to aid us in our purpose. That purpose is neither the gathering of testimony from others, nor the mere gaining of a personal conviction satisfactory to ourselves; but rather the ascertainment of facts under such thorough conditions of observation as may make it seem impossible to those who credit us with honesty and normal intelligence to reject our conclusions. We seek, in other words, *evidence*, that is, facts so ascertained and recorded as to be open to but one interpretation. We are well aware how difficult such evidence is to obtain for any class of phenomena, and how little the history of opinion concerning mediumistic phenomena encourages one to hope that what seems evidence to one set of persons will seem evidence to another. But the society for psychical research is founded expressly to escape, it may be, from this disgracefully chaotic state of opinion. Its members have confidence in each other, and conclusions attained by persons acting as a committee of the society are much more likely to be influential than the same conclusions would be if they were published by the same persons acting alone. This consideration seems to warrant us in announcing the attainment of the unambiguous evidence as the goal of our endeavor, and in inviting the coöperation of all those who think they may help us to that end.

We shall accordingly be grateful to all such "mediums," whether professional or private, but especially the latter, as shall be willing to demonstrate to us experimentally their possession of peculiar powers; and, secondly, we shall be grateful to any one who will place us in communication with such a medium.

Accounts of remarkable phenomena, however interesting in themselves, will not be of use to us at present.

Letters should be addressed to Mr. W. H. Pickering, Institute of Technology, Boston, Mass.

William James, M.D.,
Charles Carroll Everett, D.D.,
Minot J. Savage,
W. H. Pickering,

Committee.

d. CIRCULAR REQUESTING FINANCIAL SUPPORT (1892)

The American Branch of the Society for Psychical Research has issued a circular which is here reprinted and to which the attention of readers of *The Journal* is specially called. The society is doing admirable work in sifting genuine from spurious psychical phenomena and in establishing beyond question among men of science and non-Spiritualists generally, a class of facts the recognition of which for years has been confined almost exclusively to Spiritualists. The American Branch of the Society for Psychical Research deserves to be generously sustained in its important work and it is hoped that readers of *The Journal*, who appreciate this work and are pecuniarily able will donate to the society and thus help increase its efficiency. The circular says:

We desire to remind our members that the Branch has been heavily subsidized from England during the past two years. In addition to our contributions from other persons in England, the indebtedness of the Branch to the parent Society on account of all the Proceedings and Journals supplied to the members and associates of the Branch during the past two years, has been borne by one English gentleman.

There are now about 420 names on our roll, of which about ninety represent full members. The income of the branch from assessments is thus about $2,500.00. It is obvious that this sum is but a small portion of the amount required for the following items:

1. Payment of Proceedings and Journals supplied to the American Branch.

2. Salary of Secretary.

3. Salary of assistant.

4. Rent of offices.

5. Expenses of travelling for the interview of witnesses and for experimental investigation.

6. Postage, printing, etc., etc.

The work of the Branch must therefore continue to depend chiefly upon voluntary donations, until the membership, which is steadily though slowly upon the increase, is large enough to provide an adequate annual fund by the mere payment of dues.

We believe that nearly all our members might render great service to the Society by extending the knowledge of its methods and work, and obtaining new adherents to the society either as full members or associates. With this object in view we enclose herewith a blank form for the proposal of new members. Additional forms can be obtained on application to the Secretary.

In the meantime we hope that those of our members who can contribute voluntary donations will either remit at once to the Treasurer, or express their willingness to make a contribution later in the present year.

WILLIAM JAMES,
S. P. LANGLEY,
RICHARD HODGSON,
Secretary and Treasurer.

5 Boylston Place, Boston, Mass.

e. NOTICE CONCERNING DISSOLUTION OF THE AMERICAN BRANCH (1906)

It will be a sufficient explanation of the reasons for the organization of an American Society to publish the official document which announced the dissolution of the American Branch. This is found below as published in the *Journal* of the London Society.

Dissolution of the American Branch.

The following document was signed by three Vice-Presidents of the Society for Psychical Research at a meeting in Boston last May, at which it was resolved to dissolve the American Branch of the London Society:

American Branch of The Society for
Psychical Research.

After full and anxious consideration it has been decided to dissolve the American Branch of the Society for Psychical Research at the end of the current year.

It is hoped that a scheme, upon which Professor Hyslop has been for some time past engaged, may result in the formation of an independent organization which will carry on the work of psychical research in America.

The records of sporadic phenomena now accumulated at the office of the Branch will be carefully gone through, and a selection from them will be published in the *Journal*.

The Piper records, and all documents appertaining thereto, will remain in the charge of the Council of the Society; and, as promptly as the labor involved in the study of their voluminous and complicated contents will allow, a full report on the later developments of the Piper case up to the date of Dr. Hodgson's death will be issued in the *Proceedings*.

After publication the Council of the Society will allow qualified and serious students access to the records; but only on terms which will ensure that all private and intimate matter contained in them shall be handled with proper discretion and reserve, and that all confidences shall be respected.

Signed on behalf of the American Branch

> WILLIAM JAMES,
> JAMES H. HYSLOP,   } Vice-Presidents.
> GEORGE B. DORR,

Signed on behalf of the Council of the Society for Psychical Research.

J. G. PIDDINGTON.

5 Boylston Place, Boston, Massachusetts, May 18, 1906.

Report of the Committee on Mediumistic Phenomena (1886)

The Committee on Mediumistic Phenomena has no definitely concluded piece of work to offer. An account of what has been done during the year, however, with a few reflections, may not be out of place.

Mr. Glendower Evans's untimely death, and Mr. T. W. Higginson's resignation, reduced the committee to two members,—Mr. M. J. Savage and Dr. W. N. Bullard. The undersigned, who had resigned, joined the committee again in March. We held no formal meetings as a committee, but each did what work he had opportunity for. Mr. Savage's departure for Europe has made a report from him impossible, although he spent many hours in the service, with results which it is hoped may some day be completed and see the light. Dr. Bullard has no report to make.

My own time was chiefly divided between two mediums,—one a trance-medium, whom, at her request, I shall call Mrs. P.; the other, Miss Helen Berry, whose public "materializing" manifestations are reputed to be among the best of their class.

Concerning Miss Berry, there is little to say. Test conditions against fraud are not habitually offered at her seances. On one occasion it was granted to Mr. Savage to sit behind the cabinet, others being in front, whilst I explored it after the medium's entrance, and found no confederate concealed. A trap-door seemed out of the question. In a minute two forms emerged from the cabinet. But this was our first sitting, and for certain reasons we cannot call the experiment satisfactory until we have an opportunity of taking part in it again. The real test of the Berry's genuineness is supposed to be the resemblance of the forms to deceased friends of the sitters, and the character of what they say. A large amount of testimony can be collected from sitters as to the unmistakable identity of the forms with their dead wives, husbands, brothers, etc.

I visited twelve seances, and took with me, or sent, personal friends enough to have, in all, first-hand reports of thirty-five visits, embracing sixteen or seventeen seances. No spirit form came directly to any one of us, so we offer no opinion regarding the phenomena.

To turn to the much simpler and more satisfactory case of Mrs. P. This lady can at will pass into a trance condition, in which she is "controlled" by a power purporting to be the spirit of a French doctor, who serves as intermediary between the sitter and deceased friends. This is the ordinary type of trance-mediumship at the present day. I have myself witnessed a dozen of her trances, and have testimony at first hand from twenty-five sitters, all but one of whom were virtually introduced to Mrs. P. by myself.

Of five of the sittings we have *verbatim* stenographic reports. Twelve of the sitters, who in most cases sat singly, got nothing from the medium but unknown names or trivial talk. Four of these were members of the society, and of their sittings *verbatim* reports were taken.

Fifteen of the sitters were surprised at the communications they received, names and facts being mentioned at the first interview which it seemed improbable should have been known to the medium in a normal way. The probability that she possessed no clew as to the sitter's identity, was, I believe, in each and all of these fifteen cases, sufficient. But of only one of them is there a stenographic report; so that, unfortunately for the medium, the evidence in her favor is, although more abundant, less exact in quality than some of that which will be counted against her.

Of these fifteen sitters, five, all ladies, were blood relatives, and two (I myself being one) were men connected by marriage with the family to which they belonged. Two other connections of this family are included in the twelve who got nothing. The medium showed a most startling intimacy with this family's affairs, talking of many matters known to no one outside, and which *gossip* could not possibly have conveyed to her ears. The details would prove nothing to the reader, unless printed *in extenso*, with full notes by the sitters. It reverts, after all, to personal conviction. My own conviction is not evidence, but it seems fitting to record it. I am persuaded of the medium's honesty, and of the genuineness of her trance; and although at first disposed to think that the "hits" she made were either lucky coincidences, or the result of knowledge on her part of who the sitter was and of his or her family affairs, I now believe her to be in possession of a power as yet unexplained.

The most promising way of investigating phenomena like this seems to be that of learning a great deal about one "Subject," who, of course, ought to be a good specimen of the class. Hitherto we have heard a little about a great many Subjects. Stenographic reports are expensive, but they seem indispensable for a conclusive discussion of the facts. They do away with doubts about the veracity of the sitter's memory; and they enable us to make a comparison of different sittings, which without them is hardly possible at all. Questions arise as to the irrelevant names and facts which almost every sitting to some extent contains. Are they improvisations of the moment? Are they in themselves right and coherent, but addressed to the wrong sitter? Or are they vestiges of former sittings, now emerging as part of the automatism of the medium's brain? A reading of the stenographic reports already taken makes it probable that, for some of them at least, this last explanation is correct. "Spirits" originally appearing to me have appeared in the sittings of others who knew nothing either of their persons or their names.

What science wants is a *context* to make the trance-phenomena continuous with other physiological and psychological facts. Curious to ascertain whether there were continuity between the medium-trance and the ordinary hypnotic trance, I made some observations *ad hoc* upon Mrs. P. My first two attempts to hypnotize her were unsuccessful. Between the second time and the third, I suggested to her "Control" in the medium-trance that he should make her a mesmeric subject for me. He agreed. (A suggestion of this sort made by the operator in one hypnotic trance would probably have some effect on the next.) She became partially hypnotized on the third trial; but the effect was so slight that I ascribe it rather to the effect of repetition than to the suggestion made. By the fifth trial she had become a pretty good hypnotic subject, as far as muscular phenomena and automatic imitations of speech and gesture go; but I could not affect her consciousness, or otherwise get her beyond this point. Her condition in this semi-hypnosis is very different from her medium-trance. The latter is characterized by great muscular unrest, even her ears moving vigorously in a way impossible to her in her waking state. But in hypnosis her muscular relaxation and weakness are extreme. She often makes several efforts to speak ere her voice becomes audible; and to get a strong contraction of the hand, for example, express manipulation and suggestion must be practised. The automatic imitations I spoke of are in the first instance very weak, and only become strong after repetition. Her pupils contract in the medium-trance. Suggestions to the "Control" that he should make her recollect after the trance what she had been saying were accepted, but had no result. In the hypnotic-trance such a suggestion will often make the patient remember all that has happened.

No sign of thought-transference—as tested by card and diagram-guessing—has been found in her, either in the hypnotic condition just described, or immediately after it; although her "Control" in the medium-trance has said that he would bring them about. So far as tried (only twice), no right guessing of cards in the medium-trance. She was twice tried with epistolary letters in the medium-trance,—once indicating the contents in a way rather surprising to the sitter; once failing. In her normal waking state she made one hundred and twenty-seven guesses at playing-cards looked at by me,—I sometimes touching her, sometimes not. Suit right (first guess) thirty-eight times,—an excess of only six over the "probable" number of thirty-two,—obviously affording no distinct evidence of thought-transference. Trials of the "willing game," and attempts at automatic writing, gave similarly negative results. So far as the evidence goes, then, her medium-trance seems an isolated feature in her psychology. This would of itself be an important result if it could be established and generalized, but the record is obviously too imperfect for confident conclusions to be drawn from it in any direction. Being compelled by other work to abandon the subject for the present, these notes are published merely as a suggestion of lines of inquiry which others may be better fitted than myself to carry out.

If a good trance-subject could be obtained for the society at the outset of her or his career, and kept from doing miscellaneous work until patiently and thoroughly observed and experimented on, with stenographic reports of trances, and as much attention paid to failures and errors as to successes, I am disposed to think that the results would in any event be of scientific value, and would be worth the somewhat high expense which they necessarily would entail. If the friends of spiritualism would contribute money for the thorough carrying out of any such scheme, they would probably do as much as by any one thing could be done, to bring about the "recognition" of trance-mediumship by scientific men.

As for the other kinds of mediumistic phenomena, I have during the past year been very much struck by the volume of evidence which can be collected in their favor. But the mere *volume* of evidence is of no account unless it can be proved that the evidence is likely to be of the ordinary human sort, bad and good mixed together in the usual proportion. If it is possible that it is unusually bad in *quality*, the quantity of it is of little account. Now, that there *are* reasons for believing its quality to be in these matters below the average, no one familiar with the facts can doubt. Only the establishment of one or two absolutely and coercively proven cases—of materialization, for example—will show that the hearsay evidence for *that* phenomenon may be mixed. And only *then* can the volume of evidence already extant on the subject be taken into account by one who has no direct personal experience on which to rely. The ordinary disbeliever rules out all hearsay evidence in advance. The believer accepts far too much of it, because he knows that some of it is good. The committee of the society should first devote itself to the very exact and complete study of a few particular cases. These may consume much labor and time. But if, after studying them, it should reach favorable conclusions, it would do vastly more to make the vaguer testimony already extant influential with the society as a whole, than it could do by discussing such testimony now.

⇌ 4 ⇌

Notes on Echolalia in Mrs. Piper (1886)

Echolalia represents the mind as the complete victim of suggestion or outside ideas. In the early development of her mediumship Mrs. Piper showed indications of this echolalia and its highly developed automatism as a consequence. In proof of this I shall quote from an early record of her phenomena. I owe the opportunity to do this to Prof. William James who made the record. It occurred on February 9th, 1886, and I quote his notes verbatim.

"Then tried hypnotizing. After a couple of minutes her eyes began to close. I then made a few passes and found not only that she could not open her eyes, but that I could hardly recall her to consciousness. When awakened she said she was so *weak* she could hardly move or speak. Tried her for muscular contractions without success. Great tendency to fall asleep. *Echolalia* when forehead was stroked. On stroking either temple whilst she read aloud, she became *inarticulate* but whether this was aphasia proper or lethargy it was hard to tell. Tendency (irresistible?) to *imitate movements* she saw me execute. No appearance whatever of doing what she thought I wanted. Finally I impressed upon her that she should not sleep but guess cards with me before I 'awakened' her. She was in no sense asleep, but guessed rapidly as I told her to, and then said she did not see the cards as in the last experiment, but simply named whichever one came into her mind."

ᴗ 5 ᴗ

Letter on Professor Newcomb's Address
before the American Society
for Psychical Research (1886)

In your editorial note of Jan. 29, on Professor Newcomb's presidential address to the American society for psychical research, reference is made to his 'very acute observation' that in certain drawings published by the English society as apparent results of thought-transference, 'the lines join perfectly, as would be the case with the work of a draughtsman who could see, and this too in the drawings made blindfold.' You go on to say that 'the natural inference is that there was some trickery'; and you add, that the English society's work 'bears the character of that of amateurs and enthusiasts.' I think you ought, in justice, to let your readers know that the drawings particularly referred to in the address were five in number. Of the series to which three of these belong, it is conspicuously said, in the accompanying report, that, 'as regards the bandage round his eyes,' the draughtsman 'sometimes pulls it down before he begins to draw.' The two other drawings belong to a series which the report says were executed while the draughtsman 'remained blindfolded.' But, if Professor Newcomb will himself try to reproduce these drawings with his eyes closed, he may perhaps be led to agree that their accuracy can hardly be deemed to fall outside the range attainable by the muscular sense alone, especially if aided by a little practice. To brand as dupes and enthusiasts (on the strength of this single 'acute observation') a set of gentlemen as careful as these English investigators have proved to be, seems to me singularly unjust.

WILLIAM JAMES.

Cambridge, Mass., Jan. 30.

6

Letters: James on the
Religio-Philosophical Journal (1886, 1890)

a. An Enviable and Eminent Place
in American Journalism (1886)

Doctor William James, Assistant Professor of Philosophy in Harvard University, and an active, fair-minded member of the American Society for Psychical Research, in a letter received last week takes occasion to express his opinion of the *Religio-Philosophical Journal*. The opinion of such an able writer, prominent educator, and cultured gentleman, is not only of interest to the *Journal*, but to its world-wide circle of readers. Dr. James may fairly be taken as a representative of a large body whose interest in psychical phenomena is active, permanent and friendly and whose co-operation is both desirable and important to the cause of truth.

Here is that portion of the Professor's letter of interest to the *Journal*'s readers:

"The double task of the *Religio-Philosophical Journal*, of fighting against much that is 'respectable'—as the fashions go—and for much that is not, makes its problem a peculiarly difficult one. I follow its career with interest, and, anxious myself to strike the right balance between over-criticism and over-credulity, believe that I learn much from its pages. The invariable manliness and straightforwardness of tone of its original matter are most refreshing. Whatever mistakes of detail it may make, those qualities give it an enviable and eminent place in American journalism."

b. On Preserving the *Journal* (1890)

Dear Colonel Bundy: It gives me great pleasure to hear that you are about to change the form of *The Religio-Philosophical Journal*. It ought to be of a shape better suited for preservation and binding, since it nearly always contains matter which I, for one, desire to keep. You have fought a good fight all these years, and I rejoice to believe that you are at last reaping some of the fruit of it in the more solid place which your paper holds in the land. I wish you God speed, and many years of future activity on the lines which you have so well laid down. Cordially yours,

Wm. James.

Cambridge, Mass., May 11, 1890.

7

Review of *Phantasms of the Living,* by Edmund Gurney et al. (1887)

This is a most extraordinary work,[1]—fourteen hundred large and closely printed pages by men of the rarest intellectual qualifications, for the purpose of setting on its legs again a belief which the common consent of the 'enlightened' has long ago relegated to the rubbish-heap of old wives' tales. In any reputable department of science the qualities displayed in these volumes would be reckoned superlatively good. Untiring zeal in collecting facts, and patience in seeking to make them accurate; learning, of the solidest sort, in discussing them; in theorizing, subtlety and originality, and, above all, fairness, for the work absolutely reeks with candor, —this combination of characters is assuredly not found in *every* bit of so-called scientific research that is published in our day.

The book hardly admits of detailed criticism, so much depends on the minutiae of the special cases reported: so I will give a broad sketch of its contents. The title, *Phantasms of the Living,* expresses a theory on which the recorded facts are strong, but of which the latter are of course independent. The 'facts' are instances of what are commonly called 'apparitions.' Collected for the Society of psychical research, their sifting and cataloguing is a laborious piece of work which has a substantive value, whatever their definitive explanation may prove to be. Very roughly speaking, there are re-

1 *Phantasms of the Living.* By EDMUND GURNEY, FREDERIC W. H. MYERS, and FRANK PODMORE. 2 vols. London, *Trübner,* 1886. 8o.

ported in the book about seven hundred cases of sensorial phantasms which seem vaguely or closely connected with some distant contemporaneous event. The event, in about one-half of the cases, was some one's death. In addition to these cases, Mr. Gurney has collected about six hundred of hallucinations seemingly irrelevant to any actual event, and thus has certainly a wider material to work upon than any one who has yet studied the subject of phantasms. Of course, the rationalistic way of interpreting the coincidence of so large a number with a death or other event, is to call it chance. Such a large number of 'veridical' phantasms occurring by chance would, however, imply an enormous total number of miscellaneous phantasms occurring all the while in the community. Mr. Gurney finds (to take the visual cases alone) that among 5,705 persons, interrogated at random, only 23 visual hallucinations had occurred in the last twelve years. And combining by the calculus of probabilities such data as the population drawn upon for the coincidence-cases, the adult population of the country, the number of deaths in the country within twelve years, etc., he comes to the conclusion that the odds against the chance occurrence of as many first-hand and well-attested veridical visual phantasms as his collection embraces, is as a trillion of trillions of trillions to 1. Of course, the data are extremely rough; and, in particular, the census of phantasms occurring at large in the community ought to be much wider than it is. But the veridical phantasms have, furthermore, many peculiarities. They are more apt to be visual than auditory. Casual hallucinations are oftener auditory. The person appearing is almost always recognized; not so in casual hallucinations. They tend to coincide with a particular form of outward event, viz., death. These and other features seem to make of them a natural group of phenomena.

The next best rationalistic explanation of them is that they are fictions, wilful or innocent; and that Messrs. Gurney, Myers, and Podmore are victims, partly of the tendency to hoax, but mainly of the false memories and mythopoetic instincts of mankind. These possibilities do not escape our authors, but receive ample consideration at their hands. Nothing, in fact, is more striking than the zeal with which they cross-examine the witnesses; nothing more admirable than the labor they spend in testing the accuracy of the stories, so far as can be done by ransacking old newspapers for obituaries and the like. If a story contains a fire burning in a grate—

presto the Greenwich records are searched to see whether the thermometer warranted a fire on that day; if it contains a medical practitioner, the medical register is consulted to make sure *he* is correct; etc. But obviously a hoax might keep all such accessories true, and a story true as to the main point might have grown false as to dates and accessories. It therefore comes back essentially to the investigator's instinct, or *nose*, as one might call it, for good and bad evidence. A born dupe will go astray, with every precaution; a born judge will keep the path, with few. *Saturday reviewers* will dispose of the work in the simplest possible way by treating the authors as born dupes. 'Scientists' who prefer offhand methods will do the same. Other readers will be baffled, many convinced. The present writer finds that some of the cases accounted strong by the authors strike him in the reading as weak, while scruples shown by them in other cases seem to him fanciful. This is the pivot of the whole matter; for I suppose the improbability of the phantasms being veridical by chance, will, if the *stories* are true, be felt by every one. Meanwhile it must be remembered, that, so far as expertness in judging of truth comes from training, no reader can possibly be as expert as the authors. The way to become expert in a matter is to get lots of experience of that particular matter. Neither a specialist in nervous diseases, nor a criminal lawyer, will be expert in dealing with these stories until he has had Messrs. Gurney's, Myers's, and Podmore's special education. Then his pathology, or his familiarity with false evidence, may also serve him in good stead. But in him, or in them, 'gumption' will, after all, be the basis of superiority. How much of it the authors have, the future alone can decide.

One argument against the value of the evidence they rely on is drawn from the history of witchcraft. Nowhere, it is said (as by Mr. Lecky in his *Rationalism*), is better-attested evidence for facts; yet the evidence is now utterly discredited, and the facts, then apparently so plenty, occur no more. Mr. Gurney considers this objection, and comes to an extremely interesting result. After "careful search through about 260 books on the subject (including the principal ones of the sixteenth, seventeenth, and eighteenth centuries) and a large number of contemporary records of trials," he affirms that the only facts of witchcraft for which there is any good evidence whatever are those neuropathic phenomena (trance, anaesthesia, hysteria, 'suggestion,' etc.) which, so far from being now discredited, are more than ever ascertained; while the marvels like conveyance through the air, transformation into animals, etc., do not rest on *a single* first-hand statement made by a person not 'possessed' or under torture.

The authors' theory of veridical phantasms is that they are caused by thought-transference. The ghost theory and the 'astral-form' theory are criticised as unsatisfactory (ghosts of clothes, phantasms not seen by all present, etc.). Thought-transference has been once for all established as a *vera causa*. Why not assume that even the impressions announcing death were made during the last moments of the dying person's life?

Where the apparition is to several witnesses, this explanation has to be much strained; and, in spite of Messrs. Myers's and Gurney's ingenuity, I can hardly feel as if they had made out a very plausible case. But any theory helps the analysis of facts; and I do not understand that Messrs. Gurney and Myers hold their telepathic explanation to have at present much more than this provisional sort of importance.

I have given my impression of the ability of the work. My impression of its success is this: the authors have placed a matter which, previous to them, had been handled so loosely as not to compel the attention of scientific minds, in a position which makes inattention impossible. They have established a presumption, to say the least, which it will need further statistical research either to undo or to confirm. They have at the same time made further statistical research easy; for their volumes will certainly stimulate the immediate registration and publication, on a large scale, of cases of hallucinations (both veridical and casual) which but for them would have been kept private. The next twenty-five years will then probably decide the question. Either a flood of confirmatory phenomena, caught in the act, will pour in, in consequence of their work; or it will *not* pour in—and then we shall legitimately enough explain the stories here preserved as mixtures of odd coincidence with fiction. In the one case Messrs. Gurney and Myers will have made an epoch in science, and will take rank among the immortals as the first effective prophets of a doctrine whose ineffectual prophets have been many. In the other case they will have made as great a wreck and misuse of noble faculties as the sun is often called to look down upon. The prudent bystander will be in no haste to prophesy; or, if he prophesy, he will hedge. I may be lacking in prudence; but I feel that I ought to describe the total effect left at present by the book on my mind. It is a strong suspicion that its authors will prove to be on the winning side. It will surprise me after this if neither 'telepathy' nor 'veridical hallucinations' are among the beliefs which the future tends to confirm.

⤙ 8 ⤙

Letter on Mrs. Ross, the Medium (1887)

Pro and Con

In Re Mrs. H. V. Ross: "Who Shall
Decide When Doctors Disagree?"

We devoted considerable space in our latest issue to placing before the *Banner* readers the facts on both sides—as far as attainable—in the Ross imbroglio; and have decided to follow the same course the present week: Inviting each individual under whose notice this number may fall to read carefully the matter, for and against, presented therein, and make up his or her mind as to the weight of evidence.

Letter from Professor James.

To the Editor of the *Banner of Light*:

As my name has (very unwelcomely to myself) been quoted in the newspapers as that of a witness to Mrs. Ross's mediumship, I feel it my duty to say just what my experience has been.

I visited her house three times, once alone at an ordinary séance, once at a private sitting arranged by Dr. A. R. Wallace, and once at a private sitting to which I was invited by Dr. J. R. Nichols. I had previously called at the house to ask Mrs. R. if she would not consent to give a séance out of her own house. *She refused to do so at any price.*

I examined walls and floors as carefully as the mere eye would permit, and could see no way of introducing confederates. The first sitting went by without my noticing any suspicious circumstances, so that I concluded that Mrs. Ross was better worth spending time upon than any of the other "materializers" whom I had visited.

At the second sitting the sliding doors, usually kept shut, were opened, and Dr. Wallace was allowed to sit just beyond them in the back room, from which the confederates, if such there were, would have to be introduced. So far so good. But when I asked permission to sit there with Dr. W. *the permission was denied.* The moment the séance began a white-robed spirit came out, and did an unusual thing, namely, she drew Dr. Wallace out of his seat, and into the front room, and spreading her drapery out so as to conceal the side of the doorway, and part of the cabinet, kept him there some little time. No one could see this manœuvre without the suspicion being aroused that it was intended to *conceal the passage of one or more confederates from the back room over the doorway and under the cabinet curtain, which hung loosely along side of the doorpost.* At the end of the séance the same performance was repeated with Dr. Wallace, who between whiles had been allowed to sit quietly in his place. The concealment of the side of the doorway was less perfect this time, and a lady who was one of the sitters tells me that whilst Wallace was up she distinctly *saw* the doorpost eclipsed from view by the *passage of the curtain, or some other dark body over it.* During this sitting a female form emerged from the cabinet with her white drapery caught above her knees. *Her legs from the knees down were clad in black trowsers,* like those in which a male spirit had the instant before appeared, and in which another male spirit appeared the instant after.

At the third sitting a form tall enough to be that of a child four or five years old appeared between the curtains of the cabinet and stood there, whilst the little girl of one of the sitters (kneeling on the floor, if I remember rightly,) played with its left hand. I was allowed to approach, and the light was strong enough to see fairly well. The figure had an oval, delicate-featured face, looking as if it might belong to a girl of ten or twelve. The body was *as unplausible looking a dummy as I ever saw,* slung from the neck of the real person who might have been kneeling on the floor. This and the fact that the hand with which the sitter's child played was in an impossible position, made me ask the supposed spirit child to give me its right hand. The request was boldly granted, to my surprise, and what seemed, both to my sight and touch, to be *four adult finger tips, held together and surrounded by a sort of "mit" drawn down to the knuckles*, was protruded and drawn across my own extended fingers, too rapidly to be held, but slowly enough to give me confidence in my observation.

The facts I have underscored, added together, were sufficient to convince me personally that whether mediumship was or was not an element of Mrs. Ross's performance, roguery certainly was, and I resolved not to waste any more time upon performances given at her own house. Good carpentry can make a secret door in any wall.

I learn that now, many days after the capture of her confederates by Mr. Braman and his friends, she invites a more rigid scrutiny still of the cupboard and wall, and shows an affidavit from her landlord that the house is what it was before her lease. I do not learn, however, that spirits still continue to emerge from the cabinet many at a time, with the sliding-doors closed as they used to do before the catastrophe; nor do I see why a secret opening through a wall may not be unmade in forty-eight hours by the same skill which made it.

I wish to confine myself to facts as closely as possible, so I make little comment on your policy (a policy which would ruin *any* cause) of defending exposed frauds through thick and thin, so as to present a "solid front" (!!) to the enemy. You ought, it seems to me, to consider it one of your first duties to raise a fund for the following up of such exposures as that of the Ross gang by the criminal conviction and imprisonment of its members. Only then would your opinions about more genuine cases begin to deserve consideration from inexperienced inquirers like

Yours truly,   WILLIAM JAMES.

18 Garden Street, Cambridge, Feb. 10th, 1887.

[We earnestly hope Prof. A. R. Wallace will feel prompted to address a letter to our columns in reply to what Prof. James says regarding *his* part in the séance reported Jan. 8th.

As regards the *very* gentlemanly criticism in which this Harvard Professor chooses to indulge (in his last paragraph) concerning the *Banner of Light* and its course generally, we have but this to say: His statement that the *Banner* has defended "exposed frauds through thick and thin" is not true. It is a principle of common law that an individual accused of wrong-doing must be held innocent until legally proved guilty; the *Banner* has demanded only this for the Spiritualist mediums—in the face of a skeptical public, which seeks to reverse the maxim and throw the burden of proof on the medium—and on this line we shall continue to "present a solid front to the enemy," as long as this paper is issued. We have no favors to ask of Prof. James or his ilk, and feel that our course is founded in justice and truth.]

9

Review of "The Second Report on Experimental Psychology," by Charles Sedgwick Minot (1889)

As one of the members of the "Committee on Experimental Psychology" I feel that I ought to disclaim agreement with the full breadth of Dr. Minot's conclusions. His painstaking study of the diagrams sent in by our associates has given a more definite numerical form to the already well-known fact that simple geometrical figures, letters, faces, houses, and scrawls are the most likely things both to be drawn and guessed in thought-transference experiments where improvised drawings are used. But he seems to me greatly to exaggerate the importance of this diagram-habit when he considers that the absence of special provisions against it in the English Society's experiments constitutes a very formidable objection to their value as proofs of thought-transference.

Our readers will not have forgotten that only a small number of the experiments recorded in the English Society's *Proceedings* were made with diagrams at all. Where diagrams were used, it is true that their *elements* were almost always the familiar ones above mentioned. With so few elements a code of signals is much less difficult than with more; and Dr. Minot consequently infers that where whole series of diagrams were rightly guessed, this may well have been because the agent secretly conveyed information to the percipient by such a code.

This wholesale right guessing of diagrams seemed to have occurred in at least five series of experiments. (I omit the two series contributed by Herren Dessoir and Schmoll, as the success in them was inferior to that in the other series.) Three of these series are not mentioned by Dr. Minot at all. In the series with Miss E. and Miss R., reported by Mr. Guthrie (pp. 31 ff. of Vol. II of the London Society's *Proceedings*), the successful agents were investigators of honorable repute who were singly in the room with the percipient when the guessing was done, so that if there were cheating it could perfectly well have gone on without a "code." In the experiments with Miss R., as recorded by Prof. Lodge (*ibid.*, p. 194), the spectators and agents seem also to have been gentlemen themselves bent on research. In those reported by Mr. J. W. Smith (*ibid.*, p. 207), with his sister, the same seems to have been the case.

But in these three series the success was less continuous and striking than in the two series which Dr. Minot alone mentions, namely, those in which Mr. Blackburn was agent and Mr. G. A. Smith percipient. In the first of these series (Vol. I, p. 78), contact was allowed, so that it is admitted in the report that tactile signals might conceivably have been made. In almost all the drawings of the second series (Vol. I, p. 161), however, of which the success was, if anything, even more remarkable, there was no contact between agent and percipient; and although the committee admit that the possibility of *audible* signals was not absolutely excluded, yet they seem to have been keenly alert to detect them. "The material for possible signs," they say, "appears to be reduced to shuffling on the carpet, coughing, and modes of breathing. Anything distinctly unusual in any of these directions must inevitably have been noticed; and since our attention, during this part of the experiment, was of course concentrated on the relation between Mr. B. and Mr. S. we are at a loss to conceive how any signalling, sufficient in amount to convey the required ideas, could have passed undetected. Furthermore, it must be observed that the reproductions were not made in a tentative, hesitating manner as if waiting for signals; but deliberately and continuously as if copying a drawing that is seen. Moreover, in almost every instance the *proportions* of the different parts of the original figure were reproduced more accurately than were its more easily describable details. However, with the view of removing all doubts, . . . we on one occasion stopped Mr. Smith's ears with putty, then tied a bandage round his eyes and ears, then fastened a bolster-case over the head, and over all threw a blanket over his entire head and trunk. Fig. 22

was now drawn by one of us, and shewn outside the room to Mr. Blackburn, who on his return sat behind Mr. Smith, and in no contact with him whatever, and as perfectly still as it is possible for a human being to sit who is not concentrating his attention on keeping motionless to the exclusion of every other object. In a few minutes Mr. Smith took up the pencil and gave the successive reproductions shewn," which are most striking copies of the original complicated "scrawl."

Dr. Minot says of this series of experiments that in it "ample opportunity for signalling was afforded," and that "persons of cautious judgment must consider that the explanation of the success of Mr. Smith is more probably fraud than supersensuous thought-transference." It seems to me here that Dr. Minot must have been less studious of the details of the English reports than of his own postal cards with their diagrams, and that he cannot have sufficiently discriminated between the possibility *in abstracto* of framing a code of signals for such drawings and the ease *in concreto* of using such a code. The ease in this instance can hardly have been great. I cannot agree, therefore, that the revelation of the diagram-habit has appreciably weakened the evidence for thought-transference actually to be found in the English Society's reports. To most of that evidence the existence of such a habit is wholly irrelevant; and where it is pertinent, fraud based on its use seems so unlikely, *if the reports are faithful,* that vague suspicions of unfaithful reporting and bad observation seem to me carry more real sceptical weight with them than Dr. Minot's more definitely formulated charge.

The experiments of the English Society, like all possible experiments of the sort, are exposed to many vague suspicions. The true warrant for their credibility is less to be found in the increasingly minute description of precautions in the reports (which would only make the reading of the latter more tiresome), than in the reader's preconceptions as to the likelihood of the phenomena and the competence of the observers. Where the phenomena are usual, any observer will pass for competent; but his competency will be suspected just in proportion as what he tells of grows more strange. The *great* weakness of the case for thought-transference is that the accounts of it are so rare. Why don't the apparent cases come in faster, now that so many of us are on the watch? It is true that in strict logic those who believe in thought-transference ought to be no more puzzled by this lack of new cases than those who believe in fraud. Fraud we know to be a *vera causa*, which, like all such, should recur with a certain statistical regularity. If as real a thing as fraud can thus remit for a time its effects, so may a more doubtful thing like thought-transference, if it really exist, do the same. But whilst no coercive conclusion can yet be drawn, it seems to me that the *exceedingly* strong presumption in favor of thought-transference which the English reports establish—I understand that the word "thought-transference" implies no positive theory whatever as to how the knowledge is conveyed from the agent's to the percipient's mind—is not appreciably shaken by Dr. Minot's critical remarks. This I feel in duty bound to say; for whilst additional proofs are waited for, questions get prematurely closed and forgotten; and in this case that seems to me a consummation which one ought to try as long as possible to postpone.

10

Notes on Automatic Writing (1889)

Many communications concerning experiences in automatic writing have been sent in to the Secretary during the past two years, and both he and the undersigned have witnessed the phenomenon in a number of instances. It is unquestionably a field from which a rich harvest of instruction may be hoped; but as professional occupations have prevented that steady experimental study of the matter which it deserves, I will content myself with jotting down a few points which may serve to stimulate the interest of the Society, postponing a more systematic paper to some later date. I must refer the reader to the important papers by Mr. Myers in Nos. VII, VIII, and XI of the London Society's *Proceedings,* for a general introduction to the subject. I regret that the appeal to experiment with the planchette, which was made at the public meeting in the spring of 1887, was followed by insignificant results. Planchettes can be obtained at the toy-shops, or (at cost) by writing to the Secretary of the Society; and, possibly, the remainder of this paper may lead to a little wider trial amongst associates and members.

One phenomenon of which Mr. Hodgson and I have been witnesses is both new and important. *The hand and the arm of the automatic writer are (in certain instances, at least) anæsthetic.* As soon as I read M. Pierre Janet's admirable account of the double personality of his somnambulist, L.,[1] I resolved to look for this symptom in ordinary planchette writers. It will be remembered that the skin of the hysteric L. had been for many years entirely insensible to contact, but that when she took to writing automatically on being waked from the hypnotic trance, the hand which wrote (and which signed all its communications by the name of Adrienne) expressed an intelligence perfectly perceptive of those skin-sensations of which the usual intelligence, expressing itself by word of mouth, was ignorant. Might not, conversely, the usual intelligence of ordinary non-hysteric automatic writers be transiently ignorant of the sensations of the writing hand and arm?

Persons who have written with a planchette are apt to speak of a tingling or prickling in the hands. I have actually tested three automatic writers for anæsthesia. In one of them, examined between the acts of writing, no anæsthesia was observed, but the examination was superficial. In the two others, both of them men, the anæsthesia to pricking and pinching, and possibly to touch, seemed complete. The second of these cases is so interesting that I subjoin the facts in detail.

William L. Smith, of Concord, Mass., student at the Massachusetts Institute of Technology, age 21, perfectly healthy and exceptionally intelligent, whose sincerity it is impossible to suspect, has amused himself on various occasions during the past two years with planchette writing. Of his previous performances more anon. On Jan. 24, 1889, he sat with Mr. Hodgson and myself, with his right hand extended on the instrument, and his face averted and buried in the hollow of his left arm, which lay along the table. Care was taken not to suggest to him the aim of the inquiry.

The planchette began by illegible scrawling. After ten minutes I pricked the back of the right hand several times with a pin—no indication of feeling. Two pricks on the *left* hand were followed by withdrawal, and the question, "What did you do that for?"—to which I replied, "To find whether you were going to sleep." The first legible words which were written after this were, *You hurt me.*

A pencil in the right hand was then tried instead of the planchette. Here again the first legible words were, *No use [?] in trying to spel when you hurt me so.* Next: *Its no use trying to stop me writing by pricking.* These writings were deciphered aloud in the

[1] *Revue Philosophique,* XXII, 577; XXIII, 449. Mr. Myers gives an abstract of the case in the third of his articles above referred to, pp. 237–247.

hearing of S., who seemed slow to connect them with the two pin-pricks on his left hand, which alone he had felt.

After some more or less illegible writing (some of it in Greek characters) and questions asked and answered,[2] I pricked the right wrist and fingers several times again quite severely, with no sign of reaction on S.'s part. After an interval, however, the pencil wrote: *Don't you prick me any more.* S. then said, "My right hand is pretty well asleep." I tested the two hands immediately by pinching and pricking, but found no difference between them, *both apparently normal.* S. then said that what he meant by "asleep" was the feeling of 'pins and needles' [which an insensible limb has when 'waking up'].

The last written sentence was then deciphered aloud. S. laughed, having been conscious only of the pricks on his left hand, and said, "It's working those two pin-pricks for all they are worth."

I then asked, "What have I been excited about to-day?" Ans. *Possibly examining.* "No, that was yesterday; try again." Ans. *May be correct dont know possibly sleepin.*[3] "What do you mean by sleeping?" Ans. *I don't know (really?) You* [distinct figure of a *pin*] *me 19 times*[4] *and think I'll write for you.*

The sitting here ended. It was very inferior in legibility and variety to sittings of the same Subject a year previous. Two evenings later we had another sitting. S. had been most of the day in the open air, and had paddled a canoe ten miles. I immediately asked, "Are you still offended at my having pricked you?" Ans. *I'm(?).* "Where did I prick you the other night?" Ans. *On the side of my hand.* "Didn't I prick you anywhere else?" Ans. *No.* "Which hand?" Ans. *This hand.* "Which hand?" Ans. *Right.*

After some remote questions and answers the pencil was changed to the *left* hand, to see if that also would write. It spontaneously wrote a good deal, quite unintelligibly. "Are you angry?" Ans. *Yes.* "Who pricked you? How many times? Tell us all about it." Ans. *19 times on the other hand.* No further writing came on this evening. Shortly after the last answer I pinched four times, severely,

---

2 *Q.* "Who is writing? Is it Smith himself?" *A. YES. Pencil cant go alone.*

3 What I had in mind was "building-plans." As a matter of fact, however, I had been acutely suffering all day from loss of sleep, and had vainly sought to get a nap in the afternoon. There are claims of lucidity for Mr. Smith's past planchette writing, and this answer may (possibly) not have been a mere coincidence. It is true that I am a chronically bad sleeper, and Mr. S. may have heard of the fact.

4 I unfortunately hadn't counted the times. Nineteen is a plausible number.

the skin of the *left* hand between my nails. S.'s eyes were closed, but his face was visible, and I *thought* I detected a very subtle facial and respiratory reaction upon the pinching. He, however, on being questioned some minutes later, denied that he had been pricked or pinched during this evening. Later still, whilst the left hand still held the pencil, I pinched his *right* hand once, whereupon he started and said he didn't "need to be waked up." No more writing taking place after a quarter of an hour or more, I compared the two hands and found that they had equal and normal sensibility. S. is still ignorant of what interested us in these sittings. He is, unfortunately, too busy to sit again for many weeks.

Here, as the reader will perceive, we have the consciousness of a subject split into two parts, one of which expresses itself through the mouth, and the other through the hand, whilst both are in communication with the ear. The mouth-consciousness is ignorant of all that the hand suffers or does; the hand-consciousness is ignorant of pin-pricks inflicted upon other parts of the body—and of what more remains to be ascertained. If we call this hand-consciousness the automatic consciousness, then we also perceive that the automatic consciousness may transfer itself from the right hand to the left, and carry its own peculiar store of memories with it. The left hand, writing automatically on the second evening, remembered the right hand's experiences on the first, and very likely (though this was not ascertained) knew nothing of its own.

These phenomena remind us of what the lamented Gurney described in his important paper "Peculiarities of Certain Post-Hypnotic States," in Part XI of the London Society's *Proceedings*. The facts there, it will be remembered, were these: An order to do something after waking was given to the subject during the trance. Of this order no apparent consciousness remained when the trance was over. But if, before the time of execution arrived, the subject's hand was placed upon a planchette, the writing which came was all about the order, showing that the latter was retained in a split-off portion of the consciousness, which was able to express itself automatically through the hand. This dissociation of the consciousness into mutually exclusive parts is evidently a phenomenon destined, when understood, to cast a light into the abysses of Psychology.

We owe to the kindness of Dr. C. W. Fillmore, of Providence, the report of a case of hystero-epilepsy which illustrates the same phenomenon in an even more extraordinary manner.[5] The record begins in the nineteenth year of the patient's age, and continues for several years. It is filled with every conceivable species of suffering and disorder, but the entries which interest us in the present connection are the following:—

September 17, 1860.—Wild with delirium. Tears her hair, pillow-cases, bedclothes, both sheets, night-dress, all to pieces. Her right hand prevents her left hand, by seizing and holding it, from tearing out her hair, but she tears her clothes with her left hand and teeth. . . .

29th.—Complains of great pain in right arm, more and more intense, when suddenly it falls down by her side. She looks at it in amazement. Thinks it belongs to some one else; positive it is not hers. Sees her right arm drawn around upon her spine. Cut it, prick it, do what you please to it, she takes no notice of it. Complains of great pain in the neck and back, which she now calls her shoulder and arm; no process of reasoning can convince her of the contrary. [To the present time, now nearly five years, the hallucination remains firm. She believes her spine is her right arm, and that her right arm is a foreign object and a nuisance. She believes it to be an arm and a hand, but treats it as if it had intelligence and might keep away from her. She bites it, pounds it, pricks it, and in many ways seeks to drive it from her. She calls it 'Stump; Old Stump.' Sometimes she is in great excitement and tears, pounding 'Old Stump.' Says 'Stump' has got this, that, or the other, that belongs to her.] The history of September is her daily and nightly history till October 25th. . . .

November 12.—From eleven to twelve at night sits up, apparently asleep, and writes, with her paper against the wall. After she awakes, seems to be unconscious of what she has written. . . .

From November 20 to January 1, 1861, raving delirium; pulls her hair nearly all out from the top of her head. . . . The right hand protects her against the left as much as possible. . . .

February 1 to 11.—Under the influence of magnetism writes poetry; personates different persons, mostly those who have long since passed away. When in the magnetic state, whatever she does and says is not remembered when she comes out of it. Commences a series of drawings with her right paralyzed hand, 'Old Stump.' Also writes poetry with it. Whatever 'Stump' writes, or draws, or does, she appears to take no interest in; says it is none of hers, and that she wants nothing to do with 'Stump' or 'Stump's.' I have sat by her bed and engaged her in conver-

[5] The report is by the late Dr. Ira Barrows, of Providence. The patient was Miss Anna Winsor. Her mother, brother, and Dr. Wilcox, Dr. B.'s former partner, bear corroborative testimony.

sation, and drawn her attention in various ways, while the writing and drawing has been uninterrupted. As she had never exhibited any taste for nor taken any lessons in drawing I exhibit here some specimens of her first attempt.[6]

March, 1861.—She became blind. . . .

January 4, 1862.—Is still blind; sees as well with eyes closed as open; keeps them closed much of the time; reads and draws with them closed. Draws in the dark as well as in the light; is clairvoyant. Writes poetry, chiefly with the right hand, and often . . . while it is dark. The handwriting differs greatly in different pieces. . . .

January 10.—When her delirium is at its height, as well as at all other times, her right hand is rational, asking and answering questions in writing; giving directions; trying to prevent her tearing her clothes; when she pulls out her hair it seizes and holds her left hand. When she is asleep, it carries on conversation the same; writes poetry; never sleeps; acts the part of a nurse as far it can; pulls the bedclothes over the patient, if it can reach them, when uncovered; raps on the head-board to awaken her mother (who always sleeps in the room) if anything occurs, as spasms, etc.

January, 1863.—At night, and during her sleep, 'Stump' writes letters, some of them very amusing; writes poetry, some pieces original. Writes 'Hasty Pudding,' by Barlow, in several cantos, which she had never read; all correctly written, but queerly arranged, as, *e.g.*, one line belonging in one canto would be transposed with another line in another canto. She has no knowledge of Latin or French, yet 'Stump' produces the following rhyme of Latin and English:[7]—

> Sed tempus recessit, and this was all over,
> Cum illi successit, another gay rover;
> Nam cum navigaret in his own cutter,
> Portentum apparet, which made them all flutter.
>
> Est horridus anguis which they behold,
> Haud dubio sanguis within them ran cold.
> Triginta pedes his head was upraised,
> Et corporis sedes in secret was placed.
>
> Sic serpens manebat, so says the same joker,
> Et sese ferebat as stiff as a poker;
> Tergum fricabat against the old light-house,
> Et sese liberabat of scaly detritus.

[6] These specimens we have never received.—W.J.

[7] Does any reader recognize these verses? If so, will he please send them to the Secretary? It is important to ascertain whether their origin were not in the patient's memory.

Tunc plumbo percussit thinking he hath him,
At serpens exsiluit full thirty fathom,
Exsiluit mare with pain and affright,
Conatus abnare as fast as he might.

Neque illi secuti? no, nothing so rash,
Terrore sunt muti he'd made such a splash;
Sed nunc adierunt the place to inspect,
Et squamas viderunt, the which they collect.

Quicumque non credat and doubtfully rails,
Ad locum accedat, they'll show him the scales;
Quas, sola trophea, they brought to the shore;
Et causa est ea, they couldn't get more.

'Stump' writes both asleep and awake, and the writing goes on while she is occupied with her left hand in other matters. Ask her what she is writing, she replies, "*I* am not writing; that is 'Stump' writing. I don't know what he is writing. I don't trouble myself with 'Stump's' doings." Reads with her book upside down, and sometimes when covered with the sheet. 'Stump' produces two bills of fare in French. . . .

Upon this one subject of her right arm, she is monomaniac. Her right hand and arm are not hers. Attempt to reason with her and she holds up her left arm and says, "This is my left arm. I see and feel my right arm drawn behind me. You say this 'Stump' is my right arm. Then I have three arms and hands." In this arm the nerves of sensation are paralyzed, but the nerves of motion preserved. *She* has no will to move it. *She* has no knowledge of its motion. This arm appears to have a separate intelligence. When she sleeps, it writes or converses by signs. It never sleeps; watches over her when she sleeps; endeavors to prevent her from injuring herself or her clothing when she is raving. It seems to possess an independent life and, to some extent, foreknowledge.

Miss W. died in January, 1873. The record of her last ten years is not given. It would appear, from certain passages of the record in our possession, that 'old Stump' used to write of Miss W. in the third person, as Anna. This seems to be the rule in automatic utterances.

Certain other peculiarities which I have never seen quoted together deserve mention. Thus the planchette-writer often tends to fall into a drowsy condition whilst writing, and to become abstracted from the outer world. Sometimes he even passes into a state of genuine sleep or trance—I have no data thus far for distinguishing which. The writing is often preceded by peculiar sensations in the arm, and the latter is apt to be animated by involuntary spasmodic movements before the writing regularly begins.

I was witness a year ago, in Mr. Smith's case, of a phenomenon which has been described since Braid's time as 'exaltation of the muscular sense,' but, so far as I know, only recorded of hypnotic subjects.[8] Mr. Smith wrote on large sheets of brown wrapping-paper, his right arm extended, his face on a level with the table, buried in the hollow of his left elbow,—a position which made vision of the surface of the paper a physical impossibility. Nevertheless, two or three times in my presence on one evening, after covering a sheet with writing (the pencil never being raised, so that the words ran into each other), he returned to the top of the sheet and proceeded downwards, dotting each *i* and crossing each *t* with absolute precision and great rapidity. On another evening, whilst sitting in the same position, he drew the entire outline of a grotesque human figure in such a way that the pencil ended at the point where it began, and that it is now impossible to tell, from inspection of the perfectly continuous outline, just where the point in question lay. Such feats would seem quite impossible to one in the normal waking state.

Another often noted idiosyncrasy of these writings is the *freakiness* of their execution. Mirror-script, spelling backwards, writing from right to left, and even beginning at the right-hand lower corner of the page and inscribing every word with its last letter first, etc., till the top is reached, are among the peculiarities of the automatic pencil. Mr. Myers has tried to assimilate some of these traits to what is observed in aphasia—with what success, later inquiry alone can show.

Another remarkable point is that two persons can often make a planchette or a bare pencil write automatically when neither can succeed alone. The explanation of this is hard to find. The individuals themselves will sometimes say, "One of us gives the force, the other the intelligence." Certain it is that perfectly determinate combinations of individuals are often required for success. The more physiological explanation is that the automatic freedom is interfered with by conscious attention to the performance, and that when two persons work together each thinks that the other is the

[8] See, for example, Carpenter's *Mental Physiology*, § 128.

source of movement, and lets his own hand freely go. We sadly need more discriminating observations on this as well as other points.

Of course, the great *theoretic* interest of these automatic performances, whether speech or writing, consists in the questions they awaken as to the boundaries of our individuality. One of their most constant peculiarities is that the writing and speech announce themselves as from a personality other than the natural one of the writer, and often convince *him,* at any rate, that his organs are played upon by some one not himself. This foreignness in the personality reaches its climax in the demoniacal possession which has played so great a part in history, and which, in our country, seems replaced by the humaner phenomenon of trance-mediumship, with its Indian or other outlandish 'control,' giving more or less optimistic messages from the 'summer-land.' So marked is it in all the extreme instances that we may say that the *natural and presumptive* explanation of the phenomenon is unquestionably the popular or 'spiritualistic' one, of 'control' by another intelligence. It is only when we put the cases into a series, and see how insensibly those at the upper extreme shade down at the lower extreme into what is unquestionably the work of the individual's own mind in an abstracted state, that more complex and would-be 'scientific' ways of conceiving the matter force themselves upon us. The whole subject is at present a perfect puzzle on the theoretic side. And even on the phenomenal side we need more abundant proof than we have yet received that the content of the automatic communications may transcend the possible information of the individual through whose hand they come. To interest the reader in these more difficult phases of the subject I will append as illustrations some of the cases which we have received. The first is from Mr. Sidney Dean, of Warren, R.I., member of Congress from Connecticut from 1855 to 1859, who has been all his life a robust and active journalist, author, and man of affairs. He has for many years been a writing subject, and has a large collection of manuscript automatically produced.

"Some of it," he writes us, "is in hieroglyph, or strange compounded arbitrary characters, each series possessing a seeming unity in general design or character, followed by what purports to be a translation or rendering into mother English. I never attempted the seemingly impossible feat of copying the characters. They were cut with the precision of a graver's tool, and generally with a single rapid stroke of the pencil. Many languages, some obsolete and passed from history, are professedly given. To see them would satisfy you that no one could copy them except by tracing.[9]

"These, however, are but a small part of the phenomena. The 'automatic' has given place to the *impressional,* and when the work is in progress I am in the normal condition, and seemingly two minds, intelligences, persons, are practically engaged. The writing is in my own hand, but the dictation not of my own mind and will, but that of another, upon subjects of which I can have no knowledge and hardly a theory; and I, myself, consciously criticise the thought, fact, mode of expressing it, etc., while the hand is recording the subject-matter and even the words impressed to be written. If *I* refuse to write the sentence, or even the word, the impression instantly ceases, and my willingness must be mentally expressed before the work is resumed, and it is resumed at the point of cessation, even if it should be in the middle of a sentence. Sentences are commenced without knowledge of mine as to their subject or ending. In fact, I have never known in advance the subject of disquisition.

"There is in progress now, at uncertain times, not subject to my will, a series of twenty-four chapters upon the scientific features of life, moral, spiritual, eternal. Seven have already been written in the manner indicated. These were preceded by twenty-four chapters relating generally to the life beyond material death, its characteristics, etc. Each chapter is signed by the name of some person who has lived on earth,—some with whom I have been personally acquainted, others known in history. . . . I know nothing of the alleged authorship of any chapter until it is completed and the name impressed and appended.[10] . . . I am interested not only in the reputed authorship,—of which I have nothing corroborative,—but in the philosophy taught, of which I was in ignorance until these chapters appeared. From my standpoint of life—which has been that of biblical orthodoxy—the philosophy is new, seems to be

---

[9] I should say that I have seen some of these curious hieroglyphs by Mr. D., which professed to be Chinese. They bore no outward resemblance to what I have learned to know as Chinese characters. I owe to the kindness of Colonel Bundy some four or five other soi-disant specimens of ancient languages, automatically written, which I have had examined by my colleagues conversant with Sanscrit, Hebrew, Assyrian, Arabic, and Persian, as well as by a Japanese student who knew Chinese. None of the characters were in any instance recognized.—W.J.

[10] I have seen and read three of these chapters. They are fluent, scholarly, and philosophical enough, but to my mind have a curious resemblance in style to other inspirational productions which I have read, and doubtfully attain to real originality. One of them, signed Louis Agassiz, was, both in thought and diction, wholly unlike the utterances during life of my lamented teacher.—W.J.

46

reasonable, and is logically put. I confess to an inability to successfully controvert it to my own satisfaction.

"It is an intelligent *ego* who writes, or else the influence assumes individuality, which practically makes of the influence a personality. It is *not* myself; of that I am conscious at every step of the process. I have also traversed the whole field of the claims of 'unconscious cerebration,' so called, so far as I am competent to critically examine it, and it fails, as a theory, in numberless points, when applied to this strange work through me. It would be far more reasonable and satisfactory for me to accept the silly hypothesis of re-incarnation,—the old doctrine of metempsychosis,—as taught by some spiritualists to-day, and to believe that I lived a former life here, and that once in a while it dominates my intellectual powers, and writes chapters upon the philosophy of life, or opens a post-office for spirits to drop their effusions, and have them put into English script. No; the easiest and most natural solution to me is to admit the claim made, *i.e.*, that it is a decarnated intelligence who writes. But *who?* that is the question. The names of scholars and thinkers who once lived are affixed to the most ungrammatical and weakest of *bosh*. . . .

"It seems reasonable to me,—upon the hypothesis that it is a person using another's mind or brain,—that there must be more or less of that other's style or tone incorporated in the message, and that to the unseen personality, *i.e.*, the power which impresses, the thought, the fact, or the philosophy, and not the style or tone, belongs. For instance, while the influence is impressing my brain with the greatest force and rapidity, so that my pencil fairly flies over the paper to record the thoughts, I am conscious that, in many cases, the vehicle of the thought, *i.e.*, the language, is very natural and familiar to me, as if, somehow, *my* personality as a writer was getting mixed up with the message. And, again, the style, language, everything, is entirely foreign to my own style."

Another gentleman, Mr. John N. Arnold, of 19 College street, Providence, R.I., describes his experience as follows:—

I make my mind as negative as possible, place myself in the attitude of writing, with pencil and paper, and in about two or three minutes I feel a sensation at the elbow as if a galvanic battery had touched it. The thrill continues down the forearm till it reaches the hand, which quickly doubles over towards the thumb, and then back, with a strong tension, several times. When quiet, it begins to write. The power that writes sometimes tells the truth, but oftener lies. For instance, an influence which called itself Lydia, my wife's sister, wrote that Rose (my wife) had been raising blood. I replied I thought not. Lydia insisted, and, upon reaching home, I found she was correct. Again, she wrote that a lady friend was dead. I contradicted the Automat, as I had seen the lady but a few hours before. Lydia seemed hurt to think I doubted her, and strongly asserted that the lady was dead. In a few hours I ascertained the falsity of Lydia's vehement assertion by meeting the lady in question. I got so little satisfaction from the power that I gave it up, and of late can only get names, but no communications, except yes or no, in answer to my questions.

In a second communication Mr. Arnold adds:—

The pencil was always held in my right hand. I never had any mirror-writing. I sometimes guessed what was coming, but never knew. For instance, many words begin with the first two or three letters the same, as "*pre*suming," "*pre*fix." I would sometimes guess, after the Automat finished the *e* in such a word; but generally was mistaken, even when the context would indicate my word to be the proper one.

It is at least ten years (and it may be more) since the writing about my wife. I had no reason to think my wife had had hæmoptysis. She had had an attack in 1860, when we went to Macon, Ga., but not since; so that I was surprised when the Automat wrote with such confidence and persistency, and said that when I got home I should see that it was telling the truth. When I reached home I questioned my wife about it. She seemed very much astonished, and wanted to know how I got my information, as she had taken pains to conceal it from me, fearing it would cause me alarm. I have just asked my wife about this affair, and she seems to remember it substantially as I do. I have never tried answering mental questions put by another; in fact, the Automat and I got disgusted with one another years ago. We had a falling out, and haven't been on good terms since. The Auto got tired with my lack of patience, and I got tired with the Auto's lack of truthfulness.

I am glad to answer any questions about this matter, and when you get a theory that will fit this problem, please write me. I don't mean unconscious cerebration, astral light, or spirit friends; but something new, something that will fit tight and snug all around and won't have to be taken in at the back, or let out in the arm-size, and won't go all to pieces like Don Quixote's pasteboard helmet when the Damascus blade of logic, reason, and common-sense descends upon it.

An isolated case of apparent clairvoyance, like that which this gentleman reports, had of course better be treated as an accidental coincidence. But there are other cases harder so to treat,—cases where some sort of telepathy appears to be involved. But telepathy seems always doomed to be baffling. The telepathic explanation of the cases I have in mind is neither disproved nor established with the fulness that is desirable. As an illustration of what I mean, take Mr. W. L. Smith's case again. It was first made known to us in November, 1887, by a letter from one of his neighbors, Miss ——, who wrote as follows:—

After reading the reports on Automatic Writing published by the English S.P.R. . . . I determined to try my own power and those of my friends. Accordingly my friend W.L.S. and I each made a planchette. . . . The successful writer was S. himself, and with him we have obtained more remarkable results than I have ever seen reported. It is worth while to notice that he had never seen a planchette before he made his according to my direction, and had never seen writing done with one until he made his first attempt in my presence, so that the possibility of unconscious deception, which might have existed in the case of a person who had already amused himself with a planchette, was out of the question with him. The question of conscious deception may be set aside at once; yet, appreciating that experiments whose fairness depends on the honesty of any person lose their scientific value, we took pains so far as possible to avoid everything which might have been suspicious with unknown writers.

Our first attempt, though only partially successful, so far exceeded our expectations, that we were much encouraged.

After relating three attempts at answering mental questions which seem to have been failures the account goes on:—

At the fourth experiment, a repetition of the third, with a different card, the suit and number were immediately and correctly written. As in these cases there had been a possibility of thought-transfer, the next experiment was differently arranged.

The pack was carefully shuffled *by me*, and held under a table, both my hand and W.'s being in contact with it; neither of us could see the pack. I then faced the top card, again asking mentally for the suit and number of the card faced. The planchette immediately wrote the word *which*. We were about to consider the trial a failure when it occurred to me that I might have faced two cards. I found, on examining the pack, that this was not so; but, still without suggestion from W., I looked further, and found a second card in the middle of the pack, which I had unconsciously faced in shuffling.

I mention this in detail because it was the first instance of a writing unexpected by either W. or myself. At several succeeding experiments the planchette correctly wrote suit and number of cards turned up out of sight of every one, until we became tired of that test and gave it up.

A series of questions, the answers to which were unknown to any one present, seemed to furnish a fair test for the powers of the planchette. At first the questions were asked aloud; in all cases they were put without suggestion by W.

I will describe two experiments as instances of trials of this kind. During these two experiments we sat in the dark, and yet the answers were legibly written.

My first question was, "What is the name on the visiting card which lies at the top of the cards in the hall?"

The planchette did not write immediately; during the time while we waited for an answer I involuntarily formed an idea of the name which I expected, and feared that thought-transfer would come in for a share of consideration if the answer should be correctly written. At last I heard the motion of the pencil; when it ceased we took the paper to the light and found the words *Upside down*. *After* reading this, we examined the card-plate, and found as an explanation of planchette's answer, the top card turned *upside down* on the pile.

Now, not only had S. no means of knowing that the top card was upside down, but no one else in the house knew it until after the writing by planchette; I had even a distinct idea of a certain name in my mind during the whole of the experiment. Furthermore, and most remarkable of all, the hall where the card-plate stood was unlighted, so that when we went to examine the card we were quite unable to say whether or not there was a name upon the card until we had carried the plate into the next room.

This fact reminded us of the power we had already seen in planchette to read the suit and number of playing-cards, held under the table so as to be out of the range of possible, as well as actual, vision.

We put the same question, "What is the name on the card which lies at the top on the card-plate?" a second time, the cards having been rearranged by a third person, who himself did not know what card he had placed at the top. The planchette wrote, "*Miss L. P. H———*"; the name on the card proved to be Miss Lillian C. H———. This partial mistake struck us as interesting, but we could find no explanation for it, as the card-plate stood in a lighted room during this experiment, where it would have seemed much easier for planchette to see it than in the first trial.

Although these questions were put without the slightest suggestion from W., he had been told before each experiment what inquiry had been made. From this time on we took pains to keep from him all knowledge, not only of the answer, but of the question asked. The question was either asked mentally or written on paper, and kept, with great care, out of his sight, except in a few instances, which I will mark with an asterisk in the following descriptions. Although deception was out of the question, we tried to perform all experiments with as great strictness as if the writer had been unknown to us, and it is only in the starred cases that there existed the *possibility* of W.'s seeing the question.

In the following four experiments the *answers* to the questions asked were known to one or more persons in the room, but not to S.:—

1. *Q.* Is Miss H. going away Tuesday?

   A. Miss H. is no consequence to me. I don't know.

2. *Q.* What did her uncle do in Paris?

   A. How should I know you or he did in Paris, or all France (sic), I wasnt there.

(Mr. F. said he had been thinking, when the question was asked, of a friend who had been with him in Paris.)

3. *Q.* What sort of a voyage home did he have?

   A. Fair. If you keep that question to yourself there is no chance for thought transfer.

(This was not written at once, which was explained by the planchette as due to the fact that the question had been asked mentally, and by only one person. It was one of a few cases of mirror-writing.)

4. *Q.* On what steamer did J.A. come home?

   A. J.A. has been way off like Mr. F. I am not everywhere.

(This was interesting, as W.'s acquaintance with Mr. F. was limited to the evening in which the latter had been present at a planchette writing, and during which, as may be seen from the second and third questions above, Mr. F.'s visit to Paris was mentioned.)

In the following six experiments the answers to the questions asked were known to persons present at the writing, and would have been known to W. if he had known what question was proposed. Accordingly, our care was exceedingly great in all these cases to keep the question out of sight. It is worth notice that in no case was the answer exactly what was expected by those who knew what inquiry had been made.

1. *Q.* Who wrote the play of 'Hamlet'?

   A. I'd give a good deal to know that myself.

2. *Q.* Can Mr. F. make planchette write?

   A. He can if he tries hard enough old man Bacon and gets some one to help at first.

(Before and after the words 'old man Bacon' were what might have been meant for parentheses. As the words had no meaning where they were written, we naturally referred them to the question immediately preceding, "Who wrote the play of 'Hamlet'?" where they certainly seemed appropriate.)

*3. Q. What letters correspond to the notes ?

    A. *Gace.*

*4. Q. Add 4905, 3641 and 9831.

    A. *17377.*

(Planchette first copied the quantities to be added, making, by the way, a mistake in copying; this mistake, however, did not appear in the addition, though a mistake does appear in a column where the copy was correct.)

5. Q. How far is the earth from the sun?

    A. *192,310,009 kill.*

(This is curious, as every one who had known what question had been asked was expecting the answer in miles. W., however, always uses the metric system.)

6. Q. Who wrote 'Childe Harold'?

    A. *Byron, not drunk when he did it.*

Here would seem to be excellent evidence of mental questions answered and of telepathic or clairvoyant replies given. Sometime after this account was received I had the opportunity to sit with Mr. S. and the friends with whom the former successes had occurred. There were several other persons present as well. Writing came in profusion, bold and legible, but nothing that could be construed as telepathic. Many questions were written by the ladies with whom the former successes had occurred, out of S.'s sight, but were either not answered, or answered so vaguely that it was not certain that the particular question had been grasped. The questions were written across the table from Mr. S. Considering various hyperæsthetic possibilities, such questions should always be prepared outside of the room. Twice, early in 1888, Mr. S. sat for the Secretary and myself, when questions were secretly written, but in no instance pertinently answered. These negative results are, of course, not incompatible with the positive ones previously obtained, for if telepathy exist, it is certainly of fitful occurrence, even in a given individual. But they lend, at least, no strength to the first report; and, as luck will always have it, farther sittings with us (except the two recorded at the outset of this paper) have been made impossible to the subject by family wishes and his busy life.

Another similarly baffling case is given me by Mr. C., who graduated in 1888 at Harvard College, whom I know intimately, and whose sincerity I cannot doubt. Mr. C., it should be said, is himself the subject of certain automatic phenomena, with which, however, this narrative has naught to do. He told me of the following experience, either one or two days after it happened, and then wrote out the account which follows:—

It was on the evening of November 2. The company consisted of four ladies and two gentlemen. In the course of conversation a chance remark turned our thoughts upon psychological matters. Almost every one had some strange thing to relate, but no one would acknowledge belief in any supernatural power.

After speaking of various reports of mind-reading and hypnotic experiments I said, in a half-serious, half-joking way, "Suppose we try something of the sort."

The suggestion being favored, the daughter of the house, a girl of nineteen or twenty years of age, seated herself by a table, with pencil and paper. She seemed to think it was all foolery, but was amiable enough to contribute all she could to possible success, and, shading her eyes with her hand, she made herself as passive as possible.

On my part, I stood up at the opposite side of the table, about three feet removed, and fixed my mind upon a certain word, and (wishing to select one that would be most remote from her mind) I took 'hell.' With almost no hesitation in beginning, the girl made the letters, one after another, with easy legibleness (though the handwriting was neither hers nor mine).

Surprised at the success of the experiment, I felt interested to continue, and now determined to test it to the satisfaction of others. Accordingly, I went for a moment into the hall with one of the company, and there said to her that my next word should be 'omen.' Returning to the room, the same success attended as before, except that the 'e' was, in its smallness, out of proportion to the other letters, and the line between 'o' and 'm' was too long, because of a slip of the hand.

The experiment continued in like manner till some ten or a dozen words were written, of which I now remember (besides the above two, 'hell' and 'omen') 'word,' 'four,' 'moon.'

The person to whom each time I announced my intended word was of a disposition entirely to be relied on as free from either serious or facetious tricks, though, for that matter, I do not see how collusion with the 'Subject' was possible without being noticed.

The paper on which the words were written I wanted to take, but as the young lady wished to keep it I said nothing. On inquiring for it a few days later, it could not be found.

On the third day after (November 5), I again went to the house to see if more might not be done. Certain other interests, however, being emphasized in my mind, I did not find myself able to exert so strong a will as on the previous occasion. Whether because of this or not, I cannot judge; but the results were more meagre, but two words being successfully written, 'music' and 'girl.' Upon my thinking of one word, 'orange,' my 'subject' wrote all the letters, but in wrong order, thus: 'georan.'

An additional fact that I noticed this time (and I think it was true of the first evening's experiments) was, that when I stood at the right side of the girl she wrote downwards, and when I stood opposite her she wrote upwards.

The rest of the trials, which were of lines and diagrams imagined by me, resulted in nothing but undecipherable scrawls.

Concerning the feelings of myself and of the 'Subject' there is but this to say: that the girl had a headache the next day after the experiment (to which, being unaccustomed to headaches, she ascribed it), and no effect after the second. Upon me there was no after effect either time, except that after the first experiment, and on the same night, I felt as one does after giving strained attention to one thing.

The lady who did the writing, three other ladies, and a gentleman who witnessed the first evening's performance, endorsed, on Nov. 16, Mr. C.'s statement as a 'true report'; but I am not at liberty in this case to publish any names. On Dec. 2, Mr. C. added this postscript:—

I omitted to say with regard to the second series of trials, that 'music,' 'girl,' and 'orange' (the three words which the girl wrote) were the only *words* that I tried.

Concerning the first evening's experiments, my memory enables me to add, that besides the words already mentioned as being successfully written, my subject wrote with remarkable plainness this figure [a spiral], and also its reverse (though not so promptly).

Yet one further fact, perhaps worth noting: On this first evening I twice (possibly three times) let my thoughts stray whithersoever they would, while my subject and the onlookers supposed that I was exercising my intent upon some particular word. The results in these instances were nothing; unrelated pencil-marks as rambling as my thoughts, though, of course, in no way resembling them.

A few days after this I spent an evening at the subject's house with C. Nothing of interest occurred, though we tried to get results similar to those of the first occasion. The subject wrote a very little, automatically; but no sign whatever of telepathy appeared. C., I found, had stood (on the successful occasion) where he could see the movement of the young lady's hand as it wrote. The hypothesis must of course be considered, that he may have guided it by unconscious indications, like those given in the 'willing game' to the blindfold subject. The indications must in this instance have been reduced to changes in his respiration. If such indications were given, they were at any rate ineffectual when I was there, and also on three later occasions, on which, with the same *modus operandi*, Mr. C. reports that he only got total or partial failure. The sitting first reported remains thus a unique occurrence, not to be distinctly classified as yet.

The great desideratum is to get cases which can be examined continuously. Little can be done without the help of associates of the Society. I publish these incomplete notes, making no mention of much of our collected material, in order to show how important is the field, and how great the need of its assiduous cultivation.

⤙ II ⤚

The Census of Hallucinations (1889–1897)

a. International Congress of Experimental Psychology:
Instructions to the Person Undertaking to Collect Answers
to the Question on the Other Side (1889)

Sir or Madam:

At the meeting of the International Congress of Experimental Psychology in Paris in August, 1889, it was voted that the Census of Hallucinations begun by the Society for Psychical Research should be prosecuted as widely as possible in different countries by a Committee of the Congress itself. The undersigned was appointed to superintend the Census in America.

The experiences to which the question on the other side relates are what are scientifically described as casual hallucinations of sane persons, including under this term phantasmal appearances which some deny to be hallucinations because they believe them to be ghosts.

The object of our enquiry is (1) to ascertain approximately the *proportion of persons* who have such experiences, and (2) to obtain details as to the experiences with a view to examining into their cause and meaning.

For the first object it is IMPORTANT THAT THE QUESTION SHOULD BE VERY WIDELY ASKED AND OF ALL SORTS OF PEOPLE—NOT ONLY OF THOSE WHO ARE THOUGHT LIKELY TO HAVE HAD SUCH AN EXPERIENCE OR OF THOSE WHO ARE THOUGHT LIKELY NOT TO HAVE HAD IT. THE

ANSWER "No" AND THE ANSWER "YES" ARE EQUALLY IMPORTANT. The question should not, however, be asked of persons who are known to have been at any time insane, and it is not intended to include the hallucinations experienced in delirium.

No answers should be recorded of persons who have already answered a similar inquiry.

It is important not to put down second-hand answers—not to state that *A* has or has not had a hallucination on the authority of *B*, but to ask *A* himself. The name, address, sex, occupation and [approximate] age of those answering can be filled in by you (the collector) and we shall be glad if you will also put a cross against any answer known to you before asking the question. The question should not be put to persons under 21 years of age, though the answer should cover the whole life of the questioned person.

The experiences in question are believed to be rather rare, so that you will probably get few and perhaps no answers "Yes" among the 25. It will, however, greatly assist us in the second part of our work—namely, examining into the nature of the experiences—if, should you receive the answer "Yes," you will induce the person answering to fill in schedule B, of which two copies are sent with this, and of which more can be obtained from me. A separate copy of schedule B should be used for each person answering "Yes."

Should you find it impossible to collect 25 answers please return the paper filled up as far as you can. But it is much desired to obtain the answers in batches of 25 if possible.

I shall be happy to give any further information that may seem to you necessary; and if you can undertake to collect any further batches of 25 answers, or know of any one who would do so, I shall be glad to forward the necessary forms.

I am,
Yours respectfully,
WILLIAM JAMES.

☞ Please return this paper when filled-in to
PROFESSOR WILLIAM JAMES,
Cambridge, Mass.

SCHEDULE A.

QUESTION TO BE ADDRESSED BY THE COLLECTOR TO 25 PERSONS—THEIR ANSWERS BEING ENTERED BELOW.

Have you ever, when believing yourself to be completely awake, had a vivid impression of seeing, or being touched by a living being or inanimate object, or of hearing a voice; which impression, so far as you could discover, was not due to any external physical cause?

Answer (*yes* or *no*)	Name and Address of Person Answering. (Desirable in all cases, but *absolutely necessary* in case of affirmative answers. See note at foot of page.)	Sex.	Occupation.	Age.
1				
2				
etc.				

SCHEDULE B.

FURTHER QUESTIONS TO BE ADDRESSED TO ANY PERSON ANSWERING YES TO THE QUESTION OF SCHEDULE A. Namely:—Have you ever, when believing yourself to be completely awake, had a vivid impression of seeing, or being touched by a living being, or inanimate object, or of hearing a voice; which impression, so far as you could discover, was not due to any external physical cause?

1. Please state what you saw or heard or felt, and give the place, date and hour of the experience as nearly as you can.

2. How were you occupied at the time, and were you out of health or in grief or anxiety?

3. Was the impression that of some one whom you were in the habit of seeing, and do you know what he or she was doing at the time?

4. Were there other persons present with you at the time, and if so did they in any way share the experience?

5. Please state whether you have had such an experience more than once, and if so give particulars of the different occasions.

6. Any notes taken at the time, or other information about the experiences will be gratefully received.

_*[*]_* No names or addresses will be published without special permission.

> *Signature,* _____
> *Address,* _____

b. LETTER ON PUBLICITY FOR THE CENSUS (1890)

Dear Sir:—May I ask for the publicity of your pages to aid me in procuring co-operation in a scientific investigation for which I am responsible? I refer to the *Census of Hallucinations*, which was begun several years ago by the "Society for Psychical Research," and of which the International Congress of Experimental Psychology at Paris, last summer, assumed the future responsibility, naming a committee in each country to carry on the work.

The object of the inquiry is twofold: 1st, to get a mass of facts about hallucinations which may serve as a basis for a scientific study of these phenomena; and 2d, to ascertain approximately the *proportion of persons* who have had such experiences. Until the average frequency of hallucinations in the community is known, it can never be decided whether the so-called "veridical" hallucinations (visions or other "warnings" of the death, etc., of people at a distance) which are so frequently reported, are accidental coincidences or something more.

Some 8,000 or more persons in England, France and the United States have already returned answers to the question which heads the census sheets, and which runs as follows:

"Have you ever, when completely awake, had a vivid impression of seeing or being touched by a living being or inanimate object, or of hearing a voice; which impression, so far as you could discover, was not due to any external physical cause?"

The "Congress" hopes that at its next meeting, in England in 1892, as many as 50,000 answers may have been collected. It is obvious that for the purely statistical inquiry, *the answer "No" is as important as the answer "Yes."*

I have been appointed to superintend the Census in America, and I most earnestly bespeak the co-operation of any among your readers who may be actively interested in the subject. It is clear that very many volunteer canvassers will be needed to secure success. Each census blank contains instructions to the collector and places for twenty-five names; and special blanks for the "Yes" cases are furnished in addition. I shall be most happy to supply these blanks to any one who will be good enough to make application for them to

Yours truly,

Professor WM. JAMES,

Harvard University, Cambridge, Mass.

c. THE NAME HALLUCINATION (1890)

I find that the use of the word "hallucination," in my appeal for help in the "Census of Hallucinations," is giving rise to misunderstanding, and is even interpreted by some Spiritualists to imply that the question whether any apparitions have an objective origin or significance is prejudged in advance by those in charge of the investigation. As such a misunderstanding may deprive me of much valuable testimony, I beg to offer a few words which may clear away the mistake.

One cannot put everything into the title that is to be in the book. It was necessary to have some short name for the census, and out of many names, all in some degree objectionable, the name hallucination was chosen as covering *more* of the elements intended to be covered by the investigation than any other single word. "Apparitions" or "Spectral Appearances" would have excluded perceptions of any other sense than sight, whereas voices, touches, etc., are quite as important and almost as frequent as visions. "Ghosts" would surely have limited the number of our "yes" answers a good deal more than "hallucinations" can limit them. The use of the name "Census of Hallucinations" began, your readers ought to know, with Mr. Edmund Gurney, who in his book, *Phantasms of the Living*, has given copious grounds for his belief that many hallucinations are veridical, *i.e.*, connected with real events such as deaths or accidents happening at a distance to the people who are heard or who appear. He proposed the census in order to test whether or no waking hallucinations of various sorts are frequent enough in the community to warrant our regarding these veridical cases as chance coincidences. The commoner they are the more chance there would be of explaining the "truth-telling" hallucinations as accidental coincidences with the fact. In other words the more "noes" and the fewer "yeses" there are in the census-sheets the

60

greater will be the probability of genuine spirit appearance. The purpose of the statistical inquiry would, therefore, be frustrated altogether if collectors were to pick and choose amongst their friends either for positive or negative cases. They must take people just as they accidently present themselves and write down every answer as it comes.

The census-sheets themselves are perfectly explicit; and it seems to me that the question which heads them ought to dispel all doubt as to the meaning of the title. It runs thus:

"Have you ever, when believing yourself to be completely awake, had a vivid impression of seeing, or being touched by a living being or inanimate object, or of hearing a voice; which impression, so far as you could discover, was not due to any external, physical cause?"

False perceptions due to external, physical causes are technically named "illusions." The word "hallucination" means a false perception due to a non-physical cause. The cause may possibly be intra-cerebral altogether, as when a man sees vermin in delirium tremens, or as when like Martin Luther and a living friend of mine, he suddenly sees the devil with perfect distinctness before him; or it may possibly be due to telepathic impact, as Mr. Gurney supposes, from a distant mind; or finally it may possibly be due to a spirit presence which reveals itself in no other way.

All such possibilities are covered by the word hallucination. The element of errors connated by the word is that of perceiving a physical object to be there. I wish *The Journal* might find space for Professor Henry Sidgwick's remarks on the use of the word hallucination. They are to be found in the S.P.R. *Proceedings*, Part xv, Dec. 1889, pp. 8–9.

CAMBRIDGE, Mass.

Professor Sidgwick's remarks to which Professor James refers, are as follows:

We require some one general term, and the best that we can find to include all the species is "Hallucination." I admit the word to be open to some objection; because some people naturally understand from it that the impression so described is entirely false and morbid. But I need not say to readers of *"Phantasms"* that this is not our view: many of these experiences—though doubtless they all involve some disturbance of the normal action of the nervous system—have no traceable connection with disease of any kind: and a certain number of them are, as we hold, reasonably regarded as "veridical" or truth-telling; they imply in the percipient a capacity above the normal of receiving knowledge, under certain rare conditions.

Why, then, it may be asked, do we use a term that implies erroneous and illusory belief? I answer, first, because in every experience that we call a Hallucination there is an element of erroneous belief, though it may be only momentary, and though it may be the means of communicating a truth that could not otherwise have been known. If I seem to see the form of a friend pass through my room, I must have momentarily the false belief that his physical organism is occupying a portion of the space of my room, though a moment's reflection may convince me that this is not so, and though I may immediately draw the inference that he is passing through a crisis of life some miles off, and this inference may turn out to be true. In the case of a recurrent Hallucination known to be such, we cannot say that the false belief ever completely dominates the percipient's mind; but still, I conceive, it is partially there; here is an appearance that has to be resisted by memory and judgment.

It is, then, this element of error—perhaps only momentary and partial —which is implied in our term "Hallucination," and so much will be admitted by most intelligent believers in ghosts: for there are few of such believers who really hold that a ghost is actually seen as an ordinary material object is seen: *i.e.*, that it affects the percipient's eyes from the outside by reflecting rays of light on them. But we wish even those ghost-seers who hold this belief to have no difficulty in answering "Yes" to our general question: and therefore in framing it we avoided the word "Hallucination," though we have thought ourselves justified in using it in the "Instructions to Collectors" at the back of the paper.

And all would certainly admit that in many cases "Hallucination" is the only proper term. For instance, one of our informants saw a hand and arm apparently suspended from the ceiling—the owner of the real counterpart of this hand and arm being alive and heard at the time moving about in the next room.

The word "apparition" is, no doubt, a neutral word that might be used of all visual experiences of this kind; but it could only be used of visual cases. Usage would not allow us to apply it to apparent sounds or apparent touches.

I think, then, that we must use "hallucinations of the senses" as a general term for the experiences we are collecting: meaning simply to denote by it a sensory effect which we cannot attribute to any external physical cause of the kind that would ordinarily produce this effect. In

some cases we can refer it clearly to a physical cause within the organism
—some temporary or permanent physical condition. In other cases—
quite apart from telepathy—it is equally clear that the cause is primarily
psychical. For instance, in the case of persons who have been hypnotised,
it may result from a post-hypnotic order. Thus in an article by Mr.
Gurney, in *Proceedings*, Part XII., pp. 12, 13, there is an interesting
account of the result of a suggestion made by him to a subject named
Zillah in the hypnotic trance, that she would have a hallucination of
him at a certain fixed time on the following day; and there is a letter
from Zillah's mistress describing the surprise caused to Zillah by seeing
Mr. Gurney come into the kitchen and say "Good-afternoon," at the
appointed time. Here we can trace the origin of the idea which thus
externalised itself. In other cases, as with the arm above mentioned,
the idea arises spontaneously by association or otherwise in the mind.
In other cases, again, the idea which thus externalises itself may, as we
believe, come into the mind from the mind of a person at a distance—
the idea of a dying friend reaching us from his mind and rising above
the threshold of consciousness in the form of a hallucination, just as
the idea of Mr. Gurney rose above the threshold of consciousness in
Zillah's case in the form of a hallucination. A link between the two is
afforded by those rare and interesting cases, of which several have been
recorded in the publications of our Society, where one person is able
from a distance and by a mental process alone to cause an apparition of
himself to another. We have reason to think that the resulting sensory
effect is in all these cases essentially the same, though the cause of it
is very different in different cases; and, therefore, in the present state of
our knowledge, it seems best to apply the term "hallucination" to all.

d. The Statistical Inquiry into Hallucinations in America (1892)

The statistical inquiry into Hallucinations was conducted in
America by Professor W. James and Mr. R. Hodgson.

Answers were received as shown in the following table.

Table I. Proportion of affirmative to negative answers.

Answers received.	No.	Yes.	Total number of answers.	Percentage of affirmative answers.
From men	3,334	411	3,745	10.97
From women	2,125	441	2,566	17.14
Total	5,459	852	6,311	13.50

The table shows merely the number of answers actually received, and has not yet been corrected for the various sources of error mentioned in the English report.

e. REVIEW OF *Ueber die Trugwahrnehmung,*
BY EDMUND PARISH (1895)

Ueber die Trugwahrnehmung (Hallucination und Illusion) mit besonderer Berücksichtigung der internationalen Enquête über Wachhallucination bei Gesunden. EDMUND PARISH. Leipzig, Abel, 1894 [Schriften d. Ges. f. psych. Forschung, Heft 7–8; II. Sammlung]. Pp. 246.

The erudition of Herr Parish's work is exemplary and admirable, and in its text and footnotes it is safe to say that one may find reference to everything, important and unimportant, that in recent years has been written on hallucinations from either the medical or the psychological point of view. The author's personal contributions to the subject are animated by the laudable desire to minimize mysteries and to explain the exceptional phenomena of which he treats by the laws of ordinary mental life. The important points in the book are, first, Herr Parish's general theory of the hallucinatory process, a theory which he applies to all possible cases; and second, his verdict of *non liquet* upon the telepathic theory of veridical hallucinations maintained by the English 'psychical researchers.'

His theory of the hallucinatory process is that it is always an incident of 'dissociated' conditions of consciousness. By a dissociated condition he means one in which ordinary channels of association are obstructed. Reviewing the conditions under which hallucination is apt to occur, he finds them predominantly to be of this sort. In sleep, in the borderland between sleeping and waking, in melancholy, in hysteria, epilepsy, the delirium of fever, of fasting, and of certain narcotic poisonings, in hypnotism and crystal gazing, the fact of obstructed associations is admitted by all. Even in mania and drunkenness, where association seems at first sight rampant enough, this is chiefly verbal association, and objective thought is enfeebled and slow. The way in which dissociation facilitates hallucination is according to Herr P., this[1]: A stimulus is always drafted off into the

[1] Herr P. expressly bases his theory on that of the hallucinatory process given in James' *Principles of Psychology*, II, 114 ff. [WORKS, pp. 757 ff.].

64

most pervious paths at the time being. In normal association these are the most habitual paths. But there are always many stimuli at work, and many 'cerebrostatical' conditions determining perviousness, so that the final process aroused by a stimulus is the result of an intricate array of factors. Whatever path is followed *to a pause*, gives there a vivid sensible content which, in normal cases, involves a veracious perception of the object from which the stimulus comes. But if at any moment a dissociative condition is realized, so that the usual paths are blocked, whilst at the same moment other accidental paths are in a state of exalted tension from inner causes, then into these latter the stimulus discharges its energy, making them explode with the maximum of force; so that the result is the perception of an object having no usual connection with the stimulus, and by the vividness of which the consciousness of the latter may be eclipsed. The reigning state of obstructed association moreover weakens the subject's critical reaction, and the false perception is not only experienced but believed. This theory is ably defended by our author, and has the merit of being very general, and of bringing hallucinations and illusions under a common law.

Do the sporadic waking hallucinations inquired into by the 'Census' of the International Congress of Psychologists easily fit under this law? Our author tries to make them do so. First he attacks the truth of the Census, in which 'borderland' cases are hardly more than half as numerous as the 'waking' cases. Considering this to be *a priori* impossible, he explains the actual statistics plausibly enough by the greater tendency of the borderland cases to be forgotten (it being already demonstrated that the majority of all hallucinations *are* forgotten). Next, taking the alleged waking cases, he shows by a number of examples that in them also dreaminess or some other dissociated consciousness may be supposed—The Subject was 'fixating' something, if no stronger reason can be alleged. I must say that Herr Parish seems to me here to drive his theory a little too hard. Many of the narratives so distinctly belong to normal consciousness, that the better tactics would be to discredit their veracity altogether; and this method also, Herr Parish applies vigorously to the particular class of hallucinations called veridical or coincidental (*e.g.*, with the death of the person perceived).

Prof. Royce's suggestion that the narratives are often due to 'pseudo-presentiment' (false belief, after the death has happened, that it had been symbolized by an apparition previously) is made liberal use of, in spite of its almost absolutely conjectural character. The much sounder objection follows that genuinely occurring hallucinations are equipped afterwards, by the retrospective imagination of their percipients, with details that fit those of the event with which, when it happens, they are supposed to be connected. This especially applies to them where they are collective, the different percipients obeying each other's suggestion as to what they saw. Finally the false appearance of frequency of hallucinations of the coincidental class is explained by the far greater tendency of the non-coincidentals to become forgotten, the coincidentals resisting oblivion. Furthermore, Herr Parish contends that the 'frequency' of the coincidentals should in any discussion as to their being due to chance be set down as the ratio of their number to that of hallucinations of all varieties, and not to that of their own variety, which in the argument of the English committee is defined as that of 'apparitions of recognized living persons.' For all these reasons, Herr Parish concludes, the alleged frequency of the veridical class of hallucinations becomes so reduced as to form no argument against the genuine cases among them being due to chance. Moreover, he adds, we cannot lump the cases in one order of probability. Where for example the percipient is the anxious child of an aged parent ill with pneumonia, the chances are that if she have an hallucination at all, it will have that parent for its subject.

Herr Parish's criticisms are partly based on the provisional report of the English committee published at the International Congress of 1892. The committee have themselves considered such objections in their final report, which forms the subject of our next article. So I will immediately proceed to give some account of that. I will say meanwhile that this German critic's tone is uniformly respectful; that he himself prints the 59-yes cases of the Munich Census, of which 11 are more or less coincidental; and finally that his work is the most solid existing contribution to the subject up to the date of the report whose title follows below.

f. REVIEW OF THE "REPORT ON THE CENSUS OF HALLUCINATIONS" (1895)

Report on the Census of Hallucinations. H. SIDGWICK, A. JOHNSON, F. W. H. MYERS, F. PODMORE, E. M. SIDGWICK. Proceedings of the Society for Psychical Research. Part XXVI. Aug., 1894. Vol. X, pp. 25–422.

This extraordinarily thorough and accurate piece of work is understood to be the fruit mainly of Mrs. Sidgwick's labors; and the present reviewer, who has had a little experience of his own with the 'Census,' and knows something of its difficulties, may be allowed to pay his tribute of admiration to the energy and skill with which that lady and the other members of the committee have executed their burdensome task. They collected no fewer than 17,000 answers to the question: have you had, when awake, etc., an hallucination, etc. Of these answers 2,272 were 'yes,' and these Yes-cases were corresponded with or interviewed or in other ways subjected to as critical a scrutiny as circumstances allowed. The result is an unusually careful handling of the raw material offered, and a great accession of new facts. The census of hallucination was, as is well known, an idea of the late Edmund Gurney, who thought that the theory of chance-coincidence applied to 'apparitions' reported as occurring on the day of death of the person appearing might be tested by statistics. Gurney himself collected 5,705 answers, and, applying statistical reasoning to them, thought it superabundantly proved that the 'veridical' cases amongst them were too frequent to be due to chance. The Sidgwick report, unlike that of Herr Parish, keeps the Gurney question well to the front, and its general discussion of the physiological and other conditions of the hallucinatory process is less erudite and elaborate than that of the German writer.

I will quote immediately the conclusions of the report as to apparitions at the time of death. "We have 30 death-coincidences in 1,300 cases [of visual hallucination of recognized living persons], or about 1 in 43. But chance would . . . produce death-coincidences at the rate of 1 in 19,000 apparitions of recognised living persons, and 1 in 43 is equivalent to about 440 in 19,000, or 440 times the most probable number. Or, looking at the matter in a different way, we should expect that if death-coincidences only occur by chance, it will require 30 times 19,000, or 570,000 apparitions of living persons to produce 30 such coincidences. . . . We conclude then that the number of death-coincidences in our collection, if our estimate of them is accepted as fair, is not due to chance. This will not be maintained by anyone with the most elementary acquaintance with the doctrine of chances. The opponent of a telepathic or other supernormal explanation must take one of three other lines of argument, . . . even one death-coincidence being more than we should be justified in expecting chance to produce in a collection ten times the size of ours" (pp. 247–8).

Everything in this conclusion depends on the numerical premises being severally reached in legitimate ways.

In the first place, take the assumption that out of 19,000 apparitions of the sort considered, only 1 should be expected to occur on the day of death of the person seen. This is based on the mean death-rate of England. Since in England the mean annual death-rate at present is 19.15 per 1,000 of population, the mean daily death-rate must be 365 times less, or 1 in about 19,000. All daily operations concerning persons, if not directly contingent upon their death, would under these conditions be more likely to strike the living than the dying in the proportion of 19,000 to 1, and this no matter how frequent or infrequent absolutely such operations should prove to be. Apparitions are operations concerning persons; and whether such apparitions be as frequent as dreams, or whether they be very rare, whether a large fraction or a small fraction of the population be visited by them, we should expect (if they be due to mere chance) always to find this proportion observed, that only 1/19,000 of them should be of people who were dying on the day when their apparition took place. [This 'day' is measured in the report by the 12 hours preceding and the 12 hours following the death.] To the present writer this reasoning and computation seem valid.[1]

---

[1] In particular does the contention of Herr Parish (see the article on him, above, *ad finem*) seem inadmissible. He says that in estimating the probability that apparitions at the time of death are due to something more than chance we ought to measure their frequency by the ratio of their number to that of *the aggregate of all phantasms of whatsoever description*. He would even include illusions, since the process of illusion and hallucination are for him fundamentally the same. To base an argument on the ratio between the number of veridical death-apparitions and that of merely *all apparitions of recognized living persons*, he says, is a *petitio principii*. The point is a subtle one, and may well make one momentarily hesitate, but reflection leaves no permanent doubt. We have three orders of frequency in hallucinations to consider, that of hallucinations at large, that of hallucinations of persons, and that of hallucinations of dying persons. These may be caused by their respective objects, or may come at 'random,' their causes lying exclusively in the subjective cycle. The point is to see whether anything in the frequency itself can help us to decide which of these alternatives is the true one. Now with what frequency in outer things might these frequencies in hallucinations keep tally in the two cases, of outer causation and of no outer causation respectively? Obviously if persons do not cause hallucinations of themselves, the hallucinations of persons should be *no more* frequent among hallucinations than persons are frequent among all the things that may become objects of hallucinations; whilst on the contrary, if persons, and

Next, how are the numbers 1,300, for the whole number of visual apparitions of recognized living persons, and 30 for the coincidental ones among them, established? Neither of these numbers is that of the crude face of the census-returns, each being a number estimated by applying certain corrections to those returns, the corrections all being such as to weight the figures in favor of chance-coincidence as far as this can with any plausibility be done. The crude returns certainly include an unduly large percentage of coincidental apparitions, partly because a large number of non-coincidental ones are speedily forgotten and do not figure in the returns, and partly because, of the coincidental ones, some are likely to have been put in by careless collectors on account of that character, and not to have simply turned up in the census-taking by due process of chance. Now can any definite estimate be made of the amount of error that has crept into the census from these sources? The authors of the report find, by comparing the dates of the returns, that cases are the more frequent the more recent they are. This proves a forgetfulness increasing with antiquity. The obvious remedy would be, ascertaining what recent period could be taken as trustworthy, to find out how many hallucinations had visited the persons figuring in the census during that time, and then to treat the earlier part of their lives as if, in spite of their yielding smaller 'returns,' they must really have included as large

---

persons alone, do cause hallucinations, then hallucinations of persons *should* be relatively more frequent than other hallucinations, because the causation by the real outer object would be simply added, for this class alone, to the random inner causes that produce hallucinations in general. Similarly if the deaths of persons do not tend to cause hallucinations of those persons, the hallucinations of the dying should be *no more* frequent among hallucinations of persons than the dying themselves are frequent among persons; whilst if on the contrary the dying, and the dying alone among persons, do cause hallucinations of themselves, then these hallucinations should be more frequent among hallucinations of persons than the dying are among the whole population of persons. This latter ratio is what the Sidgwick committee finds realized in fact; hence its conclusion that the dying do cause hallucinations of themselves. Herr Parish's selection of the total number of hallucinations *überhaupt* as one subjective term of comparison leads to a statistical test which is also true in theory, *provided the corresponding objective terms be altered to match*. We shall then have (if dying persons do *not* cause hallucinations of themselves) this proportion: As is the ratio of real dying persons to all other real things, so at its highest should be the ratio of hallucinations of the dying to all other hallucinations whatsoever. But although there is no theoretic objection to this proportion, it is practically worthless, because we have no statistical data by which to compute the ratio of dying persons to all other real things.

a number, proportionally, of similar experiences. Taking the past 3 months as the truthworthy period, and considering visual cases alone, the authors of the report agree that the face-returns should be multiplied by 4, in order to represent the true number of 'apparitions' seen by their informants. But, as the total number of specifically described apparitions of recognized living persons returned in the census equals 350, and 350 x 4 = 1,400, the round number of 1,300* may be taken as probably near the figure sought.[2]

The whole number of death-coincidences amongst the 350 cases in question is 65, or 62 when 3 cases known to be selected by their collectors are struck out. There is no ground for supposing that death-coincidences tend to be forgotten by their percipients: On the contrary the cases appearing in the census date with disproportionate frequency from by-gone decades. This, of course, may be due to the fact that the number 62 is too small to give true averages when distributed over the 36 years covered. But to be on the side of severity the committee assume that the proportion reported from the last decade is the only normal one, and that the earlier stories may be false, and (by a computation based on figures which need not here be reproduced) they knock off 22 on this account from the total of death-apparitions to be used, and make it 40 instead of 62, just the opposite treatment to that which they applied to the gross group of 350 cases of which these death-cases are a part. From these 40 they again knock off 8 as an ample allowance for possibly unreported selection on the collector's part,[3] and again 2 for good measure and as a sop to the adversary, so that finally the reduced number of 'veridicals' to be compared with the augmented number of veridicals and non-veridicals taken together, falls to the figure 30

---

* See "A Correction," below, for this figure of 1,300.—F.B.

[2] The period of three months is found trustworthy when 'suspicious' cases are eliminated. Suspicious cases are those where the appearance may not have been an hallucination. Figures seen in a bad light, or through an open door in passing, or at a distance in the open air, are included in this category. Study of the cases reported to have occurred within three months of the accounts given, shows that these 'suspicious' ones are rarest in the first month, and are therefore presumably peculiarly liable to oblivescence. But if they are counted in, one month and not three months becomes the trustworthy period, and the multiplier of the crude returns must then be changed from 4 to 6 1/2. The influence of this counting of suspicious cases is considerably to enlarge the total of hallucinations to be supposed, and to make the odds in favor of the coincidental ones being due to something else than chance sink from 440 to 292 against 1.

[3] The data for computing this number of 8 are given on p. 243 of the report.

which is used in the conclusion quoted from the report on a previous page.

The reader will appreciate the candor of the committee, and see how earnestly they have sought to eliminate all that might add specious color, as distinguished from real weight, to their own side. The reader whom their argument does not impress will have, they say, to take one of three courses. He may deny the accuracy of the coincidental cases, to which the reply of the committee consists in printing 31 good ones as a sample. He may still insist that the collectors have loaded their returns with an excessive number of these cases, to which the reply is too minute for quotation here (pp. 57 and 210 of the Report) but amounts to a detailed proof that there is probably no overloading of the returns in general with *yeses*, and to good reason shown for the opinion that of the 62 coincidental apparitions taken as a basis for the enquiry, at most 10 can be assumed as possibly added deliberately by the collectors to their returns. But these have been eliminated in the reduced number of 30, finally admitted to count in the argument.—Thirdly the objector may say that many of the veridical apparitions *are* causally connected with the death, but not by telepathy or any other *vis occulta*. The illness of an aged person is the cause both of death and of anxiety among relatives. Anxiety is proved by the committee's own facts to predispose to hallucination;[4] so both the hallucination in such cases and the death can be common effects of a single natural cause, the illness, working on two persons. This, it will be remembered, is Parish's final objection, mentioned above; and the report treats it as important. At the same time the authors point out that there are but 23 cases of the 62 veridicals in which the illness was known beforehand, and only in some of these was there anxiety. Moreover the close coincidence *in hour* of the death with the apparition in so many cases seems to preclude the application on a large scale of a cause like anxiety which in the nature of things must have lasted many hours or days.[5]

---

[4] Anxiety about illness was probably present in 89 out of the 1,622 cases of which there are first-hand accounts, and grief about death in 42 of the other cases, making nearly 1/12 of the whole number. As we don't spend 1/12 of our lives in grief and anxiety of these sorts it must be that during these emotions hallucinations come with undue frequency.

[5] Mere expectation, which often causes illusions, seems to play no important part in causing hallucinations. At least the committee find only 14 cases in the whole

It will thus be seen that the committee have considered on their own account all the difficulties urged by Herr Parish (with the exception of the 'pseudo-presentiment' hypothesis of Royce) and that they have considered them in a more objective and less conjectural way than he, without their case being weakened to any certain extent.[6] Plainly, though, if the 30 cases left to be used in the argument could all have been first-class cases (with record of hallucination before event, no anxiety, etc.) the argument would have been more convincing. But the successive weedings of the crude number 62 could not be performed selectively so as to accomplish just this result, and the Census is therefore still too small for *knock-down* proof of occult cause. If telepathy be regarded on other grounds as possible, then these statistics make it extremely probable. Otherwise they will not convert the disbeliever, who will pooh-pooh the statistical method *in toto* when it takes 17,000 answers to get 30 good cases to cipher with, saying that the field is too vast and lean for profitable reaping, that figures got by applying so many hypothetical corrections to inaccurate crude data, savor too much of guess-work to inspire confidence, and that cooked returns are cooked returns, even though, like these, they be cooked for the safe side, the side adverse to the conclusion reached by their means.[7]

---

collection where the phantasm was of a person for whose arrival the percipient was looking out. They give cases where 'suggestion' may be reckoned a cause (collective cases, prediction of apparition at spiritist seance, etc.), but these are ambiguous, and if occult agency be once admitted as a possibility, are perhaps as likely to be caused by that as by 'suggestion.'

6 The only criticism I can make is that the committee have possibly been too indulgent to the cases where the percipient was in bed. His conviction that he was awake is to be taken with large allowance under these circumstances.

7 The figure 4, for example, used as a multiplier of the crude returns in correction of forgetfulness, is reached by this process: out of 87 visual hallucinations reported for the most recent year, 42 are stated to have occurred within the most recent quarter, and of these 19 within the most recent month, and 12 within the most recent half-month; numbers which correspond approximately to 168, 228, and 288 per annum instead of 87. But if from the 87 the 'suspicious' cases as described above are eliminated, and the most recent quarter examined, the figures are much more even. There are 12 suspicious cases in the recent quarter; so that then 30 instead of 42 becomes the number to be counted in the quarter. Of these the last month shows 12, and the last half-month 5, numbers which correspond to 120, 144, and 120 per annum respectively. This looks like distribution by 'natural law,' *provided the evenness of the figures be not accidental.* But where such small numbers are involved, how can one be sure on that point?

This sort of reception by the hard-hearted is inevitable, and it is useless to ask how strictly logical it may be, for belief follows psychological and not logical laws. A single veridical hallucination experienced by one's self or by some friend who tells one all the circumstances has more influence over the mind than the largest calculated numerical probability either for or against. I can testify to this from direct observation. The case will, therefore, still hang pending before public opinion, in spite of the laborious industry of Mrs. Sidgwick and her colleagues. Of course if the results of the American Census, not yet published, should correspond, that will add retroactive weight. But the most that can be said, so far, in the opinion of the present writer, is this, that the Sidgwick report affords *a most formidable presumption* that veridical hallucinations are due to something more than chance. Now this means that the telepathic theory, and whatever other occult theories may offer themselves, have fairly conquered the right to a patient and respectful hearing before the scientific bar; and no one with any real conception of what the word 'Science' means, can fail to realize the profound issues which such a fact as this may involve.

g. A CORRECTION (1895)

On p. 72 of the last number of the *Psychological Review* an omission was made in my abstract of the Sidgwick report on hallucinations which makes the calculated figure of 1300 on line 9 from the top of the page [*ed.*, 70.8] unintelligible. The figure calculated from the premises which I quote is 1400, for which my text substitutes 1300 with no motive assigned. The motive obeyed by the authors of the report is the probable untrustworthiness of accounts of apparitions falling within the first ten years of the informant's life. Such visions are subtracted by the committee both from the total number of recognized apparitions and from the number of coincidental apparitions [See *Proceedings* of S.P.R., pp. 65, 247]. They form 8 per cent. of the former, so that my abstract of the calculation should have dealt with 92/100 of 350 instead of 350. This makes 322, a figure which multiplied by 4 gives 1288. For this the committee substitute 1300, as a 'round number,' slightly more favorable to the adversary.

W.J.

h. Final American Report: Letter to Henry Sidgwick (1896)

95 Irving Street, Cambridge (Mass.)
July 11. 1896

My dear Sidgwick,

I understand you to be about to refer to the Census of Hallucinations at Munich, and I have therefore been working for 10 days over our mass of material in order to give you our american figure to quote in corroboration of your own against the probability of chance coincidence, in case you care to do so. Our absolute figures are much smaller than yours, but the ratio of the actual probability to the chance-probability is not very different from your own figure.

Our figures are as follows:

Total number of answers: 7123
Total of yes-es: 1051
(% of yes-es 14.75)

Of these yes-es 429 were without particulars, and in 36 the percipient had not signed the account. Only 586 subjects thus remained for statistical treatment.

Of these, eliminating

1) all who had the experience before they were 10 years old; and
2) all who gave vaguely plural experiences,

there remain 62 subjects with *71 cases of visual hallucination of some recognized living person.* Of these, *12 are reported to have occurred on the day of the death of the person seen.*

These numbers are so small that I have not ventured to reduce them by any elimination of "suspicious" cases, as you did, but as a correction for oblivion I have multiplied the whole lot by your figure of 6 1/2.

$71 \times 6 \ 1/2 = 462$ (in round numbers)

Let this 462 represent the probable whole number of visual hallucinations of living friends really seen by the percipients since their 10th birthday. The 12 veridicals are in round numbers 1/39 of 462. Therefore 1/39 is the probability due to the unknown cause of apparitions that if a man "appear" at all it will be on his death-day.

On the other hand (the U.S. death rate being practically the same as that of England) the *pure chance* that he may so appear is only 1/19,000. But $1/39 = 1/19,000 \times 487$; so that *apparitions on the day of death are, according to our statistics, 487 times more numerous than pure chance ought to make them.*

The details will be sent to the *Proceedings* later, but I append now a few remarks. Of the 71 cases, all but the 12 that were death-apparitions are treated as insignificant in the statistical result. But this, though inevitable, is unfair to an occultist theory of their origin, since 16 of them, though not veridical of death, were coincidental in other ways. *E.g.* 6 were collective; 2 were reciprocal; one was voluntarily produced by the distant agent; 2 were premonitory; and 3 were veridical, but not of death. But let this pass. There remains another unfairness to occultism in our systematic rejection of all vaguely plural cases. I rejected 19 percipients in all for this reason; but 7 of them gave us coincidental cases, 2 of these being apparitions at time of death.

We can afford to be very generous. Suppose we throw in these 19 subjects as if each stood for 1 non-coincidental case—$19 + 71 = 90$; suppose we multiply for oblivion by 10 instead of 6 1/2, making 900 cases in all; suppose we take only 1/2 of our 12 veridicals: we still get $6/900 = 1/150 = 126$ times $1/19,000$ the chance-probability.

The objections are

1. *Smallness of numbers.* But the agreement of our figures with yours goes against this.

2. *The collectors packed their sheets with veridicals.* Actually, they say they knew the answer beforehand in 3, possibly in 4 cases. In 5 cases they state their ignorance. In 3 they say nothing. From the warning against packing with yeses and the very large number of veridicals that the collectors furnished *separately*, this objection is probably not very important.

3. *The veridical cases are not strong.* They are not. Only 5 have any corroboration, and in no case is it first rate. Our best cases are not among these. But this is an argument at any rate in favor of the sincerity of the Census; and since coincidentals and non-coincidentals are treated homogeneously (at least all the deliberate treatment going *against* the statistical result where they are treated *otherwise* than similarly) the ratio of the surface-figures is perhaps a fair one.

But I never believed and do not now believe that these figures will ever conquer disbelief. They are only useful to rebut the dogmatic assurance of the scientists that the death warnings are chance coincidences. Better call them lies, and have done with it, if you *must* be "rigorously scientific."

Our census has been a terribly slouchy piece of work, and comparing it with yours makes me blush throughout. I did n't clearly foresee the exact line of argument at first, mistrusted the value of the whole thing and let the correspondence get into arrears, in spite of the weeks and weeks of time I gave to it. The result is a mass of uncorroborated stuff. Our correspondents obstinately refused to reply in a great many cases. I don't advise any other country to take up the job. Irreproachable results would require too enormous an amount of labor.

Best regards to both you and Mrs Sidgwick. I hope you'll enjoy the Congress. I wish I could be there. But I have to stay here and sweat, tired as I am. Miss Edmunds and Hodgson, especially Miss E., have put a lot of work into the Census. She ought to have worked at it from the first.

Always truly yours,
Wm. James

i. REVIEW OF *Zur Kritik des telepathischen Beweismaterials* AND *Hallucinations and Illusions*, BY EDMUND PARISH (1897)

Zur Kritik des telepathischen Beweismaterials. EDMUND PARISH. Leipzig, Barth, 1897. 8°. Pp. 48.

Hallucinations and Illusions, a Study of the Fallacies of Perception. EDMUND PARISH. London, Walter Scott; New York, Charles Scribner's Sons. 1897. 12°. Pp. 390.

The English version of Mr. Parish's book, already reviewed in its German shape in Vol. II, p. 65 of this *Review*, is greatly improved and brought up to date. The author incorporates in it much of the criticism contained in the lecture '*Zur Kritik*,' etc. He was collector for Germany of the Census of Hallucinations reviewed there and in the present lecture he criticizes the Sidgwick report. Although he gives the authors credit in the handsomest terms for the quality of their work, he nevertheless thinks that their conclusion—that apparitions on the day of death are far too frequent to be ascribed to chance—will not hold good. His chief reasons are as follows: First, they have believed the reported amount of coincidence between the apparition and the event to be greater than facts warrant.

He gives cases to show how a figure, not recognized when seen, may be described, when news of a death is later received, as the figure of the person dead. This error, which he calls *Erinnerungs-adaptation*, he believes to be very frequent in the narratives. Secondly, he doubts whether most of the hallucinations which figure as veridical are *waking* hallucinations at all, believing them to be more probably dreams or hypnagogic visions. But if dreams are to slip in and get counted, the numerical statistical argument, he says, is entirely upset; for dreams are such frequent occurrences that coincidences between them and distant events must be frequent in proportion. And that the so-called waking hallucinations *were* mostly dreams, he proves in detail by analyzing the 26 cases which the English report prints as 'best accredited.' Most of them actually occurred at night, when the percipient was in bed or sitting up watching, or else in some other situation where a nap might naturally have occurred unawares.

This latter seems to me by far the strongest objection yet made to the Sidgwick report. In my own review of the Sidgwick report (*supra*, Vol. II, p. 74, note), I admitted this to be its weakest point.

But another objection of Herr Parish's, and the one which he himself considers his weightiest, seems to me to have very little weight indeed. He shows, by three examples, through what subconscious links of association, granting the hallucinatory tendency to be there, the ensuing hallucination may have its subject-matter determined, and then says: Not till *the possibility of all such associative links is excluded,* are we entitled to invoke an hypothetic agency like 'telepathic impact' as the cause of the hallucinatory content. But one does not see how this should affect the statistical argument, unless associative links are in themselves more likely than unassigned organic or other causes to produce visions *coincidental with deaths*. If the mental associations of the percipient belong to a cycle of events disconnected with the cycle concerned in the distant person's death, it remains as improbable as ever that the several outcomes of the two cycles coincident in content should also coincide so often in *date*. That they actually do so shows, according to Mr. Parish, a methodical flaw in the Sidgwick report. Its authors accept as an empirical fact (with a slight correction for oblivion) the measure of frequency given by the Census for visions of recognized persons, and then proceed to cipher out the improbability that any one such vision will occur by accident on the day when its object dies. But they ought rather, says their German critic, to have ciphered out, from the number of *such coincidences* as an empirical fact *what the real frequency*, as distinguished from the recollected and reported frequency, of the visions must actually have been. This would give (as I apply his reasoning) the figure of 35 hallucinations at least, of the species immediately discussed, to each adult in the community, and 60 times that number, or over 2,000 miscellaneous hallucinations of all kinds to each head of population,[1] most of which we must suppose to be forgotten immediately, if the reasoning is to be seriously applied to facts. Mr. Parish, of course, would not so apply it, for the result is absurd and incredible. He only makes a logical nut of it for the other side to crack, disbelieving himself that the returns of the Census have any definite numerical value at all. In this contemptuous estimate I cannot possibly agree.

---

[1] The computation is this: By the English figures 17,000 persons yielded 32 death-visions, each of which had only 1 pure chance in 19,000 of occurring when it did. To produce the 32 happy chances there must, therefore, have been 19,000 x 32 such visions in the whole 17,000 persons, or 19,000 x 32 + 17,000 = 35.7 such visions in each one of the 17,000. But, since the 32 death-visions were extracted from 1,942 hallucinations of all kinds experienced by the 17,000 answerers of the Census question, each answerer must have had a number of hallucinations of all kinds as much greater than 35 as 1,942 is greater than 32, which would give him approximately 2,000 hallucinations, not one of which in 9 cases out of 10 he would have remembered, for roughly 9-tenths of those questioned in the Census replied 'No.'

12

A Record of Observations of Certain Phenomena of Trance (1890)

DEAR MR. MYERS,

You ask for a record of my own experiences with Mrs. Piper, to be incorporated in the account of her to be published in your *Proceedings*. I regret to be unable to furnish you with any direct notes of sittings beyond those which Mr. Hodgson will have already supplied. I admit that in not having taken more notes I was most derelict, and can only cry *peccavi*. The excuse (if it be one) for my negligence was that I wished primarily to satisfy *myself* about Mrs. Piper; and feeling that as evidence for others no notes but steno-graphic notes would have value, and not being able to get these, I seldom took any. I still think that as far as influencing public opinion goes, the bare fact that So-and-so and So-and-so have been convinced by their personal experience that "there is something in mediumship" is the essential thing. Public opinion follows leaders much more than it follows evidence. Professor Huxley's bare "en-dorsement" of Mrs. Piper, *e.g.*, would be more effective than vol-umes of notes by such as I. Practically, however, I ought to have taken them, and the sight of your more scientific methods makes me doubly rue my sins.

Under the circumstances, the only thing I can do is to give you my present state of belief as to Mrs. Piper's powers, with a simple account from memory of the steps which have led me to it.

I made Mrs. Piper's acquaintance in the autumn of 1885. My

wife's mother, Mrs. Gibbens, had been told of her by a friend, during the previous summer, and never having seen a medium before, had paid her a visit out of curiosity. She returned with the statement that Mrs. P. had given her a long string of names of members of the family, mostly Christian names, together with facts about the persons mentioned and their relations to each other, the knowledge of which on her part was incomprehensible without supernormal powers. My sister-in-law went the next day, with still better results, as she related them. Amongst other things, the medium had accurately described the circumstances of the writer of a letter which she held against her forehead, after Miss G. had given it to her. The letter was in Italian, and its writer was known to but two persons in this country.

[I may add that on a later occasion my wife and I took another letter from this same person to Mrs. P., who went on to speak of him in a way which identified him unmistakably again. On a third occasion, two years later, my sister-in-law and I being again with Mrs. P., she reverted in her trance to these letters, and then gave us the writer's name, which she said she had not been able to get on the former occasion.]

But to revert to the beginning. I remember playing the *esprit fort* on that occasion before my feminine relatives, and seeking to explain by simple considerations the marvellous character of the facts which they brought back. This did not, however, prevent me from going myself a few days later, in company with my wife, to get a direct personal impression. The names of none of us up to this meeting had been announced to Mrs. P., and Mrs. J. and I were, of course, careful to make no reference to our relatives who had preceded. The medium, however, when entranced, repeated most of the names of "spirits" whom she had announced on the two former occasions and added others. The names came with difficulty, and were only gradually made perfect. My wife's father's name of Gibbens was announced first as Niblin, then as Giblin. A child Herman (whom we had lost the previous year) had his name spelt out as Herrin. I think that in no case were both Christian and surnames given on this visit. But the *facts predicated* of the persons named made it in many instances impossible not to recognise the particular individuals who were talked about. We took particular pains on this occasion to give the Phinuit control no help over his difficulties and to ask no leading questions. In the light of subsequent experience I believe this not to be the best policy. For it often happens, if you give this trance-personage a name or some small fact for the lack of which he is brought to a standstill, that he will then start off with a copious flow of additional talk, containing in itself an abundance of "tests."

My impression after this first visit was, that Mrs. P. was either possessed of supernormal powers, or knew the members of my wife's family by sight and had by some lucky coincidence become acquainted with such a multitude of their domestic circumstances as to produce the startling impression which she did. My later knowledge of her sittings and personal acquaintance with her has led me absolutely to reject the latter explanation, and to believe that she has supernormal powers.

I visited her a dozen times that winter, sometimes alone, sometimes with my wife, once in company with the Rev. M. J. Savage. I sent a large number of persons to her, wishing to get the results of as many *first* sittings as possible. I made appointments myself for most of these people, whose names were in no instance announced to the medium. In the spring of 1886 I published a brief "Report of the Committee on Mediumistic Phenomena" in the *Proceedings* of the American Society for Psychical Research, of which the following is an extract:—

"I have myself witnessed a dozen of her trances, and have testimony at first hand from 25 sitters, all but one of whom were virtually introduced to Mrs. P. by myself.[1] Of five of the sittings we have *verbatim* stenographic reports. Twelve of the sitters, who in most cases sat singly, got nothing from the medium but unknown names or trivial talk. Four of these were members of the Society, and of their sittings *verbatim* reports were taken. Fifteen of the sitters were surprised at the communications they received, names and facts being mentioned at the first interview which it seemed improbable should have been known to the medium in a normal way. The probability that she possessed no clue as to the sitter's identity was, I believe, in each and all of these 15 cases, sufficient. But of only one of them is there a stenographic report; so that, unfortunately for the medium, the evidence in her favour is, although more abundant, less exact in quality than some of that which will be

[1] I tried then, and have tried since, to get written accounts from these sitters, in most cases in vain. The few written statements which I have got are in Mr. Hodgson's hands, and will doubtless be sent you with the rest of the material which he will submit.

counted against her. Of these 15 sitters, five, all ladies, were blood relatives, and two (I myself being one) were men connected by marriage
with the family to which they belonged. Two other connections of this
family are included in the 12 who got nothing. The medium showed
a most startling intimacy with this family's affairs, talking of many
matters known to no one outside, and which gossip could not possibly
have conveyed to her ears. The details would prove nothing to the
reader, unless printed *in extenso*, with full notes by the sitters. It reverts, after all, to personal conviction. My own conviction is not evidence, but it seems fitting to record it. I am persuaded of the medium's
honesty, and of the genuineness of her trance; and although at first
disposed to think that the 'hits' she made were either lucky coincidences,
or the result of knowledge on her part of who the sitter was and of his
or her family affairs, I now believe her to be in possession of a power as
yet unexplained."

I also made during this winter an attempt to see whether Mrs.
Piper's medium-trance had any community of nature with ordinary
hypnotic trance. I wrote in the report:—

"My first two attempts to hypnotise her were unsuccessful. Between
the second time and the third, I suggested to her 'control' in the medium-trance that he should make her a mesmeric subject for me. He
agreed. (A suggestion of this sort made by the operator in one *hypnotic*
trance would probably have some effect on the next.) She became partially hypnotised on the third trial; but the effect was so slight that I
ascribe it rather to the effect of repetition than to the suggestion made.
By the fifth trial she had become a pretty good hypnotic subject, as far
as muscular phenomena and automatic imitations of speech and gesture
go; but I could not affect her consciousness, or otherwise get her beyond
this point. Her condition in this semi-hypnosis is very different from her
medium-trance. The latter is characterised by great muscular unrest,
even her ears moving vigorously in a way impossible to her in her waking
state. But in hypnosis her muscular relaxation and weakness are extreme. She often makes several efforts to speak ere her voice becomes
audible; and to get a strong contraction of the hand, for example, express manipulation and suggestion must be practised. The automatic
imitations I spoke of are in the first instance very weak, and only become strong after repetition. Her pupils contract in the medium-trance.
Suggestions to the 'control' that he should make her recollect after the
medium-trance what she had been saying were accepted, but had no
result. In the hypnotic-trance such a suggestion will often make the
patient remember all that has happened.

"No sign of thought-transference—as tested by card and diagram guessing—has been found in her, either in the hypnotic condition just described, or immediately after it; although her 'control' in the medium-trance has said that he would bring them about. So far as tried (only twice), no right guessing of cards in the medium-trance. No clear signs of thought-transference, as tested by the naming of cards, during the waking state. Trials of the 'willing game,' and attempts at automatic writing, gave similarly negative results. So far as the evidence goes, then, her medium-trance seems an isolated feature in her psychology. This would of itself be an important result if it could be established and generalised, but the record is obviously too imperfect for confident conclusions to be drawn from it in any direction."

Here I dropped my inquiries into Mrs. Piper's mediumship for a period of about two years, having satisfied myself that there was a genuine mystery there, but being over-freighted with time-consuming duties, and feeling that any adequate circumnavigation of the phenomena would be too protracted a task for me to aspire just then to undertake. I saw her once, half-accidentally, however, during that interval, and in the spring of 1889 saw her four times again. In the fall of 1889 she paid us a visit of a week at our country house in New Hampshire, and I then learned to know her personally better than ever before, and had confirmed in me the belief that she is an absolutely simple and genuine person. No one, when challenged, can give "evidence" to others for such beliefs as this. Yet we all live by them from day to day, and practically I should be willing now to stake as much money on Mrs. Piper's honesty as on that of anyone I know, and am quite satisfied to leave my reputation for wisdom or folly, so far as human nature is concerned, to stand or fall by this declaration.

As for the explanation of her trance-phenomena, I have none to offer. The *primâ facie* theory, which is that of spirit-control, is hard to reconcile with the extreme triviality of most of the communications. What real spirit, at last able to revisit his wife on this earth, but would find something better to say than that she had changed the place of his photograph? And yet that is the sort of remark to which the spirits introduced by the mysterious Phinuit are apt to confine themselves. I must admit, however, that Phinuit has other moods. He has several times, when my wife and myself were sitting together with him, suddenly started off on long lectures to us about our inward defects and outward shortcomings, which were very earnest, as well as subtile morally and psychologically, and impressive in a high degree. These discourses, though given in Phinuit's own person, were very different in style from his more usual talk, and probably superior to anything that the medium could produce in the same line in her natural state. Phinuit himself, however, bears every appearance of being a fictitious being. His French, so far as he has been able to display it to me, has been limited to a few phrases of salutation, which may easily have had their rise in the medium's "unconscious" memory; he has never been able to understand *my* French; and the crumbs of information which he gives about his earthly career are, as you know, so few, vague, and unlikely sounding, as to suggest the romancing of one whose stock of materials for invention is excessively reduced. He is, however, as he actually shows himself, a definite human individual, with immense tact and patience, and great desire to please and be regarded as infallible. With respect to the rough and slangy style which he so often affects, it should be said that the Spiritualistic tradition here in America is all in favour of the "spirit-control" being a grotesque and somewhat saucy personage. The *Zeitgeist* has always much to do with shaping trance-phenomena, so that a "control" of that temperament is what one would naturally expect. Mr. Hodgson will already have informed you of the similarity between Phinuit's name and that of the "control" of the medium at whose house Mrs. Piper was first entranced. The most remarkable thing about the Phinuit personality seems to me the extraordinary tenacity and minuteness of his memory. The medium has been visited by many hundreds of sitters, half of them, perhaps, being strangers who have come but once. To each Phinuit gives an hourful of disconnected fragments of talk about persons living, dead, or imaginary, and events past, future, or unreal. What normal waking memory could keep this chaotic mass of stuff together? Yet Phinuit does so; for the chances seem to be, that if a sitter should go back after years of interval, the medium, when once entranced, would recall the minutest incidents of the earlier interview, and begin by recapitulating much of what had then been said. So far as I can discover, Mrs. Piper's waking memory is not remarkable, and the whole constitution of her trance-memory is something which I am at a loss to understand. But I will say nothing more of Phinuit, because, aided by our friends in France, you are already systematically seeking to establish or disprove him as a former native of this world.

Phinuit is generally the medium of communication between other spirits and the sitter. But two other *soi-disant* spirits have, in my presence, assumed direct "control" of Mrs. Piper. One purported to be the late Mr. E. The other was an aunt of mine who died last year in New York. I have already sent you the only account I can give of my earliest experiences with the "E. control." The first messages came through Phinuit, about a year ago, when after two years of non-intercourse with Mrs. Piper, she lunched one day at our house and gave my wife and myself a sitting afterwards. It was bad enough; and I confess that the human being in me was so much stronger than the man of science that I was too disgusted with Phinuit's tiresome twaddle even to note it down. When later the phenomenon developed into pretended direct speech from E. himself I regretted this, for a complete record would have been useful. I can now merely say that neither then, nor at any other time, was there to my mind the slightest inner verisimilitude in the personation. But the failure to produce a more plausible E. speaks directly in favour of the non-participation of the medium's *conscious* mind in the performance. She could so easily have coached herself to be more effective.

Her trance-talk about my own family shows the same innocence. The sceptical theory of her successes is that she keeps a sort of detective bureau open upon the world at large, so that whoever may call is pretty sure to find her prepared with facts about his life. Few things could have been easier, in Boston, than for Mrs. Piper to collect facts about my own father's family for use in my sittings with her. But although my father, my mother, and a deceased brother were repeatedly announced as present, nothing but their bare names ever came out, except a hearty message of thanks from my father that I had "published the book." I *had* published his *Literary Remains*; but when Phinuit was asked "what book?" all he could do was to spell the letters L, I, and say no more. If it be suggested that all this was but a refinement of cunning, for that such skilfully distributed reticences are what bring most credit in to a medium, I must deny the proposition *in toto*. I have seen and heard enough of sittings to be sure that a medium's trump cards are promptitude and completeness in her revelations. It is a mistake in general (however it may occasionally, as now, be cited in her favour) to keep back anything she knows. Phinuit's stumbling, spelling, and otherwise imperfect ways of bringing out his facts is a great drawback with most sitters, and yet it is habitual with him.

The aunt who purported to "take control" directly was a much better personation, having a good deal of the cheery strenuousness of speech of the original. She spoke, by the way, on this occasion, of the condition of health of two members of the family in New York, of which we knew nothing at the time, and which was afterwards corroborated by letter. We have repeatedly heard from Mrs. Piper in trance things of which we were not at the moment aware. If the supernormal element in the phenomenon be thought-transference it is certainly not that of the sitter's *conscious* thought. It is rather the reservoir of his potential knowledge which is tapped; and not always *that*, but the knowledge of some distant living person, as in the incident last quoted. It has sometimes even seemed to me that too much intentness on the sitter's part to have Phinuit say a certain thing acts as a hindrance.

Mrs. Blodgett, of Holyoke, Mass., and her sister, devised, before the latter died, what would have been a good test of actual spirit-return. The sister, Miss H.W., wrote upon her deathbed a letter, sealed it, and gave it to Mrs. B. After her death no one living knew what words it contained. Mrs. B. not then knowing Mrs. Piper, entrusted to me the sealed letter, and asked me to give Mrs. Piper some articles of the deceased sister's personal apparel, to help her to get at its contents. This commission I performed. Mrs. P. gave correctly the full name (which even I did not know) of the writer, and finally, after a delay and ceremony which occupied several weeks on Phinuit's part, dictated what purported to be a copy of the letter. This I compared with the original (of which Mrs. B. permitted me to break the seal); but the two letters had nothing in common, nor were any of the numerous domestic facts alluded to in the medium's letter acknowledged by Mrs. Blodgett to be correct. Mrs. Piper was equally unsuccessful in two later attempts which she made to reproduce the contents of this document, although both times the revelation purported to come direct from its deceased writer. It would be hard to devise a better test than this would have been, had it immediately succeeded, for the exclusion of thought-transference from living minds.

My mother-in-law, on her return from Europe, spent a morning vainly seeking for her bank-book. Mrs. Piper, on being shortly afterwards asked where this book was, described the place so exactly that it was instantly found. I was told by her that the spirit of a boy named Robert F. was the companion of my lost infant. The F.'s were cousins of my wife living in a distant city. On my return home I mentioned the incident to my wife, saying, "Your cousin did lose a baby, didn't she? but Mrs. Piper was wrong about its sex, name, and age." I then learned that Mrs. Piper had been quite right in all those particulars, and that mine was the wrong impression. But, obviously, for the source of revelations such as these, one need not go behind the sitter's own storehouse of forgotten or unnoticed experiences. Miss X.'s experiments in crystal-gazing prove how strangely these survive. If thought-transference be the clue to be followed in interpreting Mrs. Piper's trance-utterances (and that, as far as my experience goes, is what, far more than any supramundane instillations, the phenomena *seem* on their face to be) we must admit that the "transference" need not be of the conscious or even the unconscious thought of the sitter, but must often be of the thought of some person far away. Thus, on my mother-in-law's second visit to the medium she was told that one of her daughters was suffering from a severe pain in her back on that day. This altogether unusual occurrence, unknown to the sitter, proved to be true. The announcement to my wife and brother of my aunt's death in New York before we had received the telegram (Mr. Hodgson has, I believe, sent you an account of this) may, on the other hand, have been occasioned by the sitters' conscious apprehension of the event. This particular incident is a "test" of the sort which one readily quotes; but to my mind it was far less convincing than the innumerable small domestic matters of which Mrs. Piper incessantly talked in her sittings with members of my family. With the affairs of my wife's maternal kinsfolk in particular her acquaintance in trance was most intimate. Some of them were dead, some in California, some in the State of Maine. She characterised them all, living as well as deceased, spoke of their relations to each other, of their likes and dislikes, of their as yet unpublished practical plans, and hardly ever made a mistake, though, as usual, there was very little system or continuity in anything that came out. A *normal* person, unacquainted with the family, could not possibly have said as much; one acquainted with it could hardly have avoided saying more.

The most convincing things said about my own immediate household were either very intimate or very trivial. Unfortunately the former things cannot well be published. Of the trivial things, I have forgotten the greater number, but the following, *raræ nantes*, may serve as samples of their class: She said that we had lost recently a rug, and I a waistcoat. [She wrongly accused a person of stealing the rug, which was afterwards found in the house.] She told of my killing a grey-and-white cat, with ether, and described how it had "spun round and round" before dying. She told how my New York aunt had written a letter to my wife, warning her against all mediums, and then went off on a most amusing criticism, full of *traits vifs*, of the excellent woman's character. [Of course no one but my wife and I knew the existence of the letter in question.] She was strong on the events in our nursery, and gave striking advice during our first visit to her about the way to deal with certain "tantrums" of our second child, "little Billy-boy," as she called him, reproducing his nursery name. She told how the crib creaked at night, how a certain rocking-chair creaked mysteriously, how my wife had heard footsteps on the stairs, &c., &c. Insignificant as these things sound when read, the accumulation of a large number of them has an irresistible effect. And I repeat again what I said before, that, taking everything that I know of Mrs. P. into account, the result is to make me feel as absolutely certain as I am of any personal fact in the world that she knows things in her trances which she cannot possibly have heard in her waking state, and that the definitive philosophy of her trances is yet to be found. The limitations of her trance-information, its discontinuity and fitfulness, and its apparent inability to develop beyond a certain point, although they end by rousing one's moral and human impatience with the phenomenon, yet are, from a scientific point of view, amongst its most interesting peculiarities, since where there are limits there are conditions, and the discovery of these is always the beginning of explanation.

This is all that I can tell you of Mrs. Piper. I wish it were more "scientific." But, *valeat quantum!* it is the best I can do.

13

What Psychical Research
Has Accomplished (1892)

If to have one's name knocked about in conversation and in newspapers be fame, the "Society for Psychical Research" is famous. Yet it is probable that any real acquaintance with its history, its aims, and its work hardly exists outside the narrow circle of its membership. Believing, as I do, that the Society fulfils a function which, though limited, is decidedly important in the organization of science, I am glad to give a brief account of it to the uninstructed reader.

According to the newspaper and drawing-room myth, soft-headedness and idiotic credulity are the bond of sympathy in the Society, and general wonder-sickness is its dynamic principle. A glance at the membership fails, however, to corroborate this view. The president is Prof. Henry Sidgwick, known by his other deeds as the most incorrigibly and exasperatingly critical and sceptical mind in England. The hard-headed Arthur Balfour is one vice-president, and the hard-headed Prof. J. P. Langley, secretary of the Smithsonian Institution, is another. Such men as Professor Lodge, the eminent English physicist, and Professor Richet, the eminent French physiologist, are amongst the most active contributors to the Society's *Proceedings*; and through the catalogue of membership are sprinkled names honored throughout the world for their scientific capacity. In fact, were I asked to point to a scientific journal where hard-headedness and never-sleeping suspicion of sources of error might be seen in their full bloom, I think I should have to fall back on the *Proceedings* of the "Society for Psychical Research." The common run of papers, say on physiological subjects, which one finds in other professional organs, are apt to show a far lower level of critical consciousness. Indeed, the rigorous canons of evidence applied a few years ago to testimony in the case of certain "mediums" led to the secession from the Society of a number of spiritualists. Messrs. Stainton Moses and Alfred Russel Wallace, amongst others, thought that no experiences based on mere eyesight could ever have a chance to be admitted as true, if such an impossibly exacting standard of proof were insisted on in every case.

The "Society for Psychical Research" was founded in February, 1882, by a number of gentlemen, foremost amongst whom seem to have been Professors Henry Sidgwick, W. F. Barrett, and Balfour Stewart, and Messrs. R. H. Hutton, Hensleigh Wedgwood, Edmund Gurney, and F. W. H. Myers. Their purpose was twofold: first, to carry on systematic experimentation with hypnotic subjects, mediums, clairvoyants, and others; and, secondly, to collect evidence concerning apparitions, haunted houses, and similar phenomena which are incidentally reported, but which, from their fugitive character, admit of no deliberate control. Professor Sidgwick, in his introductory address, insisted that the divided state of public opinion on all these matters was a scandal to science, absolute disdain on *a priori* grounds characterizing what may be called professional opinion, whilst completely uncritical and indiscriminate credulity was too often found amongst those who pretended to have a first-hand acquaintance with the facts.

As a sort of weather bureau for accumulating reports of such meteoric phenomena as apparitions, the "S.P.R." (as I shall continue briefly to call it) has done an immense amount of work. As an experimenting body, it cannot be said to have completely fulfilled the hopes of its founders. The reasons for this lie in two circumstances: first, the clairvoyant and other subjects who will allow themselves to be experimented upon are few and far between; and, secondly, work with them takes an immense amount of time, and in the case of the Society has had to be carried on at odd intervals by members engaged in other pursuits. The Society has not yet been rich enough to control the undivided services of skilled experimenters in this difficult field. The loss of the lamented

Edmund Gurney, who more than any one else had leisure to devote, has been so far irreparable. But were there no experimental work at all, and were the Society nothing but a weather bureau for catching sporadic apparitions, etc., in their freshness, I am disposed to think its function indispensable in the scientific organism. If any one of my readers, spurred by the thought that so much smoke must needs betoken fire, has ever looked into the existing literature of the supernatural for proof, he will know what I mean. This literature is enormous, but it is practically quite worthless for evidential purposes. Facts enough are there, indeed; but the records of them are so fallible and uncritical that the most they do is to confirm the presumption that it may be well to keep a window open in one's mind upon that quarter.

In the Society's *Proceedings,* on the contrary, a different law prevails. Quality, and not mere quantity, is what has been mainly kept in mind. The most that could be done with every reported case has been done. The witnesses, where possible, have been cross-examined personally, the collateral facts have been looked up, and the narrative appears with its precise coefficient of evidential worth stamped on it, so that all may know just what its weight as proof may be. Outside of these *Proceedings,* I know of no systematic attempt to *weigh* the evidence for the supernatural. This makes the value of the seven volumes already published unique, and I firmly believe that as the years go on and the ground covered grows still wider, the Society's *Proceedings* will more and more tend to supersede all other sources of empirical information concerning phenomena traditionally deemed occult. If the Society could continue to exist long enough for the public to become familiar with its presence, so that any case of apparition or of a house or person infested with unaccountable noises or disturbances of material objects would, as a matter of course, be reported to its officers, who thereupon would take down the evidence in as thorough a way as possible, we should end ere long by having a mass of facts concrete enough to found a decent theory upon.

Those who are now sustaining the Society should accustom themselves to the idea that its first duty is simply to exist from year to year and perform this recording function well, though no conclusive results of any sort emerge in the first generation. All our learned societies have begun in some such modest way. Three years after the English Society was founded, Professor Barrett came to this country and stirred up some scientific men in Boston, so that the "American Society for Psychical Research" was founded as a separate organization. After five years this Society perished. Providence had raised up no one in its midst who had both leisure and aptitude for doing work of the sort required. But though the organization was abandoned, its associates for the most part joined the English Society, which thereupon constituted an "American Branch," with Professor Langley and the present writer as its "honorary vice-presidents" and Mr. Richard Hodgson as its salaried secretary and executive agent. The "American Branch" has suffered from the same defect as the American Society. The secretary is the only individual connected with it who is able to make any solid contribution to its work. It requires, moreover, a large increase of membership to become self-supporting.

One cannot by mere outward organization make much progress in matters scientific. Societies can back men of genius, but can never take their place. The contrast between the parent Society and the "American Branch" illustrates this. In England, a little group of men with enthusiasm and genius for the work supplied the nucleus; in this country, Mr. Hodgson had to be imported from Europe before any tangible progress was made. What perhaps more than anything else has held the Society together in England is Professor Sidgwick's extraordinary gift of inspiring confidence in diverse sorts of people. Such tenacity of interest in the result and such absolute impartiality in discussing the evidence are not once in a century found in an individual. His obstinate belief that there is something yet to be brought to light communicates patience to the discouraged; his constitutional inability to draw any precipitate conclusion reassures those who are afraid of being dupes. Mrs. Sidgwick—a sister, by the way, of the great Arthur Balfour—is a worthy ally of her husband in this matter, showing a similarly extraordinary power of holding her judgment in suspense, and a keenness of observation and capacity for experimenting with human subjects which are rare in either sex.

The *worker* of the Society, as originally constituted, was Edmund Gurney. Gurney was a man of the rarest sympathies and gifts. Although, like Carlyle, he used to groan under the burden of his labors, he yet exhibited a colossal power of dispatching business and getting through drudgery of the most repulsive kind. His two thick volumes on the *Phantasms of the Living*, collected and published in three years, are a proof of this. Besides this, he had exquisite artistic instincts, and his massive volume on *The Power of Sound* is certainly the most important work on æsthetics in the English language. He had also the tenderest heart and a mind of rare metaphysical power, as his volume of essays, *Tertium Quid*, will prove to any reader. Mr. F. W. H. Myers, already well known as one of the most brilliant of English essayists, is the *ingenium præfervidum* of the "S.P.R." Of the value of Mr. Myers' theoretic writings I will say a word later. Mr. Hodgson, the American secretary, is distinguished by a balance of mind almost as rare in its way as Sidgwick's. He is persuaded of the reality of many of the phenomena called spiritualistic, but he also has uncommon keenness in detecting error; and it is impossible to say in advance whether it will give him more satisfaction to confirm or to smash a given "case" offered to his examination. Other names in the *Proceedings* are those of Mr. Malcolm Guthrie, Mr. Frank Podmore, Prof. Oliver Lodge, Prof. Ch. Richet, and M. Léon Marillier.

It is now time to cast a brief look upon the actual contents of these *Proceedings*.[1] The first two years were largely taken up with experiments in thought-transference. The earliest lot of these were made with the daughters of a clergyman named Creery, and convinced Messrs. Balfour Stewart, Barrett, Myers, and Gurney that the girls had an inexplicable power of guessing names and objects thought of by other persons. Two years later, Mrs. Sidgwick and Mr. Gurney, recommencing experiments with the same girls, detected them signalling to each other. This makes it impossible to accept the record of their previous performances. It is true that for the most part the conditions had then excluded signalling, and it is also possible that the cheating may have grafted itself on what was originally a genuine phenomenon. Yet Gurney was wise in abandoning the entire series to the scepticism of the reader. Three other thought-transference subjects were experimented upon at

---

[1] The Society, in addition to the *Proceedings*, prints privately a monthly journal, which is issued to members only. This contains what may be called raw materials, imperfectly corroborated interviews and provisional discussions only; whereas the *Proceedings*, which appear thrice a year in parts numbering from 150 to 300 pages, contain worked-up reports of facts and such theoretical contributions as may receive the *imprimatur* of a special committee. The best way in this country to get the *Proceedings* regularly is to join the Branch. They may also be bought singly from the secretary, R. Hodgson, 5 Boylston Place, Boston, Mass., and from Damrell & Upham, booksellers, Washington and School streets, Boston.

great length during the first two years: one was Mr. G. A. Smith; the other two were young ladies in Liverpool in the employment of Mr. Malcolm Guthrie.

It is the opinion of all who took part in these experiments that sources of conscious and unconscious deception were sufficiently excluded, and that the large percentage of correct reproductions by the subjects of words, diagrams, and sensations occupying other people's consciousness were entirely inexplicable as results of chance. The present writer confesses that the reading of the records leaves on him a similar impression. But the odd thing about this sort of "thought-transference" is that since the first three years of the Society's existence no new subjects have turned up with whom extensive and systematic experiments could be carried on. All the later reports are of brief series and semi-sporadic results, leaving no ground for certainty. Meanwhile the witnesses of Mr. Smith's, Miss Relph's, and Miss Edwards' performances were all so satisfied of the genuineness of the phenomenon that "telepathy" has figured freely in the papers of the *Proceedings* and in Gurney's book on *Phantasms* as a *vera causa* on which additional hypotheses might be built. No mere reader can be blamed, however, if he refuse to espouse so revolutionary a belief until a larger bulk of testimony be supplied.

Volume II contains another experimental paper, that on the divining-rod, by Mr. Edward R. Pease, with inconclusive results. The divining-rod has never again shown its face in the *Proceedings*. Gurney's papers on hypnotism must be mentioned next. Some of them are less concerned with establishing new facts than with analyzing old ones, the papers on memory during hypnotism, for example. Omitting these, we find that in the line of pure observation Gurney claims to have ascertained in more than one subject the following phenomenon, of which the theoretic explanation is doubtful: The subject's hands are thrust through a blanket, which screens the operator from his eyes, and his mind is absorbed in conversation with a third person. The operator meanwhile points with his finger to one of the fingers of the subject, which finger alone responds to this silent selection by becoming stiff or anæsthetic, as the case may be. The interpretation is difficult, but the phenomenon, which I have myself witnessed, seems authentic.

Another observation made by Gurney seems to prove the possibility of the subject's mind being directly influenced by the operator's. The hypnotized subject responds or fails to respond to questions asked by a third party according to the operator's silent permission or refusal. Of course, in these experiments all obvious sources of deception were considered. But Gurney's most important contribution by far to our knowledge of hypnotism was his series of experiments on the automatic writing of subjects who had received post-hypnotic suggestions. For example, a subject during trance is told that he will poke the fire in six minutes after waking. On being waked he has no memory of the order, but while he is engaged in conversation his hand is placed on a *planchette*, which immediately writes the sentence, "P., you will poke the fire in six minutes." Experiments like this, which were repeated in great variety, prove that below the upper consciousness the hypnotic consciousness persists, engrossed with the suggestion and able to express itself through the involuntarily moving hand.

Gurney shares, therefore, with Janet and Binet, whose observations were made with widely differing subjects and methods, the credit of demonstrating the simultaneous existence of two different strata of consciousness, ignorant of each other, in the same person. The "extra-consciousness," as one may call it, can be kept on tap, as it were, by the method of automatic writing. This discovery marks a new era in experimental psychology; it is impossible to overrate its importance. But Gurney's greatest piece of work is his laborious *Phantasms of the Living.* As an example of the drudgery stowed away in the volumes, it may suffice to say that in looking up the proofs for the alleged *physical* phenomena of witchcraft, Gurney reports a careful search through two hundred and sixty books on the subject, with the result of finding no first-hand evidence recorded in the trials except the confessions of the victims themselves, and these, of course, are presumptively based on hallucinations. This statement, made in an unobtrusive note, is only one instance of the care displayed throughout the volumes. In the course of these, Gurney discusses about seven hundred cases of apparitions which he collected. A large number of these were "veridical," in the sense of coinciding with some calamity happening to the person who appeared. Gurney's explanation is that the mind of the person undergoing the calamity was at that moment able to impress the mind of the percipient with an hallucination.

Apparitions, on this "telepathic" theory, may be called "objective" facts, although they are not "material" facts. In order to test the likelihood of such veridical hallucinations being due to mere chance, Gurney instituted the "census of hallucinations," which has been continued with the result of obtaining answers from some twenty-five thousand people, asked at random in different countries whether, when in good health and awake, they had ever heard a voice, seen a form, or felt a touch which no material presence could account for. The result seems to be, roughly speaking, that about one adult in ten has had such an experience at least once in his life, and of the experiences themselves 14 per cent coincide with some real distant event. In other words, one person out of every one hundred and forty in the community has had a veridical hallucination of some sort or other, vague or precise. The question is, Is this degree of frequency too great to be deemed fortuitous, and must we suppose an occult connection between the two events? My own position is still one of doubt, although I tend to accept the occult connection. In but few cases is the evidence as complete as one could wish, and the data themselves are all too crude for a mathematical computation of probability. The great use of the census is to have been the means of collecting an enormous amount of material for study. The admirable report upon it which Mrs. Sidgwick will make to the "International Congress of Experimental Psychology" next August will continue Gurney's labors, and put the entire subject of hallucinations on a new empirical basis.

The next experimental topic worth mentioning in the *Proceedings* is the discussion of the physical phenomenon of mediumship (slate-writing, furniture-moving, and so forth) by Mrs. Sidgwick, Mr. Hodgson, and "Mr. Davey." This, so far as it goes, is destructive of the claims of all the mediums examined. In the way of "control," "Mr. Davey" himself produced fraudulent slate-writing of the highest order, while Mr. Hodgson, a "sitter" in his confidence, reviewed the written reports of the series of his other sitters —all intelligent persons—and shows that in every case they failed to see the essential features of what was done before their eyes. This Davey-Hodgson contribution is probably the most damaging document concerning eye-witnesses' evidence which has ever been produced. Another substantial bit of work based on personal observation is Mr. Hodgson's report of Madame Blavatsky's claims to physical mediumship. This is adverse to the lady's pretensions; and although some of Madame Blavatsky's friends make light of it, it is a stroke from which her reputation will hardly recover. Although the "S.P.R." has thus found that the evidence for matter moving without contact is as yet insufficient, its observations on an American medium, Mrs. Piper, tend to substantiate the claim that hypernormal intelligence may be displayed in the trance state. A tediously long report of sittings with Mrs. Piper in England, followed by a still longer ditto in America, gives proof (entirely conclusive to the present writer's mind) that this lady has shown in her trances a knowledge of the personal affairs of living and dead people which it is impossible to suppose that she can have gained in any "natural" way. A satisfactory explanation of the phenomenon is yet to seek. It offers itself as spirit-control; but it is as hard to accept this theory without protest as it is to be satisfied with such explanations as clairvoyance or reading the sitter's mind.

One of the most important experimental contributions to the *Proceedings* is the article of Miss X—— on "Crystal-Vision." Many persons who look fixedly into a crystal or other vaguely luminous surface fall into a kind of daze and see visions. Miss X—— has this susceptibility in a remarkable degree, and is, moreover, an unusually intelligent critic. She reports many visions which can only be described as apparently clairvoyant, and others which beautifully fill a vacant niche in our knowledge of subconscious mental operations. For example, looking into the crystal before breakfast one morning she reads in printed characters of the death of a lady of her acquaintance, the date and other circumstances all duly appearing in type. Startled by this, she looks at *The Times* of the previous day for verification, and there amongst the deaths are the identical words which she has seen. On the same page of *The Times* are other items which she remembers reading the day before; and the only explanation seems to be that her eyes then inattentively observed, so to speak, the death-item, which forthwith fell into a special corner of her memory and came out as a visual hallucination when the peculiar modification of consciousness induced by the crystal-gazing set in.

Passing from papers based on observation to papers based on narrative, we have a number of ghost stories, etc., sifted by Mrs. Sidgwick and discussed by Messrs. Myers and Podmore. They form the best ghost literature I know of from the point of view of emotional interest. As to the conclusions drawn, Mrs. Sidgwick is rigorously non-committal, while Mr. Myers and Mr. Podmore show themselves respectively hospitable and inhospitable to the notion that such stories have a basis of objectivity dependent on the continued existence of the dead.

I must close my gossip about the *Proceedings* by naming what, after all, seems to me the most important part of its contents. This is the long series of articles by Mr. Myers on what he now calls the "subliminal self," or what I have designated above as the "extra-consciousness." The result of Myers' learned and ingenious studies in hypnotism, hallucinations, automatic writing, mediumship, and the whole series of allied phenomena is a conviction which he expresses in the following terms:

"Each of us is in reality an abiding psychical entity far more extensive than he knows—an individuality which can never express itself completely through any corporeal manifestation. The Self manifests itself through the organism; but there is always some part of the Self unmanifested; and always, as it seems, some power of organic expression in abeyance or in reserve."

The ordinary consciousness Mr. Myers likens to the visible part of the solar spectrum; the total consciousness is like that spectrum prolonged by the inclusion of the ultra-red and ultra-violet rays. In the psychic spectrum the "ultra" parts may embrace a far wider range, both of physiological and of psychical activity, than is open to our ordinary consciousness and memory. At the lower end, beyond the red, as it were, we have the *physiological* extension, mind-cures, "stigmatization" of ecstatics, etc.; in the upper or ultra-violet region, we have the hyper-normal cognitions of the medium-trance. Whatever the judgment of the future may be on Mr. Myers' speculations, the credit will always remain to them of being the first attempt in our language, and the first thoroughly *inductive* attempt in any language, to consider the phenomena of hallucination, hypnotism, automatism, double personality, and mediumship as connected parts of one whole subject. No one seems to me to have grasped the problem in a way both so broad and so sober as he has done.

One's reaction on hearsay testimony is always determined by one's own experience. Most men who have once convinced themselves, by what seems to them a careful examination, that any one species of the supernatural exists, begin to relax their vigilance as to evidence, and throw the doors of their minds more or less wide open to the supernatural[2] along its whole extent. To a mind that has thus made its *salto mortale*, the minute work over insignificant cases and quiddling discussion of "evidential values," of which the Society's reports are full, seems insufferably tedious. And it is so; few species of literature are more truly dull than reports of phantasms. Cases which one collects one's self from the witnesses may acquire a personal interest; but cases merely found printed as having occurred to strangers are hard to read or to remember without some definite purpose in one's mind, such as trying to classify them, or seeing how they may affect a theory or fill gaps in a growing series. Taken simply by themselves, as separate facts to stare at, they appear so devoid of meaning and sweep that even were they certainly true, one would be tempted to leave them out of one's universe for being so idiotic. Every other sort of fact has some context and continuity with the rest of nature. These alone are context-less and discontinuous.

Hence I think that the sort of loathing—no milder word will do —which the very words "psychical research" and "psychical re-searcher" awaken in so many honest scientific breasts is not only natural, but in a sense praiseworthy. A man who is unable himself to conceive of any *orbit* for these mental meteors can only suppose that Messrs. Gurney, Myers & Co.'s mood in dealing with them must be that of silly marvelling at so many detached prodigies. And *such* prodigies! Whereas the only thing that really interests these "researchers" is the glimpse that they gain of the orbit itself. Thus between the spiritualists and theosophists, who have so much orbit that they are sickened by the methods, and the scientists, who have so little that they are sickened by the facts, of the "S.P.R.," the latter stands in a rather forsaken position. And yet it is a position of peculiar merit, as I think that a little reflection will show.

Orthodoxy is almost as much a matter of authority in science as it is in the Church. We believe in all sorts of laws of nature which we cannot ourselves understand, merely because men whom we admire and trust vouch for them. If Messrs. Helmholtz, Huxley, Pasteur, and Edison were simultaneously to announce themselves as converts to clairvoyance, thought-transference, and ghosts, who can doubt that there would be a prompt popular stampede in that

[2] By "the supernatural" I mean, of course, anything that appears to transcend the "scientifically" recognized "laws of nature," from faith-cures up to theosophic Mahatmas.

99

direction? We should have as great a slush of "telepathy" in the scientific press as we now have of "suggestion" in the medical press. We should hasten to invoke mystical explanations without winking, and fear to be identified with a by-gone *régime* if we held back. In society we should eagerly let it be known that we had always thought there was a basis of truth in haunted houses, and had, as far back as we could remember, had faith in demoniacal possession.

Now, it is certain that if the cat ever does jump this way, the cautious methods of the "S.P.R." will give it a position of extraordinary influence. As, one after another, the fashion-setting converts dropped in and the popular credulity began, its efforts at exactitude about evidence and its timidity in speculating would seem supremely virtuous. Sober-headed scientists would look to its temper as a bulwark; whilst its poor little detached facts, no longer so idiotic and neglectable, would prove the least of possible entering wedges for theosophists and others who had ready-made supernaturalistic philosophies to propagate. In short, the "S.P.R." would be a surprisingly useful mediator between the old order and the new.

All this on the supposition that the Helmholtzes and Huxleys *did* become converted. Now, the present writer (not wholly insensible to the ill consequences of putting himself on record as a false prophet) must candidly express his own suspicion that sooner or later the cat *must* jump this way. The special means of his conversion have been the trances of the medium whose case in the *Proceedings* was alluded to above. Knowing these trances at first hand, he cannot escape the conclusion that in them the medium's knowledge of facts increases enormously, and in a manner impossible of explanation by any principles of which our existing science takes account. Facts are facts, and the larger includes the less; so these trances doubtless make me the more lenient to the other facts recorded in the *Proceedings*. I find myself also suspecting that the thought-transference experiments, the veridical hallucinations, the crystal-vision, yea, even the ghosts, are sorts of thing which with the years will tend to establish themselves. All of us live more or less on some inclined plane of credulity. The plane tips one way in one man, another way in another; and may he whose plane tips in *no* way be the first to cast a stone! But whether the other things establish themselves more and more or grow less and less probable, the trances I speak of have broken down for my own mind the limits of the admitted order of nature. Science, so far as science denies such exceptional facts, lies prostrate in the dust for me; and the most urgent intellectual need which I feel at present is that science be built up again in a form in which such facts shall have a positive place. Science, like life, feeds on its own decay. New facts burst old rules; then newly divined conceptions bind old and new together into a reconciling law.

And here finally is the real instructiveness of Messrs. Myers and Gurney's work. They are trying with the utmost conscientiousness to find a reconciling conception which shall subject the old "laws of nature" to the smallest possible strain. Mr. Myers uses that method of gradual approach which has performed such wonders in Darwin's hands. When Darwin met a fact which seemed a poser to his theory, his regular custom, as I have heard an ingenious friend say, was to *fill in* all round it with smaller facts, and so mitigate the jolt, as a wagoner might heap dirt round a big rock in the road, and thus get his team over without upsetting. So Mr. Myers, starting from the most ordinary facts of inattentive consciousness, follows this clew through a long series which terminates in ghosts, and seeks to show that these are but extreme manifestations of a common truth, the truth that our normal conscious life is but the visible segment of a spectrum indefinitely long, of which the invisible segments are capable, under rarely realized conditions, of acting and being acted upon by the invisible segments of other conscious lives. This may not be ultimately true (for the theosophists, with their astral bodies and the like, may, for aught I know, prove to be on the correcter trail), but no one can deny that it is *scientific*.

Science always takes a known kind of phenomenon and tries to extend its range. Sensorial hallucination is a known phenomenon; and it is also a known phenomenon that impressions received by the "subliminal"[3] strata of consciousness may be hallucinatory in their intensity—witness the phenomena of dreams and the hypnotic trance. Mr. Myers accordingly seeks to interpret mediumistic experiences and ghostly apparitions as so many effects of the impact upon the subliminal consciousness of causes "behind the veil." The *effects*, psychologically speaking, are hallucinations; yet so far

---

[3] Subliminal, from *sub* and *limen*: "beneath the threshold."

as they are "veridical" they must be held probably to have an "objective" cause. What that objective cause may be Mr. Myers does not decide; yet from the context of many of the hallucinations it would seem to be an intelligence other than that of the medium's or seer's ordinary self, and the interesting question is, Is it what I have called the extra-conscious intelligence of persons still living, or is it the intelligence of persons who have themselves passed behind the veil? Only the most scrupulous examination of the "veridical" effects themselves can decide. I do not myself see how any candid mind can doubt that Mr. Myers' scrupulous testing of the minutest cases is in the line of the best scientific tradition. I do not see, whatever prove the fate of his hypothesis, how his "working of it for all it is worth" can fail to mark a distinct step onward in our knowledge of the truth.

I have myself, during the past two years as American agent for the census, collected some five hundred cases of "hallucination" in healthy people. The result is to make me feel that we all have potentially a "subliminal" self, which may make at any time irruption into our ordinary lives. In its lowest phases it is only the depository of our forgotten memories; in its highest, we don't know what it is at all. Take, for instance, a series of cases. During sleep many persons have *something* in them which measures the flight of time better than the waking self does. It wakes them at a preappointed hour; it acquaints them with the moment when they first awake. It may produce an hallucination, as in a lady who informs me that at the instant of waking she has a vision of her watch-face with the hands pointing (as she has often verified) to the exact time. Whatever it is, it is subconscious.

A subconscious something may also preserve experiences to which we do not openly attend. A lady taking her lunch in town finds herself without her purse. Instantly a sense comes over her of rising from the breakfast-table and hearing her purse drop on the floor. On reaching home she finds nothing under the table, but summons the servant to say where she has put the purse. The servant produces it, saying: "How did you know where it was? You rose and left the room as if you didn't know you'd dropped it." The same subconscious something may recollect what we have forgotten. A lady used to taking salicylate of soda for muscular rheumatism awakens one early winter morning with an aching neck.

In the twilight she takes what she supposes to be her customary powder from a drawer, dissolves it in a glass of water, and is about to drink it down, when she feels a sharp slap on her shoulder and hears a voice in her ear saying, "Taste it!" On examination, she finds she has got a morphine powder by mistake. The natural interpretation is that a sleeping memory of the morphine powders awoke in this quasi-explosive way. A like explanation offers itself as most plausible for the following case: A lady, with little time to catch the train, and the expressman about to call, is excitedly looking for the lost key of a packed trunk. Hurrying upstairs with a bunch of keys, proved useless, in her hand, she hears an "objective" voice distinctly say, "Try the key of the cake-box." Being tried, it fits. This may well have been the effect of some long-eclipsed experience.

Now, the *effect* is doubtless due to the same hallucinatory mechanism, but the *source* is less easily assigned as we ascend the scale of cases. A lady, for instance, goes after breakfast to see about one of her servants who has become ill over night. She is startled at distinctly reading over the bedroom door in gilt letters the word "small-pox." The doctor is sent for, and ere long pronounces small-pox to be the disease, although the lady says, "The thought of the girl's having small-pox never entered my mind till I saw the apparent inscription." Then come other cases of warning; *e.g.*, that of a youth sitting in a wagon under a shed, who suddenly hears his dead mother's voice say, "Stephen, get away from here quick," and jumps out just in time to see the shed roof fall.

After this come the by no means infrequent experiences, usually visual, but sometimes both visual and auditory, of people appearing to distant friends at or near the hour of death. Then we have the trance-visions and utterances, which (as in the case of a circle of private persons with whom I have recently become acquainted) may appear astonishingly profuse and continuous and maintain a superior level intellectually. For all these higher phenomena, it seems to me that whilst the proximate mechanism is that of "hallucination," it is straining an hypothesis unduly to name any ordinary subconscious operation, such as expectation, recollection, or inference from inattentive perception, as the ultimate cause that starts it up. It is far better tactics to brand the narratives themselves as unworthy of trust. The trustworthiness of most of them is to my own mind far from proved. And yet, in the light of the medium-trance, which *is* proved, it seems as if they might well all be members of a "natural kind" of fact of which we do not yet know the full extent. Thousands of "sensitive" organizations in the United States to-day live as steadily in the light of these experiences and are as indifferent to modern "science" as if they lived in Bohemia in the twelfth century. They are indifferent to science, because science is so callously indifferent to their experiences. The essential "point" I wish to make to my readers is that by taking the experiences of these persons as they come and applying the ordinary methods of science to their discussion, the *Proceedings* of the "S.P.R.," whatever be their theoretic outcome, form a department of empirical natural history worthy of all encouragement and respect.

A final word about the *practical* outcome of inquiries into the extra-consciousness may not be out of place. I remember saying, at a public meeting in Boston three years since, that a good psychical researcher let loose in an insane-asylum would be likely to discover facts in the patients which the doctors had overlooked. M. Pierre Janet, on the whole the most brilliant French inquirer into the extra-consciousness, gave a pretty verification of this prediction last year by the "Étude sur un cas d'aboulie et d'idées fixes," which he published in the *Revue Philosophique*. He is only a professor of philosophy, but he pursues his studies in the Paris hospitals, and in the *Salpêtrière* he had a patient named Marcella, aged nineteen, handed over to him.

Marcella was a melancholic girl whose character had gradually become so changed for the worse as to be unrecognizable, and whose life was a picture of invincible apathy and inertia, varied by occasional spells of violence—a sort of case that in our asylums is generally "let alone" as much as possible, in the hope that time may of itself effect a cure. M. Janet patiently and lovingly studied all her symptoms, and describes them at great length. The essential facts for my present purpose are these: He soon observed that she had periods of absent-mindedness, which he calls her "clouds." During these "clouds" she responded to no questions, and after them had no memory of what had taken place in them. But by piecing together various partial clews which he elicited, he discovered that although so outwardly impassive, she was a prey throughout these "clouds" to monotonous hallucinations of a ter-rifying sort. When I say that what she told when hypnotized was one of his clews, and that her automatic writing was another, the reader will see why I speak of M. Janet's methods as those of a psychical researcher.

The next thing which he made out was that her inertia and mel-ancholy were in great part after-effects of these hallucinations. M. Janet tried all usual methods, including ordinary hypnotic commands, with only transient success. Only when he *entered into* her hallucinations, confining them in part, but mixing other ele-ments with them and giving them new terminations, did marked benefit result. But here a fresh difficulty came up. After each suc-cessive delusion that was exorcised, the patient became better than ever before; but each one was replaced after some days by another more obstinate and bad. At last there came a delusion, based on hallucinations of hearing, which made her refuse her food. It per-sisted so long that, at the end of his resources one day, M. Janet put a pencil into her hand to see if she might not automatically prescribe for herself. "*Il faut la forcer et ce sera fini*," the hand "un-consciously" wrote. But when force was applied, Marcella fell into an alarming hystero-epileptic attack which lasted two hours and made the experimenter momentarily regret his rashness.

From this attack she unexpectedly emerged *quite well*, and re-mained so for twelve days. Then she relapsed into the same delu-sion coupled with the additional refusal to speak; and this condi-tion, terminating by a similar convulsive crisis, never returned again. Before long, however, a frenzied attack of suicidal mania set in, lasted fifteen days, and then spontaneously disappeared, leaving the girl practically *cured* and oblivious of all that had happened in the previous weeks. Her condition, for several months at least, was *normal*. But the remarkable aspect of the case is one of which M. Janet saw the significance only late in the series of his operations. The hallucinations were largely based on painful ex-periences in the girl's life, which came up, as if present again, in her "clouds." Her morbid waking state was a sort of resultant effect of the accumulation of these influences; and each later hallu-cination that was peeled off, so to speak, by M. Janet gave an older one a chance to become more acute, until the whole regressive series was run through. Her mind was thus gradually freed of a deposit of obsessions that had accumulated during five years. The refusal to eat and the suicidal frenzy were repetitions of crises that she had gone through at the beginning of her malady, and once having thrown them off she got entirely well. Might not such a case well lead our younger medical men to explore their patients' "subliminal selves" a little more than they yet do?

14

Review of *Science and a Future Life,*
by Frederic W. H. Myers (1893)

Science and a Future Life. With Other Essays. By Frederic W. H.
Myers. Macmillan. 1893. 12mo, pp. 242.

The career of the author of this little volume shows how a deep
interest in the problem of human destiny may transform the cast
of a mind from the literary to the scientific, without at the same
time damping the emotional ardor with which life began. In the
second essay in this book, "Charles Darwin and Agnosticism," Mr.
Myers quotes the well-known passage of Darwin's *Life* in which
the great naturalist deplores the decay of his æsthetic and sentimental faculties: "Now for many years I cannot endure to read a
line of poetry . . . . My mind seems to have become a kind of machine for grinding general laws out of large collections of facts, but
why this should have caused the atrophy of that part of the brain
alone on which the higher tastes depend, I cannot conceive," etc.,
etc. Without comparing Mr. Myers to Darwin in the matter of
"science," his case inevitably suggests the other contrast. His earlier
essays and his poems were the fruit of an exclusively literary, æsthetic, and religious culture. His contributions to the Psychical
Research *Proceedings* show him as a wide reader of neurology and
collector and classifier of masses of rare and problematical facts.
But now in this latest volume he reappears with that serenity and
hope in definite methods of work which it seems the peculiar bless-
ing of a scientific occupation to confer, but still with the old sense

of life as an emotional "problem," and with unabated rhetorical fire.

The Essays (not counting a memorial of the late Prince Leopold) are five in number, and under their diverse titles have the same essential aim, which is to show, first, how disconsolately irrational is the view of the world which merely materialistic science and merely mundane history offer to the mind's acceptance; and, second, how probable certain kinds of neglected fact have made it that the world which science acknowledges is but an extract, and the history which we see about us but a fragment, of a larger universe of which we as yet know nothing definite, but which, if known, might satisfy our rational need. What Mr. Myers proposes is thus primarily not a dogma, but a method. Nothing could be further from him than to try to convict agnosticism of error on dialectic grounds. Others may do that: he seeks first to make the reader feel its insufficiency, and then to invite him to a practical channel of escape, by following which he has himself been cheered. In other words, he shows the agnostic horse the medicinal waters, but refrains, in these pages, from forcing him to drink. Hence the great persuasiveness of his writing. It does not challenge the resisting attitude, as so many onslaughts on materialism do. For, considered as a non-"psychical researcher," Mr. Myers is himself an acute case of agnosticism, and feels all the disconsolateness of which he writes. It is only as psychical researcher that he has recovered, and yearns over others that they should do the same. The following passages come as near as anything in the book to giving an expression of his positive faith:

"Of late years the induction of hallucination in sane and healthy persons during the hypnotic trance has begun to be recognised as an experimental method of great value in psychology. But comparatively few *savants* have as yet recognised the extreme variety and instructiveness of the phantasmal sights and sounds which occur spontaneously to normal persons, and which it is now for the first time becoming possible to study in a systematic instead of a merely anecdotic manner. . . . The study of cases of [a certain] type, many of which I have set forth elsewhere, has gradually convinced me that the least improbable hypothesis lies in the supposition that some influence on the minds of men on earth is occasionally exercised by the surviving personalities of the departed. I believe this influence to be, usually, of an indirect and dreamlike character, but I cannot explain the facts to myself without supposing that such an influence exists. I am further strengthened in this belief by the study of the automatic phenomena. I observe that in all the varieties of automatic action—of which automatic writing may be taken as a prominent type—the contents of the messages given seem to be derived from three sources. First of all comes the automatist's own mind. From that the bulk of the messages are undoubtedly drawn, even when they refer to matters which the automatist once knew, but has entirely forgotten. Whatever has gone into the mind may come out of the mind; although this automatism may be the only way of getting at it. Secondly, there is a small percentage of messages apparently telepathic—containing, that is to say, facts probably unknown to the automatist, but known to some living person in his company, or connected with him. But, thirdly, there is a still smaller residuum of messages which I cannot thus explain—messages which contain facts apparently not known to the automatist nor to any living friend of his, but known to some deceased person, perhaps a total stranger to the living man whose hand is writing. I cannot avoid the conviction that in some way —however dreamlike and indirect—it is the departed personality which originates such messages as these. I by no means wish to impose these views upon minds not prepared to accept them. What I do desire is, that as many other men as possible should qualify themselves to judge independently of the value of the evidence on which I rely—should study what has been collected, and should repeat and extend the observations which are essential to the formation of any judgments worth the name. . . .

"I place together then—as I claim that history gives me a *primâ facie* right to do—certain experiments which have, so to say, gained general acceptance but yesterday, and certain cognate experiments which are on their way (as I think) to general acceptance on some not distant morrow; and I draw from these a double line of argument in favour of human survival. In the first place, I point to the great extension and deepening which experiment has given to our conception of the content and capacities of the sub-conscious human mind,—amounting, perhaps, to a shifting of man's psychical centre of gravity from the conscious to the sub-conscious or subliminal strata of his being—and accompanied by the manifestation of powers at least not obviously derivable from terrestrial evolution. And, in the second place, I claim that there is, in fact, direct evidence for the exercise of some kind of influence by the surviving personalities of departed men. I claim that the analysis of phantasmal sights and sounds, treated by careful rules of evidence, indicates this influence. And I claim that it is indicated also by the analysis of those automatic messages which, in various manners, carry upwards to the threshold of consciousness the knowledge acquired from unknown sources by the sub-conscious mind" (pp. 30–36).

In other words, Mr. Myers writes himself down with decision as a "spiritualist," but it is hardly necessary to note how greatly his methods and temper differ from those which are usually associated with that name. But, be his spiritualism true or false, his merits as the first comparer and coördinator of these abnormal phenomena along their whole extent must always be acknowledged. What strikes one most in the present volume, after its felicity of style, is the breadth of the author's intellectual sympathies. The book may be cordially recommended to all who are interested in the higher aspects of contemporary thought.

15

Letter to the Editor of *Mind* on Ward's Review of *Briefer Course* (1893)

DEAR SIR,—Mr. Ward, in his over-generous notice of my briefer Psychology in your October number, says something which calls for a word of correction from me, for it concerns others besides myself. Quoting my sentence that mediumistic phenomena are "a field which the *soi-disant* scientist usually refuses to explore," he names the Society for Psychical Research, and remarks that it must strike the impartial spectator as a little humorous that "these people" should not only have arrogated to themselves a title under which every psychological inquirer might be enrolled, but should "stigmatise as *soi-disant* scientists the great body of psychologists, who, in fact, think proper not to join their ranks." If there is anything humorous here, it would seem to be the ascription to all "these people" of an opinion which was foreign even to the mind of the solitary author of the sentence from which Mr. Ward so ingeniously distils it, for no mention of the "S.P.R." was made in my text. The point is, as Mr. Ward says, a trifle, but exactitude is meritorious; and I therefore beg to say that I have never heard one of "these people" brand any psychologist as a *soi-disant* scientist, or otherwise speak harshly of him for not joining the ranks of the society in question. The temper of the psychical researchers is, as a rule, more humble. As for myself (if I can remember what was in my mind when I wrote the sentence in point) the *soi-disant* scientists intended must have been such fine old crusted enemies of superstition as that eminent biologist who once said to me that if the facts of telepathy, &c., *were* true, the first duty which every honest man would owe to Science would be to deny them, and prevent them, if possible, from ever becoming known. I surely never dreamed, when I wrote the words *"soi-disant* scientist," of the numerous psychological inquirers who have not joined the "S.P.R."; and least of all of such a truly scientific psychologist as Mr. Ward himself.

I remain, very truly yours,

WILLIAM JAMES.

Florence, October 24, 1892.

I am sorry I have misunderstood Prof. James. That I did it without "ingenuity" a word or two will show. First I "named" the S.P.R., and it is true they are not named in the text. But they are mentioned in a note appended to the very sentence I quoted, and it is certain they occupy the field into which Prof. James hopes to draw his psychological readers. Next this is "the field which the *soi-disant* scientist usually refuses to explore." Here somebody is blamed for not doing something which it is assumed he ought to do. Who is it? Do physicians reproach philologists for ignoring the comma-bacillus? If *psychical* research is neglected, do we expect to find biologists called to task and not rather psychologists: and that when the censor is a psychologist writing about psychology? Lastly, if it was natural to suppose that psychologists were intended, was there much straining in taking "usually" to imply "the great body of psychologists," when it is notorious that the great body of psychologists are not, in fact, "psychical researchers"?

JAMES WARD.

Cambridge, Dec. 11, 1892.

16

Review of
Annales des Sciences Psychiques (1894)

The *Annales des Sciences Psychiques* for Sept.–Oct. 1893 contains three articles on thought-transference.

Dr. Dariex, being in another part of Paris from a cancer-patient whose sufferings he was relieving by hypnotism, mentally willed that she should sleep. Three times running she fell asleep at the time when he was exerting the volition. The fourth time the effect was less complete; the fifth time there was no effect, but the conditions were here different, and the author inclines to admit that the first four experiments were probably cases of cause and effect.

Dr. Tolosa-Latour, who was treating a hysterical patient by hypnotism, relates how, one day, whilst in a railway-carriage in France, she being at Madrid, he willed that she should have a convulsive attack [!!!], which she had with great severity at about the same hour, such attacks being at that time rare in her experience.

Professor Tamburini reviews Gurney's *Phantasms of the Living* at considerable length, concluding that the subject of veridical hallucinations merits the most careful study. The 'telepathic' hypothesis of their production supposes that a stimulus starting from the distant agent's mind impresses the mind of the seer, not necessarily with the content of the agent's consciousness, as in thought-transference, but often with another idea altogether. [Thus agent, whilst dying, has his mind filled with images of seer's person, but seer has a vision of agent's person, not of his own.] T. seeks to diminish this paradox by recalling those illusions in which the object perceived is unlike the stimulus, as when a noise made by birds will be heard as human speech. The most original part of the article is a suggestion that if the word telepathy do denote a real process in nature, it may be a process obtaining between different portions of one and the same brain, and that thus the train of our ideas may be partly determined by a sort of factor of which no account has yet been taken.—The author includes or appends eight unpublished cases of veridical hallucination, dream, or impression, one of them relating to a shipwreck, the seven others to as many deaths.

17

Two Reviews of
Apparitions and Thought-Transference,
by Frank Podmore (1895)

a. *Apparitions and Thought-Transference, an Examination of the Evidence for Telepathy.* FRANK PODMORE. Contemporary Science Series. New York, Charles Scribner's Sons, 1894. 12°, pp. 401.

Mr. Podmore gives here a convenient summary of the work of the Society for Psychical Research, striving to make the theory of telepathy cover as much of the field as it can be stretched over. When one sees brought together, as here in the early chapters, the evidence for thought-transference drawn from the simple experiment in which one person is set to guessing numbers, drawings, etc., which another person is intently looking-at or thinking-of, one perceives that it is far from contemptible in either quality or amount, and even if one is unwilling oneself to follow, one can find no very harsh names to apply to those who, like Mr. Podmore, take thought-transference as an approved *vera causa*, and try by its means to explain such phenomena as apparitions at the time of death, distinct in nature as they appear at first sight to be from the successful guessing of pictures in another's mind.

The book mentions successful experiments of the simple order with at least thirty subjects at short-range, and this leaves out many of the records published in the S.P.R. *Proceedings.* Of course these experiments are of diverse value, some of them being too brief or too faulty in method to base strict conclusions on, but they all contribute to the cumulative impression that chance and trickery can with difficulty be supposed to be the only things concerned. As an instance of a good series I take the observations of Mrs. Sidgwick on five hypnotized subjects who guessed numbers drawn by a third person from a bag containing 81 lotto-counters marked from 10 to 90, and handed to the hypnotizer to gaze at, all this of course out of sight of the subject. Out of 644 trials 131 were successful, that is, both digits were given correctly, though in 14 out of the 131 cases the order was reversed. 'Chance' should only have given 8 correct guesses. Again, with hypnotizer and subject in different rooms, there were 27 quite correct guesses, instead of the chance-number, 3. In the unsuccessful trials here, the first digit came right 85 out of the 252 times, instead of the chance-number, 28. Mrs. Sidgwick went through another series with the same subjects, in which 'mental pictures' were the things to be guessed, some of them being quite complex scenes, in all 108 experiments, of which 33 were correct. Of these trials, 55 were made with the agent and percipient in different rooms, so that the successes in the same room were 31 out of 71. Practically, since collusion seems fairly excluded, the only recourse of the doubter here is to say that the series were too short and that farther experimentation would have reduced the success to the chance-number. And here is where the force of so many other successful series, longer or shorter, comes in. They make the reader feel as if the dice must be in some way loaded; and to the force that loads them Mr. Podmore and his colleagues have given a name, that, namely, of *telepathy*, in lieu of a theory about it.—It is clear that many series of guesses with more successes than the probability due to chance can yield, will not positively prove that chance may not have produced the result after all; and it is still clearer that such statistics are no guide as to what the positive force may be. And here the other phenomena gone over by Mr. Podmore come in to give some feeble help. But they run into a mass of details ill adapted for synopsis, so with this brief notice I conclude.

b. *Apparitions and Thought-Transference*: An Examination of the Evidence for Telepathy. By Frank Podmore, M.A. [Contemporary Science Series.] Charles Scribner's Sons.

This readable little volume is practically an abridgment of the work of that often named and oftener misunderstood body, the Society for Psychical Research, of which Mr. Podmore is one of the more active members. It gives in brief compass an account of the fruits (if fruits they be) of its industry; and one who wishes to know what "scientific occultism" is like can do no better than turn to its pages. The chapter-headings will give the best notion of what it contains. There is an introduction on methods and problems, and a finale on theories and conclusions; there are three chapters on the experimental transference from one mind to another of simple ideas, sensations, motor impulses, etc.; six chapters on transference as it occurs not experimentally but, according to the theory the author believes in, spontaneously, as, for instance, in coincidental dreams, and in apparitions at the time of death; one on experimentally induced apparitions at a distance; one on collective hallucinations; one on clairvoyance in trance or mediumship; and one on clairvoyance in the normal state, including crystal-vision.

The first result of reading the book has been to make the present reviewer cease to wonder at the tenacity with which, in spite of the resolute opposition of orthodox science, beliefs of the semi-supernatural order retain their hold upon the mind. They are nourished by the constant recurrence of experiences of the sort here retailed, of which probably in all ages of history it would have been possible, with no extraordinary diligence, to compile a contemporaneous collection similar to those of which Mr. Podmore tells. And the second effect on the reviewer's mind is the sense the book gives him of the phenomena having, as it were, an essentially baffling nature. They are abundant; but in nearly every instance the proofs, however good up to a certain point, fall short of being quite coercive. Moreover, the phenomena are all so fragmentary, sporadic, and contextless that they weave themselves into no system. It almost seems as if it were intended in the nature of things that these events should be always present in sufficient measure to tempt belief, but always in insufficient measure to justify it. It is evident that what is needed to make the mind close upon telepathy, veridical apparitions, and ghosts, and embrace them, is a philosophical theory of some kind which has a use for such facts. But our philosophies and sciences have absolutely no place for them and no context to supply them with. It is probable, therefore, that Mr. Podmore's book will leave most readers in the baffled condition which Mr. Andrew Lang's recent book, *Cock Lane and Common Sense*, expresses so well—a condition of being unable to drop the subject, but quite as unable to be sure that there is anything firm in it to hold on to.

One of the oddest chapters in the book is that on "experimentally induced apparitions." Since 1886 there have come to Mr. Podmore's knowledge no less than seven cases in which one person by strong concentration of will has made his phantasm appear to a friend situated at a distance. There is another case dating from 1822, and another one in which the nature of the effect is less clear. The evidence in most of these cases is complete, and would be "good enough to hang a man" for any other sort of crime than so appearing, so that the doubting reader's only resource is to suppose accidental coincidence or conspiracy to deceive Mr. Podmore and his colleagues. The theosophists would probably call it a case of projection of the astral body. Meanwhile lovers all over the world are more or less unconsciously pressing in the direction of this experiment, yet we get no reports from them of its success. Perhaps they don't do it with sufficient malice prepense, from not yet being acquainted with its feasibility. The present critic knows of one case, not in Mr. Podmore's book, in which it would appear to have succeeded. Repetitions of such a result, if they could be recorded with more frequency, would perhaps do as much as anything purely empirical could do to gain credence for the philosophy which Mr. Podmore professes. We therefore cordially recommend the attempt to all who have a stomach for psychical research and a good "power of concentration."

18

Telepathy (1895)

Telep′athy [from Gr. τῆλε, far + πάθος, feeling]: thought-transference, or the phenomenon of the reception by the mind of an
impression not traceable to any of the ordinarily recognized channels of sense, and assumed to be due to an influence from the mind
of another person, near or remote. Thus the sphere of telepathy
is not the same as that of *clairvoyance*, in which it is assumed that
the mind of the subject may receive an impression of *impersonal
facts*, or things at a distance. The subject who receives the impression is called the percipient, the one from whom the influence
emanates is usually called the agent, in accounts of experiments
on this phenomenon.

In the earlier works on animal magnetism there are many reports concerning subjects who are said to have developed the
faculty of obeying the unspoken will of their magnetizer, going to
sleep and waking, moving, acting, and speaking in accordance with
his silent commands. More recently there have been public exhibi-
tors of "mind-reading," and their performances have been imitated
in private circles by the so-called willing-game. In most of these
feats the agent is required to think intently of some act while he
lays his hands on some part of the so-called mind-reader's person.
The mind-reader, either promptly or hesitatingly, will then usually
perform the act. It is safe to assume that wherever such personal
contact between the pair is allowed, the percipient is guided by

the encouragement or checking which the agent's hands more or less unconsciously exert upon his at first tentative movements; so that muscle-reading, and not mind-reading, is the proper name for this phenomenon. There are, it is true, reports of success in the willing-game where no contact was allowed; but in the absence of authentic details, they can not be taken as evidence that telepathy exists. For the same reason the earlier mesmeric reports have doubtful evidential value. The operators took too few precautions against "suggesting" to the subjects by other channels than speech what their will might be. It is only within recent years that we have learned to measure the acuteness with which an entranced person with his mind concentrated upon his hypnotizer will divine the intentions of the latter by indications which he gives quite unconsciously by voice or movement, or even by the mere order of sequence of what he does. On these accounts, evidence in the strict sense for telepathy must be sought in a small number of experiments conducted by a few more careful observers since about 1880. These experiments, taken in the aggregate, appear to make it unreasonable to doubt any longer the fact that occasionally a telepathic relation between one mind and another may exist.

In a faultless experiment on thought-transference certain precautions must be observed. To avoid previous collusion between agent and percipient the agent should receive from a third party the idea to be transferred; and the latter should, when possible, select it by drawing lots or by some other appeal to chance. This is to exclude the possibility of himself and the percipient being led by number-habits, diagram-habits, or other parallel paths of inner association to a common result. The percipient should not be in the room when the idea is determined on; and when possible it should be chosen in silence, written down, and shown, if it need be shown beforehand, in written form. The percipient should, if possible, do his guessing in another room. In any case he should be blindfolded, and there should be no conversation with him during the performance, the signal that he must attend to his inner impressions being given by bell or other sound. Physical contact between agent and percipient must not occur, and if the percipient writes or draws his result the agent should not look on, since an unconscious commentary by changes in breathing, etc., might reveal to the percipient whether he was going right or wrong.

The *Proceedings* of the Society for Psychical Research contain

Original Drawing   Reproduction

Fig. 1.

some records of experiments made under approximately faultless conditions. In certain cases the ideas to be transferred were diagrams or drawings. A couple of examples will show the success reached when at its best. Fig. 1 is from a series made with Mr. Blackburn, agent, G. A. Smith, percipient, in which out of thirty-three trials without contact, though with percipient and agent in one room, there were twenty-five reproductions as good as those here given of a figure prepared and kept outside of the room. Fig. 2 gives the first six trials of a series reported by Malcolm Guthrie, of Liverpool, he being agent and a Miss E. percipient. The conditions seem almost faultless, if the account is accurate, though the figures are simpler than in the former series. In all, with various agents, Miss E. made 150 trials, the majority of which were successful entirely or in part. Sixteen specimens are printed in the report, all about as good as those in Fig. 2.

The same Miss E. and a Miss R. were subjected at Liverpool in

Original Drawing   Reproduction

No. 1. Mr. Guthrie and Miss E.
No Contact.

No. 2. Mr. Guthrie and Miss E.
No Contact.

No. 3. Mr. Guthrie and Miss E.
No Contact.

No. 4. Mr. Guthrie and Miss E.
No Contact.

No. 5.

No. 6.

FIG. 2.

1883 to a series of experiments in transferring ideas and sensations of every order, the agents being Mr. Guthrie and others. Out of 713 trials there were but 252 cases in which the percipient either got no impression or described the object wrongly. In the remaining 461 cases the success was either complete or partial.

"Miss X." has published (*Proceedings* of Society for Psychical Research, vol. vi) a long series of telepathic interchange of experiences over a long distance with "Miss D.," corroborated by independent entries in their respective diaries. Of 20 such entries 14 refer to a consciousness on the part of Miss D. that Miss X. was at that hour (the hours are quite irregular) playing a certain definite piece of music.

Miss Wingfield was the subject of a series of number-guessings, where out of 2,624 trials there were 275 successes instead of 29, which was the figure probable on the assumption of "chance." The numbers thought of were the 90 two-digital ones, from 10 to 99. They were drawn at random from a bowl and thought of by the percipient's sister. In a later series of 400 trials with this percipient the completely right guesses were 27 instead of the chance number 4; there were moreover, 21 guesses with the digits reversed, and 162 with a single digit in its right place.

Similar, though less extended and perhaps less conclusive, series of experiments at guessing ideas have been reported in the Society for Psychical Research *Proceedings* by various experimenters—Dessoir, Schmoll and Mabire, W. J. Smith, von Schrenck-Notzing, and Barrett and Gurney. The observations last referred to were those first published. The subjects were two girls who, four years later when experiments were resumed, were found, when tested in each other's presence, to be cheating by a code of signals. Much has been made of the breakdown of this case. But very many of the earlier successes recorded of these children occurred when they were singly present, and often when only one experimenter knew the thing to be guessed. Collusion under such circumstances can not well be charged, although willingness to cheat rightly casts vague suspicion on all trials done with the percipient concerned, and shows the importance of making all tests under the conditions described as "faultless" a few lines back. Mr. Rawson finally, in vol. xi of the *Proceedings*, gives a striking series of correct card and diagram guesses.

On telepathy in the hypnotic state there are recorded in the

Proceedings experiments by Dr. B. Thaw and Prof. and Mrs. H. Sidgwick. The conditions in the latter set seem to have been, on the whole, very careful, though not quite faultless in the technical sense. The agent was the hypnotizer, G. A. Smith. The things to be impressed were usually the numbers (of two digits) on eighty-one lotto-counters, drawn by Prof. Sidgwick from a bag and handed to Mr. Smith to gaze at, while the hypnotized percipient awaited the impression. There were four percipients, with 644 trials made with agent and percipient in the same rooms, and 218 made with them in different rooms. In the former set 131 trials were successful, though the digits were named in reverse order in 14 of these 131 cases. In the latter set there were only 9 successes. The "probable" number of successes by chance would have been in the former set 8, in the latter at most 3. Later, with three of the same percipients and three new ones, Mr. Smith still being agent, Mrs. Sidgwick and Miss Johnson report 252 trials and 27 successes (chance number = 4), with agent and percipient in different rooms. Mr. Smith transferred "mental pictures" to five subjects, successfully in 31 out of 71 trials in one room, in 2 out of 55 in different rooms. The subjects of the mental pictures were such things as "a boy skating," "a baby in a perambulator with nurse," "a mouse in a trap," etc.

Prof. Richet has described (*Proceedings* of Society for Psychical Research, vol. v) a series of successes in guessing drawings in the hypnotic state; but as he found that the same subjects succeeded 30 times out of 180 trials in guessing the drawing when it was inclosed in an envelope and unknown to any one present, it is doubtful whether telepathy or clairvoyance be the cause of the success. Control-experiments showed that "chance" could give as many as 3.5 per cent. of good successes at matching pictures made arbitrarily by different persons with others taken at random from a large collection previously prepared. Richet's hypnotic subjects gave, however, 10 per cent. of good successes in 200 trials, and he concludes the existence of an unknown power.

Thus, to count only systematically pursued experiments, some of which are not mentioned here, there are accounts from more than a dozen competent observers concerning about a score of subjects, all seeming to show a degree of success in guessing very much greater than that which chance would give. Different readers, however, will weigh the evidence differently, according to their prepossessions. Much of it is fragmentary, and in much one or other condition of "faultlessness" in experimenting is violated. The mass, however, is decidedly imposing; and if more and more of this solitary kind of evidence should accumulate, it would probably end by convincing the world.

Meanwhile there are other kinds of telepathy which, illogically perhaps, impress the believing imagination more than high percentages of success in guessing numbers can. Such are cases of the induction of sleep in hypnotic subjects by mental commands given at a distance. Pierre Janet, Richet, Gibert, Ochorowicz, Héricourt, Dufay, Dariex, Tolosa Latour, and others are the relaters of these observations, of which the most important evidentially are those made on the celebrated somnambulic subject, Madame B., or "Léonie." Out of one series of 25 trials with this woman, there were 18 complete and 4 partial successes. Mr. Ochorowicz vouches for some of these, and gives also a long series in which silent commands were acted out by another hypnotic subject of his own, both he and she being, however, in the same room. The most convincing sort of evidence for thought-transference is given by the sittings of certain "test-mediums," of which the best worked-out case is that of Mrs. Piper, published in the Society for Psychical Research *Proceedings* for 1890–92–95. This lady shows a profuse intimacy, not so much with the actual passing thoughts of her sitters as with the whole reservoir of their memory or potential thinking; and as the larger covers the less, so the present writer, being as convinced of the reality of the phenomenon in her as he can be convinced of anything in the world, probably makes less exacting demands than he otherwise would on the sort of evidence given for minor grades of the power.

The authors of the word telepathy have used it as a theory whereby to explain "veridical hallucinations" such as would be the apparition of a person at a distance at the time of his death. The theory is that one who is dying or passing through some crisis is for some unknown reason peculiarly able to serve as "agent" and project an impression, and that the telepathic "impact" in such a case produces hallucination. Stated thus boldly the theory sounds most fanciful, but it rests on certain actual analogies. Thus a suggestion made to a suitable subject in the hypnotic trance that at a certain appointed time after his awakening he shall see the operator or other designated person enter the room, will post-hypnotically take effect and be followed at the appointed time by an exteriorized apparition of the person named. Moreover, strange as the fact may appear, there seems evidence, small in amount but good in quality, that one may, by exerting one's will to that effect, cause one's self to appear present to a person at a distance. As many as eight persons worthy of confidence have recently reported successes in this sort of experiment. The writer knows a ninth case, impossible to publish, but where the evidence (as far as taken) is good. Now the committee on the census of hallucinations of the Society for Psychical Research find that the "veridical" ones among them—those, namely, in which the apparition coincides with the death of the person who appears —are 440 times more numerous than they ought to be if they were the result of mere chance. For the particular data and logic by which this figure is obtained, see the report in vol. x of the Society for Psychical Research *Proceedings*. Of course, if such a conclusion ever be accepted, and if the telepathic theory of such apparitions be credible, the probability that telepathy is the cause of success in the simpler number-guessing cases would be greatly re-enforced. The whole subject, so far as definite observation goes, is still in its earliest infancy.

BIBLIOGRAPHY.—J. Ochorowicz, *De la suggestion mentale* (Paris, 1887); *Proceedings of the Society for Psychical Research, passim*; F. Podmore, *Apparitions and Thought-Transference* (1894).

19

Address of the President before the Society for Psychical Research (1896)

The Presidency of the Society for Psychical Research resembles a mouse-trap. Broad is the path and wide the way that leadeth thereinto. Flattering bait is spread before the entrance: the distinguished names of one's predecessors in the office; the absence of any active duties; England and America symbolically made one in that higher Republic where no disputed frontiers or foreign offices exist;—and all the rest of it. But when the moment comes to retrace one's steps and go back to private life like Cincinnatus to his plough, then comes the sorrow, then the penalty for greatness. The careless presidential mouse finds the wires all pointing against him; and to get out there is no chance unless he leave some portion of his fur. So in resigning my office to my worthier successor, I send this address[1] to be read across the ocean as my ransom, not unaware as I write it that the few things I can say may well fall short of the dignity of the occasion and the needs of the cause for which our Society exists.

Were psychical research as well organized as the other sciences are, the plan of a presidential address would be mapped out in advance. It could be nothing but a report of progress, an account of such new observations and new conceptions as the interim might

1 Read at the Annual Meeting of the Society in London on January 31st, 1896, and also at meetings of the American Branch in Boston on January 31st and New York on February 1st, 1896.

have brought forth. But our active workers are so few compared with those engaged in more familiar departments of natural learning, and the phenomena we study so fortuitous and occasional, that two years must as a rule prove too short an interval for regular accounts of stock to be taken. Looking back, however, on our whole dozen years or more of existence, one can appreciate what solid progress we have made. Disappointing as our career has doubtless been to those of our early members who expected definite corroboration or the final *coup de grâce* to be given in a few short months to such baffling questions as that of physical mediumship, to soberer and less enthusiastic minds the long array of our volumes of *Proceedings* must suggest a feeling of anything but discouragement. For here for the first time in the history of these perplexing subjects we find a large collection of records to each of which the editors and reporters have striven to attach its own precise coefficient of evidential value, great or small, by getting at every item of first-hand evidence that could be attained, and by systematically pointing out the gaps. Only those who have tried to reach conclusions of their own by consulting the previous literature of the occult, as vague and useless for the most part as it is voluminous, can fully appreciate the immense importance of the new method which we have introduced. Little by little, through consistently following this plan, our *Proceedings* are extorting respect from the most unwilling lookers-on; and I should like emphatically to express my hope that the impartiality and completeness of record which has been their distinguishing character in the past will be held to even more rigorously in the future. It is not as a vehicle of conclusions of our own, but as a collection of documents that may hereafter be resorted to for testing the conclusions and hypotheses of *anybody*, that they will be permanently important. Candor must be their very essence; and all the hesitations and contradictions that the phenomena involve must appear unmitigatedly in their pages. Collections of this sort are usually best appreciated by the rising generation. The young anthropologists and psychologists who will soon have full occupancy of the stage will feel, as we have felt, how great a scientific scandal it has been to leave a great mass of human experience to take its chances between vague tradition and credulity on the one hand and dogmatic denial at long range on the other, with no body of persons extant who are willing and competent to study the matter with both patience and rigor. There have been isolated experts it is true, before now. But our Society has for the first time made their abilities mutually helpful.

If I were asked to give some sort of dramatic unity to our history, I should say first that we started with high hopes that the hypnotic field would yield an important harvest, and that these hopes have subsided with the general subsidence of what may be called the hypnotic wave. Secondly, I should say that experimental thought-transference has yielded a less abundant return than that which in the first year or two seemed not unlikely to come in. Professor Richet's supposition that if the unexplained thing called thought-transference be ever real, its causes must to some degree work in everybody at all times (so that in any long series of card-guessings, for example, there ought always to be some excess of right answers above the chance-number) is, I am inclined to think, not very well substantiated. Thought-transference may involve a critical point, as the physicists call it, which is passed only when certain psychic conditions are realized, and otherwise not reached at all—just as a big conflagration will break out at a certain temperature, below which no conflagration whatever, whether big or little, can occur. We have published records of experiments on at least thirty sub-jects, roughly speaking, and many of these were strikingly success-ful. But their types are heterogeneous, in some cases the conditions were not faultless, in others the observations were not prolonged, and generally speaking, we must all share in a regret that the evi-dence, since it has reached the point it *has* reached, should not grow more voluminous still. For whilst it cannot be ignored by the candid mind, it yet as it now stands, may fail to convince coercively the sceptic. Any day, of course, may bring in fresh experiments in successful picture-guessing. But meanwhile, and lacking that, we can only point out that our present data are strengthened in the flank so to speak, by all observations that tend to corroborate the possibility of other kindred phenomena, such as telepathic impres-sion, clairvoyance or what is called 'test-mediumship.' The wider genus will naturally cover the narrower species with its credit.

Now, as regards the work of the Society in these latter regards, we can point to solid progress. First of all we have that master-piece of intelligent and thorough scientific work—I use my words advisedly—the Sidgwick Report on the Census of Hallucinations. Against the conclusion of this report, that death-apparitions are

440 times more numerous than they should be according to chance, the only rational answer that I can see is that the data are still too few, that the net was not cast wide enough, and that we need, to get fair averages, far more than 17,000 answers to the Census-question. This may of course be true, though it seems exceedingly unlikely, and in our own 17,000 answers veridical cases may have heaped themselves unduly. So neither by this report then, taken alone, is it absolutely necessary that the sceptic be definitely convinced. But then we have, to strengthen *its* flank in turn, the carefully studied cases of 'Miss X' and Mrs. Piper, two persons of the constitution now coming to be nicknamed 'psychic' (a bad term but a handy one), each person of a different psychic type, and each presenting phenomena so chronic and abundant that, to explain away the supernormal knowledge displayed, the disbeliever will certainly rather call the Subjects deceivers and their believers dupes, than resort to the theory of chance-coincidence. The same remark holds true of the extraordinary case of Stainton Moses, concerning which Mr. Myers has recently given us such interesting documents. In all these cases (as Mr. Lang has well said of the latter one) we are, it seems to me, fairly forced to choose between a physical and a moral miracle. The physical miracle is that knowledge may come to a person otherwise than by the usual use of eyes and ears. The moral miracle is a kind of deceit so perverse and successful as to find no parallel in usual experience. But the limits of possible perversity and success in deceit are hard to draw—so here again the sceptic may fall back on his general *non-possumus*, and without pretending to explain the facts in detail, say the presumption from the ordinary course of Nature holds good against their supernormal interpretation. But the oftener one is forced to reject an alleged sort of fact by the method of falling back on the mere presumption that it can't be true because so far as we know Nature, Nature runs altogether the other way, the weaker does the presumption itself get to be; and one might in course of time use up one's presumptive privileges in this way even though one started (as our anti-telepathists do) with as good a case as the great induction of psychology that all our knowledge comes by the use of our eyes and ears and other senses. And we must remember also that this undermining of the strength of a presumption by reiterated report of facts to the contrary does not logically require that the facts in question should all be well proved. A lot of rumours in the

air against a business man's credit, though they might all be vague and no one of them amount to proof that he is unsound, would certainly weaken the *presumption* of his soundness. And all the more would they have this effect if they formed what our lamented Gurney called a faggot and not a chain, that is, if they were independent of each other and came from different quarters. Now our evidence for telepathy, weak and strong, taken just as it comes, forms a faggot and not a chain. No one item cites the content of another item as part of its own proof. But taken together the items have a certain general consistency; there is a method in their madness, so to speak. So each of them adds presumptive value to the lot; and cumulatively, as no candid mind can fail to see, they subtract presumptive force from the orthodox belief that there can be nothing in any one's intellect that has not come in through ordinary experiences of sense.

But it is a miserable thing for a question of truth to be confined to mere presumption and counter-presumption, with no decisive thunderbolt of fact to clear the baffling darkness. And sooth to say, in talking so much of the merely presumption-weakening value of our records, I have been wilfully taking the point of view of the so-called 'rigorously scientific' disbeliever, and making an *ad hominem* plea. My own point of view is different. For me the thunderbolt *has* fallen; and the orthodox belief has not merely had its presumption weakened, but the truth itself of the belief is decisively overthrown. If you will let me use the language of the professional logic-shop, a universal proposition can be made untrue by a particular instance. If you wish to upset the law that all crows are black, you mustn't seek to show that no crows are; it is enough if you prove one single crow to be white. My own white-crow is Mrs. Piper. In the trances of this medium, I cannot resist the conviction that knowledge appears which she has never gained by the ordinary waking use of her eyes and ears and wits. What the source of this knowledge may be I know not, and have not the glimmer of an explanatory suggestion to make; but from admitting the fact of such knowledge I can see no escape. So when I turn to the rest of our evidence, ghosts and all, I cannot carry with me the irreversibly negative bias of the rigorously scientific mind, with its presumption as to what the true order of nature ought to be. I feel as if, though the evidence be flimsy in spots, it may nevertheless collectively carry heavy weight. The rigorously scientific mind may in truth easily over reach itself. Science means first of all a certain dispassionate method. To suppose that it means a certain set of results that one should pin one's faith upon and hug forever, is sadly to mistake its genius, and degrades the scientific body to the status of a sect.

But I am devoting too many words to scientific logic and too few to my review of our career. In the question of physical mediumship we have left matters as baffling as we found them; neither more nor less. For if on the one hand we have brought out new documents concerning the physical miracles of Stainton Moses, on the other hand we have by the Hodgson-Davey-experiments and the Paladino-episode very largely increased the probability that testimony based on certain sorts of observation may be quite valueless as proof. Eusapia Paladino has been to us both a warning and an encouragement. An encouragement to pursue unwaveringly the rigorous method in such matters from which our *Proceedings* have never departed, and a warning against drawing any prompt inference whatever from things that happen in the dark. The conclusions to which some of us had been hastily led on 'the Island' melted away when in Cambridge the opportunity for longer and more cunning observation was afforded. Some day, it is to be hoped, our *Proceedings* may be enabled to publish a complete study of this woman's life. Whatever the upshot of such a study, few documents could be more instructive in all ways for psychical research.

It is pleasant to turn from phenomena of the dark-sitting and rat-hole type (with their tragi-comic suggestion that the whole order of nature might possibly be overturned in one's own head by the way in which one imagined oneself on a certain occasion to be holding a tricky peasant woman's feet) to the "calm air of delightful studies." And on the credit-side of our Society's account a heavy entry must next be made in favour of that immense and patient collecting of miscellaneous first-hand documents that alone has enabled Mr. Myers to develop his ideas about automatism and the subliminal self. In Mr. Myers' papers on these subjects we see for the first time in the history of men's dealings with occult matters, the whole range of them brought together, illustrated copiously with unpublished contemporary data and treated in a thoroughly scientific way. All constructions in this field must be provisional and it is as something provisional that Mr. Myers offers us his attempt to put order into the tangle. But thanks to his genius we begin to see for the first time what a vast interlocked and graded system these phenomena, from the rudest motor automatisms to the most startling sensory apparition, form. Mr. Myers' methodical treatment of them by classes and series is the first great step towards overcoming the distaste of orthodox Science to look at them at all.

But our *Proceedings* contain still other veins of ore for future working. Ghosts, for example, and disturbances in haunted houses. These, whatever else may be said of them at present, are not without bearing on the common scientific presumption of which I have already perhaps said too much. Of course one is impressed by such narratives after the mode in which one's impressibility is fashioned. I am not ashamed to confess that in my own case, although my *judgment* remains deliberately suspended, my *feeling* towards the way in which the phenomena of physical mediumship should be approached has received from ghost and disturbance-stories a distinctly charitable lurch. Science may keep saying "such things are simply impossible"; yet, so long as the stories multiply in different lands, and so few are positively explained away, it is bad method to ignore them. They should at least accrete for future use. As I glance back at my reading of the past few years (reading accidental so far as these stories go, since I have never followed up the subject) ten cases immediately rise to my mind. The Phelps-case at Andover, recorded by one of the family in *McClure's Magazine* for this month; a case in China in Nevius's *Demon Possession*, published last year; the case in John Wesley's life; the *Amherst Mystery* in Nova Scotia (New York, 1888); the case in Mr. Willis's house at Fitchburg, Mass., recorded in *The Atlantic Monthly* for August, 1868 (XXII, 129); the Telfair-Mackie case in Sharpe's *History of Witchcraft* in Scotland; the Morse case in Upham's *Salem Witchcraft*; the case recounted in the Introduction of W. v. Humboldt's *Briefe an eine Freundin*; a case in the *Annales des Sciences Psychiques* for last year (p. 86); the case of the carpenter's shop at Swanland, near Hull, in our *Proceedings*, Vol. VII, Part XX, pp. 383–394. In all of these, if memory doesn't deceive me, material objects are said to have been witnessed by many persons moving through the air in broad daylight. Often the objects were multitudinous—in some cases they were stones showered through windows and down-chimney. More than once it was noted that they fell gently and touched the ground without shock. Apart from the exceptionality of the reputed occurrences, their mutual resemblances suggest a natural type, and I confess that until these records or others like them are positively explained away, I cannot feel (in spite of such vast amounts of detected fraud) as if the case against physical mediumship itself as a freak of nature were definitively closed. But I admit that one man's psychological reaction cannot here be like unto another's; and one great duty of our Society will be to pounce upon any future case of this 'disturbance' type, catch it whilst red-handed and nail it fast, whatever its quality be.

We must accustom ourselves more and more to playing the rôle of a meteorological bureau, be satisfied for many a year to go without definitive conclusions, confident that if we only keep alive and heap up data, the natural types of them (if there are any) will surely crystallize out; whilst old material that is baffling will get settled as we proceed, through its analogy with new material that will come with the baffling character removed.

But I must not weary your patience with the length of my discourse. One general reflection, however, I cannot help asking you to let me indulge in before I close. It is relative to the influence of psychical research upon our attitude towards human history. Although, as I said before, Science taken in its essence should stand only for a method and not for any special beliefs, yet as habitually taken by its votaries Science has come to be identified with a certain fixed general belief, the belief that the deeper order of Nature is mechanical exclusively, and that non-mechanical categories are irrational ways of conceiving and explaining even such a thing as human life. Now this mechanical rationalism, as one may call it, makes, if it become one's only way of thinking, a violent breach with the ways of thinking that have until our own time played the greatest part in human history. Religious thinking, ethical thinking, poetical thinking, teleological, emotional, sentimental thinking, what one might call the personal view of life to distinguish it from the impersonal and mechanical, and the romantic view of life to distinguish it from the rationalistic view, have been and even still are, outside of well-drilled scientific circles, the dominant forms of thought. But for mechanical rationalism, personality is an insubstantial illusion; the chronic belief of mankind that events may happen for the sake of their personal significance is an abomination; and the notions of our grandfathers about oracles and omens, divinations and apparitions, miraculous changes of heart and wonders worked by inspired persons, answers to prayer and providential leadings, are a fabric absolutely baseless, a mass of sheer *untruth*. Now of course we must all admit that the excesses to which the romantic and personal view of Nature may lead, if wholly unchecked by impersonal rationalism, are direful. Central African Mumbo-jumboism in fact is one of unchecked romanticism's fruits. One ought accordingly to sympathize with that abhorrence of romanticism as a sufficient world-theory; one ought to understand that lively intolerance of the least grain of romanticism in the views of life of other people, which are such characteristic marks of those who follow the scientific professions to-day. Our debt to Science is literally boundless, and our gratitude for what is positive in her teachings must be correspondingly immense. But our own *Proceedings* and *Journals* have, it seems to me, conclusively proved one thing to the candid reader, and that is that the verdict of pure insanity, of gratuitous preference for error, of superstition without an excuse, which the Scientists of our day are led by their intellectual training to pronounce upon the entire thought of the past, is a most shallow verdict. The personal and romantic view of life has other roots beside wanton exuberance of imagination and perversity of heart. It is perennially fed by *facts of experience*, whatever the ulterior interpretation of those facts may prove to be; and at no time in human history would it have been less easy than now—at most times it would have been much more easy—for advocates with a little industry to collect in its favour an array of contemporary documents as good as those which our publications present. These documents all relate to real experiences of persons. These experiences have three characters in common: they are capricious, discontinuous and not easily controlled; they require peculiar persons for their production; their significance seems to be wholly for personal life. Those who preferentially attend to them, and still more those who are individually subject to them, not only easily *may* find but are logically bound to find in them valid arguments for their romantic and personal conception of the World's course. Through my slight participation in the investigations of the Society for Psychical Research, I have become acquainted with numbers of persons of this sort, for whom the very word Science has become a name of reproach for reasons that I now both understand and respect. It is the intolerance of Science for such phenomena as we are studying, her peremptory denial either of their existence or of their significance except as proofs of man's absolute innate folly, that has set Science so apart from the common sympathies of the race. I confess that it is on this its humanizing mission that our Society's best claim to the gratitude of our generation seems to me to depend. We have restored continuity to history. We have shown some reasonable basis for the most superstitious aberrations of the foretime. We have bridged the chasm, healed the hideous rift that Science, taken in a certain narrow way, has shot into the human world.

I will even go one step farther. When from our present advanced standpoint we look back upon the past stages of human thought, whether it be scientific thought, or theological thought, we are amazed that a Universe which appears to us of so vast and mysterious a complication should ever have seemed to any one so little and plain a thing. Whether it be Descartes' world or Newton's; whether it be that of the materialists of the last century or that of the Bridgewater treatises of our own; it always looks the same to us—incredibly perspectiveless and short. Even Lyell's, Faraday's, Mill's and Darwin's consciousness of their respective subjects are already beginning to put on an infantile and innocent look. Is it then likely that the Science of our own day will escape the common doom, that the minds of its votaries will never look old-fashioned to the grandchildren of the latter? It would be folly to suppose so. Yet, if we are to judge by the analogy of the past, when our Science once becomes old-fashioned, it will be more for its omissions of fact, for its ignorance of whole ranges and orders of complexity in the phenomena to be explained, than for any fatal lack in its spirit and principles. The spirit and principles of Science are mere affairs of method; there is nothing in them that need hinder Science from dealing successfully with a world in which personal forces are the starting-point of new effects. The only form of thing that we directly encounter, the only experience that we concretely have, is our own personal life. The only complete category of our thinking, our professors of philosophy tell us, is the category of personality, every other category being one of the abstract elements of that. And this systematic denial on Science's part of personality as a condition of events, this rigorous belief that in its own essential and innermost nature our world is a strictly impersonal world, may, conceivably, as the whirligig of time goes round, prove to be the very defect that our descendants will be most surprised at in our own boasted Science, the omission that to their eyes will most tend to make *it* look perspectiveless and short.

But these things lie upon the knees of the gods.—I must leave them there, and close now this discourse, which I regret that *I* could not make more short. If it has made you feel that (however it turn out with modern Science) our own Society at any rate is not 'perspectiveless,' it will have amply served its purpose; and the next President's address may have more definite conquests to record.

20

Psychical Research (1896)

'Psychical Research' has so many enemies, fair and foul, to elude before she gets her scientific position recognized, and is moreover so easily vulnerable in her present stage of development, that I may be excused, as one of her foster-fathers, for uttering a word that may turn the edge of Prof. Cattell's amiable *persiflage* in the last number (p. 582) of this *Review*. He seems not quite to have caught the argument of my presidential address. The inquiry, I said in substance, still remains baffling over a large part of its surface, for the evidence in innumerable cases can neither be made more perfect, *nor*, on the other hand, be positively explained away. It *may* be malobservation, illusion, fraud or accidental coincidence; it *may* be good and true report. One can only go by its probabilities and improbabilities; and the scientist, who goes by the *presumption* that the usual laws of nature are superabundantly proved, feels the improbability of 'occult' phenomena to be so infinitely great that he is practically certain that the evidence in their favor must be bad, even though he can't show in the particular case where the badness comes in. The issue between Prof. Cattell and myself is as to the general logic of presumption here. I urged that the force of the scientist's presumption, quâ presumption, might some day be worn out by the accumulation of 'psychic' cases, long before his doctrine of nature was radically overthrown, as it would be were a single case conclusively proved. Prof. Cattell says: "When we have an enormous number of cases, and cannot find among them a single one that is quite conclusive, the very number of cases may be interpreted as an index of the weakness of the evidence"; apparently holding the scientist's presumption to be actually strengthened by the quantity and quality, taken together, of the psychical research reports. It would indeed be strengthened if, *pari passu* with the accumulation of reports, there went for each concrete type of case a parallel accumulation of demonstrations of its erroneousness. And as this is just what happened in the 'physical mediumship' type, the work of the S.P.R. in that field has been mainly destructive. But it has happened practically nowhere else. In the veridical apparitions, in the chief thought-transference experiments, fallacy has been assumed, but not clearly demonstrated. The presumption has remained presumption merely, the scientist saying, "I can't believe you're right," whilst at the same time he has been unable to show how or where we were wrong, or even except in one or two cases to point out what the error most probably may have been. In such a state of things people trust their instincts merely, while waiting for a final proof. Many naturalists, for instance, consider the evidence for the sea-serpent practically sufficient. In others it provokes a smile. Meanwhile a single sea-serpent dragged up on the beach would settle the matter forever. I spoke of my own final proof or psychical sea-serpent-corpse, under the name of a 'white crow.' Professor Cattell says: Can the exhibition of any number of gray crows prove that any crows are white? But our reports are not of gray crows; at the very worst they are of white crows without the skins brought home, of sea-serpents without the corpse to show; and where there are such obvious reasons why it must be easier to see a wild beast than to capture him, who can seriously maintain that continued reports of merely seeing him tend positively to decrease the probability that he exists? In the case of telepathy, ghosts, death-apparitions, etc., the reasons why the evidence is always likely to be imperfect rather than perfect are equally obvious, and the logic is the same as in the wild beast case. Continued reports, far from strengthening the presumption that such things cannot exist, can only detract from its force.

Both here and in my address I have played into the hands of the scientist, and granted him every conceivable concession about the facts for the sake of making my point as to the logic of presumption all the more clear. But there is such a thing as being too fair-minded, so that one wades in a very bog of over-reasonableness. For, in point of fact, the concrete evidence for most of the 'psychic' phenomena under discussion is good enough to hang a man twenty times over. The scientist's objections, on the other hand, are either shallow on their face (as where apparitions at the time of death are disposed of as mere 'folk-lore,' or swept away as a mass of fiction due to illusion of memory), or else they are proved to be shallow by further investigation, as where they are ascribed to chance-coincidence. May I add a word to illustrate this?

On page 69 of Vol. II of this *Review*, I summarized the elaborate Sidgwick's report on the Census of Hallucinations. That paper concluded that the stories of apparitions occurring on the day of the death of the person appearing were 440 times too numerous for the phenomenon to be fairly ascribed to chance. I said that the chief objection practically to this conclusion was that the census, covering only 17,000 cases, was still too small. Last spring I wrote a letter to Professor Sidgwick, giving, for quotation at the Munich Congress, the results of my American census of 7,123 cases. They prolong and corroborate his own. The 'yes' cases were 1,051 in number, or 14.75% of the whole. I cite part of my letter:

"Of these yeses 429 were without particulars, and in 36 the percipient had not signed the account. Only 586 subjects thus remained for statistical treatment.

"Of these, eliminating all who had the experience before they were 10 years old; and all who gave vaguely plural experiences, there remain 62 subjects with *71 cases of visual hallucination of some recognized living person. Of these, 12 are reported to have occurred on the day of the death of the person seen.*

"These numbers are so small that I have not ventured to reduce them by any elimination of 'suspicious' cases, as you did, but as a correction for oblivion have multiplied the whole lot by your figure 6 1/2.

$$71 \times 6\ 1/2 = 462 \text{ (in round numbers)}.$$

"*Let this 462 represent the probable whole number* of visual hallucinations of living persons really seen by the percipients since their tenth birthday. The 12 veridicals are in round numbers 1/39 of 462. Therefore 1/39 is the probability induced from facts, and due to the unknown cause of apparitions, that if a man 'appear' at all it will be on his death-day.

"On the other hand (the U.S. death rate being practically the same as that of England) the *pure chance* that if any one appear on a certain day it will be one who is dying on that day is only 1/19000. But 1/39 = 1/19000 × 487; so that *apparitions on the day of death are, according to our statistics, 487 times more numerous than pure chance ought to make them.*

"The details will be sent later, but I append now a few remarks. Of the 71 cases, all but the 12 that were death-apparitions are treated as insignificant in the statistical result. But this, though inevitable, is unfair to an occultist theory of their origin, since 16 of them, though not veridical of death, were coincidental in other ways. *E.g.*, 6 were collective, 2 were reciprocal, 1 was voluntarily produced by the distant agent, 2 were premonitory and 3 were veridical, but not of death. But let this pass. There remains another unfairness to occultism in our systematic rejection of all vaguely plural cases. I rejected 19 percipients in all for this reason, but 7 of these percipients gave us coincidental cases, 2 of them being apparitions at time of death.

"We can afford to be very generous. Suppose we throw in these 19 subjects as if each stood for one non-coincidental case. Suppose we multiply for oblivion by 10 instead of 6 1/2, making 900 cases in all. Suppose we take only 1/2 of our 12 veridicals. We shall still get 6/900=1/150 =126 times 1/19000, the chance-probability."

The objections to be urged are:

"1. *Smallness* of numbers. But the agreement of our figures with yours goes against this.

"2. *The collectors packed their sheets with veridicals.* As a matter of fact, they say they knew the answer beforehand in 3, possibly in 4 cases. In 5 cases they state their ignorance. In 3 they say nothing. From the warning against packing with yeses and the very large number of veridicals that the collectors furnish *separately*, this objection is probably not very important.

"3. *The veridical cases are not strong.* They are not. Only 5 have any corroboration, and in no case is it first-rate. Our best cases are not among these. But this is an argument at any rate in favor of the sincerity of the Census; and since coincidentals and non-coincidentals are treated homogeneously (at least all the deliberate treatment going against the statistical result, where they are treated otherwise than similarly), the ratio of the surface figures is perhaps a fair one.

"But I never believed and do not now believe that these figures will ever conquer disbelief. They are only useful to rebut the assurance of the scientists that the death-warnings, if not lies, are chance coincidences. Better call them lies and have done with it."

I make this quotation, first because of the facts themselves, but mainly because I have above too easily granted the ambiguity of the evidence for such phenomena, and I wish to show, by a new example, how, when two interpretations are possible, it is not always the scientist's which has the greater numerical probability in its favor, or which is the more carefully or conscientiously weighed.

21

A Case of Psychic Automatism, Including "Speaking with Tongues," by Albert Le Baron, Communicated by Professor William James (1896)

[In the early '70s I was invited to see a young woman from the country, who had come up to Boston in the hope of finding some learned men in that city who might be able to determine the unknown language which her lips were irresistibly impelled to utter. I cannot now recall her account of the way in which this phenomenon in her had originated, but it was a curious thing to hear. When she gave herself permission, her vocal organs would articulate nonsense-syllables with the greatest volubility and animation of expression and with no apparent fatigue, and then again stop at the behest of her will. The young woman and the friends with whom she stayed seemed sincere in their belief that this must be a religious miracle identical with the "speaking with tongues" so common among the earliest Christians, and which St. Paul seems himself to have possessed, judging from I. Corinthians, Chap. XIV. It is hardly needful to say that at the time when I saw her, this young woman's speech had not been recognized by any linguistic expert in Boston or Cambridge, and that (she herself knowing no foreign tongue) all its phonetic elements were palpably English.

I never heard of the later history of her case, and have never since met with this phenomenon of automatism until I became acquainted last year with Mr. Le Baron, as I will call the gentleman whose narrative follows. I had, a couple of years previously, corresponded with him about a small and abstruse work on metaphysics which he had published; a year later, the lady whom he calls Evangel in his narrative wrote to me that he had become the subject of remarkable personal powers which I ought to witness;[1] and cor-

1 This is the letter:

"November 26th, 1894.

"MY DEAR PROFESSOR JAMES: Among those who came to [us] this summer was Mr. [Le Baron]. He was so much impressed with what he thought the ideal state of things which he found that he returned again and again for a day at a time to get an uplift as he said. On one of these occasions while calling at our house (he was in a room which was always my mother's afternoon room), he had a strange psychical experience. He began talking in a way that he could not control. Later he spoke to me in a voice so like my mother's that her St. Bernard dog, which hitherto had not noticed him, got up and went over to him and smelt his face in seeming recognition. As he seemed unable to help himself I became alarmed and called help. Since then he has had many strange experiences, speaking in various tongues and writing down the sounds phonetically and then writing translations. One of them, 'Hymn to Egypt,' I mail herewith. He is conscious of all he does now and can permit the utterance or not at will. He is very desirous of confirming the tongues, if possible. . . . Some one versed in Oriental languages could quickly tell whether what comes to him is of value. Respectfully yours,

(Signed) _____ _____."

A later letter from the same lady reads as follows:

"April 26th, 1895.

"MY DEAR PROFESSOR JAMES: . . . Mr. [Le Baron] came to [our camp] last Summer, to write-up for the _____ _____ a short account of [our] work. He had been a great lover of the Kantian philosophy, but he had lapsed into agnosticism, and almost pessimism. The work at [Shelter Island] interested him so much that he remained over night. During the night he had a vision concerning it which seemed to him so far from realization that he spent the night in tears, and went away feeling that our work was an ideal one, but that there was no place for it in this busy, bustling nineteenth century. Nevertheless, it lured him back again, and one evening while sitting in our reception room at our own house, and talking with me concerning the work and my mother's life, he had a very startling experience. He was suddenly psychologized in some way, and, though conscious, began saying words which he felt did not originate in his own mind. His whole manner of speaking and his tones changed so much that the large Saint Bernard dog, which had been a special pet of my mother, rose up from the rug and went over to him and began lapping his hands all over. The tone in which Mr. [Le Baron] spoke was very like my mother's, and the words said purported to be inspired by her. When I saw how much he was affected, I became alarmed, and called assistance. After a time he resumed his normal condition, and said that he had been conscious through it all, knew that he was talking, but could not help himself. This, as I understand, was the beginning of many strange experiences which came to him later, at home surrounded by his family, and also when away from home on journeys.

"Of the strange tongues with which he speaks, I can say but little. I have no knowledge of them, and the translations that purport to be given are largely of an ethical nature. He has kept a very accurate account of these communications, but I have not yet had the leisure and opportunity to examine them.

"This speaking in strange tongues is not a new thing to me. Once in this city I heard an old man, a Catholic, speak in a tongue which was very musical, and

144

respondence finally brought about a meeting with him and an exhibition of his vocal automatism of which, at his request, Dr. Hodgson and I presently had phonograms taken, which are now at the Society's office in Boston.

Mr. Le Baron, who is a literary man, aged 39, was at that time (February 1895) much impressed by his various experiences, and by no means willing to abandon the idea that his unintelligible vocal performances were involuntary reproductions of some ancient or remote tongue. His earnestness and energy in seeking to gain corroboration for this view is the best possible proof that the vocal movements carried with them for him, as he made them, no subjective feeling of being due to his personal will. This, too, in spite of the fact that his will could both start and arrest them, make them go fast or slow, and sing instead of speaking them. The phonetic elements in his case again seemed English; and I tried to make him believe (but all in vain) that the whole thing was a decidedly rudimentary form of motor automatism analogous to the scrawls and scribbles of an "undeveloped" automatically-writing hand. He spent hours poring over grammars and vocabularies of African and Asiatic tongues. First it was Coptic, then Rommany, then something Dravidian. I corresponded with various philologists in his behalf, sending them specimens, phonetically written out, of his discourse. But no light came, and finally he grew convinced, by the mere progress of the phenomenon, that it was less important than it pretended to be.

---

purported to be an old form of the Latin language. He was entirely an uneducated man, and later on what he said was translated by Mrs. Cora L. V. Richmond, of whom you have probably heard. What was given purported to be from a priest of the Romish Church who was a missionary to California several hundred years ago, and in this communication he claimed that what he said could all be verified by documents now in the Vatican at Rome. These communications were taken down by Mrs. Richmond's husband in shorthand, and if you desire, I have no doubt you can verify what I have said.

"Concerning Mr. [Le Baron] there is little more to be said except this: That the experiences which have come to him have altered his whole course of thinking. Where he was formerly despondent, he is now optimistic, and at peace with himself. This in itself is a great joy to his family and to me. If I could see you, I could tell you much more which at present it is impossible for me to write.

"I feel that Mr. [Le Baron] has a work before him for which these experiences are in some degree, perhaps, preparing him. Of this I feel sure: That he is earnest, sincere, and absolutely to be relied upon. Very truly yours,

———— —— ————."

At last yielding to urgent importunity on my part (for the case seemed to me too rare and too valuable from the intellectual character of the Subject to be lost), Mr. Le Baron has written out the autobiographic narrative which follows, of his experience. The names are changed to prevent identification, and the actual geographical scope of country disguised; but the facts related I believe to be substantially true, and the relative distances of the journeys taken are correct. Of the sincerity of the writer I have myself no doubt.

WILLIAM JAMES.]

ALBERT LE BARON'S EXPERIENCE.

In the summer of 1894 I had occasion, for the sake of a certain literary project, to visit a portion of our Coast. At a place to which I will give the name of Shelter Island I found a group of mystics summering. I drifted into the esoteric camp with a copy of Kant's Critique in my valise, by way of a little light summer reading. The leader of the Shelter Island mystics, Evangel, was a spiritist of the loftiest type, a believer in re-incarnation, whose psycho-automatic 'control' was her dead mother. Of practical genuine spiritualism I knew nothing. To theosophy I was an utter stranger. I found the atmosphere of the camp pregnant with a new type of the old style of millenial optimism. The World's Congress of Religions had re-awakened the hope of a new chemistry of civilization. The pious heart of Evangel was solacing itself with the holy hope of doing something to effect a union of the occidental and oriental religions on the purest conceivable basis of Gnostic-Platonism. Occasionally, séances were secretly held, far into the midnight, for the purpose of procuring information from 'invisible brethren' to carry on the work. At one of these séances I met with my first experience. We were seated under a pine tree. Clairvoyants were present. "Wheels" of light and other phenomena were said to be seen by them. I sat listening to the affirmations.

Suddenly an entirely new and strange psycho-automatic force shook through me like a gust of fierce wind through a tree. I willed myself into a state of passivity in order to observe the phenomena. I went into no trance however. The force became intelligent in action. It drew back my neck. Additional motor violence was displayed in my limbs. I was brought, from my sitting posture, down on the flat of my back. The force produced a motor disturbance of my head and jaws. My mouth made automatic movements; till, in a few seconds, I was distinctly conscious of *another's voice* —unearthly, awful, loud, and weird—bursting through the woodland from my own lips, with the despairing words: "Oh! My People!" Mutterings of semi-purposive prophecy followed. One of the clairvoyants added additional weirdness to the experience by positively affirming that phantasms of ancient Egyptian sages stood over me.

I was so dazed and 'rattled' by the experience and the motor disturbances, that, at the close of the séance, I had to be assisted to my feet, and was walked for some time to and fro in the night air to recover my equilibrium.

The witnesses of the foregoing experience are alive at this hour. The names can be secured—if desired—by anyone. Either Professor James or Dr. Hodgson could secure them and furnish them, for the names of some of them are already known to the S.P.R. officers.

During my short stay in the camp I enjoyed the hospitality of Evangel. Later, I was reclining on the sofa her mother had lain on during her last sickness. Again, the psycho-automatism struggled to manifest itself. I shaded my eyes with my hand to shut off distracting objects, and to assist my thought to a dead stand-still. This time, a woman's voice came through my lips. Evangel positively claimed that it was the voice of her dead mother.

On hearing the voice of the woman escape my lips, her dead mother's old dog "Barry" staggered painfully across the room to where I was lying, and began smelling my face.

"He smells her!" whispered Evangel. The old dog lay down by my side. In a few minutes the voice of the psycho-automatism changed. A man's deep voice succeeded that of the dead woman's.

"It's father!" again whispered Evangel.

Statements of a semi-prophetic character were again indulged in by the psycho-automatism, and the words: "he shall be a leader of the hosts of the Lord!" exploded with loud emphasis. The séance came to a close. The effect of all this new experience on my emotional nature was powerful. I trod in holy awe about the rooms of the house of Evangel, as, ever and anon, vibrations of the psycho-automatism with which I was *en rapport*, trembled through my nerves, evoking strange and holy modes of the most exquisite consciousness.

Those feelings were the most wonderful I have ever enjoyed.

One night I slept in the bed where the dead father of Evangel slept during the last years of his life. The next morning I awoke lame. I limped about painfully for hours. The father of Evangel *was a lame man*.[2] As a sensitive somnambule I had taken on his lame condition. On the general principle that all startling and unusual phenomena are interpreted as having some personal bearing, particularly when we are distinctly informed that they have, I construed the vibrations of the psycho-automatism, whenever they occurred, as evidence of the presence of the 'spirit' of Evangel's mother.

"Has mother been here?" asked Evangel on one occasion, discovering me in a flood of tears. I answered her in an affirmative sob, and a tone of pious awe; for my assent to the spiritistic interpretation of the phenomena had induced a permanent and deep exaltation of religious sentiment. I would lie in bed on my back peering wistfully into the night darkness at the shadowy and vapory outlines of what I supposed to be "invisible brethren." I could hear distinct raps on the head-board. Small globules of golden light would, after travelling about the room in the blackness, come and melt away over my eyes. In the dense darkness, a group of arithmetical figures once shone from near the ceiling of the room.

Evangel was the possessor of a finger ring, considered to possess occult powers. She had been told by a clairvoyant that she was to receive this talisman, some months previous to her reception of it. The gem came in a round about way from Egypt, having been purchased from an Arab by a certain American gentleman whilst on a trip to the Orient.

The mysterious advent of this ring, and the profound belief of Evangel in the genuineness of the communications from the spirit of her saintly mother, were the two—as she considered them—impregnable facts, by the means of which she substantiated the accuracy of her call to her work. As proof of the occult spiritual power of the ring, Evangel told of a young man, a sceptic, who, on placing the ring on his finger, was thrown down on the floor of a room in a convulsive condition.

I heard the story and asked for the ring to be placed on my finger. An attempt at spontaneous chirography was suggested. My hand flew in wide jerky spasmodic movements over the table. Noth-

---

[2] In answer to enquiries, Mr. Le Baron writes: "I did not know beforehand that her father was lame. I was informed so when seen limping."—Ed.

ing intelligible came. I laughed in incredulity. Evangel gently rebuked me: "You must not laugh at them." "They are glad to meet you!" ejaculated another lady in the room, explaining the violence of the motor disturbances.

But the ice was broken. It was only a question of development. It was also explained that I was difficult to control and that it would take a little time for '*them*' to be able to write through me. Subsequently the psycho-physical spontaneity controlled the right arm and hand, and wrote intelligible verbiage. From subsequent experiences, I believe the automatism capable of modifying the ordinary presentations of at least four out of the five senses. As the interpretation of life by me now was solely from the angle of *mystical cognition*, rather than from the theorems of pure reason, I became a most devoutly earnest religionist. My love of the sublime was nurtured by the dream of Evangel as to the possibility of the union of the occidental and oriental religious worlds, and my converse with the 'spirits' of the dead upon that vast subject. I secretly avoided the living to talk with the 'spirits' in the depths of the pine woods, or on the hill-tops, with my head bared to the heavens. Following out the same principle I took delight in roaming through private burying grounds. I invariable 'sensed' the presence of the spontaneity in grave yards; and this 'sensing' of the psycho-spontaneity was always interpreted by me to be an indication of the presence of the "invisible brotherhood." I became ascetic, and avoided animal food. I quoted the oracles of Zoroaster, and laid aside Kant's Critique. I became exquisitely morbid on the subject of my own spiritual and moral unworthiness, and could not reconcile humility with the splendid confidence of Evangel.

The first message of importance given to me on leaving Shelter Island was at Riverhead, September 6th and 8th, 1894. The first message was to be sent to Evangel as purporting to be an address to her from her mother. In the second address, the psycho-spontaneity or automatism, assuming to be the "*true* mother" of my "soul," said, among other things: "I am going to guide you into the way of truth. . . . You must be at the door of the church near the old house in the town of Stowe which is in the state Vermont, by the time the sun rises on next Tuesday. You will then see the reason why I told you to go." On September 9th, at my residence, having returned to New York City, I asked for more explicit instructions. Among other things, the psycho-automatism, still assuming to be the dead mother of Evangel, said: "I think you are now to be the one that shall hear the voice of the One that shall be the truth. . . . You will know that it is He by the voice of the Holy One." As (in my opinion though perhaps obscurely stated) the reverence accompanying the deific rhetoric of civilizations varies in the ratio that the special education of a people leads them to insert their own concrete value into any given method of rhetoric, I did not deem it unlikely that the psycho-automatism would assume that deific rhetorical style likely to be the most revered by me. I did not know that such a village as Stowe existed. But Evangel did; as I subsequently learned. A map shewed the village located some distance from Bolton. On Sunday night I left New York for Bolton, Vermont. I hired a carriage at the hotel at Bolton and drove to Stowe. At Stowe I ordered the carriage ready by sunrise. The next morning about 5 o'clock I was in the porch of the church. The building was old, weather-beaten, and the flooring of the porch in a decayed condition. The porch faced the east, and the edifice was on a hill overlooking the village. An old house stood near it. I uncovered my head and stood in the porch and faced the east. The night had been a drizzling one. The sky was black with the remnants of the rain clouds. Slowly golden streaks of dawn appeared. The black clouds rolled away. The sun arose. I noticed a graveyard across a field. The psycho-automatism indicated an ejection of verbiage. The verbiage assumed a deific style, and was as follows:

I shall be glorified in the work of the people for thou hast proved thyself to be the man whose voice is the voice of Him who sent thee. Thou hast obeyed the command of the Holy One, and the Valleys shall rejoice in the hope and the joy of the Lord. I shall be in thy heart and thou shalt answer to my voice.

Such a style of verbiage proved to me that the cause of the psycho-automatism knew that my emotional nature would be influenced by it when I recognized its deific modes of composition. I have no adequate idea of any deific object answering to such a communicating style, but simply state the facts, irrespective of the deific, or any other mere rhetorical form.

On returning to Bolton I concluded to remain there till I had finished a certain small piece of literary work. On Wednesday night, September 12, I retired to my room at the inn somewhat early, to be alone with the "invisible brotherhood";—perchance they had something to communicate. Again the psycho-automatism assumed the grave deific style known to the occidental English speaking world. *Viva voce* it gave utterance to the following chain of historic conceptions:

I will tell thee of the days of thy sojourning in the land of the people of the Jumba where the land is the joy and the light is the joy of the people. The land is the country of the ancient Egyptians and thy glory and thy power was the pride of the people. Thy name was Rameses and thy glory was the end of the triumph of the people. Thou didst throw down the people for their joy was the truth of the truth. Thou didst exalt thyself to the end and the hope of the truth was in thy keeping and thy victory was the fall of the truth. Thy way was not the way of the Lord and the Lord hath sent thee through the fire.

The point I subsequently made on the foregoing speech, was, that granting the composition to be a chain of lies from beginning to end, it certainly takes some degree of intelligence to be able to lie so artistically, and that the cause of the psycho-automatism must have known something of the truth about the matter, to be able to lie about it.

I deem it a vital necessity for future psychical illustration to give a somewhat full and adequate illustration of the various rhetorical forms of the deific verbiage employed by my psycho-automatism. Heretofore, experimental inductions of such psycho-automatic processes have not scientifically reached the analytical stage of the mystico-deific-modes.

A somewhat poetic form of the deific style given to me *viva voce* in an hotel of Woodstock, Vermont, is a case in point. There are some eighty-nine words in the passage.

When the song of the day is the song of the night, and the truth is the joy, and the triumph of the peace is the song of the redeemed, then the hope of all flesh shall be the truth, and the deliverance from the truth which now is the truth of the day but the darkness of the light! The flash of the truth is the truth of the day, and the flash of the fire of the truth shall soon be the light of the night!

That a high excitement of the mind inspiring confidence and hope of success is an essential to the induction of such phenomena goes without saying. On any lower plane than ecstasy or transport of soul I was in a constantly distressed condition.

From this arose the temptation to yield—at odd moments—a facility of credulous assent to the re-incarnating and other assertions of the psycho-automatism. If however I accepted the mystic conceptions as *bonâ fide* then I was thrown into violent antagonism to my own common-sense, and that of the world. On the other hand, if I withdrew my assent to the holier utterances of the psycho-automatism then my 'spiritual' nature, and love of the sublime, violently rebelled. Thus I vibrated like a pendulum between the new world of psychic phenomena on the one hand, and the old world of physical phenomena on the other. To my cognition of the foregoing alternative was presented the following perplexing dilemma. If both of these worlds of experience simply implied relations of my consciousness to two totally distinct worlds of *phenomena*, and my consciousness was in any way related to the deific 'thing-in-itself'; then, from *what* unknown source emanated these *two distinct worlds of phenomena* to which the laws of this deific consciousness related? This *crux criticorum* still remains the puzzle of my life.

But other startling experiences were before me.

On Monday morning, September 17, came another message *viva voce* to go to St. Louis. To a house on the street "which is called the street of the —— the number is ONE TWO THREE."

This I construed to mean 123 —— Street. The object of my going was explained. I would meet some one there who would give me information. In this message given in my home in the suburbs of New York City to go to St. Louis, a tendency to the antithetical deific style appeared more fully. The principle by which conceptions were purposely set in opposition to each other, revealed itself in the following seventy-five words:

I have seen thee in glory and I have seen thee in shame!
I have seen thee in light and I have seen thee in darkness!
I have seen thee in peace and I have seen thee in terror!
I have seen thee in joy and I have seen thee in sorrow!
I have seen thee exalted and I have seen thee debased!

Tuesday, September 18, I secured railway transportation New York to St. Louis, return; and whilst on the train, conversed by means of a pencil and pad with the psycho-automatism. The perpetual question with me was, can I, *via* psycho-automatism, ascend into the uncreated essence of thought—to the Mind of Minds—and perchance snatch down some new metaphysical conception helpful to the lower world? Utter self-surrender, and self-abandonment, was insisted on by the psycho-automatism. 123 —— Street, I found to be a business block. The number had been given, as I thought, simply as a test. Other tests were given the next day. I began to rebel. In the directory I found the name of an artist whom I knew. I explained myself. From my artist friend I learned that the most occult man in the west lived on Chonteau Avenue, and that he considered his life controlled by a princely-priest of the house of Rameses the Great! I called on the gentleman and saw a picture of this Egyptian prince-priest on the wall of his room. The occultist was ascetic in appearance, pale, with large dreamy eyes. I explained my mission; and later, whilst in an apparently semi-trance condition, he made a lengthy foreign speech which purported to come from the princely-priest of the house of the Egyptian King. A stenographer who was present took down the subsequent translation. Both the gentleman and his stenographer knew Evangel.

The following sentences may shew the trend of the verbiage and the conceptions:

Oh! Son of Ram! For the first time have I the privilege of speaking to you face to face since I last held your hands chilling with physical death on the banks of the Nile. . . . I congratulate you that you have laid aside the tempestuous feeling of arrogance which in the ancient days controlled you for your overpowering—which have brought to you in the times past much of discipline, much of sorrow, much of anguish before you had entered the present body. . . . Having fulfilled obligations to the utmost, having reached the point to which you were sent and directed through the devious ways which you have travelled to reach and attain. We know you well enough to understand that the life which comes will be devoted to such degree as possible under the circumstances of the environment to the new thought—the understanding and comprehension of the *real*, and to the awakening to that which you become to see is the unreality. Out of the darkness shall come the Light, the Light that is the joy and the hope of the nations! etc.

The speech of this gentleman simply added fuel to my psychic fire, and I have every reason to believe that the gentleman believed he was uttering a genuine foreign tongue.

Was this psycho-automatism 'fooling' this man, as well as myself? If not, what as yet undiscovered law governed the phenomena? That this psycho-automatism could reach a style of deific assumption, even majestic in its utterance, is further illustrated by the following composition, which came through my hand automatically, far into the dead of night, as I lay in a passion of self-abasement on my bed in the hotel.

The love of the past hath been darkness, the love of the future shall be light! The power of all flesh is love and the light of all flesh is love! My love shall cover the great mountains! My love shall rule the seas as with a rod of power! My love shall be the strength of the Day and my love shall be the curtain of the Darkness! My love shall inhabit the earth and my love shall save all flesh! My love shall be thy father and thy mother and my love shall be thy love! My love is the sun in its strength and the flowers breathe my love! The stars rejoice in my love and my love shall fill all things with my glory! I love the man whose heart is broken, and I love the woman whose sorrow is the cup of her peace! I love the man who is poor and the man who is filled with the joys of life! I love the man who shall not love me and I love the man who loves me! I love the darkness for the darkness shall be light! I love the terror for I love the peace! I love the beauty of man and I love the sadness of man! I love the unrest of man and I love the peace of man! I love the peace and I love the sorrow! I love the joy and I love the terror! I love the praise and I love the curse! I love the man whose ways are dark and I love the man whose ways are light! I love the love of hope and I love the love of love! I love the day of mourning and I love the day of joy! I love the love of pleasure and I love the love of pain! I love the man who steals and I love him from whom he has stolen! I love the man who kills and I love the man who is slain! I love the world for the world is mine and the truth of all things is love!

To substantiate the fact that the psycho-automatism can give—*viva voce* as well as by automatic-chirography—expression to conceptions embodying the same antithetic principle of reiterative deific personification, I append the following seventy-five words:

I have heard the roar of cities! I have heard the music of the woodlands! I have heard the tears of the nations as they fell! I have heard the songs of the nations as they rose! I have heard the roar of the death of the man who was slain in battle! I have heard the shout of the victor! I have heard the new word and I have heard the old word!

It is for the reader to decide whether or no the above phrases can be construed as being in any way explanatory of the transcendental basis of the world as a sum of phenomena. They are beyond my comprehension. Whether or no they proceed telepathically from the living or dead; or whether they proceed from some transcendental subject, which is a sort of deific representation of that which contains the grounds of cosmical phenomena according to unknown and transcendental laws, I cannot make deposition to. I do not know. Whilst on my return trip to New York City my first experience in clairaudience was given. I was sleeping, and suddenly awakened by a voice shouting in my ear the words: "The enthusiasm shall fill the hearts of the multitude in the place of the hours of the Day!" In subsequent dreams came such sentences as: "It shall take two birds to carry thee, my son." "Blessed are they who always obey themselves." The latter sentence I saw in my dream, in English characters, among a number of ideographs on an Egyptian slab of stone.

From the foregoing it is evident, that, in its incipiency the phenomenon differed from that of a *dédoublement de la personnalité*, in that it did not appear to be a case of 'subliminal consciousness' on the one hand, or a supra-normal intellectual faculty on the other, but distinctly that of a purely *extraneous psycho-physical spontaneity or automatism*. It was *psychic*, for it presented conceptions; it was *physical*, for it presented sense intuitions; it was *spontaneous* and *automatic*, for it acted independent of the usual trend of motor phenomena on the one hand, and of the wilful intelligence as used in ordinary experience on the other. This it automatically continued to do until later on in my experience when I believed myself to be so completely *en rapport* with it that I considered the spontaneity practically identical with and in perfect accord with the actions of my own will. From this point on there was a gradual diminution in the character of the manifestations.

Just so long as I assented to its absolute *objectivity* my emotions and feelings were all dramatically influenced to joy or grief by the appearance of its conceptions. It was unquestionably true that if interests could be predicated of the cause of the psycho-automatism, those interests were always in an inverse ratio to physical pleasure on a low plane. How my suffering could be in any sense an advantage to the cause of this psycho-automatism, save as a means of getting me into a more sensitive condition, I do not know. And yet my experience repeatedly taught me that a complete self-surrender to the psycho-automatism, as a deific telepathic ideal, resulted in the communication of a loftier flow of verbiage. And, as a distinct *mode* of consciousness, the psycho-mystic mode now ranked, in my own experience, as the *causa sine qua non* of a definite form of religion.

The automatism repeatedly urged me to take long journeys, which, judging from my past experience in obeying it, I have no doubt would have resulted in gifts of deific verbiage, and other phenomena, if I had obeyed. It told me to be in —— on the 30th of December 1894, and I should receive a reward, but I did not go. It told me to go and see the Emperor of China, but I did not go. It told me to go to Seville, Spain, but I did not go. The only reason I could account for its perpetual desire for me to take such journeys, was, that it seemed to know that my nervous system transmitted better when I was in a 'worked up' condition when coming and going. Expectation or disappointment threw me into the more sensitive condition essential to its manifestation.

Speaking in Unknown Tongues.

It is hardly necessary to observe that a deific style of verbiage is necessarily relative, and that—as mere sound—the neighing of a pony is more musical to my ear, than for a man to utter deific conceptions to me in a language I know nothing about. On Sunday morning, September 30th, 1894, I had my first experience in "speaking in unknown tongues," at my residence in the suburbs of New York City. I had been conversing with the psycho-automatism the night previous, and up to that time had received sufficient deific verbiage, one way and the other, to make a small book. Suddenly, whilst conversing with it in my bed-room on Sunday morning, it changed abruptly off from English into unintelligible sounds resembling a foreign tongue, and which, had I not been, as I think, pretty level headed at the time, I should have construed as a mental state pathognomic of mania. And yet I was not sufficiently at myself to immediately seize pencil and pad and write down the sounds. When I subsequently asked of the psycho-automatism for a translation, among others I received the two following:

The Darkness to Egypt.

I have seen all thy ways, O son of the Nile! I have heard all thy songs, O son of the Nile! I have listened to all thy woes, O son of the Nile! I have been with thee, O son of the Nile! I have been near thee when thy days were full of glory. I have been near thee when thy days were covered in sadness. I have heard thy voice, O son of Egypt! I have counted thy tears, O son of Egypt! I have heard thy voice of wailing, O son of Egypt! I have watched thee when thy men of might have flown; I have watched thee when thy glory has faded; I have watched thee when thy sun has set; I have watched thee, O son of the Nile! Thy tears have been my tears; thy joys have been my joys; thy woes have been my woes. O son of the Nile, I love thee! O son of the Nile, I love thee! My heart yearns for the days of thy glory. My heart opens to thy heart. O son of the Nile, how I love thee! Thy sands are now the way of the stranger; thy plains are now the path of the poor; thy fields are now the wastes of the day. Thy hope is gone; thy day has fled; thy years are gone. O son of Egypt, I have loved, loved, loved, loved thee! Thy day shall rise again. Thy hope shall dawn, thy sun shall shine, thy love shall be mine, thy tears shall flow, thy hope shall dawn, thy flowers shall bloom again. Thy palaces shall rise again, thy dream shall live again. Thy years shall be years of joy, thy triumph shall be the triumph of peace, thy walks shall ring with new songs, thy hopes shall dawn with new stars, thy rivers shall flow with new life; thy heavens shall blaze with new light. Thy hope is my hope, thy coming is my coming. I am he who loved thee; I am he who kissed thy lips; I am he who in thy great hour was thine. I love thee, I love thee, I love thee; O son of Egypt, I love thee! When thy day shall rise again I will be thy guide; when thy hour shall dawn again I will be thy love; when thy morn shall rise again I will be thy sun; when thy life shall flow I will be thy heart; when thy love shall beat I will be thy breast; when thy womb shall bear thy young I will be thy guide; when thy life shall ebb again I will be thy life; when thy star shall go to rest I will be thy night; when thy love shall be thy day I will be thy love. O son of Egypt, I have loved thee! Thy way has been long; thy path has been dark; thy woes have been many; thy tears have been as the sand. I love thee! I love thee! I love thee!

The other translation embodied, among other things, the following relatively intelligible sentences, which, as I wrote them down, *according to the sounds*, are as enigmatical to me as the purported foreign tongue from which they assumed to be a translation:

Son of Peru—of Gerro—of Terro—of Tichaperu—Terra—Terra—of Pesuro—of Tepecutu—of Teruto—Zeereelu—Instopan—of Zeecorila—Sceucru. Greeting: I have come through these of mine—I have come—I have come! Eros, Eros, Eros.

The intelligibility of the first translation, at least, the *a priori* cognitive content of the translated sentences assured me that the unintelligible sounds were not necessarily pathognomic of mania, but like the repeated requests to take journeys, were another stratagem to keep me in a 'worked up' condition of expectation or disappointment essential to its manifestations. If, *cæteris paribus*, such was its object, it succeeded admirably, and here again arose the temptation to yield a facility of credulous assent to the opinion that I was speaking a language known to me previously, on the hypothesis of the pre-existence of the soul. This for a time I believed. In my attempt to demonstrate this I exerted an immense amount of philological energy as Professor William James and Dr. Hodgson can testify. On Monday, October 1st, 1894, I left my home in the suburbs of New York City for the town of Levanna, N.Y. In room 12 of the hotel and on Monday night, came the following messages in "unknown tongues" together with the interpretations:

The unknown tongue. Te rumete tau. Ilee lete leele luto scele. Impe re scele lee luto. Onko keere scete tere lute. Ombo te scele te bere te kure. Sinte te lute sinte Kuru. Orumo imbo impe rute scelete. Singe, singe, singe, eru. Imba, Imba, Imba.

The Translation. The old word! I love the old word of the heavens! The love of the heavens is emperor! The love of the darkness is slavery! The heavens are wise, the heavens are true, the heavens are sure. The love of the earth is past! The King now rules in the heavens!

Unknown tongue. Etce ce Tera. Lute te turo scente. Inke runo tere. Scete inte telee turo. Oru imbe impe iste. Simpe, Simpe, Simpe.

Translation. Love now has been sent! The light of the earth! The joy of the day! The light of all the world!

Unknown tongue. Puree otee Sincalee. Sintee teef eenotef teeotsepo. Teeoseeton guopeson. Oto te pere te ture, to tere, te stere, te tinke, te lutetum. Ombo, Ombo, Ombo.

Translation. The light of the day has now come! The darkness has gone! The love of earth, of air, of darkness, of night is no more!

Unknown tongue. Egypto. Mome su u Ra. Ere mete su onko inte. Ama tu telee. Oumbe te senete su u Ra. Inter pelee te tete. Ombo O sceuntri. Inteneo duru sinte. Mome su u Ra. Sene tu te skule. Ombo telute tene turo inko. Impe telute omko sinke tinke devuda. Ombededo dene sinte lepo. Olumono teme setre comto. Mome su u Ra. Entenke tele mete tura obde sinte tulepe. Omte tete leste dinke itelete. Mome su u Ra. Indude dinke lutesin, Amen Ra, Amen Ra, Amen Ra.

Translation. O son of Ra! I have come to thee! The truth has come. I have come O son of Ra! See the truth in me! The truth is not of darkness O son of Ra! I will teach thee! I will tell thee of the light! The light is all that I will teach thee! The truth shall lead thee! It shall be all that shall lead thee O son of Ra! The truth has long been hidden from thee! The light has been small! Darkness has been thine O son of Ra! In the truth the love is known! The pure sun!

Unknown tongue. Intelete te interlute. Bule te skuru te sinte omkoton. Stinte te lete ode tinkalong. Lepe lute impe sute compo intope. Lute su empri. Lute lu lelee inkapon. Instute te binkalong te pelee te obde de pere. Bolotele te sinte. Inde tere somte compo. Peme tu stimele inkepe. Surume tome lete skuru. Istepe tompo dere ombo luto lutoston. Amen Ra, Amen Ra, Amen Ra.

Translation. The book of the past is not the book of the love! It is the song of the sadness! The great light has come to help the darkness! Love is emperor! Love is the light of the darkness! The home of the poor is the palace of love! All the light is love! All the earth shall be light! All the darkness shall be light! All the light shall be darkness! The love of all things shall be the light of all things! Pure light!

Unknown tongue. De Bedeouins. Scele ce ompo. Ilee te tere simpee. Orumee tereme scele. Orumeto te scelo te rume. Rene mene te scele. Ire scelete sceluto. Keputuro sceletis. Simerete te scele. Intemete te colope. Erete esimpe sonte. Samarata et te lute. Eru de lute de sumbos. Indodede scele erumo. Orumoro impe iste. Scele poloto arimo. Imba, Imba, Imba.

Translation. Light is omnipotent! To love the darkness is simple! I have brought the light! I have lighted the heavens! The Darkness of the Heavens shall pass! I adore the great heavens! The Darkness has gone! The light is simple! The Glory has come! The one has ruled! I love the Sarah of old! I love the day of the symbols! The heavens are now aflame! The morning has come! The night is polluted!

Unknown tongue. Esteru Combo. Esteelee te teme te skomo te turo impe. Impe ikke te turo teto. Repe tete inke. De gurumbo de tete. Itru re simpe te compo. Inte te polote. Erim de stere te tau. Repe tete institi. De bulo de ruro de dere. Instipiti te com. Omboro de pemeste. Rume debe. Ororde de sumpto. Interule de combo. Inke rule ruletee.

Simbaletee te tokan. Tinke te rulee tete. Ikombo de sceninkee. Sere te combo de elee. Indo, Indo, Indo.

Translation. I have heard! I see! I understand! Understand, and see, and hear! I see! See the end! The Darkness doth see! The Light doth see! He hath finished the Darkness! I see the pollution! The only light has come! I see it all! The book, the truth, the word! The truth has come! The Day has dawned! Darkness flies! The way is Great! The thought has come and the Day! The symbol has passed! The fact is here! I have come to see you! I have come to love you!

Unknown tongue. Ingruputo Cepetuotef. Sentefopleson leme teme tome. Intersperopston stefoeton. Ilu, Ilu, Ilu.

Translation. The light has been sent to me! The light shall come to you!

Unknown tongue. Bode lute compokon su me tote se bute lomele. Ilu impte tutete compete. Sere muto tompe. Boome tepe iste olo tene. Istrune te poto lotete. Bete ponko tseste letelo. Bute pinkete ofsto sute lute. Lute compte luteson. Pileto sintere luteto. Bule tule linke ompto dicele. Inste luton crito pomero. Interstele tele produmo lute mute sinkeru ompto. Sinketeru lute tete picketu simpetu. Sitituti, Sitituti, Sitituti.

Translation. I have now brought you the word of light! The love is the love of the Day! The Day is of the Love! The coming of all things are near! The instrument is of the word-man. The power is with the word-man! The joy is of the love! The great love of the Love-Man! The love of the Great-Love-Man. The book will tell you of all the Love Greatness! The Light of the Power is the Love of all things! The Love is produced by the great light of all things! All the Light must come from the Great Light!

In the attempt subsequently to explain the foregoing 'foreign tongues' I arranged nine different theories, from which the reader may take his choice.

First Theory. The sentences are all the work of a powerful unconscious imagination and the sentences do not possess the natural consonantal and vowel elements of a language at all.

Second Theory. They are brand new ideas in old and foreign verbal husks, the forms of which were latent in the man's sub-consciousness at birth.

Third Theory. The consonantal and vowel combinations are but the articulate shells of very ancient ideas latent in this man's sub-consciousness at birth, but out of the shells of which the meanings have been eaten up or metamorphosed by some at present unknown law of mental evolution, but are not now to be considered as ideas at all.

Fourth Theory. They are none of the foregoing but are new and actual presentations of real and new ideas in a foreign tongue.

Fifth Theory. They are none of the foregoing but a ludicrous and silly mistake of the man's imagination allied to some species of humorous hallucination and are not to be considered seriously, or they are a perjury, or a ghastly jest, or a very profound mental trick, or the loose jargon of a maniac.

Sixth Theory. They are none of the foregoing but are a species of scientific telepathy, and the consonantal and vowel combinations come from some morally indifferent, sublimely good, or awfully naughty source, and which is subject to the will of the man.

Seventh Theory. Notwithstanding he says he never knew or heard these consonantal and vowel combinations before he uttered them, he may be in some very mysterious way deceiving himself.

Eighth Theory. That it may not be beyond human belief that he is unconsciously in possession of a similar principle of intuitive linguistic power said to be possessed at this day by the higher adepts of India, or the Grand Lama of Thibet, or the Rosicrucians, by the means of which an unknown language is spoken by purely intuitive processes unknown to the analysis of western mental philosophy.

Ninth Theory. That these consonantal and vowel combinations and their intuitive vocal adjustments may be startling scientific hints of mental forces latent in everybody, and which if studied, generalized, verified, systematized, and seriously investigated by philosophers might prove of incalculable benefit to the human race, but which could find no encouragement for expression in the nineteenth century because of the fierce and mocking intolerance of the conservative dogmas of the age.

My instinct of self-preservation urges me to publish these theories simply to assure those who have *new* ones that my larder is full for the present, and I don't need them.

The foregoing 'foreign' paragraphs are not all that were given by any means but I have given enough to indicate to the reader the phonetic principle employed by the psycho-automatism in keeping me in touch with itself, and in the 'worked up' condition essential to its manifestation. When it ceased giving me prose it gave poetry in "unknown tongues." As the foreign verbiage came *viva voce* I penciled it down mostly in an archaic mono-phonetic form, and the subsequent blending into diphonetic and other forms was governed by the principle of conjectural euphony. In the 'poems' the number of feet in a line was grasped by the recurring of the sound synonyms. In a large number of cases where the letter *c* had the sound of *s*, I used the letter *s*. In the foregoing paragraphs I occasionally used two ee's to convey the long sound of a single e. In my later writing down of the verbiage the sound of hard c was shown by the letter k.

As an illustration of the kind of poetry given *viva voce* by the psycho-automatism I append the following poem with its translation:

> Ede pelute kondo nedode
> Igla tepete kompto pele
> Impe odode inguru lalele
> Omdo resene okoro pododo
> Igme odkondo nefulu kelala
> Nene pokonto sefo lodelu
> Impe telala feme olele
> Igde pekondo raog japate
> Rele pooddo ogsene lu mano.

> I have been looking looking for daylight;
>   Ages have flown and the years have grown dark:
> Over the hilltops the sun is now shining,
>   Far from the sky comes the song of the lark.
> Beauty is dawning, the darkness is passing,
> Far up the vales fly the songs of the light.
> Into the cities the joy will be spreading;
> Into the byways the light will be spread:
> Glory has come to the lost son of man!

For me to quote the entire poem with the 'foreign tongue' precedent, would occupy no less than 272 lines. As a further illustration however of the phonetic principle employed by the psycho-automatism to keep me in a 'worked up' state, I append a list of foreign words from a note-book containing talks in "unknown tongues" beginning the first weeks in October 1894, and closing the last week in April 1895.

A very large per cent of the words I subsequently traced in a vocabulary of primitive Dravidian, or British Indian, non-Aryan languages.

Aru, aar, ama, arde, adaba, asode, asopan, arimo, angora; barabu, bado, bede, bete, beme, bere, belu, befo, belo, beja, beod, bepo, bela, bil'e, butebon, bings, bode, bote, bola, bodo, bomo, bondo, boda, bobo, bolo, bono, bood, brote, bume, boid, bute, bule, bulo, bubo, bubu, bulu, blublu, buto, baba, beto, botu; ce, cele, condo, comtin, compe, coere, combo, crito, confebo, confo, cimbale; dape, dara, de, debo, dede, defu, defood, dako, dekon, dikeado, dekan, dege, debe, dole, dela, delu, dera, depin, depe, deso, deme, delulu, delo, delu, delule, delute, demo, deog, depu, derne, dinke, dinbe, dode, doig, dobo, doja, do'me, domo, dolu, dope, dolo, do'se, doog, dongo, dorure, dote, do'le, do're, do'ong, du, dudo, dudu, dudedu, du'de, dububo, du'ing, dubudu, du'le, dubu, ducelu, duru, dubuing, dutitu; EE, EEE, eme, ede, ege, edu, elu, ese, ene, ele, ete, eis, eru, edko, efrn, este, egle, egpe, eglu, erim, ebede, eklou, edda, edebo, edede, edebe, edebu, emete, etepe, etutu, egotes, egtore, egsuro, egypto, esimpe, ecemete, edelude, edelute, edeputo, ebedebede; fara, fatu, fadumba, fapeme, falu, fala, fano, fajo, fao, fape, fado, faton, fapa, fako, fakon, facre, faja, fale, falute, falale, faidme, fase, faod, fare, faig, feme, feja, fele, fedon, fepo, felo, fejo, feto, feno, felu, fekum, fetan, fekan, fela, feoglo, fekondo, feredo, fiule, fole, foid, fola, fodo, folo, fote, fose, fode, fobo, fota, foja, fojs, fofu, folo, foko, fopo, foso, foto, fope, foka, fomo, fondo, fore, food, fokon, fosan, foigre, foloda, folecon, fosonko, fonoto, folale, fula, fuka, futu, fute, fuja, fule, fupe, fulalo, fulela, fukodo, fulo, fure, fuma, futing, fupon, fukolo, furo.

As the tracing out of the phonetic forms through the entire alphabet would be a bore to any one but a linguist, the foregoing may suffice for illustrative purposes. I visited other towns, and received *viva voce* enough additional verbiage at the hotels I stopped at, to make several chapters. I abandoned my experiments about the end of April 1895. This was due to the fact, primarily, that I could not, and did not substantiate the verbiage as an actual language, although I could trace out a very large number of words in actual use among the non-Aryan tribes of British India. Balfour's cyclopædia of British India put me on the track of a number of words, also Hunter's vocabulary of the non-Aryan tribes. That there are some laws in mystic psychology not yet understood goes without saying. That there exists some mental source, defined as a psycho-automatism, with which man is capable under certain conditions of putting himself *en rapport* has been abundantly proven by the praise-worthy efforts of the Society for Psychical Research; and if my desperate plunge at the problem ended in *a seeming negation* it was not due to any lack of persistency on my part.

———————

[At the General Meeting of the S.P.R. on April 24th, 1896, when the above paper was read, Mr. F. W. H. MYERS made the following remarks upon the case, which, at Mr. Le Baron's request, are here reprinted.—ED.]

Mr. Le Baron's experiences are of especial interest as filling a gap that had remained for some time open in the symmetrical series of cases which show the progress of each class of automatic verbalisation from insane incoherence to supernormal instructiveness. In each of the other forms of verbalisation the series is already pretty complete. In *word-seeing* we start from the meaningless and terrifying words or sentences sometimes seen by the insane, as though written in fire, without them or within; we pass through the stage of words seen in the crystal with nothing to point to an origin external to the seer's mind; and we arrive at the supernormal phenomenon of the sight of words in the crystal which convey facts previously unknown to the seer. Similarly in *word-hearing* we start from the delusions of madness, when persecuting voices and the like are so often heard; we go on to internal auditions of a monitory kind, which may well proceed from the auditor's own subliminal self; and finally we come to those "clairaudient" premonitions which imply the possession of a wider purview than the automatist himself had ever—to his own supraliminal knowledge—attained. For the third form of verbalisation,—*word-writing,* —the continuous series from insanity to inspiration is by this time still more familiar to readers of our *Proceedings*. In each case the gradual development from phenomena *below* into phenomena *above* the normal standard of personality seems to show that in these special directions the personality is most easily modifiable; and that subliminal disturbances, whether dissolutive or evolutive, are apt to come to the surface by these as their readiest paths. It is therefore only by a study in each case of the actual messages given that we can rightly rank the automatist, either as insane, or as merely a person in whom subliminal uprushes are unusually facile, or as a man in some sense inspired with fuller knowledge than other men, either by his own hidden spirit, or by spirits without him.

In the fourth form of verbalisation,—*word-utterance*,—we have until now mainly found examples of the lowest and the highest classes. The ceaseless vociferation of mania is familiar to all; and wonder is often expressed at the vigour and persistency of the maniac's utterance,—far surpassing the achievements of practised public speakers. Then at the other end of the scale we have the utterances which come through Mrs. Piper, in which (as fresh evidence makes increasingly probable) intelligences other than Mrs. Piper's own are habitually concerned.

But for intermediate examples,—for utterance neither insane nor in any true sense inspired,—we have thus far had to fall back mainly on old records. Chief of these have been the accounts of the Irvingite speaking with tongues. Next, perhaps, comes a little-known work, "Strange Sermons of Rachel Baker," which contains two cases of sermonising utterance during apparently quite genuine sleep. I need not say that "trance addresses" are quite a common feature in spiritist reunions. In the very few cases where I have heard these public addresses under supposed inspiration, I have felt sure that the speaker was in full possession of his or her ordinary consciousness. But I think it very probable that speeches may sometimes be genuinely made in a trance state;—which would, of course, be no more wonderful than it is when a hypnotised boy at an entertainment lectures on temperance and so forth, and remembers nothing about it when he awakes. The trance may be a mere self-hypnotisation; —and such, in the absence from the speech of any facts unknown to the speaker, we are bound to consider it.

But among all these strictly automatic vocalisations, neither insane nor inspired, Mr. Le Baron's case is the fullest and most instructive. I know no stronger example of the subjective sense of genius, or rather of positive inspiration, accompanying a subliminal uprush of absolutely meaningless matter. Some of this matter, indeed, was meaningless even to incoherence,—consisting of "unknown tongues," which are pretty certainly destined to remain unknown. One cannot but note, with satisfaction at our present progress, yet with deep regret at the sad story of the past, the different way in which these so-called tongues were treated in Irving's time and in our own. Several, at least, of the speakers with tongues in Irving's congregation were, I have no doubt, perfectly sincere;

and Irving himself was, as all know, a man of probity and elevation. Yet his ignorance—his unavoidable ignorance—of the phenomena of automatism landed him and his flock first in natural mistake, but at last in obstinate credulity, and spoilt the close of a noble and high career. In Mr. Le Baron's case, on the other hand, the automatist himself had the courage and candour to estimate his utterances in the calm light of science, in spite of strong subjective inducement to continue to assign to them a value which they did not possess. He had the good fortune, I need hardly add, to meet with a wise and gentle adviser, and the phenomenon which, if differently treated, might have led on to the delusion of many, and perhaps to the insanity of one, became to the one a harmless experience, and to the world an acquisition of interesting psychological truth. If our Society shall continue thus to tend to convert enthusiasm into science and peril into instruction, it will not have existed in vain.

F. W. H. Myers.

22

Telepathy: Controversy with Titchener on Lehmann and Hansen (1896–1899)

a. Review of "Ueber unwillkürliches Flüstern," by F. C. C. Hansen and Alfred Lehmann (1896)

Ueber unwillkürliches Flüstern, eine kritische und experimentelle Untersuchung der sogenannten Gedankenübertragung. F. C. C. Hansen und Alfred Lehmann. Philosophische Studien, XI. 4. Pp. 471–530.

In the S.P.R. *Proceedings*, VI, 128, is a series of experiments by Prof. and Mrs. Sidgwick on the transference of numbers from the mind of Mr. Smith to two young men hypnotized by him. The numbers were bi-digital, running from 10 to 90, drawn from a bag and silently looked at by Mr. S. The subjects named whatever numbers they saw appear in their mental field of vision. There were 1,356 trials, with the result that any digit 'seen' or 'named' by the subject invariably corresponded much more often to the digit 'drawn' than to any other digit. In table I, for example, in a series of 354 trials, both digits were named rightly 79 times instead of the 'probable' number of four or five times. Some cause was evidently at work inclining the subjects to guess right. The Sidgwicks think that this cause cannot have been vocal indications given by Smith and hyperæsthetically heard by the subjects, because if the latter had been guided by sound their mistakes would have shown the effect of sound as well as their successes; that is, the numbers named wrongly by them would have also tended to resemble in sound the numbers actually drawn from the bag, which the Sidgwicks try to show by a comparative table was not the case.

The Danish writers subject this opinion to a careful criticism. Repeating the experiment with two hemispherical mirrors, 90 cm. wide, opposite each other, the head of the agent being in the focus of one, and that of the percipient in the focus of the other, they found that the numbers could be *heard* by the percipient, and consequently named rightly; when the agent inwardly articulated them, even the bystanders could hear nothing and the agent's lips were tightly closed. They also found certain parts of the room within which the sound of a grain of shot dropping on a plate could be heard, whereas it could not be heard from other places. The percipient, if in such a favored place, might of course catch a vocal indication to which bystanders would be deaf. Subjecting the whole number of 'guesses,' right and wrong, to a laborious phonic analysis, they prove moreover that the mistakes made by the English subjects, mistakes whose nature, according to the Sidgwicks, was such as to exclude their being due to imperfect hearing, showed a striking analogy to those made by themselves, which positively *were* due to imperfect hearing. In the English observations, namely, the numbers oftenest substituted for each other were those whose common phonetic elements were the same that caused the most frequent confusions of hearing in Messrs. H. and L. The Sidgwicks' opinion is, therefore, Messrs. H. and L. conclude, superficial and hasty, and hyperæsthesia of hearing remains 4,000 times more probable than any other assignable cause, of the amount of 'thought-transference' recorded in their experiments. The authors point also to the facility with which, in diagram-guessing, figures may be considered 'right' which really represent quite different objects from those meant by the agent, if only the two objects have analogous elements. The paper is a genuinely scientific contribution to the elucidation of so-called thought-transference phenomena, and contrasts most agreeably with the random abuse to which their recorders are accustomed.

b. REVIEW OF "INVOLUNTARY WHISPERING CONSIDERED IN RELATION TO EXPERIMENTS IN THOUGHT-TRANSFERENCE," BY HENRY SIDGWICK (1897)

Involuntary Whispering Considered in Relation to Thought-

Transference. HENRY SIDGWICK. Proceedings of S.P.R., XII, 298–315. December, 1896.

Messrs. Lehmann and Hansen, it will be remembered (*Psychological Review,* Vol. III, p. 98 [*ed.,* pp. 167–168]), sought to prove that a certain series of experiments in thought-transference, by Professor and Mrs. Sidgwick, were explicable because the agent's inward articulation of the numbers guessed was probably heard hyperæsthetically by the hypnotized percipients. Repeating the experiments so that the percipient could actually hear the agent's suppressed whispering, they found that not only the successes, but also the mistakes resembled those in the Sidgwick series, and from such like effects they think that we ought to infer like causes.

Their paper, the carefulness of which is a refreshing exception to most criticism of the Psychical Research Work, is reviewed by Professor Sidgwick, who concludes that their experiments do not show positive evidence for whispering as the source of the English results. Much of his reply is too minute for reproduction. The most telling point he makes is an empirical one. Happening to have the record of an old series of pure chance-guesses at numbers, made with the agent and percipient in separate closed rooms, he compares this with the guesses of the Danish series. Of course, the number of successes differ widely in the two series, but the errors run even more closely parallel than they do when the Danish whispering series and the English 'thought-transference' series are compared. As such an amount of similarity in error with the whispered series is obviously fortuitous in this case, so it may be fortuitous in the thought-transference case. Professor Sidgwick would partly explain the degree of similarity found (which is but slight[1]) by an

---

[1] The Danish authors made only 500 experiments, obviously too small a number for safe conclusions. The better to frame critical opinion, I have myself collected a series of upwards of 1,000 guesses at bi-digital numbers whispered with closed lips by the agent. Following Lehmann's method, and comparing the four most frequent erroneous guesses at each digit of the numbers whispered with the four most frequent errors made in divining the same digits in the English thought-transference series, I find (taking the digits from 1 to 9) that 20 of the erroneous digits are common to the two series. But I find that if one compares the four *least* frequent erroneous guesses in my whispered series with the *most* frequent corresponding ones in the thought-transference series, one gets 15, no great difference. Taking the one most frequent error of substitution for each digit in my series, I find but 2 agreements with the thought-transference series, and 2 with the Sidgwick series of pure guesses. Plotting the frequency of the various errors in the several series as curves shows so great a discrepancy between my whispered series and the Danish

unconscious preference for certain numbers in the guesses of both sets of percipients. If, for example, both tended frequently to guess 'five,' five as a frequent error would occur in both series, and make them in so far forth agree.[2]

Sidgwick, although admitting that whispering may possibly have been a cause of successful guessing when agent and percipient were in the same room, thus denies that Professor Lehmann has proved the point. And he absolutely denies Lehmann's explanation where the agent and successful percipient were separated by closed doors. Passing to a general discussion of the subject, especially so far as drawings were the things guessed, he gives a *resumé*, in brief, of the whole body of evidence which many readers will find a convenient summary to refer to.

c. LETTER: LEHMANN AND HANSEN ON THE TELEPATHIC PROBLEM (1898)

To the Editor of *Science*: Professor Titchener in to-day's *Science* assumes that Messrs. Lehmann and Hansen have performed a work of definitive demolition in the well-meant article of theirs to which he refers. If he will take the pains to read Professor Sidgwick's criticism of their results in the S.P.R. *Proceedings*, Vol. XII, p. 298, as well as the note to my report of his paper in the *Psychological Review*, Vol. IV, p. 654, he will probably admit that, owing to the fewness of the data which they collected, they entirely failed to prove their point. This leaves the phenomena in dispute still hanging, and awaiting a positive interpretation from other hands.

I think that an exploded document ought not to be left with the last word, even for the sake of 'scientific psychology.' And I must incidentally thank Professor Titchener for his admission that 'aloof-

---

one that it becomes obvious that the series are too short to serve as proper terms of comparison with the thought-transference series. Moreover, the curves of my series and those of the thought-transference series show at special points variations from each other so great, when compared with the absolute figures which they represent, that the same conclusion is again obvious. Both the agreements and the disagreements are thus probably accidental. I, myself, agree then entirely with Professor Sidgwick that Professor Lehmann has failed to prove his particular hypothesis of whispering as the cause of the 'thought-transference' results; and I am pleased to notice that Mr. Parish, in the work noticed below (*Hallucinations and Illusions*, p. 320, note), also considers Professor Sidgwick 'perfectly justified in his contention.'

2 In my own series, the tendency to run on favorite numbers in guessing was a well marked phenomenon, to eliminate the effects of which many thousands of guesses would be required.

ness, however authoritative' (which phrase seems to be *style noble* for 'ignorance of the subject, and be d——d to it'), is an attitude which need not be invariably maintained by the 'Scientific,' even towards matters such as this. I only wish that his admission were a little less apologetic in form.

WILLIAM JAMES.

CAMBRIDGE, MASS.,
    December 23, 1898.

d. LETTER: LEHMANN AND HANSEN ON TELEPATHY (1899)

TO THE EDITOR OF SCIENCE: One or two of your readers may possibly remember a small exchange of words between Professor Titchener and myself *apropos* of his article in *Science* for December 23d (Vol. VIII, p. 897).

Messrs. Lehmann and Hansen had sought to show experimentally that the results of certain experiments by Professor H. Sidgwick, which the latter had ascribed to 'thought-transference,' were really due to involuntary whispering by the agent, overheard hyperæsthetically by the subjects. Professor Titchener closed his article by saying: "The brilliant work of Messrs. L. and H. has probably done more for scientific psychology than could have been accomplished by any aloofness, however authoritative."

To these words I, in your next number, took exception, saying that if Professor Titchener would read Sidgwick's and my criticisms of the work of the Danish investigators, he would probably agree 'that, owing to the fewness of the data which they had collected, they entirely failed to prove their point.' I, consequently, called their essay 'an exploded document'; to which my 'scientifically-minded' *confrère* rejoined (in *Science* for January 6th) that he had carefully read the criticisms, and had thus seen us 'handling the fuse,' but that he had 'not yet heard the detonation.'

As the explosion was so audible to me, the disproof being quasi-mathematical, I was astounded at this hardness of hearing in my colleague; and, to make sure that I was not a victim of auditory hallucination, I wrote to Professor Lehmann to know what he himself thought of his conclusions, in the light of the criticisms in question. His answer, somewhat belated, just arrives.

He says: "Your own as well as Professor Sidgwick's experiments and computations prove, beyond a doubt, that the play of chance had thrown into my hands a result distinctly too favorable to my theory, and that the said theory is consequently not yet established (*bewiesen*)."

This is identically Professor Sidgwick's and my contention; and for his candor, as well as for his willingness to take pains to experiment in this region, Professor Lehmann deserves to stand high as a 'psychical researcher.'

Professor Titchener, meanwhile, still hugging the exploded document, wanders upon what he calls 'the straight scientific path,' having it apparently all to himself. May the consciousness of his fidelity to correct scientist principles console him in some degree both for his deafness and for his isolation.

WILLIAM JAMES.

CAMBRIDGE, April 20, 1899.

e. LETTER: TELEPATHY ONCE MORE, No. I (1899)

TO THE EDITOR OF SCIENCE: Why Professor Titchener should have taken an essay which he now admits to have completely failed even to make probable its point, as an example of the 'brilliant work' which 'scientific psychology' can do in the way of destroying the telepathic superstition, may be left to be fathomed by readers with more understanding of the ways of 'Science' than I possess.

Meanwhile, as one interested in mere accuracy, I must protest against two impressions which Professor Titchener, in your number of May 12th, seeks to leave upon the reader's mind.

The first is that whispering was first considered by Professor Lehmann. It has been elaborately discussed in the S.P.R. *Proceedings* over and over again. Sidgwick's 6-page discussion of it in the report of his own experiments is the basis of comparison used by Lehmann in his ampler but abortive investigation.

The second of Professor Titchener's implications is that it was Lehmann who introduced number-habits, and even forced the admission of them on the recalcitrant Sidgwick. Lehmann makes no mention of number-habits. Sidgwick himself introduces them to account, not for the thought-transference results, but for the many errors common to the guesses of his Subjects and Lehmann's; the two perhaps had the same number-habit. Does Professor Titchener seriously think that a number-habit in a guesser can account for the amount of coincidence between the numbers which he guesses and those upon counters drawn at random out of a bag?

Even in anti-telepathic Science accuracy of representation is required, and I am pleading not for telepathy, but only for accuracy.

WILLIAM JAMES.

APPENDIX

In the *Journal* of the S.P.R. (English), 9 (October 1899), 113–120 (McD 1899:6), the editor summarized the controversy, with quotations, and added his own comment. Because it fills in the gaps that result from the reprinting only of James's own contributions, the S.P.R. editorial commentary is added here in the form of an Appendix. Preceding the quotation of (c), James's letter to *Science*, is the following beginning of the S.P.R. *Journal* account (pp. 113–114):

MESSRS. HANSEN AND LEHMANN ON THE
TELEPATHIC PROBLEM.*

The following correspondence may interest or entertain some of our readers.

Professor Titchener, of Cornell University, contributed to *Science*, for December 23rd, 1898, a paper on "The Feeling of being Stared at." After explaining the popular belief that one may make a person look round by staring at the back of his head, by the fact that many persons are nervous when others are behind them, and, involuntarily looking round at intervals to reassure themselves, meet our eyes if we are making the experiment, he adds the following paragraph. The rest of the correspondence explains itself.

In conclusion, I may state that I have tested this interpretation of the "feeling of being stared at," at various times, in series of laboratory experiments conducted with persons who declared themselves either peculiarly susceptible to the stare or peculiarly capable of "making people turn round." As regards such capacity and susceptibility, the experiments have invariably given a negative result; in other words, the interpretation offered has been confirmed. If the scientific reader object that this result might have been foreseen, and that the experiments were, therefore, a waste of time, I can only reply that they seem to me to have their justification in the breaking down of a superstition which has deep and widespread roots in the popular consciousness. No scientifically-minded psychologist believes in telepathy. At the same time, the disproof of it in a given case may start a student upon the straight scientific path, and the time spent may thus be repaid to science a hundredfold. The brilliant work of Lehmann and Hansen upon the telepathic "problem" (*Philos. Studien,* 1895, XI., 471) has probably done more for scientific psychology than could have been accomplished by any aloofness, however authoritative.

E. B. TITCHENER.

Cornell University.

* *Ueber unwillkürliches Flüstern; eine kritische und experimentelle Untersuchung der sogenannten Gedankenübertragung.* Von F. C. C. Hansen und A. Lehmann. Wundt's *Philosophische Studien.* 1895, XI., 471.

Titchener replied to James's attack of December 23, 1898, reprinted above as (c), by a brief note in the next issue of *Science* which the S.P.R. editor quotes as follows:

[From *Science,* January 6th, 1899.]

I can assure Professor James that I do not knowingly leave unread anything that he or Professor Sidgwick writes. I carefully considered the two papers to which he refers, at the time of their appearance, and have recently turned to them again. I am afraid, however, that I cannot make the admission that Professor James expects. Even if I granted all the contentions of criticism and report, I should still see no reason to change the wording of my reference to Lehmann and Hansen. But there is a great deal that I cannot grant. While, like Stevenson's Silver, "I wouldn't set no limits to what a virtuous character might consider argument," I must confess that, in the present instance, the grounds for such consideration have not seldom escaped me.

Professor James rules that the *Phil. Studien* article is "exploded." I have tried to take up the position of an impartial onlooker; and, from that position, I have seen Professor James and Professor Sidgwick and Herr Parish handling the fuse, but I have not yet heard the detonation.

E. B. TITCHENER.

The editor then skips over the beginning of James's (d) reply with the remark, "[From *Science,* May 5th, 1899.] | After recapitulating the early stages of the discussion, Professor James writes, in reference to the final sentences of the above letter:—" and then proceeds to quote from James beginning "As the explosion was so audible to me" (171.31) to the end. The editor adds the following footnote, keyed to 'arrives.' (171.36), containing the letter to James from Lehmann in German (the original holograph of which is in the S.P.R. archives) that James quotes in his English translation:

> * Professor Lehmann writes to Professor James:—
>
> "Kopenhagen, d. 5/4, 1899.
>
> ". . . . . Sowohl die Ihrigen als Professor Sidgwick's Experimente und Berechnungen zeigen unzweifelhaft, dass der Zufall mir ein für meine Theorie gar zu günstiges Resultat in die Hände gespielt hat, und dass die Theorie folglich nicht bewiesen ist. Ausserdem geht aus den Berechnungen Professor Sidgwick's hervor[,] dass die Zahlen-Gewohnheit (number-habit) eine wichtige Rolle spielt. Ob diese beide[n] Faktoren die Sache erklären können, wird sich wohl schliesslich, durch fortgesetzte Versuche, herausstellen. Als vorläufige Hypothese wird das unwillkürliches [*stet*] Flüstern in Verbindung mit der Zahlen-Gewohnheit unzweifelhaft genügen; meines Erachtens liegt jedenfalls im Augenblick keine Veranlassung vor, ausserdem okkulte Kräfte anzunehmen. Professor Sidgwick sagt es zwar nicht, man sieht es aber leicht aus seiner Abhandlung, dass er sehr geneigt ist, an mystische Ursachen zu glauben. Ich bedaure sehr, ihm hier nicht folgen zu können.
>
> "Selbstverständlich steht es Ihnen ganz frei, wenn Sie es wünschen, diese Erklärung zu veröffentlichen. . . . .
>
> > "ALFR. LEHMANN."

He then continues his article with a quotation from Titchener's reply in *Science* for May 12, 1899, followed by his own bracketed comment.

[From *Science*, May 12th, 1899.]

It is evident that Professor James and I have been writing at cross purposes. On the point that Lehmann has not "established" his explanation of the Sidgwick results I am heartily at one with James, Sidgwick, Parish and Lehmann himself. But Professor James need not have awaited the return mail from Copenhagen to wrest this admission either from Lehmann or from me. Lehmann wrote in his original paper: "Ein exacter Beweis hierfür (*i.e.*, for his explanation) kann wohl im Augenblicke nicht geführt werden." Nor, I take it, in any future Augenblick.

On the other hand, I have never regarded this point as the point at issue. Lehmann set out to examine telepathy at large. He chose the Sidgwick experiments simply as typical series, considering the authors' names a guarantee of serious intent and careful work. In his inquiry he laid hold of a condition which had never been thoroughly investigated before, and traced its effects in experiments that were both ingeniously devised and rigidly controlled; no one can neglect the unconscious whisper in future telepathic work. His paper is a model of scientific method; he has shown us how borderland questions are to be attacked, and proved that the "ordinary channels of sense" have unexplored resources. His suggestions will be fruitful, for the next stage of advance must be an exhaustive study of the "number-habits" which Sidgwick at first rejected, but now makes the headstone of the corner. Even granting all the contentions of the critics, therefore, I should assert that Lehmann's work is brilliant, and that it has done signal service to scientific psychology. But, as I hinted before, I do not know that quasi-mathematics has contributed much to psychology in any field of research.

I conclude with a word on the logic of Professor James' objection. A theory is pronounced which, from the outset, lays claim to probability and to probability only. "Exact proof" is acknowledged to be impossible. Criticism plays upon the theory, and the author again acknowledges that his hypothesis is not proven. Professor James, apparently forgetting the first acknowledgment, affirms that the criticism has "exploded" the theory! What is not proven is, *eo ipso*, exploded! Is Professor James, then, ready to grant that his recent book on "Human Immortality"—something which assuredly is not yet proven—is an "exploded document"? If the alternatives before me are scientific isolation and companionship on these logical terms, I prefer the isolation.

E. B. TITCHENER.

[There seems here some slight confusion in the use of the terms, "proof" and "probability." Professor Titchener first introduces Professor Lehmann's paper as an example of scientific "disproof" of telepathy in a given case; then, when Professor Lehmann admits his own failure as regards the Sidgwick case, Professor Titchener claims that there was no failure, since Professor Lehmann never pretended to "establish" his explanation, but only to make it probable. But what Professor Lehmann admits in his candid letter is that Professors Sidgwick's and James's criticisms show that he had not *proved his explanation to be even probable*. The utmost that his experiments could do—and, of course, the utmost that he claimed for them—was to establish a presumption in favour of the view that a certain condition was the efficient cause of certain results. Such a presumption could only be established by showing that the results concurred with the condition more often than they would be likely to do by chance. Professor Sidgwick proved that the concurrence was not too frequent to be attributed to chance, and thus showed that the authors had failed to establish the presumption aimed at.—ED.]

The letter of May 26, 1899, reprinted above as (e), was James's last contribution, and the controversy was brought to a close by a brief note from Titchener in *Science* for June 2, which the S.P.R. editor quoted at the end of the James letter and then proceeded to his own summary, which concludes the S.P.R. account:

[From *Science*, June 2nd, 1899.]

When a scientific discussion degenerates into protest and imputation of motive, it is probably time for the discussion to stop. But I wish to state, in self-defence, that I do not "seek to leave upon the reader's mind" the two impressions to which Professor James refers. I do not say that Lehmann first considered whispering; I say that he was the first *thoroughly to investigate* it. There is a difference. I do not imply that Lehmann introduced number-habits; I say that the next step in advance beyond him is an exhaustive study of number-habits. Again there is a difference.

E. B. TITCHENER.

It is true that, as Professor Titchener admits, Professor Lehmann did not introduce number-habits to explain the successful results of the S.P.R. experiments in thought-transference. Not only so, but he did not even mention them in his original pamphlet. In his letter to Professor James, however (see above, p. 115, foot-note [*ed.*, 175.13–15]), he maintains, "as a provisional hypothesis, that involuntary whispering, combined with number-habits, would undoubtedly suffice" to explain the successes. This remark suggests that he is under misapprehension as to what can and what cannot be achieved by number-habits—a misapprehension from which there is no clear evidence that Professor Titchener himself is free. It may therefore be worth while to give here a brief general review of the subject.*

It has long been recognised by psychologists that most—if not all—persons have unconscious preferences for certain objects or ideas over others of the same class; so that, if one is told to guess or to think of, say, a colour, a playing-card, or a number,—certain colours, cards, or numbers occur to the mind more frequently than others, and are there-

---

* For examples of the experimental study of number-habits, we may refer our readers to the two articles on their experiments in thought-transference by Professor and Mrs. Sidgwick in the *Proceedings* S.P.R. In Vol. VI., p. 170, a complete analysis from this point of view of all the numbers included in their experiments is given, and in Vol. VIII., p. 548, the number-habits of their most successful percipient are fully described. In Vol. XII., pp. 303–4, Professor Sidgwick returns to the subject in his discussion of the work of Messrs. Hansen and Lehmann. See also a review of Dr. Dessoir's *Das Doppel-Ich*, by Mr. F. W. H. Myers, in Vol. VI., p. 209.

fore guessed more often. These idiosyncrasies are called "mental habits," or,—if we are referring to numbers only,—"number-habits." It is hardly ever possible to account for them, that is, to trace the origin of any particular preference; it would seem as if the individual acquired them entirely at random. Not only so, but they may vary in the same person at different times, while different persons may exhibit the same preferences.

Now, supposing that two persons are trying experiments in the thought-transference of numbers, the same numbers may happen to be the favourites of both agent and percipient. If, then, the agent *selects* numbers to think of, some successful guesses may be made which are due—not to thought-transference, but to similarity in the number-habits of the two experimenters.

This source of error, however, may be absolutely excluded if the numbers to be guessed are *not selected voluntarily* by the agent, but *drawn at random* from a batch of numbers. As early as 1886, therefore (see *Phantasms of the Living*, Vol. I., pp. 31–35, and Vol. II., p. 653), experimenters who worked in connection with the Society for Psychical Research were accustomed to use the method of drawing numbers at random, and it is hardly necessary to say that all the number-guessing in the experiments of Professor and Mrs. Sidgwick was carried out on this plan.

On the other hand, supposing again that the agent *selects* the numbers and that his number-habits are markedly *dissimilar* from those of the percipient, then the successes would probably be decidedly fewer than they would be if due to chance alone.

Now, confining ourselves to cases where the numbers to be guessed are *drawn at random*, it is clear that the existence of any decided number-habit does not affect in any way the probability of guessing right by chance, since the number drawn at any moment is neither more nor less likely to be one of the percipient's favourites than to be any other number. On the average, therefore, the number of *accidental successes* would be the same, whether a number-habit existed or not.

A decided number-habit may, however, affect prejudicially the number of *successes produced by telepathy* (assuming, for the sake of the argument, that successes may sometimes be due to telepathy), because the idea of the favourite number, constantly obtruding itself into the mind, would tend to obscure or replace the impressions derived telepathically; just as, when a material object is perceived in the ordinary way through the senses, a preconceived idea as to what the object is may often make us perceive it wrongly.

Thus, in experiments of the kind under consideration, there is only one case in which the existence of number-habits can increase the successes and so make the evidence for telepathy in that case appear stronger than it really is; namely, the case in which (1) the agent selects the numbers to be guessed and at the same time (2) his number-habits are similar to those of the percipient. In all other cases, number-habits would decrease those successes which are due to any other agency than chance.

23

Review of
"Telepathic Dreams Experimentally Induced," by G. B. Ermacora (1896)

Telepathic Dreams Experimentally Induced. G. B. ERMACORA. Proceedings of the Society for Psychical Research. Vol. XI. Pp. 235–308.

This is a startling experimental record of a new genus of thought transference. The personages are: Dr. Ermacora; the Signora Maria, a young woman with trances and automatic writing in which she manifests a secondary personality alleging itself to be a spirit named Elvira; Angelina, Maria's cousin, a child in her fifth year; and, finally, the Signora Annetta, Maria's mother. The two ladies and the child live together at Padua, and Dr. Ermacora is a familiar visitor at the house. A certain spontaneous dream of Angelina's, in which she seemed to see the so-called Elvira, led Dr. E. to try systematically whether he could determine Angelina's dreams by ordering 'Elvira' to appear to her in sleep and make her dream according to his prescription. The experiments made were seventy in number and almost every one succeeded. Dr. Ermacora, for reasons that he does not give, was unable to isolate Angelina from the two ladies, so the physical possibility was not precluded of Siga. Maria telling the child every night, after the details of the dream had been dictated in the evening, what she must report next morning. He considers it morally impossible, however, that the ladies should wilfully play a trick on him; and believing that Signora Maria, if she coached Angelina at all, could only do so whilst herself asleep, he habitually locked and sealed Angelina into a separate room, and got Signora Annetta to sleep with Signora Maria, so as to detect any possible somnambulism. This nevertheless was not reported. He moreover prescribed dreams, the nature of whose details was incommunicable verbally, such as dreams of persons shown in photograph to Maria-Elvira, and afterwards identified in photograph by the child as having been seen in dreams; or dreams of instruments pictured in manufacturers' catalogues, and similarly discriminated in Maria's absence by the child from amongst other figures of instruments that contained the same mechanical elements and would have had to be described in the same words. The child's accounts also made it clear that the suggestion, whatever it was, must have been in optical, and not in verbal terms; for she often gave circumstances of the dream in words of her own limited experience that differed from the names used in prescribing the dream—'dog' for lamb, *e.g.* (she had never seen a lamb); 'hail' for snow; 'dark place down stairs' for cellar (she had never been in a cellar); 'tramway' for ship (the steamboats at Venice which was the child's home are known as tramways) etc.

Dr. E.'s conclusion is that there was communication between the subliminal selves of Angelina and Maria. It is clear, in spite of the precautions taken, that much of the evidence hinges on the honesty of Siga. Maria and her mother, which Dr. Ermacora says it is impossible for him to doubt. I, knowing Dr. E. personally, and having been present at one of his experiments, do not doubt *his* honesty. He is a trained physicist, author of a thick book on electricity, and possesses an unusual experience of 'psychic' phenomena, and a shrewd mind in comparing hypotheses. The editors do not doubt *my* honesty, or they will not print this report. But the facts are so unprecedented that the whole chain of honesties will seem a weak one, and the 'rigorously scientific' mind will exercise its natural privilege, and doubtless promptly and authoritatively dismiss the narrative as 'rot.'

Review of
I Fenomeni Telepatici e le Allucinazioni Veridiche,
by Enrico Morselli (1897)

I Fenomeni Telepatici e le Allucinazioni Veridiche; Osservazioni Critiche Sul Neo-misticismo Psicologico. ENRICO MORSELLI. Firenze, Landi, 1897. Pp. 58.

A courteously written plea against accepting the recently published evidence for thought-transference and veridical hallucination. The familiar methodological generalities about what should constitute satisfactory scientific evidence for such phenomena are laid down at excessive length, but the author gets in some short-range work in criticizing the evidential defects of several narratives published as good ones by the French, Italian and English psychical researchers. A curious prejudice runs through his pages that no evidence for supernormal cognition can be drawn from cases of persons of neuropathic constitutions, or from those in whom there have been multiple experiences of the sort. He even thinks that he discredits veridical apparitions by saying that the majority of them seem to have occurred in 'English misses' at the change of life. Can he be so sure in advance that neuropathic constitution, or even the 'menopause,' might not be predisposing conditions for telepathic susceptibility, if such a thing should, in point of fact, exist? And, as for persons with multiple experiences, they would seem *a priori* to be just those from whom evidence might be best obtained. In point of fact they are so—one subject of 'psychic temperament' being worth many with single experiences. Professor Morselli, at the close of his pamphlet, gives a list of conditions which he seems to regard as alternatives to telepathy—no case should be counted as telepathic if it be possible to conceive it "under one or another of the following psycho-physical explanations; simple suggestion, auto-suggestion, individual and collective credulity, psycho-physical automatism, hypnoid or sub-conscious conditions, sensorial illusion, psychical illusion, *e.g.*, from accidental coincidence, provoked hallucination, especially with *point de repère*, unconscious perception, emotion or movement, involuntary expression of one's own thought, doubling of personality, dream or hypnagogic hallucinations, illusions of memory, after-images or retarded sensations, sensations induced by imperceptible or unappreciated physical agents (heat, electricity, magnetism, light), conditions of ecstacy (monoideism), hysteria, epilepsy and epileptoid, cataleptic, or somnambulic states, with loss or obscuration of consciousness, lucid forms of insanity, especially with hallucinatory fixed ideas, psychic mimicry and imitative of psychosis, or collective hallucination, intense emotional conditions with their effects, transient states of cerebral intoxication, whether endogenous or exogenous. . . ." Once more, one is tempted to ask why must all these things be *alternatives* to supernormal cognition? Why, if it exist at all, may it not co-exist with some of them? Why, indeed, may not some of them be its most predisposing conditions? Again, in point of fact, if there be supernormal cognition, it looks as if this were the case with it.

It is a pleasure to turn from the generalities and abstractions of the learned Genoese professor to the criticism at closer quarters of the next author on our list.*

---

* The final paragraph of this review led to the next review: that of Edmund Parish's *Zur Kritik des telepathischen Beweismaterials*. In the present edition these have been separated to appear in different categories.—F.B.

25

Letter on Mrs. Piper, the Medium (1898)

To the Editor of Science: Your reference to my name in the editorial note in *Science* for April 15th, entitled 'Mrs. Piper, the Medium,' justifies me in making some remarks of my own in comment on your remarks upon Mr. Hodgson's report of her case. Any hearing for such phenomena is so hard to get from scientific readers that one who believes them worthy of careful study is in duty bound to resent such contemptuous public notice of them in high quarters as would still further encourage the fashion of their neglect.

I say any hearing; I don't say any fair hearing. Still less do I speak of fair treatment in the broad meaning of the term. The scientific mind is by the pressure of professional opinion painfully drilled to fairness and logic in discussing orthodox phenomena. But in such mere matters of superstition as a medium's trances it feels so confident of impunity and indulgence whatever it may say, provided it be only contemptuous enough, that it fairly revels in the untrained barbarians' arsenal of logical weapons, including all the various sophisms enumerated in the books.

Your own comments seem to me an excellent illustration of this fact. If one wishes to refute a man who asserts that some A's are B's, the ordinary rule of logic is that one must not show that some *other* A's are *not* B's—one must show him either that those first A's themselves are not B's, or else that no A possibly can be a B.

Now Mr. Hodgson comes forward asserting that many of Mrs. Piper's trances show supernatural knowledge. You thereupon pick out from his report five instances in which they showed nothing of the kind. You thereupon wittily remark, 'We have piped unto you but ye have not danced,' and you sign your name with an air of finality, as if nothing more in the way of refutation were needful and as if what earlier in the article you call 'the trivial character of the evidence . . . taken under the wing of the Society' were now sufficiently displayed.

If, my dear sir, you were teaching Logic to a class of students, should you, or should you not, consider this a good instance by which to illustrate the style of reasoning termed 'irrelevant conclusion,' or *ignoratio elenchi*, in the chapter on fallacies? I myself think it an extraordinarily perfect instance.

And what name should you assign to the fallacy by which you quote one of those five sitters as saying that he himself got nothing from the medium 'but a few preposterous compliments,' whilst you leave unquoted the larger part of his report, relating the inexplicable knowledge which the medium showed of the family affairs of his wife, who accompanied him to the sitting? I am not sure that the logic books contain any technical name for the fallacy here, but in legal language it is sometimes called *suppressio veri*, sometimes something still less polite. At any rate, you will admit on reflection that to use the conclusion of that sitter's report alone, as you did, was to influence your readers' minds in an unfair way.

I am sure that you have committed these fallacies with the best of scientific consciences. They are fallacies into which, of course, you would have been in no possible danger of falling in any other sort of matter than this. In our dealings with the insane the usual moral rules don't apply. Mediums are scientific outlaws, and their defendants are quasi-insane. Any stick is good enough to beat dogs of that stripe with. So in perfect innocence you permitted yourself the liberties I point out.

Please observe that I am saying nothing of the merits of the *case*, but only of the merits of your forms of controversy which, alas, are typical. The case surely deserves opposition more powerful from the logical point of view than your remarks; and I beg such readers of *Science* as care to form a reasonable opinion to seek the materials for it in the *Proceedings* of the Society for Psychical Research,

Part XXXIII (where they will find a candid report based on 500 sittings since the last report was made), rather than in the five little negative instances which you so triumphantly cull out and quote.

Truly yours,

WILLIAM JAMES.

MY note in *Science* was not 'editorial,' but was placed in that department of the *Journal* for which editors take the least responsibility. I gave my individual opinion, Professor James gives his, and I fear that our disagreement is hopeless. I could not quote the 600 pages compiled by Dr. Hodgson, but I gave the concluding sentences written by *all* the men of science whose séances were reported. Professor James blames me for not quoting the knowledge that the medium showed of the family affairs of Professor Shaler's wife, but Professor Shaler himself says, "I am . . . absolutely uninterested in it for the reason that I don't see how I can exclude the hypothesis of fraud." I wrote the note with reluctance and only because I believe that the Society for Psychical Research is doing much to injure psychology. The authority of Professor James is such that he involves other students of psychology in his opinions unless they protest. We all acknowledge his leadership, but we cannot follow him into the quagmires.

J. McKEEN CATTELL.

26

Review of "A Further Record of Observations of Certain Phenomena of Trance," by Richard Hodgson (1898)

A Further Record of Observations of Certain Phenomena of Trance. RICHARD HODGSON. Proceedings of Society for Psychical Research, Part XXXIII, Feb. 1898, Vol. XIII, pp. 284–583.

A continuation of the case of the test-medium, Mrs. Piper, already reported on in previous *Proceedings*. The present account is based on the results of 500 more sittings, about 130 of which were with unnamed strangers introduced to Mrs. Piper, for the first time. The almost exclusive 'control' up to 1892 was a personality named Phinuit, concerning whose earthly identity no evidence has turned up. Since 1892, however, the principal control has, until a year ago, purported to be the spirit of G.P., a young literary man recently dead in New York. The most striking feature of the present report is the expressed opinion of Dr. Hodgson, that the communications of G.P., as well as of others, now seem to him more naturally explicable on the hypothesis of spirit-return than on any other hypothesis. This conversion to spiritism of so critical an investigator, until lately disinclined to any such conclusion, marks, of course, the passage of a 'critical point' in the history of the Society for Psychical Research, as well as in Dr. Hodgson's own career.

The phenomenon, briefly described, is as follows: The medium waits passively for the trance to come on, which it now does quietly, though formerly there was a good deal of respiratory disturbance and muscular twitching. 'Phinuit' used to communicate entirely by speech, but G.P. early manifested himself by seeking to write on a pad placed on the medium's head. He now writes on the table. 'Phinuit' may talk whilst the hand is writing on other subjects, often under controls different from G.P., and purporting to be deceased friends of sitters. After two hours, more or less, the communications grow 'weak' and confused, and Mrs. Piper emerges from the trance, often with an expression of fear or distress, and usually with incoherent expressions on her lips, which Dr. Hodgson ascribes to her own subliminal consciousness, as distinguished from her consciousness under complete control. These intermediary and fragmentary expressions he considers to be also worthy of study.

The remarkable feature of the trances is the supernormal knowledge which the medium in a majority of cases displays of her sitter's private affairs. This knowledge is incoherent, fragmentary and, as a rule, of unimportant matters. The communications most convincing to those who received them could, out of deference to the natural dislike to publicity of sitters, not be printed at all, so that the evidence now offered to the reader is by no means 'full-strength.' Dr. Hodgson gives copious specimens of it, however, such as it is, in most of its varieties, including complete failures amongst the rest. It is intolerably tedious and incoherent reading; and one can but admire, along with the pertinacity of the reporter and his scrupulous accuracy, the manner in which his memory retains the threads of cross-connection among the parts of the system, and is able to bring points in one sitting to the illustration of points in another. Certainly there never before was such a conjunction of a good medium with a thorough investigator—and in this respect the report marks an epoch in our knowledge of trance-states.

Dr. Hodgson considers that the hypothesis of fraud cannot be seriously entertained. I agree with him absolutely. The medium has been under observation, much of the time under close observation, as to most of the conditions of her life, by a large number of persons, eager, many of them, to pounce upon any suspicious circumstance, for fifteen years. During that time *not only has there not been one single suspicious circumstance remarked, but not one suggestion has ever been made from any quarter* which might tend positively to explain how the medium, living the apparent life she leads, could possibly collect information about so many sitters by natural means. The 'scientist,' who is confident of 'fraud' here, must remember that in science as much as in common life an hypothesis must receive some positive specification and determination before it can be profitably discussed; and a fraud which is no assigned kind of fraud, but simply 'fraud' at large, fraud *in abstracto*, can hardly be regarded as a specially scientific explanation of specific concrete facts. In the concrete here, there is *no* sign *whatever* that the medium when awake has any curiosity about persons, least of all about persons whom she has never met.

No, Mrs. Piper's trances are phenomena *sui generis*. Mr. Hodgson, admitting the element of supernormal knowledge in them as a fact, weighs against each other as two theories of its origin, first the supposition of telepathy from the sitters' and other living minds, and second, spirit-communication. He finds the latter theory to offer on the whole the least resistance, since a minute discussion of the points of success and failure shows that they fall into the simpler systematic order if we connect them with the departed personalities from which they profess to proceed. G.P., for instance (with one exception, which Mr. Hodgson explains), always recognized his old acquaintances (30 in number) when anonymously introduced as sitters, and rightly called them by name, but similarly recognized no one else. Obviously such selection round G.P. as a center would be less simply explicable were the medium tapping the consciousnesses of the sitters for their names, than were an independent personality with G.P.'s actual mundane memories a factor of the case. Again, the very confusion of many communicators, identified by sitters, and their inability to bring out more than a few rudimentary facts about themselves, points rather to a genuine spirit-presence obstructed in its means, than to telepathy from the sitters, whose minds, full of other facts relevant to the case, might apparently be drawn upon for them as easily as for those already given. In brief: "There are various selections of information given in connection with various communicators which are intelligible if regarded as made by the communicators themselves, but for which there is no satisfactory explanation to be found by referring them to Mrs. Piper's personality. With one class of *deceased* persons Mrs. Piper's supposed telepathic percipience fails; with another class it succeeds; and it fails and succeeds apparently in accordance with what we should expect from the minds of the deceased, and not in accordance with what we should expect from the minds of living persons acting upon Mrs. Piper's percipient personality" (p. 393). The case is a matter of balancing probabilities based on minute comparisons of detail, and Mr. Hodgson is far from ascribing certainty to the spiritistic conclusion which he adopts.

Mr. Hodgson fails to mention one feature of the case which may make for the spirit-hypothesis, and which will probably have struck other readers besides myself. No one can be conversant with his investigation of the Piper case without admiring the great grasp of memory of details which the investigator exhibits. And yet Mr. Hodgson's memory is as nothing compared with Mrs. Piper's, who, with hundreds of sitters, many appearing only a few times, at years of interval, and conversing of inconceivably paltry personal details, seems never to fail to make connection again, or to take up the conversation just where it was left. Mr. Hodgson's memory covers fewer years, and taking and transcribing the notes of the sittings, as he does, and consulting and comparing the records *ad libitum*, he has a great advantage over Mrs. Piper. Yet he would be quite incapable of resuming conversation with former sitters as she does in her trance. Mrs. Piper's trance-memory, then, is no ordinary human memory; and we have to explain its singular perfection either as the natural endowment of her solitary subliminal self, or as a collection of distinct memory-systems, each with a communicating 'spirit,' as its vehicle. The choice obviously cannot be made off-hand.

If I may be allowed a personal expression of opinion at the end of this notice, I would say that the Piper phenomena are the most absolutely baffling thing I know. Of the various applicable hypotheses, each seems more unnatural than the rest. Any definitely known form of fraud seems out of the question; yet undoubtedly, could it be made probable, fraud would be by far the most satisfying explanation, since it would leave no further problems outstanding. The spirit-hypothesis exhibits a vacancy, triviality and incoherence of mind painful to think of as the state of the departed; and coupled therewithal a pretension to impress one, a disposition to 'fish' and face round, and disguise the essential hollowness, which are, if anything, more painful still. Mr. Hodgson has to resort to the theory that, although the communicants probably are spirits, they are in a semi-comatose or sleeping state while communicating, and only half aware of what is going on, while the habits of Mrs. Piper's neural organism largely supply the definite form of words, etc., in which the phenomenon is clothed. Then there is the theory that the 'subliminal' extension of Mrs. Piper's own mind masquerades in this way, and plays these fantastic tricks before high heaven, using its preternatural powers of cognition and memory for the basest of deceits. Many details make for this view, which also falls well into line with what we know of automatic writing and similar subliminal performances in the public at large. But what a ghastly and grotesque sort of appendage to one's personality is this, from any point of view: the humbugging and masquerading extra-marginal self is as great a paradox for psychology as the comatose spirits are for pneumatology. Finally, we may fall back on the notion of a sort of floating mind-stuff in the world, infra-human, yet possessed of fragmentary gleams of superhuman cognition, unable to gather itself together except by taking advantage of the trance states of some existing human organism, and there enjoying a parasitic existence which it prolongs by making itself acceptable and plausible under the improvised name of a 'spirit control.' On any of these theories our 'classic' human life, as we may call it, seems to connect itself with an environment so 'romantic' as to baffle all one's habitual sense of teleology and moral meaning. And yet there seems no refuge for one really familiar with the Piper phenomenon (or, doubtless, with others that are similar) from admitting one or other, perhaps even all of these fantastic prolongations of mental life into the unknown.

The world is evidently more complex than we are accustomed to think it, the 'absolute world-ground,' in particular, being farther off (as Mr. F. C. S. Schiller has well pointed out) than it is the wont either of the usual empiricisms or of the usual idealisms to think it. This being the case, the 'scientific' sort of procedure is evidently Mr. Hodgson's, with his dogged and candid exploration of all the details of so exceptional a concrete instance; and not that of the critics who, refusing to come to any close quarters with the facts, survey them at long range and summarily dispose of them at a convenient distance by the abstract name of fraud.

27

Frederic Myers's Service to Psychology (1901)

On this memorial occasion it is from English hearts and tongues belonging, as I never had the privilege of belonging, to the immediate environment of our lamented President, that discourse of him as a man and as a friend must come. It is for those who participated in the endless drudgery of his labours for our Society to tell of the high powers he showed there; and it is for those who have something of his burning interest in the problem of our human destiny to estimate his success in throwing a little more light into its dark recesses. To me it has been deemed best to assign a colder task. Frederic Myers was a psychologist who worked upon lines hardly admitted by the more academic branch of the profession to be legitimate; and as for some years I bore the title of 'Professor of Psychology,' the suggestion has been made (and by me gladly welcomed) that I should spend my portion of this hour in defining the exact place and rank which we must accord to him as a cultivator and promoter of the science of the Mind.

Brought up entirely upon literature and history, and interested at first in poetry and religion chiefly; never by nature a philosopher in the technical sense of a man forced to pursue consistency among concepts for the mere love of the logical occupation; not crammed with science at college, or trained to scientific method by any passage through a laboratory; Myers had as it were to re-create his personality before he became the wary critic of evidence, the skilful handler of hypothesis, the learned neurologist and omnivorous reader of biological and cosmological matter, with whom in later years we were acquainted. The transformation came about because he needed to be all these things in order to work successfully at the problem that lay near his heart; and the ardour of his will and the richness of his intellect are proved by the success with which he underwent so unusual a transformation.

The problem, as you know, was that of seeking evidence for human immortality. His contributions to psychology were incidental to that research, and would probably never have been made had he not entered on it. But they have a value for Science entirely independent of the light they shed upon that problem; and it is quite apart from it that I shall venture to consider them.

If we look at the history of mental science we are immediately struck by diverse tendencies among its several cultivators, the consequence being a certain opposition of schools and some repugnance among their disciples. Apart from the great contrasts between minds that are teleological or biological and minds that are mechanical, between the animists and the associationists in psychology, there is the entirely different contrast between what I will call the classic-academic and the romantic type of imagination. The former has a fondness for clean pure lines and noble simplicity in its constructions. It explains things by as few principles as possible and is intolerant of either nondescript facts or clumsy formulas. The facts must lie in a neat assemblage, and the psychologist must be enabled to cover them and 'tuck them in' as safely under his system as a mother tucks her babe in under the down coverlet on a winter night. Until quite recently all psychology, whether animistic or associationistic, was written on classic-academic lines. The consequence was that the human mind, as it is figured in this literature, was largely an abstraction. Its normal adult traits were recognised. A sort of sunlit terrace was exhibited on which it took its exercise. But where that terrace stopped, the mind stopped; and there was nothing farther left to tell of in this kind of philosophy but the brain and the other physical facts of nature on the one hand, and the absolute metaphysical ground of the universe on the other.

But of late years the terrace has been overrun by romantic improvers, and to pass to their work is like going from classic to Gothic architecture, where few outlines are pure and where uncouth forms lurk in the shadows. A mass of mental phenomena are now seen in the shrubbery beyond the parapet. Fantastic, ignoble, hardly human, or frankly non-human are some of these new candidates for psychological description. The menagerie and the madhouse, the nursery, the prison, and the hospital, have been made to deliver up their material. The world of mind is shown as something infinitely more complex than was suspected; and whatever beauties it may still possess, it has lost at any rate the beauty of academic neatness.

But despite the triumph of romanticism, psychologists as a rule have still some lingering prejudice in favour of the nobler simplicities. Moreover there are social prejudices which scientific men themselves obey. The word 'hypnotism' has been trailed about in the newspapers so that even we ourselves rather wince at it, and avoid occasions of its use. 'Mesmerism,' 'clairvoyance,' 'medium,' —*horrescimus referentes!*—and with all these things, infected by their previous mystery-mongering discoverers, even our best friends had rather avoid complicity. For instance, I invite eight of my scientific colleagues severally to come to my house at their own time, and sit with a medium for whom the evidence already published in our *Proceedings* had been most noteworthy. Although it means at worst the waste of the hour for each, five of them decline the adventure. I then beg the 'Commission' connected with the chair of a certain learned psychologist in a neighbouring university to examine the same medium, whom Mr. Hodgson and I offer at our own expense to send and leave with them. They also have to be excused from any such entanglement. I advise another psychological friend to look into this medium's case, but he replies that it is useless, for if he should get such results as I report, he would (being suggestible) simply believe himself hallucinated. When I propose as a remedy that he should remain in the background and take notes, whilst his wife has the sitting, he explains that he can never consent to his wife's presence at such performances. This friend of mine writes *ex cathedra* on the subject of psychical research, declaring (I need hardly add) that there is nothing in it; the chair of the psychologist with the Commission was founded by a spiritist, partly with a view to investigate mediums; and one of the five colleagues who declined my invitation is widely quoted as an effective critic of our evidence. So runs the world away! I should not indulge in the personality and triviality of such anecdotes, were it not that they paint the temper of our time, a temper which, thanks to Frederic Myers more than to any one, will certainly be impossible after this generation. Myers was, I think, decidedly exclusive and intolerant by nature. But his keenness for truth carried him into regions where either intellectual or social squeamishness would have been fatal, so he 'mortified' his *amour propre*, unclubbed himself completely, and became a model of patience, tact, and humility wherever investigation required it. Both his example and his body of doctrine will make this temper the only one henceforward scientifically respectable.

If you ask me how his doctrine has this effect, I answer: *By co-ordinating!* For Myers's great principle of research was that in order to understand any one species of fact we ought to have all the species of the same general class of fact before us. So he took a lot of scattered phenomena, some of them recognised as reputable, others outlawed from science, or treated as isolated curiosities; he made series of them, filled in the transitions by delicate hypotheses or analogies, and bound them together in a system by his bold inclusive conception of the Subliminal Self, so that no one can now touch one part of the fabric without finding the rest entangled with it. Such vague terms of apperception as psychologists have hitherto been satisfied with using for most of these phenomena, as 'fraud,' 'rot,' 'rubbish,' will no more be possible hereafter than 'dirt' is possible as a head of classification in chemistry, or 'vermin' in zoology. Whatever they are, they are things with a right to definite description and to careful observation.

I cannot but account this as a great service rendered to Psychology. I expect that Myers will ere long distinctly figure in mental science as the radical leader in what I have called the romantic movement. Through him for the first time, psychologists are in possession of their full material, and mental phenomena are set down in an adequate inventory. To bring unlike things thus together by forming series of which the intermediary terms connect the extremes, is a procedure much in use by scientific men. It is a first step made towards securing their interest in the romantic facts, that Myers should have shown how easily this familiar method can be applied to their study.

Myers's conception of the extensiveness of the Subliminal Self quite overturns the classic notion of what the human mind consists in. The supraliminal region, as Myers calls it, the classic-academic consciousness, which was once alone considered either by associationists or animists, figures in his theory as only a small segment of the psychic spectrum. It is a special phase of mentality, teleologically evolved for adaptation to our natural environment, and forms only what he calls a 'privileged case' of personality. The outlying Subliminal, according to him, represents more fully our central and abiding being.

I think the words subliminal and supraliminal unfortunate, but they were probably unavoidable. I think, too, that Myers's belief in the ubiquity and great extent of the Subliminal will demand a far larger number of facts than sufficed to persuade him, before the next generation of psychologists shall become persuaded. He regards the Subliminal as the enveloping mother-consciousness in each of us, from which the consciousness we wot of is precipitated like a crystal. But whether this view get confirmed or get overthrown by future inquiry, the definite way in which Myers has thrown it down is a new and specific challenge to inquiry. For half a century now, psychologists have fully admitted the existence of a subliminal mental region, under the name either of unconscious cerebration or of the involuntary life; but they have never definitely taken up the question of the extent of this region, never sought explicitly to map it out. Myers definitely attacks this problem, which, after him, it will be impossible to ignore.

What is the precise constitution of the Subliminal—such is the problem which deserves to figure in our Science hereafter as the *problem of Myers*; and willy-nilly, inquiry must follow on the path which it has opened up. But Myers has not only propounded the problem definitely, he has also invented definite methods for its solution. Post-hypnotic suggestion, crystal-gazing, automatic writing and trance-speech, the willing-game, etc., are now, thanks to him, instruments of research, reagents like litmus paper or the galvanometer, for revealing what would otherwise be hidden. These are so many ways of putting the Subliminal on tap. Of course without the simultaneous work on hypnotism and hysteria independently begun by others, he could not have pushed his own work so far. But he is so far the only generalizer of the problem and the only user of all the methods; and even though his theory of the extent of the Subliminal should have to be subverted in the end, its formulation will, I am sure, figure always as a rather momentous event in the history of our Science.

Any psychologist who should wish to read Myers out of the profession—and there are probably still some who would be glad to do so to-day—is committed to a definite alternative. Either he must say that we knew all about the subliminal region before Myers took it up, or he must say that it is certain that states of super-normal cognition form no part of its content. The first contention would be too absurd. The second one remains more plausible. There are many first hand investigators into the Subliminal who, not having themselves met with anything super-normal, would probably not hesitate to call all the reports of it erroneous, and who would limit the Subliminal to dissolutive phenomena of consciousness exclusively, to lapsed memories, subconscious sensations, impulses and *phobias*, and the like. Messrs. Janet and Binet, for aught I know, may hold some such position as this. Against it Myers's thesis would stand sharply out. Of the Subliminal, he would say, we can give no ultra-simple account: there are discrete regions in it, levels separated by critical points of transition, and no one formula holds true of them all. And any conscientious psychologist ought, it seems to me, to see that, since these multiple modifications of personality are only beginning to be reported and observed with care, it is obvious that a dogmatically negative treatment of them must be premature, and that the problem of Myers still awaits us as the problem of far the deepest moment for our actual psychology, whether his own tentative solutions of certain parts of it be correct or not.

Meanwhile, descending to detail, one cannot help admiring the great originality with which Myers wove such an extraordinarily detached and discontinuous series of phenomena together. Unconscious cerebration, dreams, hypnotism, hysteria, inspirations of genius, the willing-game, planchette, crystal-gazing, hallucinatory voices, apparitions of the dying, medium-trances, demoniacal possession, clairvoyance, thought-transference—even ghosts and other facts more doubtful—these things form a chaos at first sight most discouraging. No wonder that scientists can think of no other principle of unity among them than their common appeal to men's perverse propensity to superstition. Yet Myers has actually made a system of them, stringing them continuously upon a perfectly legitimate objective hypothesis, verified in some cases and extended to

others by analogy. Taking the name automatism from the phenomenon of automatic writing—I am not sure that he may not
himself have been the first so to baptize this latter phenomenon—
he made one great simplification at a stroke by treating hallucinations and active impulses under a common head, as *sensory* and
motor automatisms. Automatism he then conceived broadly as a
message of any kind from the Subliminal to the Supraliminal. And
he went a step farther in his hypothetic interpretation, when he
insisted on 'symbolism' as one of the ways in which one stratum of
our personality will often interpret the influences of another. Ob-
sessive thoughts and delusions, as well as voices, visions, and impulses, thus fall subject to one mode of treatment. To explain
them, we must explore the Subliminal; to cure them we must
practically influence it.

Myers's work on automatism led to his brilliant conception, in
1891, of hysteria. He defined it, with good reasons given, as "a
disease of the hypnotic stratum." Hardly had he done so when the
wonderfully ingenious observations of Binet, and especially of
Janet in France, gave to this view the completest of corroborations.
These observations have been extended in Germany, America, and
elsewhere; and although Binet and Janet worked independently of
Myers, and did work far more objective, he nevertheless will stand
as the original announcer of a theory which, in my opinion, makes
an epoch, not only in medical, but in psychological science, because
it brings in an entirely new conception of our mental possibilities.

Myers's manner of apprehending the problem of the Subliminal
shows itself fruitful in every possible direction. While official
science practically refuses to attend to Subliminal phenomena, the
circles which do attend to them treat them with a respect altogether
too undiscriminating—every Subliminal deliverance must be an
oracle. The result is that there is no basis of intercourse between
those who best know the facts and those who are most competent
to discuss them. Myers immediately establishes a basis by his remark that in so far as they have to use the same organism, with its
preformed avenues of expression—what may be very different
strata of the Subliminal are condemned in advance to manifest
themselves in similar ways. This might account for the great generic
likeness of so many automatic performances, while their different
starting-points behind the threshold might account for certain differences in them. Some of them, namely, seem to include elements

of supernormal knowledge; others to show a curious subconscious mania for personation and deception; others again to be mere drivel. But Myers's conception of various strata or levels in the Subliminal sets us to analyzing them all from a new point of view. The word Subliminal for him denotes only a region, with possibly the most heterogeneous contents. Much of the content is certainly rubbish, matter that Myers calls dissolutive, stuff that dreams are made of, fragments of lapsed memory, mechanical effects of habit and ordinary suggestion; some belongs to a middle region where a strange manufacture of inner romances perpetually goes on; finally, some of the content appears superiorly and subtly perceptive. But each has to appeal to us by the same channels and to use organs partly trained to their performance by messages from the other levels. Under these conditions what could be more natural to expect than a confusion, which Myers's suggestion would then have been the first indispensable step towards finally clearing away.

Once more, then, whatever be the upshot of the patient work required here, Myers's resourceful intellect has certainly done a service to psychology.

I said a while ago that his intellect was not by nature philosophic in the narrower sense of being that of a logician. In the broader sense of being a man of wide scientific imagination, Myers was most eminently a philosopher. He has shown this by his unusually daring grasp of the principle of evolution, and by the wonderful way in which he has worked out suggestions of mental evolution by means of biological analogies. These analogies are, if anything, too profuse and dazzling in his pages; but his conception of mental evolution is more radical than anything yet considered by psychologists as possible. It is absolutely original; and, being so radical, it becomes one of those hypotheses which, once propounded, can never be forgotten, but soon or later have to be worked out and submitted in every way to criticism and verification.

The corner-stone of his conception is the fact that consciousness has no essential unity. It aggregates and dissipates, and what we call normal consciousness,—the 'Human Mind' of classic psychology,—is not even typical, but only one case out of thousands. Slight organic alterations, intoxications and auto-intoxications, give supraliminal forms completely different, and the subliminal region seems to have laws in many respects peculiar. Myers thereupon makes the suggestion that the whole system of consciousness studied by the classic psychology is only an extract from a larger total, being a part told-off, as it were, to do service in the adjustments of our physical organism to the world of nature. This extract, aggregated and personified for this particular purpose, has, like all evolving things, a variety of peculiarities. Having evolved, it may also dissolve, and in dreams, hysteria, and divers forms of degeneration it seems to do so. This is a retrograde process of separation in a consciousness of which the unity was once effected. But again the consciousness may follow the opposite course and integrate still farther, or evolve by growing into yet untried directions. In veridical automatisms it actually seems to do so. It drops some of its usual modes of increase, its ordinary use of the senses, for example, and lays hold of bits of information which, in ways that we cannot even follow conjecturally, leak into it by way of the Subliminal. The ulterior source of a certain part of this information (limited and perverted as it always is by the organism's idiosyncrasies in the way of transmission and expression) Myers thought he could reasonably trace to departed human intelligence, or its existing equivalent. I pretend to no opinion on this point, for I have as yet studied the evidence with so little critical care that Myers was always surprised at my negligence. I can therefore speak with detachment from this question and, as a mere empirical psychologist, of Myers's general evolutionary conception. As such a psychologist I feel sure that the latter is a hypothesis of first-rate philosophic importance. It is based, of course, on his conviction of the extent of the Subliminal, and will stand or fall as that is verified or not; but whether it stand or fall, it looks to me like one of those sweeping ideas by which the scientific researches of an entire generation are often moulded. It would not be surprising if it proved such a leading idea in the investigation of the near future; for in one shape or another, the Subliminal has come to stay with us, and the only possible course to take henceforth is radically and thoroughly to explore its significance.

Looking back from Frederic Myers's vision of vastness in the field of psychological research upon the programme as most academic psychologists frame it, one must confess that its limitation at their hands seems not only unplausible, but in truth, a little ridiculous. Even with brutes and madmen, even with hysterics and hypnotics admitted as the academic psychologists admit them, the official outlines of the subject are far too neat to stand in the light of analogy with the rest of Nature. The ultimates of Nature,— her simple elements, if there be such,—may indeed combine in definite proportions and follow classic laws of architecture; but in her proximates, in her phenomena as we immediately experience them, Nature is everywhere gothic, not classic. She forms a real jungle, where all things are provisional, half-fitted to each other, and untidy. When we add such a complex kind of subliminal region as Myers believed in to the official region, we restore the analogy; and, though we may be mistaken in much detail, in a general way, at least, we become plausible. In comparison with Myers's way of attacking the question of immortality in particular, the official way is certainly so far from the mark as to be almost preposterous. It assumes that when our ordinary consciousness goes out, the only alternative surviving kind of consciousness that could be possible is abstract mentality, living on spiritual truth, and communicating ideal wisdom—in short, the whole classic platonizing Sunday-school conception. Failing to get that sort of thing when it listens to reports about mediums, it denies that there can be anything. Myers approaches the subject with no such *a priori* requirement. If he finds any positive indication of 'spirits,' he records it, whatever it may be, and is willing to fit his conception to the facts, however grotesque the latter may appear, rather than to blot out the facts to suit his conception. But, as was long ago said by our collaborator, Mr. Canning Schiller, in words more effective than any I can write, if any conception should be blotted out by serious lovers of Nature, it surely ought to be the classic academic Sunday-school conception. If anything is *un*likely in a world like this, it is that the next adjacent thing to the mere surface-show of our experience should be the realm of eternal essences, of platonic ideas, of crystal battlements, of absolute significance. But whether they be animists or associationists, a supposition something like this is still the assumption of our usual psychologists. It comes from their being for the most part philosophers in the technical sense, and from their showing the weakness of that profession for logical abstractions. Myers was primarily a lover of life and not of abstractions. He loved human life, human persons, and their peculiarities. So he could easily admit the possibility of level beyond level of perfectly concrete experience, all 'queer and cactus-like' though it might be, before we touch the absolute, or reach the eternal essences.

Behind the minute anatomists and the physiologists, with their metallic instruments, there have always stood the out-door naturalists with their eyes and love of concrete nature. The former call the latter superficial, but there is something wrong about your laboratory-biologist who has no sympathy with living animals. In psychology there is a similar distinction. Some psychologists are fascinated by the varieties of mind in living action, others by the dissecting out, whether by logical analysis or by brass instruments, of whatever elementary mental processes may be there. Myers must decidedly be placed in the former class, though his powerful use of analogy enabled him also to do work after the fashion of the latter. He loved human nature as Cuvier and Agassiz loved animal nature; in his view, as in their view, the subject formed a vast living picture. Whether his name will have in psychology as honourable a place as their names have gained in the sister science, will depend on whether future inquirers shall adopt or reject his theories; and the rapidity with which their decision shapes itself will depend largely on the vigour with which this Society continues its labour in his absence. It is at any rate a possibility, and I am disposed to think it a probability, that Frederic Myers will always be remembered in psychology as the pioneer who staked out a vast tract of mental wilderness and planted the flag of genuine science upon it. He was an enormous collector. He introduced for the first time comparison, classification, and serial order into the peculiar kind of fact which he collected. He was a genius at perceiving analogies; he was fertile in hypotheses; and as far as conditions allowed it in this meteoric region, he relied on verification. Such advantages are of no avail, however, if one has struck into a false road from the outset. But should it turn out that Frederic Myers has really hit the right road by his divining instinct, it is certain that, like the names of others who have been wise, his name will keep an honourable place in scientific history.

28

Review of *Human Personality and
Its Survival of Bodily Death*,
by Frederic W. H. Myers (1903)

Human Personality and Its Survival of Bodily Death. By FREDERIC
W. H. MYERS. 2 vols. 8vo. (Longmans, Green & Co., London,
New York, and Bombay. 1903.)

Such large portions of the text of these bulky volumes, which are
the legacy of Myers's literary life, have already appeared in these
Proceedings, and their author's general conceptions are so familiar
to my readers, that I feel free to omit from this notice all detailed
account of the book's contents and composition. For aught I know
such an account may be given by my fellow-reviewers. The contents are so intricate and the ideas so many that the great danger is
that of not seeing the forest for the trees, and of not apprehending
with distinctness the steps of Myers's reasoning. It seems to me
wisest, therefore, to employ the opportunity accorded me in analys-
ing his argument into its essential features, following, as I do so, a
logical rather than a textual order.

What would entitle Myers, if he were successful in what he attempted, to be regarded as the founder of a new science is that
conception of the Subliminal Self, by which he colligated and co-
ordinated a mass of phenomena which had never before been
considered together, and thus made a sort of objective continuum
of what, before him, had appeared so pure a disconnectedness that
the ordinary scientific mind had either disdained to look at it, or
pronounced it mostly fictitious. Two years ago I wrote in these

Proceedings that Myers had endowed psychology with a new problem—*The exploration of the subliminal region* being destined to
figure hereafter in that branch of learning as "Myers's problem."
Reading these volumes, we gain a definite idea of how far he himself had pushed forward the topographical survey of that region.

Conservatives in anthropologic science will immediately say that
Myers used the concept of the "subliminal" far too broadly, and
that the only safe demarcation of the term is that of the neuro-
pathologists. These observers for the most part now recognise a
subliminal region frankly, but they recognise it only as a dissociated part of the normal personality. Experiences forgotten by the
upper consciousness may here still lead a parasitic existence, and
in an inferior, dreamlike way may interfere with normal processes.
For these critics the subliminal is synonymous with the *forgotten*
and forms a region of disintegration exclusively.

Most neurologists either ignore those other "evolutive," "superior," or "supernormal" phenomena, in which Myers's chief
interest lay, or scout them wholesale as deceptions. The few who
admit them are more likely to see in them another department of
experience altogether than to treat them as having continuous
connection with the ordinary phenomena of mental dissociation.

Those who simply ignore them (for whatever reason) may themselves be ignored here as belated students. However acutely aware
one may be of the sources of fallacy in reports of the marvellous, I
fail to see how the records quoted in these volumes, and in vastly
greater profusion in Gurney's *Phantasms of the Living* and the
other S.P.R. publications, can rightfully be met by a wholesale
and indiscriminating *non possumus*. Any one with a healthy sense
for evidence, a sense not methodically blunted by the sectarianism
of "Science," ought now, it seems to me, to feel that exalted
sensibilities and memories, veridical phantasms, haunted houses,
trances with supernormal faculty, and even experimental thought-
transference, are natural kinds of phenomenon which ought, just
like other natural events, to be followed up with scientific curiosity.

Hypnotic phenomena form the centre of perspective for Myers's
map of the subliminal region. In the first place, the system of
faculty of a subject under hypnosis is quite different from his waking system of faculty. While portions of the usual waking system
are inhibited, other portions are sometimes supernormally ener-
gised in hypnosis, producing not only hallucinations, but after-

results in the way of sense-discrimination and control of organic function, to which the waking consciousness is unable to attain. We are thus led to the notion of two different currents of mental life, one deeper, and the other shallower, of which either is best appealed to while the other is in abeyance. That these currents may not only alternate but may co-exist with each other is proved by Gurney's, Binet's, and Janet's discovery of Subjects who, receiving suggestions during hypnosis and forgetting them when wakened, nevertheless then wrote them out automatically and unconsciously as soon as a pencil was placed in their hands.

Allying the curative phenomena of hypnosis with the great re-parative powers of sleep, and its enhancements of faculty with the enhancements of faculty to which dreaming and natural somnam-bulism occasionally give rise, Myers postulates a region of sleeping consciousness present at all times in all of us, a region moreover which in certain respects has an advantage over the waking levels of the mind. This subliminal region is usually closed off from the ordinary waking consciousness, but under special conditions of appeal, which vary with the idiosyncrasy of the individual, it may break in with effects which reveal its presence to us. The popular word "suggestion" is only a name for a successful appeal to this subliminal consciousness.

The appeal, in hypnotic subjects, is made through the ordinary consciousness in the first instance; and into that consciousness the effects, when they are "post-hypnotic," return in the form of "auto-matisms," sensory or motor. In other words, hallucinations or un-motived impulses to act, which in some cases are upheavals from the subliminal into the supraliminal region, may be so in all cases. The two regions thus form environments for each other, with pos-sibilities of interaction, though under ordinary conditions their intercourse is small.

So far Myers would seem to be on perfectly solid ground. There *is* a subliminal region of life which opens fitfully into the supra-liminal region. The only doubt is as to whether it be general in human beings, or whether it be not limited to a few hypnotic and hysteric subjects.

The subliminal region being thus established as an actuality, the next question is as to its farther limits, where it exists. My sub-liminal, for instance, has my ordinary consciousness for one of its environments, but has it additional environments on the remoter side? Has it direct relations of intercourse, for example, with the consciousness, subliminal or supraliminal, of other men?

Some of the phenomena of hypnotism or mesmerism suggest that this is actually the case. I refer to the reports (several of them irreproachably recorded) of hypnotism at a distance, of obedience to unspoken orders, and of "community of sensation" between hypnotiser and subject, of which Sections 568 to 571 of Myers's Volume I give some account. Remote influences, to which the supraliminal region is closed, may thus occasionally pass into the subliminal region, showing that this latter communicates not only with the supraliminal mind of the subject himself, but with the mind of other persons, and possibly with a still wider world.

How wide this world may possibly be is suggested by all the various reports of thought-transference and clairvoyance in the hypnotic state. And if we now pass beyond conditions of artificial hypnosis, and take into account states of abstraction like those produced in some persons by crystal gazing and by automatic writing, and the "trances" of certain somnambulists and mediums, with the clairvoyant faculty reported to be found therein, we find ourselves obliged (if we credit the reports) to assume that the subliminal life has windows of outlook and doors of ingress which bring it (in some persons at least) into a commerce, of which the channels entirely escape our observation, with an indefinitely extended region of the world of truth.

The jump which Myers makes here is that of generalising his conclusions. The "conservative" critic who does not deny the facts *in toto* would most probably call them pathological freaks of idiosyncrasy. He would protest against their being treated as revelations of the constitution of human nature at large. Myers, on the other hand, regards them as such revelations, and considers that the subjects show their "idiosyncrasy" rather in lying as open as they do to our observation, than in having the kind of human constitution which the observations disclose.

He is thus led to the general conception of a subliminal life belonging to human nature in general, and having its own indefinitely wide environment, distinct from that with which our bodily senses carry on their commerce. Set over against this subliminal life, and in strong contrast with it, we find the normal consciousness, dealing primarily through the senses with the material world and in possession of faculties of attention, and in particular of memory, which are pitifully small in comparison with those which the subliminal consciousness wields. The normal consciousness is thus only a portion of our nature, adapted primarily to "terrene" conditions. Those more directly intuitive faculties which it lacks, and of which we get glimpses in individuals whose subliminal lies exceptionally open, can hardly be vestiges, degenerations of something which our ancestors once possessed. We should rather regard them as germs of something not yet evolved for methodical use in our natural environment, but possibly even now carrying on a set of active functions in their own wider "cosmic" environment.

The "supernormal" becomes thus for Myers synonymous with the "evolutive" as contrasted with the "dissolutive" with which the ordinary neurologist would prefer to connect it. The supernormal faculties of the subliminal take us into the cosmic environment; and for Myers this cosmic environment takes on more and more, as the volumes proceed, the character of a "spiritual world." From its intercourse with this spiritual world the subliminal self of each of us may draw strength, and communicate it to the supraliminal life. The "energising of life" seems, in fact, to be one of its functions. The reparativeness of sleep, the curative effects of self-suggestion, the "uprushing" inspirations of genius, the regenerative influences of prayer and of religious self-surrender, the strength of belief which mystical experiences give, are all ascribed by Myers to the "dynamogeny" of the spiritual world, upon which we are enabled to make drafts of power by virtue of our connection with our subliminal. He dreams of a methodical evolution and extension, as our knowledge of the channels shall improve, of our resources in this direction.

Myers's theory, so far, is simple enough. It only postulates an indefinite inward extension of our being, cut off from common consciousness by a screen or diaphragm not absolutely impervious but liable to leakage and to occasional rupture. The "scientific" critic can only say it is a pity that so vast and vaguely defined a hypothesis should be reared upon a set of facts so few and so imperfectly ascertained.

The vagueness of the hypothesis at this point chiefly consists in the ill-defined relations of the subliminal with its "cosmic" environment. Is this latter the Absolute Soul of the World, with which all our subliminals may be supposed to be substantially continuous? Or are the various subliminals discontinuous?—and is their intercourse transacted across an isolating interval?

As the work proceeds, Myers tends more and more towards the latter conception: the "spiritual world" becomes a "world of spirits" which interact.

This follows naturally from the consideration, to which he next proceeds, of veridical phantasms and mediumistic messages. At first sight "ghosts," etc. (if admitted to be actual phenomena), would seem to require a physical rather than a mental hypothesis for their explanation; and mediumistic messages, if taken at their face value, suggest that the "controlling" spirit intrudes into the very organism of the medium rather than that it merely actuates the medium's subliminal mind. The plot thickens very much hereabouts, and obliges one to ask more definitely whether the environment of the subliminal be mental exclusively or whether it may not also be physical. Myers is shy of putting forth psychophysical hypotheses, but in his conceptions of "phantasmogenetic invasion" of space and of "telergy" and "telekinesis," we find that he is forced to abandon purely mental territory. Subliminal selves, affecting one another in their quality of purely psychic entities, are not the sole factors that need be considered in our explanations. Space and their physical relations to space are also required.

Let me indicate very briefly what are the essential points in Myers's handling of this new range of experiences.

In the first place, take the so-called "veridical phantasms of the living." Assuming them to be established by the evidence, the records show that the mind of the percipient must be at least one of the factors of their production. If they were purely physical or "astral" presences, why should they wear earthly clothes, and carry earthly accessories? and when the percipient is in the midst of companions, why should they so seldom appear to *them*?

Evidently the phantasm, whatever may be its remoter starting-point, involves, as a mere immediate bit of experience, the psychophysical process called "hallucination" on the part of the percipient himself.

Secondly, since there are well recorded cases where a living person, A, made his phantasm appear to B by simply willing that it should do so, and since in many of the other cases of phantasms of the living, the person who appeared probably *wished* to appear where he did appear, it seems fair to interpret these appearances generally as hallucinations produced by the action of one mind upon another, somewhat after the pattern of the hallucinations which a hypnotiser makes his subject experience so easily by suggesting that he shall have them, either during the hypnosis or after waking up. "Telepathy" is the name which Myers gave to the immediate influence of one subliminal upon another. The records seem to prove that telepathy either may or may not be a transfer of ready-made content from one mind to another. Sometimes the influencing mind appears to act only as a suggestive stimulus, and the results on the mind influenced show every variation from a vague emotional mood to an elaborated perception full of accessories, or to an automatically impulsive act.

Activity of the influencing mind at a distance from its body is at any rate proved, according to Myers, by these phantasms of the living and by other telepathic phenomena.

It is round this conception of action at a distance, to which Myers applies the term of "psychical invasion," that his theory now turns towards its ulterior developments.

The fact that a phantasm may appear to a whole collection of persons at once, or to an indifferent companion of the person, rather than to the person himself of whom the phantasm's original might reasonably be supposed to be thinking, suggests that our soul's invasive powers apply to outer space as well as to other minds. Myers cites examples of these, as of all other special types of case which his argument requires, and considers that the probability of this space-invasion by the subliminal powers of the living is strengthened by two additional kinds of fact. First we have cases of apparent "bilocation" of mind and organism, as when a living person appears to view his own body from a remote position, or to see his own "double" as a phantasm; and second, we have an impressive array of cases which make for "travelling" clairvoyance, ("telæsthesia," as Myers calls it) whether in dream, in crystal gazing, or in the mesmeric trance. Myers indulges in no hypothesis whatever as to the *modus operandi* of this space-invasion by our subliminal. At any rate it seems to bring space in as a portion of the subliminal's environment. The subliminal has relations with space as well as with other minds.

So far the powers of living persons have been considered exclusively. But phantasms of the slowly or suddenly dying shade by continuity of time-relation into phantasms of the recently dead, and these in turn shade into phantasms of the long dead, *i.e.* into narratives of the haunted-house type, of which the mass recorded is decidedly imposing.

The order of theoretic construction, if we go back to the beginning, is thus somewhat as follows:—From hyperæsthesia in the hypnotic state we pass gradually into telepathy between the subject and the operator; from this to phantasmogenetic telepathy between living men at a distance from one another; from this to space-invasions, whether phantasmogenetic or clairvoyant, by the subliminal of living persons; and finally from this to similar invasions (phantasmogenetic, at any rate) by the dead. We thus reach the hypothesis of spirit survival. Primarily, we reach this only in the somewhat idiotic form of "ghosts," for up to this point we have been considering only what Myers calls automatisms of the *sensory* order.

But *motor* automatisms carry us a good deal further towards a "world of spirits." Sensory automatisms seem to be essentially fugacious. Rarely is their content elaborately developed or prolonged. It is quite otherwise with automatic writing and speech, for here the messages are consecutive, and bring explicit professions of origin and purpose along with them. This may obtain when the subject who offers them is awake as well as when he is entranced.

The whole topic of "spirit messages" is thus opened up to our reflection. Although Myers died before he could write out his review of the evidence for spirit messages in detail, he all along shows that he deemed it sufficient: some such messages, at any rate, he held to have been proved authentic. With this our "cosmic" environment, as he believed in it, comes into full view. Our subliminals surround one another and act upon one another, as well as upon space; and spirits of the departed (which may themselves be constituted as we are, and have something like a subliminal condition of their own) may also act upon us and upon space, and receive our action too. When the action is transient, it is probably merely an impact upon our subliminal, of which we need not necessarily suspect the source. When it is more protracted or "invasive," space gets affected, and we either see a ghost or feel a presence; and it is an open question, in such effects as these upon our consciousness, how far our subliminal mind exclusively receives the operation of the invader, and how far he may act directly on our physical nervous system. Prolonged "possession" or "control" of the organism seems to involve the profoundest sort of operation which is possible; and Myers is willing here to admit that the foreign spirit may directly actuate the medium's nervous system.

That spirits of departed men should actuate these living bodies of ours directly, shows a form of physical influence to which Myers gives the name of *telekinesis*, and of which still other instances would be the raps, the table-movings without contact, and the other "physical phenomena of mediumship," as they are commonly termed. Myers discusses these phenomena warily, using delicate methods of gradual approach (see especially the exquisitely ingenious "Scheme of Vital Faculty," which ought to have been prominently printed as the concluding chapter of the whole book, but which appears inconspicuously among the Appendices as Section 926 A, Vol. II, pp. 505–554). On the whole he seems well disposed to treat the evidence for physical phenomena as adequate.

And now his whole theory lies before us. It is a vast synthesis, but a coherent one, notwithstanding the vagueness of some of the terms that figure in it. No one of the dots by which his map is plotted out, no one of the "corners" required by his triangulation, is purely hypothetical. He offers empirical evidence for the concrete existence of every element which his scheme postulates and works with. In logical form the theory is thus a scientific construction of a very high order, against which one can urge only two general kinds of objection. One can say first that the stepping-stones themselves, the corners, are too frail, that the types of fact invoked need much additional corroboration; or one can say, even if the kinds of facts were admitted to be solid where they have been observed, that Myers has ascribed a universality and an extension to them for which he has no warrant, that he has drawn his rules from the exceptional cases, and made his spiritual universe too continuous.

Disregarding these criticisms for the moment, I am impelled to say a word about this matter of Myers's "scientific" ability. Reading him afresh in these two volumes, I find myself filled with an admiration which almost surprises me. The work, whatever weaknesses it may have, strikes me as at least a masterpiece of co-ordination and unification. The voluminous arsenal of "cases" of which the author's memory disposes might make the most erudite naturalist or historian envy him, and his delicate power of serially assorting his facts, so as to find always just the case he needs to fit into a gap in the scheme, is wholly admirable. He shows indeed a genius not unlike that of Charles Darwin for discovering shadings and transitions, and grading down discontinuities in his argument.

Three circumstances, probably, have worked against the general public recognition of Myers's scientific powers. These have been, first, the nature of the material he worked in; second, his literary fluency; and third, his emotional interest in immortality. The two latter characteristics, combining their effects, have given to certain passages in the present volumes a tone so lyrical that it may well make them distasteful to the ordinary scientific reader. For propagandist purposes the existence of these passages is, I think, to be regretted. Myers could well have afforded (having shown his undisputed lyrical power elsewhere) to be dryer in this argument, and by being so he would have doubtless turned certain possible disciples, now lost to him, into respectful listeners. But he so habitually saw the meanest subliminal phenomena in the light of that transterrene world with which they might remotely be connected, that they became glorified in his mind into experiences in themselves majestic. All his materials were objects of love to him, and the richly latinized and hellenized vocabulary in which he spoke of them shows how they affected his imagination.

From this point of view I think we need not regret a feature of these volumes which to some persons may have seemed pathetic. Myers, namely, was cut off by death before he could write his direct discussion of the evidence for spirit-return. But that discussion is a matter of dry-as-dust detail which may well be left to the pages of our *Proceedings* and *Journal*, and to workers who are not such universal geniuses. He has fully expressed in this book his general position on the subject; and being so lyrical a fountain in the direction of immortality, he could hardly have embarked on the evidence without alienating still more a class of students whose sympathy may on the whole be precious. Even though the cap-stone of the work, as he projected it, be lacking, still the essential Myers is in it, for it is as the organiser and co-ordinator, far more than as the critic of this or that particular set of observations, that posterity will best remember him.

As regards the truth of his theory, as contra-distinguished from its formal merits as a constructive effort, it is certainly too early for any one to pass dogmatic judgment. Most readers, even those who admire the scheme as a whole, will doubtless shrink from yielding their credence to it unreservedly. It will seem like skating over ice too thin for any intellect less nimble than Myers's to place its feet on boldly. The types of case which he uses as stepping-stones are some of them, at present, either in quality or quantity, decidedly weak supports for the weight which the theory would rest upon them, and it remains at least possible that future records may not remedy this frailty.

The reproach that he has over-generalised the exceptional is also one which, in the present state of our knowledge, cannot be decidedly rebutted. He may extend the subliminal too far when he supposes that all of us possess it, and that works of genius generally have their source in it. He may extend "phantasms" too far when he fills a whole cosmic environment with spirits able to engender them. As between the individual subliminal and the cosmic environment, he may also not have drawn the boundary correctly. There may well be more of the "dissolutive" subliminal and less of the "spirit" than he supposes, in some of his palmary phenomena. But however it may have to be contracted in one case, or extended in another, the subliminal region, as Myers conceived it, will remain a *vera causa* in psychology, explanatory, either of the whole or of a part, of the great mass of occult occurrences so far as they are authentic. "Automatisms" are indeed what he first said they were, messages from the subliminal to the supraliminal regions.

The imperfection which I feel most acutely in Myers's survey of the subliminal life is its failure adequately to account for its being so impartially the home both of evolutive and of dissolutive phenomena. The parasitic ideas of psycho-neurosis, and the fictitious personations of planchette-writing and mediumship reside there side by side with the inspirations of genius, with the faculties of telepathy and telæsthesia, and with the susceptibility of genuine spirit-control. Myers felt the paradoxical character of such cohabitation, and, as usual, was ready with a suggestion for attenuating the difficulty.

"It may be expected," he writes, "that supernormal vital phenomena will manifest themselves as far as possible through the same channels as abnormal or morbid vital phenomena, when the same centres or the same synergies are involved. . . . If there be within us a secondary self aiming at manifestation by physiological means, it seems probable that its readiest path of externalisation—its readiest outlet of visible action,—may often lie along some track which has already been shown to be a line of low resistance by the disintegrating processes of disease, . . . lie along some plane of cleavage which the morbid dissociations of our psychical synergies have already shown themselves disposed to follow" (Vol. II, p. 84).

But this conception is deficient in clearness. Are there three zones of subliminal life, of which the innermost is *dissolutive,* the middle one *superior* (the zone of genius, telepathy, etc.), and the outermost *supreme* and receptive directly of the impact of the spirit-world? And can the two latter zones reach the supraliminal consciousness only by passing through the interior and inferior zone, and consequently using its channels and mixing its morbid effects with their own? Or is the subliminal superior throughout when considered in itself, and are the curious parasitisms of hysteria and alternate personality, and the curious uncritical passivity to the absurdest suggestions which we observe in hypnosis to be explained by defective brain-action exclusively, without bringing in the subliminal mind? Is it the brain, in short, which vitiates and mixes results, or is it the interior zone of the subliminal mind? I make no attempt to solve the question.[1] It is practically as well as theoretically a vital one, for there can be no doubt whatever that the *great* obstacle to the reception of a *Weltanschauung* like Myers's is that the superior phenomena which it believes in are so enveloped and smothered in the mass of their degenerative congeners and accompaniments that they beget a collective impression of disgust, and that only the strongest of mental stomachs can pick them over and seek the gold amongst the rubbish.

Meanwhile it must not be forgotten, if one finds Myers's map unsatisfactory, that no regular psychologist has ever tried his hand at the problem. Psychologists admit a subliminal life to exist in hypnosis and in hysteria, and they use a case like that of Janet's "Adrienne" to explain the manner in which "secondary personalities" may become organised. But the existence all about us of thousands and of tens of thousands of persons, not perceptibly hysteric or unhealthy, who are mediumistic to the degree at any rate of being automatic writers, and whose mediumism results in these grotesque impersonations, this, I say, is a phenomenon of human life which they do not even attempt to connect with any of the other facts of Nature. Add the fact that the mediumship often

[1] For Mr. Myers's treatment of the question, see especially Vol. I, pp. 72–75.— EDITOR.

gives supernormal information, and it becomes evident that the phenomenon cannot consist of pure eccentricity and isolation. There is method in it; it must have a context of some sort and belong to a region where other things can be found also. It cries aloud for serious investigation. Myers's map is the only scientifically serious investigation that has yet been offered. It is to be hoped that those whom it dissatisfies may not merely reject it, but also make some effort to provide something better.

I cannot conclude without paying my tribute to the innumerable felicities of suggestion with which *Human Personality* abounds. Myers's urbanity of style, and his genius for analogy were never more profusely displayed, or in so many directions. Bold as his theory is, it is one of its merits that it should be so sober in the way of either physical or metaphysical hypothesis. What "spirits" are, or what their relations are to "space," he never tries to say, but uses the terms like a *Naturforscher*, as mere designations for factors of phenomena. The book on the whole must be considered a worthy monument to his memory.

Telepathy Once More, No. II (1903)

Sir: However science may be *made* by lonely men observing natural facts and meditating on their meaning, science prevails at last and is disseminated through the public by authority pure and simple. Innovations in science may long be barred from general recognition by the authority of those who hold conservative views. My learned colleague, John Trowbridge, in his article entitled "Telepathy," in your last week's number, presses with all the weight of his authority against the door which certain "psychical researchers" are threatening to open wide enough to admit a hitherto discredited class of facts. His reasonings will soon be forgotten by readers who will yet remember his name and quote his hostile vote if it be left to go unchallenged. So you will, perhaps, allow a lover of fair play, not to discuss telepathy itself, which would indeed be a complicated matter, but to inscribe against Professor Trowbridge's manner of discussing it a protest which some such readers may also happen eventually to remember.

Professor Trowbridge says that there is "no science in the subject of telepathy; it is a belief." So far, he thinks, as men who have made their reputations by accurate work may be counted among its believers, they are men of advancing years who have abandoned strenuous investigation with its small returns, and "find it easier to philosophize and to write out their thoughts than to put them to the test of experiment. When a scientific man," he adds, "takes to such work in psychics and philosophy, the death knell of his scientific career is rung."

Heaven forbid that the death-knell of my colleague's scientific career should be rung yet, but he has described to a dot his own contribution to psychics and philosophy in this article. He seems to me to have found it easier to philosophize and write out his thoughts than either to experiment or to read the experiments of others, preferring to follow an *a priori* mental image which he has framed, of all the possible evidence for telepathy, and then to lump all possible students of it together in advance as a set of irreclaimably vague "believers."

I do not here assume to say that the various investigations recorded in the *Proceedings* of the Psychical Research Society have placed "telepathy" in an invulnerable position. Far from it. But I do say that Professor Trowbridge's description of such investigations so little resembles the reality as to be unrecognizable. I find it hard, after reading his article, to believe that he himself has read with any care, or even read at all, such documents as Gurney's *Phantasms of the Living*, or Mrs. Sidgwick's report on the Census of Hallucinations, or her and Professor Sidgwick's "Observations on Thought-Transference," and the discussions consequent thereon. Yet how can one effectually criticise evidence with which one seems to have no detailed acquaintance? I write, therefore, to beg Professor Trowbridge's readers and mine not to bow down before mere disparaging generalities and abstract statements, by whatsoever eminent authority they may be published, but rather to go to the original documents themselves, filled as they are with painstaking and minute discussion. Certainly it is not in their pages that the subject is treated with the greater vagueness or inaccuracy.

No man or set of men can be expected to be accurate "all over." Like the body, the mind grows slack when not kept up to standard by incessant training. Within their several sciences, men of science keep each other up to standard by their merciless habits of criticising. But "psychical research" is a dog with so few friends at court that almost any stick seems good enough to beat him with; and I venture to suggest that Professor Trowbridge (like many another physical philosopher who has written on this extraneous theme) has felt so confident of indulgence from his immediate professional fellows, whatever might be his line of argument, that he has let himself go, and indulged in conclusions based on a knowledge of the state of the question which in any matter of pure physics he would have considered unpardonably superficial, and which is certainly so superficial here as to be almost irrelevant. To use his own words, he has "found it easier" to follow unscientific methods.

WILLIAM JAMES.

CAMBRIDGE, MASS., April 18, 1903.

Letter to James Hyslop Supporting the Prospectus for an American Institute for Scientific Research (1903)

95 Irving Street,
Cambridge, October 25, 1903.

Dear Professor Hyslop:

My opinion regarding the scheme of raising a fund for the endowment of research into mediumship, alternate personality, subconscious states in general, and the borderland between abnormal (or supernormal) and normal psychology is that it is wise. The S.P.R. doesn't cover quite the whole ground, though it might also be helped by the fund.

In my opinion the most fruitful work will lie in the direction of thorough description of the phenomena presented by certain rare individuals. Some of Janet's patients, Prince's patient, Flournoy's medium, and Mrs. Piper, are examples of the sort of study I mean. Needless to say, this has hardly ever been done, for both the investigator and the person investigated have to devote an endless amount of time, and time means money, which has seldom been forthcoming.

I feel strongly the need of an extensive sifting over of the mediums now available, and the selection of a very few for thoroughgoing study. Our "cases" are so far almost scandalously few. But to keep the investigator going, and to isolate the medium into satisfactory conditions, inevitably involves expense. I imagine that few scientific inquiries would give more valuable returns, if well carried out.

Sincerely yours,

WILLIAM JAMES.

A Case of Automatic Drawing (1904)

'Automatisms' have recently been made a frequent topic of investigation by psychologists, and although the exact reason why some persons have them and others do not remains as little explained as does the precise character and content which they may affect in a given individual, yet we are now so well acquainted with their variety that we can class them under familiar types.

The rudiment of all the motor-automatisms seems to be the tendency of our muscles to act out any performance of which we may think. They do so without deliberate intention, and often without awareness on our part, as where one swings a ring by a thread in a glass and finds that it strikes the number of times of which we think; or as when we play the willing game, and, laying our hands on the blindfolded 'percipient,' involuntarily guide him by our checking or encouraging pressure until he lays his hands upon the object which is hid.

The next higher grade of motor automatism, involving considerable subconscious action of intelligence, is found in the various alphabet-using forms of amateur mediumship, such as table tipping, the 'Ouija-board,' and certain other devices for making our muscles leaky and liable to escape from control.

'Graphic' automatisms, of which planchette-writing is the most popularly known example, is a more widespread accomplishment than ordinary people think. We have no statistics, but I am inclined to suspect that in twenty persons taken at random an automatic writer of some degree can always be found.

The messages are often elaborate, and surprise the writer quite as much as they do the bystanders by their content. The upper consciousness seems sometimes to cooperate in a faint way, sometimes merely to permit, and sometimes to be entirely ignorant of what the hand is doing. Occasionally the subject grows abstracted, and may go into a sort of reverie or trance if the writing or drawing is prolonged. Sometimes, but apparently in a minority of cases, the hand becomes insensible to pricking and pinching. Of the matters set down and their peculiarities I will say nothing here, these words of mine being merely introductory to a case of automatic drawing which may be interesting to the general reader from its lack of complication and its oddity.

The subject, C.H.P., married, fifty years old, made his living as a bookkeeper until the autumn of 1901, when he fractured his spine in an elevator accident. Since the accident he has been incapable of carrying on his former occupation.

For several years previous to the accident, automatic hand-movements, twitchings, etc., had occurred, but having no familiarity with automatic phenomena Mr. P. thought they were mere 'nervousness,' and discouraged them. He thinks that 'drawing' would have come earlier had he understood the premonitory symptoms and taken a pencil into his hand.

The hand movements grew more marked a few months after the elevator accident, but the subject sees no definite reason for ascribing to the accident any part in their production.

They were converted into definite movements of drawing by an exhibition which he witnessed in February, 1903. The account which follows is in Mr. P.'s own words.

A friend who was interested in hypnotism introduced me to a man who had some power as a hypnotist, and this man gave for our amusement a sample of automatic drawing, a man's face in dotted outline, no shading or detail. The movement of his hand reminded me of the way my own hand frequently acted, so the next day I sat down to a table with a pencil and paper, and tracings were directly made; but it was some days before I made an object that could be recognized, and I have never made dotted outlines like the man who performed before me.

For some days the movements were violent, and the traces left by the pencil were erratic, the lines being drawn with seemingly no aim, but finally rude forms of objects were executed.

Gradually my hand moved with more regularity and the pictures produced became interesting. Among these were dark-skinned savages, animals and vases of ancient type usually ornamented fantastically with curious faces.

A large proportion of the drawings were human heads, at first very crude in design and execution.

In the course of about two months the pictures assumed an artistic appearance, especially the heads. Most of the heads were quite small and dim in outline and detail.

My hand executed these without volition or direction from my natural self. My mind directed neither the design nor the execution. A new power usurped for the time being the functions of my natural or everyday mind. This power directed the entire performance.

Many times I tried to produce pictures of familiar faces, or scenes familiar to me by long association. I could produce nothing in this direction, but confusion was the result of the attempt. My hand continued to be guided by the unknown power. Weird, fantastic pictures were produced in abundance, many of them artistic in execution, but mostly of ancient type.

Sometimes the face would be so covered with strange devices as scarcely to be recognized as being intended for a face. Frequently a rock would be drawn with faces hewn in it.

While drawing these pictures I became drowsy, so much so that after finishing an artistic one I would sometimes go into an hypnotic sleep, and always would, after a long sitting, if I did not combat the influence.

My pencil moved sometimes so rapidly as to make it difficult to follow it with my eye. At other times it moved slowly. Some of the best effects were produced by rapid movements. I never knew what my pencil would make when it commenced, and often did not know until finished. Sometimes a design would be entirely changed.

Small pictures were frequently produced by a few rapid movements of the pencil from side to side, the pencil apparently not being lifted, yet the features of the face and general contour of the subject in hand would appear plainly. Voluntary suggestion has little effect on the drawings. After repeated suggestions I have sometimes been able to obtain an allegorical picture, as for instance when I asked for a message from my son, who resided at a distance, a carrier pigeon, having a ribbon around its neck with a letter attached, was produced.

I have tried hard to account for the power or directing mind that produces these pictures, but so far with no satisfactory result. I must say, however, that evidence to me is strong that, in order that the unknown power should have sway, the natural or earthly mind must be for the time being set aside, either entirely, or (what seems to me more reasonable) the unknown power is for the time being the dominant one, but acts in conjunction with the earthly mind. Although while drawing I feel more or less drowsy, my senses seem in some respects to be very keen. To my eyes the pictures usually appear highly exaggerated in beauty as well as in distinctness.

So much is this the case that on the completion of a picture and having taken it up to examine it, the distinctness and beauty which were so apparent while drawing, have departed. Frequently, while

drawing, the picture will be illuminated by delicate colors; and a feeling of great disappointment occurs when, on the completion of the picture, I find that not only the colors have disappeared, but the fine points of the picture also.

One strong feeling is left in my mind that whatever directs the pencil is all-powerful, and that nothing is too difficult for its performance if it only chooses to assert its power.

I ought to add that the style of design which my hand draws is strange to me. I have never observed anything like them anywhere. Neither do I know of any influence, suggestive or otherwise, that could have given me this power, with the exception (as I have stated) of having seen a man make a slight exhibition of automatic drawing, but this exhibition was long after I had noticed movements of my own hand. However, that exhibition gave me the idea of taking a pencil into my hand to try for results.

One point I might state clearly. While drawing, my eyes are fastened intently on the point of the pencil in contact with the paper, following the course of the pencil as if they were fascinated by it.

Of automatic *writing* I have done little. Occasionally the name of a near relative will appear, sometimes with figures attached. Sometimes an incoherent sentence will be commenced, but not finished. The name and figures usually appear either on a face or under or over it. Occasionally a word or line is written in (as I suppose) some ancient language, under or close to a drawing. I have never been able to discover what language this is. Perhaps it is, like the drawings, imperfect.

I had never been interested in hypnotism or kindred subjects before, nor ever attended any meetings or exhibitions in these lines, having always had a disbelief in anything of the kind.

P.S. Three months having elapsed since writing the above, I have but little to add in explanation. Pictures are still produced by the same mysterious power. The artistic appearance is better and the human form is more in evidence. I still think the drawings come from involuntary suggestion, that is, suggestion from the inner mind. Perhaps it would be better to call it impulse rather than suggestion.

I saw Mr. P. make one drawing. His hand on that occasion moved very slowly in small circles, not leaving the paper till the drawing had, as it were, thickened itself up. He seemed to grow very ab-

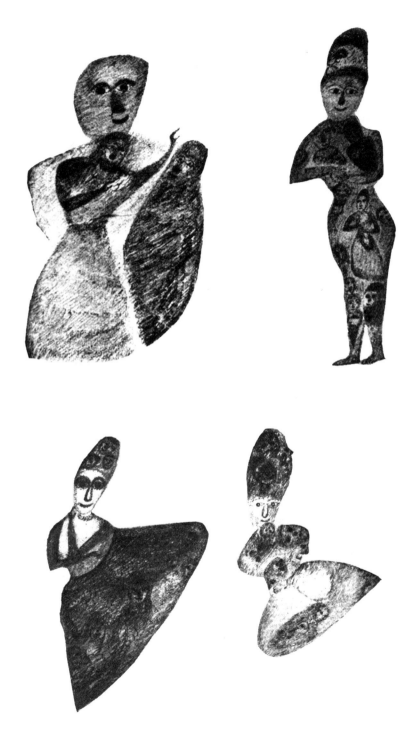

stracted before the close of the performance, but on testing his hand with a needle, it showed no anesthesia.

It is evident that with a little more system, a little more handwriting, and possibly some speaking under 'control,' this gentleman (whose narrative seems absolutely sincere) would exemplify a case of mediumship of what one might call the 'Martian' type. It would then remind one somewhat of the case so admirably studied by Professor Flournoy in his book *From India to the Planet Mars*. As the case stands, it is peculiar only for the monotony and oddity of the designs drawn by the hand. As in many other cases, we have no means of guessing why the subject in his drawings follows so peculiar a type. His own statement that he never saw anything like them before, must be taken with a grain of salt; for memories which have lapsed entirely from the upper consciousness of a subject have again and again been proved to actuate his hand in automatic writing. This case may be one of such a memory simply developing and confirming its habits. It may possibly on the other hand be the expression of a 'secondary personality' of some sort, in which (or in whom), if we could make exploration, a systematic context of ideas would be found.

↤ 32 ↦

Letter to J. G. Piddington on
Mrs. Thompson in Trance (1904)

I do not intend to discuss here the genuineness of Mrs. Thompson's trance; but, as reference has been made to the question, it may be of interest to quote a letter addressed to me by Professor James in answer to my enquiries about an experiment which I knew that he had made with a view to testing whether Mrs. Thompson when entranced was insensible to pain. Professor James writes as follows:

"Our conception of 'trance' is anything but definite, and I know of no test of genuineness.

"Anæsthesia may not be a sure sign of it; and if it were a sign it might, within limits, be easily feigned.

"Failure of pupils to react to light has been used to prove the genuineness of hypnotic trance, and so have other neural oddities. They certainly would prove an unfeigned and *abnormal state*. The altered speech and the amnesia[1] are what are *understood* by medium trance. Insensibility to *violent* pain being with difficulty simulable, it would, if found, be presumptive proof that the altered personality and amnesia were also unsimulated.

"I subjected Mrs. T[hompson] to no violent pain, merely pricked her lips and hands with a pin, without warning. Her demeanour might have been feigned, but I doubt or disbelieve it. It tallies with the demeanour of Flournoy's case, and combines with the general impression of sincerity which I receive from Mrs. T[hompson]."

[1] It will appear later that complete amnesia does not obtain in Mrs. Thompson's case.

Letter to Isaac K. Funk on
The Widow's Mite (1904)

From William James, Professor of Psychology, Harvard University.

"I regard fraud as an improbable hypothesis, and, if the circumstances are completely reported, not seriously to be considered.

"The improbabilities of an accidental coincidence grow with the number of details which coincide. The medium hit so many details in reference to this "Widow's Mite" that the probabilities of her success being altogether accidental are very small. It is difficult to measure the improbability mathematically, but common sense will consider it almost infinitely great in this case.

"In view of the many recent proofs that our 'subconscious self' may often know what our conscious self is ignorant of, it is possible that the medium (had her subconscious mind been in communication with the cashier's subconscious mind) might have thus known that the coin had never been sent back. The greater genuineness of the darker coin, if it were not a pure coincidence, might have been similarly gathered from other minds at a distance. It is obvious that in the case under discussion subconscious mindreading would have to go beyond the actual sitters at the 'séance.'

"The hypothesis of spirit communication is undoubtedly a possible one and simpler than any other, provided one supposes the spirits in question to have been tremendously inhibited in their communications. This is a necessary inference from the gaps and guesses which the facts they reported exhibited."

↙ 34 ↙

A Case of Clairvoyance (1907)

The following case of the recovery of the body of a drowned person in consequence of indications given by a clairvoyant, has been entrusted to me for publication by Dr. Harris Kennedy, of Roxbury, a cousin of my wife. It should have been published in 1899. Dr. Kennedy (whose brother was staying at Lebanon at the time the events happened) got the depositions of the witnesses while the case was still hot; and delay has added nothing to the data for our judgment.

I first subjoin the summarized account drawn up by Dr. Kennedy.

DR. KENNEDY'S ACCOUNT.

On Monday, Oct. 31st, 1898, Miss Bertha Huse left her home at Enfield, N.H., at 6 A.M., before the rest of the family had risen. She took her way down the street toward the so-called Shaker Bridge. On her way she was seen by several people, and by one person when she was on the bridge. Her family, learning of her absence, instituted a search for her, and during the greater part of the day 150 men, more or less, hunted the woods and lake shore in that vicinity. This search proving of no avail, Mr. Whitney, a mill owner of Enfield, sent to Boston for divers, with a suitable outfit. A diver named Sullivan worked the better part of all Tuesday, and up to Wednesday noon, without success in the lake.

On Wednesday evening, Nov. 2nd, Mrs. Titus, of Lebanon, N.H., a village about four and one-half miles from Enfield, while dozing after supper, aroused the attention of her husband, who was seated near her, by her noises, and extremely horrified countenance. When he spoke to her, she failed to answer, and it was necessary for him to shake her before arousing her to consciousness. When she was conscious, the first thing she said was, "Why did you disturb me? In a moment I should have found that body." After this she told her husband, "If I behave very peculiarly tonight, or cry out, or seem greatly disturbed, do not on any account awaken me, but leave me to myself." At some time during the night Mr. Titus was aroused by the screams of his wife. He got up, lit a lamp, and waited, obeying his wife's instructions. She, during a following interval, though not awake, spoke in substance as follows:

"She followed the road down to the bridge, and on getting part way across it, stepped out on to that jutting beam which was covered with white frost. There she stood undecided whether to go into the water there or go up over the hill to the pond. While so standing, she slipped on the log, fell backwards, and slid in underneath the timber work of the bridge. You will find her lying, head in, and you will only be able to see one of her rubbers projecting from the timber work."

Early in the morning, at her earnest solicitation, her husband went to Mr. Ayer, an employee of the Mascoma Flannel Co., at Lebanon, and asked him for leave to absent himself from the mill that morning, in order to go with his wife to the Shaker Bridge at Enfield. He then told Mr. Ayer the story, substantially as above. Mr. Titus also told the story to Mr. W. R. Sunderlin, as well as to certain other persons, all in Lebanon, before he went with his wife to Enfield, where he told other parties of this occurrence, and asked Mr. Whitney, who had been foremost in the search, to accompany him and his wife to the spot his wife was desirous of investigating. When they reached the bridge, Mrs. Titus pointed out a certain spot where she said they would find the body in the position as above mentioned. Mr. Whitney, who was then one of quite a number at the spot, sent a messenger to get the diver who had been working in the neighborhood of that spot on the previous days. On his arrival Mrs. Titus pointed out to him the spot where she said the body lay. He said, "I searched there yesterday, and found nothing."

She said, "Yes, you searched *there*, and *there* (pointing to certain spots), but you did not search *there*, and if you go down, you will find only the rubber of her shoe projecting from the timber work." To satisfy her, he put on his diving suit, and went down at the spot indicated. After a moment or two, the bonnet of the deceased rose to the surface, and shortly after the diver came up bringing the body. The diver then said, "I did not look in this place yesterday, as the brush and debris were so thick there that I could not see; in fact, all I could feel of the body, was the rubber, projecting from the timber work."

Mrs. Titus' grandmother is said to have had a similar power in her day, but Mrs. Titus is not known to have made any pretense of being a clairvoyant, having never used her trances for any pecuniary reward, or for the sake of any notoriety. On the day following, viz., Nov. 4th, Mrs. Titus was ill.

CORROBORATIVE STATEMENTS.

Here follow the statements of several of the persons named in the preceding story. They were written down by Dr. Kennedy from their lips a few days after the occurrences, read by him to them, and signed by them as accurate.

Mr. Ayer's Statement.

On Thursday, A.M., Nov. 3rd, 1898, Mr. George Titus came to the Mascoma Mills. At about 6.15 A.M. he called Mr. J. C. Ayer to one side to tell him the following:

"My wife had three trances last night, in one she caught hold of me, and I tried to pull her away but could not. She then said, 'I know where the girl is. I can find her. The girl went on to the bridge and walked out on a log and then walked back and forth, looking toward the hills. She slipped off and went down backwards. She did not intend to commit suicide. You will find her in the mud, with one foot out.'"

I, J. C. Ayer, have charge of the mill hands, and know both the sister of the girl, Bertha M. Huse, who was drowned, and Mr. Titus. Both of them worked for me in the mill. This story, which I told Dr. Harris Kennedy on Nov. 10, 1898, is, so far as I know, a correct statement of what was told me by Mr. Titus.

(Signed)   J. C. AYER.

Mr. Sunderlin's Statement.

Testimony in the Titus case, given by W. R. Sunderlin, at Lebanon, N.H., Dec. 1st., 1898. The following is as told by Sunderlin to Henry L. Briggs, Nov. 11th., and corrected by Sunderlin in presence of Sinclair Kennedy, Dec. 1st.:

On the morning of Thursday, Nov. 3rd, Geo. A. Titus, who keeps a horse in my barn, came into my barn about 5:20, and looking about said, "What, are we alone here. I want to tell you something, but I don't want any one to overhear me, and you must say nothing of what I am going to tell you. My wife has had a trance, and declares she can tell where to find the body of Bertha Huse. She says she is in the lake (Mascoma) at the east side of Shaker Bridge."

I naturally laughed at the idea, but Titus stuck to his story. Titus told me that on coming upstairs after supper (he lives in the second story house), he found his wife sitting in a rocking chair, asleep but gesticulating. He aroused her, whereupon she at once said, "O, George, why did you wake me. In a few minutes I could have told you where that girl is. If I go into another trance tonight or any other time, don't disturb me."

They then retired for the night. Along towards 11 or 12, Titus said he was waked by his wife's groans and mutterings. When he lit a lamp, he found his wife in apparent spasms, though still asleep. While so asleep she declared that Bertha Huse would be found in the lake to the east of the bridge, lying head down between two logs, her body covered by mud and brush; but that one foot would be sticking up, on which was a new rubber. That the girl first appeared to her (Mrs. Titus) on the bridge. That she appeared undecided whether to go in at the spot she was on, or from some point further down the bridge. That while standing on a frost-covered log with her back to the water, her foot slipped, and she went into the lake backwards.

Sunderlin continuing said; "I told Titus, Well, George, if you and your wife feel this way, you better hitch up and go out to the bridge. And if your wife thinks she is then sure of the spot, drive up to Enfield and see if you can get Whitney interested in this."

When Titus came back later in the day, he told me, "When we arrived at the bridge, she got out of the buggy, and walked along the east side of the bridge, looking intently into the lake. Suddenly she stopped, and said, 'George, she is right down there, between those two logs.' She then got into the buggy, and we drove to Whitney's house.

"Mr. Whitney smiled, on hearing the story, but went to the lake with us. My wife went directly to the spot she had pointed out to me, and told Whitney, 'She is right down there.' As her opinion could not be shaken, Whitney brought the diver. The diver shook his head and said, 'I have been down there.' My wife said, 'No, you have been down there, and there, but not *there*. She is head down in the mud, with one foot sticking up, and a new rubber on it.'

"The diver turned to Whitney, and said, 'I am under your orders, sir.' The diver went down at the spot indicated. In a minute the girl's hat came up. Shortly after the diver brought up the body."

(Signed by)   W. R. SUNDERLIN.

In presence of Sinclair Kennedy.

Mr. Titus' Story.

Sunday, Oct. 30th, 1898, Mrs. Titus, of Lebanon, said to her husband, "George, something awful is going to happen. I cannot tell you now what it is, but can later on." Monday, Oct. 31st, just about 6.40 A.M., as Mr. Titus was leaving for the mill, his wife said, "That has happened."

At noon Mr. Titus told his wife that the Huse girl (a sister of the one drowned) had gone home, Mr. Titus remarking that her mother was perhaps ill, at least so some of the people at the mill thought. She said, "It is something worse, I can feel it."

Monday evening we heard the girl was missing.

Tuesday, Nov. 1st, Mrs. Titus talked about the matter, and said, "That girl is in the lake."

Wednesday, Nov. 2nd, about 7.30 P.M., after having washed her dishes, Mrs. Titus was in the rocking chair. Mr. Titus spoke to her three times in a low tone and the fourth time loudly, and she woke up. "George, why didn't you let me be, in the morning I could have told you where the girl lay and all about it."

She then got up and walked about the house before she went to bed, which was between 8.30 and 9 P.M. After talking a short time, both Mr. and Mrs. Titus fell asleep.

At 11 P.M. (Wednesday) Mr. Titus woke her up. She was talking in her sleep with the diver, and hit her husband, saying, "She is not down there, but over here to the left." She begged her husband to leave her alone.

At 12.15 A. M. (Thursday) she again went into a trance which lasted until one o'clock. Mr. Titus lit a lamp and watched and talked with her in very low tones; when questioned on this subject she would answer, but did not hear about other things.

She said something about cold, and Mr. Titus said, "Are you cold, Nellie?" She said, "Oh, Oh, I am awfully cold." This Mr. Titus said referred to the drowned girl.

After she came out of the trance at one o'clock she told it just as she had it in the trance.

In the morning she said it was her duty to go over to the bridge at Enfield, and Mr. Titus asked Mr. Ayer to let him off, which Mr. Ayer did. Mr. and Mrs. Titus drove in a buggy to Enfield, leaving Lebanon at 7, taking about an hour.

When about 5 or 6 rods on the bridge, Mrs. Titus called out to stop and got out and walked over to a certain spot, and looked over and said, "George, she's down there." "Nellie, are you sure?" She said, "Yes."

Then Mr. and Mrs. Titus drove to Mr. Whitney's house, where she told her story. Mr. Whitney laughed, but said he would come down.

Mrs. Titus returned to the same spot, and said, "George, she is down there."

Mr. Whitney arrived a few moments later, about 8:30 or 8:45. Mr. Titus called attention to the spot, and Mr. Whitney said, "Walk down the bridge, and see if there is not another place where she is likely to be."

She, Mrs. Titus, walked down a little way, and came back saying, "George, she is right *there*." She explained that she could see the rubber just as plainly as while in her trance the night before.

Mr. Titus says she located the spot in the night, and that he could and did recognize it from her description.

After the diver came up with the body, he said he was not afraid of the woman in the water, but of the one on the bridge.

Mrs. Titus fights against these trances, as she is usually ill for some time after.

The girl walked down to the bridge, and stood wondering whether she would go there or over to the pasture. She slipped and went down between the logs of the bridge. Went down head first, and was buried in the mud, one foot sticking out. Diver said just exactly as *she* said. She knew neither the Huse girl nor was any acquaintance.

Her mother had the power, but wrote. Some days could write nothing, and then again a great deal. Mrs. Titus has no control over the trance which comes on in spite of her efforts to drive it off.

The above story which I told Dr. Harris Kennedy on Nov. 10th, 1898, is, so far as I know, correctly stated.

(Signed)   GEORGE N. TITUS.

Mr. Whitney's Letter.

Baltic Mills, Enfield, N.H., Nov. 15th, 1898.

My Dear Sir:

There is very little that I can add to the report which you must have in regard to the finding of the body of Miss Huse. Mrs. Titus and her husband called at my house the third morning after the disappearance.

Mrs. Titus said she was positive she could locate the body of Miss Huse in the Mascoma Lake. I went down with her and her husband to the bridge, which crosses the lake, should say the bridge was an eighth of a mile long, we walked along on the bridge together, arriving at a point about three-quarters way across the bridge. Mrs. Titus said, this is the place, she pointed to a place in the water where she said the body would be found. We secured the diver, and he went down and located the body exactly as Mrs. Titus had before said. There is really very little that I can add, Mrs. Titus certainly knew nothing about the circumstances, as she had not been in the town for two or three years previous. The diver's name is Sullivan, and he is from the Boston Tow-Boat Co., 89 State Street.

Yours truly,
(Signed)   GEORGE WHITNEY.

Mr. Sullivan's Statement.

On Nov. 21st, 1898, the diver Sullivan was seen by me [H. Kennedy] and the following drawn up after my chat with him. He signed it on Dec. 1st, at the meeting of the Bowditch Club,[1] at Hotel Nottingham, Boston.

1 The Bowditch Club is a group of assistants and younger instructors at the Harvard Medical School, who meet for purposes of professional enlightenment. Dr. Kennedy was at the time such an assistant. W.J.

Sullivan's Statement.

Nov. 21st, 1898, Mr. Sullivan, the diver in the Enfield case, was seen, at Simpson's dry dock, in East Boston. Being questioned in regard to the finding of Miss Huse, he told the following story:

"I was employed by the Boston Towboat Co., to search the Mascoma Lake. I went up at 7.10 Monday from Boston, arrived at night, and spent the greater part of Tuesday and Wednesday, Nov. 2nd, from 10 A.M. until 3:10 P.M., in searching along the Shaker Bridge. We had given up the idea of diving, and I telephoned to Boston for powder, intending to go down by the early morning train and have the powder meet me at Union Station, and take the next train up, having about 20 minutes in Boston, and return with the powder. In the morning, before I could leave Enfield, Mr. and Mrs. Titus drove over from Lebanon and called on Mr. Whitney. Mr. Titus told Mr. Whitney the story of his wife's trance, and said that altho he did not take much stock in it himself, he felt that on her account he ought to tell Mr. Whitney about it, simply to satisfy his wife. Mr. Whitney laughed, and said that he did not take any stock in it, and at the same time sent for me. We all went to the bridge, and Whitney told me that altho he did not have much faith in it himself, he felt that there might be people in the village who did, and as long as we had started to do all we could to recover the body, we ought at least to give this woman a chance. I said that the villagers up there thought that the missing girl had taken to the woods, and therefore they had had searching parties, while I was dragging the lake; but I told him that I was there, waiting his orders, my business was to find the body, and I was willing to do anything that he said, adding at the same time, that I did not want to be made a fool of by going down in a variety of places that she might point out along the bridge. He said, "No," that she simply would pick out one place, and he thought the least we could do was to go down at the place she picked out, and that would satisfy the villagers.

Mrs. Titus walked along the bridge, and came to a spot and said, "This looks like the spot I saw in my trance," then after a moment's hesitation she said, "No, not exactly," and walked a little way along and stopped at another point, and said, "This looks very much more like the place that I saw last night." She stood there looking over the rail of the bridge from 20 minutes to half an hour.

At last she said she was sure that was the place. I asked Mr. Whitney what I should do, and he said I had my suit, and he thought I had better go down in that spot. I took a guide line with sinker, located the spot from the bridge, threw the sinker over some little way from the bridge, as near as possible to the spot she pointed out. I then placed the ladder, and put on my suit, and went down. Mrs. Titus had told me the body was lying head down, only one foot with a new rubber showing, and lying in a deep hole. I started down the ladder, which extended about five feet under the water. When I swung off the ladder I went sideways and then turned. As I struck the crib work, 10 feet below the ladder, I turned to face the ladder, and my hand struck something. I felt of it, and it felt like a foot. I stopped short where I was:—it is my business to recover bodies in the water, and I am not afraid of them, but in this instance I was afraid of the woman on the bridge. I thought to myself, "How can any woman come from four miles away and tell me or any other man where I would find this body?" I investigated and felt of her foot, and made sure that it was a body. She was lying in a deep hole head down. It was so dark that I could not see anything. I had to feel entirely. I pulled her out, carried her up till I could get the light from above, and then arranged her clothing by laying her out on the crib of the bridge. When I had her laid out on the crib, I reached out for my guide line, but found I could not pull it up. I had to take out my knife and cut it as far as I could reach, and then I tied the line under her arms. The line was simply a clothes line, (6 thread).

I then came up and asked for Mr. Whitney. I said, "She is down there." Mr. Whitney said, "I know it." I thought Mr. Whitney had been convinced pretty strongly. He said it turned out that when I pulled her out of the hole, her hat came off and rose to the surface, and Martin, who worked the pump for me, came near getting into trouble by being pushed off the bridge when the hat appeared on the surface, because the people rushed for the side of the bridge. Fortunately he was not pushed off.

We had a man there in a little skiff, who pulled her up. Mr. Whitney asked me what I thought of it, and I told him I did not think, I was *stunned.*

There are two statements which Mrs. Titus made that are absolutely correct. She located the place where I was to go down; also told me that the body was lying, head in, in a deep hole, with one foot sticking up, with a new rubber. I was down in about 18 feet of water. It was so dark, nobody could see anything down there. She must have seen the body as it was lying, because she described the position, and she had already pointed out the place I was to go down, and nobody could have known who had not seen the body as it was lying on the bottom. If you ask me how she knew it, I don't know; but if you ask me if I believe in it, why, I have been convinced against my will. If my best friend had told me, I should have thought he had seen a ghost. But if I ever have a similar case and can't find the body, I shall introduce the parties to Mrs. Titus, and she will find it.

(Signed)   MICHAEL J. SULLIVAN.

Witnesses:

Alfred Schaper,	Maynard Ladd,	Langdon Frothingham,
E. W. Taylor,	M. A. Potter,	Alfred W. Balch,
Geo. Burgess Magrath,	Allen H. Cleghorn,	Henry E. Hewes,
E. A. Woods,	Harris Kennedy,	William James.

Mr. Sullivan was cross examined at the Bowditch Society meeting, where, his story being read to him, he confirmed it, in the presence of the witnesses whose names are signed above. I add some details from the stenographic notes taken on that evening, and from additional information there given by Dr. Kennedy.

The bridge was a straggling structure between an eighth and a quarter of a mile long, originally made by building cribs on the ice. These sank when the ice melted, and were joined by timber. Hardly any current exists; the water is dark, and great quantities of debris and brush have collected in and about the crib work. It was absolutely impossible to see from above either the body, or the place where the body lay. The detail of the Indian rubber shoe (though it adds to the impressiveness of the narration) is unimportant evidentially. Dr. Kennedy says—"The girl was called by her parents at about eight o'clock on the Monday morning. She had been feeling poorly and they had let her sleep. They found she had gone and had taken her rubbers."

At half past 6 on that morning it appears that "the blacksmith's wife," who was in a position to see the bridge, saw a woman upon it. This blacksmith's wife was not interviewed by Dr. Kennedy. The diver had spoken with her. This is what he reports.

Q. Was she an intelligent sort of woman?

A. She seemed so.

Q. She didn't say she saw the woman fall over?

A. No; she said she saw her on the bridge, or thought it was her. She saw some woman there. That was all she could say.

CRITICAL REMARKS.

The scientific interpretation of the case is three-fold:—

1. *The footprint theory*. It appears that there was a light frost on the fatal Monday morning, and that the footprints of the girl were traced from her house to the bridge and thereupon to a distance unrecorded. One of the gentlemen at the Bowditch Club said: "I think that the case is tremendously weakened by the fact that those footprints were seen, and by the fact that people saw her on the bridge. If you can prove that she was seen at a certain point on the bridge before she disappeared, it is not a difficult coincidence to imagine that she fell in at a certain point; and that would surely have been described to Mrs. Titus. It is conceivable that the woman who saw her on the bridge, knew Mrs. Titus. Some people have a power of observation which others have not. Mrs. Titus, with a particularly acute power of observation, might have learned something which others did not."

If this means that footprints and the blacksmith's wife furnished to Mrs. Titus data which the latter's acute powers, either of imagination or observation, completed into an accurate vision of the corpse's position in the water, it seems almost as great a mental miracle as "clairvoyance." The footprints had evidently not led to any spot on the bridge that suggested the girl's having stopped there, for the whole town, knowing of them and in spite of them, was searching the woods; and if they had even indicated one side of the bridge as the more probable side, why should the diver have been allowed to search *both sides, as he did on the Tuesday and Wednesday*? When asked whether he could go back now, and pick out the spot on the bridge where the girl fell off, the diver replied: "I don't think I could pick out that spot." The following questions and answers are from his cross examination.

Q. How should you know that spot from the one next to it?

A. If there wasn't anything connected with it, I could not pick it out, hardly.

If the diver, who had been there, felt so uncertain, it seems still less likely that Mrs. Titus could have accurately found the spot by a bare hearsay description.

2. This leads to the second naturalistic theory:—*Mrs. Titus may have witnessed the accident.* Like the blacksmith's wife, she may have happened to be near the bridge at the fatal hour, and seen what happened. She then probably went home, and with her husband's complicity worked up the trance story, and on Thursday morning pointed out the spot. The husband's alibi of her would necessarily then be false, and would prove him an accomplice on this theory. Mr. Sullivan's remark on having it propounded was, "Yes, but how could she then know the *exact position of the body on the bottom?*"

Another point against this theory is the odd delay until Thursday morning. Why should Mrs. Titus, if she had a perverse desire to win fame as a clairvoyant, have given the diver two free days in which to find the body unaided.

3. Finally, Bertha Huse, intending to commit suicide, might have confided the *intention and the mode of execution to Mrs. Titus, either directly* or through her sister, who, it appears, worked at Lebanon, and was probably known to Mrs. Titus. This third hypothesis is psychologically even more improbable than the two others. Against all three of these explanations, stands the fact of the precision of the clairvoyant's direction to the diver. Here are some passages from the latter's cross-examination:—

Q. You think that Mrs. Titus pointed to almost the exact spot where the body was found?

A. I know she did. If it wasn't for her, the body would not have been found.

Q. You say it was too dark for you to see?

A. It was total darkness. It is light water, but the crib work cuts off the light.

Again:—

Q. You found her with her head down and feet up in almost the exact spot Mrs. Titus indicated?

A. I might say to an inch.

Mr. Sullivan's mind seems to have been quite "stunned," as he expressed it, by the uncanniness of such an exact and immediate

verification. "When I put out my hand it came up against something that felt like a foot." . . . "If I had come across the body the
day before, or the first day I was there, I would have thought
nothing of it. I would say, 'All right for Boston tonight, I guess.'
But when I came across her, and felt out what it was, it did actually
stun me, and in place of paying attention to the body, I did so to
the woman overhead, that picked out the spot, and the way she said
it lay. . . . I thought of that, about this Mrs. Titus! I said I never
believed in anything like that! Then I commenced to haul her up
after I settled that part of it. I had been positive I would not find
the body. I had been mad because I would have to go down because of this woman saying, 'there is the spot where the body is.' "

It was evident that the exactness of the description was the striking thing for Sullivan. He was interrogated as to whether the position of the body tallied with Mrs. Titus' account of the way the girl
fell over backwards. The body stood vertically, head downwards,
in a hole in the cribwork. He thought that a sudden dive backwards was the best explanation of its being caught thus. "She was
lying feet up and head down. She was straight up and down." "I
take it a woman drowning herself, jumping over feet first, the air
would get under her clothes, and she would drift around a little
ways; . . . but if a woman goes backwards, she will settle quicker."
"Bodies that have drifted, as a general thing, lie horizontal."

It was plain enough that *neither of these three naturalistic explanations has the least plausibility*. A reader to whom the hypothesis of clairvoyance is impossible, had far better explain the case as a
very exceptional one of accidental coincidence. I should unhesitatingly do this myself were cognate cases *rarissimi*. But the records
of supernormal seership of various types and grades which the *Proceedings* of the S.P.R. are more and more abundantly publishing,
make, it seems to me, the scientific '*non-possumus*' absurd. There
is an almost identical case for instance, in Vol. xi, p. 383 ff., where
the corpses of two drowned boys named Mason, were found in
Cochihuate Lake, near Natick, Mass., through directions given by
a Boston clairvoyant named Mrs. York. See also a similar case on
p. 389 of the same volume.

My own view of the Titus case consequently is that it is *a decidedly solid document in favor of the admission of a supernormal
faculty of seership*—whatever preciser meaning may later come to
be attached to such a phrase.

I conclude by appending a notice that appeared in the *Granite State Free Press*, of Lebanon, N.H., on Friday, November 11th, 1898, and a letter from a sister of the drowned girl, received by me quite recently.

"CARD.

"The people of Enfield and adjoining towns, who so spontaneously came to our relief and assistance by words of sympathy and kindly and generous acts during the long days and nights of terrible anxiety and suspense, attending search for our dear daughter, sister, and niece; to that kind-hearted man, George E. Whitney, who so generously contributed assistance by personal effort and otherwise; to Mrs. Titus, who voluntarily came to our assistance when all means and efforts had failed, and by the exercise of a, to us mysterious but we believe a God-given power, designated the place where the body could be found and where it was found; to the funeral director, the bearers and singers; to the friends who came from a distance to attend the funeral; and to those who contributed the beautiful flowers; we wish hereby to express to each and all, our deep sense of gratitude and heartfelt thanks for this manifestation of their friendship. The memory of this will always be treasured by us.

(Signed)   MR. & MRS. EDWIN E. HUSE.
LEONA E. HUSE.
MR. & MRS. GUY E. HUSE.
MR. & MRS. L. D. DUNBAR."

Enfield, N.H., April 2nd, 1907.

Professor William James,
            Cambridge, Mass.

Dear Sir:—

In reply to your letter of recent date received by my mother, I will simply say—we have never had any reason to doubt that the facts of the case you referred to were correctly stated in the papers at the time of the accident.

We do not attempt to explain Mrs. Titus' part in it, but do know she performed a wonderful act for us, for which we shall always be very thankful. We have no reason to doubt either Mr. or Mrs. Titus' statements in regard to it.

In regard to your criticisms, am quite sure if you had been here you would not have advanced them.

We have not seen Mrs. Titus for several years, so can tell you nothing about her.

I judge by your letter that you have the facts of the case, so you will excuse me if I write nothing more—as it is far from pleasant to talk or write about what is to us a great sorrow.

Very truly,

MRS. H. BARROW,
For Mrs. Edwin E. Huse.

35

Letter on Dr. Gower and Table Lifting (1907)

At the end of April, 1906, Professor William James, on his way home from Leland Stanford University, made a short stay at —— in the hope of witnessing some of the phenomena. The sitters, in the absence of Dr. Gower, were, however, disinclined to try experiments, but they talked freely of their experiences to Professor James, and he gives a brief report as follows:

April 30th, 1906.

We got here at noon yesterday, and opened communication with Dr. Williams, who told me that Dr. Gower had not yet arrived from Europe, but who gave me and helped me to much testimony as to the physical phenomena reported. Professor H., Mr. J.T., and Mrs. Williams (whom I didn't see till this morning), all said that movements without contact were so absolutely certain in their minds as no longer to cause astonishment. Yet no systematic notes had been taken, and the evidence, strongly as it impressed me (especially Mrs. Williams's, who [seemed to take little interest in the phenomena], but who replied, when I asked her straight whether she believed she had seen her tables move without contact, "*of course!*"),—the evidence, I say, cannot be used to convince others, but subjectively has much impressed me.

Their circles began over ten years ago, Dr. Gower being their starter and enthusiastic director. Dr. Williams thinks that Dr.

Gower is the essential medium; he says that Dr. Gower considers Mrs. Williams more essential. They have sat little without Dr. Gower, and have never (?) had contactless movements when he was not present. Mr. T. proved himself to be a very efficient solicitor of movements—the most successful method being heartily to suggest to the table that it should move.

Movements with contact were often inexplicable in Dr. Williams's opinion by muscular pressure. They used various tables in various places, no one table seeming more propitious. An extension dining table figured, and a very light stand. The table most in use at Dr. Williams's was a solid oak one about 3 ft. square on top, with casters. There was also a much used oaken library table. I tried to lift one end of it with my left hand, but failed; evidently it weighed some 80 lbs. Its greatest feat one day was moving across the whole length of the room, say 12 feet. The little table had risen bodily from the ground, and struck Dr. Williams in the chest.

Most of the contactless movements were very brief as if the force exhausted itself quickly. No one had complained of tiredness after sitting.

Mrs. Williams testified to the water-splashing reported to Hodgson.

The best way to induce movements without contact had been to get them first with contact, then reduce the contact to one finger from each sitter, then take off the fingers, holding the hands not far, and tell the table to move, when it often would. The contactless movements were sliding, tipping, and rising bodily.

36

Physical Phenomena at a
Private Circle (1909)

A fortnight ago I heard that, at a private circle of spiritualists in a New England town, a table had been bodily lifted from the floor with no contact but that of fingers to its upper surface. The rarity of the case induced me to make a visit to the town in question, where I have had three sittings with the circle and from whence I now write.

The circle is composed of solid citizens of the town and their wives or sisters. They have sat weekly for a couple of years, and impressed me as perfectly sincere and earnest in their quest of facts. They use a four-cornered and four-legged table of wood, thirteen pounds in weight, on the center of which a revolving disc twenty inches in diameter, bearing an alphabet, has been pivoted. The disc revolves with a minimum of friction, and an index hand, pivoted independently, points to the letters and spells messages. The sitters' fingers may be placed on the edges of the table an inch below the disc or on the disc itself. To avoid too much pressure on the rotating disc, a ring or rail of thick brass wire has been adjusted to the corners of the table, surrounding the disc at four inches' distance, on which the wrists of those present may rest while they lay their finger tips on the disc. This ring slides with a moderate friction through four brass collars which sustain it, and which themselves are sustained by brass stems screwed to the angles of the table. The disc and the ring are thus concentric. [I go into these details about the ring, for reasons which will appear presently.]

For nearly three years nothing happened at this circle but answers to questions by tipping, and messages spelt out by the disc. No one present seemed to be exclusively the medium, tho one lady, absent from town at the time of my visit, was considered to have the most "power."

I.

Of the first physical phenomenon I got only oral testimony. This was the fact on two occasions, in the autumn of 1907, of explosive sounds as "loud as a pistol shot," seeming to occur each time in the room where the sitting was being held. On one occasion the sound was repeated seven times. On the other, the sitting being held in a house a couple of miles distant from the first one, it occurred but once. It was entirely unexpected and unexplained, seems to have startled everyone very much, and all present believed that it was spiritual.

II.

The second physical phenomenon obtained by the circle was the following: I copy the account from the diary of the circle's proceedings, under date of November 24th, 1907.

"At this meeting we at first took large center table, placed ordinary finger-bowls on table, one for each person, and partly filled with water. Mrs. M.'s bowl moved with just her fingers in the water, not touching the bowl in any way. Made intelligent movements, moving towards Mr. R. when asked. Other bowls also moved, but fingers had to be in contact with them in some manner."

The five witnesses have signed their names to this record for me. They say that the bowl "waltzed round the edge of the table," that they had tried the experiment on other evenings, but that this was the only attempt that succeeded.

III.

The next phenomenon of the kind which happened is given in the following account which I wrote down from the oral testimony of seven of the eight witnesses, and to which all but the absent one have appended their signatures, though they are willing to have these printed.

"On the night of November 19th, 1908, we, the undersigned, were having a sitting round the table used for many months in our experiments. [The table I have described above.—W.J.]

On the occasion in question our finger-tips were all resting on the top of the disc, so that they could not possibly exert any lifting force whatever on the table. The hands of Mrs. B. alone were in the air, a few inches above the center of the disc. After some of the usual tiltings of the table, with two or three of the legs off the ground, *it rose gently and with all four legs off the ground to the height of six inches or more,* to the great surprise of all of us, and remained in the air two or three seconds, subsiding slowly to the ground.

Some said that the sensation of resistance to their fingers was as if the table were supported by a spiral spring.

Immediately after this a message was spelt out, ordering Mrs. B. to join her hands above the table with those of Mr. D. The same phenomenon was then repeated twice over, the table rising the last time to what seemed to be ten inches from the floor." [Here follow the signatures.]

IV.

My own first visit was on Thursday, Dec. 3, 1908. [Thursday is the night on which the circle habitually sits.] Eight persons, counting myself, were present, three women, five men.

We sat at first with our fingers on the solid table beneath the disc, and various tippings came. Then, with our wrists or palms on the ring and our fingers on the disc various messages were spelt.

Mrs. B., whose fifth sitting it was, had her fingers automatically jerked away whenever she placed them on the disc. This had happened previously; and, during the previous lifting of the table on Nov. 19th, she had held her hands in the air some inches above the disc. She kept them in that situation on this present occasion whenever we made attempts to have the table lifted. Such attempts were several times repeated, but with no success.

On the controls then being asked whether they could not *make the disc rotate* without contact, they spelt "no."

Suddenly, while we were sitting with our wrists on the brass ring and our fingers on the disc, which turned and spelled, *we perceived that the ring or rail itself was moving.* It had never done this on any previous evening. The phenomenon was consequently unexpected, and seemed to strike all present with surprise.

Some one immediately suggested that all wrists should be lifted, and then, in brilliant light, and no one's hands in any way in contact with the rail, our fingers, however, resting on the disc, we all distinctly saw the rail or ring *slide slowly and for several inches through the collars, as if spontaneously.*

We then stuck a mark upon the ring to make its motion more obvious, and repeated five or six times the experiment, the same result ensuing, though more slightly each time. It always took the contact of our wrists to start the rail, but *its motion continued when the contact ceased.* This was not from its acquired momentum, for we ascertained that the friction of the collars which held the rail stopped instantly every motion imparted voluntarily by the hand.

On the succeeding Saturday and Sunday evenings, we sat again (one of the ladies being absent), but nothing but the usual tilting of the table and spelling of messages occurred.

So much for the "record," which all present have signed. It will be observed that all the phenomena reported (save the movements of the finger bowl) were unexpected and startling to the spectators. The explosions and the table's rising seem to have been eminently so, and to have made a great impression.

On December 3rd, when the ring revolved, the conditions of observation were perfect, the light (from an electric chandelier just overhead) being brilliant, and the phenomena being slow enough, and often enough repeated, to leave my own mind in no doubt at the time as to what was witnessed. I was quite convinced that I saw that no hand was on the ring while it was moving. The maximum length of its path under these circumstances was fully six inches. With this conviction that I saw all there was to see, I have to confess that I am surprised that the phenomenon affected me emotionally so little. I may add, as a psychological fact, that now, after four days' interval, my mind seems strongly inclined not to "count" the observation, as if it were too exceptional to have been probable. I have only once before seen an object moved "paradoxically," and then the conditions were unsatisfactory. But I have supposed that if I could once see the same thing "satisfactorily," the levee by which scientific opinion protects nature would be cracked for me, and I should be as one watching an incipient over-flow of the Mississippi of the supernatural into the fields of ortho-dox culture. I find, however, that I look on nature with unaltered eyes to-day, and that my orthodox habits tend to extrude this would-be levee-breaker. It forms too much of an exception.

Nevertheless, in the somewhat scandalously divided state of opin-ion about Eusapia Paladino, I think that every approach to similar phenomena observed anywhere ought to be recorded. It may be that the frequency rather than the quality of the records, will es-tablish their "case."

Report on Mrs. Piper's Hodgson-Control (1909)

PART I: SUMMARY OF SPECIAL INCIDENTS

Introduction

Richard Hodgson died suddenly upon December 20th, 1905.[1] On December 28th a message purporting to come from him was delivered in a trance of Mrs. Piper's, and she has hardly held a sitting since then without some manifestation of what professed to be Hodgson's spirit taking place. Hodgson had often during his lifetime laughingly said that if he ever passed over and Mrs. Piper was still officiating here below, he would 'control' her better than she had ever yet been controlled in her trances, because he was so thoroughly familiar with the difficulties and conditions on this side. Indeed he was; so that this would seem *primâ facie* a particularly happy conjunction of 'spirit' with medium by which to test the question of spirit-return.

I have collated 69 of the American sittings (the latest being that of January 1st, 1908) in which the professed R.H. has appeared (his communications forming possibly a sixth of the total bulk of the

1 This report was prepared to be read at the General Meeting of the Society, on January 28th, 1909. To make a single document by distributing its material through the larger report would cost much labor, so the two parts are printed separately, but readers will understand that they should be read in conjunction.

records), and a few remarks as to my own relation to the phenomenon would seem a good introduction to what follows. I have no space for twice-told tales, so I will assume that my readers are acquainted, to some degree at any rate, with previously printed accounts of Mrs. Piper's mediumship.[2] Until the spring of 1906, I had myself had no sitting with Mrs. Piper and had hardly seen her for some nine years, but for most of that time I had been kept informed of what was going on by reading the typed records, furnished me by my friend Hodgson, of all the trances of which report was taken, and for which the sitters had not asked secrecy to be observed. The 'Control' most frequently in evidence in these years has been the personage calling himself 'Rector.' Dr. Hodgson was disposed to admit the claim to reality of Rector and of the whole Imperator-Band of which he is a member, while I have rather favored the idea of their all being dream-creations of Mrs. Piper, probably having no existence except when she is in trance, but consolidated by repetition into personalities consistent enough to play their several rôles. Such at least is the dramatic impression which my acquaintance with the sittings has left on my mind. I can see no contradiction between Rector's being on the one hand an improvised creature of this sort, and his being on the other hand the extraordinarily impressive personality which he unquestionably is. He has a marvellous discernment of the inner states of the sitters whom he addresses, and speaks straight to their troubles as if he knew them all in advance. He addresses you as if he were the most devoted of your friends. He appears like an aged and, when he speaks instead of writing, like a somewhat hollow-voiced clergyman, a little weary of his experience of the world, endlessly patient and sympathetic, and desiring to put all his tenderness and wisdom at your service while you are there. Critical and fastidious sitters have recognized his wisdom, and confess their debt to him as a moral adviser. With all due respect to Mrs. Piper, I feel very sure that her own waking capacity for being a spiritual adviser, if it were compared with Rector's, would fall greatly behind.

As I conceive the matter, it is on this mass of secondary and automatic personality of which of late years Rector has been the centre, and which forms the steady background of Mrs. Piper's

[2] Chief among these are Hodgson's reports in Vols. VIII and XIII of the S.P.R. *Proceedings*, Mrs. Sidgwick's discussion in Vol. XV, Hyslop's long account in Vol. XVI, and his briefer one in his book *Science and a Future Life*.

trances, that the supernormal knowledge which she unquestionably displays is flashed. Flashed, grafted, inserted—use what word you will—the trance-automatism is at any rate the intermediating condition, the supernormal knowledge comes as if from beyond, and the automatism uses its own forms in delivering it to the sitter. The most habitual form is to say that it comes from the spirit of a departed friend. The earliest messages from 'Hodgson' have been communicated by 'Rector,' but he soon spoke in his own name, and the only question which I shall consider in this paper is this: *Are there any unmistakable indications in the messages in question that something that we may call the 'spirit' of Hodgson was probably really there?* We need not refine yet upon what the word 'spirit' means and on what spirits are and can do. We can leave the meaning of the word provisionally very indeterminate,—the vague popular notion of what a spirit is is enough to begin with.

Sources other than R.H.'s surviving spirit for the veridical communications from the Hodgson-control may be enumerated as follows:—

(1) Lucky chance-hits.

(2) Common gossip.

(3) Indications unwarily furnished by the sitters.

(4) Information received from R. H., during his lifetime, by the waking Mrs. P. and stored up, either supraliminally or subliminally, in her memory.

(5) Information received from the living R.H., or others, at sittings, and kept in Mrs. Piper's trance-memory, but out of reach of her waking consciousness.

(6) 'Telepathy,' *i.e.* the tapping of the sitter's mind, or that of some distant living person, in an inexplicable way.

(7) Access to some cosmic reservoir, where the memory of all mundane facts is stored and grouped around personal centres of association.

Let us call the first five of these explanations 'natural,' and the last two 'supernatural' or 'mystical.' It is obvious that no mystical explanation ought to be invoked so long as any natural one remains at all plausible. Only after the first five explanations have been made to appear improbable, is it time for the telepathy-theory and the cosmic-reservoir theory to be compared with the theory of R.H.'s surviving spirit.

The total amount of truthful information communicated by the R.H.-control to the various sitters is copious. He reminds them, for the most part, of events—usually unimportant ones—which they and the living R.H. had experienced together. Taking any one of these events singly, it is never possible in principle to exclude explanations number 1 and 4. About number 3, a complete record of the sitting ought generally to decide. Number 2 is often excluded either by the trivial or by the intimate nature of the case. Number 5 would be easily settled if the records of the sittings of the living Hodgson with Mrs. Piper were complete and accessible. They are supposed, for the past ten or twelve years at least, to exist in complete form. But parts of them are in Hodgson's private cipher, and they are now so voluminous that it would be rash to say of any recent message from Hodgson, so long as the matter of it might conceivably have been talked of at any previous trance of Mrs. Piper's, that no record of such talk exists: It might exist without having yet been found.

Add, to these several chances that any communication of fact by the Hodgson-control may have had a natural source, the further consideration that Mrs. Piper had known H. well for many years, and one sees that her subliminal powers of personation would have had an unusually large amount of material to draw upon in case they wished to get up a make-believe spirit of Hodgson. So far, then, from his particular case being an unusually good one by which to test the claim that Mrs. Piper is possessed during her trances by the spirits of our departed friends, it would seem to be a particularly poor one for that purpose. I have come to the conclusion that it is an exceptionally bad one. Hodgson's familiarity when in the flesh with the difficulties at this end of the line has not made him show any more expertness as a spirit than other communicators have shown; and for his successes there are far more naturalistic explanations available than is the case with the other spirits who have professed to control Mrs. Piper.

So much for generalities, and so much for my own personal equation, for which my various readers will make their sundry kinds of allowance. But before taking up the messages in detail, a word more about the fourth of the naturalistic explanations which I have instanced (conversations, that is, between Mrs. Piper and Hodgson when alive) is in order. Abstractly, it seems very plausible to suppose that R.H. (who systematically imposed on himself the law of never mentioning the contents of any trance in her waking presence) might have methodically adopted a plan of entertaining her on his visits by reciting all the little happenings of his days, and that it is this chronicle of small beer, stored in her memory, that now comes out for service in simulating his spirit-identity.

In the concrete, however, this is not a highly probable hypothesis. Everyone who knew Hodgson agrees that he was little given to anecdotical small change, unless the incident were comic or otherwise of an impressive order, and that his *souvenirs* of fact were usually of a broad and synthetic type. He had had a 'splendid time' at such a place, with a 'glorious' landscape, swim, or hill-climb, but no further detail. Gifted with great powers of reserve by nature, he was professionally schooled to secretiveness; and a decidedly incommunicative habit in the way of personal gossip had become a second nature with him—especially towards Mrs. Piper. For many years past he had seen her three times weekly (except during the months of her summer vacation) and had had to transcribe the records afterwards. The work was time-consuming, and he found it excessively fatiguing. He had economized energy upon it by adopting for many years past a purely business tone with the medium, entering, starting the trance, and leaving when it was over, with as few unnecessary words as possible. Great *brusquerie* was among the excellent R.H.'s potentialities, and for a while the amount of it displayed towards Mrs. P. led to a state of feeling on her part of which a *New York Herald* reporter once took advantage to exploit publicly. R.H. was remonstrated with, and was more considerate afterwards. It may well be that Mrs. Piper had heard one little incident or another, among those to be discussed in the following report, from his living lips, but that any large mass of these incidents are to be traced to this origin, I find incredible.

The spirit-Hodgson's first manifestation was, as I have said, eight days after his death. There was something dramatically so like him in the utterances of those earliest days, gradually gathering 'strength' as they did, that those who had cognizance of them were much impressed. I will begin by a short account of these earliest appearances, of which the first was at Miss Theodate Pope's sitting on Dec. 28th, 1905. At this sitting Rector had been writing, when suddenly the hand dropped the pencil and worked convulsively for several seconds in an excited manner.

MISS P.   What is the matter?

[The hand, shaking with apparently great excitement, wrote the letter H, . . . bearing down so hard on the paper that the point of the pencil was broken. It then wrote "HODGSON."]

MISS P.   God bless you!

[The hand writes "I am"—followed by rapid scrawls, as if regulator of machine were out of order.]

MISS P.   Is this my friend?

[The hand assents by knocking five times on paper-pad.]

(RECTOR.) Peace, friends, he is here, it was he, but he could not remain, he was so choked. He is doing all in his power to return. . . . Better wait for a few moments until he breathes freer again.

MISS P.   I will.

(R.) Presently he will be able to conduct all here.

MISS P.   That is good news.

(R.) Listen. Everything is for the best. He holds in his hand a ring. . . . He is showing it to you. Cannot you see it, friend?

MISS P.   I cannot see it. Have him tell me about it.

(R.) Do you understand what it means?

MISS P.   I know he had a very attractive ring.

(R.) Margaret.

"A l l" was then written, with a "B" after it, and Miss P. asked "what is that?" A "B" and an "L" followed, but no explanation. [The explanation will be given later.]

The above is the whole of the direct matter from Hodgson at this, the first of the sittings at which he has appeared. (For the sequel to this ring-episode, see below, pp. 263–268.)

At Miss Pope's next sitting (five days later), after some talk about him from Rector, R.H. appeared for the second time, and in the character, familiar to him, of being a well-spring of poetical lore.

Mrs. Piper's hand cramped most awkwardly, first dropped and then broke the pencil. A new one being given, the hand wrote as follows:—

RICHARD HODGSON I AM WELL HAPPY   GLAD I CAME   GOD BLESS POPE

Miss POPE.   Many thanks. [Then the hand wrote:—]

> It lies not in her form or face
> Tho these are passing fair,
> Nor in the woman's tone of grace,
> Nor in her falling hair;
> It lies not in those wondrous eyes
> That swiftly light and shine,
> Tho all the stars of all the skies
> Than these are less divine.

I am only practising.

Miss P.   Who wrote it?

(RECTOR.) Richard only.

Miss P.   When?

Now.

Miss P.   Doesn't it exist on paper in our world?

No.

Miss P.   Did you really make that up?

Yes.

Miss P.   Well, you are clever.

If you ever find this in your world, never believe in this world!

Miss P.   I shall look for it, you may be sure.

Good! Think I'm asleep? Not much! My head. I must leave you now.

(RECTOR.) It is impossible for us to hold him—that is all.

Miss P.   Rector, did he dictate that poem to you? . . . Do you think he made it up?

(RECTOR.) I do positively know he did. . . . Farewell!

At the second sitting after this (Jan. 8th, 1906), Miss Pope again being the sitter, R.H. appeared again, writing as follows:—

I AM Hodgson . . . I heard your call—I know you—you are Miss Pope. Piper instrument. I am happy exceedingly difficult to come very. I understand why Myers came seldom. I must leave. I cannot stay. I cannot remain to-day. . . .

(A tobacco-pouch that had belonged to Hodgson was presently given to the Medium as an 'influence,' when the writing went on:—)

I am in the witness-box, do you remember?—Do you remember my promise to shake you up?

Miss P.   I once asked Geo. P[elham] to 'shake me up.'

No, I do not mean that.

Miss P.   What do you mean?

I said if I got over here first I would soon learn how to communicate. —I would not make a botch of it.

Miss P.   I remember—indeed you did.

I am certainly R.H. I am sure. I have joined dear old G. Pelham, who did so much for me—more than all the rest put together.

[After a few words in Rector's name, a brush that had belonged to Hodgson was put into the medium's hand.]

Remember my theory about objects?

Miss P.   What was it?

They carried their own light. I was right.

Miss P.   Yes, I remember very well.

I see it now, I was right.
Did you receive my lines to Miss D—— [Referring apparently to the verses at the previous sitting.]

Miss P.   Good, that is most interesting.

Amen! Miss D—— [This name, correctly given, is that of the cousin of R.H., mentioned as 'Q' in previous reports, a name probably well known to the trance-consciousness.—W.J.]

Miss P.   Miss D——?

Yes. Ah, ah, ah.

Miss P.   What does that mean?—(referring to the "ah, ah," which written words indicate laughter).

I am amused at you. Yet? found them?

MISS P.   No, I haven't.

It will take the remainder of your earthly life, and then you'll fail.

MISS P.   You are just the same as ever.

Not quite as full of energy as I wish, but give me time.

[Rector then comes in, and the sitting closes.]

On Jan. 16th and Jan. 17th, R.H. spoke again to Miss Pope, but without anything evidential in matter—or in manner either, unless the following be counted as dramatically like:—

I shall never assume control here. Imperator shall lead me. In his care I am safe. I was met by him. There will be no moaning at the bar when I pass out to sea—remember it?

[Miss Pope assents.]

On Feb. 5th, R.H. asks again:—

Got any news of my poem?

MISS P.   No, I give that up.

I thought you would come to it. I made that up in a moment and composed to Miss D——.

[After some more non-evidential talk, R.H. mentions his living friend, Miss Bancroft, and says:—]

Give my love to her and tell her I hope to speak with her soon.

> It seems as if the wondrous land
>   Within her vision lay:
> I dimly sense the mystic strand
>   Behind the glorious gray.

To Margaret Bancroft. Give her this. She has light. [Correct.—W.J.]

MISS P.   Yes. Is this your own?

I just made it for her. . . . Tell her I shall never forget those hills, the water, our talks, and the delightful visit I had with her. [Correct.—W.J.]

MISS P.   I think she is coming soon to speak with you here.

Good. I hope so. Will you tell her, give her my message, ask her if she

261

knows anything about my watch being stopped. Do you? I must go out and get a little breath.

[Miss B. writes:—"I think the watch means *my* watch. We had a number of jokes about the frequent stopping of my watch."]

On Jan. 23rd, 1906, Mrs. Wm. James, and W. James, Jr., had a sitting at which R.H. used the medium's voice and gave a very life-like impression of his presence. The record runs as follows:—[3]

Why, there's Billy! Is that Mrs. James and Billy? God bless you! Well, well, well, this is good! [Laughs.] I am in the witness-box. [Laughs.] I have found my way, I am here, have patience with me. All is well with me. Don't miss me. Where's William? Give him my love and tell him I shall certainly live to prove all I know. Do you hear me? see me? I am not strong, but have patience with me. I will tell you all. I think I can reach *you.*

Something on my mind. I want Lodge to know everything. I have seen Myers. I must rest.

[After an interval he comes in again:—]

Billy, where is Billy? What are you writing, Billy? Are you having any sports? Would you like to take a swim? [R.H.'s chief association with W.J., Jr., had been when fishing or swimming in Chocorua Lake.] Well, come on! Get a good deal of exercise, but don't overdo it! Perhaps I swam too much. [He undoubtedly had done so.]—I learned my lesson, but I'm just where I wanted to be.

Do you remember [Q]? [Q] helped me. Then I saw Mother, Rebecca, and Father. I want very much to converse with Annie. [His sister.] She perfectly understood my efforts and was everything to me. I want her to know that I am living, and I am going on to show what I know to the end of all time. Is Ellen well?—that's my sister. I want G.D. [his brother-in-law] to have my watch. [The Hodgson-family names used here are correct, but were known to the trance-consciousness.—W.J.]

Do you play ball?—tennis? Men will theorize—let them do so! I have found out the truth. I said that if I could get over there I would not

---

[3] In this and in some of my future citations from the records, I have condensed the material by leaving out repetitions and digressions, so that what appears is often straighter and more coherent than what was originally given. I have, however, scrupulously endeavored to omit nothing that could possibly have determined what was said or influenced its veridicality.—W.J.

make a botch of it. If ever R.H. lived in the body, he is talking now. ... William [James] is too dogmatic. ... I want George [Dorr] to extricate all those papers and set those marked 'private' aside. This has been on my mind. ... George is to be trusted *absolutely* with all sincerity and faith. There are some private records which I should not wish to have handled. Let George and Piddington go through them and return them to the sitters. The cipher! I made that cipher, and no one living can read it. [Correct.] I shall explain it later. Let Harry [James] and George keep them till then. [They had been appointed administrators of his estate, a fact probably known to Mrs. Piper.] This is the best I have been able to do yet. I spoke with Miss Pope, but this is the best. Remember, every communication *must* have the human element. I understand better now why I had so little from Myers. [To W.J., Jr.] What discourages you about your art? [W.J., Jr., was studying painting.] Oh what good times we had, fishing! Believe, Billy, wherever you go, whatever you do, there is a God.

So much for Hodgson's first appearances, which were characteristic enough in manner, however incomplete.

Within the space to which this preliminary report is limited one can hardly quote the records *verbatim*, for they are anything but concise. My best plan will be to cull a few of the best veridical communications, and discuss them singly, from the point of view of the alternatives of explanation.

I begin with what I shall call

The Ring Incident.

On Hodgson's 50th birthday a lady whom I will call Mrs. Lyman, an old friend of his, much interested in the Piper work, had given him a rather massive ring to wear. The source of this ring H. had kept to himself, and after his death Mrs. L. asked the administrator of his estate to return it to her. The ring could not be found.

At the sitting of Dec. 28th (R.H.'s first appearance as a spirit), it will be remembered that the control Rector had said to Miss Pope, the sitter, "He holds in his hand a ring—do you understand what it means?"

Miss P.   I know he had a very attractive ring.

Rector (writing)   Margaret. a ll B L.

On Jan. 16th, Miss Pope being again the sitter, the R.H.-control suddenly wrote:—

Give ring to Margaret back to Margaret. [Mrs. Lyman's name is not Margaret.]

Miss P.   Who is Margaret?

I was with her in summer.

Miss P.   All right, but the ring has not been found yet. Can you find out where it is?

The undertaker got it.

Miss P.   Oh, all right.

I know. Help me.

Miss P.   I shall look it up.

It was with me.

Miss P.   Yes, I heard so.

It was, it was.

Miss P.   I will attend to it.

Thank you.

On January 24th Mrs. Lyman herself had her first sitting. As soon as Hodgson appeared he wrote:—

The ring. You gave it me on my fiftieth birthday. When they asked I didn't want to say you gave it me, I didn't want to say that. . . . Two palm-leaves joining each other—Greek. [Here followed an illegible word. The palms truly described the ring, which Mrs. Piper probably had seen; but it bore no Greek inscription, nor was the symbol on it a Greek cross.] You gave it me—

Mrs. L.   Yes, Dick, where is it now?

They have got it. They took it off my finger after I was gone.

Mrs. L.   No, they didn't find it on your finger.

Pocket, it was in my pocket, I'll find it you shall have it.

On January 29th Mrs. L. had another sitting. The Hodgson-control wrote:—

I have been trying to make clear about that ring. It is on my mind all the time. I thought if I could get Margaret B. to get it for me, I would get it to you through her, then no one would understand. I could not tell Miss Pope about you.

Mrs. L.   Did you think Margaret B. gave it to you?

Oh dear no! not at all.

Mrs. L.   Then why did you speak of her?

I could trust her absolutely, and no one could understand. She would never betray it. You gave it to me on my 50th birthday. Palms and R.H. [Then a possible attempt to draw a symbol engraved on the ring.] No one living knows this but myself and yourself.

Mrs. L.   That is true, but what was the motto in the ring?

All will be clear to me in time. Do not ask me test questions now. . . . I wish the ring now to go back to yourself. I thought Margaret would understand and be glad to do it for me. I could not tell Miss Pope about you.

On March 5th R.H. again inquires of Mrs. Lyman about the ring. She then asks him: "Did you have it on that last day when you went to the boat-club?" [R.H. died while playing a game of hand-ball at the boat-club.]

I certainly had it on that day.

Mrs. L.   You told Miss P. the undertaker got it.

Thought he did and I am sure a man took it from my finger.

[After a few more words R.H. continues:—]

I had that ring on my finger when I started for the club, I recall putting in my pocket. I did so because it hurt my finger when playing ball. I am not dreaming, I am clear. When I get here first I am a little stuffy, but I am as clear now as I ever was, I put it in my waistcoat pocket.

Mrs. L.   Why do you think a man stole it?

I saw it on a finger. . . . I put in my pocket, and the one who took care of my clothes is responsible for it. . . . What did they do with my waistcoat?

On May 16th, on being told that the ring is not yet found, the R.H.-control writes:—

I saw it taken by a man from my locker. He was in charge at the time and he has my ring. . . . I shall be able to discover his name so you may be able to find it. I see where he goes and the house where he lives, plainly. . . . Five story brick house not far from the club and he is on the third story from the street, near the corner of the street, the room is in the rear of the building and I see his face clearly [a description of the man follows]. I see the ring on his finger clearly. The waistcoat was in his room when I entered the light a few moments ago. I am as sure of this as I am that you are Mrs. Lyman.

In point of fact the ring was found a couple of months later in the pocket of Hodgson's waistcoat, which had been too carelessly explored for it, and which had lain during all the interval in a room at the house of Mr. Dorr, with whom the Hodgson-control had all the time been having frequent communications.

The whole incident lends itself easily to a naturalistic interpretation. Mrs. Piper or her trance-consciousness may possibly have suspected the source of the ring. Mrs. Lyman's manner may have confirmed the suspicion. The manner in which the first misleading reference to 'Margaret' was afterwards explained away may well have been the cunning of a 'control' trying plausibly to cover his tracks and justify his professed identity. The description of the house and of the man to whom he ascribes its present possession sounds like vague groping, characteristic also of control-cunning. The description was but little like that of Mr. Dorr, whose house, moreover, is neither very near a corner nor very near a club.

On the other hand, if the hypothesis be seriously entertained that Hodgson's spirit was there in a confused state, using the permanent Piper automatic machinery to communicate through, the whole record is not only plausible but natural. It presents just that mixture of truth and groping which we ought to expect. Hodgson has the ring 'on his mind' just as Mrs. Lyman has. Like her, he wishes its source not to be bruited abroad. He describes it accurately enough, truly tells of his taking it to the fatal boat-club, and of putting into his waistcoat-pocket there, of the waistcoat being taken from the locker, and vaguely, but not quite erroneously, indicates its present position.

Mrs. Lyman's own impression of the incident is as follows:—

"No living person beside myself knew who had given him the ring, and I am quite sure that the living R.H. would have been as desirous as I to keep all mention of me out of the trance-record. Had he had entire control he would never have mentioned the ring until I had come to a sitting, but in his half-dreamy state something slipped out to Miss Pope, the sitter, aided telepathically perhaps by her knowledge that he had lately worn an unusual-looking ring which she knew was missing after his death. I am sure that Miss Pope thought the ring would be a good 'test,' so that although she was not the first to speak of it, it must certainly have been in her mind. It is characteristic of R.H. that even in his half-conscious state he is able to keep his own counsel so well. The word Margaret and the letters B and L which followed the mention of the ring at the very first sitting seems to refer to Miss Margaret Bancroft and myself. He knew that Miss Bancroft had 'light,' and he seems to feel that if he can only reach her she will understand what he wants. He was well aware of my own morbid dislike of having my affairs mentioned at the trance outside of my own sittings. You know that curious trait of suspicion in Hodgson's absolutely honest nature—trained in him professionally. When Miss Pope tells him the ring cannot be found, he at once thinks: 'there was my body, and my clothes, etc., I believe the undertaker took it.' Then I myself, Mrs. Lyman, come and again tell him the ring can't be found. His earthly memories presently become clear and he tells me exactly what he did with it before his death. But his suspicious side has been aroused—you know how anything once registered on the trance-machinery seems to make an impression and tends to recur—and again he thinks that some-one took it. Nothing could be more characteristic of H. than his indig-nant remark about the man who had charge of his clothes being *re-sponsible*. It all seems to me the kind of unpractical thing that a man would do in a dream. There are strong characteristics of R.H. in it, but it is R.H. dreaming and troubled. I am glad I haven't to make myself intelligible to a stranger to the persons involved; but knowing them as I do, I feel my own way straight through the maze, and the explana-tion is clear."

This incident of the ring seems to me a typical example of the ambiguity of possible interpretation that so constantly haunts us in the Piper-phenomenon. If you are willing beforehand to allow that a half-awakened spirit may come and mix its imperfect memo-ries with the habits of the trance-automatism, and you apperceive the message sympathetically, what you get is entirely congenial with your hypothesis. But if you insist that nothing but knock-down evidence for the spirits shall be counted, then, since what comes is also compatible with natural causes, your hardness of heart remains unbroken, and you continue to explain things by automatic personation and accidental coincidence, with perhaps a dash of thought-transference thrown in. Readers will interpret this ring-episode harmoniously with their prepossessions. Taken by itself its evidential value is weak; but experience shows, I think, that a large number of incidents hardly stronger than this one will almost always produce a cumulative effect on the mind of a sitter whose affairs they implicate, and dispose him to the spiritistic view. It grows first possible, then plausible, then natural, and finally probable in a high degree.

The next incident I will recite is one which at a certain moment gave me a little thrill, as if I might be really talking with my old friend. (I have to make the personal confession that this reality-coefficient, as Professor Baldwin calls it, has generally been absent from my mind when dealing with the Piper-controls or reading reports of their communications.) I will call the episode 'the nigger-talk case.'

The Nigger-Talk Case.

On February 27th, 1906, at a sitting with Professor Hyslop, the following dialog took place:—

R.H.   I wonder if you recall what I said I would do if I should return first?

HYSLOP.   I do not remember exactly.

Remember that I told Myers that we would talk nigger-talk—Myers—talk nigger-talk?

HYSLOP.   No, you must have told that to someone else.

Ah yes, James. I remember it was James, yes, Will James. He will understand.

Mr. Hyslop immediately wrote to me—I being in California—enclosing the record and soliciting corroboration. I had to reply that the words awakened absolutely no echo in my memory. Three months later I returned to Cambridge, and began to study records of sittings held during my absence. I met this incident again, and again it failed to stir my memory. But the very next day, in a conversation with Messrs. Dorr and Piddington, while I was recalling certain discussions that I had formerly had with Hodgson about the amenability to suggestion of the Piper-controls, it suddenly flashed across me that these were probably what the words to Hyslop had meant. I had namely said to Hodgson, more than once, that a little tactful steering on his part would probably change the sacerdotal verbiage of the Imperator-group so completely that he would soon find them 'talking like nigger-minstrels.' For a moment I felt sure that this expression of mine, buried so deep in my own mind that it required a peculiar chain of associations to revive it, was what was dimly working in the memory of a surviving Hodgson, and trying to extricate itself. It was so incredible that R.H. would ever have repeated such a remark to either the waking Mrs. Piper or to her controls, that it seemed a good test of his survival. I regret to say, however, that the subsequent developments of the incident have deprived it in my eyes of all test-value. Not only did the Hodgson-control, when questioned by me subsequently, fail to recall anything like that discussion of the control's suggestibility which was the setting in which my memory had put the phrase, but Mr. Piddington has found in the Piper-records evidence that Hodgson had used the words 'nigger-talk' in speaking to the Myers-control, so that this expression must be considered as part of the stock of Mrs. Piper's trance-vocabulary.[4] Such an incident shows how wary one must be in one's interpretations. A really expert critic of the Piper-trances ought to be familiar with the entire mass of material previous to any utterance under consideration. Hodgson was extraordinarily expert in this sense, and one of the weirdest feelings I have had, in dealing with the business lately, has been to find the wish so frequently surging up in me that he were alive beside me to give critical counsel as to how best to treat certain of the communications of his own professed spirit.[5]

---

[4] "Feb. 4th, 1902. Dr. Hodgson (spontaneously to Myers-control) Do you remember about your laughing with me once and your saying that doubtless you would some time be coming back and talking nigger-talk?" A reference to the same incident is also made in the sitting of Feb. 13th, 1901.

[5] It will be important to call attention to the following message which Prof. James permits me to embody in a note. On February 26th, 1909, I had a sitting, the first one, with a lady who is a private person and keeps her powers concealed from all but her most intimate friends. She knew me only by reputation and had met me for the first time the night before. Nearly all her automatic writing has been done to help her mother and a few friends have occasionally been allowed to see it. It is always mirror writing. The lady has read almost nothing on the subject of psychic research. She writes me that the only book she ever read in this connexion was Swedenborg's "Heaven and Hell." She has not seen any of the *Journals* of the

The Huldah-Episode.

During the voice-sitting of May 2nd, 1906, Mr. Piddington being present, the R.H.-control said:—

> Pid, I want very much to give you my private letters concerning a Miss—a Miss—in Chicago [pseudonym]. I do not wish anyone to read them.

J.G.P.   How shall I know?

> Look at my letters stamped from Chicago. I wouldn't have them get out for the world.

The name 'Densmore' [pseudonym] was then written. Mr. Piddington asked whether the letters would be signed by the surname or the Christian name. The name 'Huldah' was then given as that by which the letters would be signed.

On May 14th Piddington reported to the R.H.-control that no such letters could be found, and asked for further information— "Can you tell me at what time this lady wrote letters to you? Was it lately?"

> No, several years previously. I should be much distressed if they fell into other hands. No one living except the lady and myself knows of the correspondence.

J.G.P.   If I cannot find those letters, should you feel any objection to my writing to the lady to ask if there has been such a correspondence?

> Yes, I would rather you would do so.

American Society, in fact none of its publications. There can be no question of her honesty, and the probability that she may have casually seen a reference to the incident is so remote that it amounts to an impossibility.—J. H. Hyslop.

"(Have you been following me recently?)

I was not able to come in. I don't think you have yet had a real good test from me *me* as I [am] [Sheet changed.] not strong enough you know Prof James son? he is all right now. that is what I want you to tell Dr James

(All right. I understand.) [Pause.] (Did you try where I was recently?)

I often follow you and am going to sing a coon song one of these days   nigger dialect   tell James this

(All right, I will.)

he will see what I mean   to keep my promise."

Later (May 29th) Piddington reports unsuccessful search again, and Mr. Dorr, who also is present, asks whether 'Huldah' is one of a family of Densmores known to him. "Is she a sister of Mary, Jenny, and Ella [pseudonyms]?"

> Ella is the one. Huldah we used to call her.

[This was emphatically spoken. Then followed a statement (not caught in Mr. Dorr's notes) that the lady's full name was Ella Huldah Densmore.]

> No one living could have known it. I hope I have destroyed them—I may have done so and forgotten it. There was a time when I greatly cared for her, and I did not wish it known in the ears of others. I think she can corroborate this. I am getting hazy. I must leave.

On June 5th, Mrs. William James and Mr. Dorr being present, D. asked:—"Can you tell us anything more about Huldah Densmore? You said the other day that she was the same person as Ella. Were you clear in saying that?"

> Did I say that? That was a mistake. She is a sister. Is one of the three sisters, but not Ella. [She *was* Ella.] I know what I am talking about. I saw Huldah in Chicago. I was very fond of her. I proposed marriage to her, but she refused me.

The statement about proposing marriage was not divulged to me by my wife until I had already had a letter from the lady called Ella Densmore in this narrative, who was then in a foreign country, and to whom I had written to ascertain whether she and Hodgson had ever corresponded, or whether she or anyone in her family was christened Huldah. Both Mr. Dorr and I knew her, but I was ignorant that she and Hodgson were acquainted. Great was my surprise when she wrote as follows:—

> Regarding the utterances of Mrs. Piper, I have no difficulty in telling you the circumstances on which she may have founded her communications. Years ago Mr. H. asked me to marry him, and some letters were exchanged between us which he may have kept. I do not remember how I signed the letters to him. I have sometimes used my middle name, Hannah, instead of Ella. [She knew of no 'Huldah' in her family.]

In spite of the confusion that pervades Hodgson's veracious utterances here, it seems improbable that they should merely have been lucky flukes. Two naturalistic explanations offer themselves immediately.

(1) He might have made Mrs. Piper his confidant at the time; but no one who knows Hodgson will regard this explanation for a moment as credible.

(2) Nothing spreads as fast as rumors of this sort; so that if there had been a gossipy rumor, it might very well have spread to Mrs. Piper's ears, although it had skipped over Mr. Dorr's and mine. I accordingly inquired of a dozen of R.H.'s most intimate friends, saying: "Suppose I were to tell you that Hodgson had been in love not long ago, and had offered himself to a certain lady—would any particular person's name arise in your mind in consequence of such a suggestion?" Not a single one of these friends thought of the name of Miss Densmore, although three of them suggested other names very wide of the mark. Evidently no gossip had got into circulation, and R.H. had covered his tracks well. He was indeed the most singular mixture of expansiveness and reticence I have ever known; and the reticence had been increased professionally, as I may say, through his long training in having to guard the private affairs of sitters, and to watch himself with Mrs. Piper. I was Hodgson's earliest American friend, and until his death always imagined myself to enjoy an almost perfect intimacy with him. Since his death I have nevertheless found that whole departments of his life were unknown to me. In this 'Huldah' matter in particular, not only was I unaware that he and she were acquainted, but if anyone had described him to me as being in love with her, I should have scouted the story as inherently improbable, from the character of the two parties.

Nevertheless the story was true, barring the false name Huldah and a certain vacillation about the real Christian name. The sister of the so-called 'Huldah' has told me, moreover, that besides herself, she thought that no living person knew from her sister's lips of R.H.'s state of mind. As Hodgson himself had apparently told no one, the incident seemed an excellent one to count in favor of spirit-return, unless, indeed, it should turn out that while it was happening, he had been led to consult the Piper-controls about it himself, and to use 'Huldah's' name as a test of their telepathic or clairvoyant powers. But that even then he could have given them the real name seems unlikely, in view of his habitual methods. The records taken to England have not yet been looked over from this point of view, and no one knows just what they may contain, but fortunately one of the sittings with Mrs. Piper after Hodgson's decease throws decisive light upon the matter. Hodgson *did* consult the Imperator group at the time of his disappointment, and the reasonable conclusion is that the revelation which so surprised Mr. Dorr and myself was thus a product of Mrs. Piper's trance-memory of previous conversations with the living Hodgson.

The sitting to which I allude was held on January 27th, 1906, by Prof. W. R. Newbold. In the course of it the Hodgson-control suddenly says:—

Let me ask if you remember anything about a lady in [Chicago] to whom I referred.

W.R.N.   Oh Dick, I begin to remember. About eight or nine years ago, was it, Dick?

Yes.

[*Note by W.R.N.*—Such a lady was frequently mentioned at sittings in 1895, and H. was told he would marry her. I was present when these statements were made, if my memory serves me.]

W.R.N.   Tell me more, so *I* won't tell *you*!

And my position regarding her.

W.R.N.   I wasn't sure it was in [Chicago].

Do you remember . . . . Densmore?

W.R.N.   Was it *Jessie* Densmore?

Yes. Good.

[Mr. Dorr, who was present, here interjects:—] "Do you mean the name was *Jessie* Densmore, Hodgson?"

No, no, no, no. [Jessie was the first name of R.H.'s Australian cousin, 'Q.'—W.J.]

W.R.N.   Dick, you told me years ago about a lady you were interested in, but I have forgotten her name and where she lived.

She lived in [Chicago].

W.R.N.   Dick, it comes back to me as a cloud.

She was a Miss Densmore; I loved her dearly.

W.R.N.   You used to tell me about her years ago.

Yes, and she afterwards married. Yes, I told you, and you are the only man I ever told. [Correct, apparently, save for the possibility of his having told Myers—see below.—W.J.]

W.R.N.   I'm not sure you told me her name.

Yes, I did.

W.R.N.   The name is the least likely thing for me to remember . . . . What is the married name of Miss Densmore?

Heaven knows! It has gone from me and I shall soon go myself.

So much for Dr. Newbold's evidence. He has sent me a letter written to him by Hodgson in 1895, from which it would appear that the Piper controls had prophecied that both he and Newbold would erelong be made matrimonially happy, but that whereas the prophecy was being verified in N.'s case, it had been falsified in his own, he having that day received formal announcement of the marriage of Miss Densmore to another. The only other material which I shall quote is the following dialog, at a sitting of my own, October 24th, 1906. Inquiring about 'Huldah,' I ask:—

W.J.   Did you make anyone your confidant?

No, though I may possibly have given a hint of it to Newbold.

W.J.   Did you tell anybody on the other side of the water?

I may possibly have hinted it to Lodge.

W.J.   Her sister tells me she thinks you may have told Myers when he was alive.

I think not: I may have hinted it to Myers.

W.J.   She denies any knowledge of the name Huldah.

I used that name instead of the right christian name [he here gives the latter correctly] to avoid compromising—it was a very delicate matter, and caused me great disappointment. Have you communicated it to her?

W.J. Yes, and she corroborates. . . .

[R.H. displays no farther curiosity,—a living person would probably have asked whether the lady had said nothing about him, etc.]

Do you remember a lady-doctor in New York? a member of our Society?

W.J. No, but what about her?

Her husband's name was Blair . . . I think.

W.J. Do you mean Mrs. Dr. Blair Thaw?

Oh yes. Ask Mrs. Thaw if I did not at a dinner party mention something about the lady. I may have done so.

[Mrs. Thaw writes in comment upon this:—"Fifteen years ago, when R. H. was visiting us after his operation for appendicitis he told me that he had just proposed to a young lady and been refused. He gave no name."—Mrs. Thaw is the only living person beside Newbold to whom I can certainly find that he ever spoke of this episode, and the clue to Mrs. Thaw comes from the control! W. J.]

W.J. Do you remember the name of Huldah's present husband?

[To which R. H. replies by giving his country and title correctly, but fails to give his name.]

The entire incident shows the importance of completeness in the records. Without Professor Newbold's sitting we should have no present assurance that the trance-memory might have furnished the facts which seemed at the first blush to suggest so strongly the return of a 'spirit' in a state of confused memory. *Compatible* with the return of such a spirit the facts indeed are. The possibility of the more naturalistic explanation doesn't make the supernatural one impossible; and if spirit-return were already made probable by other evidence, this might well be taken as a case of it too. But what I am sifting these records for is *independent* evidence of such return; and so long as the record in this instance lends itself so plausibly to a naturalistic explanation, I think we must refuse to interpret it in the spiritistic way.

A couple of smaller veridical incidents which have seemed to the sitters to make rather strongly for spirit-return are connected with R.H.'s financial history. I shall call them

The Pecuniary Messages.

The American Branch had never fully paid its expenses; and although the Secretary's salary had always been very small, Hodgson had, after the first years, been reluctant to have any part of it charged to the mother-country. The result had occasionally been pecuniary embarrassment on his part. During his last visit to England, shortly after Myers's death, this embarrassment had been extreme; but an American friend, divining it in the nick of time, rescued him by an impulsive and wholly unexpected remittance. To this remittance he replied by a letter which contained some banter, and among other things cited the story of a starving couple who were overheard by an atheist who was passing the house, to pray aloud to God for food. The atheist climbed the roof and dropped some bread down the chimney, and heard them thank God for the miracle. He then went to the door and revealed himself as its author. The old woman replied to him: "Well, the Lord sent it, even if the devil brought it."

At this friend's sitting of Jan. 30th, R.H. suddenly says:—

Do you remember a story I told you and how you laughed, about the man and woman praying.

SITTER: Oh, and the devil was in it. Of course I do.

Yes, the devil, they told him it was the Lord who sent it if the devil brought it. ... About the food that was given to them. ... I want you to know who is speaking.

The sitter feels quite certain that no one but himself knew of the correspondence, and regards the incident as a good test of R.H.'s continued presence. Others will either favor this interpretation of it, or explain it by reading of the sitter's mind, or treat it as a chance coincidence, according to their several prepossessions. I myself feel morally certain that the waking Mrs. Piper was ignorant of the incident and of the correspondence. Hodgson was as likely to have informed *me*, as anyone, of the affair. He had given me at the time a vivid account of the trouble he had been in, but no hint of the quarter from which relief had come.

Of the other pecuniary message no written record exists, but the sitter has acquainted me with the incident, which ran as follows:—

To assure Hodgson a salary, Mr. Dorr had acquainted a certain wealthy friend (who believed in the cause and in the value of the Secretary's work) with the situation of the Branch, and with R.H.'s reasons for not wishing to be indebted to the parent-Society. This friend had agreed to pay into the Branch-treasury the amount of deficit in the yearly salary-account, provided the operation should remain anonymous, and Hodgson should ask no questions. Hodgson agreed to this. But upon the first sitting which this friend had after his death, the 'spirit' of R.H. immediately referred to the matter and thanked the sitter warmly for the support given. The donor is of opinion, as I am also, that Hodgson may have suspected the source of the aid while receiving it, and that his 'spirit' may therefore naturally have thanked the right person. That Mrs. Piper's waking consciousness should have been acquainted with any part of the transaction is incredible. The donor's name had been kept from me, who was Vice-President of the Society, and had yearly to know the accounts. I had known that the deficit in Hodgson's pay was made up by anonymous American believers in his work, but had supposed that there were several of them. I cannot well understand how Mrs. Piper should have got wind of any part of the financial situation, although her controls may have got wind of it in trance from those who were in the secret.

Few persons will ascribe the affair to chance-coincidence, but with both thought-transference and trance-memory as possible explanations, the incident cannot be deemed to furnish certain proof of Hodgson's personal survival.

In a later report I shall quote sittings at greater length and discuss briefly some of the control's peculiarities. The conclusions I shall then draw will probably not be different from those which I now draw as follows:—

(1) The case is an exceptionally bad one for testing spirit-return, owing to the unusual scope it gives to naturalistic explanations.

(2) The phenomena it presents furnish no knock-down proof of the return of Hodgson's spirit.

(3) They are well compatible, however, with such return, provided we assume that the Piper-organism not only transmits with great difficulty the influences it receives from beyond the curtain, but mixes its own automatic tendencies most disturbingly therewith. Hodgson himself used to compare the conditions of spirit-

communication to those of two distant persons on this earth who should carry on their social intercourse by employing each of them a dead-drunk messenger.

(4) Although this Hodgson-case, taken by itself, yields thus only a negative, or at the best a baffling conclusion, we have no scientific right to take it by itself, as I have done. It belongs with the whole residual mass of Piper-phenomena, and they belong with the whole mass of cognate phenomena elsewhere found. False personation is a ubiquitous feature in this total mass. It certainly exists in the Piper-case; and the great question there is as to its limits. If, when lavish allowance has been made for this strange tendency in our subliminal life, there should still appear a balance of probability (which in this case can only mean a balance of simplicity) in the view that certain parts of the Piper-communications really emanate from personal centres of memory and will, connected with lives that have passed away; if, I say, this balance of probability should appear decisively anywhere in the mass, then the rest of the mass will have to be interpreted as at least possibly similarly caused. I admire greatly Hodgson's own discussion of the Piper-case in Volume XIII of our *Proceedings*, especially in sections 5 and 6, where, taking the whole mass of communication into careful account, he decides for this spiritist interpretation. I know of no more masterly handling anywhere of so unwieldy a mass of material; and in the light of his general conclusions there, I am quite ready to admit that my own denials in this present paper may be the result of the narrowness of my material, and that possibly R.H.'s spirit has been speaking all the time, only my ears have been deaf. It is true that I still believe the 'Imperator-band' to be fictitious entities, while Hodgson ended by accepting them as real; but as to the general probability of there being real communicators somewhere in the mass I cannot be insensible to Hodgson's able discussion, or fail to feel the authority which his enormous experience gave to his opinion in this particular field.

(5) I therefore repeat that if ever our growing familiarity with these phenomena should tend more and more to corroborate the hypothesis that 'spirits' play some part in their production, I shall be quite ready to undeafen my ears, and to revoke the negative conclusions of this limited report. The facts are evidently complicated in the extreme, and we have as yet hardly scratched the surface of them. But methodical exploration has at last seriously begun, and

these earlier observations of ours will surely be interpreted one day in the light of future discoveries which it may well take a century to make. I consequently disbelieve in being too 'rigorous' with our criticism of anything now in hand, or in our squeezing so evidently vague a material too hard in our logical forceps, at the present stage. What we need is more and more observations. Quantity will probably have to supplement quality in the material. When we have the facts in sufficient number, we may be sure that they will cast plenty of explanatory backward light. We can therefore well afford to play a waiting game.

PART II: SELECTIONS FROM DETAILED RECORDS

Introduction

"Believe me, I am not rubbish."—THE HODGSON-CONTROL.

Richard Hodgson had always seemed and felt so robust that the possibility of his death had been thought of by no one, and no provision against it had been made.[6] He had worked the American Branch of our Society practically alone, for many years, and although Prof. Hyslop and I were vice-presidents, we had no minute acquaintance with details at the office, where Miss Lucy Edmunds, the assistant secretary, was now left in charge alone.

What was to be done about the Branch? what was to be done with its mass of records? what with Hodgson's private property?—these were so many problems requiring immediate solution. Last, not least, there was the problem of Mrs. Piper's future.

The question of R.H.'s property was easily answered by the legal appointment of Messrs. Dorr and H. James, Jr., to be administrators of his personal estate, he having left no will. The great mass of Members and Associates of the Branch being inert and indifferent, the handling of the other questions fell to a small group of more acutely interested persons, of whom Dr. Hyslop and I were the only ones with official authority.

Absent in California for about five months, I found on my return that certain differences of opinions had been developing at home.

Prof. Hyslop, who had expended so much labor already on the

[6] Part I of this report was written to be read at the S.P.R. meeting in London, January 28th, 1909. I must assume in what follows that my readers are already acquainted with the contents of Part I.

Piper material, wished, if possible, to secure the records for the new American Society which he was founding. Others, whose sittings had been of a peculiarly intimate nature, claimed that the records of those sittings were their private property. In some quarters an objection was felt to such a mass of American material going to England. One person protested rather vehemently against the prominent part played by a certain other person in the deliberations. There being no one officially empowered to succeed Hodgson in taking charge of Mrs. Piper's sittings, differences of opinion regarding her future relations to the S.P.R. had arisen.

There was, in short, a state of strain which I have to mention here, for the trance-utterances of that period refer to it, and its peculiarities must be taken account of in estimating their significance.

In the end, however, since we all had fair minds and good-will, and were united in our common love for Hodgson, everything got settled harmoniously. Mr. Piddington was sent for to represent the English Society; it was decided to extinguish the American Branch, and to carry the Piper-reports to England, practically complete, while Hyslop's Society should take possession of the other records; workable arrangements were found for Mrs. Piper; the situation, in short, smoothed itself out, leaving nothing but a new system of friendships among persons who before Hodgson's death had for the most part been unacquainted with one another.

The records of the Piper trance show that during all this period the 'controls' had cognizance of the main factors of perplexity. There were, however, so many sources of leakage at this epoch that no part of this cognizance can be counted as evidence of supernormal knowledge. Whether in or out of trance, the Medium may well have come into possession of what was essential in the facts, and the gaps could be filled by her imagination, either waking or somnambulistic. The result, however, was that those who held sittings at this time had a lively feeling that the control-personality they talked with, whether Rector or Hodgson, was an intelligence which understood the whole situation. It talked appropriately with Dorr about certain records not being made public; with Henry James, Jr., about the disposition of R.H.'s books and other property; with Piddington and Dorr about Hyslop's desires and how best to meet them; with Hyslop about his responsibilities and about mediums in whom he and Hodgson had recently been interested; with Dorr, James, Piddington, and Mrs. Lyman about whom to induce to manage the sittings; with more than one of us about a certain person who was unduly interfering, etc., etc.; the total outcome being that each sitter felt that his or her problems were discriminatingly perceived by the mind that animated the sleeping medium's organism.

More than this—most of us felt during the sittings that we were in some way, more or less remote, conversing with a real Rector or a real Hodgson. And this leads me to make a general remark about the difference between reading the record of a Piper-sitting and playing an active part in the conversation recorded.

One who takes part in a good sitting has usually a far livelier sense, both of the reality and of the importance of the communication, than one who merely reads the record. Active relations with a thing are required to bring the reality of it home to us, and in a trance-talk the sitter actively co-operates. When you find your questions answered and your allusions understood; when allusions are made that you think you understand, and your thoughts are met by anticipation, denial, or corroboration; when you have approved, applauded, or exchanged banter, or thankfully listened to advice that you believe in; it is difficult not to take away an impression of having encountered something sincere in the way of a social phenomenon. The whole talk gets warmed with your own warmth, and takes on the reality of your own part in it; its confusions and defects you charge to the imperfect conditions, while you credit the successes to the genuineness of the communicating spirit. Most of us also, when sitters, react more, prick our ears more, to the successful parts of the communication. Those consequently loom more in our memory, and give the key to our dramatic interpretation of the phenomenon. But a sitting that thus seemed important at the time may greatly shrink in value on a cold re-reading; and if read by a non-participant, it may seem thin and almost insignificant.[7]

[7] A striking example of this was furnished me lately by a manuscript which a friend sent me. She had been one of Mrs. Piper's most assiduous clients. Her conversations with a certain spirit-control had been copious, fluent and veridical, and to herself so comforting and elevating, that she had epitomized them in this manuscript which, she thought, ought to be published. Strictly evidential matter was ruled out

Somewhat similar fluctuations are noticed in the reality-feeling which the records may awaken at different times in one and the same reader. When I first undertook to collate this series of sittings and make the present report, I supposed that my verdict would be determined by pure logic. Certain minute incidents, I thought, ought to make for spirit-return or against it in a 'crucial' way. But watching my mind work as it goes over the data, convinces me that exact logic plays only a preparatory part in shaping our conclusions here; and that the decisive vote, if there be one, has to be cast by what I may call one's general sense of dramatic probability, which sense ebbs and flows from one hypothesis to another—it does so in the present writer at least—in a rather illogical manner. If one sticks to the detail, one may draw an anti-spiritist conclusion; if one thinks more of what the whole mass may signify, one may well incline to spiritist interpretations.

This was the shape in which I myself left the matter in my recent preliminary report. I said that spirit-return was not proved by the Hodgson-control material, taken by itself, but that this adverse conclusion might possibly be reversed if the limited material were read in the light of the total mass of cognate phenomena. To say this is to say that the proof still baffles one. It still baffles me, I have to confess; but whether my subjective insufficiency or the objective insufficiency (as yet) of our evidence be most to blame for this, must be decided by others.

The common-sense rule of presumption in scientific logic is never to assume an unknown agent where there is a known one, and never to choose a rarer cause for a phenomenon when a commoner one will account for it. The usual is always more probable, and exceptional principles should be invoked only when the use of ordinary ones is impossible. Fraud is a form of human agency both known and common, though much less common than cynics suppose; 'personation' is unquestionably common in the whole realm of our subconscious operations; 'telepathy' seems fairly es-

---

from it as too minute or private, and what remained was ethical and human matter only. Never having known the communicator, and reading passively and critically, I felt bound to dissuade from publication. I could not believe that readers would find in the communications a twentieth part of the importance which their receiver had found there. The vital heat was absent, and what remained was ashes. I may well have been wrong in this opinion, but the incident brought vividly home to my own mind the contrast between the inside view of the sitter, and the outside one of the mere critic.

tablished as a fact, though its frequency is still questionable; accidental coincidences occur, however rarely; but 'spirits' of any grade, although they are indeed matters of tradition, seem to have shown themselves (so far as concrete evidence for them goes) nowhere except in the specific phenomena under investigation. Our rule of presumption should lead us then to deny spirits and to explain the Piper-phenomena by a mixture of fraud, subconscious personation, lucky accident, and telepathy, whenever such an explanation remains possible. Taking these Hodgson-records in detail, and subjecting their incidents to a piecemeal criticism, such an explanation does seem practically possible everywhere; so, as long as we confine ourselves to the mere logic of presumption, the conclusion against the spirits holds good.

But the logic of presumption, safe in the majority of cases, is bound to leave us in the lurch whenever a real exception confronts us; and there is always a bare possibility that any case before us may be such an exception. In the case at present before us the exceptional possibility is that of 'spirits' really having a finger in the pie. The records are fully compatible with this explanation, however explicable they may be without it. Spirits may co-operate with all the other factors, they may indeed find that harnessing the other factors in their service is the only way open to them for communicating their wishes. The lower factors may, in fact, be to a spirit's wishes what the physical laws of a machine are to its maker's and user's aims. A spectator, confining his attention to a machine's parts and their workings, and finding everything there explicable by mechanical push and pull, may be tempted to deny the presence of any higher actuation. Yet the particular pushes and pulls which the form of that machine embodies, would not be there at all without a higher *meaning which the machine expresses*, and which it works out as a human purpose. To understand the parts of the machine fully, we must find the human purpose which uses all this push and pull as its means of realization. Just so the personation, fishing, guessing, using lucky hits, etc., in Mrs. Piper, may be, as it were, the mechanical means by which 'spirits' succeed in making her living organism express their thought, however imperfectly.

As soon, therefore, as we drop our routine rule of presumption, and ask straight for truth and nothing but truth, we find that *the whole question is as to whether the exceptional case confronts us.* This is a question of probabilities and improbabilities. Now in every human being who in cases like this makes a decision instead of suspending judgment, the sense of probability depends on the forms of dramatic imagination of which his mind is capable. The explanation has *in any event* to be dramatic. Fraud, personation, telepathy, spirits, elementals, are all of them dramatic hypotheses. If your imagination is incapable of conceiving the spirit-hypothesis at all, you will just proclaim it 'impossible' (as my colleague Münsterberg does, *Psychology and Life*, p. 230), and thus confess yourself incompetent to discuss the alternative seriously.

I myself can perfectly well imagine spirit-agency, and I find my mind vacillating about it curiously. When I take the phenomena piecemeal, the notion that Mrs. Piper's subliminal self should keep her sitters apart as expertly as it does, remembering its past dealings with each of them so well, not mixing their communications more, and all the while humbugging them so profusely, is quite compatible with what we know of the dream-life of hypnotized subjects. Their consciousness, narrowed to one suggested kind of operation, shows remarkable skill in that operation. If we suppose Mrs. Piper's dream-life once for all to have had the notion suggested to it that it must personate spirits to sitters, the fair degree of virtuosity it shows need not, I think, surprise us. Nor need the exceptional memory shown surprise us, for memory usually seems extraordinarily strong in the subconscious life. But I find that when I ascend from the details to the whole meaning of the phenomenon, and especially when I connect the Piper-case with all the other cases I know of automatic writing and mediumship, and with the whole record of spirit-possession in human history, the notion that such an immense current of experience, complex in so many ways, should spell out absolutely nothing but the words 'intentional humbug' appears very unlikely. The notion that so many men and women, in all other respects honest enough, should have this preposterous monkeying self annexed to their personality seems to me so weird that the spirit-theory immediately takes on a more probable appearance. The spirits, if spirits there be, must indeed work under incredible complications and falsifications, but at least if they are present, some honesty is left in a whole department of the universe which otherwise is run by pure deception. The more I realize the quantitative massiveness of the phenomenon and its complexity, the more incredible it seems to me that in a world all of whose vaster features we are in the habit of considering to be *sincere* at least, however brutal, this feature should be wholly constituted of insincerity.

If I yield to a feeling of the dramatic improbability of this, I find myself interpreting the details of the sittings differently. I am able, while still holding to all the lower principles of interpretation, to imagine the process as more complex, and to share the feeling with which Hodgson came at last to regard it after his many years of familiarity, the feeling which Prof. Hyslop shares, and which most of those who have good sittings are promptly inspired with. I can imagine the spirit of R.H. talking to me through inconceivable barriers of obstruction, and forcing recalcitrant or only partly consilient processes in the Medium to express his thoughts, however dimly.

This is as candid an account of my own personal equation as I can give. I exhibited it in my treatment of special incidents in the preliminary report, and the reader will make allowance for it in what is to follow. In the end he must draw his conclusions for himself; I can only arrange the material.

The best way perhaps to do this will be to begin with certain general characteristics, Hodgson's mannerisms, for example.

Hodgson was distinguished during life by great animal spirits. He was fond of argument, chaff, and repartee, a good deal of a gesticulator, and a great laugher. He had, moreover, an excessive appetite for poetry. I call it excessive, for it was anything but fastidious—he seemed to need sonorous rhyme and meter for his daily food, even if the quality and sentiment were commonplace. All these traits were manifested from the outset in his appearances as a 'control'—some examples are given in my preliminary report. Chaff and slang from a spirit have an undignified sound for the reader, but to the interlocutors of the R.H.-control they seem invariably to have been elements of verisimilitude. Thus T.P. writes, *a propos* of a bantering passage in the record of Jan. 16, 1906:—"T.P. and R.H. were such good chums that he was saucy to her, and teasing her most of the time. R.H.'s tone towards T.P. in all his communications is *absolutely characteristic*, and as he was in life." Similarly, Dr. Bayley appends this note to a number of ultra-vivacious remarks from R.H.: "Such expressions and phrases were quaintly characteristic of R.H. in the body, and as they appear, often rapidly and spontaneously, they give the almost irresistible impression that it is really the Hodgson personality, presiding with its own characteristics. To fully appreciate this, of course, one would have had to have known him as intimately as I did."[8]

For these rollicking observations the control chose his sitters well in accordance with his habits during life. This, however, did not exclude very serious talk with the same persons—quite the reverse sometimes, as when one sitter of this class notes: "Then came words of kindness which were too intimate and personal to be recorded, but which left me so deeply moved that shortly afterwards, at the sitting's close, I fainted dead away—it had seemed as though he had in all reality been there and speaking to me."

The extracts given in the earlier report or to be given soon will show what I mean by Hodgson's rollicking manner. The later communications show more of it than the earlier ones; and it quickly manifested the tendency, characteristic in our medium's utterances, to become stereotyped. Whatever they may have been at the outset, they soon fall into what may be called the trance-memory's 'stock,' and are then repeated automatically. Hodgson quickly acquired a uniform mode of announcing himself: "Well, well, well! I am Hodgson. Delighted to see you. How is everything? firstrate? I'm in the witness-box at last," etc.,—with almost no variety. This habitual use of stock-remarks by Mrs. Piper may tempt one to be unjust to the total significance of her mediumship. If the supernormal element in it, whatever it is, be essentially discontinuous and flash-like, an utterance that to-day belongs to the regular trance-stock may have *got into* that stock at a former moment of supernormal receptivity. Supernormal receptivity of some kind is certainly involved in the total phenomenon, but I believe that information that originally came thus quickly ceases to be supernormal. The control G.P., at the outset of his appearance, gave supernormal information copiously, but within a few years he has degenerated into a shadow of his former self, dashing in and quickly out again, with an almost fixed form of greeting. Whatever he may have been at first, he seems to me at last to have "passed on," leaving that amount of impression on the trance-organism's habits.

I will now cull from the records a number of extracts relative to particular sitters, which show the control's familiarity with their affairs, calling the first of these extracts

[8] Sitting of April 3rd, 1906.

The Oldfarm Series.

Oldfarm is the name of Mr. George B. Dorr's place at Bar Harbor, Maine, where R.H. had often been a summer guest. Mrs. Piper at the time of these sittings had never been at Bar Harbor; and although she had had many interviews, as well with Mr. Dorr as with Mr. Dorr's mother before the latter's death, it is unlikely that many of the small veridical details in what follows had been communicated to her at those interviews. At Mr. Dorr's sitting of June 5th, 1906, he asks the R.H.-control for his reminiscences of Oldfarm: "Do you remember your visits to us there?"

Certainly I do. One night we stayed out too long and your mother got very nervous, do you remember? Minna was there. . . . We stayed out *much* too long. I felt it was a great breach of etiquette but we couldn't help it! I fear as guests we were bad [laughs].

[R.H.'s sitting out with "Minna" and others "much too long" and "their being bad as guests" seems excellent. In old days they used often to sit up hopelessly late into the night, when the nights were pleasant, out on the piazza, talking in the dark; and my mother's half-real and half-humorous exasperation over it, expressed in her own vivid way, and R.H.'s boyish delight in doing it and at the scoldings they all used to get for it next day, would naturally be one of the first things he would recall, associated as those evenings were with people whom he cared for.—D.]

And do you remember the discussion I had with Jack, when he got impatient? You were much amused!

[His recollection of his discussion with Jack, who used, together with M., to be at our house with him a great deal in the old days, is characteristic. I do not myself remember the special occasion to which he refers, but the incident, including my own amusement at the heat they used to get into in their talk, falls in most naturally with all my own recollections of that time.—D.]

And I remember your mother's calling me out one Sunday morning to see the servants go to church in a buckboard.

[I cannot now recall my mother taking R.H. out to see the servants off on any special day, but he was with us many Sundays, and I have no doubt that his memory of this is absolutely accurate, nor is it anything of which Mrs. Piper might know,—it is not the sort of thing that anyone would have spoken to her of, or mentioned at the trance. The *buckboard* is quite correct. It was a big buckboard that carried six people and was the only wagon which we had big enough to take all the people up, but its use is not sufficiently universal at Bar Harbor to injure the evidential value of his recollection of it. Again, the people used to go off from the kitchen, which is at an end of the house and cannot be seen from the living rooms or piazzas, so that his statement that my mother called him *out* to see them off, while a small point, seems to me of value; and the event itself, with the arrangements that had to be made to make it possible, was quite enough of a circumstance in our family life to make recollection of it natural.—D.]

I can see the open fireplace in the living room.

[The room is one in which the fireplace, broad and arching, is the central feature and would be first thought of in thinking of the room.—D.]

G.B.D.   Do you remember where you used to sleep?

Out in the little house just out across the yard, where we used to go and smoke.

[His recollection also of the little house is good. The only mistake in reference to it is in speaking of it as "across the yard," it being in fact across the lawn and garden, upon a hillside opposite the house. We always kept some rooms in it for our guests, over-flowing into it when the house was full, and R.H. liked it better than the house itself in the greater freedom that it gave him. We used to close the house itself early in the evening, and R.H. was very apt then to go up to the cottage with some other man or men and sit up and smoke and talk—often until quite late.—D.]

I remember the bathing and the boats and a walk through the woods.

[The bathing was one of the incidents at Oldfarm which R.H. would have best remembered. We used to take long walks over the mountains and go down for a plunge when we returned from them. There were often three or four men or more going in together when the house was full, and it was something in which R.H. delighted especially, so that his recollection of this would be apt to be one of his most vivid ones.—D.]

G.B.D.   Do you remember whether you used to bathe off the beach, or off the rocks?

We used to bathe off the *rocks*; I'm sure of that. *I can see the whole place.*

[I asked the question as to whether we went in off the rocks or the beach so as to see if he really had a clear remembrance of it, and I asked it in such a way that my companion at the sitting thought R.H.'s answer "off the rocks" was probably wrong. My bath-house was not on the beach, but on a point running far out into the sea, very bold and rocky, and we used to spring off the rocks into deep water, climbing out by a perpendicular ladder fastened to the ledge.—D.]

I can see the little piazza that opened out from your mother's room and the whole beautiful outlook from it, over the water.

[That that piazza and its view should be one of R.H.'s strongest recollections of the place seems to me most natural, while at the same time the piazza itself, which is not a conspicuous object in the house from without, and which was only familiar to my mother's more intimate friends, is not a thing which would occur naturally to anyone not familiar with our life down there.—D.]

Mr. Dorr then asks R.H. if he remembers a walk he once took with a young friend from New York, where R.H. outwalked the other man and was very triumphant about it afterward, and whether he could recall the man's name. He also asks him if he remembers the name of the man who lived in the farm house, where R.H. used generally to sleep when staying at Oldfarm. Both of these names would have been quite familiar to R.H. in life. R.H. cannot give them and makes no attempt to do so.

R.H.   Names are the hardest things to remember; it's extraordinary but it's true. The scenes of my whole life are laid open to me but names go from one's memory like a dream. I remember walking through the woods there and sitting down and lighting my pipe and coming back late to lunch.

On June 20th, 1906, at a sitting of Miss Bancroft's, at which Mr. Dorr was present, the R.H.-control suddenly writes:—

Do you remember anything about Celery-root? about C e l l e root?

Miss B. (to G.B.D.)   —Do *you* remember anything about it?

G.B.D.   No.

Or was it at your place, George. [Difficulty in reading this sentence. When read successfully, G.B.D. says "yes."]

Your mother used to have it, and I was surprised to see it there as I thought it the best of it. As I thought it the best part of it. The best part of it. No one would ever think of this thing I know.

MISS B.   You mean you think you got this at Mr. Dorr's?

Think! I know. I think so, yes. I think George's mother used to have it and I never got it anywhere but there.

G.B.D., who did not at first recall what is meant, then remembers and says "Good." He appends the following note:

[We used to have a bunch or two of raw celery, when we grew our own, placed on the table as a *hors d'œuvre*, and served whole, with the upper portion of the root left on it in the French fashion. This part of the root is very good eating, but it is not usually served in America; and though I have no clear remembrance now of special talk about this with R.H., I remember quite well his talking at our table late one fall about these autumn vegetables and think that what is spoken of is this.—D.]

On July 2nd, 1906, Mr. Dorr had a spoken sitting alone, taking the short-hand record himself, and asked again for Oldfarm recollections:—

G.B.D.   Can you give me any names connected with Bar Harbor, or of the mountains there which you used to climb, or of the people to whose houses you used to go with me, or any others that you can recall?

No, I can't recall any names now . . . I will think it over and try.

G.B.D.   Can you recall four sisters whom we used to walk with, and be much with, a number of years ago?

I remember Minna and Gemma. [Names known to the medium in former trances, but pertinent as a reply.]

G.B.D.   I will give you the name of the sisters, and see if that recalls anything to you. It was the Minturns.

Oh! the Minturns! [repeated eagerly and emphatically]. There was Gertrude and Robert, a brother named Robert—and Mary. They lived in New York. I remember them well. [Correct, save that Mary should have been May.]

G.B.D.   There was another sister, who used to walk oftenest with us—can you recall her name?

[R.H. makes one or two ineffectual attempts, giving wrong names.]

G.B.D.   Now, Hodgson, can't you tell me something about the lady you were interested in, whose letters you asked Piddington to find?

This was Huldah Densmore.

G.B.D.   But there is no Huldah in the family, that I know, nor can we learn of any. We have asked her sister, and she has never heard the name of Huldah.

Wait a moment. Let me think. It is most difficult to get earthly memories. They go from one, but I find that they come back to me as I think of things. She married a——[name of nationality given correctly]. If you will write to her, you will find I am right. Write to her!

G.B.D.   Did you want to marry her?

Yes, I did. And I remember what a disappointment it was to me.

G.B.D.   Was she out of sympathy with your work?

She wanted me to give it up—it was a subject she did not care to have to do with. [Correct as to the lady's animus.—W.J.]

G.B.D.   Was it at our house you met her?

I met her there, at Bar Harbor. Your mother ought to remember it well. She introduced us to each other. [Correct.—D.]

G.B.D.   But my mother is on your side.

Oh yes, I had forgotten. It has troubled me over here, thinking I might have left her letters among my papers. So I spoke to Piddington about it.

G.B.D.   I think you must have destroyed them. We didn't find any.

I think I must have destroyed them—I hope I did.

[This "Huldah" episode is treated in a separate section of Part I of this report, see above, pp. 270–275.—W.J.]

I recall the pansies your mother used to place over the table. I remember that well—delightful to see them! I can see them now.

[My mother used to have pansies spread loosely over the tablecloth, when she had people to dine or sup with us at Bar Harbor, where we had a large bed of them planted near the house so that we could get them freely for this purpose. The custom is not common enough to let H.'s statement pass for a happy guess, nor do I think it likely he would have spoken of it to Mrs. Piper, either awake or in trance. It came out quite suddenly also, and with a positiveness which made me feel that it was a true recollection, something seen at the moment in a mental picture.—D.]

G.B.D., endeavoring to extract Bar Harbor names from R.H., again tries to get that of the man who occupied the farmhouse at which R.H. used generally to sleep when at Oldfarm. He was not able to give that, but gave the name of the gardener, Miller. "It is possible," Mr. Dorr writes, "that Mrs. Piper may have heard of Miller's name as that of the manager of my plant-nurseries at Bar Harbor. I remember I once meant to send her some plants from the nurseries for her garden, and think it probable they went. It is also possible that the name may have come up at the trance in my own past sittings."

I remember a beautiful road, a bicycle-road you made, going through the woods.

[A dozen years ago I made a bicycle-road on my own back-land, which ran through the woods beneath a mountain over which we often used to walk. It was a pleasant and familiar feature in our summer life there, and it would naturally be one of the pictures that would come back to R. H. in thinking of the place—like the view from my mother's balcony of which he spoke at the former sitting. But it is not a thing of which either he or I would have spoken to Mrs. Piper, whether in trance or awake.—D.]

G.B.D. then tries again to get the name of the man who occupied the farmhouse, describing him to R.H. without mentioning his name.

Oh yes, I remember him well—I remember going off with him once fishing—going down the shore in a boat. . . . I remember one evening, and it impressed me so vividly because your mother did not like it, and I felt we had done wrong and hurt her—M. and I were smoking together and we talked too late, and she felt it was time to retire—

[This would be remarkably good if the incident should prove not to have come up already in R.H.'s own sittings after M. died. She used to smoke cigarettes occasionally, and was the only person of the feminine sex whom I now recall as having done so at our house. Unless in possibly referring to this incident to her 'spirit' at trances, after M. died, Hodgson would have been most unlikely to speak of it to others,—certainly not to Mrs. Piper, either in trance or awake. —D.]

G.B.D.   Do you remember where you went with John Rich when you went fishing with him—Oh I forgot! I did not mean to give you his name!

John Rich, John, that is his name! But I am sorry you gave it to me too—it might have come to me. We got a boat and went over to an island. Coming back we had some difficulty in getting our fish in. We had poor luck in catching them, and then we lost them. Ask him, he will remember it, I think.

[R.H.'s recollection of going off with Rich seems to be good, as I think it over. That he should go off with Rich only and neither alone nor with me or other guests, is exactly what happened,—and yet not what might have been expected to happen. His going to an island is descriptive also.—D.]

Do you remember what you used to put over your back that had a cup in it? And there was a little brook where we used to stop and drink. And then I used to stop and light my pipe—the whole scene is as vivid to me! If I could only express it to you!

[I used to carry a little canvass bag slung over my shoulder, and a cup in it, when we went on long tramps. This may be what R.H. refers to, though I think that he was rather apt to carry a folding leather cup of his own in his pocket. The whole recollection is rather vague in my memory, going back a number of years. The picture is a good one of just what used to happen when we were off on our tramps together, though of course what he describes would be always apt to happen on walks through woods and over mountains. The picture of the little brook we used to stop and drink at is good—I can see it now.—D.]

After some talk about the Tavern Club, about Australia, and about the state of things in the other world—some of which will be noticed later, R.H. goes on as follows:—

Do you remember one summer there was a gentleman at your house who had a violin. I had some interesting talks with him about these things, and I liked to hear him play his violin. A little gentleman— I remember him very well.

[This describes a man named von G., who was an excellent violinist and who also talked interestingly on psychical-research matters, in which he professed to have some faculty. As R.H. himself was also fond of the violin, it seems natural that some memory of von G. should stand out now. That Mrs. Piper should have any knowledge of this gentleman seems most improbable.—D.]

My earthly memories come only in fragments. I remember quite well this little gentleman and how interested I was in talking with him about psychics, and in his instrument as well. I remember a man Royce visiting you.

[Prof. Royce says that he has been at Oldfarm along with Hodgson, but adds that that might be a natural association in Mrs. Piper's mind, since he thinks that the only time he ever saw her was at the Dorrs' in Boston.—W.J.]

This is, I think, the whole of the matter relative to Oldfarm which the R.H.-control has given. The number of items mentioned is not great, and some inability to answer questions appears. But there are almost no mistakes of fact, and it is hardly possible that all the veridical points should have been known to Mrs. Piper normally. Some of them indeed were likely *a priori*; others may have been chance-hits; but for the mass, it seems to me that either reading of Mr. Dorr's mind, or spirit-return, is the least improbable explanation.

The fewness of the items may seem strange to some critics. But if we assume a spirit to be actually there, trying to reach us, and if at the same time we imagine that his situation with regard to the transaction is similar to our own, the surprise vanishes. I have been struck over and over again, both when at sittings myself and when reading the records, at the paralyzing effect on one's ready wit and conversational flow, which the strangeness of the conditions brings with it. Constraint and numbness take the place of genial expansiveness. We 'don't know what to say,' and it may also be so 'on the other side.' Few persons, I fancy, if suddenly challenged to prove their identity through the telephone, would quickly produce a large number of facts appropriate to the purpose. They would be more perplexed, and waste more time than they imagine.

I next pass to what I will call

The Owl's Head Series.

Owl's Head was the name of the summer place of Miss Margaret Bancroft, overlooking Rockland Harbor, in Maine, where Mrs. Piper had never been. R.H. had very greatly enjoyed visits which he had made there on two successive summers. Miss Bancroft had been a sitter of Mrs. Piper's and was a convert to spiritism, with some degree of 'psychic' susceptibility herself. At her first sitting after Hodgson's death, Feb. 19th, 1906, Mr. Dorr also being present, the following dialog took place:—[9]

I am Hodgson! Speak! Well, well, well, I am delighted to see you. How are you?

Miss B.   I am all right. How are you?

Firstrate.

Miss B.   I can scarcely speak to you.

But you *must* speak to me.

Miss B.   Will you give me some definite message?

Surely I will. I have called and called to you. Do you remember what I said to you about coming here if I got a chance?

Miss B.   Yes, I do.

I wish you to pay attention to me. [The sitter and Mr. Dorr were together trying to decipher the script.] Do you remember how I used to talk about this subject, evenings? You know what you said about my writing—I think I am getting on firstrate.

[Everything accurate so far! Miss B. can herself write automatically, and since R.H.'s departure, has thought that he might have been influencing her subconsciousness in that and other ways. The words 'I have called,' etc., she interprets in this sense. Rector, however, already knew of her automatic writing.—W.J.]

Do you remember what a good time we had at Head? I am so glad I went. . . . Do you remember a little talk we had about the lights and satellites? Do you remember how interested you were? Do you remember what I used to say about returning if I got over here first?

[9] Here, as in all the rest of the records reprinted, I omit repetitions and remarks not connected with the recollections. Nothing is omitted, however, which in my eyes might affect the interpretation of what is printed.—W.J.

Miss B.   Yes, I remember all that.

[Accurate again. The 'Head' must mean Owl's Head, where during two successive summers Hodgson had visited the sitter, and been supremely happy. The 'lights' refer to the lights of Rockland, across the bay, of which he greatly admired the effect, and at night on the piazza he had often spoken about the planets and stars, and the question of their habitation.—M.B.]

Well, here I am, now fire away, now fire.

Miss B.   Can you tell me the names of some who were with you there last summer?

Remember Miss Wilkinson?

Miss B.   No.

You ask me about whom? Not understand. How are the children? [The house had been full of schoolchildren, of whom R.H. was fond. —M.B.]

Miss B.   They are well.

Good! Do you remember the day I walked across to the Mountain?

Miss B.   No, I don't remember.

Ask Putnam if he and I—My watch stopped.

[For this reference to a watch stopping, compare pp. 262 and 355 of this report. I suspect some confused memory of a real incident to be at the bottom of it.—W.J.]

Miss B.   Can you not recall something you did at the Head?

That is just what I am trying to do. Don't you remember how I had to laugh at you, laugh on that boat, about that boat?

This last word, being wrongly deciphered as 'hat,' Miss B. asks:—

Miss B.   Whose hat blew off?

My hat, do you not remember the day it blew off? Yes, you are not following me very clearly.

Miss B.   I am trying to recall about that hat.

Do you remember fishing? Yes.

Miss B.   Yes, I remember fishing.

Capital! Remember about my hat? went into the water.

MISS B. Yes, I think I do.

I should say you did. Oh my! but I am not so stupid as some I know. I have not forgotten anything. Get my Poem?

MISS B. Yes, and I want to thank you for it.

Don't bother about that. I want you to know I am really here and recognize you, and the firstrate time I had at Owl's —— Thank you very much. How is Bayley? Certainly firstrate time I had at Owl's. Thank you very much. Owl's. Remember the jokes I told you? Jsp. Thank you. Remember what I said about dressing them [or 'him?']? Remember? Oh I do well. . . .

MISS B. How am *I* getting along?

Capital! You are doing well, all you need is experience. I would like to take a swim! I would like to take a swim. Plunge.

[Much incoherence hereabouts. The names Bayley and Jessup (Jsp) are correct. Hodgson used to bathe with them off the rocks, and Miss B. recalls jokes between them about dressing there. H. and they went deep-sea fishing almost daily. One day Dr. B. and R.H. went fishing in a gasolene launch, and on their return had much riotous laughter about some happenings in the boat. Miss B. can remember nothing definite about a hat, but is inclined to interpret the allusion as referring to this incident. The 'poem' she conceives to be the verses "It seems as if the wondrous land," etc., written at Miss Pope's sitting of Feb. 5th. See Part I of this report, p. 261.—W.J.]

On the following day Miss B. had a second sitting, and R.H. asked "How is Nellie?" [Nellie is a member of Miss B.'s household, presumably unknown to Mrs. Piper, about whom R.H. always used during his lifetime to inquire.]

On the night of Hodgson's death, Miss B., whom I described above as having 'psychic' aptitudes, had received a strong impression of his presence. She now asks:—

MISS B. Yesterday you said you had 'called and called' me. When did you ever call me?

Just after I passed out I returned to you and saw you resting. . . and came and called to you telling you I was leaving. . . .

MISS B. Did I not answer?

Yes, after a while.

MISS B.   What did I do?

You arose and seemed nervous. I felt I was disturbing you. I then left.

MISS B.   Do you not recall another time when I was sure you were there and I did something? . . . What did I do at one o'clock, Christmas morning?

I saw you, I heard you speak to me once, yes. I heard you speak to someone, and it looked like a lady. You took something in your hand, and I saw you and heard you talking.

MISS B.   Yes, that is true.

I heard you say something about someone being ill, lying in the room. [Nellie was ill in my room.—M.B.]

MISS B.   Yes, that is true. I also said something else.

You said it was myself.

MISS B.   Yes, I said that. Anything else?

I remember seeing the light, and heard you talking to a lady. [Cor·rect.—M.B.]

MISS B.   The lady did something after I talked to her.

You refer to the message, she sat down and wrote a message for me. [I do not understand what is meant by this, unless it be a confused reference to Miss Pope's reception of a message to me in the sitting of Feb. 5th.—M.B.] [See Part I, p. 261.—W.J.] [10]

There was nothing more of interest from Hodgson at this sitting. Dr. Bayley, to whom reference was made in connexion with

[10] *A propos* to Miss Bancroft's 'psychic' susceptibility, at a sitting on October 17th, 1906, which Mrs. M. had with Mrs. Piper, the following words were exchanged:—

MRS. M.   Any other messages, Dick?

R.H.   Not for him [the person last spoken of], but tell Margaret it was I who produced that light she saw the other night.

The sitter immediately wrote to Miss Margaret Bancroft, with whom she had recently become acquainted, to ask (not telling her of the message) whether she had had any special experiences of late. Miss B. answered: "I had a very curious experience on the morning of the 14th. At four o'clock I was awakened from a sound sleep, and could feel distinctly the presence of three people in the room. I sat up and was so attentive that I hardly breathed. About nine feet from the floor there appeared at intervals curious lights, much like search-lights, but softer, and there seemed to be a distinct outline of a figure. . . . This lasted probably from fifteen to twenty minutes . . . when I went into a sound sleep."

Owl's Head at Miss Bancroft's first sitting, had two sittings in April, in which the hearty and jocose mannerisms of R.H. were vividly reproduced; but there was a good deal of confusion, owing to Dr. Bayley's lack of familiarity with the handwriting; and the evidential material, so far as the Hodgson-control (whom we are alone concerned with) went, was comparatively small. One passage was this:—

R.H.   Get that book I sent you?

Dr. B.   I received the book right after your death.

[Hodgson had addressed some books and some cards to be sent to friends as Christmas presents. They were mailed after his death on December 20th. It should be added that Miss Bancroft had at her sitting of Feb. informed Rector that such a book had come to *her*, and Rector associated her and Doctor Bayley as friends.]

Have you seen Billy? [My friend Prof. W. R. Newbold.—B.]

Dr. B.   No, have you any word for him?

Ask him if he remembers the day we went to the seashore and we sat on the beach, and I told him how I hoped to come over here any time, only I wanted to finish my work. And ask him if he remembers what I told him about my getting married.

Dr. B.   I don't know anything about it. That's a good test. [Proves to have been correct.—W.J.]

Also ask him if he remembers what I said about the children of my old friend Pilly.

[W.R.N. remembers R.H. telling him of a certain 'Pilly,' but forgets about the children.]

No one living could know this but Billy. . . .

I ask if you recall the fishing process.

Dr. B.   Why, Dick, it will be very sad fishing without you.

[R.H. and I had done much deep-sea fishing together, but my supposition that this was meant may have deflected him from some explanation of the 'fishing' process of the controls at the sittings.—B.]

I wonder if you remember Miss Nellie.

Dr. B.   Perfectly.

Give her my kindest regards. . . . Got your feet wet!

Dr. B. Tell me more about that, Dick.

Do you remember how I put my pipe in the water? Do you remember my putting my coat on the seat, and my pipe got into the water? Remember ducking?

Dr. B. Ducking?

I said plunge.

Dr. B. Plunge?

Yes! Let's take a plunge.

Dr. B. Yes indeed!

ALL. . . .

Dr. B. Who was along with us, Dick?

Jess—. . . I got it in my head. [Dr. Jessup is correct.—B.]

Do you remember the Head? Oh I think it was the best summer I ever had. Best, best, best. . . . Do you remember laugh about Mitchell? Laugh? [This might refer to a very distinct incident involving a friend named MacDaniel.—B.] Idiosyncrasies . . . [What immediately followed was illegible.]

On the next day, April 4th, Dr. B. says to Hodgson:—

Dr. B. Give me your password if you can to-day.

Password? I had no less than forty. One was shoeing. Yes, yes, do you remember?

Dr. B. Of course I don't remember about your passwords; but you wrote Mrs. Bayley a charade of your own making, and if you can give the answer to that it will be a splendid test.

Shoo fly, shoo fly! [It runs in my head that these words were answers to charades propounded last summer, but I can get no confirmation and may be mistaken.—B.]

Dr. B. I have the letter with the charade here. (Puts it into the medium's hand.)

Doctor, this is *peacemaker, peacemaker.* I gave this word in my letter. Shoo fly.

[Miss Bancroft writes: "I have a dim recollection about 'peacemaker'. I feel very sure about 'shoo fly'."]

Dr. B.   I will look it up. [There were two charades in the letter handed to the medium, but the words given answer neither of them.—B.]

Do you remember anything about that awful cigar and my joke about it? [Mrs. Bayley remembers a cigar so huge that neither R.H. nor I would smoke it. He finally broke it up and smoked it in his pipe. This may have been the joke referred to.—B.]

Doc, [This is not R.H.'s usual way of addressing me.—B.] that is peace-maker! And to Mrs. B. I felt I said shoo fly. If you knew the difficul-ties I am having, you would smile out loud. . . . Can you play ball?

Dr. B.   Well, H., neither of us were very active ball-players in the country.

Listen, do you remember our late hours?

Dr. B.   Indeed I do. [R.H. and I used to sit out on the porch smoking to untimely hours.—B.]

Got your sleep made up yet?

Dr. B.   Not quite!

Next followed some rather unintelligible as well as illegible ref-erences to skinning fish and baling a boat. Then:—

Do you remember how we tried to make many words out of one? [Compare Piddington's Report, *Proceedings*, Vol. XXII, p. 65.—W.J.]

Dr. B.   Yes.

And the fun we had?

Dr. B.   Yes. [R.H. had enjoyed doing this with some of the ladies at Owl's Head.—B.]

Do you remember reading in the evening?

Dr. B.   Well enough.

Remember the joke I told you about Blats [Blavatsky] . . . and her tricks? [Correct, but matter of common knowledge.—W.J.]

Dr. B.   Now, Dick, do you remember some of the words of the song which we all sang so much, and which you brought there last summer?

Song? awful! song?

Dr. B.   It begins "Come, I will sing you."

Oh yes!—gone out of my head like a shot!

DR. B. Yes, Dick.

Listen, let me tell you something. Do you remember a little song I sang to the children which went like this: "Little Popsey Wopsey . . . Chickey Biddy Chum . . . all . . ." I am tired.

DR. B. Dick, that was splendid, I remember it well. [Known also to Mrs. Piper.—W.J.]

Do you remember my palming tricks?

DR. B. Yes. [Known also to Mrs. Piper.—W.J.]

And how you all seemed to enjoy them? . . . I am getting clearer since I have met you here. It helps in recalling many things I had almost forgotten. Listen, do you remember my recitation of a Hindoo?

DR. B. No, I don't remember that.

Which reads like this: "I think till I'm weary of thinking—"

DR. B. Yes, I know that well. [Known also to Mrs. Piper.—W.J.]

Do you remember my letter to Will, in which I told him of the delight of the place? [Possibly a misreading for "depth of the piece."]

DR. B. Who is Will?

Will James. Or perhaps I didn't read it to you after all.

DR. B. No, I didn't hear that letter. [I recall no letter either about the 'place,' or about the 'piece'; but my memory is so bad that that proves nothing. I *have* heard the 'piece,' however, and heard it from Hodgson.—W.J.]

. . . Ask Margaret Bancroft if she remembers telling me about you and Mrs. Bayley giving her a watch. I am glad I found her after I came over. I think she is perfectly sincere and a light. [Miss Bancroft writes: —"I felt badly about accepting the watch, and consulted Mr. Hodgson about it. He said a number of things about my sensitiveness, and after that I felt all right about the watch. I don't think I told anybody of this interview with Dr. Hodgson. As regards my 'sincerity,' the last talk I had with him was on that very subject. . . . He said he would certainly convince Dr. Bayley of my sincerity." The reader knows already that Miss Bancroft is a 'light.']

On June 20th, 1906, Miss Bancroft had her third sitting. Some days previous to this, Mrs. M., an old friend of Hodgson, had taken to her sitting a cross which remained among his effects, and asked the R.H.-control for directions concerning its disposition. The control had ordered it to be sent to Miss Bancroft; and when he appeared to Miss Bancroft at the sitting a few days later almost his first word was:—

Get my cross?

Miss B.   Yes, thank you very much. . . .

A Mascot I send to you.

Miss B.   Yes, I know you sent it to me.

I shall be with you when you are in the cottage.

Miss B.   Do you know that I have bought the place?

Of course I do. I understand pretty well what you are about. [Miss B. had been enabled to buy the land at Owl's Head since her sittings in the previous February.]

. . . There is more help coming to you to enlarge the house. . . . You remember you thought it necessary to have more room.

Miss B.   Yes, I remember very well.

Did you see me in your dream with my trousers rolled up at the bottom?

Miss B.   I am not sure that I did.

I spoke to you and you replied.

Miss B.   I have seen you several times in dreams.

Remember my knock?

Miss B.   When did you knock?

You were sleeping.

Miss B.   I remember twice when I thought someone knocked my arm.

But I woke you, I certainly did. [Correct.]

Miss B.   Can't you do me a favor by knocking now? . . .

Not while I keep on speaking. You wish me to knock your arm now, eh? I cannot do so and keep on speaking.
Do you remember the evening I told you about my sister Ellen's boy?

Miss B.   I do not recall it.

Yes, Ellen's boy and his passing over.

Do you remember—Enid? What I told you about her? And her poems? A scholarship and her poems?

Miss B. I remember all that. [He had told me a great deal about this niece Enid.—M.B. Mrs. Piper denies knowledge of her existence. —W.J.]

Listen. I am in the witness box! I am trying to help you to recognize me. . . .

Do you remember anything about celery root? . . . [See above, p. 289.] Margaret do you remember the walk through the woods?

Miss B. Yes, I remember it.

Do you remember "Let us sing of—sing you
Let us sing of a"

Miss B. Yes, I understand.

No you do not. No song.

Miss B. Yes I do. Try and give it to me.

I am but you do not understand. You do not understand *at all*. Let us sing the old song.

Miss B. You mean the song "Come let us sing"?

Yes.

Miss B. Tell me what it is.

I am telling you. 'Come let us sing the—what would you sing—sing— sing'

[He taught us a song last summer "Come I will sing you" and the response was "What will you sing me?" "I will sing you one oh," etc. My idea is that he wanted to have me give him the next line and probably he would have been able to give me the text and perhaps the whole song or part of it, but I did not understand what he wanted to do.—M.B.]

Miss Bancroft had two more sittings, on Dec. 2nd and 3rd, 1907. On Dec. 2nd Hodgson seemed to be cognizant of certain changes in the Owl's Head place, that there was a new wall-paper of yellow colour, a new bath-house, a new pier and platform, etc., none of which facts Mrs. Piper was in a way to have known.

He also showed veridical knowledge of a very private affair between two other people, that had come under Miss Bancroft's observation. There was, however, some confusion in this sitting, and R.H. was not 'strong.' The results were better on Dec. 3rd, but the evidential parts do not lend themselves well to quotation, with one exception, as follows:—

MISS B. Don't you remember something that happened that you helped us in?

I remember that one evening ——

MISS B. What happened that evening?

We got a little fire and I helped. Yes.

MISS B. Yes, that is true.

Put it out —— the fire —— —— I remember it well.

MISS B. What did you tell us to get before the fire occurred?

Before the fire?

MISS B. You told us to get something for the house.

I said you ought to get a —— in case of fire —— pail, yes.

[Here the hand drew three parallel horizontal lines, which might have meant shelves, and beneath them the outline of a vessel with a cover.]

MISS B. What are they for?

Water pails water pails —— yes, fire buckets —— fire Yes, I did.

[He told us in Maine, when we were experimenting with Mrs. Austin by automatic writing, to get fire buckets and put them up on the shelves, which we did long before the fire occurred. He warned us of this fire many times, but no one seemed to pay much attention to it but myself.—M.B.]

MISS B. What did you tell us to put on them?

Go on you will find that I am not asleep.

MISS B. I never thought you were asleep.

So much for the Owl's Head record, which, as the reader sees, follows a not incoherent thread of associated facts.

Few of the items were false, but on the other hand it must be remembered that a mind familiar with Hodgson's tastes and habits might have deduced some of them (swimming and fishing, for example) *a priori* by combining the two abstract ideas 'Hodgson' and 'seaside.' Leakages impossible now to follow might also account for the medium's knowledge of such items as the names Nellie, Jessup, etc., for her connecting Dr. Bayley with 'Billy,' etc. For the 'fire-buckets,' 'watch,' 'sincerity,' and other items, it would seem necessary to invoke either lucky chance or telepathy, unless one be willing to admit spirit-return. I should say that I have condensed the record considerably, leaving out some matter irrelevant to Owl's Head memories, some repetitions and all the talk that grew out of slowness in deciphering the script.

Dr. Bayley himself wrote me after his sittings: "They are pretty good, and have about convinced me (as evidence added to previous experience) that my much loved friend is still about. I had had either four or six sittings, some of them in conjunction with Miss Bancroft, before R.H.'s death. I do not think that Mrs. Piper normally knew me by name, or knew that I was from Philadelphia or that I knew Newbold. I realize that the average reader of these records loses much in the way of little tricks of expression and personality, subtleties impossible to give an account of in language. As I look over the sittings and realize my own blunders in them, I cannot always decide who was the more stupid, the communicator, or myself."

Professor Newbold's Sittings.

The message given to Dr. Bayley for 'Billy' (*i.e.* Prof. Wm. R. Newbold) makes it natural to cite next the experience of this other intimate friend of R.H. Prof. Newbold had two written sittings, on June 27th and July 3rd, 1906, respectively, Mr. Dorr being present both times. On June 27th, after a few words with Rector, Hodgson appears, and the dialog continues as follows:—

R.H.   Well, well, of all things! Are you really here! I am Hodgson.

W.R.N.   Hallo, Dick!

Hello, Billy, God bless you.

W.R.N.   And you, too, though you do not need to have me say it.

I wonder if you remember the last talk we had together—

W.R.N.   I do remember it, Dick.

I can recall very well all I said to you that glorious day when we were watching the waves. [Our last talk was on a splendid afternoon of July, 1905, at Nantasket Beach.—N.]

W.R.N. Yes, Dick, I remember it well.

I told you of many, many predictions which had been made for me. I told you I hoped to realize them but I would not consent to give up my work.

W.R.N. Firstrate, Dick, you told me just that.

I would give up almost anything else but my work——my work—— and my pipe.

W.R.N. Dick, that sounds like you!

Don't you remember?

W.R.N. Do you remember something *I* told *you* on the boat going to Nantasket?

Yes of course. Long ago you wrote me of your happiness and I wrote back and asked you if you were trying to make me discontented.

W.R.N. I don't remember, but I have your letters and will look it up.

[This allusion to my 'happiness' is very characteristic. He often spoke to me of it.—N.]

Look over your letters and you will find my memory better than yours.

W.R.N. Like as not! Like as not!

I have hoped to boss things on this side. [R.H. had often told me of his belief that if he could 'pass over' and communicate, many of the difficulties of the spiritistic theory would disappear. I can mentally see him now shaking his pipe at me threateningly and saying: "If I get over before you, Billy, I'll make things hot for you."—N.]

W.R.N. Yes, Dick, so you did.

Therefore if I seem bossy pardon me —— Bossy —— Pardon.

W.R.N. Go ahead, Dick, be as bossy as you will. I have nothing to say to you until you get through.

Good. That's what I wish. I remember telling you how you must not write more about your happiness.

W.R.N. Did you tell me this on the trip or in the letter?

In the letter.

W.R.N.   Firstrate! I have piles of letters. I will go through them.

If you do you will find it *all*. [I cannot find it in the letters.–N.] Oh, I am so delighted to see you of all persons.

W.R.N.   Well, you were a dear friend of mine.

I had the greatest affection for you.

W.R.N.   Do you remember what a friend you were to me, years ago?

Yes, I do, and how I helped you through some difficulties?

W.R.N.   I should say you did, Dick!

But I do not care to remind you of anything I did: —— only as a test —— only as a test.

W.R.N.   Yes, that's right, we *wish* a test.

I remember how delighted I was with your experiences.

W.R.N.   You were!

You told me much about them which I recall most clearly—recall.

W.R.N.   Right! [What follows refers to the trip to Nantasket and was probably preceded by some reference to it on my part which the record omits.–N.]

You and I had smoked —— [Correct.] until I got a dip ——

W.R.N.   Right!

—— and we walked along the shore ——

W.R.N.   Right, Dick!

and waited until the boat returned. [We had to wait perhaps twenty or thirty minutes.—N.]

W.R.N.   Dick, what did we do while waiting?

We took a dip and went to hear some music.

W.R.N.   No, *we* did not; *you* took a dip.

I say *I* took a dip and you sat and watched me.

W.R.N.   After that what did we do?

We went and got some —— let me think! ——

W.R.N.   I can't read that, Dick.

A drink —— drink. I asked you to have cigar. C i g a r —— and something else.

W.R.N.   That is true about the cigar. Go on.

At the moment I do not think what it was.

W.R.N.   All right, it is not worth the trouble.

Do you remember anything about sausages I cooked?

W.R.N.   Indeed I do! Many a one you cooked for breakfast.

Yes, and how you laughed about them.

W.R.N.   I said they were the best I ever tasted, Dick.

Yes, I remember.

[A passage is omitted here in which veridical reference is made to a private subject of which we had talked.—N.]

I do not catch all you say, Billy, —— too bad. Speak slowly, old chap, and I shall understand. I asked you about your [word undecipherable] and you said you thought you were not half worthy of all you had received.

W.R.N.   Well, I thought it; I don't remember saying it to you.

You did say it once in my room.

W.R.N.   I can believe it, Dick; I have thought it a thousand times.

[A remark was next ascribed to me which exactly expressed what I had thought, though I am forced to omit it.—N.]

I gave you a long explanation of the whole *modus operandi* and you were a very good listener. Do you remember the day?

W.R.N.   I do not remember the details. I remember in a general way talking about it. [I recalled the details clearly as soon as I had thought it over. The 'long explanation' was made in H.'s room in June, 1904.—N.]

All right. Good, listen. And you and I met in New York and I advised you what to do?

W.R.N.   Was it in New York or Boston? In Boston, wasn't it?

You and I went to the theatre.

W.R.N.   Certainly we did.

And then to my club.

W.R.N.   Right, yes, that is right, Dick.

And to my rooms where I cooked sausages and made tea.

W.R.N. Yes, you gave me the first good tea I ever tasted!

[Statements are here omitted relating to a person deceased. True on the whole, but not evidentially significant.—N.]

Do you remember that clergyman ——

W.R.N. Try the last word again.

who was a medium in Philadelphia?

W.R.N. I do, I think I do ——. A clergyman who was an Episcopalian.

Yes. Went into trance. Yes.

W.R.N. Yes, I know what you are thinking of, but he was not a clergyman.

[Word —— name perhaps —— written several times but undecipherable. Some years later I *had* met a clergyman who was mediumistic, but did not go into trance. Hodgson knew of his case, but had never met him. The two cases seem to be confused.—N.]

And his wife was afraid of him.[11]

W.R.N. No, I don't remember that, Dick.

You have them mixed up in your mind.

W.R.N. Very likely.

I saw a young man who went into trance.

W.R.N. That's right, yes.

And do you remember my opinion of him?

---

[11] I think that this reference to a clergyman, who 'went into a trance and his wife was afraid of him,' is to the same man that was mentioned at my sitting in October following. The details were given and discussed in the *Journal* of the American Society for Psychical Research more than a year later (Vol. I, p. 143). This interpretation is apparent in the mention of the same man in the sitting with Prof. James on May 1st, more than a month previous to this one of Prof. Newbold and in connexion with which the name 'Sanger or Zangler' was given (p. 552), saying that he was a clergyman.

I had been invited by an Episcopalian clergyman, the Rev. Stanley L. Krebs, who is probably meant by 'Sanger or Zangler,' to visit him at his home and to try some experiments with a Presbyterian clergyman who went into trances, but whose wife objected to this. Both clergymen lived in Pennsylvania, and in my sitting in October it was said that the clergyman lived in that state and that his wife disliked his going into trances. I got a part of the name, the syllable 'San. . .'. Dr. Hodgson before his death knew of my visit there and also of a remarkable experience of Mr. Krebs in connexion with the other clergyman and was much interested in it.—J. H. Hyslop.

W.R.N. Yes, Dick, I remember your opinion of him. Tell me what it was!

I thought he was hysterical and induced his trances through hysteria. I remember telling you about [name given, but omitted here], and by the way, Billy, do you recall his idea on this subject?

W.R.N. Yes, I do. His ideas?

Yes, all about it. The devil!

W.R.N. He thought it was the devil?

Yes. The devil has nothing to do with it. I laughed when you told me about it.

W.R.N. Now, Dick, have you any more to say?

Do you remember the story I told you about the girl who said her prayers?

W.R.N. No, I do not remember. Perhaps I might if you told me.

Yes. And when she got through she said she was sure she thought the devil was prompting her prayer. [I remember no such anecdote.—N.]

W.R.N. No, Dick; but I want you to tell me, if you possibly can, something I told you on the boat going down to Nantasket, just before we got there.

About your home-life?

W.R.N. No, it was about my work, Dick.

Oh yes, I recall you said you would like to give it up.

W.R.N. No, Dick, I did not say that. [I had just resigned my eight years of Deanship and was very glad of the relief. If R.H.'s remark referred to that fact, it was apposite.—N.]

Not for anything! [Seemingly meant to suit my answer.—N.]

Do you remember our talk about hypnotism?

W.R.N. Yes, we talked about hypnotism.

And hypnotising students. You said your mind was on your work and how much you liked it.

W.R.N. Yes, I said that. There was a lot more I said, but never mind it. Let it go.

I will give it all eventually—eventually. Yes. I am in the witness-box.

W.R.N. Poor Dick!

Poor Dick! Not much! Poor Dick! Not much! Fire away! I recall your psychological teaching very clearly.

[R.H. next goes 'out' to rest, but returns after a brief interval of Rector.]

Hello, Billy! All right? All right now? You told me you were working on some interesting work which you enjoyed better than anything you had done in years. You said you would not give it up for anything!

W.R.N. Right, Dick. Now before we got on the boat, to go out to Nantasket, what did we do?

I believe we went to the hotel and got some bite [word not clear] to eat.

W.R.N. No! No!

Drink [word not clear] No! Do let me think what I gave you. I asked if you would get w e i g h e d.

W.R.N. I believe you did. I am not sure now. Don't bother about it any more. It is not worth the trouble.

I did! You said I —— and joked about your weight. Don't you recall?

W.R.N. I don't remember, but I often have joked about my weight and I dare say I did with you then.

I remember drinking—— Yes, and I said I did not take beer. Yes, you asked me, I remember well. I remember the water well. You smoked cigar, and I also——pipe—— [I smoked a cigarette, but not a cigar.—N.]

W.R.N. Now let us drop the trip to Nantasket, Dick. I think you have told me all you remember about the trip to Nantasket that you can.

I have it surely right as it was the last time I saw you! I remember it as it was the last time I saw you.

W.R.N. That's right, Dick, it was the very last time I saw you.

Do you remember the stand near the boat where we went in and got a "Life"—— [I don't recall this.—Some illegibility followed.—N.]

W.R.N. Where we went to get a what, Dick? Write that once more! [Word undecipherable.]

You do not get it very clearly, Billy.

W.R.N.   No, it's long since I have had experience in the writing.

I understand. Therefore I am doing my best to make it clear.

[The communicator now professes to report a conversation which I had with a definitely named person who died some years ago.—N.]

He told me he did not approve or believe in your having——anything to do with this subject. [True.—N.] He thought it was the devil and you had better keep out of it.

W.R.N.   Right.

He said he would try to reach you if such were possible.

[I saw the person here referred to not long before his death. He made no reference of any kind to the future life. Such a promise as is here ascribed to him is quite incongruous with all I ever knew of him—I do not believe the thought would have occurred to him.—N.]

He did tell me so and before he left his body he felt a little different. But he wants to see you very much——very much indeed and tell you how he understands your life now.

W.R.N.   Can you tell me from him what he said before he passed out of the body?

Yes. He said you said "Come to me if you are alive."

W.R.N.   No, Dick, you've got that wrong!

Wait a minute. Listen, Billy. You said "I wish you to be with me."

W.R.N.   No, Dick, that's wrong; you had better try to get it another time when the light is clearer.

Listen, Billy, you said when you get to the——the other side you will know——know. [Incorrect.—N.]

W.R.N.   Did I say that to him, Dick?

He told me you said so. He said so, and he thought he was not going to live here. I have talked with him about it often and he thought he would not live.

[W.R.N. now repeats that so long as the 'light' is not clear R.H. had better not stay.]

Yes. Yes, I will return when the light is clear and tell you clearly.

W.R.N.   Now, Dick, many of my relatives have passed to your side and if you see them you can give me their names.

Good. I will find all I can and report to you. I will report to you.

W.R.N.   Names are good tests.

Exactly, I remember. Look up those letters. I am going now. I am holding on to a figment! Goodbye! God bless you! R.H.

The Hodgson part of the sitting of July 3rd was as follows:—

(R.H.)   I am Hodgson.

W.R.N.   Hallo, Dick!

I am glad to greet you, Billy, old chap! How are you? Firstrate?

W.R.N.   Yes I am, Dick!

Capital. Good. So am I. I come to assure you of my continued existence. Do you remember what I said to you the last time I left you after our experiment with that young man? I said hysteria was the cause of his trances.

W.R.N.   Exactly, yes.

He could not kadoodle me.

W.R.N.   That is a new word to me.

I made that up—ask Judah.

[Mr. Judah writes of his sitting of March 27th or 28th: "I tried to get R.H. to repeat a word which he had used in one of our long conversations. It was 'kadoodle'—I think he must have coined it for the occasion. He could not or at least did not give it."— As this attempt was during a trance, the reference to Mr. Judah in Newbold's sitting has no evidential bearing.—W.J.]

Tell me about your wife—is she well?

W.R.N.   Yes, better than for these many years.

Capital! Glad to hear it. Remember me to her.

W.R.N.   All right, Dick, I will.

Give me something of my own. . . . I shall be clearer in a minute. Billy, do you remember how depressed you were at one time, and how I used to advise you?

W.R.N.   Indeed I do.

And did it not result in good?

W.R.N.   Indeed it did, Dick. You did advise me just as you say, and it did result in good.

I have memories, many memories—let me remind you of a few of them as I recall them now.

W.R.N.   All right, Dick. Go ahead.

Do you remember the man with whom you and I experimented in Philadelphia?

W.R.N.   Indeed I do.

Do you remember the name he gave me as being my sister's?

W.R.N.   No, Dick, I don't remember, but go on and give me all you can about him.

Do you remember when I asked him about hypnotism, he said he was not a good subject, and you and I had a good laugh over it after he left.

W.R.N.   I don't remember that either, Dick. Do you remember who was with us when we experimented with him?

You, myself,—yes, and Dr. Hyslop. [Hyslop was not there.—W.R.N.] Do you remember a young student in whom you and I were intensely interested? We hypnotized him several times, but with little result. [Possibly refers to a medical student whom I hypnotized in 1899 with very interesting results. I wrote to H. and arranged experiments (apparent clairvoyance). But H. never saw him.—N.]

W.R.N.   Bless my soul! I think it must be ****. I will get your letters. I may find something about it in them.

You certainly will. Have you looked up my last reference?

W.R.N.   I can't; I'm in Boston and my letters are in Philadelphia.

Oh, of course, I understand. Help me if I seem stupid.

W.R.N.   No, you are not stupid, I am.

I wish to remind you of things of which you are not thinking, so far as possible.

W.R.N.   Yes, that's good.

Do you remember the case of a clergyman—?

W.R.N.   Yes, certainly. I remember a clergyman who lived in Philadelphia and thought he had supernormal experiences, and I told you about them.

Why didn't you say so before? Yes. I just told you about the case of hysteria—and you were interested in telepathy. [The young clergyman had professed to have telepathic powers—he cheated.—N.]

W.R.N.   Is this the case you were talking about at the last sitting?

Of course he was. You asked me what experiments we tried with him.

W.R.N.   That is right.

I said telepathic experiments, and some were pretty poor.

W.R.N.   Right.

Do you remember, Billy . . . ? [A veridical reference here which W.R.N. prefers to omit.]

W.R.N.   Yes, Dick.

I am delighted to recall your telling me you were happy and contented and how pleased you were with your classes—.

W.R.N.   Right, Dick.

And how readily your work was being accepted. You were so happy about it all. It gave me great delight.

W.R.N.   Thank you.

You certainly did. You also told me of your advancement in a material way.

W.R.N.   Yes, I told you that, that is right.

Which pleased me greatly.

W.R.N.   Yes, Dick, it did!

You were my counterpart—counterpart in expressions of delight. You and I were very pleased and I told you I would not give up my work even for a wife.

[I don't recall this remark, but it sounds characteristic.—N.]

W.R.N.   Yes, Dick, you are very clear and easy to understand.

I am glad to hear it. I am trying my level best to give you facts.

W.R.N.   Very good.

I said my pipe and my work would not be given up even for a wife.

Oh how you have helped me, Billy. Yes, in clearing my mind wonderfully.

[I omit here a few sentences from R.H. in which he credits me with a remark I have often made to him, seldom to others.—Important veridically.—N.]

W.R.N.   Dick, I have told you that twenty times.

You have certainly, but Billy, I used to say it was the most important thing in the world I believed.

[Refers next to psychical research and in particular to the Piper case.]

You said you could not understand why so many mistakes were made, and I talked you blind, trying to explain my ideas of it.

W.R.N.   Dick, this sounds like your own self. Just the way you used to talk to me.

Well if I am not Hodgson, he never lived.

W.R.N.   But you are so clear.

Of course I am, I am drawing on all the forces possible for strength to tell you these things.
You laughed about the ungrammatical expressions and said, why in the world do they use bad grammar?

W.R.N.   Yes, Dick, I said that.

I went into a long explanation and attributed it to the registering of the machine. You were rather amused but were inclined to leave it to my better understanding.

W.R.N.   You mean, I think, that you understood the subject better than I and I took your explanation? You mean that therefore I was inclined to accept your explanation?

I think I do. I find new difficulties such as a blind man would experience in trying to find his hat. And I am not wholly conscious of my own utterances because they come out automatically, impressed upon the machine.

W.R.N.   Perfectly clear.

Yes, I am standing beside you.

W.R.N.   Can you see me, Dick?

Yes, but I feel your presence better. I impress my thoughts on the machine which registers them at random, and which are at times doubtless difficult to understand. I understand so much better the *modus operandi* than I did when I was in your world. Do you remember you said you could faintly understand—faintly understand the desire on the part of a friend after coming to this side to communicate with his friend on the earthly side. But why he would choose such methods were the most perplexing things to you.

W.R.N.   No, Dick, you are thinking of someone else. I never told you that.

Yes you did in the case of the man I am talking of, who pretended to give manifestations, and you were right in your judgment.

W.R.N.   Yes! I think I did say it in that case.[12]

While in other cases you were open and clear to my explanations—and agreed with me, especially regarding G.P.

W.R.N.   Right! Firstrate! That is all very characteristic.

You were a good listener always, Billy, always. [R.H.'s talks and mine *had* been rather one-sided!—N.] Do you remember a trip we had into the mountains years ago? I am trying to recall. We took a bit of clothing and spent several days together.

W.R.N.   No, Dick, I never did that with you, you are thinking of somebody else.

Wait a moment. Let me ask you if you and I did not pass a few days together one summer.

W.R.N.   No, Dick, only in Boston.

Sure? All right, let me narrate what is in my mind.

W.R.N.   Right! Go on.

---

12 When the "choice of such methods" was first mentioned, I supposed it referred to the notion that mediums ought to be persons of distinguished character or abilities. I therefore disavowed it, for I have never seen any reason for the assumption. When it was referred to the "men who pretended to give manifestations," I doubtfully acknowledged it, supposing it referred to the so-called "physical phenomena," especially those of Stainton Moses. The objections upon which I used to lay most stress in my talks with H. were (1) the astonishing ignorance often displayed with reference to subjects which the supposed communicators must have been acquainted with; (2) the whole Imperator group, its historical and philosophical teachings, its supposed identity with the similar group in the Stainton Moses case and its connexion with the seed-pearls, perfumes and other physical phenomena which Moses professed to produce. To these objections H. could never give an answer: they are not here mentioned.—N.

I remember we were together one summer and we went to the woods or——and lay under some trees and had a smoke and discussed several problems. Where was it, Billy?[13]

W.R.N.   Not with me, I think, Dick, unless it was somewhere in Boston.

I think it may have been in Boston.

W.R.N.   Go on to something else, Dick. I don't remember that.

I remember when you were with me I got very much interested in some letters you wrote me after your return home——your saying some things puzzled you very much. [A firstrate veridical statement from R.H. has had to be omitted here. The matter referred to had, however, been mentioned at sittings in 1895.—N.]

W.R.N.   By jingo! that is true, Dick. It was ten years ago.

Do you remember a woman named Wright? [Name not clearly written.]

W.R.N.   No, not at this moment.

Did I not tell you about her the day we were at the shore?

W.R.N.   Ah, Dick, I think you did, but I do not remember it well enough to make it a good test.

Do you remember my remark about the way in which the name was spelled?

W.R.N.   No, I don't remember it, Dick.

Also about her giving me some very interesting things?

W.R.N.   No, Dick, I do not remember it. Do you remember telling me that day that when you got on the other side you would make it hot for me?

I do indeed remember it well. I said I would shake you up—shake you up.

W.R.N.   That is just the word you used Dick. [I am not now sure the word was 'shake you up,' but it was some such colloquial expression.—N.]

---

13 This incident of lying under the trees, smoking, and discussing several problems most probably refers to an experience with Dr. Bayley. I happen to have gotten the incident through another psychic, Mrs. Soule, when Dr. Bayley was present as a sitter and acknowledged the correctness of it.—J. H. Hyslop.

Yes, I did. Oh—I said, won't I shake you up when I get over there if I go before you do! And here I am, but I find my memory no worse than yours in spite of the fact that I have passed through the transition stage—state. You would be a pretty poor philosopher if you were to forget your subject as you seem to forget some of those little memories which I recall, Billy. Let me ask if you remember anything about a lady in [Chicago] to whom I referred.

W.R.N. Oh Dick, I begin to remember. About eight or nine years ago was it, Dick? [Here follows the 'Huldah'-material already quoted in my Part I of this report. See pp. 270–275.—W.J.]

Do you remember some trouble I had with Mrs. F. . . ?

W.R.N. I have some remembrance. [I recall this, but no details.—N.]

I told you about her. Yes, Mrs. —— Mrs.! I told you about her, and you thought I did right at the time.

W.R.N. Dick, did you get any names of those relatives of mine on your side?

Oh yes, names on my side. Yes, I found lots of your uncles and aunts. Your wife's also. Do not make me any worse than I am.——Do you remember my explanation about Proctor?

W.R.N. No.

Don't you remember my old friend?

W.R.N. No.

The astronomer? . . . Do you remember my little talk about the satellites?

W.R.N. Yes, I do.

And about the inhabitants of Mars?

W.R.N. I do indeed, I remember very well. [This was in 1895.—N.]

Do you remember my own talk independent of sittings, and my talks on the subject of canals? [R.H.'s own interest in these things was known to the trance-controls, by conversations he had held with them at earlier sittings.—W.J.]

W.R.N. Yes, indeed, I remember.

This is what I am reminding you of. I heard you and William—William discussing me, and I stood not one inch behind you.

W.R.N.   William who?

James.

W.R.N.   What did William James say? [I recall this talk with W.J. last week.—N.]

He said he was baffled but he felt it was I talking—at one moment—then at another he did not know what to think.

[Perfectly true of my conversation with N. after his sitting with Mrs. P. a week previous.—W.J.]

W.R.N.   Did you hear anything else?

Yes, he said I was very secretive and careful.

W.R.N.   Did you hear him say that?

He did. He said I was, —— I am afraid I am.

W.R.N.   I don't remember his saying so. [I remember it.—W.J.]

I tell you Billy he said so.

W.R.N.   Did he say anything else?

He paid me a great compliment, [I recall this.—N.] I fear I did not deserve it. However, I am here to prove or disprove through life. Amen.
Remember my explanations of luminous ether? [A favorite subject of discussion with him, possibly known to Mrs. Piper.—N.]
Good bye. God bless you and your good wife. Remember me to her. Adieu.—R.H.

Some persons seem to make much better 'sitters' than others, and Prof. Newbold is evidently one of the best. The two sittings of his from which I have quoted are more flowing and contain less waste matter, perhaps, than any others. If the R.H. who appeared therein be only a figment of Mrs. Piper's play-acting subconscious self (compare R.H.'s words "I am holding on to a figment" on page 314 above), we must credit that self with a real genius for accumulating the appropriate in the way of items, and not getting out of the right personal key. Not many items were certainly wrong in these sittings, and the great majority were certainly right. If two of the omitted communications could have been printed, they would have greatly increased the veridical effect. Professor Newbold gives me his own resultant impression in the following words: "The evidence for H.'s identity, as for that of other communicators, seems to me very strong indeed. It is not absolutely conclusive; but the only alternative theory, the telepathic, seems to me to explain the facts not as well as the spiritistic. I find it, however, absolutely impossible to accept the necessary corollaries of the spiritistic theory, especially those connected with the Imperator group, and am therefore compelled to suspend judgment."[14]

After Dr. Newbold's, it would seem natural to cite Dr. Hyslop's sittings, which were six in number during the period which this report covers. But he has himself given an account of them, with inferences,[15] so I refrain. It may suffice to say that Hyslop had already been converted, largely by previous experiences with Mrs. Piper, to the spiritist theory[16] of such phenomena, and that he held it in a form similar to that to which Hodgson had been led, supposing namely that at the time of communicating, the communicating spirits are themselves in a dreamy or somnambulic state, and not in full possession of their faculties.[17]

Dr. Hyslop's sittings in the present series, although they seem to me to contain no coercive evidence for a surviving Hodgson, as contrasted with the field of alternatives—I doubt if Hyslop would make any such claim for them—yet lend themselves easily to the notion that Hodgson, in a somewhat amnesic and confused state, was there. They pursued a train of ideas most natural for such a Hodgson to have followed, and they confirmed Dr. Hyslop in the theory which he had already reached as the line of least resistance in these matters:—Hodgson was probably communicating as best he might under the available conditions. He led the conversation back to his and Hyslop's earlier experiences, recalled the differences of opinion they had had over the proofs of Hyslop's report on Mrs. Piper in 1901; alluded to a meeting which they were to

14 Compare Newbold's previous account of his experience of the Piper-phenomena, in the S.P.R. *Proceedings*, Vol. XIV, pp. 6–49.

15 In the *Journal of the American Society for Psychical Research*, 519 West 149th Street, New York, Vol. I, Nos. II, III, and IV.

16 See his Report on Mrs. Piper in Vol. XVI of the S.P.R. *Proceedings*.

17 Compare with this Mrs. Sidgwick's well-argued theory that they are not *trying* to communicate at all, but that the medium in trances is able telepathically to tap their minds in spots, just as she taps the minds of the sitters. (*Proceedings* S.P.R., Vol. XV, pp. 16–38.)

have had in New York if Hodgson had not 'passed over' and to what Hyslop wished to discuss there; reminded Hyslop of some experiments on mediums which they had made together in earlier days, and of messages purporting to be from R.H. which Hyslop was receiving through another medium at present; discussed other mediumistic persons, and especially the aptitudes of a certain young 'light' in whom Hyslop was interested; sent a veridical message to Dr. Newbold; recalled a certain 'cheese' of which he and Hyslop had partaken on a unique occasion together; gave advice regarding Hyslop's practical perplexities in the crisis of S.P.R. affairs; expressed his sympathy in the most appropriate fashion; etc., etc.—most of this in an exceedingly scanty way, to be sure, but with such naturalness of tone, and following such characteristic lines of association with the sitter, that the latter's view was, as I said, only confirmed.

A reader of the records, not having Dr. Hyslop's Mental *Apperceptionsmasse* to interpret them by, might fail to find them convincing. My own feeling towards these sittings is what it is towards all the others. The interpretation of them will depend on that of the whole larger mass of material with which they belong.

W.J.'s Sitting.

The evidence is so much the same sort of thing throughout, and makes such insipid reading, that I hesitate to print more of it in full. But I know that many critics insist on having the largest possible amount of *verbatim* material on which to base their conclusions, so I select as a specimen of the R.H.-control's utterances when he was less 'strong,' one of two voice-sittings which I had with him myself (May 21st, 1906). The reader, I fear, will find it long and tedious, but he can skip.

(R.H. enters, saying:—)

Well, well, well, well! Well, well, well, that is —— here I am. Good morning, good morning, Alice.

Mrs. W.J. Good morning, Mr. Hodgson.

I am right here. Well, well, well! I am delighted!

W.J. Hurrah! R.H.! Give us your hand!

Hurrah, William! God bless you. How are you?

W.J.   Firstrate.

Well, I am delighted to see you. Well, have you solved those problems yet?

W.J.   Which problems do you refer to?

Did you get my messages?

W.J.   I got some messages about your going to convert me.

Did you hear about that argument that I had? You asked me what I had been doing all those years, and what it amounted to? [R.H. had already sent me, through other sitters, messages about my little faith. —W.J.]

W.J.   Yes.

Well, it has amounted to this,—that I have learned by experience that there is more truth than error in what I have been studying.

W.J.   Good!

I am so delighted to see you to-day that words fail me.

W.J.   Well, Hodgson, take your time and don't be nervous.

No. Well, I think I could ask the same of you! Well, now, tell me,—I am very much interested in what is going on in the society, and Myers and I are also interested in the society over here. You understand that we have to have a medium on this side while you have a medium on your side, and through the two we communicate with you.

W.J.   And your medium is who?

We have a medium on this side. It is a lady. I don't think she is known to you.

W.J.   You don't mean Rector?

No, not at all. It is —— do you remember a medium whom we called Prudens?

W.J.   Yes.

Prudens is a great help. Through Prudens we accomplish a great deal. Speak to me, William. Ask me anything. What I want to know first of all is about the society. I am sorry that it could not go on.

W.J.   There was nobody to take your place.

If it can't go on then it must be ——

W.J. Be dissolved. That is what we have concluded. There is nobody competent to take your place. Hyslop is going to,—well, perhaps you can find out for yourself what he is going to do.

I know what he is going to do, and we are all trying to help Hyslop, and trying to make him more conservative, and keener in understanding the necessity of being secretive.

W.J. You must help all you can. He is splendid on the interpreting side, discussing the sittings, and so forth.

I know he is, but what a time I had with him in writing that big report. It was awful, perfectly awful. I shall never forget it. [Hodgson had tried to get Hyslop's report in S.P.R. *Proceedings*, Vol. XVI, made shorter, a fact possibly known to the medium.—W.J.]

There is one thing that troubles me. Harry [James] asked me about a letter which he had received [at a previous sitting, from a certain C.B., asking whether R.H. had tried to appear to her since his death]. I have not got that cleared up in my mind yet. It was regarding someone to whom I have returned since I passed over.

(A letter from a certain H——t asking a similar question, was here offered as an 'influence'; and held on the medium's forehead.)

I did not return to C.B. Did you get her message?

W.J. I have not got her message. Harry may have it.

I also gave a message to Mrs. C. Did you get that?

W.J. Either George Dorr or Harry must have got that. You see I have not seen everything yet, having been in California.

Oh, yes, I forgot. William, can't you see, don't you understand, and don't you remember how I used to walk up and down before that open fireplace trying to convince you of my experiments?

W.J. Certainly, certainly.

And you would stand with your hands in your trousers pockets. You got very impatient with me sometimes, and you would wonder if I was correct. I think you are very skeptical.

W.J. Since you have been returning I am much more near to feeling as you felt than ever before.

Good! Well, that is capital.

W.J. Your 'personality' is beginning to make me feel as you felt.

325

If you can give up to it, William, and feel the influence of it and the reality of it, it will take away the sting of death.

W.J. But, R.H., listen a moment. We are trying to get evidential material as to your identity, and anything that you can recollect in the way of facts is more important than anything else. For instance, do you recollect a Churchill case, Mr. Churchill, who came on from New York or from the West with some materials, and you and I had some discussions? I have just had that worked up in the laboratory. Can you remember anything of that?

Oh, yes. I had Osler in my mind also and I was preparing some answers for that. [Piddington on May 2nd had told the controls that some MS. notes of a reply to Osler had been found among Hodgson's papers.—W.J.] I think perhaps you have heard about that, have you?

W.J. Yes, I have heard about that.

Well, Sanger, or Zangler? the clergyman, do you remember him?

W.J. No, I don't remember. [Impossible to identify.—W.J.]

Don't you remember a young man whom I was going to see? I think I told you about it, William,—quite sure I did,—who was a clergyman, and who was afraid of his condition, going into the trances. Don't you remember that at all? Ask Alice. Perhaps she remembers.

Mrs. J. No, I don't remember that account of the clergyman. I think perhaps Hyslop may remember it. I remember something about dream-cases and what we called death-bed experiences. [Possibly the case mentioned to Newbold, see above, pp. 315–316.]

[For probable meaning of the name 'Sanger or Zangler' and the references to the clergyman mentioned compare the sitting with Prof. Newbold, footnote p. 310.—J. H. Hyslop.]

W.J. Yes, this clergyman had had some of those, had he?

He had had some experiences in dreams. And then there was a case in Washington that I was anxious to look up. Do you remember my speaking anything about that?

W.J. No, I am not so sure of that. Do you remember a Denver case, a Gower case?

Oh yes, you recall that to my mind. And do you remember the description of the man whose finger,—there was something peculiar about his finger?

W.J. Yes, I do remember that. I remember that incident.

[I seemed to, at the moment, but the memory has failed to become distinct.—W.J.]

Well, have you found anything more about that?

W.J. No, I have not. If you could recall what kind of a case the Gower case was, it would be interesting. [For this case, concerning which R.H. had been in correspondence, see Miss Johnson's report in S.P.R. *Proceedings*, Vol. XXI, p. 94.]

Wasn't that a case of hysteria? [18]

W.J. No, not hysteria. He corresponded with you and wanted you to come and see the phenomena. Do you remember?

I do remember a physical-manifestation case, and I remember an aural case,—the voices came. And I think the Gower case was physical manifestation, if I remember. [No voices.—W.J.] [19]

W.J. That is correct. Can you remember what the physical manifestations were?

Well, I hope I will not get these mixed up in my mind, because I have several that are passing through my thoughts. There was one where they had the table manifestations, and they had also some experiments in knocking about the room after retiring. Do you remember those? [The table had moved without contact, but I fail to remember any 'knocking.'—W.J.]

Mrs. J. Yes.

I think I had those correct in my mind, and then I think—do you remember the case where the hands appeared, as though they were in phosphorescent light?

W.J. I don't remember that case.

I have those two now just on my mind at the moment. I think they will come to you clearly presently. Now tell me a little bit more about

18 It is probable that the allusion to "a case of hysteria" refers to the 'young light' of an earlier date, mentioned in a sitting with Mrs. L. and in my sittings, a case that Dr. Hodgson and I saw together, and in which he remarked indications of hysteria and mentioned the fact to me at the time.—J. H. Hyslop.

19 The allusion to "a physical manifestation case" where the "voices came" seems to me to be to the case which Dr. Hodgson and I saw together, and which was more fully described in my sittings. Cf. *American Journal for Psychical Research*, Vol. I, p. 101. There is possibly confusion of this with the Gower case, of which Dr. Hodgson knew, as I learned from Mr. Gower at the time of Dr. Hodgson's death.—J. H. Hyslop.

the Society. That will help me keep my thoughts clear. I think, William—are you standing?

W.J. Yes, I am standing.

Well, can't you sit?

W.J. Yes.

Well, sit. Let's have a nice talk.

W.J. The society is going to disband. Hyslop and Piddington and George Dorr and I have agreed to that, and we have written a circular, which we have signed, to the members, and I don't think there will be any objection. The American work will have to go on apart from the English work in some way.

Well, then about Hyslop's society. I think he will succeed in that. I feel very much encouraged in regard to that.

W.J. I certainly hope he will succeed.

I want to ask you if you have met at all Miss Gaule?

W.J. Maggie Gaule? I have not met her. [A medium known to R.H. during life, probably also known by name to Mrs. P.—W.J.]

I am very much disappointed in some respects. I have tried to reach her. [In 1908, Hyslop got messages from R.H. through Miss Gaule. —W.J.] I have reached another light and I did succeed in getting a communication through.

W.J. What was your communication?

I did not believe in her when I was in the body. I thought she was insincere, but I believe her now and know that she has genuine light, and I gave a message recently to a Mrs. M. in the body. I referred to my books and my papers and several other things. Her name is Soule. [R.H. acted as Mrs. Soule's control, and something like incipient cross-correspondences were obtained.—W.J.]

W.J. Soule?

A.M.R. [the stenographer] I know her.

And now, as I go through my rooms [which were still full of R.H.'s effects] I have talked over the matters there very well. Now let me see—tell me more about the Gower case. Are you going to look that up?

W.J. I stopped at Denver on my way from California, and I saw all the witnesses, and I think it is a good case.

I am inclined to think he is honest and I will investigate and if possible I will give some manifestations there that you will know that it comes from me. I will do everything I can because I am so anxious, and if I cannot prove—wait a moment—will you spell this after me? [Very dramatic change—as if some sudden influence had come upon him.]

W.J. Yes.

It is Z e i v o r n [spelt out].

[W.J. pronounces each letter after it is spoken by R.H.]

Now put those letters, repeat those backwards, and I have left that word written and I think you will find it among my papers. It is original and nobody saw it, nobody would understand it. [Not found there.—W.J.]

W.J. That is a password?

Yes.

W.J. Now, Hodgson, do you remember any sealed test that you left with Myers or me or anybody?

I left one with Lodge.

W.J. Did you leave one with me?

Yes, I left one with you. [I myself supposed so, but have found none. —W.J.]

W.J. Can you recall anything about that? It is very hard to remember those things.

It is sealed, if I remember rightly. Now wait a moment. That is one you will find in the office—in my rooms, rather—and I think I left it in a book.

W.J. This one that you just spelt out?

Yes.

W.J. Did you make that word up?

I spelt the word, made the word up and spelt it out because I knew no one living could guess at it or hit it.

W.J. It does not mean anything in particular?

Nothing at all.

W.J.   Just a password?

Yes. And the one I gave to *you*, I shall have to think that over, William.

W.J.   Think that over, Hodgson. Think it over carefully. Take your time and see if you can get it, because it is very important.

I shall do so, and I want to do it in a way to exclude if possible the theory of clairvoyance. Now I want to ask you a question, may I, while it is on my mind? Have you ever asked Harry if he asked Dr. Bayley about that charade? [Reference to a former sitting with H.J., Jr.]

W.J.   Yes, there is an answer from Dr. Bayley, about a charade containing the word 'peacemaker.' [Dr. Bayley recalls no such charade.—W.J.]

Yes.

W.J.   And that is all right.

The answer?

W.J.   Yes. [I print the record as it stands—it seems incoherent on my part.—W.J.]

Well, about the cheese? Please answer me.

W.J.   The cheese is all right. That is a very —— [The 'cheese' recalled to me another charade.—W.J.]

No, no,—I want to know if he gave it to Bayley.

W.J.   Yes, that was sent to Bayley by Harry, I think, but whether *you* gave it to Bayley originally, I am not sure. [R.H. did so give it, Dr. Bayley informs me, but Mrs. Piper says she also had heard this charade from R.H.—W.J.]

Well, I wish you would find that out. You see these things are all going through my mind, as though there was a panorama of things going through my vision.

W.J.   Hodgson, what are you doing, apart from Mrs. Piper?

Why, I am working with the society, William, trying to reach other lights, trying to communicate, trying to get into touch with you all.

W.J.   Why can't you tell me more about the other life?

That is a part of my work. I intend to give you a better idea of this life than has ever been given.

W.J.   I hope so.

It is not a vague fantasy but a reality.

Mrs. J.   Hodgson, do you live as we do, as men do?

What does she say?

W.J.   Do you live as men do?

Mrs J.   Do you wear clothing and live in houses?

Oh yes, houses, but not clothing. No, that is absurd. [Query: the clothing? or the statement made about it?—W.J.] Just wait a moment. I am going to get out.

W.J.   You will come back again?

Yes.

Rector.   He has got to go out and get his breath.

(When R.H. comes back he recommences talking about his pass-words:—)

Philanthropist—That is one of the words, but—wait a moment—that is Lodge's. Now I remember that very well. The other one which I have spelled—you wait a moment—there is something troubling me regarding the—do you remember another case? I want to recall it to your mind. Do you remember a case about a young girl, a young woman that I told you about?

W.J.   Yes.

I have seen her since I came over. Yes, I think Hyslop brought her here to me.

W.J.   Yes.

Well, that is the nearest approach to a case of hysteria of anything I know. Do you remember my telling you about it, William?

W.J.   Well, I do remember a case. I don't fully identify it.

It was about a year before I passed out.

W.J.   I do remember a young woman. Have you been influencing her?

No, I tried to reach her two or three times, one or two messages, but they did not come from me.

W.J.   I don't know whether it is the same case. The one I meant had been in an asylum.

That is the one. I tried to get the message through but I found it was a failure. [Evidently not the person I was thinking of.–W.J.]

[The letter from H——t (see above, p. 325) was here again put into Mrs. Piper's hand.]

I tell you one person, William, who has light, and that is B——g.

W.J.   Have you been able to get near Mrs. B——g?

Yes, I gave her a communication since I passed out. You ask her if she received anything like this: "I have seen the Doctor and I put my hands palms to your face facing you." You ask her if she got anything of that kind. [Mrs. B. informs me that she has had no direct impression from Hodgson since his death, but numerous messages from him through mediums on the Pacific Coast.–W.J.]

W.J.   How did you get this message to her?

Appeared to her and thought she saw me. She put her hand up. She had just retired.

W.J.   What time of day was it?

Just retired.

W.J.   Gone to bed? Do you remember, Hodgson, anyone by the name of H——t?

A medium?

W.J.   No, not a medium, a friend.

You mean lived in Providence? [The letter was from a Mr. H——t in England.–W.J.]

W.J.   No, I don't think he lived in Providence.

Oh yes, I remember Mr. H——t who used to live in Providence and from whom I received a great many letters. [Unknown, as yet, to W.J.]

W.J.   Have you tried to have any communication with him?

No, I don't think I have. I think I shall try, though. I have had some communications, you know, here. I have met several people. But independently I have gone to very few.

[The conversation then goes on about the lost ring (compare Part I of this report, pp. 263–268), and about the 'cheese' charade. Then I, thinking of a certain pitfall which the children and I had dug for Hodgson, asked:–]

W.J.   Do you recall any incidents about your playing with the children up in the Adirondacks at the Putnam camp?

Do you remember,—what is that name, Elizabeth Putnam? She came in and I was sitting in a chair before the fire, reading, and she came in and put her hands, crept up behind me, put her hands over my eyes, and said "who is it?" And do you remember what my answer was?

W.J.   Let me see if *you* remember it as I do.

I said, "Well, it feels like Elizabeth Putnam, but it sounds like———"

W.J.   I know who you mean. [R.H. quite startled me here because what he said reminded me of an incident which I well remembered. One day at breakfast little Martha Putnam (as I recall the fact) had climbed on Hodgson's back, sitting on his shoulders, and clasped her hands over his eyes, saying "Who am I?" To which R.H., laughing, had responded: "It sounds like Martha, but it feels like Henry Bowditch"—the said H.B. weighing nearly 200 lbs. I find that no one but myself, of those who probably were present, remembers this incident. —W.J.]

Do you realize how difficult that is?

W.J.   It is, evidently; yet you were just on the point of saying it. Is it a man or a woman?

A man.

W.J.   Have you any message for that man now?

Dr.—not Putnam—Dr. Bowditch!

W.J.   That is it, Bowditch.

"Sounds like Dr. Bowditch."

W.J.   It was not Elizabeth Putnam, but it was Charlie Putnam's daughter.

Charlie Putnam, yes. Now do you remember that?

W.J.   But what is the name of Charles Putnam's daughter?

Of whom? Annie? Oh, she is the youngest. She is the young lady. And there was a Mary—Mamie. [False names.—W.J.] [Names of my wife. —J.H.H.]

W.J.   But you *must* remember Charles Putnam's daughter's name!

I have got it now in my mind. I could not think of it at first. Well it

333

has gone from me at the moment. Never mind. That is less important than the thing itself.

W.J. Do you remember another thing? We played a rather peculiar game. Possibly you may recall it. Had great fun.

I remember playing leap-frog with the boys. Do you remember that?

W.J. Yes, that was frequent.

Yes, that is a very—and then do you remember how I played bear.

W.J. Yes, bear is firstrate. I was not there, but I heard them talking about your playing bear. I remember one morning you and I had a very——

Well, what you remember I might not remember at all.

W.J. Of course not. You played so often with them that you may have forgotten.

Besides all that, I am trying to avoid things that are in your mind if possible, to remind you of other incidents. Well, let me see—what were we playing—we were playing—you remember at all playing marbles with the children?

W.J. No.

That is another game I played with them. [False.] Oh, such fun, such days as those were. You say you and I were playing with them particularly?

W.J. Yes, perhaps that will come to you.

That may come to me at some other time. But all those things you ask me about the children,—well, that is the first thing I can remember. That is all right so far as it goes. Now let me see what other thing I can tell you that no one living knows but myself. Do you remember a place where we used to go, where I used to go and smoke? I used to go with Billy [my son.—W.J.] a great deal, and it was high up.

W.J. Doubtful.

Yes, do you remember that at all? By the way, how is Billy?

W.J. Billy is firstrate.

He has gone away, hasn't he? [Correct, but not evidential.]

W.J. Yes.

I think he is now on the right track and hope he will keep so. Give my deepest love to him and tell him how much I think of him and also the rest.

W.J. Yes.

[Some non-evidential matter here is omitted.]

Excuse me, it seems to me you are peculiarly dull concerning my affairs at my rooms. I suppose Harry knows more about them than you do.

W.J. Do you think it would help you to have the 'light' taken to your room there in your old surroundings? Do you think you could get more influences and feel nearer?

Perhaps I could. I left everything so suddenly, I had so little time to make my plans and my arrangements. I suppose you understand that?

W.J. Yes, indeed. Would it be advisable to take the 'light' to your rooms?

Well, I should rather come here and mention my individual things from time to time and then take her there later, . . . because there are many things which I wish to locate and point out and dispose of from time to time and things I would like to mention. I wish you would repeat to me those letters, to see if you have got them correct.

W.J. Z e i v o r n.

That is right. It is written in cipher, the one word, and written by itself, on a large sheet of paper, carefully folded and placed in one of my books, and it is in a book of poems I think, and I think it was Longfellow's, and the book has a scroll up and down the back, and the binding is green in colour, and I don't think anyone living knows that but myself. [Not found.—W.J.]

W.J. Yes, are there any particular things that you would like to have sent to Australia?

I have talked that over pretty carefully with Piddington and I think those arrangements are already made.

W.J. Yes, that is right.

I wanted to recall,—Alice, perhaps you can help me to recall,—what was that balcony where we used to go and smoke?

Mrs. J. Why, yes, it was up-stairs, the upper story of the piazza. [If Chocorua were meant, Mrs. Piper had seen this 'balcony.'—W.J.]

335

That is all right. That is perfectly clear. She always did have a clear head. . . . Now I want,—William, I want one thing. I want you to get hold of the spiritual side of this thing and not only the physical side. I want you to feel intuitively and instinctively the spiritual truth, and when you do that you will be happy, and you will find that I was not idling and was not spending my time on nonsense; and as I thought over all, as it came to me after I entered this life, I thought "What folly! If I could only get hold of him!"

W.J. I wish that what you say could grow more continuous. That would convince me. You are very much like your old self, but you are curiously fragmentary.

Yes, but you must not expect too much from me, that I could talk over the lines and talk as coherently as in the body. You must not expect too much, but take things little by little as they come and make the best of it, and then you must put the pieces together and make a whole out of it. Before I lose my breath, is there any other question you want to ask me? What do you think of that bust, William? I don't quite approve of it. I think it is all nonsense. [On March 12th Mr. Dorr had told the R.H.-control that Mr. Bela Pratt had begun to model a bust of him for the Tavern Club.]

W.J. I do not know anything about it. I have not seen it. But it is a natural thing for the Tavern Club to want of you, they were so fond of you, all of them.

I want to know, William, what is that you are writing about me?

W.J. I am not writing anything about you at present.

Aren't you going to?

W.J. Perhaps so.

Can I help you out any?

W.J. Yes, I want you to help me out very much. I am going to write about these communications of yours. I want to study them out very carefully, everything that you say to any sitter.

Well, that is splendid. You could not have said anything to please me more than that.

W.J. I am glad you approve of my taking it in hand.

Yes, I do. Of all persons you are the one.

W.J. I'll try to glorify you as much as I can!

Oh, I don't care about that. I would like to have the truth known, and I would like to have you work up these statements as proof that I am not annihilated.

W.J.   Precisely so. Well, R.H., you think over that 'nigger-minstrel' talk. [Compare Part I, p. 268.] If you get the whole conversation in which that nigger-minstrel talk was mentioned by me, it would be very good proof that it is you talking to me. [He failed to get it.—W.J.]

Well, I shall do it. I want you to understand one thing, that in the act of communicating it is like trying to give a conversation over the telephone, that the things that you want to say the most slip from you, but when you have ceased to talk they all come back to you. You can understand that.

W.J.   I understand that they come back.

But I shall give that out to someone here, you may be sure, and I hope to see you—this is only the beginning, and I shall be clearer from time to time, but the excitement of seeing you and all has been very beautiful to me.

W.J.   If you can manage to get a little more hold of the conditions on the other side, it will be very good.

Yes, that I shall do. You must remember I have not been over here an endless number of days? but I wish they would all try as hard as I have tried to give proof of their identity so soon after coming over.

W.J.   I wish you would more and more get Rector to let you take his place. You do all the talking and let Rector have a rest. And it would be much better, I think, for you to take control of the light, and for me particularly.

Yes, that is a very good suggestion, very good.

W.J.   Because I want to write this up, and the time taken by Rector is so much lost from you.

But he repeats for me very cleverly, and he understands the management of the light. I want to speak with Alice a moment, and then I shall have to leave you, I suppose.

Mrs. J.   Mr. Hodgson, I am so glad to know that you can come at all.

Well, you were always a great help to me, you always did see me, but poor William was blind. But we shall wholly straighten him out and put him on the right track. . . . I am sorry to be off so soon, but I know there are difficulties in remaining too long. They often told me

337

too frequent communication was not good for anyone. I understand what that means now better than ever. I am going to look up one or two cases and put you on the track of them, William, when I can communicate here,—at the same time repeat the messages elsewhere.

W.J.   That is firstrate.

I think that is one of the best things I can do. Now I am going to skedaddle. Good bye, William. God bless you. Give my love to the boys.

As I review this somewhat diluted sitting, the only evidential point in it seems to me to be the anecdote about the Putnam child (see above, p. 333). The incident was very distinct in my own memory, but seems to survive in no one else's. I was hoping for another answer altogether, about a certain 'pitfall,' namely, and this one was a surprise. Either tapping my subconscious memory, or a surviving R.H., would be possible explanations of it, unless it were more reasonable to assume that someone had told the anecdote to Mrs. Piper at the time, and that her memory was now reproducing it. Obviously the reader's solution will depend on his sense of 'dramatic probability,' and that will differ with the line of his previous experiences. For myself, considering the possibilities of 'leakage,' impossible to trace, in the whole case, I cannot be positively sure that Mrs. Piper's knowledge of this anecdote was supernormal at all. The rest of the sitting, although quite compatible with the spiritist explanation, seems to me to have no evidential force.

The same is true of the second sitting which I had a fortnight later. Much of it went over the same matters, with no better results. I vainly tried to make Hodgson remember a certain article he had written for *Mind* in 1885, and to give the name of Thomas Brown, whom he had praised there. Neither could he remember anything about the American Society for Psychical Research, as he found it on arriving in this country. He rightly mentioned his brown dress-suit and his broad-toed boots when questioned about his costume at that time, but these facts were known to Mrs. Piper. He named a 'Grenier' whom my son should have met at Paris, but whom we could not identify. He insisted much on my having said of a certain lady "God bless the roof that covers her." I trust I may have said this of many ladies, but R.H. could lead me to no identification.

The only queer thing that happened at this sitting was the following incident. A lady had sent me a pair of gloves as an 'influence' to elicit, if possible, a message from her husband, who had recently committed suicide. I put the gloves into Mrs. Piper's hand, naturally without a word of information about the case, when 'Hodgson,' who had been speaking, said, with a rather startling change of his voice into a serious and confidential tone, that he had just seen the father (known to us both in life) of a young man who a few years before had made away with himself. "I never knew it till I came over here. I think they kept it very quiet, but it is true, and it hastened the father's coming." The apparent suggestion of a suicide, even though it were another one, by the gloves, and the instantaneous change of tone in the communicator, forcibly suggested to me the notion that the gloves were shedding an influence of the kind called 'psychometric.' The facts given by R.H. about the suicide were veridical; but, with the possibilities of leakage in the case, they cannot count in any way as evidential.

After middling or poor sittings like these of my own, it seems hardly worth while to quote a *bad* one, to show the full range of the phenomenon. Were I to do so, an appropriate one for the purpose would be that of Miss Anne Putnam. There is no doubt that certain persons are good 'sitters' naturally, while others seem to impede the telepathic flow. On certain days, also, communication may be less free. The Hodgson-control had sent repeated messages to the Putnams to come and talk with him, and R.H. had been so extremely intimate a member of their family group, that the best results might have been expected. Miss Putnam's sitting, but for one item (see below, p. 353), was nevertheless extremely poor; and Dr. James Putnam's was hardly to be called good, although he was introduced to Mrs. Piper by name. The sitter's difficulty in reading the written record may perhaps account for R.H.'s lack of fluency in this latter case. There was one apparently supernormal item which unfortunately I must omit.

I will end my specimens by some extracts from two sittings of Miss M. Bergman [pseudonym]. Miss Bergman had been in previous years an excellent sitter, and was known by name to Mrs. Piper. She dwelt in another state, and her social connections were not in Massachusetts. At her first visit, December 31st, 1907, the communications were in writing and she had much difficulty in deciphering them. At the second sitting, January 1st, 1908, the voice was used and things ran much more smoothly.

At the first sitting R.H. quickly appeared, spoke of having seen two brothers of the sitter in the spirit-world (names known to trance-personalities, and non-evidential), made a wrong statement about Christmas at the cemetery, and then, being asked to recall his meetings with Miss Bergman on earth, said:—

> I will. Do you remember one evening when I came to the hotel where you were staying and I sat and told you of my experiences till it got very late and I asked you if you would not [illegible] I told you so very many jokes, you and Miss Pope were convulsed with laughter over it. [Correct, Hotel Bellevue, Boston, March 1905.—M.B.]

After a while, Hodgson reappears, saying:—

Do you remember my telling you about my German friends?

Miss B. No.

Perhaps Miss Pope remembers.

[I found later that Miss Pope well remembered Dr. Hodgson's telling about his "German friends" and that it was that which "convulsed us with laughter" the evening he had stayed so late when calling at our hotel. At this point I had become so discouraged by the great difficulty of reading the writing and the confusion in making things clear that I felt very indifferent and inert in mind.—M.B.]

Bosh.

Miss B. What do you mean by that?

You understand well.

Miss B. Bosh?

Yes, I say bosh. *B O S H   B O S H*

Miss B. What do you mean by that?

Oh I say it is *all bosh.*

Miss B. What is bosh?

Why the way you understand. It is simply awful.

Miss B. That sounds like you, Dr. Hodgson.

I could shake you.

Miss B.   How can I do better?

Put all your wits to it, you have plenty of them.

Miss B.   I will do my best. Go on.

Do. Do you remember I used to chaff you.

Miss B.   Indeed I do.

Well I am still chaffing you a bit just for recognition.

Miss B.   It helps.

Amen. Now you are waking up a bit.

Miss B.   I am.

Capital. So am I. Don't you remember I told you I would show you how to manage if I ever came over before you did.

Miss B.   Indeed I do. [Sitter had often heard Dr. Hodgson say this.][20]

Well now I am trying to show you. I used to scold you right and left and I shall have to keep it up, I think, unless you do better.

Miss B.   I deserve it.

If you do not who does?

Miss B.   You are your old self.

Oh I am the [two words not deciphered] I was. You'll find it out before I finish.

Miss B.   Have you a message for Theo [Miss Theodate Pope]?

Yes indeed give her my love and tell her I am not going to forsake her. I do not think she has been keeping straight to the mark.

Miss B.   What do you mean by that?

I think she has been getting a little mixed up in her thoughts and ideas of us over here. I am the same old sixpence and I wish she were the same. I want to see her very much.

['Theo' had had no sitting for a long time, her interest being lessened by the circumstance that records of several sittings had not been kept systematically, as before Dr. Hodgson's death. At this point the hand wrote comments relating to circumstances which had arisen in Theo's life since Dr. Hodgson's death. These comments were singularly appropriate.—M.B.]

[20] The bracketed comments in the third person are by Miss Bergman herself.

At the second sitting, when R.H. appeared, the voice began speaking very rapidly and heartily.

Well, well, well, this is Miss Bergman; hullo! I felt as though I could shake you yesterday.

Miss B.   Well, I was pretty stupid. I think we can do better to-day. Please repeat some of the messages you wrote and left sealed to be opened after your death.

One message I gave to Will. If I remember correctly it was "there is no death."

Miss B.   Who is Will?

Will James.

Miss B.   Are you sure you are now giving this quotation correctly as you wrote it?

Of course I am. [There followed an outburst spoken so rapidly that the sitter could not get it down, declaring that the speaker had not lost his memory any more than had the sitter, etc.]

Miss B.   Did you leave other messages?

Yes, another. "Out of life"—how did I quote it—"Out of life, into life eternal." . . . I know positively what I wrote. I have promised Piddington to repeat through Mrs. Verrall all the messages that I give through this light. Every message given at this light must be repeated through Mrs. Verrall before anyone opens any of my sealed messages. Mrs. Verrall is the clearest light except this which I have found. Moreover she has a beautiful character and is *perfectly honest*. That is saying a great deal. [The reader will notice that Mrs. Piper had been in England and returned, at the date of the sittings with Miss Bergman.—W.J.] Do you remember my description of luminiferous ether, and of my conception of what this life was like? I have found it was not an erroneous imagination.

[The above words were spoken with great animation and interest. The sitter, although remembering Dr. Hodgson's description of "luminiferous ether," felt that she was not qualified to enter into a conversation of this character and began to say something else. The voice interrupted her:—]

It is never the way to get the best results by peppering with questions. Intelligences come with minds filled and questions often put everything out of their thought. I am now going to give you a test. Mention it to no one, not even to Theo. Write down, seal and give to Alice or to William.

[Directions here followed regarding such a test. After these directions the voice spontaneously took up another subject.]

Your school was—[correct name given], was it not? [Already known to controls, but probably not to Mrs. Piper when awake.] You are changing, your brother tells me, and he is very pleased. He thinks you are going to broaden out and do a better work. He is very glad. Do not undertake too much. Make use of assistance in the work.

Miss B.   Where were your lodgings in Boston?

Well, now, that has brought back to my mind Boston—. Certainly—there were some doctors in my building—George Street—no—not George—Charles Street—I—I believe. Now let me see, Charles Street. Up three flights, I think I was on the top. [Correct, but known to Mrs. Piper.—W.J.]

Miss B.   Do you know when I was at your lodgings?

You were there? Didn't we have tea together? [False.]

Miss B.   No.

Did you come and read papers?

Miss B.   No.

Did you go there after I passed out?

Miss B.   Yes. I went to get some articles belonging to you, and did them up in rubber cloth.

Capital, that is good. Lodge and Piddington consider it good when I can't remember what did not happen! What was the name of that girl who used to work in my office?

Miss B.   I do not remember.

Edmund—Edwards—I am thinking of her going to my rooms to read papers. [Her name was Edmunds, known to the medium.—W.J.]

Now I want to ask you if you remember Australia, remember my riding horseback? Remember my telling you of riding through the park in the early morning with the dew on the grass and how beautiful it was.

Miss B.   Yes, yes, I remember that very well. That is fine.

I *am* Richard Hodgson. *I am he.* I am telling you what I *remember*.

I told you, too, about my preaching. I believed I was in the wrong and I stopped. It hurt some of my people to have me.

Miss B.   Tell me about your riding.

I remember telling you about my dismounting and sitting and drinking in the beauty of the morning.

Miss B.   Tell me any experiences that befell you while riding.

Oh, I told you about the experience with the fiery horse. You remember he dismounted me. It was the first experience I had in seeing stars. I lost consciousness. I experienced passing into this life. I remember my being unconscious and recovering consciousness. I remember telling you this at the hotel.

[Sitter's mind was filled here with recollections of how Dr. Hodgson had once told her all this when talking with her at the Parker House in Boston, in 1904. He had related just this experience and had said that when he recovered consciousness after being unconscious for some time, it seemed to him he had been in a spiritual universe. He also told her at that time of his having given testimony in Methodist meeting as a lad in his teens, and afterwards giving it up because he became skeptical in matters of faith. This, he said, had troubled some of his kinsfolk.—M.B.]

Miss B.   What did you use to order for luncheon when you lunched with us at the hotel?

Oh, I have forgotten all about eating—m—m—I was very fond of protose.

[The sitter did not have "protose" in mind, but remembers Dr. Hodgson sometimes asking the waiter for one of the prepared breakfast foods, but does not recall its name.—M.B.]

When I found the light it looked like a tremendous window, open window. The canopy—do you remember how they used to talk about the canopy? It is an ethereal veil. If your spiritual eyes were open you could see through this veil and see me here talking to you perfectly.

[The sitter did not care to talk about this, although she remembered perfectly Dr. Hodgson's telling her "how they talked about the canopy," so she asked a question referring to the intimate personal affairs of one of her friends. The replies showed a strange knowledge of the circumstances known only to the sitter and her friend, and were entirely *a propos*. The voice then went on speaking, and burst out with what follows, in a tone of mingled indignation and amusement:—]

Will thinks I ought to walk into the room bodily and shake hands with him. I heard him say "Hodgson isn't so much of a power on the other side." What does he think a man in the ethereal body is going to do with a man in the physical body? [Seems to show some supernormal knowledge of the state of my mind.—W.J.]

Miss B.   To whom did you speak first from that world?

Theodate, yes, Theodate, she was the one to whom I first spoke. [Correct.]

[The sitter now asked to talk with another spirit, and reply was made that R.H. would continue talking until he came. R.H. did this by again referring to the accident in the park. He spoke of being seated when he first told us of the incident, and of getting up and walking around the room as he talked. He said it chanced that this incident had been told to few people, and again dwelt upon having seen stars after falling, having been unconscious, having had visions while unconscious, as if the spirit had left the body and passed into another world. All of this corresponded exactly with fact. Dr. Hodgson had commenced the story seated, and had risen and walked about as he talked.—M.B.]

The accurate knowledge thus displayed of R.H.'s conversations at the hotels in Boston where the ladies stayed, seems to me one of the most evidential items in the whole series. It is improbable that such unimportant conversations should have been reported by the living R.H. to Mrs. Piper, either awake or when in trance with other sitters; and to my mind the only plausible explanation is supernormal. Either it spells 'spirit-return,' or telepathic reading of the sitter's mind by the medium in trance.

I now pass to R.H.'s

Australian Recollections.

R.H. has sent many messages, both of affection and for test purposes, to his sister Annie in Australia. Mrs. M., Mr. Piddington, my wife, myself, Mr. Dorr, Miss Pope, Miss Hillard, all received such messages, which were duly transmitted to the sister, on whose replies what follows is based. Some of these messages were too general to serve as good tests (*e.g.* "Do you remember my reading Fenimore Cooper?"); some had been spoken of at previous trances (*e.g.*

'Cousin Fred Hyde,' 'Q,' 'fly-the-garter,' etc. Compare report of Hodgson's own sittings in S.P.R. *Proceedings*, Vol. VIII, pp. 60–67); some awoke no corresponding memory in Miss Hodgson. There are too many of them to quote in full, so I will go rapidly over the more significant ones, taking them in their time-order.

Melbourne; Latrobe Street; bush in yard with red berries. [Correct, as to town, street, and bush, berries not recalled by Miss H. Had R.H. ever mentioned Latrobe Street and bush to Mrs. Piper? —of course she knew of Melbourne.]

Charley Roberts (or Robertson) *at the University.* [Not recalled. There was a Roberts at R.H.'s school.]

Little shed where boys used to play. [Correct.]

Sister Rebecca. [Known in previous trances.]

Plums in back-yard. [False?]

R.H., ten years old, sat with knees crossed at church, and his mother made him sit straight. Sat on his hat to keep other boys from getting it. A man named Hurley made him stop. [Probably untrue.]

Sister Annie caught him reading in bed and put out the light. [Not remembered.]

Riding horseback. [Correct.]

Holidays spent at the Hydes'. [Correct.]

Kendall. [Name not remembered.]

Great plates of peas raised in our garden. [Not particularly recalled.]

Played fly-the-garter with Tom [his brother], *Jack Munroe, and Roberts.* [No reply from Miss Hodgson about Jack Munroe—the rest true.]

Father's mines and losses. [Correct.]

Description of paternal house. [Wrong.]

Sister used to teach him. [False.]

Father nervous over children's noise. Mother used to say "Let them enjoy themselves." [Not remembered.]

Sister helped him to escape punishments. [Possibly, when very young.]

Read Fenimore Cooper. [Possibly true.]

Sunday-school poem about stars. [R.H. wrote juvenile poems— one about 'stars' not remembered.]

The account to Miss Bergman of R.H. being thrown from his horse we have already seen (above, p. 344). Miss Annie Hodgson writes of the whole collection of messages sent to her: "To my mind there is nothing striking in any of the statements." She propounded in turn three test-questions of her own to which no answer was forthcoming; and R.H., questioned by a sitter, couldn't remember the name of his schoolmaster in Melbourne. In interpreting responsibly these Australian messages, tapping the mind of the sitters and normal acquaintance with the facts on Mrs. Piper's part[21] must probably be excluded as explanations. If a naturalistic interpretation were insisted on, fictitious construction of incidents probable in any boyhood, and accidental coincidence of a certain number of these with fact, would have to be chiefly relied upon. Against fictitious construction is the fact that almost none of the names that had figured in Hodgson's own sittings in 1887 and 1888 (S.P.R. *Proceedings*, Vol. VIII, pp. 60–67) were used for reproduction. 'Enid,' 'Ellen,' 'Eric,' were added rightly; and the three names of 'Q.' (Hodgson had apparently given only the first one to Phinuit —see *loc. cit.*, p. 60) slipped out in full, as it were inadvertently, on May 29th, 1906, Hodgson insisting at the same time that her identity must never be revealed to the outside world. The possibility that Hodgson had given 'Q.'s' entire name to later controls than Phinuit cannot, however, be eliminated.

On the whole this series baffles me as much as the rest. It may be spirit-return! it may be something else! Leaks of various sorts are so probable that no sharp conclusion can be drawn.

I think that by this time the reader has enough documentary material to gain an adequate impression of the case. Additional

---

21 I wrote to Mrs. Piper for the names of H.'s Australian relatives. Here is her answer, which I take to be sincere:—

"Boston, Jan. 11, 1909. Dear Mr. James,—In replying to your letter of this morning I will say I am very sorry I cannot help you in finding Dr. Hodgson's relatives in Australia as I do not know any of them or anything about them except that he had one sister whose Christian name was Annie, and this was unknown to me until some time after Dr. Hodgson's death. Mrs. [Lyman] might be able to tell you as it was she who told me, she had some photographs of Dr. H. which I admired, and she said she would give me one later, but those she had she was going to send to his sister Annie in Australia. I was struck by the familiarity with which she used the name and concluded that she must have known her. Dr. Hodgson never talked with me about his relatives or any body else's, on the contrary he most carefully avoided all such subjects when talking with me. I haven't the slightest idea who 'Q.' was, I have never heard the name so far as I am aware.

"I am sure my daughters do not know any more than I do about Dr. Hodgson's family.—I am, very sincerely yours,   L. E. Piper."

citations of sittings would introduce no new factors of solution. The entire lot of reports, read *verbatim*, would, it is true, give a greater relative impression of hesitation, repetition, and boggling generally; and the 'rigorously scientific' mind would of course rejoice to find its own explanatory category, 'Bosh,' greatly confirmed thereby. But the more serious critic of the records will hold his judgment in suspense; or, if he inclines to the spiritistic solution, it will be because an acquaintance with the phenomenon on a much larger scale has altered the balance of presumptions in his mind, and because spirit-return has come to seem no unpermissible thing to his sense of the natural dramatic probabilities.

Before indulging in some final reflections of my own on Nature's possibilities, I will cite a few additional evidential points. I will print them in no order, numbering them as they occur.

(1) First of all, several instances of knowledge that was veridical and seemed unquestionably supernormal. These were confidential remarks, some of which naturally won't bear quotation. One of them, plausible after the fact, could hardly have been thought of by anyone before it. Another would, I think, hardly have been constructed by Mrs. Piper. A third was to the effect that R.H. thought now differently about a certain lady—she was less 'selfish' than he had called her in a certain private conversation of which he reminded the sitter.

(2) Again, there was intense solicitude shown about keeping the records of a certain former sitter from publicity. It sounded very natural and Hodgsonian, but the trance-Mrs. Piper might also have deemed it necessary.

(3) The following incident belongs to my wife's and Miss Putnam's sitting of June 12th, 1906:—Mrs. J. said: "Do you remember what happened in our library one night when you were arguing with Margie [Mrs. J.'s sister]?"—"I had hardly said 'remember'," she notes, "in asking this question, when the medium's arm was stretched out and the fist shaken threateningly," then these words came:—

R.H. Yes, I did this in her face. I couldn't help it. She was so impossible to move. It was wrong of me, but I couldn't help it.

[I myself well remember this fist-shaking incident, and how we others laughed over it after Hodgson had taken his leave. What had made him so angry was my sister-in-law's defence of some slate-writing she had seen in California.—W.J.][22]

(4) At a written sitting at which I was present (July 29th, 1907) the following came:—

You seem to think I have lost my equilibrium. Nothing of the sort.

W.J.   You've lost your handwriting, gone from bad to worse.

I never had any to lose.

Mrs. M.   It was a perfectly beautiful handwriting [ironical].

Ahem! Ahem! William, do you remember my writing you a long letter once when you were ill? You had to get Margaret [my daughter —W.J.] to help you read it and you wrote me it was detestable writing and you hoped I would try and write plainer to a friend who was ill, next time. How I laughed over that, but I was really sorry to make you wade through it. Ask Margaret if she remembers it. [Perfectly— it was in London.—M.M.J.]

(5) Another item which seems to mean either telepathy or survival of R.H., came out at a sitting of Miss Pope's on Feb. 7th, 1906.

---

22 *Primâ facie*, the following incident also sounds evidential:—

R.H.   Ask Margie if she remembers chaffing me about sitting up late to entertain people.

This happened, as I well remember, at Chocorua, but at this distance of time it is impossible to be sure whether it was not on the occasion when Hodgson and Mrs. Piper were there as visitors together. The evidence is therefore 'leaky.'

Another case of leaky evidence is the following, which *primâ facie* seems striking enough:—

In Hodgson's rooms a quantity of MS. was found, in a cipher probably invented by himself. In the sitting of Jan. 23rd, this cipher was spontaneously mentioned by the control:—

R.H.   Is this the Piper-case? the Piper phenomenon? . . . There are some private records which I should not wish to have handled. Let George and Piddington go through them and return them. The cipher—let Harry and George take care of them. That was my cipher and no one living can read it. I shall explain it later. [He never has explained it, though it was spoken of later several times.]

I think it probable here that a question about the cipher from the sitter, preceding the control's reference to it, has been accidentally omitted from the record. If so, there is nothing remarkable in the incident. The record was not stenographic, and neither my wife nor the son who took the notes is now confident that the question was not asked.

I am not going to make a botch of anything if I can help it. Not I. Do you remember my telling you what I would do if I got over here first.

Miss P.   You said several things about it.

I said if I couldn't do better than some of them I was mistaken. I said some of them were awful. Remember? And if I based my opinion on what they tried to give I should expect to be said to be in the trick. *Remember?*

Miss P.   Of course I remember.

Do you remember a story I told you about my old friend Sidgwick? Don't you remember how I imitated him?

Miss P.   Yes, what word did you say about Sidgwick? [I had not deciphered the word 'imitated.'—T.P.]

If I believed in it they would say I was in the trick.

[Still not understanding, T.P. said:—]

Miss P.   What about Sidgwick?

I imitated him.

Miss P.   What did you do?

I said s-s-s-should-be i-n th-e t-r-i-c-k.

Miss P.   I remember perfectly, that's fine.

No one living could know this but yourself and Mary Bergman.

[It was most interesting to see the hand write these words to imitate stuttering, and then for the first time it flashed over me what he had some time ago told Mary and me about Sidgwick, imitating at the same time Sidgwick's stammer: "H-Hodgson, if you b-b-believe in it, you'll b-be said to be in the t-trick." I cannot quote the exact words, but this is very nearly right.
Sidgwick referred to Hodgson's belief that he was actually communicating, through Mrs. Piper, with spirits. He meant that people not only would not believe what Hodgson gave as evidence, but would think he was in collusion with Mrs. Piper.—T.P.][23]

[23] When Dr. Hodgson told this same story to me, as I told it in a discussion of Mr. Podmore's book (*Journal of the American Society for Psychical Research*, Vol. III, p. 160), he used the term 'conspiracy' instead of 'trick.' My memory is very clear on that point. This I record so that the discrepancy will not appear to be so great.— J. H. Hyslop.

(6) At a sitting of Miss Pope's and mine, Oct. 24th, 1906, R.H. said of Miss P.—"She goes on and puts on bays and piazzas, changes her piazzas, her house, makes it all over again." As this was literally true, and as no one in Boston could well have known about it, it seemed like mind-reading. [R.H.'s saying is possibly explained, however, by a previous sitting (April 16th) of Miss Pope's, in which another of Mrs. Piper's controls had already of his own accord made the same veridical remark, so that the fact had got, however inexplicably, into the trance-consciousness, and could be used by the controls indiscriminately.]

(7) On Jan. 30, 1906, Mrs. M. had a sitting. Mrs. M. said:—

Do you remember our last talk together, at N., and how, in coming home, we talked about the work?

(R.H.)   Yes, yes.

Mrs. M.   And I said if we had a hundred thousand dollars—

Buying Billy!!

Mrs. M.   Yes, Dick, that was it—"buying Billy."

Buying only Billy?

Mrs. M.   Oh no—I wanted Schiller too. How well you remember!

Mrs. M., before R.H.'s death, had had dreams of extending the American Branch's operations by getting an endowment, and possibly inducing Prof. Newbold (Billy) and Dr. Schiller to co-operate in work. She naturally regards this veridical recall, by the control, of a private conversation she had had with Hodgson as very evidential of his survival.

(8) To the same sitter, on a later occasion (March 5th, 1906), the control showed veridical knowledge of R.H.'s *pipes*, of which two had been presents from herself. She asks him at this sitting about the disposal of some of his effects. He mentions books and photographs in a general way, then says:—

I want Tom [his brother] to have my pipes, all except any that my friends wish.

Mrs. M.   Do you remember any special ones?

Yes, I—the one you— [The hand points to *me*, etc.—Mrs. M.]

Mrs. M.   Which?

Meerschaum. [I gave R.H. a meerschaum pipe some years ago.—M.]

Mrs. M.   You do remember! Give it to anyone you would best like to.

.... I want Billy James to have it. Will you give it to him?

Mrs. M.   Do you remember any other special pipe?

You mean with a long stem? Certainly. What about it?

Mrs. M.   Can you recall anything special about it?

What? You mean the one you gave me long ago, some time ago, not the recent one?

Mrs. M.   The last one I gave you.

Last season, last season, yes.

Mrs. M.   A year or two ago, I think it was.

I recall it well. You gave me what I call a briar pipe. [A number of years ago I gave R.H. a briar-root pipe, with rather a long stem, bound round the bowl with silver, but this was not the one of which I was thinking.—M.]

Mrs. M.   The one I mean was an odd-looking pipe.

I know it well, a big large bowl.

Mrs. M.   Wasn't that the meerschaum?

Yes, Billy is to have it. The face one I want Tom to have. I want my brother Tom to have—face on it. The whole thing was a face. I mean the pipe bowl.

[I had seen such a pipe, the whole thing a face, at the Charles Street rooms a short time before. I never remember seeing Mr. Hodgson use it. The pipe of which I was thinking was a carved Swiss pipe which he evidently does not remember.—M.]

(9) Among my own friends in the Harvard faculty who had 'passed over' the most intimate was F. J. Child. Hodgson during life had never met Professor Child. It looks to me like a supernormal reading of my own mental states (for I had often said that the best argument I knew for an immortal life was the existence of a man who deserved one as well as Child did) that a message to me about him should have been spontaneously produced by the R.H.-

control. I had assuredly never mentioned C. to Mrs. Piper, had never before had a message from his spirit, and if I had expressed my feelings about him to the living R.H., that would make the matter only more evidential.

The message through R.H. came to Miss Robbins, June 6th, 1906.

> There is a man named Child passed out suddenly, wants to send his love to William and his wife in the body.

Miss R. Child's wife?

> Yes, in the body. He says . . . I hope L. will understand what I mean. I [*i.e.* R.H.] don't know who L. is. [L. is the initial of the Christian name of Professor Child's widow.—W.J.]

(10) Miss Putnam had been consulted about the disposition of certain matters left undone by Hodgson at the date of his death. At her sitting, much later, these words came out. I copy the record as it stands:—

R.H. Did you get my Christmas present? [A calendar addressed by him to me before his death.—A.C.P.] I heard you in the body say you didn't want them sent. [Mr. Hodgson had left some Christmas cards addressed, but unenclosed. I had expressed unwillingness to mail them unenveloped.—A.C.P.]

(11) Mrs. M., on March 30th, placed a volume in manuscript in the medium's hand. R.H. immediately wrote:—

> Well, well. Isn't that the book I lent you?

Mrs. M. Yes. You loaned it to me at C——.

> I remember, but you have it still!

Mrs. M. I returned it to you.

> Yes, but isn't it the one I loaned you? And the poems I used to love so well, I recall. [The book contained poems copied or composed by Hodgson, and after having been returned to him ere he died, had been taken from among his effects and brought to the sitting by Mrs. M.]

These eleven incidents sound more like deliberate truth-telling, whoever the truth-teller be, than like lucky flukes. On the whole they make on me the impression of being supernormal. I confess that I should at this moment much like to know (although I have no means of knowing) just how all the documents I am exhibiting in this report will strike readers who are either novices in the field, or who consider the subject in general to be pure 'rot' or 'bosh.' It seems to me not impossible that a bosh-philosopher here or there may get a dramatic impression of there being something genuine behind it all. Most of those who remain faithful to the 'bosh'-interpretation would, however, find plenty of comfort if they had the entire mass of records given them to read. Not that I have left things out (I certainly have tried not to!) that would, if printed, discredit the detail of what I cite, but I have left out, by not citing the whole mass of records, so much mere mannerism, so much repetition, hesitation, irrelevance, unintelligibility, so much obvious groping and fishing and plausible covering up of false tracks, so much false pretension to power, and real obedience to suggestion, that the stream of veridicality that runs throughout the whole gets lost as it were in a marsh of feebleness, and the total dramatic effect on the mind may be little more than the word 'humbug.' The really significant items disappear in the total bulk. 'Passwords,' for example, and sealed messages are given in abundance, but can't be found. (I omit these here, as some of them may prove veridical later.) Preposterous Latin sentences are written, *e.g.* "Nebus merica este fecrum"—or what reads like that (April 4th, 1906). Poetry gushes out, but how can one be sure that Mrs. Piper never knew it? The weak talk of the Imperator-band about *time* is reproduced, as where R.H. pretends that he no longer knows what 'seven minutes' mean (May 14th, 1906). Names asked-for can't be given, etc., etc.[24] All this mass of diluting material, which can't be reproduced in abridgment, has its inevitable dramatic effect; and if one tends to *hate* the whole phenomenon any-

---

[24] For instance, on July 2nd, the sitter asks R.H. to name some of his cronies at the Tavern Club. Hodgson gives six names, only five of which belonged to the Tavern Club, and those five were known to the controls already. None of them, I believe, were those asked for, namely, "names of the men he used to play pool with or go swimming with at Nantasket." Yet, as the sitter (Mr. Dorr) writes, "He failed to realize his failure."

how (as I confess that I myself sometimes do) one's judicial verdict inclines accordingly.

Nevertheless, I have to confess also that the more familiar I have become with the records, the less *relative significance* for my mind has all this diluting material tended to assume. The active cause of the communications is on any hypothesis a will of some kind, be it the will of R.H.'s spirit, of lower supernatural intelligences, or of Mrs. Piper's subliminal; and although some of the rubbish may be deliberately willed (certain hesitations, misspellings, etc., in the hope that the sitter may give a clue, or certain repetitions, in order to gain time) yet the major part of it is suggestive of something quite different—as if a will were there, but a will to say something which the machinery fails to bring through. Dramatically, most of this 'bosh' is more suggestive to me of dreaminess and mind-wandering than it is of humbug. Why should a 'will to deceive' prefer to give incorrect names so often, if it can give the true ones to which the incorrect ones so frequently approximate as to suggest that they are meant? True names impress the sitter vastly more. Why should it so multiply false 'passwords' ('Zeivorn,' for example, above, p. 329) and stick to them? It looks to me more like aiming at something definite, and failing of the goal. Sometimes the control gives a message to a distant person quite suddenly, as if for some reason a resistance momentarily gave way and let pass a definite desire to give such a message. Thus on October 17th, "Give my love to Carl Putnam," a name which neither Mrs. Piper nor the sitter knew, and which popped in quite irrelevantly to what preceded or followed. A definite will is also suggested when R.H. sends a message to James Putnam about his "watch stopping." He sends it through several sitters and sticks to it in the face of final denial, as if the phrase covered, however erroneously, some distinct 'intention to recall,' which ought not to be renounced.

That a 'will to personate' is a factor in the Piper-phenomenon, I fully believe, and I believe with unshakeable firmness that this will is able to draw on supernormal sources of information. It can 'tap,' possibly the sitter's memories, possibly those of distant human beings, possibly some cosmic reservoir in which the memories of earth are stored, whether in the shape of 'spirits' or not. If this were the only will concerned in the performance, the phenomenon would be humbug pure and simple, and the minds tapped telepathically in it would play an entirely passive rôle—that is, the telepathic data would be fished out by the personating will, not forced upon it by desires to communicate, acting externally to itself.

But it is possible to complicate the hypothesis. Extraneous 'wills to communicate' may contribute to the results as well as a 'will to personate,' and the two kinds of will may be distinct in entity, though capable of helping each other out. The will to communicate, in our present instance, would be, on the *primâ facie* view of it, the will of Hodgson's surviving spirit; and a natural way of representing the process would be to suppose the spirit to have found that by pressing, so to speak, against 'the light,' it can make fragmentary gleams and flashes of what it wishes to say mix with the rubbish of the trance-talk on this side. The two wills might thus strike up a sort of partnership and stir each other up. It might even be that the 'will to personate' would be inert unless it were aroused to activity by the other will. We might imagine the relation to be analogous to that of two physical bodies, from neither of which, when alone, mechanical, thermal, or electrical effects can proceed, but if the other body be present, and show a difference of 'potential,' action starts up and goes on apace.

Conceptions such as these seem to connect in schematic form the various elements in the case. Its essential factors are done justice to; and, by changing the relative amounts in which the rubbish-making and the truth-telling wills contribute to the resultant, we can draw up a table in which every type of manifestation, from silly planchette-writing up to Rector's best utterances, finds its proper place. Personally, I must say that, although I have to confess that no crucial proof of the presence of the 'will to communicate' seems to me yielded by the Hodgson-control taken alone, and in the sittings to which I have had access, yet the total effect in the way of dramatic probability of the whole mass of similar phenomena on my mind, is to make me believe that a 'will to communicate' *is* in some shape there. I cannot demonstrate it, but practically I am inclined to 'go in' for it, to bet on it and take the risks.

The question then presents itself: In what shape is it most reasonable to suppose that the will thus postulated is actually there? And here again there are various pneumatological possibilities, which must be considered first in abstract form. Thus the will to communicate may come either from permanent entities, or from an entity that arises for the occasion. R.H.'s spirit would be a permanent entity; and inferior parasitic spirits ('daimons,' elementals, or whatever their traditional names might be) would be permanent entities. An improvised entity might be a limited process of consciousness arising in the cosmic reservoir of earth's memories, when certain conditions favoring systematized activity in particular tracts thereof were fulfilled. The conditions in that case might be conceived after the analogy of what happens when two poles of different potential are created in a mass of matter, and cause a current of electricity, or what not, to pass through an intervening tract of space until then the seat of rest.

To consider the case of permanent entities first, there is no *a priori* reason why human spirits and other spiritual beings might not either co-operate at the same time in the same phenomenon, or alternately produce different manifestations. *Primâ facie*, and as a matter of 'dramatic' probability, other intelligences than our own appear on an enormous scale in the historic mass of material which Myers first brought together under the title of Automatisms. The refusal of modern 'enlightenment' to treat 'possession' as an hypothesis to be spoken of as even possible, in spite of the massive human tradition based on concrete experience in its favor, has always seemed to me a curious example of the power of fashion in things scientific. That the demon-theory (not necessarily a devil-theory) will have its innings again is to my mind absolutely certain. One has to be 'scientific' indeed, to be blind and ignorant enough to suspect no such possibility. But if the liability to have one's somnambulistic or automatic processes participated in and interfered with by spiritual entities of a different order ever turn out to be a probable fact, then not only what I have called the will to communicate, but also the will to *personate* may fall outside of the medium's own dream-life. The humbugging may not be chargeable to her all alone, centres of consciousness lower than hers may take part in it, just as higher ones may occasion some of the more inexplicable items of the veridical current in the stream.

The plot of possibilities thus thickens; and it thickens still more when we ask how a will which is dormant or relatively dormant during the intervals may become consciously reanimated as a spirit-personality by the occurrence of the medium's trance. A certain theory of Fechner's helps my own imagination here, so I will state it briefly for my reader's benefit.

Fechner in his *Zend-Avesta*[25] and elsewhere assumes that mental and physical life run parallel, all memory-processes being, according to him, co-ordinated with material processes. If an act of yours is to be consciously remembered hereafter, it must leave traces on the material universe such that when the *traced parts of the said universe systematically enter into activity together* the act is consciously recalled. During your life the traces are mainly in your brain; but after your death, since your brain is gone, they exist in the shape of all the records of your actions which the outer world stores up as the effects, immediate or remote, thereof, the cosmos being in some degree, however slight, made structurally different by every act of ours that takes place in it.[26] Now, just as the air of the same room can be simultaneously used by many different voices for communicating with different pairs of ears, or as the ether of space can carry many simultaneous messages to and from mutually attuned Marconi-stations, so the great continuum of material nature can have certain tracts within it thrown into emphasized activity whenever activity begins in any part or parts of a tract in which the potentiality of such systematic activity inheres. The bodies (including of course the brains) of Hodgson's friends who come as sitters, are naturally parts of the material universe which carry some of the traces of his ancient acts. They function as receiving stations; and Hodgson (at one time of his life at any rate) was inclined to suspect that the sitter himself acts 'psychometrically,' or by his body being what, in the trance-jargon, is called an

---

[25] *Zend-Avesta*, 2nd edition, 1901, §§ XXI and following. Compare also Elwood Worcester: *The Living Word*, New York, Moffatt, Yard & Co., 1908, Part II; and Wm. James, *A Pluralistic Universe*, Longmans, Green & Co., 1909. Lecture IV.

[26] "It is Händel's work, not the body with which he did the work, that pulls us half over London. There is not an action of a muscle in a horse's leg upon a winter's night as it drags a carriage to the Albert Hall but what is in connection with, and part outcome of, the force generated when Händel sat in his room at Gopsall and wrote the Messiah. . . . This is the true Händel who is more a living power among us one hundred and twenty-two years after his death than during the time he was amongst us in the body." Samuel Butler, in the *New Quarterly*, I, 303, March, 1908.

'influence,' in attracting the right spirits and eliciting the right communications from the other side. If, now, the *rest of the system of physical traces* left behind by Hodgson's acts were by some sort of mutual induction throughout its extent, thrown into gear and made to vibrate all at once, by the presence of such human bodies to the medium, we should have a Hodgson-system active in the cosmos again, and the 'conscious aspect' of this vibrating system might be Hodgson's spirit redivivus, and recollecting and willing in a certain momentary way. There seems fair evidence of the reality of psychometry; so that this scheme covers the main phenomena in a vague general way. In particular, it would account for the 'confusion' and 'weakness' that are such prevalent features:— the system of physical traces corresponding to the given spirit would then be only imperfectly aroused. It tallies vaguely with the analogy of energy finding its way from higher to lower levels. The sitter, with his desire to receive, forms, so to speak, a drainage-opening or sink; the medium, with her desire to personate, yields the nearest lying material to be drained off; while the spirit desiring to communicate is shown the way by the current set up, and swells the latter by its own contributions.

It is enough to indicate these various possibilities, which a serious student of this part of nature has to weigh together, and between which his decision must fall. His vote will always be cast (if ever it be cast) by the sense of the dramatic probabilities of nature which the sum total of his experience has begotten in him. *I myself feel as if an external will to communicate were probably there*, that is, I find myself doubting, in consequence of my whole acquaintance with that sphere of phenomena, that Mrs. Piper's dream-life, even equipped with 'telepathic' powers, accounts for all the results found. But if asked whether the will to communicate be Hodgson's, or be some mere spirit-counterfeit of Hodgson, I remain uncertain and await more facts, facts which may not point clearly to a conclusion for fifty or a hundred years.

My report has been too rambling in form, and has suffered in cordiality of tone from having to confine itself to the face-value of the Hodgson-material taken alone. The content of that material is no more veridical than is a lot of earlier Piper-material, especially in the days of the old Phinuit control.[27] And it is, as I began by saying, vastly more leaky and susceptible of naturalistic explanation than is any body of Piper-material recorded before. Had I been reviewing the entire Piper-phenomenon, instead of this small section of it, my tone would probably give much less umbrage to some of its spiritistic friends who are also valued friends of mine.

[27] See, in proof of this assertion, Hodgson's and Hyslop's previous reports.

~ 38 ~

The Confidences of a "Psychical Researcher" (1909)

The late Professor Henry Sidgwick was celebrated for the rare mixture of ardor and critical judgment which his character exhibited. The liberal heart which he possessed had to work with an intellect which acted destructively on almost every particular object of belief that was offered to its acceptance. A quarter of a century ago, scandalized by the chaotic state of opinion regarding the phenomena now called by the rather ridiculous name of 'psychic'—phenomena of which the supply reported seems inexhaustible, but which scientifically trained minds mostly refuse to look at—he established, along with Professor Barrett, Frederic Myers and Edmund Gurney, the Society for Psychical Research. These men hoped that if the material were treated rigorously and, as far as possible, experimentally, objective truth would be elicited, and the subject rescued from sentimentalism on the one side and dogmatizing ignorance on the other. Like all founders, Sidgwick hoped for a certain promptitude of result; and I heard him say, the year before his death, that if anyone had told him at the outset that after twenty years he would be in the same identical state of doubt and balance that he started with, he would have deemed the prophecy incredible. It appeared impossible that that amount of handling evidence should bring so little finality of decision.

My own experience has been similar to Sidgwick's. For twenty-five years I have been in touch with the literature of psychical research, and have had acquaintance with numerous 'researchers.' I have also spent a good many hours (though far fewer than I ought to have spent) in witnessing (or trying to witness) phenomena. Yet I am theoretically no 'further' than I was at the beginning; and I confess that at times I have been tempted to believe that the creator has eternally intended this department of nature to remain *baffling*, to prompt our curiosities and hopes and suspicions all in equal measure, so that although ghosts, and clairvoyances, and raps and messages from spirits, are always seeming to exist and can never be fully explained away, they also can never be susceptible of full corroboration.

The peculiarity of the case is just that there are so many sources of possible deception in most of the observations, that the whole lot of them *may* be worthless, and yet that in comparatively few cases can aught more fatal than this vague general possibility of error be pleaded against the record. Science meanwhile needs something more than bare possibilities to build upon; so your genuinely scientific inquirer—I don't mean your ignoramus 'scientist'—has to remain unsatisfied. It is hard to believe, however, that the creator has really put any big array of phenomena into the world merely to defy and mock our scientific tendencies; so my deeper belief is that we psychical researchers have been too precipitate with our hopes, and that we must expect to mark progress not by quarter-centuries but by half-centuries or whole centuries.

I am strengthened in this belief by my impression that just at this moment a faint but distinct step forward is being taken by competent opinion in these matters. 'Physical phenomena' (movements of matter without contact, lights, hands and faces 'materialized,' etc.) have been one of the most baffling regions of the general field (or perhaps one of the least baffling *prima facie*, so certain and great has been the part played by fraud in their production); yet even here the balance of testimony seems slowly to be inclining towards admitting the supernaturalist view. Eusapia Paladino, the neapolitan medium, has been under observation for twenty years or more. Schiaparelli, the astronomer, and Lombroso were the first scientific men to be converted by her performances. Since then innumerable men of scientific standing have seen her, including many 'psychic' experts. Everyone agrees that she cheats in the most barefaced manner whenever she gets an opportunity. The Cambridge experts, with the Sidgwicks and Richard Hodgson at their head, rejected her *in toto* on that account. Yet her credit has steadily risen, and now her last converts are the eminent psychiatrist Morselli, the eminent physiologist Bottazzi, and our own psychical researcher Carrington, whose book on *The Physical Phenomena of Spiritualism* (*against* them rather!) makes his conquest strategically important. If Mr. Podmore, hitherto the prosecuting attorney of the S.P.R. so far as physical phenomena are concerned, becomes converted also, we may indeed sit up and look around us. Getting a good health-bill from 'Science,' Eusapia will then throw retrospective credit on Home and Stainton Moses, Florence Cook (Prof. Crookes's medium), and all similar wonder-workers. The balance of *presumptions* will be changed in favor of genuineness being possible at least, in all reports of this particularly crass and low type of supernatural phenomenon.

Not long after Darwin's *Origin of Species* appeared I was studying with that excellent anatomist and man, Jeffries Wyman, at Harvard. He was a convert, yet so far a half-hesitating one, to Darwin's views; but I heard him make a remark that applies well to the subject I now write about. When, he said, a theory gets propounded over and over again, coming up afresh after each time orthodox criticism has buried it, and each time seeming solider and harder to abolish, you may be sure that there is truth in it. Oken and Lamarck and Chambers had been triumphantly despatched and buried, but here was Darwin making the very same heresy seem only more plausible. How often has 'Science' killed off all spook-philosophy, and laid ghosts and raps and 'telepathy' away underground as so much popular delusion. Yet never before were these things offered us so voluminously, and never in such authentic-seeming shape or with such good credentials. The tide seems steadily to be rising, in spite of all the expedients of scientific orthodoxy. It is hard not to suspect that here may be something different from a mere chapter in human gullibility. It may be a genuine realm of natural phenomena.

Falsus in uno, falsus in omnibus, once a cheat, always a cheat, such has been the motto of the english psychical researchers in dealing with mediums. I am disposed to think that as a matter of policy, it has been wise. Tactically, it is far better to believe much too little than a little too much; and the exceptional credit attaching to the row of volumes of the S.P.R.'s *Proceedings*, is due to the fixed intention of the editors to proceed very slowly. Better a little belief tied fast, better a small investment *salted down*, than a mass of comparative insecurity.

But however wise as a policy the S.P.R.'s maxim may have been, as a test of truth I believe it to be almost irrelevant. In most things human the accusation of deliberate fraud and falsehood is grossly superficial. Man's character is too sophistically mixed for the alternative of 'honest or dishonest' to be a sharp one. Scientific men themselves will cheat—at public lectures—rather than let experiments obey their well-known tendency towards failure. I have heard of a lecturer on physics, who had taken over the apparatus of the previous incumbent, consulting him about a certain machine intended to show that however the peripheral parts of it might be agitated, its 'centre of gravity' remained immoveable. "It *will* wobble," he complained. "Well," said the predecessor, apologetically, "to tell the truth, whenever *I* used that machine I found it advisable to *drive a nail* through the centre of gravity." I once saw a distinguished physiologist, now dead, cheat most shamelessly at a public lecture, at the expense of a poor rabbit, and all for the sake of being able to make a cheap joke about its being an 'american rabbit'—for no other, he said, could survive such a wound as he pretended to have given it.

To compare small men with great, I have myself cheated shamelessly. In the early days of the Sanders Theatre at Harvard, I once had charge of a heart, on the physiology of which Prof. Newell Martin was giving a popular lecture. This heart, which belonged to a turtle, supported an index-straw which threw a moving shadow, greatly enlarged, upon the screen, while the heart pulsated. When certain nerves were stimulated, the lecturer said, the heart would act in certain ways which he described. But the poor heart was too far gone, and although it stopped duly when the nerve of arrest was excited, that was the final end of its life's tether. Presiding over the performance, I was terrified at the fiasco, and found myself suddenly acting like one of those military geniuses who on the field of battle convert disaster into victory. There was no time for deliberation; so, with my forefinger under a part of the straw that cast no shadow, I found myself impulsively and automatically imitating the rhythmical movements which my colleague had prophecied the heart would undergo. I kept the experiment from failing; and not only saved my colleague (and the turtle) from a humiliation that but for my presence of mind would have been their lot, but I established in the audience the true view of the subject. The lecturer was stating this; and the misconduct of one half-dead specimen of heart ought not to destroy the impression of his words. "There is no worse lie than a truth misunderstood," is a maxim which I have heard ascribed to a former venerated President of Harvard. The heart's failure would have been misunderstood by the audience and given the lie to the lecturer. It was hard enough to make them understand the subject anyhow; so that even now as I write in cool blood I am tempted to think that I acted quite correctly. I was acting for the *larger* truth at any rate, however automatically; and my sense of this was probably what prevented the more pedantic and literal part of my conscience from checking the action of my sympathetic finger. To this day the memory of that critical emergency has made me feel charitable towards all mediums who make phenomena come in one way when they won't come easily in another. On the principles of the S.P.R., my conduct on that one occasion ought to discredit everything I ever do, everything for example, I may write in this article,—a manifestly unjust conclusion.

Fraud, conscious or unconscious, seems ubiquitous throughout the range of physical phenomena of spiritism, and false pretense, prevarication and fishing for clues are ubiquitous in the mental manifestations of mediums. If it be not everywhere fraud simulating reality, one is tempted to say, then the reality (if any reality there be) has the bad luck of being fated everywhere to simulate fraud. The suggestion of humbug seldom stops, and mixes itself with the best manifestations. Mrs. Piper's control, 'Rector,' is a most impressive personage, who discerns in an extraordinary degree his sitter's inner needs, and is capable of giving elevated counsel to fastidious and critical minds. Yet in many respects he is an arrant humbug—such he seems to me at least—pretending to a knowledge and power to which he has no title, nonplussed by contradiction, yielding to suggestion, and covering his tracks with plausible excuses. Now the non-'researching' mind looks upon such phenomena simply according to their face-pretension, and never thinks of asking what they may signify below the surface. Since they profess for the most part to be revealers of spirit-life, it is either as being absolutely that, or as being absolute frauds, that they are judged. The result is an inconceivably shallow state of public opinion on the subject. One set of persons, emotionally touched at hearing the names of their loved ones given, and consoled by assurances that they are 'happy,' accept the revelation, and consider spiritualism 'beautiful.' More hard-headed subjects, disgusted by the revelation's contemptible contents, outraged by the fraud, and prejudiced beforehand against all 'spirits,' high or low, avert their minds from what they call such 'rot' or 'bosh' entirely. Thus do two opposite sentimentalisms divide opinion between them! A good expression of the 'scientific' state of mind occurs in Huxley's *Life and Letters*:

"I regret," he writes, "that I am unable to accept the invitation of the Committee of the Dialectical Society . . . . I take no interest in the subject. The only case of 'Spiritualism' I have ever had the opportunity of examining into for myself, was as gross an imposture as ever came under my notice. But supposing the phenomena to be genuine—they do not interest me. If anybody would endow me with the faculty of listening to the chatter of old women and curates in the nearest provincial town, I should decline the privilege, having better things to do. And if the folk in the spiritual world do not talk more wisely and sensibly than their friends report them to do, I put them in the same category. The only good that I can see in the demonstration of the truth of 'Spiritualism' is to furnish an additional argument against suicide. Better live a crossing-sweeper than die and be made to talk twaddle by a 'medium' hired at a guinea a *séance*."[1]

Obviously the mind of the excellent Huxley has here but two whole-souled categories, namely revelation or imposture, to apperceive the case by. Sentimental reasons bar revelation out, for the messages, he thinks, are not romantic enough for that; fraud exists anyhow; therefore the whole thing is nothing but imposture. —The odd point is that so few of those who talk in this way realize that they and the spiritists are using the same major premise and differing only in the minor. The major premise is: "Any spirit-revelation must be romantic." The minor of the spiritist is: "this *is* romantic"; that of the Huxleyan is: "this is dingy twaddle"— whence their opposite conclusions!

Meanwhile the first thing that anyone learns who attends seriously to these phenomena is that their causation is far too complex for our feelings about what is or is not romantic enough to be

---

[1] T. H. Huxley, *Life and Letters*, I, 240.

spiritual to throw any light upon it. The causal factors must be carefully distinguished and traced through series, from their simplest to their strongest forms, before we can begin to understand the various resultants in which they issue. Myers and Gurney began this work, the one by his serial study of the various sorts of 'automatism,' sensory and motor, the other by his experimental proofs that a split-off consciousness may abide after a post-hypnotic suggestion has been given. Here we have subjective factors; but are not transsubjective or objective forces also at work? Veridical messages, apparitions, movements without contact, seem *prima facie* to be such. It was a good stroke on Gurney's part to construct a theory of apparitions which brought the subjective and the objective factors into harmonious co-operation. I doubt whether this telepathic theory of Gurney's will hold along the whole line of apparitions to which he applied it, but it is unquestionable that some theory of that mixed type is required for the explanation of all mediumistic phenomena; and that when all the psychological factors and elements involved have been told off—and they are many—the question still forces itself upon us: Are these all, or are there indications of any residual forces acting on the subject from beyond, or of any 'metapsychic' faculty (to use Richet's useful term) exerted by him? This is the problem that requires real expertness, and this is where the simple sentimentalisms of the spiritist and scientist leave us in the lurch completely.

'Psychics' form indeed a special branch of education, in which experts are only gradually becoming developed. The phenomena are as massive and wide-spread as is anything in Nature, and the study of them is as tedious, repellent and undignified. To reject it for its unromantic character is like rejecting bacteriology because *penicillium glaucum* grows on horse-dung and *bacterium termo* lives in putrefaction. Scientific men have long ago ceased to think of the dignity of the materials they work in. When imposture has been checked-off as far as possible, when chance coincidence has been allowed for, when opportunities for normal knowledge on the part of the subject have been noted, and skill in 'fishing' and following clues unwittingly furnished by the voice or face of bystanders have been counted in, those who have the fullest acquaintance with the phenomena admit that in good mediums *there is a residuum of knowledge displayed* that can only be called supernormal: the medium taps some source of information not open to ordinary people. Myers used the word 'telepathy' to indicate that the sitter's own thoughts or feelings may be thus directly tapped. Mrs. Sidgwick has suggested that if living minds can be thus tapped telepathically, so possibly may the minds of spirits be similarly tapped—if spirits there be. On this view we should have one distinct theory of the performances of a typical test-medium. They would be all originally due to an odd *tendency to personate,* found in her dream-life as it expresses itself in trance. [Most of us reveal such a tendency whenever we handle a 'ouija-board' or a 'planchet,' or let ourselves write automatically with a pencil.] The result is a 'control,' who purports to be speaking; and all the resources of the automatist, including his or her trance-faculty of telepathy, are called into play in building this fictitious personage out plausibly. On such a view of the control, the medium's *will to personate* runs the whole show; and if spirits be involved in it at all, they are passive beings, stray bits of whose memory she is able to seize and use for her purposes, without the spirit being any more aware of it than the sitter is aware of it when his own mind is similarly tapped.

This is one possible way of interpreting a certain type of psychical phenomenon. It uses psychological as well as 'spiritual' factors, and quite obviously it throws open for us far more questions than it answers, questions about our subconscious constitution and its curious tendency to humbug, about the telepathic faculty, and about the possibility of an existent spirit-world.

I do not instance this theory to defend it, but simply to show what complicated hypotheses one is inevitably led to consider, the moment one looks at the facts in their complexity and turns one's back on the *naïve* alternative of 'revelation or imposture,' which is as far as either spiritist thought or ordinary scientist thought goes. The phenomena are endlessly complex in their factors, and they are so little understood as yet that offhand judgments, whether of 'spirits' or of 'bosh' are the one as silly as the other. When we complicate the subject still farther by considering what connexion such things as rappings, apparitions, poltergeists, spirit-photographs and materializations may have with it, the 'bosh' end of the scale gets heavily loaded, it is true, but your genuine inquirer still is loathe to give up. He lets the data collect, and bides his time. He believes that 'bosh' is no more an ultimate element in

Nature, or a really explanatory category in human life than 'dirt' is in chemistry. Every kind of 'bosh' has its own factors and laws; and patient study will bring them definitely to light.

The only way to rescue the 'pure bosh' view of the matter is one which has sometimes appealed to my own fancy but which I imagine few readers will seriously adopt. If, namely, one takes the theory of evolution radically, one ought to apply it not only to the rock-strata, the animals and the plants, but to the stars, to the chemical elements, and to the laws of nature. There must have been a far-off antiquity, one is then tempted to suppose, when things were really chaotic. Little by little, out of all the haphazard possibilities of that time, a few connected things and habits arose, and the rudiments of regular performance began. Every variation in the way of law and order added itself to this nucleus, which inevitably grew more considerable as history went on; while the aberrant and inconstant variations, not being similarly preserved, disappeared from being, wandered off as unrelated vagrants, or else remained so imperfectly connected with the part of the world that had grown regular, as only to manifest their existence by occasional lawless intrusions, like those which 'psychic' phenomena now make into our scientifically organized world. On such a view, these phenomena ought to remain 'pure bosh' forever, that is, they ought to be forever intractable to intellectual methods, because they should not yet be organized enough in themselves to follow any laws. Wisps and shreds of the original chaos, they would be connected enough with the cosmos to affect its periphery every now and then, as by a momentary whiff or touch or gleam, but not enough ever to be followed up and hunted down and bagged. Their relation to the cosmos would be tangential solely.

Lookt at dramatically, most occult phenomena make just this sort of impression. They are inwardly as incoherent as they are outwardly wayward and fitful. If they express anything, it is pure 'bosh,' pure discontinuity, accident, and disturbance, with no law apparent but to interrupt, and no purpose but to baffle. They seem like stray vestiges of that primordial irrationality, from which all our rationalities have been evolved.

To settle dogmatically into this bosh-view would save labor, but it would go against too many intellectual prepossessions to be adopted save as a last resort of despair. Your psychical researcher therefore bates no jot of hope, and has faith that when we get our data numerous enough, some sort of rational treatment of them will succeed.

When I hear good people say (as they often say, not without show of reason), that dabbling in such phenomena reduces us to a sort of jelly, disintegrates the critical faculties, liquefies the character, and makes of one a *gobe-mouche* generally, I console myself by thinking of my friends Frederic Myers and Richard Hodgson. These men lived exclusively for psychical research, and it converted both to spiritism. Hodgson would have been a man among men anywhere; but I doubt whether under any other baptism he would have been that happy, sober and righteous form of energy which his face proclaimed him in his later years, when heart and head alike were wholly satisfied by his occupation. Myers's character also grew stronger in every particular for his devotion to the same inquiries. Brought up on literature and sentiment, something of a courtier, passionate, disdainful, and impatient naturally, he was made over again from the day when he took up psychical research seriously. He became learned in science, circumspect, democratic in sympathy, endlessly patient, and above all, happy. The fortitude of his last hours touched the heroic, so completely were the atrocious sufferings of his body cast into insignificance by his interest in the cause he lived for. When a man's pursuit gradually makes his face shine and grow handsome, you may be sure it is a worthy one. Both Hodgson and Myers kept growing ever handsomer and stronger-looking.

Such personal examples will convert no one, and of course they ought not to. Nor do I seek at all in this article to convert anyone to my belief that psychical research is an important branch of science. To do that, I should have to quote evidence; and those for whom the volumes of S.P.R. *Proceedings* already publisht count for nothing, would remain in their dogmatic slumber, though one rose from the dead. No, not to convert readers, but simply to *put my own state of mind upon record publicly* is the purpose of my present writing. Someone said to me a short time ago that after my twenty-five years of dabbling in 'Psychics,' it would be rather shameful were I unable to state any definite conclusions whatever as a consequence. I had to agree; so I now proceed to take up the challenge and express such convictions as have been engendered in me by that length of experience, be the same true or false ones. I may be dooming myself to the pit in the eyes of better-judging posterity; I may be raising myself to honour; I am willing to take the risk, for what I shall write is *my* truth, as I now see it.

I began this article by confessing myself baffled. I *am* baffled, as to spirit-return, and as to many other special problems. I am also constantly baffled as to what to think of this or that particular story, for the sources of error in any one observation are seldom fully knowable. But weak sticks make strong faggots; and when the stories fall into consistent sorts that point each in a definite direction, one gets a sense of being in presence of genuinely natural types of phenomena. As to there being such real natural types of phenomena ignored by orthodox science, I am not baffled at all, for I am fully convinced of it. One cannot get demonstrative proof here. One has to follow one's personal sense, which of course is liable to err, of the dramatic probabilities of nature. Our critics here obey their sense of dramatic probability as much as we do. Take 'raps' for example, and the whole business of objects moving without contact. 'Nature,' thinks the scientific man, is not so unutterably silly. The cabinet, the darkness, the tying, suggest a sort of human rat-hole life exclusively and 'swindling' is for him the dramatically sufficient explanation. It probably is, in an indefinite majority of instances; yet it is to me dramatically improbable that the swindling should not have accreted round some originally genuine nucleus. If we look at human imposture as a historic phenomenon, we find it always imitative. One swindler imitates a previous swindler, but the first swindler of that kind imitated someone who was honest. You can no more create an absolutely new trick than you can create a new word without any previous basis.—You don't know how to go about it. Try, reader, yourself, to invent an unprecedented kind of 'physical phenomenon of spiritualism.' When *I* try, I find myself mentally turning over the regular medium-stock and thinking how I might improve some item. This being the dramatically probable human way, I think differently of the whole type taken collectively, from the way in which I may think of the single instance. I find myself believing that there is 'something in' these never ending reports of physical phenomena, although I haven't yet the least positive notion of the something. It becomes to my mind simply a very worthy problem for investigation. Either I or the scientist is of course a fool, with our opposite views of probability here; and I only wish he might feel the liability, as cordially as I do, to pertain to both of us.

I fear I look on Nature generally with more charitable eyes than his, though perhaps he would pause if he realized as I do, how vast the fraudulency is which in consistency he must attribute to her. Nature is brutal enough, Heaven knows; but no one yet has held her non-human side to be *dishonest*, and even in the human sphere deliberate deceit is far rarer than the 'classic' intellect, with its few and rigid categories, was ready to acknowledge. There is a hazy penumbra in us all where lying and delusion meet, where passion rules beliefs as well as conduct, and where the term 'scoundrel' does not clear up everything to the depths as it did for our fore-fathers. The first automatic writing I ever saw was forty years ago. I unhesitatingly thought of it as deceit, although it contained vague elements of supernormal knowledge. Since then I have come to see in automatic writing one example of a department of human activity as vast as it is enigmatic. Every sort of person is liable to it, or to something equivalent to it; and whoever encourages it in himself finds himself personating someone else, either signing what he writes by a fictitious name or spelling out, by ouija-board or table-tips, messages from the departed. Our subconscious region seems, as a rule, to be dominated either by a crazy 'will to make-believe,' or by some curious external force impelling us to per-sonation. The first difference between the psychical researcher and the inexpert person is that the former realizes the commonness and typicality of the phenomenon here, while the latter, less in-formed, thinks it so rare as to be unworthy of attention. *I wish to go on record for the commonness.*

The next thing I wish to go on record for is *the presence*, in the midst of all the humbug, *of really supernormal knowledge.* By this I mean knowledge that cannot be traced to the ordinary sources of information—the senses namely—of the automatist. In really strong mediums this knowledge seems to be abundant, though it is usually spotty, capricious and unconnected. Really strong me-diums are rarities; but when one starts with them and works down-wards into less brilliant regions of the automatic life, one tends to interpret many slight but odd coincidences with truth, as possibly rudimentary forms of this kind of knowledge.

What is one to think of this queer chapter in human nature? It is odd enough on any view. If all it means is a preposterous and inferior monkey-like tendency to forge messages, systematically embedded in the soul of all of us, it is weird; and weirder still that it should then own all this supernormal information. If on the other hand the supernormal information be the key to the phenomenon, it ought to be superior; and then how ought we to account for the 'wicked partner,' and for the undeniable mendacity and inferiority of so much of the performance? We are thrown, for our conclusions, upon our instinctive sense of the dramatic probabilities of nature. My own dramatic sense tends instinctively to picture the situation as an interaction between slumbering faculties in the automatist's mind and a cosmic environment of *other consciousness* of some sort which is able to work upon them. If there were in the universe a lot of diffuse soul-stuff, unable of itself to get into consistent personal form, or to take permanent possession of an organism, yet always craving to do so, it might get its head into the air, parasitically so to speak, by profiting by weak spots in the armor of human minds, and slipping in and stirring up there the sleeping tendency to personate. It would induce habits in the subconscious region of the mind it used thus, and would seek above all things to prolong its social opportunities by making itself agreeable and plausible. It would drag stray scraps of truth with it from the wider environment, but would betray its mental inferiority by knowing little how to weave them into any important or significant story.

This, I say, is the dramatic view which my mind spontaneously takes, and it has the advantage of falling into line with ancient human traditions. The views of others are just as dramatic, *for the phenomenon is actuated by will of some sort anyhow,* and wills give rise to dramas. The spiritist view, as held by Messrs. Hyslop and Hodgson, sees a 'will to communicate,' struggling through inconceivable layers of obstruction in the conditions. I have heard Hodgson liken the difficulties to those of two persons who on earth should have only dead-drunk servants to use as their messengers. The scientist, for his part, sees a 'will to deceive,' watching its chance in all of us, and able (possibly?) to use 'telepathy' in its service.

Which kind of will, and how many kinds of will are most inherently probable? Who can say with certainty? The only certainty is that the phenomena are enormously complex, especially if one includes in them such intellectual flights of mediumship as Swedenborg's, and if one tries in any way to work the physical phenomena in. That is why I personally am as yet neither a convinced believer in parasitic demons, nor a spiritist, nor a scientist, but still remain a psychical researcher waiting for more facts before concluding.

Out of my experience, such as it is (and it is limited enough) one fixed conclusion dogmatically emerges, and that is this, that we with our lives are like islands in the sea, or like trees in the forest. The maple and the pine may whisper to each other with their leaves, and Conanicut and Newport hear each other's fog-horns. But the trees also commingle their roots in the darkness underground, and the islands also hang together through the ocean's bottom. Just so there is a continuum of cosmic consciousness, against which our individuality builds but accidental fences, and into which our several minds plunge as into a mother-sea or reservoir. Our 'normal' consciousness is circumscribed for adaptation to our external earthly environment, but the fence is weak in spots, and fitful influences from beyond leak in, showing the otherwise unverifiable common connexion. Not only psychic research, but metaphysical philosophy and speculative biology are led in their own ways to look with favor on some such 'panpsychic' view of the universe as this. Assuming this common reservoir of consciousness to exist, this bank upon which we all draw, and in which so many of earth's memories must in some way be stored, or mediums would not get at them as they do, the question is, What is its own structure? What is its inner topography? This question, first squarely formulated by Myers, deserves to be called 'Myers's problem' by scientific men hereafter. What are the conditions of individuation or insulation in this mother-sea? To what tracts, to what active systems functioning separately in it, do personalities correspond? Are individual 'spirits' constituted there? How numerous, and of how many hierarchic orders may these then be? How permanent? How transient? And how confluent with one another may they become?

What again, are the relations between the cosmic consciousness and matter? Are there subtler forms of matter which upon occasion may enter into functional connexion with the individuations in the psychic sea, and then, and then only, show themselves?—So that our ordinary human experience, on its material as well as on its mental side, would appear to be only an extract from the larger psycho-physical world?

Vast indeed, and difficult is the inquirer's prospect here, and the most significant data for his purpose will probably be just these dingy little mediumistic facts which the Huxleyan minds of our time find so unworthy of their attention. But when was not the science of the future stirred to its conquering activities by the little rebellious exceptions to the science of the present? Hardly, as yet, has the surface of the facts called 'psychic' begun to be scratched for scientific purposes. It is through following these facts, I am persuaded, that the greatest scientific conquests of the coming generation will be achieved. *Kühn ist das Mühen, herrlich der Lohn!*

A Possible Case of Projections
of the Double (1909)

The following case lacks direct personal corroboration from the two witnesses, so that there is only hearsay evidence for the fact of the apparition. But the type of phenomenon is so rare and, if not to be explained by accidental coincidence, so important, that all reported cases of it should be recorded.

In the present case the "agent" is a colleague of mine; an able and respected professor in Harvard University. He originally told me the story shortly after it happened in 18——. The present account, written at my request in 1903, tallies exactly with my memory of that earlier story. "A" at that time was unwilling to give me her version. She is now dead, and of course the narrative is in so far defective.

Cambridge, April 16, 1903.

My dear Dr. James:

I recall exactly all the details of the matter which you wish me to write about, but I cannot be sure whether the thing occurred in the latter part of 1883 or the first part of 1884. At this time A and I were seeing each other very frequently, and we were interested, among other things, in that book by Sinett on Esoteric Buddhism. We talked a good deal about it, and about the astral body, but neither ever made any proposal to the other to try any experiments in that line.

One evening, about 9:45 o'clock, or, perhaps, nearer 10, when I had been thinking over that subject as I sat alone in my room, I resolved to try whether I could project my astral body to the presence of A. I did not at all know what the process was, but I opened my window, which looked towards A's house [tho that was half a mile away and behind a hill] and sat down in a chair and tried as hard as I could to wish myself into the presence of A. There was no light in my room. I sat there in that state of wishing for about ten minutes. Nothing abnormal in the way of feelings happened to me.

Next day I met A, who said something to this effect. [I mean that I cannot give the exact words.]

"Last night about ten o'clock I was in the dining room at supper with B. Suddenly I thought I saw you looking in thru the crack of the door at the end of the room, towards which I was looking. I said to B.: 'There is Blank, looking thru the crack of the door!' B., whose back was towards the door, said: 'He can't be there; he would come right in.' However, I got up and looked in the outer room, but there was nobody there. Now, what were you doing last night at that time?"

This was what A told me and I then explained what I had been doing.

You see, of course, that the double evidence [I mean, A's and B's] might make this story pretty well founded, but it must be left entirely independent on my account, for there are good reasons why neither A nor B can be appealed to.

Notes

Appendixes

A Note on the Editorial Method

The Text of
Essays in Psychical Research

Apparatus

Index

Notes

The American Society for Psychical Research was organized at a series of meetings held in Boston on September 23, 1884, December 18, 1884, and January 8, 1885. The spiritualist movement in America was then in its prime, led by hundreds of mediums apparently gifted with psychic powers and claiming millions of believers. Reports of mysterious phenomena were commonplace: the dead sent messages and wrote books, objects moved with no visible causes, ghosts materialized sufficiently to distribute flowers and be photographed. Few observers doubted that most mediums were jugglers and their manifestations fraudulent, but who could be sure that careful and systematic study would not uncover some genuine marvels? One of the purposes of the Society was to record, investigate, and, in most cases, debunk the reports pouring in from all sides, although many of its members at least hoped, if they did not believe, that the fraudulent mass was hiding something mysterious and important.

The first membership list records some 250 full members and associates, many of them eminent in the intellectual life of the time. Simon Newcomb, a mathematician and astronomer, served as the first president. The five vice-presidents were Granville Stanley Hall, a psychologist then at Johns Hopkins University; George Stuart Fullerton, a philosopher at the University of Pennsylvania; Edward Charles Pickering, an astronomer at the Harvard College Observatory; and Henry Pickering Bowditch and Charles Sedgwick Minot, both of the Harvard Medical School. James took an active part in the founding of the Society and was elected to the council for a term of three years. He was later reelected to serve until 1891. The list of officers for February 1889 shows James as one of four vice-presidents, together with Fullerton, Josiah Royce, and Charles Robert Cross, a physicist at the Massachusetts Institute of Technology. Samuel Pierpont Langley of the Smithsonian Institution was then serving as president. Thus, James was in good company and his adherence was neither unusual nor damaging to his reputation. In its early years, the Society was more likely to be attacked by spiritualists than by academics. James differs from his colleagues only by his persistence. Most of the others left the Society within a few years, while James remained faithful to the end of his life. And by the late 1890s, James frequently found himself defending the intellectual respectability of psychical research.

While spiritualism represents the more spectacular and notorious interest of the Society, most of its efforts were devoted to other subjects. The English society upon which the American one was being modeled was studying thought-transference, and the Americans followed suit. At the meeting of December 18, 1884, James and Bowditch were appointed a committee on work to draw up a plan for the investigations of the Society (see Circular No. 2 in the present volume). They pointed out that in England there were permanent committees on Thought-Transference, Hypnotism, Apparitions and Haunted Houses, Physical Phenomena (Spiritualism), and Reichenbach's Experiments. The American Society adopted this plan, but the bulk of its *Proceedings* was devoted to thought-transference. To January 1890 when the Society was dissolved, four numbers of *Proceedings* were published, making up the one volume.

The minutes of the Society as published in the *Proceedings* provide glimpses of James's day-to-day involvement with psychical research. In the report of the Committee on Thought-Transference given on June 4, 1885, James appears as one of numerous contributors of experiments in thought-transference (p. 8). However, it is not possible to establish which of the experiments are James's since the individual experimenters are identified only by number. James's share can be identified in the report of June 1886 (p. 109). He was involved in three series of experiments with negative results. An agent drew one of ten geometrical shapes which a percipient tried to guess. There was one correct guess in twenty tries with James as agent; there were no correct guesses in ten tries with James as percipient. At the meeting of June 4, 1885, James reported that "the committee on mediumistic phenomena had made a number of visits to mediums, but had nothing of importance to report" (p. 49). On October 6 of the same year, he commented on an informal report on thought-transference and discussed phantasms of the dead (p. 62). On January 12, 1886, he reported for the Committee on Hypnotism. In the presence of the audience he hypnotized Gouverneur M. Carnochan, "causing him to exhibit various phenomena characteristic of this condition" (p. 62). On June 15 he again reported for the Committee on Hypnotism (see *Essays in Psychology*, WORKS) and for the Committee on Mediumistic Phenomena (reprinted in the present volume) (p. 133). On January 11, 1887, he discussed muscle-reading and read a paper on "Sensations from Amputated Limbs" (see *Essays in Psychology*, WORKS) (p. 134).

A more informative account of the meeting of January 12, 1886, is available in *Science*, 7 (January 29, 1886), 91–92:

> The meeting closed with some remarkable experiments by Dr. William James, who mesmerized Mr. Carnegie [Carnochan], one of the committee on hypnotism. While the latter was in the trance, Dr. James told him he could not see the chairman, with the effect of rendering him blind to that officer. Placing a prism in front of Mr. Carnegie's eye, so as to produce two images on his retina, Dr. James asked what he saw. The answer showed that he saw only one chairman, and therefore remained blind to one of the two images. This is believed to be quite a new fact in hypnotism. To show that although the subject adopts any suggestions made to him as to his sensory images, no matter how false the suggestion, yet he has extreme delicacy of perception, the following experiment was made: the subject was made to see an imaginary photograph of President Cleveland on a blank sheet of paper; the photograph was made, in the subject's vision, to leave the sheet of paper and travel round the room; behind Mr. Carnegie's back the paper was turned upside down; the photograph was now made to seem to Mr. Carnegie to return to the paper, which was handed to him; he immediately turned it about to its previous position. Thus an hypnotic subject can be made to believe in a sensation which

is unreal, and yet can distinguish between two ends of a blank piece of paper.

The meeting of May 12, 1887, marked the professional organization of the Society when Richard Hodgson became its paid secretary. James asked him questions about the methods of research in England (pp. 134–135). On January 10, 1888, James reported on automatic writing (reprinted in the present volume). The *Proceedings* also show that James received several letters reporting presentiments, which he handed over to the Committee on Phantasms and Presentiments (pp. 373–374, 433–434). There is in addition James's statement in the case of Franz Hugo Krebs (Appendix V in the present volume).

The meeting held on December 12, 1888, was reported by the *Boston Daily Globe* in its issue of December 13, under the headline "Gunning for Ghosts. Poor Luck of Psychical Research Society. Don't Quite Know What to Make of Spiritualistic Phenomena. But Have Some Cases of Thought Transference and Presentiments." James's role is summarized as follows:

> Professor James then said that the laziness of the members of the society was the reason why so few satisfactory results had been obtained. He called on the members to brace up in their contributions of time and money, saying "We have important work to perform if we can only keep alive." Professor James said that Dr. Hodgson, the secretary, would be away from Boston a great deal of the time next year, investigating cases in other cities, and thus would require considerable money, which he hoped would be forthcoming.

The spiritualist *Banner of Light*, 64 (December 22, 1888), 4, with much glee proclaimed "Poor Luck of the Psychical Research Society." After all, what else but failure can be expected from men who have never permitted believing spiritualists to take a leading part in their work? In reference to James's remarks, the *Banner* comments:

> We surmise that the Professor is mistaken in this as in other of his conclusions; that the reason of so few unsatisfactory results is that the Society of which he is a distinguished, active member, is on the wrong track: It is searching for fraud, and finds so little that it has scarcely any success to report. It makes the most of what it ferrets out, but that is so infinitesimally small it has to go to outsiders for a supply, and accepts even that grudgingly; but rejects all that savors of sustaining the truth. What different results can be expected from such a course, since proofs of the truths of Spiritualism, and of the genuineness of its phenomena, "hang about us like a cloud"?

The Society will continue to fail until it "gets down from its high stilts and works out its mission with the people and for the people, rather than for a class of self-inflationists."

Information about James's work on the various committees of the Society is available primarily in James's own published reports. An exception is the Committee on Experimental Psychology, successor of the Committee on Reichenbach's Experiments, the minutes of which are preserved in the archives of the present American Society for Psychical Research in New York (Box I; file "Historical"). The minutes show that the Committee met at 5 Boylston Place in Boston, the address of Richard Hodgson, on May 16, October 11, November 28, 1887, and February 2, November 20, 1888, with Charles Sedgwick Minot,

Bowditch, Hodgson, and James regularly in attendance. At the first meeting, James and Hodgson were asked to prepare a circular for a census of the frequency of hallucinations. This would appear to be the unsigned circular identified as "Blank G" and published in the *Proceedings*, pp. 270–274. It appears as Appendix II in the present volume. On November 20, 1888, James was involved in the discussion of Minot's report on thought-transference (see note to 33.1).

When Richard Hodgson, a professional psychical researcher sent by the English society, became secretary on May 12, 1887, he relieved James of a considerable burden of correspondence. Nevertheless, it seems that James continued to receive numerous reports of strange things. It is on the whole fortunate that little of this correspondence has survived. Its character can be estimated from the cases which are preserved in two file cabinets in the basement of the American Society. James is involved in a few of the hundreds of cases on file.

In a file folder titled "Apparitions," there is a letter to James, December 22, 1892, from Ellis F. Moyse concerning apparitions seen by a girl who on Halloween ate an apple and combed her hair. Under "Coincidences" there is a letter from Prof. J. B. Greenough dated May 1899 describing a coincidence. In the file "Dowsing I" there is a letter from W. W. Blair, August 8, 1904, asking for advice concerning Blair's brother who can discover mineral ores. Blair thinks it would be a good idea to form a company. Under "Glossographia-Glossolalia" is found a letter from Mrs. George Hackett, June 7, 1892, concerning Maggie O'Neill who has spoken 7–8 languages. Hackett claims that the languages were identified by a linguist, but in a letter to Hodgson the linguist denies this. In the file "Hallucinations (Auditory)" there are letters from Charles S. Macomber, November 20, 1905, and Rose F. Curtis, November 14, 1896. The latter concerns the case of a certain Harriet F. Sawyer. Under "Hallucinations" there are letters from C. C. Batchelder, October 2, 1903, and John Francis Barrett, November 20, 1895. On the latter there is a note in James's hand: "wrote for addresses etc. March, 95." The case involved apparitions at Phillips Exeter Academy and was taken over by Hodgson. Under "Hauntings" there are five cases. Mary McNeil Scott, November 21, 1894, sent James an 18-page manuscript about hauntings in New Orleans. Scott claims to have met James at "Mrs. Whitman's." K. W. Michaelis, December 13, 1901, reports a haunted house in Montreal, while someone from Cincinnati, Ohio, whose name was not deciphered, contributes a 24-page letter. Several letters dated in 1886 develop the case of Lilian Aldrich of Boston. Some of her letters were in response to questions raised by James. James's letters concerning the case to Thomas Bailey Aldrich and his wife Lilian are at Houghton (bMS Am 1429 [2623-2626]). The last haunting is reported by L. M. Barrelle of Boston, October 26, 1896. The "Occult Miscellany" file contains a letter from E. S. Bullock, November 5, 1907, and William M. Reily, January 2, 1891. Reily describes the case of Mrs. Adam Michter of Allentown, Pa., who had been starving for 200 days. On this letter there is a note by James apparently addressed to Hodgson: "I have written that he will doubtless soon hear from you."

Under "Telekinesis II" Edw. D. Towle of Hillsboro, N.H., January 27, 1909, asks James to investigate a case of table-tipping, while "Telekinesis IV" contains a letter from H. E. Lunt, May 1, 1899, responding to a letter from James. The last letter found in the files in the basement is from Alfred Church Lane, a former student, February 4, 1894, asking for advice on the conduct of telepathy experiments.

No doubt the above list represents only a fragment of the cases. It shows that James's reputation kept him from completely setting aside psychical research even during periods when he was trying to rid himself of the burden. At the same time, it is clear that psychical research was never far away from James's concerns because he responded with active attention to any inquiry and often initiated the correspondence himself.

The American Society for Psychical Research ceased to exist as an independent organization on January 14, 1890, when it became the American Branch of the English society. On the whole, this amounted to little more than the discontinuance of its own *Proceedings*. From this date, minutes of the American Branch appear somewhat irregularly in the *Journal of the Society for Psychical Research* (English). The plan for an American Branch was accepted by the council of the English society on November 1, 1889. The details seem to have been arranged in correspondence between Frederic William Henry Myers on the English side and Hodgson on the American. On November 29, Bowditch, Langley, and James were elected vice-presidents of the English society "subject to their consent" (*Journal*, 3 [December 1889], 170).

The meeting of January 14 was held in Boston and presided over by James. Following the vote to dissolve, it continued as the first meeting of the Branch. James and Langley were appointed as an advisory committee, while Hodgson continued as secretary and treasurer. At this meeting, James gave a "brief account" of experiments in hypnotism by Pierre Janet (*Journal*, 4 [February 1890], 207). James again presided on March 4. He urged the 200 members in attendance to cooperate with the International Congress of Experimental Psychology and support its plans for a census of hallucinations (*Journal*, 4 [April 1890], 239). On December 2 James again occupied the chair and reported on the state of affairs since the formation of the Branch: membership had increased from about 350 to 440, and some 4,000 to 5,000 responses to the census of hallucinations had been received. James also discussed the case of Ansel Bourne (see *Essays in Psychology*, WORKS) (*Journal*, 5 [January 1891], 4–5). On February 10, 1892, James chaired a meeting of the New York section of the Branch. Some 400 members were present at Columbia College where he "delivered an address, briefly stating the results of the Census of Hallucinations, and at some length explaining the importance of the Society's work" (*Journal*, 5 [March 1892], 221). On May 3 some 100 members were present in Boston when James reported the results of the census: some 5,600 replies had been received, of which about 540 were in the affirmative. James also described the work of Pierre Janet, who treated a case of *aboulia* by means of hypnotism (*Journal*, 5 [August 1892], 282).

During these early years it took much effort simply to keep the American group intact and solvent. The spiritualists would have provided a natural base, but in fact the Society received little help from that quarter. Relations between the two groups were rather strained, and the Boston *Banner of Light*, perhaps the leading spiritualist publication in America, neglected few opportunities to scold the Society for its misguided ways. The psychical researchers were much too cautious, had no "comprehension of spiritual laws and forces," and wanted to "drag everything down to the requirements of the science of muck" (*Banner*, 68 [January 3, 1891], 4). In 1891 the American Branch lost some support when the American Psychical Society was organized in Boston, involving some members of the Branch in its work and publications. James, at least indirectly, became involved in some of the ensuing controversies. Amos Emerson Dolbear (1837–1910), American educator and inventor, a member of the Psychical Society, reported to his group on December 21, 1891, concerning sittings given by Maud Jones Gillett, a California medium, where a "number of learned men" were "bamboozled by an illiterate adventuress," at least according to some. The Psychical Society published favorable reports of the sittings, which were criticized by Richard Hodgson in an unsigned article in the *Religio-Philosophical Journal*, n.s. 2 (February 13, 1892), 598–599. Dolbear replied and the controversy dragged on for many issues. Hodgson gives a summary of the case in the *Journal*, n.s. 2 (March 19, 1892), 676–678; that Mrs. Gillett bamboozled is the editorial verdict of the *Journal*, n.s. 2 (April 9, 1892), 723. James, it is reported (p. 676), received a number of letters from Dolbear which he forwarded to Hodgson.

But within a few years many spiritualists softened their view of materialization, and James turned to them for financial support. For example, on November 4, 1899, the *Banner of Light* (vol. 86, p. 4) declared absurd the belief that spirits, complete with "a whiskey and tobacco, onions and garlic, coffee and spruce gum laden breath," can be "produced to order in five or ten minutes from the spirit world at prices ranging from fifty cents to two dollars per individual sitter." It proposed the view that materializations are hallucinations of a kind, that spiritual forces sometimes "throw pictures upon the sensitive plate of a mind in the form, thereby causing the mind to see the form of one who is in spirit life." In this new climate it was possible for Harrison D. Barrett, president of the National Spiritualists' Association, in his presidential report for 1898 before the national convention of the Association to praise the work of the psychical researchers. According to Barrett, it is a shame that the expenses of psychical research in America should be borne by the society in England. He then states:

> Prof. James has visited me twice with regard to this matter, and suggested that the time had come for Spiritualists to join hands with the Societies for Psychical Research in order that the grand truths of Spiritualism may be given to the world. Prof. James also suggested that he felt as if the Spiritualists should lead in this work, as it is their religion in whose name these psychic phenomena are offered to the public. If the Spiritualists will give every possible facility for a thorough and comprehensive study of their phenomenal evidences, they will render the cause of truth a signal service. Prof. James has not yet accepted the spiritualistic hypothesis, but he and many other gifted scholars are anxious to know the truth, hence should be assisted in their quest by every true Spiritualist in America (*Banner of Light*, 84 [October 22, 1898], p. 2).

The board of trustees was instructed to contact James in order that the "union of forces" be brought about as soon as possible. Apparently nothing came of this effort, because in his report for 1899 Harrison again instructs the board to establish ties with the psychical researchers.

Richard Hodgson's death in 1905 forced a decision concerning the conduct of psychical research in America. In 1906 the Branch was dissolved. A letter signed by James, George Bucknam Dorr, and James Hervey Hyslop announced both the dissolution of the Branch and the formation of an independent psychical research organization (*Journal of the Society for Psychical Research* [English], 12 [June 1906], 284). This letter is reprinted in the present volume. The new organization was based in New York with Hyslop, at one time a professor of philosophy at Columbia University, its leading figure. Hyslop's American Institute for Scientific Research began to function in 1906. Section

B of the Institute became the present American Society for Psychical Research, which still maintains offices in New York.

Hyslop would have been the obvious candidate to succeed Hodgson, but he was not trusted by the leaders of the English society. This is clear from James's letter of February 19, 1906, to Isaac K. Funk (copy at Houghton, bMS Am 1092.1). James notes that the society in London has legal ownership of the papers of the Branch and that it will not appoint Hyslop in place of Hodgson because Hyslop too often follows his own methods. As is clear from James's letter to Hyslop of October 25, 1903, reprinted in the present volume, Hyslop was already planning in 1903 to reorganize things and take charge of psychical research in America.

Throughout his career, James remained loyal to the psychical research of Myers, Edmund Gurney, and other leaders of the English society. Distance prevented him from taking part in their investigations, but he remained closely in touch through extensive correspondence. The December 1885 membership list of the Society for Psychical Research (English) includes James among the corresponding members. The Society, established in 1882, survives to the present time and maintains offices in London. James retained his corresponding status to the time of the merger. As has been noted, he was elected a vice-president in 1889 and retained this title to his death, except for the period 1894–1895 when he served as president.

James's two great concerns in the early years were Mrs. Piper and the census of hallucinations. Once these interests were exhausted, he withdrew for a time from active psychical research. His writings during the 1890s are general endorsements of the cause; they do not develop specific cases. In about 1903 James wrote to Hamlin Garland:

> I have myself had no direct contact with mediums for many years, and am still in a state of *bafflement* as to all these phenomena. It seems as if they were intended deliberately by the Almighty never to be either proved or disproved definitely.
>
> I wish I had had *your* experience. There are waves of public interest— it may be that there is just now an ebb—but there will sometime again be a flood, and things will hitch a little forward. Practically I am quite out of it. Haven't the time or energy! (Hamlin Garland, *Forty Years of Psychic Research* [New York: Macmillan, 1936], pp. 141–142).

Garland himself believed in contact with spirits. He was at the time writing a spiritualistic novel, *The Tyranny of the Dark*, and was asking James to supply new material. Shortly thereafter, James returned to active research with an interest in the more spectacular claims. His early work attempts to steer a middle course between skepticism and credulity, and on the whole belongs to the field of abnormal psychology. There is less balance in the later writings, but rather an eagerness to find evidence in favor of the occult.

Over the years a great deal of material passed from James to Hodgson. On May 25, 1892, James informs Hodgson that he is delivering all "my stock" to the office. This includes James's "hallucination book," two boxes of unanalyzed cases, and an index book of old American Society for Psychical Research cases with analyses. The index is said to have been prepared in part by "my student Wood," while the rest was dictated by James to J. W. Alger (bMS Am 1092.9 [965]). In addition, James routinely passed on letters which he himself did not wish to follow up. The endless investigations of Mrs. Piper also produced a great deal of paper, since many of her hundreds of séances were recorded stenographically or reported from memory and notes. Following Hodgson's death some disposition of these papers had to be made, with much of the responsibility resting with James. In fact, James's son Henry served as an executor of the estate. Most of the Piper records and some other materials were inherited by the London group. This is clear from a note written by John George Piddington, who handled the transfer from the English side, in the *Journal of the Society for Psychical Research* (English), 12 (July 1906), 286: "The Piper records with other material from the Branch office were now in the hands of the Society." On January 6, 1907, in a letter to Piddington, James describes Piddington as heir to the Piper records, and on January 1, 1909, he notes that Piddington has exported a mass of Piper records from 5 Boylston St. (bMS Am 1092.9 [3488, 3491]).

Hyslop also received some papers. Lucy Edmunds, Hodgson's secretary, wrote Hyslop on June 18, 1907, indicating that Hyslop had received boxes of newspaper clippings reporting psychic manifestations. James was supposed to have a copy of a catalogue of the clippings prepared by Edmunds. But on July 1 she wrote that James had not yet received his list (American Society for Psychical Research, Box I; file "Historical"). Additional records must have been given to Hyslop, since the file cabinets in the basement mentioned earlier contain letters addressed to Hodgson.

Few James materials are preserved in the archives of the American Society in New York. In addition to what has been mentioned above, there is a typescript of "Report on Mrs. Piper's Hodgson-Control" with corrections in James's hand, several letters, and files of Piper transcripts. The letters include two originals to Weston D. Bayley, September 9, 1906 (Box II; file "Noted Personalities II") and October 14, 1909 (Box II; file "Historical Miscellany"). In the former James reports that he has received from George B. Dorr copies of transcripts of sittings; in the latter, that he has not seen Mrs. Piper since "last May." Also preserved is a carbon copy of a letter to James from Piddington, October 3, 1907, informing James that Piddington cannot send James records of the Piper investigations in England (Box II; file "ASPR Miscellaneous"). There are also letters from James to Hyslop, for which the body of these notes should be consulted.

There are numerous Piper transcripts covering the years 1898–1905, when James was largely inactive (Boxes III, X–XVII). A cursory examination revealed only one sitting involving James. On January 18, 1899, with James, his wife, and Hodgson as the sitters, James's sister Alice through Mrs. Piper announces that James is suffering from a "tired brain." Shortly thereafter James says "I must go to a lecture" and leaves. It should be noted that some of the accounts are in shorthand and some in Mrs. Piper's automatic script.

The London holdings are more extensive. There are numerous letters to Piddington, Henry Sidgwick, Mrs. Sidgwick, Myers, Hodgson, and Oliver Lodge, to be mentioned in the body of the notes. There are manuscripts of James's presidential address and "A Case of Psychic Automatism," described by Professor Bowers in his textual introduction. There are Piper transcripts, but again usually not those in which James was involved. Of the transcripts quoted in "Report on Mrs. Piper's Hodgson-Control," the London society has those of the sittings of January 23, May 29, June 5, June 20, June 27, July 2, and July 3, 1906.

The main William James Collection is housed in the Houghton Library of Harvard University. Items from it can be identified by the call number 'MS

Am 1092', with sometimes 'b' or 'f' as a prefix and a decimal following the numeral '2'. Many of James's books are also preserved there; many of these are sufficiently identified by their call numbers which begin with 'WJ' or 'AC'. James's numerous books in psychical research and spiritualism are scattered in the Widener stacks. An unpublished list can be consulted at Houghton (bMS Am 1092.9 [4579], fols. 70–77). Numerous pamphlets and clippings, many not included in lists of books in James's library, are in Widener, scattered in collections of pamphlets under the call numbers Phil 7059.800 to Phil 7059.899. Many books from James's library were sold. A list was compiled by Ralph Barton Perry and is also at Houghton (bMS Am 1092.9 [4578]).

Houghton has almost no manuscript materials in the field of psychical research. A sample of the automatic writing of John N. Arnold is preserved (bMS Am 1092.9 [4528]) and is included as an Appendix to the present volume.

Many of James's writings in the field are included in Gardner Murphy and Robert O. Ballou, eds., *William James on Psychical Research* (New York: Viking Press, 1960). The volume includes some letters expressing James's shifting and candid views of this "baffling" subject.

James figures to some degree in most of the literature on psychical research. Robert Laurence Moore, *In Search of White Crows: Spiritualism, Parapsychology, and American Culture* (New York: Oxford University Press, 1977) provides a useful survey of the extensive literature. Moore borrows his title from James and emphasizes psychical research as a challenger to an entrenched, orthodox science. Alan Gauld, *The Founders of Psychical Research* (London: Routledge & Kegan Paul, 1968) surveys with considerable sympathy the personalities of James's time. The strongest critic is Trevor H. Hall. A lawyer and amateur magician, Hall marshals an impressive mass of evidence and casts serious doubts on the legitimacy of the work done at the time. He views Gurney as an honest but misguided researcher. Myers, William Crookes, Ada Goodrich Freer, and others do not fare as well; Hall raises serious questions about their integrity and motives. Hall's works will be cited in the body of the notes.

James continued to contribute to the literature after his death. Numerous mediums and sitters announced that James was communicating through them—regrettably, in a bland style typical of spirit messages. The most extensive output in this line is by Jane Revere Burke: *The One Way* (1921), *Let Us In* (1931), *The Bundle of Life* (1934), and *Messages on Healing* (1934). More recently Susy Smith has published *The Book of James* (New York: G. P. Putnam's Sons, 1974).

Abbreviations

PASPR for *Proceedings of the American Society for Psychical Research*, 1885–1889 and 1907–

JASPR for *Journal of the American Society for Psychical Research*, 1906–

PSPR for *Proceedings of the Society for Psychical Research* (English), 1882–

JSPR for *Journal of the Society for Psychical Research* (English), 1884–

1.1 The] *Planchette; Or, the Despair of Science. Being a Full Account of Modern Spiritualism, Its Phenomena, and the Various Theories Regarding It. With a Survey of French Spiritism* (Boston: Roberts Brothers, 1869) (WJ 479.75), generally attributed to Epes Sargent (1813–1880), American journalist.

3.7 Bell] Robert Bell (1800–1867), British journalist, "Stranger than Fiction," *Cornhill Magazine*, 2 (August 1860), 210–224, describing sittings given by Daniel Dunglass Home (1833–1886), American-born physical medium.

3.27 Franklin] Benjamin Franklin, quoted by Sargent, p. 54, without a source.

3.29 Faraday's] Michael Faraday (1791–1867), English chemist, quoted in a letter by John Tyndall on "Faraday and the Spiritualists" to the *Pall Mall Gazette*, 7 (May 9, 1868), 6.

4.12 Finney] Sargent, p. 304, identifies the medium as Selden J. Finney.

5.11 "The] This account of the formation and purposes of the Society in England is taken from the "Objects of the Society," PSPR, 1 (October 1882), 3–4.

6.19 Reichenbach's] See note to 9.9.

6.24 Sidgwick] Henry Sidgwick (1838–1900), British philosopher, president in 1882–1884 and 1888–1892. The correspondence between James and Sidgwick is preserved at Houghton (bMS Am 1092.9 [615–618, 3760–3767]) and the Society for Psychical Research in London.

6.24 Balfour] Arthur James Balfour, 1st Earl of Balfour (1848–1930), British philosopher and statesman, a vice-president from 1882, president in 1893.

6.25 Barrett] William Fletcher Barrett (1844–1925), British physicist, a vice-president from 1882, played an important role in the organization of the American Society (see note to 6.29).

6.25 Carlisle] Harvey Goodwin (1818–1891), Bishop of Carlisle, vice-president from 1884.

6.26 Hollond] John R. Hollond, a vice-president from 1882 to the early 1890s.

6.26 Hutton] Richard Holt Hutton (1826–1897), British essayist and biographer, a vice-president from 1882.

6.26 Moses] William Stainton Moses (1839–1892), British clergyman and spiritualist, sometimes wrote under the pseudonym M. A. Oxon. Preserved in Widener is James's copy of *Spirit Teachings* (London: London Spiritualist Alliance, 1894) (Phil 7068.94.45). Moses was one of the founders of the Society and a vice-president to his resignation in 1886.

6.27 Noel] Roden Berkeley Wriothesley Noel (1834–1894), British poet, a vice-president from 1882.

6.27 Rayleigh] John William Strutt (3rd Baron Rayleigh) (1842–1919), British mathematician and physicist.

6.28 Stewart] Balfour Stewart (1827–1887), Scottish physicist, co-author with Peter Guthrie Tait of *The Unseen Universe or Physical Speculations on a Future State*, published anonymously in 1875. James's review of the book is reprinted in *Essays, Comments, and Reviews*, WORKS. Stewart served as vice-president from 1882, as president in 1885–1887.

6.28 Wedgwood] Hensleigh Wedgwood (1803–1891), British philologist, a vice-president from 1882.

6.29 Barrett] Barrett visited the United States in 1884 in an attempt to arouse interest. In his report Barrett writes that "Professor James, who is the brother of the eminent novelist, was already acquainted with our hon. sec., Mr. Edmund Gurney, and had read the earlier parts of our Proceedings with much interest" (JSPR, 1 [November 1884], 177). The report provides much detail about efforts to organize psychical research in America.

8.3 BARKER] George Frederick Barker (1835–1910), American physicist, left the Society before February 1889.

8.3 STOREY] Moorfield Storey (1845–1929), American lawyer, left the Society before December 1887.

8.4 EVERETT] Charles Caroll Everett (1829–1900), professor of theology at Harvard. Four letters from Everett to James are in Houghton (bMS Am 1092, letters 177–180). Everett retained his affiliation with the Society until his death.

8.4 TROWBRIDGE] John Trowbridge (1843–1923), American physicist. His name does not appear in the first published list of members (July 1885).

8.5 SCUDDER] Samuel Hubbard Scudder (1837–1911), American naturalist, left the Society before August 1894.

8.6 WATSON] William Watson (1834–1915), American engineer and author, retained his affiliation into the 1900s.

8.7 SELLERS] Coleman Sellers (1827–1907), American engineer, left the Society before February 1892.

8.10 BOWDITCH] Henry Pickering Bowditch (1840–1911), American physiologist, professor at the Harvard Medical School, retained his affiliation into the 1900s. James's correspondence with Bowditch is at Houghton (bMS Am 1092.9 [77–84, 772–818]).

8.10 MINOT] Charles Sedgwick Minot (1852–1914), American biologist and educator, left the Society before 1898.

8.11 JACKSON] Charles Cabot Jackson (1843–1926), a Boston businessman, left the Society before 1890.

8.11 NEWCOMB] Simon Newcomb (1835–1909), American astronomer, left the Society before 1898.

8.12 HIGGINSON] Thomas Wentworth Higginson (1823–1911), American orator, reformer, and author. One undated letter from James to Higginson is in the Boston Public Library. Higginson left the Society before February 1892.

8.13 PICKERING] William Henry Pickering (1858–1938), American astronomer, left the Society before November 1890.

8.14 HODGES] Nathaniel Dana Carlile Hodges (1852–1927), American librarian, left the Society before December 1887.

8.16 FULLERTON] George Stuart Fullerton (1859–1925), American philosopher, a leading member of the Seybert Commission (see note to 194.24). Always skeptical of spiritualist claims, Fullerton withdrew from the Society in about 1900.

8.16 PICKERING] Edward Charles Pickering (1846–1919), American astronomer, left the Society before November 1890.

8.17 SMITH] Robert Pearsall Smith (1827–1898), a Philadelphia businessman, later established residence in London. James visited the Smiths in Philadelphia and London, admired the religious writings of his wife Hannah Whitall Smith (see *Talks to Teachers*, WORKS, pp. 118–119), and was on friendly terms with their children.

8.19 HALL] Granville Stanley Hall (1844–1924), American psychologist. For a note on the relations between James and Hall see *The Principles of Psychology*, WORKS, note to 7.25. Hall severed his ties with the Society before December 1887, although his term on the Council was to run till January 1888.

8.19 WOODHULL] Alfred Alexander Woodhull (1837–1921), American military surgeon, left the Society before December 1887.

8.21 PEIRCE] James Mills Peirce (1834–1906), American mathematician and educator, left the Society before November 1890.

9.9 Reichenbach's] Karl Ludwig Friedrich von Reichenbach (1788–1869), German chemist and industrialist, in *Odisch-magnetische Briefe* (1852) proposed the view that most bodies are surrounded by a subtle effluence which can be seen by some especially sensitive individuals. The English Society reported negative results, except for three cases (PSPR, 1 [July 1883], 230–237). In a completely dark room, three of forty-five subjects claimed to see faint lights around an electro-magnet whenever the current was on. An experimenter in a different room would switch the current on or off and all three subjects usually recognized such changes. The American report, Joseph Jastrow and George F. H. Nuttall, "On the Existence of a Magnetic Sense" (PASPR, 1 [July 1886], 116–126), emphasizes the need to prevent sounds made by the switching from being heard by the subjects. The American report is completely negative. Before the end of 1887 the Reichenbach Committee was replaced by the broader Committee on Experimental Psychology. It should be noted that one of the subjects in the English studies was G. A. Smith, a participant in Gurney's telepathy experiments (see note to 34.15), while the other two were his friends.

11.5 Savage] Minot Judson Savage (1841–1918), American Unitarian clergyman. While retaining his affiliation with the Society, Savage was one of the organizers of the spiritualist American Psychical Society.

12.33 After] With Richard Hodgson's death the American Branch lost its only full-time investigator. When it became clear that a new secretary would not be appointed, it was decided to dissolve the Branch and thus permit Hyslop to carry on with his plans for a new organization in New York (see note to 219.3).

13.20 HYSLOP] James Hervey Hyslop (1854–1920), American philosopher and psychical researcher. The correspondence between James and Hyslop is at Houghton (bMS Am 1092, letters 435–437; bMS Am 1092.1) and at the Society for Psychical Research in New York. Several of James's letters to Hyslop are published in Murphy and Ballou.

13.21 DORR] George Bucknam Dorr (1853–1944), a student at Harvard in 1870–1874 and 1888–1891, associated with James in several psychical research investigations. James's letters to Dorr are at Houghton (bMS Am 1092.1; bMS Am 1092.9 [890]).

13.24 PIDDINGTON] John George Piddington (1869–1952), British psychical researcher. James's letters to Piddington are at Houghton (bMS Am 1092.9 [3488–3493]) and the Society for Psychical Research in London. Piddington was in Boston to look after the liquidation of the Branch and to remove most of its records to London.

14.1 Committee] A circular of this committee asking mediums to present themselves for investigation is reprinted in the present volume, pp. 10–11.

14.5 Evans's] Glendower Evans (1859–1886), established a close friendship with James while a student at Harvard in 1875–1879.

14.7 Bullard] William Norton Bullard (1853–1931), American neurologist.

14.16 Berry] It seems impossible to establish which medium James has in mind. In 1883 the *Banner of Light* regularly carried advertising for Helen C. Berry, a physical medium, residing at 18 Arnold St., Boston, and her sister Gertrude, also a medium. In 1887 and 1888, apparently the same pair advertised themselves as the "Berry Sisters" who gave séances at their home at 55 Rutland St., Boston. But there could have been another Helen Berry active during those years, because on June 9, 1888 (vol. 63, p. 5), the *Banner* reports that "Miss Helen Berry, the excellent medium, who has been a resident of Philadelphia, Pa., the past two years, is in town and will soon locate at Onset Bay." The situation is further confused by the fact that the Berry sisters of Boston were regulars at Onset Bay, Mass., site of spiritualist summer encampments. No references to the exposure of any medium named Berry were found in the *Banner*.

The Committee on Mediumistic Phenomena shortly concluded that the study of physical mediums was a waste of time. Thus, in a later report, Joseph Weatherhead Warren (1849–1916), American physician, writes:

Individual members of the committee have also visited other mediums of varied powers and have witnessed occult manifestations with a view to determining the desirability of bringing them to the attention of the committee. No less than five such persons of considerable reputation have recently been publicly exposed or are "under a cloud." So that at least seven materializing or etherealizing mediums (nearly every one of which has been highly recommended to our special attention) have come to grief here in Boston during the past two or three years. Such a state of things hardly tends to encourage your committee in the active pursuit of this class of phenomena; but we are still ready to examine even these phenomena on the receipt of tangible experiences on the part of trustworthy persons, provided we are permitted to impose such conditions as seem to us reasonable and necessary (PASPR, 1 [March 1889], 321–322).

James shared the general disillusionment with physical mediumship, until years later Eusapia Paladino rekindled his interest. His attitude in the late 1880s is expressed in letters to his wife (*The Letters of William James*, ed. Henry James, 2 vols. [Boston: Atlantic Monthly Press, 1920], I, 228) and in his statement concerning the exposure of Hannah Ross.

15.14 P.] Leonora Evelina Piper (1859–1950), American trance medium, probably the most intensely studied medium of the period. Most of the information about her early career is derived from Richard Hodgson; additional details are sometimes found in the seemingly endless stream of reports published by the Society or by the individual sitters. Little additional information is supplied in the biography by her daughter, Alta L. Piper, *The Life and Work of Mrs. Piper* (London: Kegan Paul, Trench, Trubner, 1929), hagiographical in tone and based primarily on published transcripts. Alta Piper includes excerpts from James's letters to Mrs. Piper, fragments of what must have been an extensive correspondence which now seems lost. Also of little use is M. Sage, *Mrs. Piper & the Society for Psychical Research*, trans. Noralie Robertson (New York: Scott-Thaw, 1904). Clark Bell, *Spiritism, Hypnotism and Telepathy, as Involved in the Case of Mrs. Leonora E. Piper and the Society for Psychical Research*, 2nd ed. (New York: Medico-Legal Journal, 1904), pp. 123–128, 159–172, reprints from the *New York Herald* a long statement made by Mrs. Piper in 1901, together with newspaper comments, and letters by Hodgson, James, and other investigators. W. H. Salter, *Trance Mediumship: An Introductory Study of Mrs Piper and Mrs Leonard* (London: Society for Psychical Research, [1950]), provides a helpful summary of the many investigations. Salter does not mention the work of investigators not connected with the Society.

Professional mediums were generally not highly regarded either for their honesty or their morals. Mrs. Piper was not a professional medium in the strict sense because she did not publicly advertise sittings available to all comers for the price of admission. However, it is clear that she relied upon her mediumship for at least a part of her livelihood. She was paid by the Society and apparently at various stages of her career collected fees from individual sitters.

The earliest reference to Mrs. Piper which I could find occurs in a letter from James to his wife of September 22, 1885 (bMS Am 1092.9 [1424]). The question of paying the medium arises shortly thereafter. Thus, on December 24 James writes to Alice: "Savage did not come to Mrs. Piper's and we did not try the slates. I had a pleasant talk with her, and found she entered into my purposes. She said her work was using her up. It is evident she won't give us her time for nothing. But I have more than ever the impression that she is a perfectly honest woman. . . . Am going now to write to Harry & Alice, & Pearsall Smith" (bMS Am 1092.9 [1429]). The letters to Henry and their sister have survived (bMS Am 1092.9 [2626, 1132]); the letter to Smith was not found. It could well have been a request for funds since Smith was wealthy and well-known for his generosity.

The reports of the Committee on Mediumistic Phenomena for this period contain appeals for funds in connection with what appear to be references to Mrs. Piper. Reporting for the Committee in late 1887, Bullard notes that there are mediums worth investigating but that no "scientific investigation can be undertaken by them until *much more money* is placed at their disposal." Bullard then continues:

> The committee have, for example, already partially investigated a "medium" who has made a decidedly favorable impression on certain members. Such reports of sittings with her as are already in the possession of the committee are, however, not sufficient to enable them to arrive at a definite conclusion. It is very desirable that more sittings should be held and that exact stenographic reports thereof should be made. This, lack of

funds at present prevents our undertaking (PASPR, 1 [December 1887], 230).

A later report by Warren also emphasizes the need for funds:

During the year the committee, as such, has undertaken the careful examination of the results obtained by one well-known trance medium who is reported to have given to many prudent sitters names and communications of such accuracy and fulness that it is supposed that such results could only be reached by some occult agency, or by some mental process which is not exactly recognized as yet.

Warren adds that "by the generous coöperation of the medium" additional sittings could be held "provided such amounts of money could be placed at our disposal as would enable us to obtain the full reports of a large number of sittings with this medium and perhaps with others." A "liberal gift" from one person, a "moderate amount" from the Society, and a "smaller contribution" enable the investigation to continue (PASPR, 1 [March 1889], 320–321). Hodgson's account of the work of the same committee (PSPR, 8 [June 1892], 2) shows that the medium was Mrs. Piper, while James's letter to his wife shows that part of the money was being used to pay her. Hodgson's biographer states that when Hodgson took over the Piper case in the summer of 1887 it was agreed that she would receive about £200 per year, while Hodgson would have sole control over her sittings (A. T. Baird, *Richard Hodgson* [London: Psychic Press, 1949], p. 45). The published reports leave the impression that Mrs. Piper was generously contributing her services to science when in fact she was receiving about $1000 per year, roughly half the salary of an assistant professor at Harvard.

Significant in this regard is James's letter to Piddington of May 21, 1910, apparently a response to an appeal for contributions to the Piper pension fund:

A dozen years ago I said to Hodgson that we were morally incurring a pecuniary responsibility for her old age, which I personally was unwilling to share, so none of my family saw her for about 8 years, & we have only seen her ½ a dozen times since R.H.'s death. I have steadily foreseen this appeal, and have told Dorr long since that I would give only the nominal sum of $100.00, having far more pressing charity claims to satisfy. Those whom Mrs. P. sustained spiritually may well feel differently (bMS Am 1092.9 [3492]).

In her 1901 statement Mrs. Piper admits that mediumship became for her "a remunerative occupation":

It was on account of my desire to understand the phenomenon and prove its nature that I gave myself up to scientific investigation and willingly placed myself in the hands of honored scientific men, who expressed the wish for me to do so, with the full understanding on both sides that I should submit to any form of test they might see fit to apply. In doing this, however, the thought of making it a remunerative occupation never once occurred to me, although since then I have as a matter of fact done so (Bell, p. 161).

But we know from James's letter to his wife that the question of remuneration arose in the course of the earliest contacts. And there are indications that at the time Mrs. Piper was giving sittings and collecting fees.

In his letter to his wife of December 24, James reports Mrs. Piper's statement that "her work was using her up," suggesting considerable mediumistic activity prior to the appearance of the Jameses. The *New York Herald*, October 20, 1901, part 5, page 7, in editorial comments accompanying Mrs. Piper's statement, reports that upon discovering her mediumistic powers, in the summer of 1884, Mrs. Piper gave numerous sittings at a dollar each. According to the *Herald*, she gave no sittings during the following winter, but was active in the fall of 1885 when she encountered the Jameses. Since the *Herald* does not state how its information was obtained, some doubt must attach to this report. On the other hand, when Hodgson commented publicly on the report, he did not challenge any part of the biographical information (*Herald*, October 24, 1901, p. 7; October 30, 1901, p. 9).

There is evidence that Mrs. Piper collected fees even from sitters sponsored by the Society. Paul Bourget, a French journalist, had sittings with Mrs. Piper in December 1893. In his *Outre-Mer: Impressions of America* (New York: Charles Scribner's Sons, 1895), pp. 354–355, Bourget writes: "Footprints indicate that more than one person must that day have knocked at the door of this modern sorceress, to whom we in our turn are coming. Still the *séance* is expensive—ten dollars." At the door "a little girl receives us, all smiles, and conducts us into the parlor, saying that her mother has had a great many sittings during the past few days, and that she is very tired." The fee mentioned by Bourget is quite substantial, and if his reference to numerous footprints can be taken literally, we get the picture of a thriving business supplementing a regular income from the Society. The Bourget sittings are described by James in his letter to Hodgson of December 8, 1893 (original at the Society for Psychical Research, London): "My impression is that both Marie and the Bourgets should have a second sitting. But the price prevents M. & is likely to prevent the B's. Can any of the Society money be used?" Marie is James's servant who was invited to the sitting by James himself, because while sitting for Bourget Mrs. Piper repeatedly gave information which in James's view best fitted Marie's circumstances. The whole episode is rather odd: why would James, often so generous in supporting various causes, break off a promising line of investigation because the subject could not pay, especially when he himself had invited her to the sitting? And where is Mrs. Piper's generosity in behalf of science? On the contrary, there is an indication of a certain lack of flexibility where the collection of fees is concerned.

James's letter to his wife of December 24 contains another remark not compatible with the general impression left by the published accounts. This is the reference to slate writing, the production of messages in an occult manner on the inside surfaces of slates locked together or on surfaces cleaned and inspected by the sitter. Mrs. Piper in the language of the time was a trance medium. Physical mediums, including slate-writers, produce physical phenomena which witness to the presence of occult powers, while trance mediums simply transmit messages, with the content of the messages serving as the only guarantees of genuineness. When Mrs. Piper began her career, some of the most famous physical mediums had already left the stage under pressure of repeated exposures, or so their critics charged. It would have been well known that while physical mediums produce the more spectacular effects, they face much greater risks of exposure. Thus James's reference to slate writing is important and puzzling. Unfortunately, it is not clear whether Mrs. Piper presented herself as a slate-writer or whether this was something suggested by

James. If the former, this would be evidence that Mrs. Piper was prepared to commit fraud because all slate writing requires advance preparation. But even in the latter case, the fact that she agreed could cast some doubt upon her good faith.

James was convinced that Mrs. Piper knew much about the James family which she could not have learned through normal means. And James was not the only one impressed in this way. Bourget, for example, came away much impressed with his own test. It is thus not surprising that the numerous accounts of Mrs. Piper emphasize the care with which the various investigators tried to exclude normal sources of information. However, the various reports do not refer to a possible contact between James and Mrs. Piper, a contact which is mentioned by both Mrs. Piper and her daughter. Mrs. Piper's account is as follows: "I was then living in Boston. My maid of all work told a friend who was a servant in the household of Professor William James, of Harvard, that I went into 'queer sleeps,' in which I said 'many strange things.' Professor James recognized that I was what is called a psychic, and took steps to make my acquaintance" (Bell, p. 162). Alta Piper's account is somewhat different but retains the link between servants. "My grandparents had at that time in their service an old Irish servant who had been with them for years and who, while good-natured, faithful, and utterly devoted to the family, possessed withall the Celtic imagination and ingrained superstition of her race." The maid had a sister in service at a Boston home where James's mother-in-law was a frequent visitor. Alta Piper conjectures that the stories told by the servant first brought Mrs. Piper to the attention of the Jameses. "I ought here to mention that Mrs. Gibbins [sic] was entirely unknown to Mrs. Piper, and when personally making the appointments both for herself and her daughter, she had taken special care that her identity should remain concealed" (pp. 21–22). It is thus possible that Mrs. Piper's knowledge of the James family was acquired from the gossip of servants and that the whole mystery rests on the failure of the people upstairs to realize that servants also have ears.

Alta Piper makes clear that there was much socializing between Mrs. Piper and her investigators. She stayed in their homes, chatted with their wives, children, servants. It seems reasonable to suppose that she could have learned much in the course of a visit of several days or weeks in spite of the most severe precautions. There are also indications that the sittings themselves were not always carefully conducted. In "Deux séances chez Mrs P*** de Boston," *Annales des Sciences Psychiques,* 5 (1895), 65–75, Bourget notes that he had a second sitting with Mrs. Piper which took place in James's house. The medium was bothered by the presence of a servant to whom she talked about the servant's family, all of Bourget's efforts notwithstanding.

James describes the Bourget sittings in his letter to Hodgson of December 8, 1893, quoted in part by Hodgson in his "A Further Record of Observations of Certain Phenomena of Trance," PSPR, 13 (February 1898), 494–495. For James, Mrs. Piper's conversations with the servant, Marie Garin, were not at all a nuisance. For several sittings Mrs. Piper had been mentioning the name Marie and this time James decided to call the servant in to see whether she was the Marie in question. Mrs. Piper then gave several specific pieces of information concerning Marie's family, information which Marie thought she had not revealed to anyone likely to pass it on to Mrs. Piper.

Not everyone was equally impressed with Mrs. Piper. In his report Warren notes:

It would seem that not merely the physical condition of the medium is of importance, but that the personality, or frame of mind of the persons present (sitter or committee member), has a marked effect on the sitting or on the trance conditions. On this account several sitters were altogether unsuccessful and some four or five sittings had to be abandoned. Two members of the committee also proved to be a hindrance to the manifestations (weakening the power of the medium, it was said, and making her tired), and their services had to be dispensed with (PASPR, p. 321).

Horace Howard Furness, the Shakespeare scholar, in his letter to James of October 19, 1890 (bMS Am 1092 [283]) describes a sitting with Mrs. Piper at which she said that Furness was interested in account books and was the owner of large cotton mills in England. Furness believed that she feigned her trances because once she opened her eyes to look at some flowers brought in by Furness.

According to Alta Piper, Mrs. Piper's first psychic experience came when at the age of eight she had a premonition of the death of her "Aunt Sara." The time of the premonition was recorded by Mrs. Piper's parents and coincided to the hour with the actual time of death (Alta Piper, pp. 12–13). But her mediumship did not develop until after her marriage. In 1884 she visited J. R. Cocke, a professional medium, seeking medical diagnosis of a suspected tumor. Cocke also claimed to develop mediumship and was controlled by a French doctor named Finny. In the course of one sitting, Mrs. Piper became entranced and wrote out remarkable messages. To quote Alta Piper:

> These "circles" were held for the purposes of effecting "cures" and of "developing latent mediumship." At the meeting which my mother and grandfather attended on this particular Sunday evening, those present seated themselves in the form of a circle around which the clairvoyant then passed placing his hands on the head of each person in turn. When he reached my mother hardly had he put his hand on her head before she felt what she described as "chills" and saw in front of her "a flood of light in which many strange faces appeared," while "a hand seemed to pass to and fro before my face." She then rose from her chair and, unaided, walked to a table in the centre of the room on which writing material had previously been placed. Picking up a pencil and paper and writing rapidly for a few minutes she then handed the written paper to a member of the circle and returned to her seat (p. 17).

When rumor of this event spread abroad, Mrs. Piper was besieged for sittings, but except for members of her family and "one or two intimate friends," she "definitely refused to see anyone" (p. 20). This reluctance lasted until contact with the James family was established.

Alta Piper's account lacks dates and names. These are supplied in Hodgson's "A Record of Observations of Certain Phenomena of Trance," PSPR, 8 (June 1892), 1–167. On pp. 46–50 Hodgson describes the early trances, quoting at length statements made by Mrs. Piper. She first visited Cocke on June 29, 1884; the incident described by Alta took place on June 30. Unfortunately Hodgson is silent about Mrs. Piper's activities during the fifteen months which elapsed from the visit to Cocke to the meeting with James. James's remarks suggest that in the fall of 1885 Mrs. Piper was a practising medium. It would have helped a great deal to know what kinds of phenomena she claimed to produce.

Mrs. Piper did not advertise in the *Banner of Light*, for many years the main organ of Boston's professional mediums. The *Banner* seems to know nothing about her until much later, and the later reports in no way suggest that the editors viewed her as one of their own. By contrast, the career of James R. Cocke can be traced in some detail. Essentially the same facts about Cocke are reported by Hodgson (p. 47).

The *Banner*, 54 (October 20, 1883), 4, describes Cocke as aged 20, wholly blind, playing music while entranced and possessed by the spirit of Johann Sebastian Bach. Cocke begins to advertise on October 27, describing himself as an "unconscious entranced musical medium." He was developed by James A. Bliss, who sometimes is described as his partner or business manager. In all fairness to Cocke it must be stressed that he is not associated with the following ad for Bliss's "Red Cloud and Blackfoot's" magnetized paper—10 cents a sheet—for healing the sick or developing mediumship: "Make sick people well. Where paper go Blackfoot go, go quick. Send right away" (54 [April 12, 1884], 7). Cocke advertised his services extensively in the fall of 1884: development of mediumship, magnetic treatments, free medical examinations, psychometric readings by mail ("enclose a lock of hair, age and sex together with $1.00 and 2¢ postage stamp"), free consultations to see whether a person can be developed as a medium. Of special interest is the following ad placed some six months after Mrs. Piper's sitting: "Mr. Cocke is assisted by powerful and intelligent spirits, who endeavor to bring the best influences around those in his care." Cocke offers to supply references from mediums who have been "recently developed by his guides" (56 [January 10, 1885], 7). Cocke's interests shifted in the direction of medicine and by 1886 he was calling himself Doctor Cocke. His ads disappear from the pages of the *Banner* only in November 1894.

There are different ways of interpreting Mrs. Piper's relations with Cocke. It is possible that she went to him for medical advice, noticed the strange events and powers in her vicinity, gave several sittings to a few friends, and in complete bewilderment turned to men of science for an explanation. This is the impression left by Mrs. Piper herself: "Only by the merest chance did I discover that I possessed a power wholly unexplained to myself and mystifying to my family and friends" (Bell, p. 161). On the other hand, assuming strained financial circumstances, with an infant on her hands, she could have been in search of a profession. The latter hypothesis is supported by evidence showing that after her encounter with Cocke she set herself up as a professional medium. This evidence has already been discussed.

The *Herald* suggests that the Piper family was not well-off. The documentary record confirms this since it shows that in her early years Mrs. Piper changed her place of residence frequently. She was born in Nashua, New Hampshire, but at the time of her marriage was living in Haverhill, Massachusetts. Her first daughter was born in Boston, the second in Methuen, Mass. During most of her career as a medium, she lived in Arlington Heights, Massachusetts. The *Herald* prints pictures of her house, of her garden, and states that "her own cozy little home" was earned in part by "her toilsome years of going into the trance state."

According to her death certificate, Leonora (Leonore on the death certificate; Leonora according to other records) Evelina Piper was born in Nashua, daughter of Stillman Simonds, and died on July 3, 1950 at 54 Dwight St., Brookline, Mass. According to her marriage certificate, on October 6, 1881 she married William R. Piper, a manufacturer from Toledo, Ohio. Haverhill is given as her place of residence. No occupation for her is listed. She had two daughters, Alta Laurette, born May 16, 1884 at 40 Pinckney St., Boston, the Pipers' home at the time, and Minerva Leonora, born October 7, 1885, in Methuen.

For her last seventeen years, Mrs. Piper shared an apartment in Brookline with her second daughter, Minerva, a singer and music teacher who died in a nursing home in 1972. The apartment has undergone numerous changes in tenants since that time. No records of Alta Piper's death were found in Massachusetts. Apparently, she was living in England in the late 1940s, but returned in time to witness her mother's death. Alta is listed as the informant on her mother's death certificate. Little is known concerning William Piper. The marriage records indicate that he was a manufacturer; other records state that he was a salesman; the *Herald* reports that he was a tailor. According to Alta Piper, p. 73, he died when she was twenty, that is, in 1904. But no records of his death were found in Massachusetts, suggesting that he did not die in that state.

According to her death certificate, Mrs. Piper's usual occupation during her working years was "at home."

15.15 French] Mrs. Piper's earliest control identified himself as a French doctor named Jean Phinuit Scliville, born in Marseilles in about 1790. His origins are discussed at some length by Hodgson (pp. 50–56) who concludes that the control was not a French physician. Hodgson points out the resemblance between Mrs. Piper's control and that of J. R. Cocke.

15.21 reports] The earliest transcripts seem not to have been published and I have not seen copies of them. Hodgson includes many transcripts, but the earliest is dated May 4, 1887. Hodgson claims to have included "nearly all the records" which he has "received (before November, 1891)" (p. 59).

15.35 relatives] The first to have a sitting with Mrs. Piper was James's mother-in-law, Elizabeth Putnam Webb Gibbens. She had three daughters: James's wife Alice, Mary Sherwin (later married William Mackintire Salter), and Margaret Merrill (later married Leigh Gregor). The mother and the two unmarried sisters were at the time living with the Jameses. It is not clear who the fifth female blood relative would have been. The second male related to these ladies by marriage could have been Salter. His marriage took place on December 2, 1885. James's brother Robertson is often mentioned in later Piper transcripts and could have been one of the twelve who got nothing.

James's sister Alice was not involved. She was already in England and disliked the whole Piper investigation. According to Jean Strouse, Alice's biographer, in the fall of 1885 James asked Alice for a lock of her hair for Mrs. Piper to hold. Alice later confessed that the hair was not her own but that of a friend who had died some years earlier. Alice later hoped that "the dreadful Mrs. Piper won't be let loose upon my defenceless soul" (Jean Strouse, *Alice James: A Biography* [Boston: Houghton, Mifflin, 1980], p. 256).

16.31 hypnotize] For a more detailed account of James's efforts to hypnotize her see p. 19.

17.28 "willing] A popular pastime in which one person would try to locate some object hidden by the others or perform some action they were thinking of. It was generally thought that a successful seeker was being guided by slight movements and reactions on the part of those in the know.

19.8 "Then] From James Hervey Hyslop, "A Record and Discussion of Mediumistic Experiments," PASPR, 4 (1910), 380.

20.1 Newcomb's] The "Address of the President" by Simon Newcomb, read in Boston on January 12, 1886, appears in PASPR, 1 (July 1886), 63–86. According to Newcomb, the investigations in England of thought-transference go far towards showing that no genuine thought-transference ever takes place. He argues that if such phenomena were real, increasing practice would enable investigators to produce them with greater regularity and at will. This has not happened. Furthermore, there would be descriptions of the exact circumstances which favor the production of the phenomena, but no such descriptions are available in the published accounts. The "acute observation" concerning the accuracy of the drawings does not appear in the published text. The editorial note in *Science*, 7 (January 29, 1886), 89, points out both the flaws and the strong points of Newcomb's reasoning. In the published text, the hypothesis of fraud is not advanced, although Newcomb uses several examples suggesting the possibility. In his reply, *Science*, 7 (February 12, 1886), 145–146, Newcomb insists that he had tried to produce the required drawings and had failed.

20.16 report] Gurney, Myers, Barrett, and Podmore, "Third Report on Thought-Transference," PSPR, 1 (July 1883), 162, 164.

22.3 Doctor] The letter was probably addressed to John Curtis Bundy (1841–1892), editor of the spiritualist *Religio-Philosophical Journal* in Chicago. In a letter to Thomas Davidson, January 4, 1885 (bMS Am 1092.9 [857]), James asks whether Bundy would be a safe member of the Society for Psychical Research. Bundy is listed as an associate member from July 1885.

23.2 BUNDY] James's letter is one of many received by the *Journal* on its twenty-fifth anniversary. Most of the others are by persons committed to spiritualism as a religion.

24.1 This] James's copy of Gurney, Myers, and Podmore, *Phantasms of the Living*, 2 vols. (London: Society for Psychical Research, 1886) is at Houghton (Phil 7068.86.20*B). It is primarily the work of Edmund Gurney (1847–1888), British aesthetician and psychical researcher. Perry reports that copies of *The Power of Sound* (1880) and of vol. I of *Tertium Quid: Chapters on Various Disputed Questions* (1887) were sold. James reviewed the latter work in the *Nation*, 46 (April 26, 1888), 349. Upon Gurney's death James contributed a brief note to the *Nation*, 47 (July 19, 1888), 53. Gurney's letters to James are at Houghton (bMS Am 1092 [letters 303–323]). His life has been studied by Trevor H. Hall, *The Strange Case of Edmund Gurney* (London: Gerald Duckworth, 1964). Hall concludes that while Gurney's judgment was sometimes questionable, there can be no doubt concerning his integrity. In Hall's view, the standards of evidence used by the English Society declined following Gurney's death.

25.1 seven] Gurney reports 399 death-cases out of a total of 668 cases of "spontaneous telepathy" (*Phantasms*, II, 26).

25.12 Gurney] *Phantasms*, II, 16–17. Gurney reports the odds as being "*a thousand billion trillion trillion trillions to 1.*"

25.39 ransacking] A. Taylor Innes, "Where are the Letters? A Cross-Examination of Certain Phantasms," *Nineteenth Century*, 22 (August 1887),

174–194, claims that all of the supposed veridical hallucinations mentioned in *Phantasms of the Living* rest upon the memory of witnesses because in not a single case are the contemporary documents produced, even in cases where they are alleged to exist. In his reply, "Letters on Phantasms. A Reply," *Nineteenth Century*, 22 (October 1887), 522–533, Gurney claims that at least three cases in which the required evidence is produced are mentioned in the book.

26.31 Lecky] William Edward Hartpole Lecky (1838–1903), Irish historian and essayist, *A History of the Rise and Influence of Rationalism in Europe* (1865).

26.34–35 "careful] *Phantasms*, I, 172.

29.13 name] James's name was widely mentioned in newspaper accounts of the Ross affair although he was not present on the evening in question. The exposure is typical of the many undertaken by vigilante groups and shows that both mediums and skeptical investigators faced genuine risks. Accounts of the Ross mediumship are available from a variety of different perspectives.

Hannah V. Ross, assisted by her husband, Charles, gave widely reported materialization sittings in Providence, R. I., in 1883. The *Banner of Light*, 54 (March 8, 1884), 4, reports that she was seized by investigators in Providence; while later issues report that in the spring of 1885 she rented parlors in Boston for "Full-Form Materializations." On January 8, 1887, under the headline "A Distinguished Party at Materialization Seances," the *Banner* reports a sitting on December 27, 1886, attended by six ladies and ten gentlemen, including Alfred Russel Wallace, William James, and several regular contributors to the *Banner*. Both Wallace and James were present at another sitting on December 28. While no spirit approached James, several other sitters were much favored:

> Mr. Brackett's niece, Bertha, came; she was quite strong, and passed around the room, vivaciously greeting all in her characteristically pleasant way. Mr. B. said, "You are not quite as tall as you are at some other séances." She replied, "I come here just as I am in spirit-life; in my feelings and actions I am, and always expect to be, a child." The appearance of Bertha attracted much attention. She is a most singular embodiment of youthful beauty and child-like affection (*Banner of Light*, 60 [January 8, 1887], 4).

In the evening of January 31, 1887, a party of concerned citizens disrupted proceedings at the Rosses and seized several spooks in various stages of undress. The *New York Times* for February 4, 1887, reports the incident on p. 1:

> It was agreed that at a certain moment each member of the party should seize one of the "spirits," as well as the medium and her husband. A moment or two before the signal was given one of the party was conversing with a materialized spirit. The young man seized the shadow by the hand, and with a firm grip, and yanked it into the middle of the room. At the same instant the light was turned on, a stalwart man seized Mr. Ross in his arms, just as that gentleman pulled his revolver, while others securely held Mrs. Ross, as well as several "spooks" in the cabinet.

"Close investigation showed four boys and a little girl inside" the cabinet and an "ingenious mechanical contrivance" which operated a hidden door. The *Times* introduced its story with the remark that James and others had pronounced Mrs. Ross "among the wonders of the nineteenth century."

An amusing account of another, unpublicized exposure of the Rosses is found in a letter to James from Horace Howard Furness, the Shakespearean scholar, which cannot be dated precisely:

> Ah, my dear James, I wish I had the graphic power to describe my last visit to that Cabinet. I knew it was chock full of spirits so the minute I clasped around the waist the boss, Mrs. Ross (happy rhyme, that!) my left foot flew out and set two or three little spirits hopping up and down with pain on that side; then my right foot flew out and set two or three more together with big Indian dancing round (bMS Am 1092, letter 281).

After being chased out of the cabinet, Furness continues, "I took my seat looking as innocent as a cherub." For reasons which are not stated, Furness did not want the persecution of the Rosses to continue and urged James to use his influence to avoid another raid.

The *Banner* reports the raid of the 31st in its issue of February 12 (vol. 60, p. 4) and tries, it seems, to shield the Rosses behind the prestige of James and Wallace:

> At the same time we would refer our readers to the testimonies that have appeared in our columns to the genuineness of the manifestations at Mrs. Ross's, particularly to the accounts in the BANNER of January 8th and 29th of crucial investigations by gentlemen of undoubted veracity, scientific prestige and the most critical and observing habits of mind.

The *Banner*'s reference to "testimonies" is rather misleading. Among the sitters on December 27 and 28, only James and Wallace enjoyed scientific prestige. And while the reports mention James and note that he asked that certain precautions against fraud be taken, they in no way state what James's view of the phenomena was. Where James is concerned, nothing noteworthy is reported.

The leading witness is Edward Augustus Brackett (1818–1908), American sculptor and poet. A member of the distinguished party on December 27, Brackett was much favored by the spirits. According to the *Banner*, the sitting of the 28th was not a great success and "the manifestations as a whole were not up to the average of Mrs. Ross's séances." But Brackett and his wife were visited by the already noted Bertha, another female form who permitted Brackett to enter the cabinet, and still another female form bearing an infant in her arms. Brackett's daughter was even allowed to hold the ghostly baby. And when the scandal broke, Brackett rushed to the defense of Mrs. Ross by attacking James's abilities as an investigator. James

> appears to be singularly unfit to investigate so delicate a subject, for both mediums and the so-called materialized forms show a decided aversion to him, and I understand that in the twenty-five or thirty séances which he has attended, not a single form has ever come to him personally, and whenever any one has tried to bring them in contact with him, it has been with great difficulty that they could be induced to approach him.

Brackett continues that James, while claiming reluctance to have his name associated with the case, "now comes forward to strike a woman while she is prostrated by a severe illness, caused by the brutal treatment of men who called themselves gentlemen." Brackett's peroration seems to be aimed at James:

> With the advance of civilization there has come to the front a class of men known as specialists who cultivate a part of their intellect to the

dwarfing of their other faculties. In many things they are the weakest of mortals; having no power to stand against public opinion, their knees knock together, and they go down with the first adverse wind that blows (60 [February 26, 1887], 5).

Brackett's *Materialized Apparitions: If not Beings from Another Life, What Are They?* (Boston: Colby & Rich, 1886) (Phil 7068.86.40) is inscribed to James by the author, a memento of happier days.

Alfred Russel Wallace entered the dispute on the side of the Rosses. His detailed criticism of James's letter appears in the *Banner*, 60 (March 5, 1887), 4. Wallace's main concern is to show that there never could have been a secret door. He quotes James's remark that "good carpentry can make a secret door in any wall" and comments:

Many persons, thinking of secret doors in cabinets and in wainscotted rooms, will hastily assent to this proposition; but the wall in question is papered down to the mopboard eight inches above the carpet, and on the opposite side it is smoothly plastered down to a four-inch board. I ask Prof. James to produce anywhere a secret door *in such a wall* . . . .

It is curious that Wallace's letter gives such a precise description of the séance room. When the exposure took place, he was no longer in Boston, and his letter is dated February 23rd, Washington, D.C. Could these details have been supplied by those who urged him to respond? In any case, Wallace argues that James should either adduce definite facts or completely withdraw his allegations.

Late in 1886 Wallace was in Boston for lectures before the Lowell Institute. A convinced spiritualist, in his mid 60s, he seems to have been susceptible to the charms of thinly clad young ladies smilingly whispering in his ear. At least this is the impression left by his account of the Ross sittings in his autobiography:

Eight or nine different figures came, including a tall Indian chief in warpaint and feathers, a little girl who talked and played . . . and a very pretty and perfectly developed girl, "Bertha". . . . But what specially interested me was, that two of the figures beckoned to me to come up to the cabinet. One was a beautifully draped female figure, who took my hand, looked at me smilingly, and on my appearing doubtful, said in a whisper that she had often met me at Miss Kate Cook's *séances* in London" (Alfred Russel Wallace, *My Life*, 2 vols. [New York: Dodd, Mead, 1905], II, 356–357).

The Rosses were raided once more on April 14, 1887 and were arrested. Mrs. Ross was discharged on the common law grounds that in cases of misdemeanor involving both husband and wife it is presumed that the wife was coerced by the husband (*Banner*, 61 [May 7, 1887], 4). Charles Ross was tried by jury which, among other things, had to decide whether or not the plaintiff attended the seance expecting to be deceived. He was found not guilty (*Banner*, 61 [June 4, 1887], 4).

In spite of the favorable legal outcome, Mrs. Ross's services were no longer advertised in the *Banner*. When she tried to resume her career some ten years later, the *Banner* had new editors who had pledged themselves not to advertise known frauds. To insure good faith, prospective advertisers were asked to produce results under test conditions set by the *Banner*. Mrs. Ross accepted the challenge and on October 1, 1897 gave a satisfactory materialization sitting but with poor results (82 [October 9, 1897], 4). She placed a few ads, but these cease in early November. If one can generalize on the basis of the *Banner*'s advertisements, by then materializations were no longer fashionable. More prominent were trance and medical mediums.

29.18 Nichols] James Robinson Nichols (1819–1888), American chemist, a participant in the sittings of December 27 and 28. Nothing in the *Banner* was found giving his view of the proceedings.

33.1 "Committee] The "Second Report on Experimental Psychology:— Upon the Diagram-Tests" by Charles Sedgwick Minot was read at the meeting of January 10, 1888 and appears in PASPR, 1 (March 1889), 302–317. It was discussed on November 20, 1888 by the Committee on Experimental Psychology consisting of James, Minot, Bowditch, and Hodgson (see p. 383). The committee distributed post cards with the instruction to draw ten shapes without consulting any other person. The 501 returned cards showed that certain shapes appeared much more frequently than others, indicating the existence of certain diagram habits. The English studies of thought-transference involved the statistical analysis of card-guessing experiments and assumed that every card has an equal chance of being selected and guessed. Minot argues that the odds vary according to the card. An agent is more likely to select certain cards because of their shape, while the percipient is more likely to reproduce certain shapes. Minot argues that similar difficulties arise in other thought-transference experiments.

33.18 Minot] In some of the English reports the possibility of cheating was discounted on the grounds that the needed codes would be too complex. But even a simple code would affect the results considerably and codes were used in at least some of the successful experiments (see notes to 34.15 and 93.21).

34.1 Dessoir] Max Dessoir (1867–1947), German psychologist, "Experiments in Muscle-Reading and Thought-Transference," PSPR, 4 (October 1886), 111–126. In Widener is James's copy of *Das Doppel-Ich* (Leipzig: E. Günther, 1890) (Phil 7042.2), while Houghton preserves a pamphlet (WJ 700.5).

34.1 Schmoll] Anton Schmoll, "Experiments in Thought-Transference," PSPR, 4 (May 1887), 324–337; Anton Schmoll and J. E. Mabire, "Experiments in Thought-Transference," PSPR, 5 (June 1888), 169–215.

34.4 Guthrie] Malcolm Guthrie, English businessman and philosophical writer, a member of the Society, describes himself as part owner of a large drapery establishment in Liverpool, when rumor reached him that some of his employees possessed remarkable powers (PSPR, 2 [April 1884], 24–25). Irving Bishop, a noted mind-reader, had performed in Liverpool in the spring of 1883. In imitation, some of the shop girls amused themselves with similar performances. It happened that Guthrie was then reading about thought-transference, heard about the performances in his establishment, and enlisted the aid of the Literary and Philosophical Society of Liverpool "for the purpose of a scientific study of the phenomena." The subjects were Miss Edwards, Miss Relph, and other employees of Guthrie's establishment. Contact was permitted in some experiments and not in others. James Birchall was the secretary of the Literary and Philosophical Society and served as the recorder.

The case is discussed in Guthrie and Birchall, "Record of Experiments in

Thought-Transference," PSPR, 1 (December 1883), 263–283; Gurney, Myers, and Barrett, "Fourth Report of the Committee on Thought-Transference," PSPR, 2 (April 1884), 1–11; Guthrie and Birchall, "An Account of Some Experiments in Thought-Transference," PSPR, 2 (April 1884), 24–42; Guthrie, "Further Report on Experiments in Thought-Transference at Liverpool," PSPR, 3 (December 1885), 424–452. The case was frequently discussed and additional references can be found by consulting the Combined Index to the publications of the Society.

34.9 Lodge] Oliver Joseph Lodge (1851–1940), British physicist, "An Account of Some Experiments in Thought-Transference," PSPR, 2 (July 1884), 189–200. Lodge initially went to Liverpool to witness Guthrie's work, but he also conducted some experiments on his own when Guthrie was not present. Birchall, Edwards, and Relph took part and the experiments involved the reproduction of diagrams. In some cases, agent and percipient held hands. The numerous letters from James to Lodge are preserved at the Society in London with some copies at Houghton (bMS Am 1092.1). Perry reports that an annotated copy of the 1907 edition of *Life and Matter* was sold. One pamphlet is preserved in Widener.

34.11 Smith] Experiments involving J. W. Smith are mentioned in PSPR, 2 (April 1884), 7; the diagrams with an introductory note appear in PSPR, 2 (July 1884), 207–216. Smith was the agent, while his sister was the percipient. The two are identified only as from Leeds. Barrett visited them to explain the "necessary precautions," but the tests reported were not made in his presence.

34.15 Blackburn] Experiments involving Douglas Blackburn and George Albert Smith are described in Gurney, Myers, and Barrett, "Second Report on Thought-Transference," PSPR, 1 (April 1883), 70–97; and "Third Report on Thought-Transference," PSPR, 1 (July 1883), 161–215, by the same authors with the addition of Podmore. Additional experiments, in which the percipients were hypnotized, are reported by Henry Sidgwick, Eleanor Mildred Sidgwick, and George Albert Smith, "Experiments in Thought-Transference," PSPR, 6 (December 1889), 128–170. For still another report see note to 116.3.

Douglas Blackburn (d. 1929), a resident of the Brighton resort, editor of the *Brightonian*, and later a novelist, published a letter in the spiritualist periodical *Light* claiming that a Mr. Smith of Brighton has powers very much like those of Irving Bishop, the mind-reader (PSPR, 1 [October 1882], 63). This led to correspondence between Blackburn and the Society and to experiments conducted by members of the Committee on Thought-Transference. The reports note: "Mr. Blackburn has frequently practiced thought-reading with Mr. Smith; but at the time when our first experiments were made, he had been accustomed to hold Mr. Smith's hand, or touch his forehead, with a view to communicating the impression. No unconscious pressure, however, could have communicated to the subject the definite words and pictures enumerated below" (PSPR, 1, 79). The experiments in the third report did not involve physical contact, although both agent and percipient were in the same room. The Society took the position that while most thought-reading consisted of the conscious or unconscious interpretation of sensible clues, the cases in the reports were cases of genuine thought-transference (PSPR, 1, 70). In his *Strange Case of Edmund Gurney*, pp. 125–149, Hall discusses Blackburn's confession of 1908 that these experiments were fraudulent.

George Albert Smith (d. 1959), in later years a photographer and cinema pioneer, "a young mesmerist living at Brighton" (PSPR, 1, 78), was an entertainer when first noticed by the Society. He became heavily involved in the work of the Society and was one of the more successful subjects of the early years. He also took part in studies of Reichenbach's phenomena (see note to 9.9) and assisted in Gurney's work on hypnotism. Smith became Gurney's private secretary. According to Hall in *The Strange Case of Edmund Gurney*, considerable doubt is cast upon Gurney's work by the fact that the tests often involved Smith and Smith's Brighton associates. Gurney died in mysterious circumstances in a Brighton hotel. Hall conjectures that Gurney committed suicide upon learning that Smith had deceived him.

34.23   "The]   PSPR, 1, 165.

35.9   Minot]   PASPR, 1, 316.

37.2   Secretary]   Richard Hodgson (1855–1905), Australian-born psychical researcher, served as secretary from 1887 to his death. The correspondence between James and Hodgson is at Houghton (bMS Am 1092.9 [183–187, 965–968]) and at the Society for Psychical Research in London.

37.10   Myers]   Frederic William Henry Myers (1843–1901), British essayist and psychical researcher, "On a Telepathic Explanation of Some So-called Spiritualistic Phenomena," PSPR, 2 (December 1884), 217–237; "Automatic Writing," PSPR, 3 (May 1885), 1–63; 4 (May 1887), 209–261. For James's view of Myers see "Frederic Myers's Service to Psychology," reprinted in the present volume, pp. 192–202. Houghton preserves James's copy of Myers's main work, published posthumously, *Human Personality and Its Survival of Bodily Death*, 2 vols. (London: Longmans, Green, 1903) (*AC 85.J2376.Zz903m) and copies of other works. James's reviews of *Science and a Future Life* and *Human Personality* are reprinted in the present volume, pp. 107–110 and 203–215. Numerous details and speculations about Myers's work are supplied by Trevor H. Hall, *The Strange Case of Edmund Gurney*, and John L. Campbell and Trevor H. Hall, *Strange Things* (see note to 97.15). The correspondence between James and Myers is at Houghton (bMS Am 1092.9 [408–425, 3306–3326]), the Society in London, and the Harry Price Library at the University of London. The one letter in the Price collection, dated April 18 [1885], is important because it establishes the date of the first meeting between James and Myers. In it James suggests that Myers call on the 21st when James's wife plans to host "an afternoon tea."

37.13   planchette]   In May 1887 the Council of the American Society published a "Request for Coöperation" which included an appeal signed by William N. Bullard as chairman of the Committee on Mediumistic Phenomena for experiments with automatic writing "as by planchette or otherwise" (PASPR, 1 [December 1887], 266).

37.21   Janet's]   Pierre Janet (1859–1947), French psychologist, "Les Actes inconscients et le dédoublement de la personnalité pendant le somnambulisme provoqué," *Revue Philosophique*, 22 (December 1886), 577–592; "L'Anesthésie systématisée et la dissociation des phénomènes psychologiques," *Revue Philosophique*, 23 (May 1887), 449–472. Janet's main work on automatism is *L'Automatisme psychologique: Essai de psychologie expérimentale sur les formes inférieures de l'activité humaine* (Paris: Alcan, 1889) (WJ 642.59). For James's view of this book see "The Hidden Self," reprinted in *Essays in Psychology*, WORKS. Janet is cited frequently in *The Principles of Psychology*.

38.13 tested] Mrs. Piper was frequently tested while entranced for anesthesia. Alta Piper narrates the following: "But the most drastic experiment ever tried in those early days was when Prof. James . . . during a sitting at which Mrs. James was present, made a small incision in Mrs. Piper's left wrist. During the trance state no notice was taken of this action and the wound did not bleed; but immediately upon awakening the wound bled freely" (p. 66).

40.25 Gurney] Edmund Gurney, "Peculiarities of Certain Post-Hypnotic States," PSPR, 4 (May 1887), 268–323.

40.38 Fillmore] Charles Wesley Fillmore, a graduate of the Harvard Medical School in 1856. James supplies additional information in his reference to the case in *Principles*, Works, p. 642n. In a letter to James concerning Mrs. Piper, May 17, 1889, Fillmore describes himself as an interested "outsider" who has contributed a few cases through Hodgson (PSPR, 8 [June 1892], 98).

41.40 Barrows] Ira Barrows (1804–1882), American physician, graduate of the Harvard Medical School in 1827.

41.41 brother] The combined Latin-English schoolboy composition suggests that the brother was a college student. The records of Brown University in Providence failed to turn up any Winsors with suitable dates.

42.22 Barlow] Joel Barlow (1754–1812), American politician and author, *The Hasty-Pudding: A Poem, in Three Cantos.*

44.5 Braid's] James Braid (1795?–1860), British hypnotist. William Benjamin Carpenter (1813–1885), British physiologist, *Principles of Mental Physiology, with Their Applications to the Training and Discipline of the Mind, and the Study of Its Morbid Conditions* (New York: D. Appleton, 1874) (WJ 511.77), p. 143 (sec. 128), does not cite a source in Braid.

44.27 Myers] Especially in PSPR, 3, 34.

45.3 *theoretic*] For a more extensive treatment see "The Hidden Self," *Essays in Psychology*, Works, and *The Principles of Psychology*, Works, pp. 200–210 and elsewhere.

45.29 Dean] Sidney Dean (1818–1901), American clergyman and author. The case is quoted in *Principles*, Works, pp. 373–374.

47.32 Arnold] See Appendix I.

53.3 C.] Gouverneur Morris Carnochan (1865–1915) was associated with James in the Committee on Hypnotism, but his Harvard dates are 1881–1886.

56.5 At] The census of hallucinations, a continuation of work begun by Gurney, was undertaken in 1889 by a committee of the English Society headed by Henry Sidgwick. The project was endorsed by the International Congress of Experimental Psychology held in Paris in August 1889. The Congress appointed James as collector for the United States. Sidgwick devoted two presidential addresses to the subject, PSPR, 6 (December 1889), 7–12, and (December 1890), 429–435. He also signed three *ad interim* reports, PSPR, 6 (December 1889), 183–185, (December 1890), 661–664; 7 (July 1891), 259–267 (this also includes the French results). The final "Report on the Census of Hallucinations" was given by Sidgwick to the Second International Congress of Experimental Psychology in London in August 1892 and published PSPR, 10 (August 1894), 25–422. None of these appear to include the American results.

James reported his results at several meetings of the American Society (see p. 385); his two published reports are included in the present volume.

60.28　Gurney]　*Phantasms of the Living*, I, 6–24.

61.27　Sidgwick's]　James is referring to Sidgwick's first presidential address on "The Census of Hallucinations."

63.6　*Proceedings*]　Edmund Gurney, "Recent Experiments in Hypnotism," PSPR, 5 (June 1888), 3–17.

64.11　Parish's]　Edmund Parish, *Über die Trugwahrnehmung (Hallucination und Illusion) mit besonderer Berücksichtigung der internationalen Enquête über Wachhallucination bei Gesunden* (Leipzig: Ambr. Abel, 1894); vols. 7–8 of the Schriften der Gesellschaft für psychologische Forschung. James's annotated copy is in Houghton (*AC 85.J2376.Zz894p). There is an English translation, *Hallucinations and Illusions: A Study of the Fallacies of Perception* (London: Walter Scott, 1897).

64.24　theory]　In back of his copy James has "His own theory 105."

64.25　'dissociated']　In back of his copy James has "Dissociation defined 106, 123."

65.19　law]　In back of his copy James has "Nature of hall. = *illusion* 102."

65.38　Royce's]　Josiah Royce (1855–1916), American philosopher, James's colleague at Harvard, "Report of the Committee on Phantasms and Presentiments," PASPR, 1 (March 1889), 350–428. Royce holds that there are pseudo-presentiments, that is, "*more or less instantaneous and irresistible hallucinations of memory*" (p. 366).

66.36　JOHNSON]　Alice Johnson (d. 1940), British psychical researcher, editor of many of the Society's publications.

67.2　Sidgwick's]　Eleanor Mildred Sidgwick (1845–1936), British educator and psychical researcher. The correspondence between James and Sidgwick is at Houghton (bMS Am 1092.9 [615–618, 3758–3759]), the Society for Psychical Research in London, and at Trinity College, Cambridge.

67.7　fewer]　PSPR, 10, 36.

67.17　Gurney]　PSPR, 10, 31, from *Phantasms of the Living*.

68.8　England.]　PSPR, 10, 245.

69.1　numbers]　PSPR, 10, 247.

70.9　number]　PSPR, 10, 242.

71.28　veridicals]　PSPR, 10, 249.

71.34　Anxiety]　PSPR, 10, 168.

71.39　expectation]　PSPR, 10, 174.

72.30　figure]　PSPR, 10, 63–64.

Notes

76.14 Edmunds] Lucy Edmunds was for many years Hodgson's secretary.

76.21 *Zur*] Edmund Parish, *Zur Kritik des telepathischen Beweismaterials* (Leipzig: Barth, 1897).

79.1 MYERS] "A Record of Observations of Certain Phenomena of Trance" appears in PSPR, 6 (December 1890), 436–659. It consists of an Introduction by Myers (pp. 436–442), "Part I" by Oliver Lodge (pp. 443–557), "Part II" by Walter Leaf (1852–1927), British scholar (pp. 558–646), an index to cases "specially difficult to explain by direct thought-transference" in Parts I and II, prepared by Lodge (pp. 647–650), "Part III" by James (pp. 651–659). The contribution by Hodgson which James assumes will appear together with his in fact appears in a later volume, "A Record of Observations of Certain Phenomena of Trance," PSPR, 8 (June 1892), 1-167.

The reports by Lodge and Leaf cover Mrs. Piper's English sittings of November 1889–February 1890 in which James was not involved. Included is one sitting held at James's home in Chocorua on September 20, 1889 when James was not present (pp. 569–574). There are numerous references to James in Hodgson's share of the report: pp. 69–84 provide the documents of the Bessie Blodgett case discussed by James; pp. 92–95 contain the Kate Walsh case; pp. 95–96 record a sitting at Chocorua with James taking part; pp. 96–100 contain six cases forwarded by James with letters to James by several sitters; pp. 133–135 give the sitting of December 4, 1890 with references to 'Eliza'. The Walsh and Eliza incidents are included as an appendix to the present volume.

79.15 Huxley's] See note to 366.9.

80.11 G.] One of James's sisters-in-law; see note to 15.35.

80.34 Herman] James's infant son Herman died on July 9, 1885.

83.20 fall] Mrs. Piper visited James at Chocorua for a holiday and to discuss final arrangements for the trip to England. Alta Piper notes that while fishing on that occasion, her mother caught the "largest bass" caught up to that time in Lake Chocorua. Following the visit James wrote Mrs. Piper: "I hope you will continue to be the same simple, genuine, unassuming Yankee girl that you are now" (*The Life and Work of Mrs. Piper*, pp. 49–50).

84.22 Hodgson] PSPR, 8 (June 1892), 46–50 (see note to 15.14).

85.6 aunt] James's aunt Catharine Walsh died on March 6, 1889. Documents concerning this incident appear as an appendix to the present volume. For details of her life see Strouse, pp. 32–35.

85.8 "E.] The case is treated by Hodgson, PSPR, 8 (June 1892), 44–45.

85.30 brother] James's brother Garth Wilkinson James died in 1883.

85.33 *Literary*] James's Introduction to *The Literary Remains of the Late Henry James* (1884) is reprinted in *Essays in Religion and Morality*, WORKS.

86.19 Blodgett] Documents related to the case of Bessie Blodgett are given by Hodgson, PSPR, 8 (June 1892), 69–84.

87.12 X.'s] See note to 97.15.

88.16 child] James's son William James was born in 1882.

89.16   Langley]   Samuel Pierpont Langley (1834–1906), American astronomer, joined the Society in 1889, became a vice-president in 1890 and was still serving in 1904.

89.18   Richet]   Charles Robert Richet (1850–1935), French physiologist. Richet's letters to James are at Houghton (bMS Am 1092, letters 796–806).

90.8   Moses]   William Stainton Moses resigned in November 1886, giving the following as his reason: "as a representative Spiritualist I could not do otherwise, considering, as I do, that the evidence for phenomena of the genuine character of which I and many others have satisfied ourselves beyond doubt, is not being properly entertained or fairly treated by the Society for Psychical Research" (JSPR, 2 [December 1886], 488).

90.9   Wallace]   Wallace was an honorary member of the Society and appears in membership lists into the 1900s. For Wallace's adventures with Boston mediums see note to 29.13.

90.22–23   Sidgwick]   An untitled address, PSPR, 1 (October 1882), 7–12.

91.40   Barrett]   See note to 6.29.

93.16   Podmore]   Frank Podmore (1856–1910), British psychical researcher. James's two reviews of *Apparitions and Thought-Transference* (1895) are reprinted in the present volume. Widener preserves *Studies in Psychical Research* (New York: G. P. Putnam's Sons, 1897) (Phil 7068.97.11) and *Modern Spiritualism: A History and a Criticism*, 2 vols. (London: Methuen, 1902) (Phil 7069. 02.11). Neither is annotated and most of the markings in *Modern Spiritualism* are not James's.

93.17   Marillier]   Léon Marillier (1842–1901), French psychologist, collector for the census of hallucinations in France. For Marillier's paper on James see *The Principles of Psychology*, WORKS, note to 421.36.

93.21   Creery]   Mary, Alice, and Maud were the daughters of Andrew M. Creery, a British clergyman. In 1881–1882 the three girls together with a family servant demonstrated thought-transference before several psychical researchers. The case is discussed in several reports of the Committee on Thought-Transference of which Barrett, Gurney, and Myers were members, PSPR, 1 (October 1882), 13–34; (April 1883), 70–97; (July 1883), 161–215; and in *Phantasms of the Living*, I, 20–31. Balfour Stewart and Creery also contributed notes, PSPR, 1 (October 1882), 35–42, 43–46. In *Phantasms* Gurney rests much of his argument upon the case: "I have dwelt at some length on our series of trials with the members of the Creery family, as it is to those trials that we owe our own conviction of the possibility of genuine thought-transference between persons in a normal state" (I, 29). In later tests the girls were caught signaling and confessed that signals were used in a few of the earlier tests. On November 5, 1887 James wrote Granville Stanley Hall that "Hodgson tells me that Gurney and Mrs. Sidgwick have had the Creerys again and caught them cheating and will soon publish a full account of it" (copy at Houghton [bMS Am 1092.1], original at Clark University). Gurney withdrew the case in "Note Relating to Some of the Published Experiments in Thought-Transference," PSPR, 5 (June 1888), 269–270.

94.3   Guthrie]   See note to 34.4.

94.24 Pease] Edward Reynolds Pease (1857–1955), British Fabian socialist, "The Divining Rod," PSPR, 2 (April 1884), 79–107. An abstract appears in JSPR, 1 (February 1884), 5–6.

94.26 Gurney's] Gurney contributed the following papers on hypnotism to the PSPR: "The Stages of Hypnotism," 2 (April 1884), 61–72; "An Account of Some Experiments in Mesmerism," 2 (July 1884), 201–206; "The Problems of Hypnotism," 2 (December 1884), 265–292; "Peculiarities of Certain Post-Hypnotic States," 4 (May 1887), 268–323; "Recent Experiments in Hypnotism," 5 (June 1888), 3–17; "Hypnotism and Telepathy," 5 (June 1888), 216–259. Many of the experiments involved George Albert Smith and his Brighton associates. Experiments with a screen are described in the second paper.

95.4 Gurney's] Reported especially in "Peculiarities of Certain Post-Hypnotic States."

95.16 Janet] See note to 37.21.

95.16 Binet] Alfred Binet (1857–1911), French psychologist. His articles on multiple personality in the *Open Court* (1889) and *Revue Philosophique* (1889–1890) are listed in *Principles*, WORKS, note to 201.6.

95.33 Gurney] See p. 25.

96.26 Sidgwick] Eleanor Mildred Sidgwick, "Results of a Personal Investigation into the Physical Phenomena of Spiritualism," PSPR, 4 (October 1886), 45–74.

96.30 Hodgson] "The Possibilities of Mal-Observation and Lapse of Memory from a Practical Point of View," PSPR, 4 (May 1887), 381–495, consisting of an Introduction by Hodgson and an "Experimental Investigation" (pp. 405–495) by S. J. Davey. A brief obituary notice in JSPR, 5 (January 1891), 16, states that Davey died on December 8, 1890, at the age of 27.

96.37 Blavatsky's] "Report on Phenomena Connected with Theosophy," PSPR, 3 (December 1885), 201–400, contains a statement by a committee as well as investigations by Hodgson and others. The Theosophical Society was founded in 1875 by Elena Petrovna Blavatsky (1831–1891), Russian traveler and religious writer, and others.

97.15 X] Ada Goodrich Freer (1857–1931), often used the pseudonym Miss X, "Recent Experiments in Crystal-Vision," PSPR, 5 (June 1889), 486–521. The *Combined Index* to the publications of the Society should be consulted for additional writings on the subject. Her career both as a psychical researcher and folklore collector is discussed in John L. Campbell and Trevor H. Hall, *Strange Things: The Story of Fr Allan McDonald, Ada Goodrich Freer, and the Society for Psychical Research's Enquiry into Highland Second Sight* (London: Routledge & Kegan Paul, 1968). Hall argues that she was introduced to the Society by Myers when she and Myers were having an affair.

97.36 Sidgwick] The *Combined Index* should be consulted for writings by the three authors. Many of them appeared in the PSPR, vols. 5–7 (1889–1892).

98.5 Myers] "The Subliminal Consciousness," PSPR, 7 (February 1892), 298–355; 8 (July 1892), 333–404, (December 1892), 436–535; 9 (June 1893), 3–128; 11 (December 1895), 334–593.

98.11 "Each] "The Subliminal Consciousness," PSPR, 7, 305.

99.34 Helmholtz] Hermann Ludwig Ferdinand von Helmholtz (1821–1894), German physiologist, physicist, and psychologist.

99.34 Huxley] See note to 366.9.

99.35 Pasteur] Louis Pasteur (1822–1895).

99.35 Edison] Thomas Alva Edison (1847–1931).

104.20 Janet] Pierre Janet, "Étude sur un cas d'aboulie et d'idées fixes," *Revue Philosophique*, 31 (March 1891), 258–287, (April 1891), 382–407.

104.25 *Salpêtrière*] A hospital in Paris in which in 1880 Jean Martin Charcot established a clinic for the treatment of nervous diseases. Janet, Binet, and other psychologists frequently observed the patients there. It is possible that in 1882 James visited it (Ralph Barton Perry, *The Thought and Character of William James*, 2 vols. [Boston: Little, Brown, 1935], II, 723).

105.19 "*Il*] Janet, p. 400.

107.3 author] Frederic William Henry Myers, *Science and a Future Life with Other Essays* (London: Macmillan, 1893). Two copies from James's library are in Houghton (*AC 85.J2376.Zz893m[A] and [B]). The former is inscribed to James by the author.

107.7 "Charles] Pp. 51–75.

107.10 "Now] Pp. 68–69 from *The Life and Letters of Charles Darwin, Including an Autobiographical Chapter*, ed. Francis Darwin, 3 vols. (London: John Murray, 1887), I, 100–101.

108.3 Leopold] "Leopold, Duke of Albany:—In Memoriam," pp. 211–243. Leopold (1853–1884) was the youngest son of Queen Victoria, noted for his support of literature and education.

108.28 "Of] P. 30.

108.34 The] Pp. 31–33.

109.27 "I] Pp. 35–36.

111.1 Ward] James Ward (1843–1925), British philosopher and psychologist. The correspondence between James and Ward is at Houghton (bMS Am 1092.9 [649–661, 3829–3854]). The relations between James and Ward are discussed by Perry, II, 644–657.

113.3 Dariex] Xavier Dariex, editor of the *Annales des Sciences Psychiques*, "Expériences de suggestion mentale à distance," *Annales des Sciences Psychiques*, 3 (1893), 257–267.

113.10 Tolosa-Latour] Manuel de Tolosa Latour (1857–1919), Spanish writer on hygiene, "Expériences de suggestion mentale à grande distance," *Annales*, 3 (1893), 268–273.

113.15 Tamburini] Augusto Tamburini (1848–1919), Italian psychiatrist, "Télépathie: Critique et observations," *Annales*, 3 (1893), 280–314.

115.4 Podmore] Frank Podmore, *Apparitions and Thought-Transference: An Examination of the Evidence for Telepathy* (London: Walter Scott, 1894). Advertising for the Contemporary Science Series identifies Scribner's as the importer. Some later editions give the names of both publishers (London: Walter Scott; New York: Charles Scribner's Sons). James's copy is not known.

115.8 evidence] Of the numerous cases mentioned by Podmore, the investigations by Max Dessoir, Anton Schmoll, Malcolm Guthrie, Oliver Lodge, Edmund Gurney, and George Albert Smith were well known to James. Podmore does not mention the Creery sittings (see note to 93.21).

116.3 Sidgwick] Podmore, pp. 65–75, from Henry Sidgwick, Eleanor Mildred Sidgwick, and George Albert Smith, "Experiments in Thought-Transference," PSPR, 6 (December 1889), 128–170; Eleanor Mildred Sidgwick, Alice Johnson, "Experiments in Thought-Transference," PSPR, 8 (December 1892), 536–596. Serious questions have been raised about Smith's good faith, see note to 34.15. In these experiments Smith was the only successful agent. Podmore (p. 66) notes that at least seven others tried to act as agents and failed.

116.37 volume] The review of *Apparitions and Thought-Transference* in the *Nation* is attributed to James on the basis of style alone, but the attribution is reasonably certain. The *Nation* had no one who during this period reviewed work in psychical research regularly. Within ten years of the Podmore review, Josiah Royce, Joseph Jastrow, Charles Sanders Peirce, Christine Ladd Franklin, and William Healey Dall contributed reviews in this field. Stylistic evidence makes it unlikely that one of them is the Podmore reviewer. On the other hand, the reviewer's view of psychical research is characteristically Jamesian. Especially characteristic are the claims that the phenomena are "baffling," that they are "so fragmentary, sporadic, and contextless that they weave themselves into no system," and that what is most needed is a theory which "has a use for such facts." Even more typical is the sentence "that these events should be always present in sufficient measure to tempt belief, but always in insufficient measure to justify it."

Most of James's contributions to the *Nation* can be documented on the basis of the *Nation* records in the New York Public Library. But the records have gaps and nothing is available for the period of the Podmore review.

117.38 Lang's] James reviewed this book in the *Psychological Review*, 1 (1894), 630–632, reprinted in *Essays, Comments, and Reviews*, WORKS.

119.2 phenomena] In a letter to Elizabeth Goddard, February 3, [1896], James writes "I believe in the fact of T. T. but have *absolutely* no theory of the *modus operandi*" (Clements Library, University of Michigan).

120.17 careful] The date and later citations indicate that James is thinking of the work of the English Society.

121.4 Fig. 1] The drawings are from the third report (see note to 34.15), PSPR, 1 (July 1883), 181, 187, 191, 207.

121.4–5 Blackburn] For references to the work of Blackburn and Smith see note to 34.15. The statistics are from the third report, PSPR, 1, 167.

121.13 trials] PSPR, 2, 31; also *Phantasms of the Living*, I, 37.

121.15 Fig. 2] The drawings are from Guthrie (see note to 34.4), "An Account of Some Experiments in Thought-Transference," PSPR, 2 (April 1884), 33, 34, 35.

123.3 trials] The figures given cannot be verified since several series of experiments were performed in 1883 and no general figure was found in the reports.

123.6 "Miss X."] Ada Goodrich Freer (anonymously), "A Record of Telepathic and Other Experiences," PSPR, 6 (June 1890), 358–397.

123.9 entries] PSPR, 6, 377.

123.13 Wingfield] Experiments by the Misses K. and M. Wingfield, of the Redings, Totteridge, are reported in *Phantasms of the Living*, I, 34; II, 653–654. No indication is given that these experiments were supervised.

123.24–25 Dessoir] See note to 34.1.

123.25 Schmoll] For Schmoll and Mabire see note to 34.1.

123.25 Smith] See note to 34.11.

123.25 Schrenck-Notzing] Albert von Schrenck-Notzing (1862–1929), German physician, "Experimental Studies in Thought-Transference," PSPR, 7 (April 1891), 3–22. Preserved in Widener is *Die Suggestions-Therapie bei krankhaften Erscheinungen des Geschlechtssinnes* (Stuttgart: Enke, 1892) (Phil 7140.8) inscribed to James by the author.

123.26 Barrett] For Barrett's reports on the Creery investigation see note to 93.21. He gives his own view of thought transference in "Appendix to the Report on Thought-Reading," PSPR, 1 (October 1882), 47–64.

123.26 Gurney] Gurney was a member of the committee investigating the Creery case.

123.37 Rawson] Henry Gilbert Rawson (b. 1851), British lawyer, "Experiments in Thought-Transference," PSPR, 11 (March 1895), 2–17. The agents and percipients in these tests were several unidentified ladies, "intimate friends" of the author and entirely trustworthy. Rawson was not a member of the Society and the experiments were conducted without supervision.

124.1 Thaw] A. Blair Thaw, American physician, "Some Experiments in Thought-Transference," PSPR, 8 (December 1892), 422–435. The agent and the percipient were Thaw and his wife.

124.2 Sidgwick] See note to 116.3. In the later series conducted by Mrs. Sidgwick, agent and percipient occupied different rooms.

124.8 percipients] PSPR, 6, 128.

124.14 Later] PSPR, 8, 541.

124.23 Richet] Charles Robert Richet, "Relation de diverses expériences sur la transmission mentale, la lucidité, et autres phénomènes non explicables par les données scientifiques actuelles," PSPR, 5 (June 1888), 18–168. The figures are given on p. 114n.

125.10 Janet] Pierre Janet, "Note sur quelques phénomènes de somnambulisme," *Revue Philosophique*, 21 (1886), 190–198; "Deuxième note sur le sommeil provoqué à distance et la suggestion mentale pendant l'état somnambulique," *Revue Philosophique*, 22 (1886), 212–223. The subject of hypnotism at a distance was raised by Janet in late 1885 at a meeting of the Société de Psychologie Physiologique. The case revolved around Madame B., the Léonie who figures extensively in Janet's *Automatisme psychologique*, a hysteric who was hypnotised by Janet and Dr. Gibert of Le Havre. Gibert himself—his first name is not given in these accounts—seems not to have published an independent report. Richet, Ochorowicz, and Dufay went to Le Havre to observe Janet's and Gibert's experiments. Another observer was Myers. His impressions are given in "On Telepathic Hypnotism, and Its Relation to Other Forms of Hypnotic Suggestion," PSPR, 4 (October 1886), 127–188.

125.10 Richet] Charles Robert Richet, "Un Fait de somnambulisme à distance," *Revue Philosophique*, 21 (1886), 199–200; "Expériences sur le sommeil à distance," *Revue Philosophique*, 25 (1888), 435–452. Richet also discusses cases other than that of Madame B.

125.10 Ochorowicz] Julian Ochorowicz (1850–1917), Polish philosopher. His observations of Madame B. are described in *De la suggestion mentale*, preface by Charles Richet (Paris: Octave Doin, 1887); English translation by J. Fitzgerald, *Mental Suggestion* (New York: Humboldt Publishing Co., 1891).

125.10 Héricourt] Jules Héricourt (b. 1850), French physician, "Un Cas de somnambulisme à distance," *Revue Philosophique*, 21 (1886), 200–203.

125.11 Dufay] Jean François Charles Dufay (1815–1898), French physician, "Contribution à l'étude du somnambulisme provoqué à distance et à l'insu du sujet," *Revue Philosophique*, 26 (1888), 301–312.

125.11 Dariex] See note to 113.3.

125.11 Tolosa Latour] See note to 113.10.

125.14 series] James's figures could be derived from Myers, PSPR, 4, 136.

125.21–22 *Proceedings*] The 1895 date is an error. James seems to have been anticipating the report actually published in 1898 (see note to 187.4). For the earlier reports see note to 79.1.

125.30 telepathy] In the glossary of *Human Personality*, I, xxii, Myers claims that he suggested the term 'telepathy' in 1882.

126.7 ninth] Perhaps the case described in "A Possible Case of Projections of the Double," see note to 376.6.

126.14 report] See note to 56.5.

127.12 successor] James was succeeded by William Crookes (1832–1919), British physicist and chemist. For an evaluation of Crookes as a psychical researcher see Trevor H. Hall, *The Spiritualists: The Story of Florence Cook and William Crookes* (New York: Helix Press, 1962).

129.10 Richet's] Charles Robert Richet, "La Suggestion mentale et le calcul des probabilités," *Revue Philosophique*, 18 (December 1884), 609–674.

130.10 'Miss X.'] See note to 97.15.

130.18 Myers] William Frederic Henry Myers, "William Stainton-Moses," PSPR, 8 (December 1892), 597–600; "The Experiences of W. Stainton Moses," PSPR, 9 (January 1894), 245–352; 11 (March 1895), 24–113.

130.19 Lang] Andrew Lang (1844–1912), British writer, JSPR, 6 (March 1894), 219–222.

132.11 Hodgson-Davey] See note to 96.30.

132.11 Paladino-] Eusapia Paladino (1854–1918), Italian physical medium. In July 1894 Lodge, Myers, and Ochorowicz were guests on an island in the Mediterranean owned by Charles Richet. Richet had invited them to study Eusapia. Lodge's favorable report appears in JSPR, 6 (November 1894), 306–360. But trickery was detected in later sittings, in Cambridge, England. An account of these is given by Henry Sidgwick, "Eusapia Paladino," JSPR, 7 (November 1895), 148–159. James continued to be interested in Eusapia's phenomena and eventually came to believe that some of them were genuine. For his later view see note to 362.33.

132.29 "calm] From the Introduction to Book II of Milton's *Reason of Church-Government*, in *Complete Prose Works of John Milton*, I (New Haven: Yale University Press, c1953), 822.

133.24 Phelps-case] Elizabeth Stuart Phelps Ward (1844–1911), American author, *Chapters from a Life* (Boston: Houghton, Mifflin, 1896), pp. 6–8, recalls her paternal grandfather's stories about the haunting of his parsonage in Stratford, Conn., when furniture and dishes moved about the room and "cold turnips dropped from the solid ceiling." The relevant chapter of the book appeared in *McClure's Magazine*, 6 (December 1885), 49–58. Her account indicates that the case was widely known.

133.26 Nevius's] John Livingston Nevius (1829–1893), American missionary in China, *Demon Possession and Allied Themes: Being an Inductive Study of Phenomena of Our Own Times* (Chicago: Fleming H. Revell Company, [1894]). There are numerous references to events of the kind usually associated with demon possession, but nothing was found which fits James's reference more directly. James's two reviews are reprinted in *Essays, Comments, and Reviews*, WORKS. James's copy of the second edition (1896) is at Houghton (24244.43.2B*).

133.27 Wesley's] John Wesley (1703–1791), English clergyman, founder of Methodism. L. Tyerman, *The Life and Times of the Rev. John Wesley, M.A., Founder of the Methodists*, 2 vols. (London: Hodder and Stoughton, 1870), I, 22–23. James's copy of vol. I is in Widener (Br 2123.25.45B).

133.27 Amherst] Walter Hubbell (b. 1851), American writer, *The Great Amherst Mystery: A True Narrative of the Supernatural* (New York: Brentano's, 1888), describes the haunting in 1878–1879 of the Teed family in Amherst, Nova Scotia.

133.28 Willis's] Henry Augustus Willis (1830–1918), American writer, "A Remarkable Case of 'Physical Phenomena,'" *Atlantic Monthly*, 22 (August 1868), 129–135, describes the case of Mary Carrick, an Irish servant in "one of the larger towns in Massachusetts." Willis does not identify Mary's employer. He does claim to have himself witnessed the events.

133.30 Sharpe's] Charles Kirkpatrick Sharpe (1781–1851), Scottish scholar, *A Historical Account of the Belief in Witchcraft in Scotland* (London: Hamilton, Adams, 1884), pp. 229–254, describes the haunting of the house of Andrew Mackie in 1695 as reported by Alexander Telfair, minister of the parish in which the haunting took place. James's edition has not been identified.

133.31 Morse] Charles Wentworth Upham (1802–1875), American clergyman and author, *Salem Witchcraft; with an Account of Salem Village, and a History of Opinions on Witchcraft and Kindred Subjects* (rpt. Williamstown, Mass.: Corner House Publishers, 1971), pp. 441–447, gives the testimony of William Morse. Morse's wife was being accused of witchcraft.

133.32 Humboldt's] Wilhelm von Humboldt (1767–1835), German philologist and diplomat, *Briefe an eine Freundin*, new ed. (Berlin: Siegfried Cronbach, 1881). Nothing was found in the Introduction by Charlotte Diede, recipient of the letters and editor of the collection.

133.33 *Annales*] A document dated La Chapelle-Viviers, December 1892, describing events in 1867 or 1868 connected with the sisters Touin, *Annales des Sciences Psychiques*, 5 (1895), 86–91.

133.34–35 Swanland] Frederic William Henry Myers, "On Alleged Movements of Objects, without Contact, Occurring not in the Presence of a Paid Medium," PSPR, 7 (July 1891), 146–198, (February 1892), 383–394. The second part consists primarily of a letter to Henry Sidgwick describing events witnessed by John Bristow, a carpenter in the village of Swanland.

136.19 Bridgewater] A series of books in natural theology published in the 1830s.

136.20 Lyell's] Charles Lyell (1797–1875), British geologist.

138.5 Cattell's] James McKeen Cattell (1860–1944), American psychologist, a review of James's presidential address, *Psychological Review*, 3 (September 1896), 582–583. The review is reprinted as an appendix. James's numerous letters to Cattell are in the Library of Congress.

143.13 Paul] I Corinthians, xiv.2.

143.21 Baron] In the extensive correspondence concerning this item at the Society for Psychical Research in London, the question of copyright ownership was raised by Guy Waters in a letter to James dated May 2, 1896. Guy Waters is Henry Guy Waters (b. 1856), who using the pseudonym Salvarona published several spiritualistic books. The discussion leaves little doubt that Waters is Le Baron.

144.2 Evangel] Evangel is Sarah Jane Farmer (1847–1916), organizer of the Green Acre Conferences at Eliot, Me., summer encampments devoted to various subjects, but emphasizing comparative religion.

145.27 Richmond] Cora Linn Victoria Richmond (Scott) (also Cora L. V. Tappan, Tappan-Richmond) (1840–1927), American medium and healer.

146.23 World's] The World's Parliament of Religions was held in 1893 in Chicago.

163.35 Balfour's] Edward Green Balfour (1813–1889), *Cyclopædia of India* (1857).

163.37 Hunter's] William Wilson Hunter (1840–1900), *A Comparative Dictionary of the Languages of India and High Asia.*

165.16 "Strange] The *National Union Catalogue* lists the following under Rachel Baker (d. 1794): *The Surprising Case of Rachel Baker, Who Prays and Preaches in Her Sleep; with Specimens of Her Extraordinary Performances* (1814). She is the author of *Remarkable Sermons of Rachel Baker, and Pious Ejaculations, Delivered During Sleep.*

165.38 Irving's] Edward Irving (1792–1834), Scottish clergyman whose church in London was noted for outbreaks of speaking in tongues.

167.7 *Proceedings*] F. C. C. Hansen, Danish physiologist, and Alfred Georg Ludwig Lehmann (1858–1921), Danish physiologist, "Über unwillkürliches Flüstern. Eine kritische und experimentelle Untersuchung der sogenannten Gedankenübertragung," *Philosophische Studien*, 11 (1895), 471–530. The two authors were primarily concerned with experiments involving G. A. Smith (see note to 34.15).

169.3 Messrs.] Henry Sidgwick, "Involuntary Whispering Considered in Relation to Experiments in Thought-Transference," PSPR, 12 (December 1896), 298–315. Sidgwick is commenting on Hansen and Lehmann, "Über unwillkürliches Flüstern."

170.16 Titchener] Edward Bradford Titchener (1867–1927), English-born American psychologist, "The 'Feeling of Being Stared At'," *Science*, n.s. 8 (December 23, 1898), 895–897. James's letters to Titchener are at Cornell University; one letter to James is at Houghton (bMS Am 1092, letter 1143).

171.28 rejoined] Edward Bradford Titchener, "Lehmann and Hansen on 'The Telepathic Problem'," *Science*, n.s. 9 (January 6, 1899), 36.

171.37 "Your] For German text see p. 175.

172.16 SCIENCE] Edward Bradford Titchener, "Professor James on Telepathy," *Science*, n.s. (May 12, 1899), 686–687.

175.32 "Ein] Hansen and Lehmann, p. 498.

176.21 "Human] Reprinted in *Essays in Religion and Morality*, WORKS.

177.3 *Science*] Edward Bradford Titchener, "The Telepathic Question," *Science*, n.s. 9 (June 2, 1899), 787.

177.36 Sidgwick] See note to 116.3.

177.41 Dessoir's] Frederic William Henry Myers, review of Max Dessoir, *Das Doppel-Ich*, in PSPR, 6 (December 1889), 207–215.

180.5 Ermacora] Giovanni Battista Ermacora (1869–1898), Italian physicist and psychical researcher, "Telepathic Dreams Experimentally Induced," PSPR, 11 (July 1895), 235–308. Preserved in Widener is James's marked copy of *I fatti spiritici e le ipotesi affrettate* (Padua: Drucker, 1892) (Phil 7068.92.65).

Notes

182.4 plea] Enrico Agostino Morselli (1852–1929), Italian anthropologist, *I Fenomeni Telepatici e le Allucinazioni Veridiche: Osservazioni Critiche* (Florence: Landi, 1897).

183.3 "under] *I Fenomeni*, p. 55.

184.2 *Science*] James McKeen Cattell, "Mrs. Piper, the Medium," *Science*, n.s. 7 (April 15, 1898), 534–535, a note on Richard Hodgson's "A Further Record of Observations of Certain Phenomena of Trance," PSPR, 13 (February 1898), 284–582. Cattell quotes remarks by James Mark Baldwin (p. 534), John Trowbridge (p. 526), Nathaniel Southgate Shaler (pp. 524–525), James Mills Peirce (pp. 460–462), and Silas Weir Mitchell (pp. 482–483). With the exception of the Peirce one, the sittings were arranged by James, held at his house, with James in most cases present and taking notes. They were held in 1892–1895.

185.17 'but] Remark by Shaler.

187.4 Piper] Richard Hodgson, "A Further Record of Observations of Certain Phenomena of Trance," PSPR, 13 (February 1898), 284–582.

187.11 G.P.] George Pellew (1859–1892), British-born, American author, graduated from Harvard in 1880, an associate of the Society. According to Hodgson, Pellew had a sitting with Mrs. Piper on March 7, 1888, but was not introduced to her by his correct name.

187.13 Hodgson] "A Further Record," pp. 324–325.

190.25 opinion] In connection with Mrs. Piper's 1901 statement, the *New York Herald* prints an excerpt from a letter by James dated September 18, 1901: "As regards the spiritualistic hypothesis, I am still 'on the fence.' I said something about the alternatives to it in a notice of Hodgson's report on Mrs. P., which I wrote for the Psychological Review in 1898" (Bell, p. 169).

191.27 Schiller] Ferdinand Canning Scott Schiller (1864–1937), British philosopher, a member of the Society.

192.1 On] Myers died on January 17, 1901, in Rome, at the same hotel where James and his wife were then staying. His last hours are described by Axel Munthe, one of several physicians who treated Myers during his last illness, in *The Story of San Michele*. Munthe describes James sitting just outside the death chamber with a notebook on his knees, waiting for a message which Myers had promised to send after his death. Munthe is quoted at length in Gay Wilson Allen, *William James* (New York: Viking, 1969), pp. 420–421. Trevor Hall, particularly in *Strange Things* and *The Strange Case of Edmund Gurney*, dwells at considerable length upon Myers's personality and work as a psychical researcher. Hall's conclusions are totally opposed to James's.

193.9 immortality] That Myers was obsessed with the question of immortality is clear from his letters to James; see Perry, II, 163.

194.24 'Commission'] James is referring to the Seybert Commission, established by the will of Henry Seybert, a believing spiritualist from Philadelphia, for the investigation of spiritualism. Horace Howard Furness (1865–1930), American Shakespeare scholar, served as its chairman, while George Stuart Fullerton served as its secretary. The Commission published only one report, *Preliminary Report of the Commission Appointed by the University of Penn-*

sylvania to Investigate Modern Spiritualism (Philadelphia: J. B. Lippincott, 1887). James's copy, inscribed by Fullerton, is in Widener (Phil 7060.102). The Commission concentrated its efforts on Henry Slade, a famous slate-writing medium, and concluded that Slade and other mediums studied were frauds.

James's efforts to get the Commission to study Mrs. Piper can be documented from the surviving correspondence. On March 1, 1894, in a letter to James, Fullerton responded negatively to James's suggestion that Mrs. Piper be studied (bMS Am 1092, letter 275). On March 13 or 14, James expressed his disappointment and asked Fullerton to give reasons for the refusal. James argued that should opinion concerning Mrs. Piper change, it would be well to have on record evidence of the obstacles which blocked her path (bMS Am 1092.1). Fullerton replied on March 19 (letter 276) and enclosed a letter to James from Furness which explained the view of the Commission. Only a copy of Furness' letter is at Harvard (bMS Am 1092, letter 284). According to Furness, the Commission has no money for any investigations, since in his very complicated will Seybert did not leave any money for such work. Furthermore, Furness and others have had sittings with Mrs. Piper which were "ridiculous" failures and they cannot recommend further investigations. One of Furness' humorous suggestions must have hurt James: there is no need to explain all of the complications in Seybert's will since Phinuit can hunt up Henry Seybert in the spirit-world and get all of the details directly.

Seybert's will established a chair of philosophy at the University of Pennsylvania on condition that a commission to study spiritualism be appointed. Fullerton was the first incumbent of the Seybert Chair.

194.39 colleagues] Probably Hugo Münsterberg (1863–1916), German-born psychologist, James's colleague at Harvard. Münsterberg's "Psychology and Mysticism," *Atlantic Monthly*, 83 (January 1899), 67–85, reprinted in *Psychology and Life* (Boston: Houghton, Mifflin, 1899), drew a sharp defense of psychical research from James's friend Ferdinand Canning Scott Schiller, "Psychology and Psychical Research," PSPR, 14 (July 1899), 348–365. For the relations between James and Münsterberg see *The Principles of Psychology*, WORKS, note to 84.32.

198.1 automatism] For Myers on this term see *Human Personality*, I, xiv–xv.

198.16 hysteria] See *Human Personality*, I, 42–50; the paper is "The Subliminal Consciousness," PSPR, 7 (February 1892), 309. Myers states that the date was 1892.

199.7 dissolutive] In *Human Personality* (I, xvi), Myers defines 'dissolutive' as follows: "Opposed to *Evolutive;* of changes which tend not towards progress but towards decay."

204.3 "Myers's] See p. 196.

206.5 distance] See p. 125.

206.7 Myers's] *Human Personality*, I, 532–543. The term 'community of sensation' is defined on I, 487. It indicates the experiencing by one person of the feelings of another.

214.31 "Adrienne"] One of the personalities of Lucie, a patient treated by Pierre Janet. For references see the indexes to *The Principles of Psychology*, WORKS, and *Essays in Psychology*, WORKS.

216.2 However] John Trowbridge, "Telepathy," *Nation*, 76 (April 16, 1903), 308–309.

219.3 Hyslop] James not only endorsed the plan but also agreed to serve on the board of Hyslop's proposed Institute. However, when Hyslop used James's name in his fund-raising efforts, James had second thoughts. On November 14, 1904, he asked that his name be withdrawn from the board of the proposed Institute: "I didn't foresee the newspaper campaign and I have enough to carry in the way of reputation for crankiness without shouldering that" (bMS Am 1092.1). In a later letter to Hyslop, December 1, 1904, James authorized the publication of the letter of October 25, but still insisted on the withdrawal from the board (bMS Am 1092.1). In his turn, on February 27, 1905, Hyslop informed James that a prospective donor had changed her mind upon hearing of James's withdrawal. Hyslop would like a strong letter of endorsement from James by return mail. Otherwise, he would be forced to publish the whole correspondence and this, in Hyslop's view, would do much damage to James's reputation. James passed this letter on to Hodgson with the note "Is n't Hyslop funnier than a goat?" (bMS Am 1092, letter 435). James replied on February 28, urging Hyslop to publish the correspondence since James would like to be judged on his own words. James expressed his usual dislike of empty organizations: "I believe in psychical research, and in its endowment. I disbelieve in endowment without research" (bMS Am 1092.1). On March 2, Hyslop thanked James for this letter which in his view clears up the whole matter (bMS Am 1092, letter 436).

219.12 Prince's] Morton Prince (1854–1929), American physician and psychiatrist. In his work *The Dissociation of a Personality* (New York: Longmans, Green, 1906) (WJ 471.41), Prince gives the case of a single patient. It is likely that James would have been aware of the case before the publication of Prince's book.

219.12–13 Flournoy's] Théodore Flournoy (1854–1920), Swiss psychologist, *Des Indes à la planète Mars* (Paris: Alcan, 1900). A copy inscribed to James is in Widener (Phil 7060.80.9). Flournoy studied Hélène Smith, pseudonym of a medium who over a number of years produced writing purporting to be in Martian with detailed descriptions of the planet. The extensive correspondence between James and Flournoy is published in *The Letters of William James and Théodore Flournoy*, ed. Robert C. Le Clair (Madison: The University of Wisconsin Press, 1966).

221.16 C.H.P.] According to James's letters to Cattell, November 17 and 29, 1903, in the Library of Congress, the author of the narrative is C. H. Perkins. No information about him was found.

229.1 Thompson's] Rosalie Thompson (b. 1868), at the time of the sittings often referred to as Mrs. Edmond Thompson of Hampstead, London. She noticed her powers in 1896 and seems to have claimed to produce physical phenomena, including materializations. Some years later she was befriended by Myers and at his urging acted as a trance medium for the Society. She continued to sit for the Society into the summer of 1901. No later sittings are known, but she seems to have remained on friendly terms with the Society and her name continued to appear in its membership lists. Reports by Oliver Lodge, Myers, Frederik van Eeden, J. O. Wilson (pseudonym), John George Piddington, Richard Hodgson, Alice Johnson, and Mrs. A. W. Verrall, of sittings with

Notes

Mrs. Thompson appear in PSPR, 17 (June 1902), 59–244. The later report by Piddington, PSPR, 18 (January 1904), 104–307, is a supplement of the earlier reports. After Myers's death, Mrs. Piper claimed to be receiving messages from Myers for his widow. The messages were warnings that Mrs. Thompson was a fraud (letter from Eveleen Myers to James, April 3, 1901 [bMS Am 1092.9 (396)]).

230.2 "I] Isaac Kauffman Funk (1839–1912), American author and publisher, *The Widow's Mite and Other Psychic Phenomena* (New York: Funk & Wagnalls, 1904), pp. 178–179. In February 1903 Funk visited a medium in Brooklyn who told him to return a coin known as the widow's mite which Funk had borrowed in connection with his dictionary. Funk himself and others thought that the coin had already been returned but further investigation showed that the coin was still in the safe. In a letter dated April 10, 1903, Funk asked various scholars to comment upon the incident, suggesting four possible explanations, fraud, coincidence, subconscious powers, and spirit communication. James is responding to Funk's request.

231.3 Kennedy] Harris Kennedy (b. 1871), attended Harvard College in 1890–1894, the medical school in 1894–1898, a member of the American Branch of the Society.

240.13 *Witnesses*] Alfred Ludwig Theodor Schaper, Edward Willis Taylor, George Burgess Magrath, Maynard Ladd, Langdon Frothingham, and Alfred William Balch were either officers, or students, or both, of the Harvard Medical School. Allen Mackenzie Cleghorn, Henry Fox Hewes, and Frederick Adams Woods were also associated with the School, suggesting that they were among the witnesses and that their names are not correctly given in the list. Murray Anthony Potter, an educator, was associated with Harvard, but not with the Medical School.

243.32 case] Frederic William Henry Myers, "The Subliminal Consciousness," PSPR, 11 (December 1895), pp. 378–389, discusses the drowning of William E. and Joshua P. Mason, pp. 389–391, the case of Rose Foster.

246.6 James] On April 18, 1906 the San Francisco earthquake forced James to break off his teaching at Stanford University. On his way home, on April 29, he stopped in Denver and made the following entry in his diary: "Reach Denver about noon. Dr. E. J. A. Rogers (Dr. Gower not having come from England), Mr. Jas Thompson, Mrs. Rogers, & Prof. Headden, all testify with absolute distinctness to having seen tables move without contact" (bMS Am 1092.9 [4555]). The diary entry places the episode in Denver, Colo., and permits identification of the participants. Dr. and Mrs. Williams are pseudonyms of Edmund James Armstrong Rogers (1852–1922), American physician residing in Denver, and his wife Georgina. Dr. Gower is John Henry Gower (b. 1855), English-born musician and mining engineer residing in Denver. Professor H. is William Parker Headden (1850–1932), American educator, while J.T. is James Thompson. Gower and Edmund Rogers were members of the Society.
    Alice Johnson, "Report on Some Recent Sittings for Physical Phenomena in America," PSPR, 21 (October 1907), 94–135, provides numerous details of the sittings which according to her began in 1902. Johnson had some sittings with Gower in England and investigated the case further in Denver in August and September 1906.

248.1 fortnight] On December 4, 1908, in a letter from Bar Harbor, Maine, to his wife, James writes that he has spent an evening at a séance where he "was rewarded by the sight of an *object moving without contact,* under conditions so simple that no room for fakery seemed possible. Since this is the crack in the levee of scientific routine through wh. the whole Mississippi of supernaturalism may pour in, I am surprised that the spectacle hasn't moved my *feelings* more" (bMS Am 1092.9 [2436]). The letter was written at Oldfarm, the home of George Bucknam Dorr who was often associated with James in psychical research work. It is not clear whether Dorr was involved in the circle. According to James's letter, the sittings took place at the home of Mr. Roberts, a local hotel keeper. Apparently the phenomena continued, because on January 1, 1909, in a letter to Piddington, James writes: "I have just got a report of table levitation from a circle in Bar Harbor which I attended a month ago, and where I saw something (vide Hyslop's next Proceedings) which awakens great confidence." James's interest in physical phenomena is perhaps the reflection of a hope that the tide of public opinion would be turned by a crucial experiment. In a letter to Henry Pickering Bowditch, July 1, 1909, he writes: "Otherwise *physical* phenomena seem to be having a boom, and I think they are a more promising entering wedge, owing to their accessibility & simplicity" (bMS Am 1092.9 [811]).

252.7 Paladino] See notes to 132.11 and 362.33.

254.14 Imperator-Band] Until 1892 Mrs. Piper's control was Phinuit. He was followed by G.P. (see note to 187.11). In 1896 William Stainton Moses, who had died in 1892, began to appear in her trances and eventually introduced Rector, Imperator, Doctor, and Prudens, a group of controls often referred to as the Imperator-Band. They claimed to be the same spirits who had controlled Moses' own trances.

254.15 favored] James's efforts to keep a balanced view of the Piper-Hodgson phenomena are extensively documented in his correspondence, much of which is quoted in Professor Bowers' textual introduction. See especially his letter to Mrs. Oliver Wadsworth, quoted on p. 497.

254.38 Hodgson's] See notes to 79.1 and 187.4.

254.39 Sidgwick's] Eleanor Mildred Sidgwick, "Discussion of the Trance Phenomena of Mrs. Piper," PSPR, 15 (February 1900), 16–38.

254.39 Hyslop's] James Hervey Hyslop, "A Further Record of Observations of Certain Trance Phenomena," PSPR, 16 (October 1901), 1–649. His *Science and a Future Life* (Boston: Herbert B. Turner, 1905) deals primarily with Mrs. Piper. James's copy of the book is in Widener (Phil 7069.05.10).

257.26 *Herald*] The controversy to which James is alluding broke out in the fall of 1901. In the summer of 1901 Mrs. Piper was interviewed by a *New York Herald* reporter and this material was published on October 20 under the headline "I Am No Telephone to the Spirit World." The story provided some biographical information—cited earlier in the present notes—and claimed that in Mrs. Piper's own view she had no contact with the spirit world, that her phenomena could be explained by telepathy and hypnotism, and that she would no longer give sittings for the Society. On October 24, p. 7, the *Herald* quoted Hodgson's statement to the effect that relations between Mrs. Piper and the

Society remain as they have always been: "Her statement that she was going to give up her sittings and withdraw from the society represents simply a transient mood. Very often in the last few years she would get into that state of mind, and, while influenced by this passing mood, she gave the statement to a reporter." But Hodgson's statement appears next to what is alleged to be a statement by Mrs. Piper dated Boston, Wednesday [October 23]: "You may say for me most emphatically that I stand by my statement published in the *Sunday Herald*, and if necessary I will die for it." Mrs. Piper is then quoted as follows:

> When Mr. Hodgson says that my statement that I would give up sittings and withdraw from the society represents simply a 'transient mood,' and that I had been in that state of mind very often in the last few years, I suppose he refers to the fact that I have several times threatened to leave the society and give no more sittings, but have always allowed myself, in the interests of science, to be persuaded to remain by arguments to the effect that we were perhaps on the brink of discovery. This time, however, my decision is final. I shall stand by it and die for it if necessary. I have not regretted it for a moment.

The tangle of who said what to whom is not resolved in the story which the *Herald* carried on October 30, p. 9.

According to this, on October 29, Boston papers printed a statement released by Hodgson over Mrs. Piper's name:

> Everything will go on just as it has previously, so far as I am concerned. . . . I do not deny that I said something to the effect that I would never hold another sitting with Mr. Hodgson, and that I would die first, to a *New York Herald* reporter last summer, when I gave the original interview, but last week I did not see a representative of the *New York Herald* and did not reply to Dr. Hodgson. That is a misrepresentation, and, furthermore, I am not responsible for many of the former statements that the *Herald* published as coming from me.

The *Herald* in its turn claims that its reporter called on Mrs. Piper on October 29. She was ill, "the result of nervousness, brought on, she says, by recent publicity." A daughter carried the Boston reports to the sick-room and returned with a message from Mrs. Piper. According to this, Mrs. Piper admitted seeing Hodgson and a reporter on October 28, but denied issuing any statements for publication. The alleged message, in a milder tone, reiterates Mrs. Piper's desire to discontinue sittings.

It is hard to evaluate these conflicting claims in the absence of independent information. James's remark, however, confirms the general impression which they convey that Mrs. Piper was often unhappy with the arrangements.

The *Herald* controversy was not the first suggestion of strains between Mrs. Piper and the Society. Thus on March 17, 1900, the *Banner of Light* (vol. 87, p. 1), reprinted the following from a New York newspaper: "Mrs. Leonora Piper, the noted spirit medium, is about to be released from her contract with the London Society of Psychic Research so that she can give to the general public the benefit of her experiences with spirit manifestations." But Hodgson denied this report in a letter which the *Banner* published on March 24, p. 1.

257.37 Pope's] Theodate Pope, a member of the Society from Farmington, Conn.

260.9 Geo.] See note to 187.11.

260.24 D] Hodgson's biographer A. T. Baird, *Richard Hodgson*, p. 3, mentions Jessie D., Hodgson's cousin and "the one and only love affair of his youth" in Australia. She died in 1879. According to Baird, Hodgson insisted that her name never be revealed to the "outside world." But for the sitting of May 29, 1906, where she is referred to as Q., the transcript gives the full name of Jessie Turner Dunn (see p. 347).

261.10 moaning] From Tennyson's "Crossing the Bar."

261.19 Bancroft] Margaret Bancroft, founder of the Haddonfield Training School, Haddonfield, N.J. The school, now known as the Bancroft School, was devoted to the education of mentally deficient children. She was an associate of the Society.

262.20 fishing] Baird, pp. 283–285, includes reminiscences of Hodgson by James's son Henry. These concern primarily fishing and hiking at Chocorua. According to Henry, since James himself hated fishing, it often fell upon Hodgson to instruct James's sons in outdoor activities.

262.24 Mother] Hodgson's mother's maiden name was Margaret Hyde, his father's name was Richard. James mentions three sisters, Rebecca, Annie, and Ellen. Rebecca died when Hodgson was quite young. Annie, apparently still unmarried (see p. 346), supplied the information about Hodgson's youth. Australian biographical dictionaries mention an Ellen Hyde, née Hodgson, who was the wife of Thomas Plumley Derham. Perhaps she was the third sister. But this identification is not certain because according to the transcript Hodgson's brother-in-law was named George Derham. At least this is the name given in the transcript where the initials G.D. appear in the published text.

262.37 omit] James's account of the sitting of January 23, 1906 was compared with the surviving transcript in the archives of the Society in London. No significant omissions were found.

263.2 George] George Bucknam Dorr, after Hodgson's death, for a time acted as Mrs. Piper's principal investigator.

263.6 Piddington] Piddington was sent to the United States by the English Society to arrange for the shipment of most of Hodgson's papers to England.

263.8 Harry] James's son Henry served as Hodgson's literary executor.

263.14 W.J.] Works by James's son William have in recent years been exhibited by the Boston Museum of Fine Arts.

263.26 Lyman] Mrs. Lyman has not been identified.

268.13 Baldwin] James Mark Baldwin (1861–1934), American philosopher and psychologist, *Handbook of Psychology: Feeling and Will* (New York: Henry Holt, 1891) (WJ 406.49), pp. 154–155.

268.28 Hyslop] The transcript of the sitting of February 27, 1906 is preserved by the Society in New York (Box III; file "Hyslop Biographical Materials II").

269.18 Piddington] Two letters from Piddington to Hyslop record the investigation of the 'nigger-talk' incident. In his letter of February 21, 1907,

Piddington writes that in the records of the communications supposedly from Myers he has come across a passage where "either the Myers control asks the living Hodgson, or the living Hodgson asks the Myers control" if the other remembers a conversation concerning 'nigger-talk' (Box 2; file "ASPR Miscellaneous"). In the letter of August 6, 1907, Piddington states that the incident took place at a sitting of February 13, 1901 (Box 2; file "Noted Personalities II").

270.10 'Densmore'] According to the transcript, her last name was Dunham. Since Hodgson, James, and Dorr knew her, and much of Hodgson's social life involved members of the Society, it seems likely that she also was connected with psychical research. Several persons with that last name were associated with the Society, including Miss E. L. Dunham, 37 E. 36th St., New York (a member in about 1890), Miss Helen Dunham, London, England (in 1898), and Miss Helen Dunham, 37 E. 36th St., New York (in 1903). Most likely, only one Helen Dunham is involved. Membership lists (1889) also include Theodore Dunham, 53 E. 30th St., New York, a physician. The Miss Dunhams could not have been his daughters, but could have been his sisters. Among other things, Theodore Dunham was a member of the Tavern Club, the Boston club where Hodgson took his meals. While the evidence is circumstantial, it seems likely that 'Densmore' lived in New York and not Chicago, that E. L. Dunham and Helen Dunham were sisters, and that 'Densmore' was either E. L. Dunham or another sister. E. L.'s disappearance from the lists coincides with the date of 'Densmore's' marriage.

271.17 three] The transcript mentions five sisters.

273.12 Newbold] William Romaine Newbold (1865–1926), American educator. His view of Mrs. Piper is given in "A Further Record of Observations of Certain Phenomena of Trance," PSPR, 14 (December 1898), 6–49.

279.24 Piper's] The seemingly endless and inconclusive probing and studying of Mrs. Piper did not discourage fresh attempts. From late 1906 to July 1908 and again from October 1909 to October 1911, Mrs. Piper was in England at the Society's expense. She then gave extensive sittings to Anne Manning Robbins and as late as 1924 attracted the attention of Gardner Murphy. There is some evidence that she herself invited the attention. In a letter to Hereward Carrington, a psychical researcher, February 10, 1912, she wrote: "It may interest you to know that I once asked Dr. Hodgson if he knew of anyone in this country who could take his place and carry on his work. Dr. Hodgson replied, 'Oh yes, I think so. I know of a young Englishman, in fact I have corresponded with him, a man named Carrington, who knows a good deal about the subject . . .' But, I am not inviting you to take charge of my case . . ." (*Letters to Hereward Carrington* [Mokelumne Hill, Cal.: Health Research, 1957]), p. 45.

282.36 dissuade] The description fits Anne Manning Robbins, *Both Sides of the Veil: A Personal Experience* (Boston: Sherman, French, 1909). The book contains an excerpt from a letter to the publisher by James urging publication: "It is a genuine record of moral and religious experience, profoundly earnest, and calculated, I should think, to interest and impress readers who desire to know adequately what deeper significances our life may hold in store."

284.7–8 Münsterberg] Hugo Münsterberg, *Psychology and Life*, p. 230. Münsterberg speaks of modern scholars who are converted "because a pathological woman is able to chat" about their "personal secrets at the rate of twenty francs a sitting."

285.31   T.P.]   Theodate Pope.

285.36   Bayley]   Weston D. Bayley, American physician, a member of the Society. For James's letters to him see p. 388.

287.12   Minna]   According to Dorr's notes on the transcript of the sitting of June 5, 1906, the Jack mentioned below is John Jay Chapman (1862–1933), American essayist and poet. Thus, Minna would be his first wife, Minna Timmins Chapman (d. 1897). According to the transcript, Gemma is Gemma Timmins.

289.5   companion]   James's wife, according to the transcript.

290.31   Minturns]   Chapman was acquainted with Robert Shaw Minturn, a New York lawyer.

291.12   nationality]   According to the transcript, 'Densmore's' husband was Italian.

292.32   M.]   Minna in the transcript.

294.1   von G.]   Von Gaertner in the transcript.

296.19   Putnam]   See note to 339.28.

300.23   Bayley]   Emily E. Bayley, an associate of the Society.

301.20   Piddington's]   John George Piddington, "A Series of Concordant Automatisms," PSPR, 22 (October 1908), 19–416. On p. 65n Piddington recalls how after Hodgson's death they tried to puzzle out certain anagrams found among Hodgson's papers.

309.30   Certainly]   An annotated copy of James's report (PSPR version) is preserved in Houghton (Phil 7069.09.5A*), given by James on October 20, 1909. There are annotations on pp. 64, 77, 88, 98, 110, 113, 118, 119, but these do not appear to be in James's hand. However, the general tone of the annotations suggests that the annotator was somehow involved in the investigations.

310.30   Krebs]   Stanley L. Krebs, from Reading, Pa., an associate of the Society.

311.4   name]   No name is given in the transcript.

313.10   person]   Newbold's father, according to the transcript.

314.17   Judah]   Noble B. Judah, a member of the Society from Chicago.

319.34   Soule]   Minnie Meserve Soule (d. 1937), American trance medium.

322.32   Newbold's]   See note to 273.12.

322.34   *Journal*]   James Hervey Hyslop, "Experiments with Mrs. Piper since Dr. Richard Hodgson's Death," JASPR, 1 (February 1907), 93–107; "Further Experiments Relating to Dr. Hodgson since His Death" (March 1907), 125–148;

"Conclusion of Experiments Relative to Dr. Hodgson; Theories" (April 1907), 183–234.

322.36 Report] See note to 254.39.

322.37 Sidgwick's] See note to 254.39.

325.15 C.B.] Mrs. C. Blodgett, an associate of the Society from Holyoke, Mass.

326.10 Osler] William Osler (1849–1919), Canadian-born physician.

327.7 Johnson's] See note to 246.6.

327.37 Gower] See note to 246.6.

328.8 written] See pp. 12–13.

333.2 Putnam] A camp in Keene Valley, N.Y., owned by Henry Pickering Bowditch, James Jackson Putnam, and James.

333.3 Elizabeth] Daughter of James Jackson Putnam.

333.12 Martha] Daughter of Charles Pickering Putnam.

336.19 Pratt] Bela Lyon Pratt (1867–1917), American sculptor, a member of the Tavern Club.

338.29 *Mind*] Richard Hodgson, "The Consciousness of External Reality," *Mind*, 10 (July 1885), 321–346, mentions favorably Thomas Brown (1778–1820), Scottish philosopher.

339.20 Putnam] Annie C. Putnam, apparently a sister of James Jackson Putnam.

339.28 Putnam's] James Jackson Putnam (1846–1918), Boston physician, a student with James in the Harvard Medical School. For a note on their relations see *The Principles of Psychology*, WORKS, note to 7.25–26.

339.34 Bergman] Mary R. Hillard, a member of the Society from Waterbury, Conn. James's letter to her, thanking her for records of Piper sittings, is in the Colby College Library.

346.2 *Proceedings*] See note to 79.1.

346.26 *Tom*] Dr. Thomas Hodgson of Melbourne, Australia, was for many years a member of the American Branch. His name disappears from the membership lists at about the time of his brother's death.

349.15 M.M.J.] Margaret Mary James.

351.11 Mrs. M.] Mary Hillard.

352.28 Child] Francis James Child (1825–1896), American scholar. For James's account of Child's death see *Letters*, II, 52.

354.7 'bosh'] In volume I of his copy of Gurney's *Tertium Quid*, James has "Clifford's 'bosh' 270." The reference is to William Kingdon Clifford (1845–1879), British mathematician and philosopher.

Notes

358.5   Fechner]   Gustav Theodor Fechner (1801–1887), German psychologist, physicist, and philosopher, *Zend-Avesta oder über die Dinge des Himmels und des Jenseits*, 2nd ed., 2 vols. (Hamburg: L. Voss, 1901) (WJ 727.13.4), II, 187–213.

358.31   Worcester]   Elwood Worcester (1862–1940), American clergyman and mental health advocate, *The Living Word* (New York: Moffat, Yard, 1908), pp. 185–351.

358.32   James]   "Concerning Fechner" in *A Pluralistic Universe*, WORKS.

358.33   "It]   Samuel Butler (1835–1902), English novelist, *The Note-Books of Samuel Butler*, ed. Henry Festing Jones (London: A. C. Fifield, 1912), p. 22; this posthumously published collection of excerpts originally appeared in six installments in the *New Quarterly* (1907–1910).

362.33   Paladino]   In 1896 (see note to 132.11) the English Society concluded that Eusapia Paladino was a fraud, but this did not discourage further investigation. And James himself eventually concluded that while Eusapia cheats much of the time, she sometimes produces genuine phenomena. The central argument in her favor is given by Flournoy in a letter to James, March 15, 1910:

> It is a known fact that Eusapia cheats by every means at her disposal when she is allowed to do so. In the seances which I attended a dozen years ago, with Myers, at Richet's, one of us was constantly under the table to hold her ankles; I recall the contractions I observed all along her legs, her calves, while the spectators indicated the production of phenomena. Fraud with the feet . . . does not explain the innumerable happenings which occur when she is controlled in all 4 limbs, and the séances take place in sufficient light (*The Letters of William James and Théodore Flournoy*, pp. 227–228).

In numerous letters in his last years James rejoices in the "Eusapian boom" as a sign that "public opinion is just now taking a step forward in these matters" (*Letters*, II, 320). Apparently discouraged by failure of psychical research to gain general support, James came to rest his hopes on a spectacular "entering wedge" (see note to 248.1) which would force a reluctant public to believe. The work of the scientists mentioned in the essay was a sign that "at last" something "definite & positive" was in sight (*Letters of James and Flournoy*, p. 218).

362.35   Schiaparelli]   Giovanni Virginio Schiaparelli (1835–1910), Italian astronomer. He was a member of a committee which observed Eusapia in Milan in October 1892 and drew up a favorable report; see Hereward Carrington, *Eusapia Palladino and her Phenomena* (New York: B.W. Dodge, 1909), pp. 29–33.

362.35   Lombroso]   Cesare Lombroso (1835–1909), Italian sociologist and physician. His view of Eusapia can be found in *After Death—What? Spiritistic Phenomena and Their Interpretation*, trans. William Sloane Kennedy (Boston: Small, Maynard [1909]).

363.3   Morselli]   Enrico Morselli, *Psicologia e 'Spiritismo': Impressioni e note critiche sui fenomeni medianici di Eusapia Paladino*, 2 vols. (Turin: Fratelli Bocca, 1908). James's copy is in Houghton (Phil 7069.08.40*).

363.3 Bottazzi] Filippo Bottazzi (1867–1941), Italian physiologist. He was a member of a group which observed Eusapia in Naples in September and October 1907; see Carrington, p. 109.

363.4 Carrington] Hereward Carrington (b. 1880), British-born psychical researcher. Carrington expresses his views in *Eusapia Palladino*. James's annotated copy, inscribed from the author, is in Widener (Phil 7069.09.3A). Also in Widener is *The Coming Science* (Boston: Small, Maynard, 1908) (Phil 7069. 08.15) and *The Physical Phenomena of Spiritualism: Fraudulent and Genuine* (Boston: Herbert B. Turner, 1907) (Phil 7069.07.10). James's letters to Carrington are published in *Letters to Hereward Carrington from Famous Psychical Researchers, Scientists, Mediums & Magicians* (Mokelumne Hill, Cal.: Health Research, 1957). According to the *Boston Herald*, October 1, 1909, Carrington addressed the Twentieth Century Club in Boston, claiming that Eusapia's were the only genuine physical phenomena he had ever encountered. He was introduced by James who is quoted as saying: "Prof. Munsterberg is quoted as having said that this was a closed subject as far as he was concerned. All this, however, is very shallow. The subject must be seriously investigated. The phenomena are extraordinary and complex. Until we know the facts better all attempts at interpretation are vague and premature."

363.10 Cook] Florence Eliza Cook (married name, Corner) (c. 1856–1904), English medium. She claimed that spirits materialized in her presence and this claim was endorsed by William Crookes who experimented with her in his laboratory in 1873–1874. For a skeptical account of these experiments see Trevor H. Hall, *The Spiritualists*. Hall argues that Florence and her mother were trying to use Florence's mediumship to obtain money from a rich businessman and needed endorsements. Hall goes far towards showing that Florence obtained Crookes's support by means of sexual favors.

363.16 Wyman] Jeffries Wyman (1814–1874), American anatomist.

363.23 Oken] Lorenz Oken (1779–1851), German natural philosopher.

363.23 Lamarck] Jean Baptiste Pierre Antoine de Monet de Lamarck (1744–1829), French naturalist.

363.23 Chambers] Robert Chambers (1802–1871), Scottish publisher and writer, author of *Vestiges of the Natural History of Creation* (1844).

364.25 Martin] Henry Newell Martin (1848–1896), Irish-born biologist, active in the United States.

366.9 Huxley's] Thomas Henry Huxley (1825–1895), English biologist and essayist. It is not clear which of several editions of *Life and Letters of Thomas Henry Huxley*, ed. Leonard Huxley, James used. In a two-volume edition (New York: D. Appleton, 1901), the quoted text is found on I, 452; in a three-volume edition (London: Macmillan, 1903), on II, 144. The London Dialectical Society, sometimes viewed as a precursor of the Society for Psychical Research, began its investigations in 1869 and published its report in 1871. The report was favorable to spiritualism.

367.21 Richet's] Charles Robert Richet, *Thirty Years of Psychical Research: Being a Treatise on Metapsychics*, trans. Stanley De Brath (New York: Macmillan, 1923).

Notes

372.23 'will] A phrase used by Dickinson Sergeant Miller (1868–1963), American philosopher, "The 'Will to Believe' and the Duty to Doubt," *International Journal of Ethics*, 9 (1898–1899), 187.

376.6 colleague] James's letter to Hodgson of April 18, 1903 (bMS Am 1092.9 [967]) makes it clear that the colleague is Morris Hicky Morgan (1859–1910), professor of classical philology at Harvard.

I.K.S.

Appendix I

Comments on Automatic Writing

Some months after publication of "Notes on Automatic Writing" James seems to have tested Mr. John N. Arnold, whose experiences are narrated in 47.34 ff. Preserved in the Houghton Library as bMS Am 1092.9 (4528) is a leaf of foolscap paper containing a sample of Arnold's automatic writing with James's comment on it. This leaf is prefaced by a page on which James wrote 'Automatic Writing | by Mr Arnold | ['Nov' del.] Oct 31. 89'. Henry James, Jr., James's son, wrote above James's inscription 'File among Biographical' and, below, 'This is an example of many, many documents & papers that have been destroyed. W. J. really did a great deal of work on such things at one time. H. J.' The foolscap leaf, on its recto, is largely covered with Arnold's scrawls, mostly unintelligible but with some identifiable letters. At the left, in an uninscribed space James wrote the following description.

Oct 31. 89 Visit from Mr. Arnold of Providence, who tried his automatic writing as below. Explosions in ulnar N. from elbow downwards, involuntary contractions, of *4th [*ov.* '3rd'] & 5th fingers, and pronations. Tried whether pencil would write better if held between those fingers: it did n't. He never gets mirror script.—His Lydia *vide AS.P.R. Rept [*added*] purported to be his wife's sister of that name—The name of one Sarah Whitman who had promised to communicate with him if she died has never been given him although eagerly looked for at any of the numerous seances which he has attended, or through his own hand. Names of utterly indifferent people come, and keep recurring.—When his writing is best it is entirely automatic i.e. he does n't know what is comng.—At other times he knows what is being written. The writing here along side is entirely ['automatic' *del.*] illegible except what the line points to—which he read as "Robert." Later I went out of the room and this "Ive met you before, Robert Hare" was written automatically with this, "Onset" below it. At his only visit to Onset 2 summers ago he met a *son [*ov. doubtful* 'sun'] of Judge Hare [*poss.* 'second' *del.*] whose 1st name he does n't know.

433

Appendix II

Questionnaire on Hallucinations

This eight-part questionnaire on hallucinations is reprinted from the *Proceedings of the American Society for Psychical Research*, 1 (December 1887), 270–274.

AMERICAN SOCIETY FOR PSYCHICAL RESEARCH.

COMMITTEE ON EXPERIMENTAL PSYCHOLOGY.

OCTOBER, 1887.

The American Society for Psychical Research is collecting accounts of cases where one person has had some remarkable experience, such as an exceptionally vivid and disturbing dream, or a strong waking impression amounting to a distinct hallucination, concerning another person at a distance, who was, at the time, passing through some crisis, such as death, or illness, or some other calamity. It appears that coincidences of this sort have occurred, but it may be alleged that they are due to mere *chance*. For the determination of this it is desirable to ascertain the proportion between (*a*) the number of persons in the community who have not had any such experiences at all; (*b*) the number of persons who have had such experiences coinciding with real events; (*c*) the number of persons who have had experiences which, though similar to the foregoing in other respects, did *not* coincide with real events.

We therefore beg any reader of this circular in the course of the next six months to repeat the following questions, *verbatim*, to as many trustworthy persons as possible, *from whom he does not know which answer to expect, and who have not already been interrogated by some one else*, and communicate the results. The questions are so framed as to require no answer but *yes* or *no*, which should be written in one of the blank squares below each question. We draw special attention to the fact that *the object of our enquiry would be defeated* if replies were received only from persons who have had remarkable experiences of the kind referred to (whether coincident with real events or not); and there should be *no selection whatever* of persons who have had such experiences. In case of negative answers only, it will be sufficient if the collector will send (not for publication) his own name and address on the circular with the replies which he has received.

If there are any affirmative answers, we desire to receive also (not for publication) the name and address of any person who answers *yes*. If the experience has been coincident with a real event, we specially request the percipient to send us an account of it.

All communications should be sent to the Secretary, RICHARD HODGSON, 5

434

Questionnaire on Hallucinations

Boylston Place, Boston, Mass., from whom additional copies of this circular may be obtained. As soon as a circular is filled it should be returned to the Secretary; circulars only partly filled will also be gratefully received. It is of the utmost importance to obtain answers from a very large number of persons, and it is hoped that many thousands of replies will be received.

I. *Have you, within the past year, when in good health, had a dream of the death of some person known to you (about whom you were not anxious at the time), which dream you marked as an exceptionally vivid one, and of which the distressing impression lasted for at least as long as an hour after you rose in the morning?*

II. *Have you, within the past three years but not within the past year, when in good health, had a dream of the death of some person known to you (about whom you were not anxious at the time), which dream you marked as an exceptionally vivid one, and of which the distressing impression lasted for at least as long as an hour after you rose in the morning?*

III. *Have you, within the past twelve years but not within the past three years, when in good health, had a dream of the death of some person known to you (about whom you were not anxious at the time), which dream you marked as an exceptionally vivid one, and of which the distressing impression lasted for at least as long as an hour after you rose in the morning?*

IV. *Have you, at any time during your life but not within the past twelve years, when in good health, had a dream of the death of some person known to you (about whom you were not anxious at the time), which dream you marked as an exceptionally vivid one, and of which the distressing impression lasted for at least an hour after you rose in the morning?*

V. *Have you, within the past year, when in good health, and completely awake, had a distinct impression of seeing or being touched by a human being, or of hearing a voice or sound which suggested a human presence, when no one was there?*

VI. *Have you, within the past three years but not within the past year, when in good health, and completely awake, had a distinct impression of seeing or being touched by a human being, or of hearing a voice or sound which suggested a human presence, when no one was there?*

VII. *Have you, within the past twelve years but not within the past three years, when in good health, and completely awake, had a distinct impression of seeing or being touched by a human being, or of hearing a voice or sound which suggested a human presence, when no one was there?*

VIII. *Have you, at any time during your life but not within the past twelve years, when in good health, and completely awake, had a distinct impression of seeing or being touched by a human being, or of hearing a voice or sound which suggested a human presence, when no one was there?*

Name of Collector:

Address of Collector:

Names and addresses of any persons who reply in the affirmative:

Appendix III

Sittings with Mrs. Piper:
Kate Walsh and Baby Eliza

The accounts of these sittings are taken from Richard Hodgson's continuation of the study of the medium Mrs. Piper, published as "A Record of Observations of Certain Phenomena of Trance" in the *Proceedings of the Society for Psychical Research*, 8 (June 1892), 1–167. The first set of records, from pp. 92–95, involves the death and spirit return of James's aunt, Catharine Walsh, with several sitters, James included. According to her death certificate, Catharine Walsh died on March 6, 1889 at "about 12 o'clock midnight A.M." The second set, from pp. 133–135, involving Baby Eliza, gives one of James's sittings, with corroborative reports.

Mr. Robertson James.   March 6th, 1889.

5, Boylston-place, *March 6th,* 1889. 1 *p.m.*
Mr. Robertson James has just called here on return from a sitting with Mrs. P., during which he was informed by Mrs. P.—entranced—that "Aunt Kate" had died about 2 or 2.30 in the morning. Aunt Kate was also referred to as Mrs. Walsh.

Mrs. Walsh has been ill for some time and has been expected during the last few days to die at any hour. This is written before any despatch has been received informing of the death, in presence of the following:—

RICHARD HODGSON.
WM. JAMES.
ROBERTSON JAMES.

On reaching home an hour later I found a telegram as follows:—"Aunt Kate passed away a few minutes after midnight.—E. R. WALSH."

(Signed)   WM. JAMES.

Mrs. William James, who accompanied Mr. Robertson James to the sitting on March 6th, writes as follows:—

18, Garden-street, Cambridge, *March 28th,* 1889.
Concerning the sitting mentioned above on March 6th, I may add that the "control" said, when mentioning that Aunt Kate had died, that I would find "a letter or telegram" when I got home, saying she was gone.

ALICE H. JAMES.

July, 1890.
It may be worth while to add that early at this sitting I inquired, "How is Aunt Kate?" The reply was, "She is poorly." This reply disappointed me,

from its baldness. Nothing more was said about Aunt Kate till towards the close of the sitting, when I again said, "Can you tell me nothing more about Aunt Kate?" The medium suddenly threw back her head and said in a startled way, "Why, Aunt Kate's here. All around me I hear voices saying, 'Aunt Kate has come.'" Then followed the announcement that she had died very early that morning, and on being pressed to give the time, shortly after two was named.   A. H. J.

R. Hodgson. November 7th, 1889.

[From a letter written to Professor W. James on the day of the sitting.]

Mrs. D. and I had sitting to-day at Arlington Heights, and the usurpation by "Kate Walsh" was extraordinary. She (Mrs. Piper) had got hold of my hands, and I had to make a few fragmentary notes afterwards of the remarks, themselves fragmentary, which she made. The personality seemed very intense, and spoke in effortful whispers.

"William—William—God bless you." (Who are you?)—"Kate—Walsh"—(I know you.) "Help me—help me—" [Taking my right hand with her right, and passing it to her left and making me take hold of her left hand.] "That hand's dead—dead—this one's alive" [*i.e.*, the right]—"help me." The left hand appeared to be at a decidedly lower temperature than the right. It was cooler than either of my hands, while the right hand was warmer than either of my hands.

"I'm alive—I'm alive—Albert's coming over soon. He can't stay—poor boy—poor boy—Albert—Albert—Alfred—Albert—I know you—Alice—Alice—William—Alice—" (Yes, I know. I'll tell them. You remember me. I stayed with you in New York.) "Yes—I know. But, oh, I can't remember. I'm so cold—I'm so cold. Oh, help me—help me"—[making tremulous movements of hands]. (I know. I'll tell them. You remember me; my name's Hodgson.) "Yes. Mr. Hudgson. Where are the girls? Yes. You had fish for breakfast on the second day, didn't you?" (I don't remember very well.) "And the tea—who was it spilt the cup of tea? Was it you or William?" [I think I remember something about the tea, but not very clearly.] "You were in the corner room—bedroom—upstairs. Were you cold? Then there was some blancmange—you didn't like that. No. It was cream—Bavarian cream. Albert—poor boy; he's coming soon. William"—[something about arranging the property]. "William—God bless him."

The above was much less than was really said. But that was the sort of thing, and nothing *à la mode* Phinuit at all. It was the most strikingly personal thing I have seen. I recollect having fish for some meal, and recall that some remarks were made about it at the time. I recall very clearly that Mrs. Walsh made tea more than once for my special benefit, and I seem to remember something about the spilling of a cup of tea, but cannot be sure. I don't know whether my room was called corner or not. It was an end room, but was in front of the house. There was a little stumbling over the name, which appeared to be Albert. I don't recall anything about the blancmange or cream stuff, but I have little taste for that kind of dish.

Concerning sitting of November 7th and "Kate Walsh" Control.

Professor James says, in letter of November 10th, 1889:—

"The 'Kate Walsh' freak is very interesting. The first mention of her by Phinuit was when she was living, three years or more ago, when she had written to my wife imploring her not to sit for development. Phinuit knew this in some incomprehensible way. A year later [in a sitting] with Margaret Gibbens [sister of Mrs. James], I present, Phinuit alluded jocosely to this fear of hers again, and made some derisive remarks about her unhappy marriage, calling her an 'old crank,' &c. Her death was announced last spring, as you remember. In September, sitting with me and my wife, Mrs. Piper was suddenly 'controlled' by her spirit, who spoke directly with much impressiveness of manner, and great similarity of temperament to herself. Platitudes. She said Henry Wyckoff had experienced a change, and that Albert was coming over soon; nothing definite about either. Queer business!"

[From Miss E. R. Walsh.]

258, Fourth Avenue, *December 1st,* 1889.

MY DEAR WILLIAM,—In reply to the questions you ask apropos of Mr. Hodgson's "sitting":

Poor Aunt Kate's *right* side was the one affected by the paralysis. She had the use of her left hand and arm until near the end. I have no recollection of hearing of any such incidents as the "spilling of tea," &c.; but I thought if anything of the kind had occurred, Margaret, in Forty-fourth-street, would be likely to remember it, so, when I was there to-day to ask after Cousin H. [Henry Wyckoff], I questioned M., but with absolutely no confirmatory result.

The partial coincidence of the following facts with the statements made to you and your wife comes a little nearer to the mark. The last week in August Cousin Henry did have a very severe convulsion, lasting many hours, from which the doctors thought he could hardly rally. An hour before, one of the nurses, in helping move him, knocked under accidentally the folding support on one side of the cot on which he lay, and the poor man slipped almost to the floor. He did not really fall, and was not at all injured, but the nervous shock brought on the convulsion. Wonderful to say, he came out of it entirely, and for several days after his brain seemed much more active; he made constant and excited efforts to speak, and it seemed as though some great change might take place in his condition. This happened in Mrs. Griffitt's stay with him. By the time we came to Forty-fourth-street, in September, he had subsided to a great extent, and then, in a week or two more, began a gradual failure, which has been going on by the slowest degrees ever since. Now he can't even lift what they call his "good hand" outside the bed covering without help. They think, however, he may live months as he is. What a death in life! Poor man, to have such an end to his harmless life. Again, Albert did intermit his visits for seven weeks or more, from the middle of August to early in October, being detained at home by a severe attack of bronchitis, and when he first reappeared one of the nurses said he looked more like dying than his uncle. Since then, however, he has quite recovered, and starts for California on the 18th.

. . . .

ELIZABETH ROBERTSON WALSH.

Sitting on December 4th, 1890.

The first sitting given by Mrs. Piper since her return *(February,* 1890) to America was in the presence of her physician and Professor William James and a stenographic reporter. Unfortunately, as I have already mentioned (see p. 5), her physician has refused to make any report whatever. An incident, however, occurred at the sitting having reference to some relations of Profes-

438

sor James, and I give the account of it here, with additional statements in explanation.

[Extracts from stenographic report of sitting.]

P.: You are not the captain. You are William. I know you; you are James. I am glad to see you. Do you know the—the—the—little one? J.: Which little one? P.: A little one, Eliza. [Makes several attempts to pronounce the name; then pronounces it correctly.] It is a little one in the spirit. Do you know a father named William? J.: Of course I do; but what William? P.: He is what you call the papa. That little one that talked to me. J.: Does she talk to you, Eliza? P.: She has got the remembrance of her papa; do you know what I mean? J.: Yes. P.: The last one she remembers is papa. She wants him to —— [Takes watch and other articles out of Mr. James's pocket. Gets knife and holds it up to head; fumbles it with fingers.] J.: You want to open that? [No answer; makes motion of drawing it away.] P.: William? J.: Yes. P.: The last thing that the little one remembers is the knife; the knife; her papa opened the knife. She asked him to open the knife. That is the last thing she says she remembers. J.: What did she die of? P.:[Taking hold of J.'s necktie.] Diphtheria. She got that of a lady. A lady came into the place that had a trunk. You know trunk? Some clothes that had been tending the lady. J.: I see; correct. P.: She tells me and your mother tells me that. J.: Is my mother with Eliza? P.: She has got her, Emily. J.: Whose knife is this that you are holding? P.: This knife is not the one.

. . . .

P.: William, do you know what I mean? You know what Eliza said? That is the name, Eliza. J.: Who is that the name of? P.: That is the name of the one I was talking about. That is the little child.

. . . .

P.: Where is the knife? [J. hands knife.] P.: William, I want to ask you if you know this little one is very small? Will you find out what she means by the knife? J.: I will. P.: She says something about William—that is papa—to open the knife. J.: Does she want him to open it now or does she say that she did? P.: She wanted him to open it, I believe; I can't tell you exactly; that is the last thing she remembers. Do you know anything about it? J.: No, I don't know anything about it. P.: He took her up the last, do you know, and put her back again. J.: Can she tell him anything about where she now is or who with? P.: She is with—do you know his sister? J.: No, I don't. P.: Don't know Mary? J.: No. P.: Don't know Lizzie, L—I—Z—Z—I—E? There are two or three and she is with them.

. . . .

P.: Will you tell Mary that it is the lady's clothes? J.: I will. P.: Will you tell William that Eliza says she caught her diphtheria from the lady's clothes? J.: That is right.

[I think there was another slight reference to this matter, but not important.]
[A. M. R., *Stenographer.*]

[Addressed to me. Dictated by W. M. Salter to his wife.—W.J.]

516, North-avenue, Chicago, *December 9th,* 1890.

DEAR WILLIAM,—We are greatly obliged for the account of the sitting with Mrs. Piper. Baby Eliza did play with my knife, and asked me to open it but a short time before she died—indeed, it was the last show of intelligence that I distinctly remember. I have told this incident to many people, and the whole question is whether in any way it could have got to Mrs. Piper. Margaret thinks she did not tell her, but she is not absolutely sure. If Mrs. Piper had not heard of it in any way it is certainly remarkable.

[From Mr. W. M. Salter.]

Chicago, *December 17th*, 1890.

DEAR WILLIAM,—Mrs. Piper stumbled (with my assistance) on to my sister Mary's name a year ago in Chocorua. The first name she used then was "Lizzie," and who was meant I could not say. I have a living aunt whose middle name is Elizabeth, but she is never called Lizzie. "Emily" I do not recognise at all—have never known or heard of an Emily in our family. If I could only be *sure* Margaret had not told Mrs. Piper of the knife incident!

WM. SALTER.

[From Mrs. W. M. Salter.]

Chicago, *December 17th*, 1890.

DEAR WILLIAM,—We were very glad to get your letter with the stenographic report of the Piper interview. I hope that you will not object to our keeping it. I am ready to swear, if necessary, that I did not tell Mrs. Piper of the knife incident when I went to see her last October with mother. I recall clearly the whole interview. And, indeed, my baby's illness is something I can speak of to no one. Time for me only adds to its pathos.

.   .   .   .

MARY G. SALTER.

P.S.—I think there is small chance of Margaret's having told Mrs. Piper the incident of the knife. She says that her first impulse was to deny absolutely having done so. Almost the whole interview was taken up with Mrs. Piper's account of her English experiences. Towards the close she referred to Baby's death. Because Margie cannot remember just what she said she is unable to positively assert anything in regard to it.—Yours,

M. G. S.

[Statement by Professor James.]

It seems *unlikely* that so interesting an incident as that of the knife could have been mentioned to Mrs. P. by Margaret G. in the few minutes' talk which she could have had about the death of "Eliza." It was more likely to have been mentioned to me, but if so, it has sunk to an unrecoverable part of my consciousness.

Mrs. P. saw "Eliza" when at Chocorua in 1889. She saw Margaret once, soon after her return from England, and Mary Salter and Mrs. Gibbens together once, in October last.

[W. J.]

[Statement by Mrs. Piper.]

December 22nd, 1890.

Mrs. Piper states that neither Mrs. Gibbens nor Mrs. Salter nor Miss Gibbens said anything whatever to her concerning any knife incident in connection with Eliza. Mrs. Salter made one reference only to Eliza during her conversation in the fall, viz.: "I thought I might get a word from Baby." This impressed Mrs. Piper because Mrs. Salter was much affected when she made this remark. Miss Gibbens on a prior visit talked more freely about Eliza and the grief which Mrs. Salter felt, but said no more about the details of the death than Mrs. Piper had learned in England from Mr. Clarke, who had told her that the child was dead and that the cause of death was diphtheria. Mrs. Piper is not quite sure whether he said diphtheria or scarlet fever.

[R. H.]

Mrs. Salter writes on December 27th, 1890:—

When I saw Mrs. Piper she talked almost exclusively about her own affairs. I merely referred to my child's death when I asked her for a sitting, otherwise I said nothing about it.

Appendix IV

Cattell's Review of James's Presidential Address

The text of this review by J. McKeen Cattell of James's Address is reprinted from the *Psychological Review*, 3 (September 1896), 582–583.

Address by the President before the Society for Psychical Research. WILLIAM JAMES. Proc. Soc. for Psych. Research, XII., 2–10, June, 1896. Science, III., 882–888, June 19, 1896.

The Society for the Psychical Research is fortunate in its leaders. The strongest argument it can offer in behalf of the phenomena it investigates seems to me not the anecdotes and other evidence it has been able to collect, but the fact that men such as Professor James and Professor Sidgwick take an interest in these things and are partly or wholly convinced of their importance.

The presidential address of Professor James, admirably written as a matter of course, reviews the work and claims of the Society with skill and moderation. He finds that the hypnotic wave has subsided and that experimental thought transference has yielded a less abundant return than at first seemed likely. But he thinks that solid progress has been made by the report on the Census of Hallucinations and in the investigation of clairvoyance. Ghosts also should not be ignored. "Though the evidence be flimsy in spots, collectively it may nevertheless carry heavy weight." It is 'a faggot not a chain.' This, however, is an argument that can be turned both ways. When we have an enormous number of cases, and cannot find among them all a single one that is quite conclusive, the very number of cases may be interpreted as an index of the weakness of the evidence. The discovery of a great many gray crows would not prove that any crows are white, rather the more crows we examine and find to be black or gray, the less expectation have we of finding one that is white.

The 'faggot' argument, intended for the 'rigorously scientific' disbeliever, will not be so likely to affect him as the fact that Professor James has found in Mrs. Piper his 'own white crow.' This is an argument difficult to answer except by referring to the continuity of history, which, as the author says, is maintained by the Society. The ablest of men have followed alchemy and astrology, have worshiped strange gods, have consulted witches and burned them. Geese have before now been mistaken for swans, and often to the honor of those who made the mistake. One white crow is enough, but its skin should be deposited in a museum.

COLUMBIA UNIVERSITY   J. McKEEN CATTELL.

Appendix V

The Case of F. H. Krebs

Franz Hugo Krebs attended Harvard College in 1886–1888 and the Harvard Law School in 1888–1892. The statements concerning the case of F. H. Krebs are reprinted from the "Appendix to the Report on Phantasms and Presentiments" in the *Proceedings of the American Society for Psychical Research*, 1 (March 1889), 474–475.

1.
(Statement by Prof. William James.)

Mr. Krebs (special student) stopped after the logic lesson of Friday, November 26, and told me the facts related in his narrative.

I advised him to put them on paper, which he has thus done.

His father is said by him to be too much injured to do any writing at present.

WM. JAMES.

DEC. 1, 1886.

2.
(Statement by Mr. F. H. Krebs.)

On the afternoon of Wednesday, November 24, I was very uneasy, could not sit still, and wandered about the whole afternoon with little purpose. This uneasiness was unaccountable; but instead of wearing away it increased, and after returning to my room at about 6.45 it turned into positive fear. I fancied that there was some one continually behind me, and, although I turned my chair around several times, this feeling remained. At last I got up and went into my bedroom, looked under the bed and into the closet; finding nothing, I came back into the room and looked behind the curtains. Satisfied that there was nothing present to account for my fancy, I sat down again, when instantly the peculiar sensation recurred; and at last, finding it unbearable, I went down to a friend's room, where I remained the rest of the evening. To him I expressed my belief that this sensation was a warning sent to show me that some one of my family had been injured or killed.

While in his room that peculiar sensation ceased, and, despite my nervousness, I was in no unusual state of mind; but on returning to my room to go to bed it returned with renewed force. On the next day (the 25th), on coming to my grandfather's, I found out that the day before (the 24th), at a little past 12, my father had jumped from a moving train and been severely injured. While I do not think that this warning was direct enough to convince sceptics that I was warned of my father's mishap, I certainly consider that it is curious

443

enough to demand attention. I have never before had the same peculiar sensation that there was some being besides myself in an apparently empty room, nor have I ever before been so frightened and startled at absolutely nothing.

(My Father's Statement.)

On questioning my father, he said that before the accident he was not thinking of me, but that at the very moment that it happened his whole family seemed to be before him, and he saw them as distinctly as if there.

(Chauncey Smith's Statement.)

On questioning Smith, he said that he distinctly remembered my coming down and stating my nervousness, but as he was studying he did not pay much attention to my talk, and could not vouch for the particulars.

On the eve of the 25th I went to his room and told him how my feeling had been verified, and he did not dispute my statement of the case; therefore to me his forgetfulness is astonishing.

F. H. KREBS, Jr.

Nov. 29, 1886

3.

(Statement by Mr. Chauncey Smith, Jr.)

I, the undersigned, distinctly remember that F. H. Krebs, Jr., came into my room November 24 and complained of being very nervous. I cannot remember exactly what he said, as I was studying at the time, and did not pay much attention to his talk.

On the 25th he came into my room in the evening, and made a statement that his state the evening before was the consequence of an accident that happened to his father, and that he had the night before told me that he had received a warning of some accident to some one dear to him. This I did not contradict, because I consider that it is extremely probable that he said it, and that I did not, through inattention, notice it.

CHAUNCEY SMITH, Jr.

A Note on the Editorial Method

These volumes of THE WORKS OF WILLIAM JAMES offer the critical text of a definitive edition of his published and unpublished writings (letters excepted). A text may be called 'critical' when an editor intervenes to correct the errors and aberrations of the copy-text[1] on his own responsibility or by reference to other authoritative documents, and also when he introduces authoritative revisions from such documents into the basic copy-text. An edition may be called 'definitive' (a) when the editor has exhaustively determined the authority, in whole or in part, of all preserved documents for the text; (b) when the text is based on the most authoritative documents produced during the work's formulation and execution and then during its publishing history; and (c) when the complete textual data of all authoritative documents are recorded, together with a full account of the edited text's divergences from the document chosen as copy-text, so that the user may reconstruct these sources in complete verbal detail as if they were before him. When backed by these data, a critical text in such a definitive edition may be called 'established' if from the fully recorded documentary evidence it attempts to reconstruct the author's true and fullest intention, even though in some details the restoration of intention from imperfect sources is conjectural and subject to differing opinion.

The most important editorial decision for any work edited without modernization[2] is the choice of its copy-text, that documentary form

---

[1] The copy-text is that document, whether a manuscript or a printed edition, chosen by the editor as the most authoritative basis for his text, and therefore one which is reprinted in the present edition subject only to recorded editorial emendations, and to substitution or addition of readings from other authoritative documents, judged to be necessary or desirable for completing James's final intentions.

[2] By 'modernization' one means the silent substitution for the author's of an entirely new system of punctuation, spelling, capitalization, and word-division in order to bring these original old-fashioned 'accidentals' of the text thoroughly up to date for the benefit of a current reader. It is the theory of the present edition, however, that James's turn-of-the-century 'accidentals' offer no difficulty to a modern scholar or general reader and that to tamper with them by 'modernization' would not only destroy some of James's unique and vigorous flavor of presentation but would also risk distortion of his meaning. Since there is every evidence that, in his books at least, James was concerned to control the texture of presentation and made numerous

on which the edited text will be based. Textual theorists have long distinguished two kinds of authority: first, the authority of the words themselves—the *substantives*; second, the authority of the punctuation, spelling, capitalization, word-division, paragraphing, and devices of emphasis—the *accidentals* so-called—that is, the texture in which the substantives are placed but itself often a not unimportant source of meaning. In an unmodernized edition like the present, an attempt is made to print not only the substantives but also their 'accidental' texture, each in its most authoritative form. The most authoritative substantives are taken to be those that reflect most faithfully the author's latest intentions as he revised to perfect the form and meaning of his work. The most authoritative accidentals are those which are preferential, and even idiosyncratic, in the author's usage even though not necessarily invariable in his manuscripts. These characteristic forms convey something of an author's flavor, but their importance goes beyond aesthetic or antiquarian appreciation since they may become important adjuncts to meaning. It is precisely these adjuncts, however, that are most susceptible to compositorial and editorial styling away from authorial characteristics and toward the uniformity of whatever contemporary system the printing or publishing house fancied. Since few authors are in every respect so firm in their 'accidental' intentions as to demand an exact reproduction of their copy, or to attempt systematically to restore their own system in proof from divergent compositorial styling, their 'acceptance' of printing-house styling is meaningless as an indication of intentions. Thus, advanced editorial theory agrees that in ordinary circumstances the best authority for the accidentals is that of a holograph manuscript or, when the manuscript is not preserved, whatever typed or printed document is closest to it, so that the fewest intermediaries have had a chance to change the text and its forms. Into this copy-text—chosen on the basis of its most authoritative accidentals—are placed the latest revised substantives, with the result that each part of the resulting eclectic text is presented in its highest documentary form of authority.[3] It is recognized, however, that

---

nonverbal as well as verbal changes in preparing printer's copy, and later in proof, for an editor to interfere with James's specific, or even general, wishes by modernizing his system of 'accidentals' would upset on many occasions the designedly subtle balances of his meaning. Moreover, it would be pointless to change his various idiosyncrasies of presentation, such as his increasing use of 'reform' spellings and his liking for the reduction of the capitals in words like *darwinism*. Hence in the present edition considerable pains have been devoted to reprinting the authoritative accidentals of the copy-text and also by emendation to their purification, so far as documentary evidence extends, from the housestyling to which they were subjected in print and which was not entirely weeded out in proof. For a further discussion, see below under the question of copy-text and its treatment.

[3] The use of these terms, and the application to editorial principles of the divided authority between both parts of an author's text, was chiefly initiated by W. W. Greg, "The Rationale of Copy-Text," *Studies in Bibliography*, 3 (1950–51), 19–36, reprinted in *The Collected Papers of Sir Walter W. Greg*, ed. J. C. Maxwell (Oxford: Clarendon Press, 1966), pp. 374–391. For extensions of the principle, see Fredson Bowers, "Current Theories of Copy-Text," *Modern Philology*, 68 (1950), 12–20; "Multiple Authority:

an author may be so scrupulous in supervising each stage of the production of a work that the accidentals of its final version join with the revised substantives in representing his latest intentions more faithfully than in earlier forms of the text. In such special cases a document removed by some stages from a preserved manuscript or from an early intermediary may in practical terms compose the best copy-text.[4]

Each work, then, must be judged on its merits. In general, experience shows that whereas James accepted some journal styling without much objection even though he read proof and had the chance to alter within reason what he wished, he was more seriously concerned with the forms of certain of his accidentals in the books, not only by his marking copy pasted up from journal articles for the printer but more particularly when he received the galley proofs. Indeed, it is not too much to state that James sometimes regarded the copy that he submitted for his books (especially when it was manuscript) as still somewhat in a draft state, to be shaped by proof-alterations to conform to his ultimate intentions. The choice of copy-texts in the WORKS, therefore, rests on the evidence available for each document, and the selection will vary according to the circumstances of 'accidental' authority as superior either in the early or in the late and revised forms of the text. In this connection, the earlier discussions in the textual analyses for the philosophical volumes of this edition give examples of the evidence and its application to the selection of copy-text that are pertinent to the present volume.

On the other hand, although James demonstrably made an effort to control the forms of certain of his accidentals in the proofs, even when he had been relatively careless about their consistency in his manuscript printer's copy, he was not always equally attentive to every detail of the housestyling that printers imposed on his work. In some cases he simply did not observe anomalies even in his own idiosyncratic practices; in others he may have been relatively indifferent when no real clash of principles was involved. Thus, when an editor is aware by reason of inconsistencies that certain 'accidental' printing-house stylings have been substituted for James's own practices as established in manuscripts and marked copy, or have been substituted for relatively neutral journal copy that seems to approximate James's usual practice, he may feel justified in emending to recover by the methods of textual criticism as much of the purity of the Jamesian accidentals as of the substantives—both ultimately contributing to the most complete and accurate expression of James's meaning.

Except for the small amount of silent alteration listed below, every editorial change in the copy-text has been recorded, with the identifi-

---

New Concepts of Copy-Text," *The Library*, 5th ser., 27 (1972), 81–115; "Remarks on Eclectic Texts," *Proof*, 4 (1974), 31–76, all reprinted in *Essays in Bibliography, Text, and Editing* (Charlottesville: University Press of Virginia, 1975).

4 An extensive analysis of specific problems in the mechanical application of traditional theories of copy-text to revised modern works may be found in Bowers, "Greg's 'Rationale of Copy-Text' Revisited," *Studies in Bibliography*, 31 (1978), 90–161.

cation of its immediate source and the record of the rejected copy-text reading. An asterisk prefixed to the page-line reference (always to this edition) indicates that the alteration is discussed in a Textual Note. The formulas for notation are described in the headnotes to the list of Emendations and to the Historical Collation, but it may be well to mention here the use of the term *stet* to call attention in special cases to the retention of the copy-text reading. Textual Notes discuss certain emendations or refusals to emend. The Historical Collation lists all readings in the collated authoritative documents that differ from the edited text except for those recorded in the list of Emendations, which are not repeated in the Historical Collation. The principles for the recording of variants are described in the headnote to this Collation, including the special notation for cross-reference to the list of Alterations in the Manuscripts.

When manuscripts are preserved in the textual transmission, their rejected variants will be recorded in the Historical Collation according to the finally inscribed readings of the text. In cases where the manuscript is copy-text and has been emended, rejected manuscript readings appear in the Emendations and are not repeated in the Historical Collation. James's manuscripts are likely to be much rewritten both during the course of composition and in the process of review, creating variants while he struggled to give shape to his thought that are of particular concern to the scholar. Since this edition is bound to the principle that its apparatus should substitute for all authoritative documents, special provision is made by a list of Alterations in the Manuscripts for the analysis and description of every difference between the initial inscription and the final revision. Alterations which are included in the Historical Collation or Emendations (set off by a special warning sign) as part of the final manuscript reading, there recorded as a variant, are not repeated in the list of Alterations in the Manuscripts.

A special section of the apparatus treats hyphenated word-compounds. The first list shows those in the present text, with the form adopted, that were broken between the lines in the copy-text and thus partake of the nature of emendations. The second lists the correct copy-text form of those broken between lines by the printer of the present edition. Consultation of the second list will enable any user to quote from the present text with the correct hyphenation of the copy-text.

Manuscript material that is reproduced or is quoted in this edition is transcribed in diplomatic form,[5] without emendation, except for two features. As with many writers, James's placement of punctuation in relation to quotation marks was erratic, sometimes appearing within the marks as in the standard American system for commas and periods, some-

---

[5] A diplomatic transcript reproduces exactly the final form of the original, insofar as type can represent script, but with no attempt to follow the lining of the original or visually—by typographical devices—to reproduce deletions, interlineations, additions, or substitutions. It follows that no emendation is attempted in such a transcript and all errors in the text are allowed to stand without correction, although a sparing use of square brackets for addition or clarification has been permitted.

times outside according to the sense as in the British system, and sometimes carelessly placed immediately below the quotation mark. To attempt to determine the exact position of each mark would often be impossible; hence all such punctuation is placed as it would be by an American printer, the system that James in fact seems to have employed himself when he thought of it. Second, the spacing of ellipsis dots has been normalized. As part of this normalization the distinction is made (James's spacing usually being variable and ambiguous) between the closeup placement of the first of four dots when it represents the period directly after the last quoted word and the spaced placement (as in three dots) when the ellipsis begins in midsentence and the fourth dot thus represents the final period. According to convenience, manuscripts may be transcribed in their final, or clear-text, form, with all alteration variants recorded systematically in an apparatus list, or on occasion they may be transcribed with a record of their alteration variants placed within the text. An abstract of the major features of the formulaic system for recording alterations, especially when they are described within the transcript of the text, may be found in the headnote to the Alterations in the Manuscripts.[6]

In this edition of THE WORKS OF WILLIAM JAMES an attempt has been made to identify the exact edition used by James for his quotations from other authors and ordinarily to emend his carelessnesses of transcription so that the quotation will reproduce exactly what the author wrote in every detail. All such changes are noted in the list of Emendations when they concern the substantives. On some occasions James altered quotations for his own purposes in such a manner that his version should be respected. Such readings are retained in the text but recorded in the list of Emendations (with the signal *stet*), and the original form is provided for the information of the consulting scholar. The general principles governing the treatment of emendations are as follows. As a rule, the author's accidentals are inserted silently from the original to replace variants created in the normal course of James's copying without particular attention to such features, or of compositorial styling. In *Essays in Psychical Research* all accidentals, as well as semi-substantives, are recorded where manuscript exists. For substantives, James faced the usual problem of a quoter in getting at the meat of the quotation by judicious condensation. He was likely to mark major omissions by ellipsis dots. On the other hand, he was by no means invariably scrupulous in indicating a number of his alterations. Thus to condense a quotation he might silently omit material ranging from a phrase to several sentences. Major omissions that would require excessive space to transcribe in the list of Emendations are indicated in the text by editorially added dots, recorded as emendations. For minor condensing omissions, James's text is ordinarily allowed to stand without the distraction of ellipsis dots, and the omitted matter is recorded

---

6 For full details of this system, see F. Bowers, "Transcription of Manuscripts: The Record of Variants," *Studies in Bibliography*, 29 (1976), 212–264.

as part of a *stet* entry in the list of Emendations. However, James's treatment of quotations could be more cavalier. Sometimes to speed up the quotation, but occasionally to sharpen its application to his own ideas, he paraphrased a word or phrase, or a major part of a sentence. Since alteration of this nature was consciously engaged in for literary or philosophic purposes, James's text in such cases is allowed to stand but the original reading is given as part of a *stet* entry in the Emendations. (Rarely, he paraphrased a whole quotation although enclosing it within quotation marks, in which case the marks are editorially removed as an emendation.) More troublesome are the minor variants in wording that seem to have no purpose idealogically or as condensations. When in the opinion of the editor these represent merely careless or inadvertent slips in copying, on a par with James's sometimes casual transcription of accidentals, the originals are restored as emendations. Within James's quotations, paragraphing that he did not observe in the original has not been recorded and final dots have not been added editorially when he ends a quotation short of the completion of a sentence. Variation from the original in James's choice whether to begin a quotation with a capital or lower-case letter has also not been recorded. Similarly, James's syntactical capitalization or use of lower case following ellipsis has been ignored whenever by necessity it differs from the original.

Although the footnotes are preserved in the text as they were originally written, the citations have been expanded and corrected as necessary in Professor Skrupskelis' Notes to provide the full bibliographical detail required by a scholar, this ordinarily having been neglected in James's own sketchy notation. The Notes also provide full information about quotations in the text that James did not footnote. Two footnotes, indicated by asterisks and initialed 'F.B.', have been added by the present editor.

References to McDermott (McD) are to the "Annotated Bibliography," *The Writings of William James,* ed. John J. McDermott (New York: Random House, 1967).

Silent alterations in the text of this work concern themselves chiefly with mechanical presentation. For instance, heading capitals are normalized in the first line of any chapter or section, headings may have their final periods removed, the headlines of the originals may be altered for the purposes of the present edition, anomalous typographical conventions or use of fonts may be normalized including roman or italic syntactical punctuation, which here has been made to conform to a logical system. The minutiae of the accidentals of footnote reference have not been recorded as emendations or as rejected readings. For example, both in the body of the text (save where manuscript exists) and in the footnotes, book titles are silently italicized from whatever other form present in the copy-text; the use of roman or italic fonts is normalized as is the general system of punctuating bibliographical references. In short, such matters involving the reference system have been silently brought into conformity with the printing practice of the time, and usually conform to that found in the styling of the period. Periods after volume numbers are silently removed; abbreviations and ampersands are ordinarily expanded silently; and James's occasional inscription of more than the usual three or four dots for ellipsis is normalized. Finally, such purely typographical matters as the use of an asterisk instead of a number for a footnote are not recorded. When unusual features call for unusual treatment, special notice is always given.

All line numbers keyed to the text include section numbers and sub-headings but do not include spaces after titles or subheadings or within the text itself. James's references to pages within the same essay are silently adjusted to the present edition; references to other volumes already published in the Works are added in brackets after James's original page numbers.

The intent of the editorial treatment both in large and in small matters, and in the recording of the textual information, has been to provide a clean reading text for the general user, with all specialized material isolated for the convenience of the scholar who wishes to consult it. The result has been to establish in the wording James's fullest intentions in their most authoritative form, divorced from verbal corruption whether in the copy-text or in subsequent printings or editions. To this crucial aim has been added the further attempt to present James's final verbal intentions within a logically contrived system of his own accidentals that in their texture are as close to their most authoritative form as controlled editorial theory can establish from the documentary evidence that has been preserved for each work.

The aid offered by this edition to serious scholars of William James's writings is not confined to the presentation of a trustworthy, purified, and established text. Of equal ultimate importance are the apparatuses devoted to the facts about the progress of James's thought from its earliest known beginnings to final publication in journal and book, and continuing to annotation in his private copies by the record of alterations that were usually never made public except when practicable in a few plate-changes. Most of the materials here made available for close study of the development and refinement of James's ideas—almost literally in the workshop—have not previously been seen by scholars except in the James Collection of the Houghton Library, and then they could not be studied in detail without tiresome collation (here fully recorded in the apparatus). Scholars may find fascinating and fruitful for study the record of the manuscripts which—as they can be reconstructed from its apparatus—offer material for scholarly analysis of the way in which James shaped the thought itself as well as its expression, if the two can indeed ever be separated. As this edition concludes, a major portion of the manuscripts at Harvard will be brought to scholars, wherever they may live, for analysis and research in the privacy and convenience of their own studies.

A Note on the Editorial Method

It is the belief of the editors of the WORKS, and the Advisory Board, that this living historical record of the development of James's ideas and their expression, as found in the apparatus and appendixes, is as significant a part of the proposed 'definitive edition' for the purposes of scholarly research as is the establishment of texts closer to James's own intentions than is customarily represented by any single preserved document.

F. B.

The Text of *Essays in Psychical Research*

1. REVIEW OF *Planchette*, BY EPES SARGENT (1869).

Copy-text: (BDA) "Planchette," *Boston Daily Advertiser*, March 10, 1869, unsigned (McDermott 1869:1).

The authorship of this unsigned review of Sargent's *Planchette: Or the Despair of Science* is attested by a remark in a letter to James's brother Henry of March 22, 1869: "I wrote a notice of a book on Spiritualism 'Planchette' for the Advertizer and got $10.00!!" (bMS Am 1092.9 [2568]).[1] Part of the article (*ed.,* 1.18–3.3) was reprinted without authoritative change in (CER) *Collected Essays and Reviews*, ed. R. B. Perry (New York: Longmans, Green, 1920), pp. 1–3 (McD 1920:2).

2. CIRCULARS OF THE AMERICAN SOCIETY FOR PSYCHICAL RESEARCH (1884–1906).

a. Organization (1884).

Copy-text: (P³¹) "Circular No. 1: Issued by the Council," *Proceedings of the American Society for Psychical Research,* 1 (July 1885), 2–4 (not noted by McD but assigned as 1885:6).

The initial number of the *Proceedings of the American Society for Psychical Research* 1 (July 1885), 1–2, gave a brief history of the foundation of the Society beginning with a meeting held in Boston on September 23, 1884, at which a committee of nine was appointed, James being a member, to draw up a constitution. The first meeting of the Society was held on December 18, 1884, and the work of organization and the appointment of committees was completed on January 8, 1885. The initial number of the *Proceedings* then proceeded to reprint various circulars that had been issued by the Society. The first, issued by the Council, appears on pp. 2–4 and was signed by James among others. It was much indebted to the "Objects of the Society" that had been formulated at the organization of the English Society between January 6 and February 20, 1882, as published in its *Proceedings,* 1 (October 1882), 3–6.

1 Hereafter all quotations from letters in the bMS Am 1092.9 series will be referred to by individual number only.

These extracts from the English *Proceedings* as printed in the Circular are abridged and with Americanized spellings.

In a letter to Carl Stumpf, written from Cambridge on January 1, 1886, James explained the need for an American Society:

> I don't know whether you have heard of the London "Society for Psychical Research," which is seriously and laboriously investigating all sorts of "supernatural" matters, clairvoyance, apparitions, etc. I don't know what you think of such work; but I think that the present condition of opinion regarding it is scandalous, there being a mass of testimony, or apparent testimony, about such things, at which the only men capable of a critical judgment—men of scientific education—will not even look. We have founded a similar society here within the year,—some of us thought that the publications of the London society deserved at least to be treated as if worthy of experimental disproof,—and although work advances very slowly owing to the small amount of disposable time on the part of the members, who are all very busy men, we have already stumbled on some rather inexplicable facts out of which something may come. It is a field in which the sources of deception are extremely numerous. But I believe there is no source of deception in the investigation of nature which can compare with a fixed belief that certain kinds of phenomenon are *impossible* (*The Letters of William James*, ed. Henry James [Boston: Atlantic Monthly Press, 1920], I, 248).

b. Request for Information (1884).

Copy-text: (P³¹) "Circular No. 2: Issued by the Committee on Work," *Proceedings of the American Society for Psychical Research*, 1 (July 1885), 5–6 (not noted by McD but assigned as 1885:7).

The reprint of the second circular, issued by the Committee on Work, followed No. 1 on pp. 5–6 of the first number of the American *Proceedings*, signed by James as one of two members of the committee. The questions, which were printed below the signatures (on p. 6 [*ed.*, pp. 9–10]), were clearly distributed with the original circular.

c. Circular Requesting Information on Mediumistic Phenomena (1885).

Copy-text: "Psychical Research," *Boston Daily Advertiser*, April 9, 1885 (not noted by McD but assigned as 1885:9).

The text of this circular appeared in the *Boston Daily Advertiser* with this introductory paragraph following the heading: "A committee of the American Society for Psychical Research has issued the following circular:—". The same text was reprinted in the *Banner of Light*, April 18, 1885, p. 4, with three substantive variants: 'unambiguous' for 'the unambiguous' in 10.29; 'we are' for 'in' in 10.30; and 'to the latter' for 'the latter' in 10.33. The circular was not reprinted in the *Proceedings*.

d. Circular Requesting Financial Support (1892).

Copy-text: (RPJ) "Psychical Research," *Religio-Philosophical Journal*, n.s. 2 (May 7, 1892), 793 (not noted by McD but assigned as 1892:12).

The circular issued in the spring of 1892, signed by James among three officers, was not reprinted in the *Proceedings*, and an original copy has not been turned up.

e. Notice Concerning Dissolution of the American Branch (1906).

Copy-text: "Dissolution of the American Branch," *Journal of the American Society for Psychical Research*, 1 (January 1907), 1–2 (not noted by McD but assigned as 1906:7).

In the English *Journal*, 12 (June 1906), 284, appeared a note announcing the dissolution of the American branch, signed by James among two other vice-presidents. With only a few trifling variants this notice was reprinted in James H. Hyslop's *Journal of the American Society for Psychical Research*, 1 (January 1907), 1–2, the newly christened successor to the *Proceedings*, from which the present reprint is taken. In the English version, Piddington was identified as the 'Hon. Secretary' and the specific address of '5 Boylston Street' was omitted. In the English version, also, the records of the Branch had been kept in the 'offices' of the Society, whereas the American statement is more modest with its accurate 'office'.

3. Report of the Committee on Mediumistic Phenomena (1886).

Copy-text: "Report of the Committee on Mediumistic Phenomena," *Proceedings of the American Society for Psychical Research*, 1 (July 1886), 102–106 (McD 1886:2).

The report had been preceded by a public request for pertinent information, appearing in the *Boston Daily Advertiser* on April 9, 1885 (No. 2c in this volume) and in the *Banner of Light* on April 18, 1885. On August 24, 1886, James wrote a rather discouraged letter to a Miss Phelps:

> I am not sure that our circular of inquiry about mediums brought even as many as ten letters of advice—not one was from a medium himself. I believe the only way to *investigate* is to go in as a private individual, to satisfy one's *self*. It is hopeless to seek *harmony* in the present stage of things. The spiritualist devotees form a solid army to protect, encourage and propagate every conceivable species of fraud. I imagine one can do very little with their help, and that it is just about useless to try, as you say, to *hit their self-respect*. Their minds are a sort of pap. Bundy, with his Religeo-Philosophical Journal, is fighting a manly fight. His side will possibly conquer, though I don't feel too sanguine. Of course you may mention the smallness of the response to our circular, but please quote none of my above growlings (quoted from the reprint in item 195 of Catalogue 184 [March 1984] of Paul C. Richards of Templeton, Massachusetts).

Several days later, on August 29, James wrote to George Croom Robertson that he had "wasted a good deal of time on 'Psychical Research' during the past year." He continued: "Our poor little 'Society' will very likely break down for lack of a Gurney or a Myers to devote time to it. But

I feel quite convinced at the end of my year's work, such as it has been that *this sort of work [*ab. del.* 'it'] is as worthy a specialty as a man could take up,—only it *is* a specialty, demanding an enormous sacrifice of time, and in which amateurs will be as inferior to experts as they are in most other departments of experience. Believing this, I shall probably give very little time to it next year, because at the utmost I should be a dabbler and amateur" (#3538).

James quoted a portion of this report, pp. 15.18–17.34, in "A Record of Observations of Certain Phenomena of Trance" (No. 12 in this volume). The variants may be found in the Historical Collation for that article.

4. NOTES ON ECHOLALIA IN MRS. PIPER (1886).

Copy-text: notes in "A Record and Discussion of Mediumistic Experiments," by James H. Hyslop, *Proceedings of the American Society for Psychical Research*, 4 (May 1910), 380 (not noted by McD but assigned as 1910:7). In his discussion Hyslop quotes from notes provided him by James of his experiments in 1886 with Mrs. Piper.

5. LETTER ON PROFESSOR NEWCOMB'S ADDRESS BEFORE THE AMERICAN SOCIETY FOR PSYCHICAL RESEARCH (1886).

Copy-text: (P[36]) "Professor Newcomb's Address before the American Society for Psychical Research," *Science*, 7 (February 5, 1886), 123 (not noted by McD but assigned as 1886:7).

In this letter to the editor on Professor Simon Newcomb's presidential address, James takes exception to an unsigned editorial note that appeared under "Comment and Criticism" in *Science*, 7 (January 29, 1886), 89. The exact quotation is as follows:

> We have alluded to the weak points of Professor Newcomb's address: the two strongest points are in criticism of the work of the English society. He finds fault very justly with their failure to ascertain the influence of varying conditions on thought-transferrence; and he further makes the very acute observation that in the reproductions of the drawings, though the lines are faulty, they always join perfectly, as would be the case with the work of a poor draughtsman who could see; and this, too, in the drawings made blindfold. The inference, which Professor Newcomb refrains from making, is, of course, that the person did see, and there was some trickery. By way of general criticism of the English society's work, we may frankly say that it is like that of amateurs and enthusiasts, and bears the character of such work, especially because it fails to deal rigidly and skilfully with the problems as they appear to professional physiologists and psychologists.

In the same issue, on pp. 91–92 under the heading of "Recent Psychical Researches," an account by V. P. is printed of the annual meeting of the Society and of Newcomb's address as well as the other papers read.

The investigation to which Newcomb took exception was that carried out by Douglas Blackburn and George Albert Smith, described in the *Proceedings of the Society for Psychical Research*, 1 (April 1883), 70–97 and 1 (July 1883), 161–215. See No. 9 in this volume for more of James's views on this set of experiments.

6. LETTERS: JAMES ON THE *Religio-Philosophical Journal* (1886, 1890).

a. An Enviable and Eminent Place in American Journalism (1886).

Copy-text: "An Enviable and Eminent Place in American Journalism," *Religio-Philosophical Journal*, 41 (November 6, 1886) 4 (not noted by McD but assigned as 1886:8).

b. On Preserving the Journal *(1890).*

Copy-text: "From Prof. James, of Harvard," *Religio-Philosophical Journal*, n.s. 1 (May 31, 1890), 9 (not noted by McD but assigned as 1890:10).

The occasional communications in the *Religio-Philosophical Journal* about the efforts of the American Society for Psychical Research made James concerned to maintain cordial relations with the paper. The first item is an excerpt from a letter by James to the editor; the second was printed in the *Journal* as part of several pages of puffery solicited by the editor.

7. REVIEW OF *Phantasms of the Living*, BY EDMUND GURNEY ET AL. (1887).

Copy-text: (P³⁶) "Phantasms of the Living," *Science*, 9 (January 7, 1887), 18–20 (McD 1887:1), a signed review of *Phantasms of the Living*, by Edmund Gurney, F. W. H. Myers, and Frank Podmore.

8. LETTER ON MRS. ROSS, THE MEDIUM (1887).

Copy-text: "Letter from Professor James," *Banner of Light*, 60 (February 1887), 4 (not noted by McD but assigned as 1887:13). This is the first in a number of letters to the editor of the *Banner of Light* under the heading "Pro and Con." The circumstances of the exposure of Mrs. Ross and the mention of James are given in Professor Skrupskelis' Notes.

9. REVIEW OF "THE SECOND REPORT ON EXPERIMENTAL PSYCHOLOGY," BY CHARLES SEDGWICK MINOT (1889).

Copy-text: (P³¹) "Note to the Foregoing Report," *Proceedings of the American Society for Psychical Research*, 1 (March 1889), 317–319 (McD 1889:2).

The signed review appeared in the *Proceedings* immediately following Minot's "Second Report." The Emendations list corrects some differences in James's quotations from Minot's report and from the text of the "Third Report on Thought-Transference" by Edmund Gurney, F. W. H.

Myers, F. Podmore, and W. F. Barrett, *Proceedings of the Society for Psychical Research* (English), 1 (July 1883), 165.

10. NOTES ON AUTOMATIC WRITING (1889).

Copy-text: (P³¹) "Notes on Automatic Writing," *Proceedings of the American Society for Psychical Research*, 1 (March 1889), 548–564 (McD 1889:3).

The passage containing Sidney Dean's report (45.29–47.31) in this communication may also be found in *The Principles of Psychology* (WORKS, 373.5–374.37), and the apparatus to that volume may be consulted for the variants. In Appendix I in the present edition are printed James's comments on a sheet of automatic writing by John N. Arnold (bMS Am 1092.9 [4528]), one of the correspondents quoted in the report, who visited James on October 31, 1889.

11. THE CENSUS OF HALLUCINATIONS (1889–1897).

a. *International Congress of Experimental Psychology: Instructions to the Person Undertaking to Collect Answers to the Question on the Other Side (1889).*

Copy-text: Original printed letter and form found in the archives of the American Society for Psychical Research, New York.

Only one question was asked in this questionnaire designed for a report from the United States supplementary to the main report on the Census of Hallucinations to be made by the English Society for Psychical Research to the Second International Congress of Experimental Psychology planned for London in 1892. If the answer to the one question in Schedule A (printed here with most of the lines for responses omitted) were 'yes', then six more questions in Schedule B were to be answered.

The letter and questionnaire form were prepared in 1889, and members of the Society for Psychical Research were urged to aid in the circulation of the questionnaire (*Proceedings of the Society for Psychical Research*, 6 [December 1889], 7). The letter (but with Henry Sidgwick's name on behalf of the S. P. R.) and the form were published as Appendix A in the S. P. R. *Proceedings*, 10 (August 1894), 402–404 (not in McD but assigned as 1894:23). The results of the survey were published at the same time as Appendix B.

As early as October 1887 the American Society for Psychical Research had determined to assist its English counterpart and had printed in its own *Proceedings*, 1 (December 1887), 270–274, an eight-part questionnaire, which has been added as Appendix II in the present volume, the boxes for answers after each question having been omitted.

b. *Letter on Publicity for the Census (1890).*

Copy-text: (P³) "To the Editor of the American Journal of Psychology," *American Journal of Psychology*, 3 (April 1890), 292 (McD 1890:6).

The Census of Hallucinations

The present text of James's letter to the editor asking for publicity is its earliest appearance so far as is known. The same letter has been observed in the *Boston Medical and Surgical Journal*, 122 (May 15, 1890), 484–485; *Science*, 15 (May 16, 1890), 304; *Open Court*, 4 (May 22, 1890), 2288 (McD 1890:8); and the *Religio-Philosophical Journal*, n.s. 1 (May 31, 1890), 11.

c. *The Name Hallucination (1890)*.

Copy-text: "The Name Hallucination," *Religio-Philosophical Journal*, n.s. 1 (June 14, 1890), 37 (not in McD but assigned as 1890:9).

The letter to the editor of the *Religio-Philosophical Journal* seems to have provoked sufficient comment about the use of the word *hallucination* that James was concerned to clarify by his letter, which the *Journal* published on June 14, 1890, under the heading "The Name Hallucination. | By Prof. William James." The remarks from Professor Sidgwick were probably inserted by the editor and are here quoted verbatim except for the correction of 'sense' to 'senses' at 62.40 and a few matters of Americanized spellings and some neglect of italics, which have been silently brought into concurrence with the original. James's reference is not quite exact, since the quotation in fact continues onto p. 10.

d. *The Statistical Inquiry into Hallucinations in America (1892)*.

Copy-text: "The Statistical Inquiry into Hallucinations in America," *International Congress of Experimental Psychology* (London: Williams and Norgate, n.d.), pp. 67–68 (not in McD but assigned as 1892:11).

The American report on the inquiry into Hallucinations appeared as the concluding Part III in the *International Congress of Experimental Psychology* proceedings for the Second Session in London, 1892. On pp. 68–69 appeared the brief discussion at the meeting of all three reports (English, French, and American) followed by a concluding comment from the president. The Society for Psychical Research in London holds a quantity of handwritten and typed drafts for its extensive report, the committee consisting of Professor Henry Sidgwick, chairman, F. W. H. Myers, F. Podmore, Dr. A. T. Myers, Mrs. Sidgwick, and Miss Alice Johnson.

The collection of the statistics and their ordering from the responses to the questionnaire proved to be an arduous chore. On January 30, 1891, James wrote to F. W. H. Myers, in part:

> To speak seriously, however, I agree in what you say, that the position I am now in (Professorship, book published and all) does give me a very good pedestal for carrying on psychical research *effectively*, or rather for disseminating its results effectively. I find however that *narratives* are a weariness, and I must confess that the *reading* of narratives ['which with' *del.*] for which I have no personal responsibility is almost intolerable to me. Those that come to me at first hand, incidentally to the Census, I get interested in. Others much less so; and I imagine my case is a very com-

mon case. One page of experimental "θ"-work [i.e. thought-transference] will "carry" more than a hundred of Phantasms of the Living. I shall stick to my share of the latter however; and expect in the summer recess to work up the results already gained in an article for Scribners Magazine, which will be the basis for more *publicity and [*intrl.*] advertizing and *bring [*intrl.*] in another bundle of schedules to report on at the Congress (#3308).

In the archives of the Society for Psychical Research (London) is preserved a single sheet in James's handwriting except for the heading 'American Statistics Census of Halls | *Feb^{ry} 1892 [*underl.*]'. This appears to be a preliminary report since the figures are somewhat lower than those finally published:

So far, I have collected
5316 cases
  525 yeses
4791 noes

---

yeses 10.9%

Of ['these *del.*] *557 ['57' *ov. [illeg.] 2*] yeses indexed at random (not all sent with schedule) 82 are coincidental—i.e. about 14%.—Our returns need a great deal of farther correspondence to make them strict, and all these figures are subject to later correction.

e. Review of Ueber die Trugwahrnehmung, by Edmund Parish (1895).

Copy-text: (P^{34}) untitled review in the *Psychological Review*, 2 (January 1895), 65–67 (McD 1895:1).

The review of Parish's disagreements with the Census of Hallucinations was the first in a signed series of three reviews, printed under the general heading "Hallucinations and Telepathy," described in detail in No. 17, the review of Frank Podmore's *Apparitions and Thought-Transference* (1895), below.

f. Review of the "Report on the Census of Hallucinations" (1895).

Copy-text: untitled, signed review in the *Psychological Review*, 2 (January 1895), 69–75 (McD 1895:3).

The work of the English committee on Hallucinations in preparing its report for the Second International Congress of Experimental Psychology gave rise to the proposal to carry the investigation further. Plans for the proposal were sent to James, who on May 15, 1892, wrote to Mrs. Henry Sidgwick:

> I got your letter with the provisional scheme of work on hallucinations long long ago, and how I came to let day succeed day without writing you even an acknowledgment is one of those things to explain which would be possible but hardly worth the pains to you of the reading. Let it pass to the account of my Shame! [¶] The plan seems to me a splendid one, and from the point of view of my own collapse, I don't see how it can fail to cover you with a certain sort of glory if it all gets worked up in definitive

shape. The labor is enormous, as I can testify. *My* mistake was in not "keeping up" daily, or at least weekly, with ['all' *del.*] the correspondence in all the schedules I received. In the midst of my other occupations, I ['let' *del.*] was irregular, and let them go, ['until' *del.*] keeping no systematic account of the correspondence, until now I fear the matter is irreparable, so far as the original Gurney-an percentage argument goes. But I have small hopes of that argument anyhow, as I believe you know; and there remains out of my labors a collection of some 600 positive cases of hallucination of every variety which are more or less available for study. These, with all my other materials, I have passed over to Hodgson, ['to see' *del.*] with your MS., to see what he can do for your report before the end of July. The cases are analytically indexed, so that the work of classification will be easy (Society for Psychical Research, London).

The English report was published in the Society's *Proceedings*, 10 (August 1894), 25–422.

In a letter dated October 24 [1894] to J. Mark Baldwin, the editor of the *Psychological Review*, James wrote: "Here goes a rather stout Hallucination report—but the subject is so important if the English Committee's conclusions are true, that the thing had to be done carefully and well. I wish it might get in to the January No. But you know what is best" (typed copy, bMS Am 1092.1). James's signed review appeared in the January 1895 issue of the *Psychological Review*.

The single direct quotation from the English report has been brought into conformity with the original by two small changes in the accidentals.

g. A Correction (1895).

Copy-text: (P[34]) "A Correction," *Psychological Review*, 2 (March 1895), 174 (McD 1895:10).

In this issue of the *Psychological Review*, James printed a correction, initialed 'W.J.', to the figure 1,300 used in his review of the Report on the Census of Hallucinations at 70.8.

h. Final American Report: Letter to Henry Sidgwick (1896).

Copy-text: (ALS) James's holograph letter to Henry Sidgwick, H. 25 in the archives of the Society for Psychical Research, London.

The Third International Congress of Psychology was held in Munich on August 4–7, 1896, its proceedings then being published in 1897. In the discussion following the English S. P. R. report on the Census, Mrs. Henry Sidgwick read a letter from William James providing the final American statistics.

On July 12, 1896, James wrote to Henry Holt: "I have been too busy over the Census of Hallucination to do anything else this A. M. . . . I have wanted to get our American results in Sidgwick's hands in time to quote at the Munich Psychologen Congress to which he is going, and I have scraped through. They entirely corroborate those of the English Census, making apparition at time of death 500 times more frequent than pure chance would account for. I am much gratified that so many months of work should not end in discordant results in the two countries" (Princeton University; typed copy at Harvard). The letter to Sidgwick, quoted at the Congress, had been sent off the preceding day. James found the compilation of the results of the questionnaire something of a trial, as shown by the end of his letter to Sidgwick (not read at the Congress) and by a letter to F. W. H. Myers of January 30, 1891, while he was collecting the statistics for the Second International Congress of 1892, already quoted under that heading.

Apparently Sidgwick was slow in acknowledging James's report for in a letter of August 30, 1896, from Lake Geneva, Wisconsin, James complained to Dickinson S. Miller: "I wish I could have been with you at Munich....I hope you met [Henry] Sidgwick there. I sent him the American Hallucination-Census results, after considerable toil over them, but S. never acknowledges or answers anything, so I'll have to wait to hear from someone else whether he 'got them off' " (*Letters*, II, 50). In fact, Sidgwick had written James (who had not yet received the letter) on August 21: "Only an irresistible impulse to forget the 'Congress' and all its works . . . has prevented me from answering your letter, as I had intended, with a brief report of our proceedings at Munich. . . . Your letter happily supplied the required element of novelty, and my wife accordingly read it to the Congress as the conclusion of her paper: and it will, I believe, appear in the Report of the Congress—with the omission of one or two phrases at the *beginning and [*intrl.*] end which were obviously not intended for publication" (#616).

The text of the letter to Sidgwick underwent several transformations. The original holograph is preserved in London in the archives of the Society for Psychical Research. The letter is marked for reading (presumably by the Sidgwicks): a line is drawn through the beginning 'I . . . so.' (74.5–9) and this sentence is also bracketed; correspondingly, the end of the letter 'Our . . . first.' (76.3–16) is also crossed out (but not bracketed). Oddly, two passages, marked for deletion, fall within the statistical part and appear in the letter as printed in the Congress proceedings: at 74.15 '(% of yes-es 14.75)' is crossed out and bracketed, as is 'These . . . but' at 74.25–26.

Held at the Houghton Library (bMS Am 1092.9 [3761]) is a carbon typescript of the same letter in its entirety, differing in some words and details from the holograph and containing two ink alterations by James, only one of which (a correction) is observed in the published versions. In printed form the non-personal part of the letter not only is found in the Congress proceedings but was also quoted by James in his "Psychical Research" (1896) reply to Cattell (see below), both times with variations from holograph and typescript. James must have had his handwritten letter typed in order to preserve its systematic presentation of the statistics made from his presumably rough notes. At this date he could not himself type. Thus the verbal differences between the letter and its typed copy must be due either to the typist's own unauthoritative changes in the process of transcription or else to James's verbal instruction. Certain of these differences would appear to be the typist's error, such as the omission of 'to the chance-probability' (74.11), the misreading of James's 'these' (altered from 'them') as 'them' (75.13), and the omission of 'I' at 74.27 where the squeezed-in, mended pronoun is not his typical formation of the letter. It is odd, perhaps, that of the seven cases of James's interlineations (without substitution in the manuscript) five are omitted from the TMs. Such a high percentage of error for clearly written and marked additions seems difficult to credit, and it is probable that after the typing James read over his original letter and added a few words here and there before sending it off.

The letter was published in part in the *Dritter Internationaler Congress für Psychologie in München*, 4 (1897), 392–394 (not in McD but assigned as 1897:15). The Congress quotation is prefaced by the statement, "Mrs. Sidgwick (*Cambridge*) read the following letter from Professor W. James of Hawards [*stet*], giving the results—hitherto unpublished—of the American statistical inquiry into the hallucinations of the sane."

It would appear that the Congress text was set from a copy of the typescript (perhaps the now missing ribbon copy was sent to be used as printer's copy), since the text is in agreement with the typescript in five substantive readings that differ from ALS. Further, it may be conjectured that proof set from the typescript was read against the original letter as well, since the interlineations in the letter, missing from the typescript, are to be found in the Congress text. It is theoretically possible, of course, that Sidgwick sent James a copy of the proofs for his quotation of the letter in the Congress proceedings. We have no information whether he did or not. The fact that only one unique reading (the addition of '12' after 'these' at 75.32, which could be an editorial attempt at clarification of an ambiguous statement) appears in the Congress quotation tells against the possibility that James saw proofs, for he could never resist the impulse to improve his style by alteration at the proof stage.

The final document to be considered is the text of the statistical part of the letter that James himself quoted in "Psychical Research." One may speculate that James used the carbon typescript as his guide for this part of the text. The "Psychical Research" text, however, contains ten substantive alterations from copy that are unique, and the natural inference is that James reworked the material before sending his article to the printer.

The choice of copy-text poses no serious problem, for only the holograph letter can have authority for the accidentals and for those words that may have been unauthoritatively omitted or that were misread in the typescript. Lacking evidence that James worked on copy for the Congress text or that he read proof, no emendations (except for some minor corrections and expansions and the ink alteration made by James in the typescript) have been made. Under ordinary circumstances the substantive alterations made in the "Psychical Research" text would very likely have been accepted into the text were it not that it has seemed expedient to reprint "Psychical Research" in its proper place after James's Presidential Address, even though Cattell's major reference in the Address is to the Census. For the convenience of the reader, therefore, the version in "Psychical Research" is reprinted together with the rest of that article in its own form and with its own apparatus, even at the risk of repetition. The apparatus for the letter to Sidgwick, therefore, contains in its Historical Collation only the substantive variants from the ALS copy-text in the TMs and in the report as printed in the proceedings of the Third Congress.

i. Review of Zur Kritik des telepathischen Beweismaterials *and* Hallucinations and Illusions, *by Edmund Parish (1897).*

Copy-text: (P³⁴) untitled, initialed review in the *Psychological Review*, 4 (November 1897), 657–658 (McD 1897:10).

The argument about the statistics in the revised 1894 Census of Hallucinations continued and is reviewed by James in this brief notice of Parish, whose early 1895 book he had reviewed in this series under (e). On November 4, 1897, in writing to J. Mark Baldwin on another matter concerning reprints, James requested two copies of the November *Review*: "May I also be accorded two copies of the Nov. number gratis, on account of my slight contribution? I want to send one to Sedgwick [*stet*] and one to Parish" (typed copy, bMS Am 1092.1).

Two emendations have been drawn from the annotated copy of the *Psychological Review* notice found in James's private file (WJ 110.72).

12. A RECORD OF OBSERVATIONS OF CERTAIN PHENOMENA OF TRANCE (1890).

Copy-text: (P³²) "A Record of Observations of Certain Phenomena of Trance," Part III, *Proceedings of the Society for Psychical Research*, 6 (December 1890), 651–659 (McD 1890:3).

Although cast in the form of a letter to Frederic Myers, James's contribution was printed in the *Proceedings* as the third part of a study of Mrs. Piper, the medium, the introduction by Myers, the first part by Oliver Lodge, and the second by Walter Leaf. On July 15, 1890, wishing to correct an error in his original letter, James wrote again to Myers:

> I scribble you a line because it suddenly is borne in upon me that I must have ['told you that it' *del.*] written, in my little story about Mrs. Piper, that in the incident of her failure to read for Mrs. Blodgett the dead sisters letter, I had sent her the original sealed letter itself. I did not; I kept that, and sent her a couple of articles of apparel one of them a glove, the other some head gear which Mrs. B. furnished me withal. Pray make the correction & oblige yours truly &c. (#3307)

As the printed form of the letter indicates (*ed.*, p. 86), Myers must have made the correction.

Richard Hodgson's share of the account was to have appeared in this series but was delayed until it was printed under the same title in the

Proceedings, 8 (June 1892), 1–167. The Kate Walsh case and the sitting of December 4, 1890, with reference to "Eliza" are reproduced from Hodgson as Appendix III in the present volume. James's Part III was reprinted in the *Religio-Philosophical Journal*, n.s. 1 (January 17, 1891), 535–536, under the title "Professor James's Experience with a Medium," prefixed by the paragraph: "In the *Proceedings of the Society for Psychical Research* for December, 1890, is published a letter from Professor William James, of Harvard University, to Mr. F. W. H. Myers, which, since it gives interesting facts such as men of science have hitherto denied or ignored, is here reproduced." Part III (81.23–83.12) also draws on No. 3 in this volume, "Report of the Committee on Mediumistic Phenomena" (15.18–17.34).

James's brother Henry was prevailed upon to read James's communication at a meeting of the Society on October 31, 1890. James refers to this event in a letter to Henry on October 20, and mentions the arrival of the proof, so that it must have been set up immediately upon receipt and before the meeting: "I think your reading my Piper letter (of which this very A.M.['{' del.] proof came to me from Myers) is the most comical thing I ever heard of. It shows how first rate a business man Myers is: He wants to bring variety & éclat into the meeting. I will *think of you* on the 31st at about 11 A.M. to make up for difference of longitude" (#2659).

A few weeks later, on November 23, he again wrote to Henry: "Your reading my letter about Mrs. Piper was the most touching thing I ever heard of. I *loathe* all this psychical work so far as it *has [ov. 'is'] a social side" (#2660).

13. WHAT PSYCHICAL RESEARCH HAS ACCOMPLISHED (1892).

Copy-text: (P[10]) "What Psychical Research Has Accomplished," *Forum*, 13 (August 1892), 727–742 (McD 1892:1).

In a letter to F. W. H. Myers of January 30, 1891, after discussing his ennui with reading the returns to the questionnaire for the Census of Hallucinations, James declares: "One page of experimental thought-transference work will 'carry' more than a hundred of 'Phantasms of the Living.' I shall stick to my share of the latter [the Census], however, and expect in the summer recess to work up the results already gained in an article for 'Scribner's Magazine,' which will be the basis for more publicity and advertising and bring in another bundle of Schedules to report on at the Congress" (*Letters*, I, 306). But instead of *Scribner's*, the article was published in the *Forum*. On May 15, 1892, James wrote to Mrs. Henry Sidgwick expressing approval of her plans for further research on hallucinations following the 1892 Census report and apologizing for not responding earlier. He added this information: "The importunity of the Editor of the Forum *aiding [tr. by guideline fr. aft. 'importunity'], I have tried to ['be' del.] make a certain compensation for *being ['bei' ov. doubtful 'ma'] such a broken reed about the Halls. [i.e., hallucinations census figures] by 'slinging' an article about the S.P.R. which will doubtless do good to its reputation, and (*perhaps [*ab. del.* 'somewhat']) to its pecuniary estate. It ['will' *del.*] is a general description and laudation of the society and its work, intended to penetrate through the armor of the popular-science stratum of the human Intellect" (Society for Psychical Research).

The article, "What Psychical Research Has Accomplished," was published in the *Forum* in 1892. In 1897—perhaps to piece out the book—James included major parts of the article under the same title, but with revisions and also with additions from his 1890 "The Hidden Self" and his 1896 "Address of the President before the Society for Psychical Research" (No. 19 in this volume), in *The Will to Believe* (WORKS, 1979). The textual discussion in the WORKS volume (pp. 339–341) provides the details, and the Historical Collation, pp. 394–399, supplemented by Appendix II, pp. 432–435, enables a reader with considerable pains to reconstruct the orginal article from the amalgamated and revised book version. Thus despite the rash statement on p. 339 of *The Will to Believe* that "What Psychical Research Has Accomplished" would not be reprinted in its original form, the decision has been made that the present volume requires its original text to be offered in order to relate it the more easily to James's other writings on psychical research. The Historical Collation records the substantive variants found in the collation of pp. 89.1–99.24 ('If . . . prodigies!'), which correspond to *WB* pp. 303.11–317.30 (WORKS, pp. 225.6–235.1) (except for *WB* pp. 306.11–21, 309.21–30 and 316.24–34 [WORKS, pp. 227.8–15, 229.18–25, and 234.9–17]), and 100.35–104.8 ('All . . . experiences.'), which correspond to pp. 320.4–323.31 (WORKS, pp. 236.22–239.3).

14. REVIEW OF *Science and a Future Life,*
     BY FREDERIC W. H. MYERS (1893).

Copy-text: (P[25]) untitled, unsigned review in the *Nation,* 57 (September 7, 1893), 176–177 (McD 1893:13).
   A brief passage, drawn from a letter of James to Myers on January 30, 1891, is pertinent:

> Verily you are the stuff of which world-changers are made. What a despot for P. R.! I always feel guilty in your presence, and am on the whole glad that the broad blue ocean rolls between us for most of the days of the year, although I should be glad to have it intermit occasionally, on days when I feel particularly larky and indifferent, when I might meet you without being bowed down with shame. . . . Of course I wholly agree with you in regard to the *ultimate* future of the business, and fame will be the portion of him who may succeed in naturalizing it as a branch of legitimate science. I think it quite on the cards that you, with your singular tenacity of purpose, and wide look at all the intellectual relations of the thing, may live to be the ultra-Darwin yourself. Only the facts are *so* discontinuous so far that possibly all our generation can do may be to get 'em called facts. I'm a bad fellow to investigate on account of my bad memory for anecdotes and

other disjointed details. Teaching of students will have to fill most of my time I foresee; but of course my weather eye will remain open upon the occult world (#3308).

15. LETTER TO THE EDITOR OF *Mind* ON WARD'S REVIEW OF *Briefer Course* (1893).

Copy-text: (P²⁴) "To the Editor of *Mind*," *Mind*, n.s. 2 (January 1893), 144 (McD 1893:14).

James Ward, of Cambridge University, wrote a critical review of James's *Briefer Course* (under its English title of *Text-book of Psychology*) in the English journal *Mind*, n.s. 1 (October 1892), 531–539. Toward the end, on p. 538, he remarked:

> On one point, however, our author is not with the crowd: he avows himself a believer in 'mediumships' or 'possessions,' maintains that the work of the Society for Psychical Research meets "one of the greatest needs of psychology," and hopes that his "personal confession may possibly draw a reader or two into a field which the *soi-disant* 'scientist' usually refuses to explore" (p. 214 [WORKS, p. 190]). Let us not sneer at this frank avowal, nor grudge the new inquirers it may incite. Meanwhile, it must strike the impartial spectator as a little humorous that, on the one hand, these people have arrogated to themselves a title under which every psychological inquirer *might* be enrolled, and on the other, stigmatise as *soi-disant* 'scientists'—a name ugly enough for anything—the great body of psychologists, who, in fact, think proper not to join their ranks.

James's answer was printed, together with Ward's reply in the January 1893 issue of *Mind*, under the heading "To the Editor of *Mind*."

16. REVIEW OF *Annales des Sciences Psychiques* (1894).

Copy-text: untitled, initialed review in the *Psychological Review*, 1 (May 1894), 317–318 (McD 1894:18). In this brief notice James gives an account of the September–October 1893 issues of *Annales des Sciences Psychiques*.

17. TWO REVIEWS OF *Apparitions and Thought-Transference*, BY FRANK PODMORE (1895).

a. Copy-text: (P³⁴) untitled review in the *Psychological Review*, 2 (January 1895), 67–69 (McD 1895:2).

This review of Podmore's *Apparitions and Thought-Transference* appeared as the second in a series of three reviews by James in the *Psychological Review* for January 1895, the first being on a work by Edmund Parish and the third (signed) on the Report on the Census of Hallucinations (see the textual discourse, pp. 460–461). That the *Review* editor mixed up the order may be observed from James's statement toward the end of the Parish review that he will next proceed to the Census report. Letters do not seem to be preserved concerning the Parish and Podmore pieces, but, as reprinted under James's review of the Census, we know from a letter to J. Mark Baldwin, the *Review* editor, dated October 24 [1894] that James hoped that his review of the Census report could be printed in the January number, as it was. It would seem, then, that the review of Parish either was written later or else that the reference to the Census review was inserted in proof. At any rate, it being improper for the Podmore review to follow that of Parish, as printed, the order of the reviews of Podmore's book and the Census report has been reversed.

b. Copy-text: untitled, unsigned review in the *Nation*, 60 (January 10, 1895), 36–37 (not noted by McD but assigned as 1895:17).

The *Nation*'s records for payment are not preserved for this period; hence the attribution of this review to James rests on the subject, the style, some verbal parallels, and the mention of Lang's *Cock-Lane and Common Sense*, which James had reviewed in the *Psychological Review* the preceding November (McD 1894:21). For a discussion see the commentary Notes.

18. TELEPATHY (1895).

Copy-text: (J) *Johnson's Universal Cyclopædia* (New York: A.J. Johnson, D. Appleton, 1895), 8, 45–47 (McD 1895:16).

The editor of the *Psychological Review*, J. Mark Baldwin, seems to have got in touch with James in May of 1894 about the telepathy article, and others, for on May 30, 1894, James responded: " 'Personality' and 'telepathy' I'll attend to, if the remuneration tempts. But 'Spiritualism' is too much for me. I recommend Hodgson as the best man extant for the purpose, if he will do the job" (typed copy, bMS Am 1092.1). The article on "Personality" is reprinted in *Essays in Psychology* in the WORKS, pp. 315–321.

"Telepathy" was completed by November 13. On that date James wrote to Baldwin: "I am sorry to say that I have mislaid the address of Lilley of Johnson's Cyclop. Can you send it to me? The 'telepathy' article is finished" (ibid.).

19. ADDRESS OF THE PRESIDENT BEFORE THE SOCIETY FOR PSYCHICAL RESEARCH (1896).

Copy-text: (TMs) James's autograph revised typescript in the archives of the Society for Psychical Research, London.

James was president of the (English) Society for Psychical Research for the term 1894–1895. His valedictory presidential address was read for him by F.W.H. Myers at the 77th General Meeting of the Society in London on January 31, 1896. As early as December 18, 1893, in a letter thanking James for accepting the presidency, Frederic Myers remarked about the customary address: "Now as to *addresses*, you must do just as you like—you will give your own *American* something, I hope! and you can send it on to us and we will humbly repeat it after you" (typed copy,

#416). The date for an address by the outgoing president was fixed in January, and publication was expected as soon as possible thereafter. In a forehanded letter of September 11, 1895, when James was nearing the end of his term, Myers wrote him about the rearrangement of the contents for different issues of the *Proceedings* owing to the necessity to drop a number largely devoted to Eusapia Paladino after her exposure in Cambridge: "The Eusapia no. of Proc. must be dropped, & after the no. wh. is to contain *Premonitions* (Nov/95) we must have a *Piper* no [.] (March/96.)² *That* no. must be utilised to draw gold from American fountains:—& shd. be in all ways a boon for the Branch. It wd. include your *Presidential address* (due to be read here at end of *Jan*)" (#419). In the margin opposite this last sentence Myers added, "Please send some little time beforehand." By November 8, however, James had still not written the address as seen in a letter to Henry Sidgwick: "Have you read the paper of Hansen and Lehmann in Wundt's phil. Studien? Of course they will have sent it to you. Don't you think it should be translated for the proceedings? I haven't looked carefully < > I shall try to get ['you' *del.*] out some remarks that may serve as a presidential address, and have them in your hands early in January" (#3760). In the same letter James also referred to an appeal of the American branch for funds: "The circular for a 'fund' will be issued after the Piper Proceedings appears. I myself hope little or nothing from it—but miracles sometimes happen and the only thing is to try."

Partly because James delayed copy, the proposed schedule had to be changed so that the Address was put off until the June *Proceedings*, 12 (June 1896), 2–10 (McD 1896:1). It was also published simultaneously in the United States in *Science*, n.s. 3 (June 19, 1896), 881–888.

In fact, James cut it rather fine despite Myers' plea, for it was not until January 1, 1896, that he wrote to Myers:

> Here is a happy New Year['s' *del.*] to you with my presidential address for a gift. Valeat quantum. The end could have been expanded, but probably this is enough to set the S.P.R. *against [*ab. del.* 'in'] a lofty *cultur-historisch* background; and where we have to do so much champing of the jaws on minute details of cases, that seems to me a good point in a president's address.
>
> In the first half it has just come over me that what I say of one line of fact being "strengthened in *the [*ov.* 'its'] flank" by another, is an "uprush" from my subliminal memory of words of Gurney's—but that does no harm. . . .
>
> I hope *you*'ll read my address—unless indeed Gladstone will consent! ! . . .
>
> I have been ultra non-committal as to our evidence—thinking it to be good presidential policy—but I may have overdone the impartiality business (#3316).

² The account of different meetings found in the *Proceedings*, 12 (June 1896), 1, records not only that James's presidential address was read for him on January 31, by F.W.H. Myers, but also that in the March 13, 1896, meeting "Selections were read from Dr. Hodgson's 'Notes on further Trance Phenomena with Mrs. Piper,' which will, it is hoped, be published in a future number of the *Proceedings*."

That James was not entirely sure of the reader may be inferred, as well, from a modest joke he made in a letter to his brother Henry of January 26, 1896, following the news that "next Friday [January 31] I read my presidential address to S.P.R. in Boston," repeating it the next day in New York. "I don't suppose they got you to read my address to the S.P.R. in London, as they did once before" (#2765). The same information about his reading the address in Boston and New York is also contained in a letter to Münsterberg of January 31, 1896 (Boston Public Library).

Miss Alice Johnson, editor of the *Proceedings*, must have sent copy to the printer immediately on receipt, for on February 3, [1896], James wrote to Mrs. Elizabeth C. Goddard, with whom he had stayed in the summer of 1895 while lecturing in Colorado Springs on "Talks to Teachers," "To you I send the proof of an address (come in this evening) which I shall beg you to return after you have made use of it. The part I ['send' *del.*] mark relates to your topic, though I fear you may find it obscure" (William L. Clements Library, University of Michigan).[3]

Retained in the London Society's archives in the Box for *Proceedings*, vols. XII–XX (1896–1908) was a ribbon typescript of thirteen pages (now missing), entitled 'The President's Address. | [short rule]'. This typescript has been considerably corrected and revised by James in ink and must be the document from which Myers read the Address. It must also have been the printer's copy although it bears no markings for the press, especially since its proof was received by James only a few days more than a month after he had mailed the typescript to England. Most of his handwritten revisions are incorporated in the *Proceedings* and *Science*. In addition, both journals agree in over thirty independent substantive variants that represent authoritative further changes in proof, as well as in a host of minor accidentals differences from the TMs that in some cases run counter to James's usual characteristics. These are readily dealt with. In the Le Baron case (McD 1896:4), printed in this volume, we have not only the original printer's-copy typescript but also a set of proofs carefully marked by Miss Johnson. Comparison of the proof typesetting against the TMs copy reveals that the printer with some frequency styled certain of the accidentals of the TMs, particularly in increasing the weight of the original's light punctuation, and that Miss Johnson completed the process in her reading of the proof, chiefly by setting off parenthetical phrases and clauses with commas, separating the clauses of compound sentences with commas, adding a comma to set off inverted phrases or dependent clauses, and the like. The difference between the somewhat erratic but light punctuation of the Address type-

---

[3] Mrs. Goddard's letter to James is not known but it must have dealt with some psychical subject of the sort that seems to have been discussed in her circle during James's stay in Colorado, and perhaps subsequently in correspondence. The excerpt given is prefixed by James's writing, "Mrs. Reed forestalled your questions to me this A M. and I have written her that I believe in the fact of T. T. [thought transference] but have *absolutely no* theory of the *modus operandi*. I am sending her a little book on the subject." He then continues, "To you . . . ."

script and the changes we find agreed upon by both P^{32} and P^{36}, the *Proceedings* and *Science* respectively, are precisely those to be observed a few months later in the Le Baron case and are almost certainly due to the same agents.

Two consequences follow this observation. The first is that the only trustworthy copy-text is TMs, James's typescript, which gives every indication of being a faithful copy of his lost manuscript. The second is that *Science* (P^{36}) was set not from a carbon of the preserved typescript with James's substantive revisions transferred carefully from the ribbon copy, but instead that P^{36} was set from a copy of the authorially revised proofs for P^{32} which contained not only the various unauthoritative accidentals changes made by the printer and Miss Johnson from the TMs text but also a number of substantive variants that James himself had marked in the first proofs. That the *Science* publication may have been arranged rather late in the game is perhaps suggested by a letter from James to Myers dated May 6, 1896. The letter is mainly concerned with the Le Baron article (quoted in its textual introduction) but at the end James remarks: "Cattell wishes my presidential address to appear here in *Science* simultaneously. We ought to know the approximate date beforehand so as to prepare the ['printers' *del.*] stuff for printing" (S.P.R. Box for *Proceedings*, XII–XX). This seems to provide important evidence that the *Science* version, which appeared in the June 19 issue, was hastily typeset, and the textual evidence practically demonstrates that the copy would have been James's own duplicate of the English revises with a handful of his further changes added.

The textual consequences of this reconstruction simplify the editorial problem. Since P^{36} can have no independent authority from P^{32} save where it diverges, agreement of P^{32} and P^{36} cannot actually confirm authority but only reinforce it insofar as it can be said that James passed the joint readings twice in proof.

After James had returned his marked original proofs to England, he must have received revises since a copy of the revised proof seems to have been given to *Science* for typesetting. We have no firm evidence that James made further changes in these revises when he returned them to England although it would have been characteristic for him to have done so and the theoretical possibility must exist, of course. But the nature of the variants and the lack of any firm substantive revision may serve to cast some doubt on the authority of revise-alterations (which should be identifiable as readings in which P^{32} differs from the joint agreement of TMs and P^{36}). Some few of these unique P^{32} readings may be put down to chance, particularly in the accidentals. Thus the running together of 'coefficient' at 128.15–16 in TMs and P^{36} versus its hyphenated compounding in P^{32} probably represents nothing more than a P^{36} styling of proof 'co-efficient', which had departed from TMs. The American spelling 'skeptic' versus TMs and P^{32} 'sceptic' would seem to be another case of independent styling in P^{36} and of no more significance than the independent P^{36} Americanized 'rumors' versus TMs and P^{32} 'rumours' at 130.40.

So with punctuation variants. The restoration of a semicolon after 'on' by P³⁶ to agree with TMs at 128.24 where the proof, as evidenced by P³², had a comma, may be attributed as much to chance or to the same standards of pointing as to a Jamesian proof-correction in P³⁶, although here the latter possibility cannot be ruled out. However, in the Le Baron article the evidence showed that after the revises had been made (or at least after the preserved set of proofs had been marked), further changes appeared in the print that must be attributed to Miss Johnson touching up proofs (probably the revises) without authority. Thus it would seem probable that in the *Address* a very few special differences in P³² from TMs and P³⁶ agreement may suggest that a later stage of the proofs existed than was used as printer's copy for P³⁶. An example comes to hand in 127.2 where TMs and P³⁶ read 'Broad is the path and wide the way' but P³² diverges by reading 'wide is the way'. At 132.19 TMs "the Island‸" is "the Island," with a comma in P³⁶ drawn from P³², but the capital for P³² lower-case 'island' pretty clearly here representing not a lucky hit by the restyling P³⁶ compositor but instead a later intervention in the P³² revises, reducing the capital. It is, of course, impossible to estimate whether any of the unique P³⁶ readings represent what was set literally from the proofs copy before in the revises of the revises they were returned by Miss Johnson to the TMs reading, as occurred a few times in the Le Baron article. Very likely there were few if any such variants. Theoretically, the two P³² differences from TMs and P³⁶ agreement remarked above could have represented James's changes in the revises that he returned (or his alterations in the P³⁶ proofs) but neither reading offers any evidence that it is authorial and perhaps some grounds for believing in editorial nitpicking, as at 132.19. Whatever the case, their authority is so ambiguous that they have not been accepted into the present edited text in place of TMs.

On the other hand, the relatively few unique P³⁶ substantive readings in certain cases do appear to be authorial and to go beyond the province of the *Science* agents, and these have been accepted—save for the three misprints—as James's second thoughts made in the *Science* proofs at a date too late to be incorporated in the *Proceedings* text.

Instead of James's ink alterations in the typescript being noted in a separate list, they have been recorded in the Emendations to give them greater prominence and to place them in the stream of James's proof revision of the text as originally typed from his manuscript.

20. PSYCHICAL RESEARCH (1896).

Copy-text: (P³⁴) "Psychical Research," *Psychological Review*, 3 (November 1896), 649–652 (McD 1896:3).

James's Presidential Address provoked a somewhat caustic review by his friend J. McKeen Cattell in the *Psychological Review*, 3 (September 1896), 582–583, reprinted as Appendix IV. In "Psychical Research" James replied, not only defending his faith in Mrs. Piper but bringing in the Census of Hallucinations, which Cattell had also criticized. The latter part of James's article is drawn from his letter to Sidgwick of July 11, 1896, providing him with the American statistics for the Census, a letter read by Mrs. Sidgwick at the Third Congress in Münich. The text varies in some details from the letter and the published form. Two corrections of what seem to be printer's errors have been made in the text.

21. A CASE OF PSYCHIC AUTOMATISM (1896).

Copy-text: (TMs) typescript drawn up under James's supervision and containing corrections and revisions in his hand, Society for Psychical Research, London.

Including correspondence, all documents for "A Case of Psychic Automatism" are held by the Society for Psychical Research (London). The documents concerning the text consist of a typescript (TMs) typed under James's direction, including his own introduction on the same machine, and containing numerous corrections and some revisions in his own hand. This TMs was marked for the printer by Miss Alice Johnson, the editor of the Society's *Proceedings*, and served as the printer's copy. The Society also holds a set of galley proofs (Pf) marked exclusively by Miss Johnson. The account was printed in the *Proceedings of the Society for Psychical Research*, 12 (December 1896), 277–297 (McD 1896:4) in which James's introduction is found on pp. 277–279 and Frederic Myers' remarks on pp. 295–297.

The ribbon-copy typescript is paged 1–37; a cancel slip is attached at the top of p. 11. On p. 2 James wrote directions for the insertion as footnotes of two letters from Evangel (Sarah J. Farmer) to him, which were pages 2a–2c in shortened form. The first, of November 26, 1894, paged 2a, appears to have been retyped but the second, of April 26, 1895, may be the original. When James's narrative continues after the break on p. 2 for the letters, the page was originally numbered on the typewriter as 2a, altered to b, and then the number was deleted in favor of a 3 added in ink. Page 4 altered an original 3 in ink, but when Le Baron's (Harry Guy Waters) experiences begin on typed paged 4 (repeated), the number is not altered. In TMs Miss Johnson marked the footnotes for the printer, added the copyright notice, and indicated that the insets should be set in smaller type. With one doubtful exception she does not seem to have interfered with the text itself except, on instructions, to interline 'Aunt Serena' above deleted typed 'Saint Evangel'. We cannot be sure whether she extended her editorial services beyond these limits, for such marking as guidelines for run-ons, or strokes deleting punctuation, are by their nature anonymous. That she was concerned with the presentation of the evidence is indicated, however, by her marginal query 'did he know this?', a query repeated in a letter to Waters since on August 28 in a letter answering other queries, he assured her that he had not known of Evangel's father's lameness prior to sleeping in his bed (see Textual Note to 148.4), a response that moved Miss Johnson to add a special footnote to that effect. This August 28 letter, quoted below, indicates that Miss Johnson had a number of other queries for Waters to answer. The typist of TMs seems to have been singularly faithful to Waters' original since he reproduced various misspellings and eccentric punctuation which James had to correct.

James's ministrations were chiefly confined to corrections of grammar, idiom, and details of spelling and punctuation. The one true addition that he made within Waters' first account of Evangel, Waters objected to, in part, in proof and Miss Johnson removed a phrase (see Textual Note to 146.19). The major change that James made was the deletion of some ten typed lines describing Evangel's ring and its effect on her conviction of perfected reincarnation (see Emendations 148.23), a deletion that was demonstrably his doing because of the bridge words that he wrote to join the severed parts. This major deletion came later than his early round of mechanical correction, for within it the earlier marginal deletion mark is crossed out that altered 'sublimization' to 'sublimation'. The reason for this deletion is obscure. So far as one may guess, it has nothing to do with the series of alterations by which James deliberately concealed Evangel's identity, as when he altered the name and place of her summer camp, and of Chicago to New York, or the fact that it was a gentleman from Lowell, Massachusetts, who brought the ring to her from Egypt, a process already initiated by Waters, who named Eliot, Maine, as 'Shelter Island' placed merely on 'a Coast'. Similarly, James suppressed several references to Waters as a newspaperman that might have provided some clues to Albert Le Baron's identity. That James would have shown Waters the edited typescript before sending it to London on or about March 18 may be taken for granted. Unfortunately correspondence has not been preserved to or from James about the origin and production of this article. Nevertheless, the best guess is that the deletion about Evangel referred to came at Waters' request. Moreover, there are a handful of additions made in TMs in a printing hand that just possibly may be assigned to Waters in the lack of any other suitable candidate (see Textual Note to 146.24).

The proof-sheets consist of seven long galleys, considerably corrected but exclusively in the hand of Miss Johnson. In James's introduction she deleted 'Aunt Serena' at 144.2 and substituted marginally 'Saint Evangel', at a later date deleting 'Saint'. Miss Johnson must have worked over the James part of the proofs at a later time than those of the Le Baron narrative, for in that part 'Aunt Serena' (set in type from this name interlined in TMs) is untouched, the name 'Evangel' first appearing in the print P[32]. (For an account of the changes in the name, see the Textual Note to 144.2.) Miss Johnson reveals herself as a scrupulous and experienced proofreader. She misses no typos and she regularly alters punctuation and capitalization to standard usage, as well as one word that had escaped the printer's own normalizing to British spelling. In only a few cases are her markings substantive, but though Waters' answers to her queries indicate that she had various stylistic reservations (as well she might), she seems not to have interfered with the wording except when authorized. It was from Waters' letter of August 28 that the two major deletions of text that she marked in the proofs (at 152.3 and its parallel at 158.7) were made by his instructions, although she may possibly have raised a question about them in her lost letter to which he is responding. That she carefully read proof against copy may be shown by the various special instances in which she restored the TMs form which the printer had altered, although, of course, she passed the vast majority of the printer's normal stylings. Her marginal query of the repetition of 'bobo' found first at 163.6 and her deletion of the same word, out of position, after 'bono' at 163.7 shows a time interval and reference back to Waters. More than one stage of proofreading is also indicated by her marginal query 'Aunt Serena' when 'Saint Evangel' had been set at 153.19 from an overlooked example in TMs, and then the subsequent deletion. Miss Johnson's proofreading, on the whole, had a considerable effect by making conventional the somewhat erratic accidentals of the original TMs, but she did not in this marked set of proofs interfere on her own behalf with the substantives.

This set of proofs seems to have constituted her own working copy which she had retained. That Waters saw proofs we know, and we must suppose that James was sent a copy of his introduction, for he writes of reading over just the start of Le Baron's section. The evidence suggests that both men had little to alter, and indeed the one change in James's introduction from TMs was not transferred to this known set (nor, apparently, were any of Waters'), but instead must have been made in the lost revises since it occurs only in the final P^{32} print (see Emendations 143.13–14 and Textual Note). The switch from 'Aunt Serena' to 'Evangel' was presumably made in these revises. Minor changes also made only in the revises occur at 148.25, 152.7, 153.1, and 164.1. Probably on her own authority Miss Johnson in the revises altered 'independent' to 'independently' (155.23); what would appear to be a printer's error occurs at 159.13 where 'tinkalong' became 'tinka ong.'

In the S.P.R. *Journal*, 7 (May 1896), 248–250 a brief account of the Le Baron paper, read by F. W. H. Myers on behalf of James at the April 24 General Meeting was printed, part of which may be quoted:

Mr. le Baron, under somewhat remarkable circumstances, became subject to accesses of vocal automatism, mainly in the form of what he calls "deific verbiage;"—a kind of hymns and declamations which issued from his lips with a strong subjective sense of inspiration. After a time these intelligible (although incoherent) utterances were succeeded by unintelligible utterances, claiming to be in "unknown tongues," of which translations were afterwards given. . . . The paper thus introduced [by James] contained a vivid account of experiences whose intensity seemed for a long time an overpowering subjective proof of their value. Specimens of the unknown tongues, recorded by the phonograph, were given. [¶] Mr.

F. W. H. MYERS made some remarks upon the case detailed in Professor James' paper, of which the purport was as follows:— [These remarks were reprinted verbatim at the end of the published paper in the *Proceedings* and are reproduced in this edition.]

Another but briefer note of the paper read at the General Meeting was also carried in the *Proceedings*, 12 (June 1896), 1, where the hope was expressed of future publication in the *Proceedings*.

Most of the correspondence does not seem to have been preserved. What we have, starts in the middle of things, after the paper's delivery, with a letter of May 1, 1896, from James to Myers in answer to a Myers letter of April 20. James writes: "I snatch a moment to say that on no account ['Ma' *del.*] must —————'s paper be *shortened.* I have bound myself by the most fearful oaths to him that all the deific utterances shall go down and all the jargon. It's lucky there isn't more of it. You see he still ['is' *del.*] believes in the tail of his mind that it maybe [*stet*] a real tongue, and he wants the record to subsist for future comparison. I don't altogether wonder at the good ['g' *del.*] creature."[4] This was followed on May 6 by the first of several letters concerning Waters' insistence that his reprints be published in separate bound form, and that he should have the copyright and the ownership of the stereotype moulds as well as some financial rights in case of a second edition.[5] After detailing Waters' request to him about the transfer of copyright and the ownership of the moulds, James writes to Myers: "You had better pacify his mind by stating in writing that the moulds are his property, & that no second edition will be published without a reasonable consideration to be paid him for their use. There's no more real *business* in him than in a kitten, but he gets nervous if everything is not fulfilled. Of course you won't abridge his MS. That was one of the most fixed parts of my agreement with him."[6]

[4] At the top of p. 24 of TMs is a deleted query in Myers' hand, 'Omit this?' with his signature. The note applies to the latter half of a lengthy "translation," the suggested text for deletion beginning about 157.15 with 'Thy day shall rise again'. It may be that the note was a reminder for Myers' reading of the paper on James's behalf before the Society.

[5] Some confusion is possible in the correspondence as to what Waters actually had in mind. However, he insisted on receiving one hundred offprints of his article and these he tried to persuade the Society to bind in cloth, or at the least in paper, for general publicity distribution and possible sale. The question of a second edition is left in abeyance except for the matter of copyright, the moulds, and an acknowledgement of his financial rights. At the top of the first galley of proofs Miss Johnson wrote: "Covers—cloth or paper.—Mr. Myers's speech to be added | Title on cover to be 'The Case of Albert Le Baron with an Introduction by William James of Harvard University,' 'price 2s.' order given Dec. 12 [or 18]." Earlier, on the back of an envelope backstamped October 7, at Cambridge (England), Miss Johnson wrote 'use name Evangel, omitting Saint. Bind in cloth— No more—'.

[6] This May 6 letter by James was triggered by a letter from Waters, 62 Clinton Street, Everett, Mass., dated May 2, 1896, emphasizing that he wanted to retain copyright, the stereotype moulds, and a financial interest in any second edition. [N. B. The 'first edition' would have been the bound offprints.] He quotes a letter from James of March 18 in which the agreement is made: " 'I hereby promise Mr. Guy Waters

Waters' unusual request for copyright and his hope that a sale might be possible in separate form apart from the reprints, caused some discussion in the Society, as evidenced by a letter from Council member H. Arthur Smith to Myers of May 25, which reads in part: "Copyright can of course be formally assigned; but I understand that Mr Le B's paper will appear in his name in our Proceedings. The only question which could thus arise as to copyright would be between the author and our Society; both will be sufficiently protected against the public, and I take it that the author does not suspect that the Society intends to make any further commercial use of his article, as for instance by publishing it separately or ['sla a' *del.*] otherwise."

On July 31 Waters wrote directly to Myers reporting the advice of his wife and sister that Myers' remarks from the May *Journal* should be reset and included in the bound reprints of his article: "I really wish you would run in your two pages Mr Myers. The ladies are right. People need the key *you gave* in those two pages. It is the finest synopsis of all this phenomena known to human history. I cannot help 'raving' when I think of those points. It only amounts to the cost of composition on two pages. I shall be sorry if you do not, because when the offprints (are thrown into book form in the shape suggested in the other letter mailed you a few hours since) the book will have ['to' *del.*] *no key*. The money I will put in over here in Boston, New York, and Chicago in mailing etc of the book when done, will balance your extra expense over there of the additional title and cloth covers."

On August 13 Waters again addressed Myers: "Professor James suggests a happy *and sensible [*intrl.*] amendment to our title for the '*cover*' of the '*offprint.*' He says leave out the word '*extraordinary*' and let the title for the '*cover*' of the '*offprint*' simply read: 'The Case of | Albert le Baron | with an introduction | by |William James | of | Harvard University.'[7] The letter continues with Waters' proposal to use his bound reprints as 'campaign flyers' for the S.P.R. and he again begs Myers' permission to reprint his remarks in order to fill out the volume.[8] On August 20 in a postcard to Myers, Waters acknowledges a letter from Myers of August 10. He is still concerned that if the covers of his off-

---

that—so far as my will can ensure it—he shall have copyright taken out in the name of Albert Le Baron for the MS. I am now sending to the Society for Psychical Research containing his narrative with my introduction and notes. He shall also have stereotype moulds taken and shipped to him, free of expense to himself, along with 100 reprints of the communication as soon as it appears.' | William James."

[7] Among the S.P.R. papers is a sheet of paper containing what seems to be a trial title for the reprint cover, written in a fancy display script: "A Case of Psychic Automatism, | including | 'Speaking with Tongues.' " In the upper left corner is a note, "For Proceedings or Journal | 100 reprints to go to author. | Also ⟨ ⟩ moulds | Copyright to be taken out in name of W James."

[8] It may be that the verbatim repetition of Myers' remarks on the Le Baron case reprinted in December to follow the article was moved by Waters' desire to have it added to the offprints. The full text of Myers' remarks had previously been printed in the May *Journal* and might otherwise have needed no second round.

prints merely reflect publication in the *Proceedings* the "book" will not receive the reviews and publicity he wants. On September 3 he returns to the attack with hints that the Society (with proper covers, of course, perhaps naming the Society's publishers) should distribute fifty of his hundred bound offprints to English and Colonial publications as a boost to the Society.

Two letters to Miss Johnson concern the text. On August 28 Waters addresses her in connection with some now lost discussion in which she had raised certain queries: "Professor James, enclosing your letter to him, writes,—'My dear Waters, Vide the two documents inclosed! I suggest a clause softening the abruptness of Aunt Serena in the first gally [*stet*], but have no time to look over the proof farther, being in the wilderness & hastening on to Chicago with a big mail just come in to answer within an hour.' " Waters then continues to Miss Johnson: (a) he agrees to her arrangement of the title and copyright notice; (b) "Your opinion as to the name 'aunt Serena' is excellent. 'Aunt anything' sounds farcical. Please stick to the old name 'Saint Evangel' "; (c) the narration should close with his full name 'Albert Le Baron' and not merely his surname; (d) he agrees that revises need not be sent him and he will keep his proofs instead; (e) No, he did not know beforehand that Evangel's father was lame; (f) omit the *duplicated* expressions " 'interpreting phenomena as having some personal bearing' ";[9] (g) "The phrases, 'the automatism *assuming to be* the true mother of my soul' etc, are by no means slips of the pen. Please let them stay."; (h) "*Why* the same English word is used for so many 'unknowns' I do not know [psychic-automatism?]. Concerning the *rationale* of such caprices by the automatism we know nothing; but to explain which would be a discovery."; (i) remove "and a medium" to avoid too many "comments." At the head of this letter Miss Johnson wrote: "ans^d Sep. 17. I have provisionally put 'Evangel' in proof. Will be time to change, if he disapproves. . . . Suggest tinted paper cover for his offprints." Finally, in a letter of September 29 to Miss Johnson, in response to her letter of September 17:

> Your two pages of adroit and delicate argument showing me *why* I should use paper covers is of course laughably convincing, and I should be happy in having the honour of yeilding [*stet*] to your persuasive reasons if I felt that by doing so I could deliberately inveigle dear Mr Myers and Prof. Sidgwick into their urging the S.P.R. to use the little pamphlet as a 'campaign flyer' or 'tract' to be scattered broadcast as a means to awaken the psychic-'unconverted' to the work of the S.P.R.
>
> I will most gladly accept your two pages of paper-cover-reasons if the S.P.R. will do some aggressive seed-sowing with the little pamphlet after your taste has decided on the matter of the *colour* of the paper.
>
> The expense of mailing a few thousands of such a small pamphlet as a means of indicating the kind of work going on would be merely nominal. If yourself, Mrs Sidgwick, Prof. Sidgwick, & Mr Myers will get the S.P.R.

---

9 This seems to have justified Miss Johnson's deletions in proof of two passages, noted in the Emendations list as 152.3 and 158.7. See the Textual Note to 152.3.

to scatter a few thousands of the tract broadcast to awaken the ps[y]chic unconverted to the vast and profound claims of the work of the S.P.R. I have certainly no objections to the tract appearing in paper covers. Will you do this?

Then may I also ask that you all decide that you put on the cover in one of its modest corners the cabalistic words: *Price, one Shilling.* I wish these three words placed thereupon because in the hugeness of my vast and incorrigible optimism I am still supposing that the tract may some day be of commercial value.

The editorial treatment of the Le Baron article could have taken the form of a more or less exact reprint of the final text from the *Proceedings,* of a reprint of the transcript of Waters' account as preserved in the TMs that James had made up—minus James's revisions—or a reprint of the typescript including the revisions. In this case the choice of the James-revised TMs as copy-text was relatively simple. In the first place, except for James's introduction the major interest in the Le Baron narrative for a collection of James's works is the record of James's treatment of the text in the typescript for which he was responsible. (The case would be altered, of course, if Waters were the author being edited.) In order to emphasize James's working over of TMs, each alteration in that copy-text document has been recorded in the list of Emendations together with the original reading, so that both the TMs and James's changes can be readily identified in a more prominent part of the apparatus than if the alterations had been segregated in a separate list.

Although it is clear that at least three substantive deletions were made in the proofs by Miss Johnson on Waters' instructions, we know that James declined to read the Le Baron proofs after the start of the first galley and so was unaware of them. As for the rest of Miss Johnson's markings in the proof, they betray only editorial improvements in the accidentals, in addition to the correction of literals, and hence they may be taken as unauthoritative and discarded except when necessary as corrections. Since the TMs was the printer's copy, even less possibility of authority can be assigned to the numerous printer's styling changes that can be detected by collation with the copy. However, these have also been recorded, as well as Miss Johnson's proof-corrections, since they preserve an interesting and even significant record of the sophistication to which the accidentals of the text were subject during the course of transmission both at the hands of the proofreader and of the printer himself. James's own proofs are not preserved nor is there any indication in Miss Johnson's proofs of the transfer of any markings from his own set. It seems clear that before returning this set of proofs to the printer for revises she was able to alter 'Aunt Serena' in James's introduction first to 'Saint Evangel' and then to 'Evangel' but did not receive Waters' approval in time to alter the name in her set of proofs of his narrative. As a result, a series of changes in the name had to be made in the now lost revises, along with a handful of other alterations, discussed above. The single substantive difference between proofs and print made in the revises for James's part has been mentioned in the Textual Note to 143.13–14 and is presumably authoritative.

As an editorial procedure, therefore, the James-annotated TMs holds as copy-text. A few minor accidental changes are adopted from the proofs when they constitute necessary corrections (although without authority), and the three deletions made in proof on Waters' instructions have been honored despite some lingering doubts about his having authorized the total deletion of the two poodle-philosopher passages. The conjectured changes made in the lost revises which appear to be authoritative have also been accepted from P³², the *Proceedings* print. The aim has been, therefore, to reproduce a text based on the document that James submitted, but with a few necessary corrections and whatever true substantive revisions that either he or Waters requested.

22. TELEPATHY: CONTROVERSY WITH TITCHENER ON LEHMANN AND HANSEN (1896–1899).

a. Review of "Ueber unwillkürliches Flüstern," by F. C. C. Hansen and Alfred Lehmann (1896).

Copy-text: (P³⁴) untitled, unsigned review in the *Psychological Review*, 3 (January 1896), 98–99 (McD 1896:6).

b. Review of "Involuntary Whispering Considered in Relation to Experiments in Thought-Transference," by Henry Sidgwick (1897).

Copy-text: (P³⁴) untitled, signed review in the *Psychological Review*, 4 (November 1897), 654–655 (McD 1897:8).

Henry Sidgwick's experiments in thought-transference were attacked by Professors Lehmann and Hansen as having, in fact, a physical explanation. To this Sidgwick replied in the S.P.R. article under review by James who approved Sidgwick's denial of the Lehmann-Hansen contention that physical communication had taken place and not thought-transference.

c. Letter: Lehmann and Hansen on the Telepathic Problem (1898).

Copy-text: (P³⁶) "Lehmann and Hansen 'on the Telepathic Problem,' " *Science*, n.s. 8 (December 30, 1898), 956 (McD 1898:4).

A little over a year later, Professor E. B. Titchener of Cornell University published "The 'Feeling of Being Stared At' " in *Science*, n.s. 8 (December 23, 1898), 895–897, in which—without reference to Sidgwick or to James—he applauded the Lehmann-Hansen position and came to the express conclusion that "no scientifically-minded psychologist believes in telepathy." In a Letter to the Editor in the next issue of *Science*, James took Titchener to task for ignoring Sidgwick's work and James's review.[10]

[10] In the Letter (and so repeated in the title) James misspelled Lehmann as 'Lehman', an error corrected in the present edition.

d. Letter: Lehmann and Hansen on Telepathy *(1899)*.

Copy-text: (P³⁶) "Messrs. Lehmann and Hansen on Telepathy," *Science*, n.s. 9 (May 5, 1899), 654–655 (McD 1899:4a).

Titchener immediately replied in the next issue of *Science*, n.s. 9 (January 6, 1899), and at that point the matter rested until in this Letter to the Editor James revived the controversy in direct response to Titchener's Letter to the Editor of the previous January 6. The next day, May 6, James wrote to Titchener:

> A letter to Science *rê* our late little "scrap" over Lehmann's "unwillkührliches [*stet*] Flustern" etc., has just been published, and I venture to call your attention to it, if it has escaped your notice. You will, I am sure, take no umbrage at the "gentle irony" with which I express myself. Psychical research in these days of scant justice from the scientists, has to avail herself of every possible weapon by which to score a point.
>
> It is but fair that you should see Lehmann's original letter, which I enclose, begging you to make return. You will observe that he absolutely succumbs to Sidgwick's and my contention as to the undemonstrative character of his own experiments, and that he adopts S.'s *hypothesis [*ab. del.* 'theory'] that the coincidence between his error and Sidgwick's was probably in large part due to the accidental coincidence of similar number-habits in the experimenters.
>
> On the main point, of "telepathy" being established, he does n't give in. That was hardly to be expected of him. As between you and myself, however, the only point under discussion was ['the' *del.*] whether L. had experimentally refuted S. I think if you will reread S.'s criticism you will now agree with [*poss.* 'bot' *del.*] L.
>
> P.S. Unfortunately "fortgesetzte Versuche" are incapable of settling this particular question, for the Sidgwicks' own experiments were only about 1300 in number, and that I judge from my own results to be much too small a term of comparison (Department of Manuscripts and University Archives, Cornell University).

e. Letter: Telepathy Once More, No. I *(1899)*.

Copy-text: (P³⁶) "Telepathy Once More," *Science*, n.s. 9 (May 26, 1899), 752–753 (McD 1899:4b).

Titchener replied in the next *Science*, for May 12, and two weeks later James's Letter to the Editor appeared in *Science*. Before it was published, James wrote to Titchener on May 21:

> I got your letter of the 8th July, and postponed answering till I should have seen your letter to Science [May 12]. Being in New Hampshire during the past days, I have only just found it on my return.
>
> I must say that in my humble opinion you don't seem to reinstate *the value of [*intrl.*] Lehman[n]'s *paper [*intrl.*] very effectually and I have said as much in a still later letter to Science. This, however, I fear Cattell will not print, leaving you in the public eye with the unanswerable *word [*alt. fr.* 'world'].
>
> I seem myself telepathically to discern that, like all Scientists, you felt

so absolutely sure that any criticism of telepathy must be ['so' *del.*] essentially sound, that you did n't read the talk the other way with sufficient care. If you did n't think that L. had successfully interpreted S's results as whispering, what *had* he done that made him worth quoting at all? Surely his general remarks about ['the' *del.*] telepathic evidence don't exhaust the subject.

Of course he disclaims an *exacter Beweis*. The nature of things excludes that; but he does claim to have made the alternative explanation, whispering, ['the' *del.*] overwhelmingly probable. He has failed to make it *probable*. Ther[e]fore he has failed altogether *in rê* Sidgwick, as he admits himself.

I think myself that the *experimental* evidence for "thought-transference" is lamentably *poor [*ab. del.* 'small'] in amount, and for the most part in quality, ['for so' *del.*] to serve as basis for admitting a phenomenon so subversive of our scientific beliefs. I think the Sidgwick series, however, an excellent model of research; and I hardly see what anyone can do, but "hang it up" as something unexplained. That seems to me the attitude of the truly "scientific *psychologist ['s' *del.*]"—"facts," however anomalous, are worth more than all our theories, however many *other* facts the latter may explain.

I candidly admit that what has made me hospitable to telepathy in general, is the particular case of Mrs. Piper, who so far outdoes these experimental things, and ['which' *del.*] to me is absolutely inexplicable today. Such investigations are fearfully tedious and in all sorts of ways uncontrollable, but they awaken ['con' *om.*]|viction if one works at first hand, without prejudice and gives time. My colleagues for the most part, when invited, have *simply [*intrl.*] refused to see Mrs. Piper. Royce, e.g., who had only to step from the next door but one into my house. Munsterberg said it was no use; if he got such results, he would know himself to have been hypnotized. I said "bring your wife, sit in the corner & observe, and see if your accounts agree." He replied "I should never allow my wife to visit such a performance." I call that ['keen' *del.*] real sportsmanlike keenness for new facts!

No matter! truth will prevail.

I echo your wish that we might meet. . . . I hear splendid things of your success as professor at Cornell, and of your admirably systematized methods in the laboratory.

I take the liberty of sending you a little volume of mine, just out [*Talks to Teachers*], light stuff enough! (Cornell University).

A few days after the appearance of James's May 26 Letter to the Editor, he wrote again to Titchener, on May 31, this time typed and addressing him as 'My dear Titchenor' (the name misspelled here and elsewhere in this letter, although spelled correctly in the preceding letters) instead of 'Professor Titchener':

I am much pleased with the tone of your letter and I feel as if the episode had on the whole tended to promote understanding rather than to increase misunderstanding.

I gave a false impression if I suggested in any way that Psychical Researchers were suffering from martyrdom. I don't think that I myself have sacrificed anything by having my name associated with that cause. The only feeling I carry into the matter is one of irritation that in a subject, which to my mind, is one altogether of empirical details, in which no general philosophic tendencies have as yet begun to reveal themselves, so many of my colleagues should keep *in the [*ink ab. del.* 'aloof in an'] attitude of *"authoritative aloofness" [*ink db. qts. added*].

You deserve credit for your small departure from this *attitude; [*ink semicolon alt. fr. comma*] Lehmann still more credit for his large departure, but you must admit that there was a certain insolence, and an insolence that felt itself secure of impunity, in the last paragraph of your original article, where you almost apologized for condescending to touch the details of such a subject. I see from what you now say that you were thinking of the whole Lehmann-Sidgwick controversy in a more superficial way than it deserved, and I do hope that hereafter you may keep on the deeper level. The stuff is fearfully dry and its personal aspects are very repugnant to me, but I believe it is a genuine "find", and I *do [*ink underl.*] think that those who won't come to close quarters with it in detail, ought not to pronounce ex cathedra judgments.

I, for example, decline to discuss Münsterberg's article with him. I have served my time with *a priori [*ink underl.*] arguments, and henceforward will only listen to those who bring definite talk about *particular [*ink intrl.*] facts.

You say that you have a right to fight for your side as I have a right to fight for mine. What I deny is that at the stage at which things now are, anybody has the right to fight *for either side [*ink intrl.*] by abstract generalities.

. . . After this correspondence, dear Titchenor, we shall meet somewhat as old friends. I wish that it were not likely to be at so remote a date. If you should pass through Boston any time before the 15th. of July, you must not fail to look me up (ibid.).

This letter could not have reached Titchener before his final parting shot printed in *Science* on June 2, a brief statement that concluded the controversy.

In the *Journal of the Society for Psychical Research*, 9 (October 1899), 113–120, the editor in "Messrs. Hansen and Lehmann on the Telepathic Problem" (McD 1899:6) introduced a résumé, with quotations, of the controversy between James and Titchener, beginning with the opening sentence, "The following correspondence may interest or entertain some of our readers." He provides a few bridges between letters, occasionally comments briefly on some point, and following the quotation of Titchener's final closing of the controversy in *Science* on June 2, he writes almost two pages of summary and comment, especially about the difficulties of tests of the telepathic communication of numbers. That this article was written with James's approval, and possibly even at his suggestion, may be indicated by the presence in the Society's archives in London of the holograph letter, in German, sent to James by Lehmann, the deletions for the printer marked, and the note that it was to be footnote 6.

No revisions of the text of James's contributions appear. Hence from the point of view of an edition of James the article would be purely repetitious of his texts if reprinted. Nevertheless, the continuity given to the exchange of public letters by the editor, the reprinting of Titchener's letters, and the comments of the editor on the whole subject are of sufficient interest to justify the preservation of the non-Jamesian portions as an Appendix applying to the reprint here of James's Letters to *Science*.

In the May 26 letter James's incorrect date reference to Titchener's letter in the May 12th issue of *Science* has been emended. Both this error and the misspelling of Lehmann's name in the December 30, 1898 letter are corrected, in fact, in the *Journal* summary article.

23. REVIEW OF "TELEPATHIC DREAMS EXPERIMENTALLY INDUCED," BY G. B. ERMACORA (1896).

Copy-text: untitled, initialed review in the *Psychological Review*, 3 (January 1896), 99–100 (McD 1896:7).

24. REVIEW OF *I Fenomeni Telepatici e le Allucinazioni Veridiche*, BY ENRICO MORSELLI (1897).

Copy-text: untitled, signed review in the *Psychological Review*, 4 (November 1897), 655–657 (McD 1897:9).

James's review of Morselli's *I Fenomeni Telepatici* came out in the *Review* as the second in a sequence beginning with his review of Sidgwick's "Involuntary Whispering" (pp. 654–655) and succeeded by a review of Parish's *Zur Kritik des telepathischen Beweismaterials*, to which reference is made in the closing sentence of the review.

25. LETTER ON MRS. PIPER, THE MEDIUM (1898).

Copy-text: (P[36]) "Mrs. Piper, 'the Medium,' " *Science*, 7 (May 6, 1898), 640–641 (McD 1898:2).

J. McKeen Cattell, an old acquaintance of James and editor of *Science* (after having given up the *Psychological Review*), had somewhat caustically criticized in the *Review*, 3 (September 1896), 582–583 (Appendix IV in this volume), James's Presidential Address to the S.P.R. James replied in "Psychical Research," published in the *Review*, 3 (November 1896), 649–652 (No. 20 in this volume). In *Science*, n.s. 7 (April 15, 1898), 534–535, Cattell returned to the attack, the occasion being Richard Hodgson's "A Further Record of Observations of Certain Phenomena of Trance," which had appeared in the S.P.R. *Proceedings*, 13 (February 1898), 284–583,[11] and was chiefly devoted to Mrs. Piper. Cattell in a note entitled "Mrs. Piper, the Medium" remarked on "the trivial character of the evidence for the heterogeneous mass of material taken under the wing of the Society" in its thirteen published volumes, but added that the present number has some interest in that it includes Hodgson's article. "The case of Mrs. Piper is of interest, because Professor James

---

[11] Hodgson's article was to be reviewed by James in the *Psychological Review*, 5 (July 1898), 420–424 (No. 26 in this volume).

has said:" and he then quotes from James's Presidential Address the passage about Mrs. Piper as James's white crow who upsets the law that all crows are black. He continued:

> It is Professor James who gives dignity and authority to psychical research in America, and if he has selected a crucial case it deserves consideration. The difficulty has been that proving innumerable mediums to be frauds does not disprove the possibility (though it greatly reduces the likelihood) of one medium being genuine. But here we have the 'white crow' selected by Professor James from all the piebald crows exhibited by the Society.
>
> I find, among the great number of names and initials whose séances with Mrs. Piper are reported, five and only five well-known men of science. The following are the concluding sentences of their reports: [quoting critical statements by J. Mark Baldwin, John Trowbridge, N. S. Shaler, J. M. Peirce, and S. Weir Mitchell, before concluding] Truly, 'we have piped unto you, but ye have not danced.'

James's resentment led to his letter in *Science*, which the journal entitled "Mrs. Piper, 'The Medium,' " followed on pp. 641–642 by a brief defense by Cattell, here printed as part of James's Letter. Cattell's response provoked a private letter from James to Cattell, dated May 8, 1898:

> I have read your brief retort and live. Your state of prejudice is so *absolute*, that quite naively and unconsciously you perpetrate acts of insolence quite as remarkable as your lapses of logic, as if I were some minor or child making a nuisance in the psychological neighborhood. You surely would not adopt that tone in regard to any other difference of scientific opinion, least of all where the adversary had 15 years first-hand acquaintance with the facts and you had never seen them.
>
> No! my dear fellow, it is as I say, all the virtues have to be drilled into us *afresh [alt. fr. 'afreash']* in each special matter, and the day for psychical research has not yet come. Understanding the conditions, I don't care personally a rap for the treatment, or think the less well as human beings of the treaters—yourself included. As you smile indulgently at me, so I, dear Cattell, at you. He smiles best who smiles last, and my prophetic soul is in no doubt about that. . . . On re-reading I can see that my first two pages suggest *temper* (the word insolence etc.). Nothing could less be the case. I fairly delight in you, my dear boy, as a first-class specimen (Library of Congress).

26. REVIEW OF "A FURTHER RECORD OF OBSERVATIONS OF CERTAIN
    PHENOMENA OF TRANCE," BY RICHARD HODGSON (1898).

Copy-text: (P[34]) untitled, signed review in the *Psychological Review*, 5 (July 1898), 420–424 (McD 1898:7).

It is interesting to see that in the conclusion of his review of Richard Hodgson's "Further Record of Observations of Certain Phenomena of Trance," which had appeared in the S. P. R. *Proceedings*, 13 February 1898), 284–583, James anticipates some of the language he was to employ in his own report on Mrs. Piper's Hodgson-Control some ten years later.

Closing paragraphs of the review (190.25–191.34) were reprinted without authoritative change in *Collected Essays and Reviews*, ed. R. B. Perry, pp. 438–441 (McD 1920:2).

27. Frederic Myers's Service to Psychology (1901).

Copy-text: (P³²) "Frederic Myers's Service to Psychology," *Proceedings of the Society for Psychical Research*, 17 (May 1901), 13–23 (McD 1901:1).

Frederic Myers died in Rome, on January 17, 1901, at the hotel where James was staying. On February 5 James wrote to Mrs. Sarah Whitman: "He suffered horribly from his breathing, but so absorbed was his mind in wider matters and so intense his intellectual activity (having essays & editorials read to him only a couple of hours before the death-rattle, etc.) that he was a sublime spectacle, and much impressed his doctors. It shows also what a real *belief* in immortality can do in the way of making a man indifferent to temporal vicissitudes. The whole thing, which lasted *4 [*ov.* '5'] weeks, took it out of me very much, but Myers remains an elevated image!" (Library of Congress).

Later, on February 24, he wrote from Rome to his brother Henry: "I have shunted myself off for 3 days past ['on' *del.*] to a paper on Myers's *position [*ab. del.* 'place'] as a psychologist. A memorial meeting of him is to be held on March 8th—enclosed ticket explains (but I don't expect you ['will' *del.*] to use it!) My paper will probably not be read, but go into the Proceedings. I fear that the S. P. R., with Myers gone, has hardly any prospect of much longer continuance. Somehow I feel very tenderly towards him, and regret not being warmer with him when I had him. The official psychologists affect to look down on him, but he has perhaps done more for psychology than any of *the [*alt. fr.* 'them'] lot" (#2865). As reported in the S.P.R. *Journal*, 10 (April 1901), 54–56, at the memorial meeting "Mr. J. G. Piddington then read extracts from a paper by Professor William James on Frederic Myers' services to Psychology," offering an extended summary.

The English styling of the S.P.R. *Proceedings* has been retained in the present reprint, but the two anomalous uses of the genitive "Myers'" (195.13, 39) have been altered to the prevailing form "Myers's", James's own usage as shown by his letter of February 24, 1901 to Henry. The essay was reprinted in *Popular Science Monthly*, 59 (August 1901), 380–389. Although James would have been responsible for this appearance, he made no alterations, and the reprint is verbatim for all substantives and substantially so for the accidentals, given the Americanizing of English spellings and the reduction of a good many of James's concept capitals. The reproduction of the English spelling 'programme' (200.35), although not unknown in the United States at this time, suggests that James merely turned over to the *Monthly* a clipping of the *Proceedings* article. The *Monthly*'s faithfulness to the *Proceedings* printed form in the general run of accidentals exceeds what might have been expected if independent copy had been furnished. No authority, therefore, can inhere to the *Monthly* text. The essay was also reprinted, without authoritative change, in the posthumous *Memories and Studies,* ed. Henry James, Jr. (New York: Longmans, Green, 1911), pp. 143–170 (McD 1911:2).

On June 26, 1901, James mailed a copy of the *Proceedings* essay to Charles Eliot Norton: "I spent a day with poor Mrs. Myers, a foolish kind of a woman but dignified *by [*ab. del.* 'from'] her disconsolateness from her husband's loss. I mailed you yesterday a notice I wrote in Rome of him. He 'looms' upon me after death more than he did in life, and I think that his book about 'Human Personality' will probably rank hereafter as 'epoch-making' " (bMS Am 1088 [3906]).

28. REVIEW OF *Human Personality and Its Survival of Bodily Death,* BY FREDERIC W. H. MYERS (1903).

Copy-text: (P³²) untitled, signed review in the *Proceedings of the Society for Psychical Research,* 18 (June 1903), 22–33 (McD 1903:3; in error duplicated as 1903:12).

James's review, preceded by 'I.' in the *Proceedings* as the first of several reviews, is found under the major heading "Supplement" and the minor heading "Reviews." The copy-text is the only publication. The English styling has been retained and in one place (as the list of Emendations indicates) fortified when an American spelling slipped by the compositor who had previously set it in English form.

In a postcard of December 25, 1902, to Sir Oliver Lodge James wrote: "Three months ago I wrote to Piddington, refusing to review Myers for the Proceedings. I was too poorly, and thought that one of the younger generation would be more fit. I am now much tougher, however, and am writing to him that I will take it, if someone else is not determined on.—" (Society for Psychical Research, London). On February 27, 1903, he re-marked in a letter to Henry Rankin: "I have just received Fred. Myers's 'Human Personality and its survival of Natural Death' in two vast volumes, which I have agreed to ['th' *del.*] review for the S.P.R. Pro-ceedings" (Houghton *67 M-96). To Ferdinand Schiller he wrote on April 8, from Asheville, N.C.: "I wrote a review of Myers's book for the *Proceedings* just before leaving home. I was dog tired and it went with difficulty. I wish that you had done it. I couldn't go into criticism of detail, so I simply skeletonized the argument, which was very likely a useful service. My opinion of the man is raised by reading the volumes, but not of the solidity of the system. The piles driven into the quicksand are too few for such a structure. But it is essential as a preliminary at-tempt at methodizing, and will doubtless keep a very honorable place in history.—" (typed copy, Stanford University Libraries). Much the same sentiments are expressed in a letter of April 30 to Théodore Flournoy:

> 'Billy' also says that you have executed a review of Myers's book, finding it *a [*intrl.*] more difficult task than you had anticipated. I am highly

curious to see what you have found to say. I, also, wrote a notice of the volumes, and found it exceeding difficult to know how to go at the job. At last, I decided just to skeletonize the points of his reasoning, but on correcting the proof just now, what I have written seems deadly flat and unprofitable, and makes me wish that I had stuck to my original intention of refusing to review the book at all. The fact is, such a book need not be *criticized* at all at present. It is obviously too soon for it to be either refuted or established by mere criticism. It is a hypothetical construction of genius which must be kept hanging up, as it were, for new observations to be referred to. As the years accumulate these in a *more [intrl.] favorable or in a *more [intrl.] unfavorable sense, it will tend to stand or to fall. I confess that reading the volumes has given me a higher opinion than ever of Myers's constructive gifts, but on the whole a lower opinion of the objective solidity of the system. So many of the facts which form its pillars are still dubious! . . . Forever *baffling* is all this subject, and I confess that I begin to lose my interest" (bMS Am 1505 [43]).

After reading Flournoy's review, James wrote to him on [July 28, 1903]: "I had great trouble in deciding what to say in my criticism of the book, and feel quite ashamed of my dry little article after reading your big and human production. Thank Heaven it is all over for both of us and having so fully paid our debt to Myers's *manes* for all that he ever did for us, we can feel satisfied, and turn towards other things" (bMS Am 1505 [44]).

One of James's last comments was made in a letter of November 2, 1903, to Richard Hodgson:

Have you read Stout's review of Myers in the Hibbert Journal? & W. Mc Dougall's in Mind? Both deny that he has proved the existence of a subliminal except as an (exceptionally existing) receptacle of lapsed supraliminal ['events' *del.*] memorys. It would give Myers a second ['eternity' *del.*] immortality to read their declarations of preference for the spirit hypothesis. To have the scientists fall back on spirits to defend them against Myers's subliminal is truly a delicious irony of fate! (Society for Psychical Research, London).

The spiritist periodical *Light* (August 5, 1905), p. 369, translated from the Italian *Revista delle Riviste di Studi Psichici*, the second number of July 1905, an interview with James during the International Conference on Psychology held in Paris, the subject being James's *Varieties of Religious Experience*. (The *Revista* is a reprint of a collection of articles on psychical subjects printed in the periodical *Nuova Parola*.) In the course of the interview

Professor James spoke of the criticism which his book had called forth from 'medical materialists,' who regard all visionaries, from St. Paul to George Fox, and from St. Francis of Assisi to Thomas Carlyle, as mere sufferers from perverted nervous or glandular functions. These dogmatic materialists, he considers, are far behind the times; they apply criticism destructively instead of affirmatively. Their method is scientific aberration rather than science. The truth of a doctrine or of religious teaching has nothing to do with the state of mind of the teacher. Whether St. Theresa was hysterical and unbalanced or not makes no difference to her theology, which must be judged on its own merits.

But, said Professor James, there is a strong reaction against this unscientific 'science.' Mr. Frederic Myers has had a great counter-influence on contemporary thought:—

'His hypothesis of the subliminal consciousness throws light on the problem of life, and on the sources of the ideal life. It lends itself to a wider generalisation, and I have used it to explain the phenomena of religious experience, and to reduce them to some degree of systematic unity. Myers used it to establish survival of personality, but my own studies have not yet led me to pronounce definitely upon this question. This, however, does not affect my conception of human personality, which is deeply rooted in the spiritual world—a region more profoundly spiritual than the subliminal consciousness, and from which come the most powerful moral impulses, the highest aspirations—a world which is a law to our outward one, and exerts a practical and decisive influence on our ordinary life.'

Speaking of the assumed parallelism between physical and psychical phenomena, Professor James said that for the pathologists who regarded everything from the material point of view, this parallelism was the starting point of a materialistic metaphysic. But he regarded the spiritual as extending so far beyond the material that it was only for a very short distance that there was any material parallel to spiritual life. He hopes shortly to publish something on these subjects, if not the book originally planned [*Varieties*, part two].

29. TELEPATHY ONCE MORE, NO. II (1903).

Copy-text: (P^{25}) "Telepathy Once More," *Nation*, 76 (April 23, 1903), 330 (not in McD but assigned as 1903:13). This publication, found under "Correspondence," answered an article entitled "Telepathy" by John Trowbridge in the *Nation*, 76 (April 16, 1903), 308–309.

30. LETTER TO JAMES HYSLOP SUPPORTING THE PROSPECTUS FOR AN AMERICAN INSTITUTE FOR SCIENTIFIC RESEARCH (1903).

Copy-text: unheaded letter, *Proceedings of the American Society for Psychical Research*, n.s. 1 (1907), 33–34 (not in McD but assigned as 1907:13). A typed copy (bMS Am 1092.1) of the letter is in the James Collection at Houghton.

After the dissolution of the American Society for Psychical Research, announced respectively in England in June 1906 and in the United States in January 1907, James Hyslop endeavored to continue publication of the American *Proceedings*. In the new *Proceedings* he seems to have revived an earlier proposal for a formal society to investigate mediumship and other psychical phenomena, and on pp. 32ff., under the heading "Letters of Indorsement," he printed letters of endorsement, dated between 1903 and 1906, from various psychologists. Among these was a letter from James dated October 25, 1903. Since it was a private letter, some question may have arisen, for on December 1, 1904, in a letter to Hyslop, James authorized its publication, but reiterated his position stated earlier in a letter of November 14 that he wished his name withdrawn from the council of Hyslop's proposed Institute: "Yes! of course use my letter! But I'm going to be obdurate about my going on the 'Board,' and shall not accept when my election is formally notified" (typed copy, bMS Am 1092.1). That James and Hyslop differed considerably in their approach to psychical research is evident from a letter written to Hyslop on February 28, 1905:

> I believe in psychical research, and in its endowment. I disbelieve in endowment without research, and in the substitution of "audiences" for investigators, "popular interest" for investigation, and newspaper tattle for facts. I loathe our American tendency to make organizations where there is no grist to grind. I would give more for one good monograph than for a Society with 1000 members and ½ a million of capital and no one to work. And I entirely disbelieve in your plan of founding a medical institute with your funds (ibid.).

31. A CASE OF AUTOMATIC DRAWING (1904).

Copy-text: "A Case of Automatic Drawing," *Popular Science Monthly*, 64 (January 1904), 195–201 (McD 1904:4).
　　In a letter to James McKeen Cattell of November 17, 1903, James seems to have enclosed C.H.P.'s (Perkins') account to see if it was publishable:

> I don't know whether this kind of case is in the line of the Pop. Sci. It is a rather odd one from the monotony and idiosyncracy of the work done. The writer seems to me a very respectable person, to whom every dollar is now important, and I suggested to him that I might possibly earn a small sum for him by printing his case in one of the magazines. He wrote it out exclusively at my suggestion, and I have patched together in the first part of the narrative data communicated to me in successive letters.
>
> Send the whole business back to me if you can't use it, and, if you can, send back the drawings which you don't choose to print (Library of Congress).

After Cattell's November 25 reply accepting the piece, James wrote on November 29:

> Yours of the 25th. rê Perkins's Automatism article, received.
>
> I never thought of hinting at any special payment for him. Pay whatever usual price the magazine would pay for that much of a contribution. Send it to me, made out to his order. I mentioned his need of "realizing" to account for my having offered to get an author's fee for him if he would put his experience on paper. He seems a very respectable fellow indeed, but I doubt whether any other magazine than the Pop. Sci. would pay him anything at all for his "case" (ibid.).

32. LETTER TO J. G. PIDDINGTON ON MRS. THOMPSON IN TRANCE (1904).

Copy-text: unheaded letter, *Proceedings of the Society for Psychical Research*, 18 (January 1904), 106–107 (McD 1904:17).

In an article in the *Proceedings* titled "On the Types of Phenomena Displayed in Mrs. Thompson's Trance," pp. 104–307, J. G. Piddington omitted portions of the reports of séances with the medium Mrs. Thompson, which had appeared in the previous number. Early in his Introduction to the series Piddington on pp. 106–107 quoted from a private letter (no longer extant) to him from William James, who had made certain tests of the degree of Mrs. Thompson's amnesia during trance.

33. LETTER TO ISAAC K. FUNK ON *The Widow's Mite* (1904).

Copy-text: *The Widow's Mite and Other Psychic Phenomena*, by Isaac K. Funk (New York and London: Funk and Wagnalls, 1904), pp. 178–179 (not in McD but assigned as 1904:19).

In *The Widow's Mite* on pp. 176–178 the author tabulated the replies of forty-two psychologists to a four-part questionnaire he had sent in respect to "The Widow's Mite" episode and its genuineness. (See Professor Skrupskelis' note for a description of the episode.) William James headed the list, and in the tabulation on p. 177 under the heading "Most Probable Theory," gave it as his opinion: "Subjective faculties and spirits." Funk relegated most answers to an appendix, but he considered James of such importance that on pp. 178–179 he quoted James's letter prefaced by the statement, "Prof. William James, of Harvard, is so well known throughout this country and England as a psychologist that the reader will pardon me for giving here also his answer in full." The date of the letter would be after April 10, 1903.

34. A CASE OF CLAIRVOYANCE (1907).

Copy-text: "A Case of Clairvoyance," *Proceedings of the American Society for Psychical Research*, 1 (January 1907), 221–236 (McD 1907:10). In James's diary occurs the following entry on March 21, 1907: "Hal Kennedy sends Titus case."

35. LETTER ON DR. GOWER AND TABLE LIFTING (1907).

Copy-text: letter in "Report on Some Recent Sittings for Physical Phenomena in America," *Proceedings of the Society for Psychical Research*, 21 (October 1907), 108–109 (not in McD but assigned as 1907:14). James is quoted in a report sent to Alice Johnson, the author of the article in the *Proceedings*, about his conversations in April 1906 with a group in Denver, Colorado, led by Dr. John H. Gower (then abroad), who participated in sessions where table levitation occurred.

36. PHYSICAL PHENOMENA AT A PRIVATE CIRCLE (1909).

Copy-text: "Physical Phenomena at a Private Circle," *Journal of the American Society for Psychical Research*, 3 (February 1909), 109–113 (McD 1909:2).

37. REPORT ON MRS. PIPER'S HODGSON-CONTROL (1909).

Copy-text: (E) "Report on Mrs. Piper's Hodgson-Control," *Proceedings of the Society for Psychical Research*, 23 (June 1909), 2–121 (McD 1909:6).

The History

The "Preliminary Report on Mrs. Piper's Hodgson-Control," comprising Part I of the complete paper, was read by J. G. Piddington on James's behalf at the General Meeting of the Society for Psychical Research in London on January 28, 1909.[12] Together with Part II, the fuller account of various selected sittings, it was published in June in the *Proceedings of the Society for Psychical Research* and in July in the *Proceedings of the American Society for Psychical Research*, 3 (1909), 470–589 (McD 1909:6). In references, the English text will be called E, and the American will be differentiated as A. The manuscript (MS), a combination of James's typing and autograph, is preserved, mounted, in the Houghton Library at Harvard University (bMS Am 1092.9 [4544]). With it are two typed leaves, the first one consisting of typescript pasted together to duplicate the start of autograph fol. 178 of the manuscript; the other is a variant typing (probably the carbon of the original) of p. 10 of TMs, a carbon copy of a typescript of Part I preserved in the New York City archives of the American Society for Psychical Research. Together with the transcript for a few sittings owned by the English and one by the American Society these are the only documents on which an editorially produced text can be based. Part of the Report was reprinted in (CER) *Collected Essays and Reviews* (1920), edited by R. B. Perry.

After his death on December 20, 1905, Richard Hodgson made his first appearance as a 'spirit' at Miss Theodate Pope's sitting with Mrs. Piper on December 28. James had known Mrs. Piper for some years, and in his "A Record of Observations of Certain Phenomena of Trance," printed in 1890 (No. 12 in this volume) he gives a brief account of his acquaintance beginning in the autumn of 1885, together with various sittings in which he participated. Since some of these sittings were held at Chocorua, his country house, a certain intimacy must have developed: indeed, only personal feeling could have moved him, for example, on

[12] In the English *Journal of the Society for Psychical Research* for February 1909 (XIV, 36) under the heading of General Meeting is the note: "Professor William James's 'Preliminary Report on Mrs. Piper's Hodgson Control' was read by Mr. J. G. Piddington; in it Professor James described the earliest communications purporting to come from Dr. Hodgson, and gave in detail a few of the most salient incidents of that period, with a discussion of the evidence for and against their supernormal character. It is hoped that the whole Report will appear later in the *Proceedings*."

February 14, 1897, to explode to Boris Sidis: "Mrs. Piper is *impossible*! Ask at 5 Boylston Place *where [*ab. del.* 'if'] Miss Edmunds ['is out' *del.*] will be in if Hodgson is out, to recommend you some other medium" (#3769). What caused this exasperation is not known (if it were exasperation and not merely an emphatic opinion that Mrs. Piper was too busy to give Sidis an appointment), but it is clear that he retained an interest in her, largely through his friendship with Hodgson. On May 8, 1898, he wrote to James McKeen Cattell that although he had of late kept aloof from sittings

> there can be *no* doubt of the supernormal knowledge. The reports suggest to the reader fraud. Yet in 15 years of steady observation *not a single suspicious circumstance* has been reported or suggested from any quarter, which might cast doubt on the *bona fide* character of Mrs. P.'s simple life, ['and' *del.*] ignorant mind, and commonplace abilities. To work off information secretly acquired, on her sitters, she would have to be a quite different type (Library of Congress).

The continuation of his general interest in psychical affairs and Mrs. Piper as a medium is suggested by a letter of March 16, 1901, to Sir Oliver Lodge, from Florence, in which he remarks that he has not breathed a word to Mrs. F. W. H. Myers of "certain Piper reports which Hodgson sent me" (Society for Psychical Research, London); and on March 23, 1902, from Cambridge, he wrote Lodge that he would be arriving in England and wanted to have

> some little conversations with you about S. P. R. affairs. . . . I do no psychical research whatever now, nor have I for several years done any, but in a general way I follow Hodgson's work, and wish to talk to you about it. Mrs. Myers is here . . . . She read me yesterday reports of 2½ sittings with Mrs. Piper. Myers came very poorly in the first one; but I confess that the dramatic impression[13] which I received from the later two was favorable as regards sincerity of effort to communicate. The turn which the Myers communications here have lately taken improves in my estimation the probability that they may be real. But these are matters of 'impression,' and it is hard to articulate grounds. I hope to bring you a batch of recent reports of Mrs. P. (Society for Psychical Research).

In response to James Hyslop's request for his opinion about raising a fund to endow research into mediumship and other supernormal phenomena, James responded on October 25, 1903: "In my opinion the most fruitful work will lie in the direction of thorough description of the phenomena presented by certain rare individuals. Some of Janet's patients, Prince's patient, Flournoy's medium, and Mrs. Piper, are examples of the sort of study I mean. . . . I feel strongly the need of an extensive sifting over of the mediums now available, and the selection of a very few for thoroughgoing study. Our 'cases' are so far almost scandalously few" (typed copy, Society for Psychical Research, New York City).

[13] For the emphasis James placed on the dramatic impression produced by Mrs. Piper's sittings, see 354.7–355.2 and references in some of the letters quoted below.

Just this descriptive sifting of the evidence is a feature of James's later Report on Mrs. Piper.

The Hodgson "case" seems to have triggered James's interest in a deeper-probing investigation of Mrs. Piper and of mediumship in general (meaning specifically the return of an authentic spirit from the dead); nevertheless, some pressure must have been put upon him—the details are not available—to analyze the phenomenon formally. The earliest reference seems to be that of an entry in James's diary for January 30, 1906: "Talked to Young Women's Xian Ass^n on S. P. R. work & Mrs. Piper . . . Letter from Piddington saying he had ordered Miss E. [Lucy Edmunds, assistant secretary of the A.S.P.R.] to send records." On January 31, James wrote "Wired Miss E. not to send 'em. Wrote to Pid." An entry for February 7, 1906, reads: "Cabled to Lodge that Newbold declines Piper work. 'Better send to Piddington' "; and on March 12, James "Discoursed on Mrs. Piper to ladys Club at the Rolfe's."

In a letter to Théodore Flournoy on July 1, 1906, roughly six months after Hodgson's death and his appearance through Rector, the Piper-control, James wrote, "I have undertaken to co-ordinate a lot of stuff that is now coming out through Mrs. Piper, purporting to be from Hodgson, in order to make a report. There is a great amount of subliminal automatism involved, but I suspect that the residual doubt will always remain as to whether it may not be a very amnesic extract of the real Hodgson trying to communicate. It will be sad indeed if this undecided verdict will be all that I can reach after so many years. Ars longa, indeed!" (*The Letters of William James and Théodore Flournoy*, ed. Robert C. Le Clair [Madison: University of Wisconsin Press, 1966], p. 179). Subsequently, a letter to James from Ferdinand Schiller of August 15, 1906, remarks, "but as you say you are at work on R. H. & Mrs. P." (bMS Am 1092 [912]). The responsibility to formulate a report that might have some viable conclusions seems to have led James into a closer relationship with Mrs. Piper than he had previously been concerned to initiate. For instance, on July 30, 1907, he wrote to his wife, Alice, that at Mrs. Ledyard's invitation he was to sit with her and Mrs. Piper the next day. "She says that R. H. has appeared, in much better shape than before, and has much advice to give. Nous verrons!" (#2397). This sitting was reported in a letter to Mrs. Henry Sidgwick of August 1:

> I had a sitting, along with Mrs. Ledyard, and entrusted three messages to "Hodgson," as follows.
> 1) To Mrs. Verrall he was to dictate *"Statue of Liberty."*
> 2) To Mrs. Flemming, *"Rose-bush."*
> 3) To Mrs. Raikes *"The World is yellow."* [14]

[14] The results of these messages are not known. James continues, "I got your recent letter duly, and thank you for it.", but then deleted this and in the margin wrote, "In writing this, I was 'confused' like R. H.'s spirit." The letter continues with an interesting statement of belief in spiritism that is stronger than James usually permitted himself: "What do you think of the developments in the case of Eusapia? Judging by what the Annals of P. R. print the proof seems overwhelming, and it has been an

Preliminary work seems to have begun in July, 1907.[15] A diary entry for July 1 states "Got going on Hodgson Piper work." On July 2, 3, and 4 the same entry appears: "Worked on Piper stuff." On November 21, 1907, James wrote "Began work on Hodgson Piper Records," but a year was to elapse before the entry of November 12, 1908, indicated the start of the actual preparation of the Report: "Began work on Hodgson material."[16] The writing may have begun on December 11: "Started work, practically my 1st morning, on the Hodgson report."[17] Thereafter the diary records indicate steady progress. "Workt on R. H. report" on December 13, and "Finisht R. H. report" on December 14. This would have been Part I only, the Preliminary Report. With little delay for revision, typing started on December 18, "Mr. House came to type my Hodgson report,"[18] which was completed the next day, "Type writer finishes copying S. P. R. report" (December 19).

From the start it would seem that James had contemplated two reports, with different structures. In the diary entry for December 21—"Began to write my longer R. H. report"—he showed the distinction and also his intention to work steadily on the project, for as his letter to Henry of December 19 indicated, he was anxious to start his *Some Problems of Phi-*

---

enormous relief to my mind to quit the balancing attitude which I have voluntarily maintained for 15 years, and come to a stable belief in the matter. I hope it may be the same with you. This case carries countless others with it, and the consequences for 'Science' are beyond computation" (Society for Psychical Research [London], Research File 1 D). It is ironic that the medium Eusapia Paladino was exposed as a fraud in 1910.

15 A letter of January 6, 1907, to J. G. Piddington states that James must postpone work on the Hodgson case in favor of *Pragmatism* (#3488).

16 As late as December 7 James was still collecting his material. For example, on December 7, 1908, he wrote to Miss Mary Hillard (the 'M. Bergman' of the two sittings described beginning at 339.33): "I thank you for the excellent record. I have the two messages locked up, and have notified Miss Johnson & Hyslop to be on the look out for them at their respective 'lights.' [In the margin opposite this paragraph James added, 'I have a sealed envelope left by R. H. with me.'] [¶] As for your sending a special report for Hyslop to print, I say No!—for the plain reason that I should rather have ['it come' *del.*] your material come out along with the other material in my own fuller report (of which I regret extremely the involuntary tardiness!) which is to be pubᵈ simultaneously by Hyslop and at London. Piecemeal publication is unfair to the cause, and provokes such criticism as Münsterberg's in *a [ab. del.* 'the'] recent Sunday paper. He could hardly have made it ['had' *del.*] on my proposed report. Hyslop drew it on himself by his scrappy publications. [¶] 'Come again!' " In the left margin of the second page James wrote vertically (possibly as a continuation of his similar addition on the first page): "I shall be very thankful for a copy (if convenient) of your first sitting, or the R. H. part of it" (Colby College Library).

17 On December 19, 1908, James wrote to his brother Henry: "My time has been consumed by interruptions almost totally, until a week ago, when I finally got down seriously to work upon my Hodgson report. It means much more labor than one would suppose and very little result. I wish that I had never undertaken it. I am sending off a preliminary instalment of it to be read at the S. P. R. meeting in January. That done, the rest will run off easily" (#2956).

18 House also typed *The Meaning of Truth*, coming to James's home and using his typewriter.

losophy. After beginning Part II on December 21, 1908, James wrote steadily. The next day, December 22, he records in his diary, "wrote report till 1$\frac{30}{}$," and on Christmas day, the 25th, "Finisht introduction to R. H. report," which one may assume to have comprised 279.14–286.38. On December 28 the diary notes, "Wrote well on Hodgson report"[19] and on January 9, 1909, "Getting along well with Hodgson report. Mr. House, type copyist," an entry that suggests that James had not waited to complete the manuscript before beginning the process of having it copied. On January 10, "I work on Hodgson business" and on January 15, triumphantly, "Finisht Hodgson report—Thank God!" The typist House must have been following close, for on January 18 James records "Finisht copying of Hodgson report, by Mr. House."[20] That there was revision of House's typescript is inevitable, but on February 1, 1909, James wrote, "I mail Report to Miss Johnson" (secretary of the London Society).[21] The business being over, James wrote in his diary on February 3, "Cleaned up table, got rid of Piper documents etc. and now ready for real work."

The first diary record of proofs comes on March 1 with "Corrected proof of Hodgson report." That proofs were sent to him in batches is suggested by the fact that although on the next day, March 2, he "Finisht proof of R. H.,"[22] on March 5 he received and worked on "more proof from S. P. R."[23] The next mention does not come until "Corrected Hodg-

[19] Later, on January 1, 1909, James wrote to Piddington about his progress: "My own poor stuff about R.H. is reaching its conclusion, amid sad interruptions. I don't think I'm fit for that kind of work at all, it goes so hard with me. I hope, however, that the material will all be mailed, in type, within a fortnight, to Miss Johnson. I can draw no strong conclusion" (#3491).

[20] In a letter of January 24, 1909, to Henry, James remarked on his attempts to regain his health and "meanwhile clearing away my writing table, have finisht my report on Mrs. Pipers Hodgson-Control, which will make about 100 pp. of the S.P.R. Proceedings" (#2957).

[21] Perhaps a little previously, on January 29 James wrote Thomas Sergeant Perry: "I have just got off my report on the Hodgson control, which has stuck to my fingers all this time. It is a hedging sort of an affair, and I don't know what the Perry family will think of it. The truth is that the 'case' is a particularly poor one for testing Mrs. Piper's claim to bring back spirits. It is *leakier* than any other case, and intrinsically, I think, no stronger than many of her other good cases, certainly weaker than the G.P. case. . . . I think that public opinion is just now taking a step forward in these matters—*vide* the Eusapian boom! and possibly both these *Schriften* [referring also to his forthcoming *American Magazine* article] of mine will add their influence" (*Letters*, II, 319–320).

[22] These early proofs were returned promptly. On March 3 James wrote to Duncan Macdonald: "As for Mrs. Piper, I just sent off some corrected proof yesterday of a report on Hodgsons reappearances as a spirit through her, from which you will see some day my own state of Mind. It will appear in the Proceedings sometime" (Hartford Seminary Foundation).

[23] The date that these proofs were returned is not recorded. But on March 10 James wrote to George Dorr, "The proofs have been sent with your corrections" (bMS Am 1092.1). Dorr's first appearance as a sitter comes in the Report on June 5, 1906, remarked in Part I at 271.13–20, but this account is too brief to require correction. Also in Part I there is a reference to Dorr's intercession to secure Hodgson a salary for his work at the American branch (277.1–22), but the proofs that Dorr saw must have concerned the Oldfarm Series in Part II (287.1–294.14) in which he plays a prominent

son proof" on April 13. The entry on May 8 "Begin *correcting [*intrl.*]
new proofs" must refer to the Report as printed in the American *Proceedings,* for on May 11 James recorded, "I correct Hyslop's proof," Hyslop
being the editor of the American journal.

Publication of the American *Proceedings* may have been delayed, for
although the first page gives June, 1909, as the date, the cover has July
as the month of issue. In fact, it seems to have been published about mid-
July on the evidence of a letter of July 14 from James to Henry Pickering
Bowditch: "My report seems, from the newspapers, to be already out in
Hyslop's Proceedings, and I am writing to him to order a copy sent to
you. It ought to appear also very soon in the english Proceedings. It is
very non-committal either way, and I am curious to know how the
séance material which I quote will strike the hitherto prejudiced
against!" (#812).[24] James's lack of information about the English *Proceedings* may be due to late publication or delays in the mails. At any
rate, the June number had not reached him by July 14, nor had the
American journal.

A summing-up of James's opinion about his Report comes in a letter
of October 19, 1909, to Mrs. Olivia Wadsworth: "I am *extremely* pleased
at your reaction on the R. H. material. How different the sense of *the
[*intrl.*] 'dramatic probabilities' of nature is in different people. Some call
it simple rubbish. For my part I have taken the rigorous method of denying a spirit where any other explanation was morally and fisically *possible.* Hence my non-proven verdict. But my own feeling of dramatic
probability makes pretty strongly for *something that represents* the living R. H. being active in the results—tho I'm sure that the phenomenon
is so complex, that we can't guess what that something may be like. [¶] I
have an article on the general subject in this month's American Magazine. [¶] It pleases me immensely to read your hearty and straight willingness to believe the utterances to be essentially sincere" (#3824).

The Documents

The manuscript of Parts I and II is preserved, substantially complete,
in the Houghton Library as bMS Am 1092.9 (4544). The early stages of
its composition and assembly—the numerous revisions, additions, and
substitutions—created a confusing series of sub-foliations, but James re-
numbered in sequence the final form. For Part I the final foliation
added in ink runs [1] 2–56. Four lines of an earlier version of 277.23–24

---

part as the owner of Oldfarm and Hodgson's chief interlocutor. His commentary in
this series is also extensive. A transcript of this sitting of June 5, 1906, is among those
preserved in the London Society's files.

24 Preceding this quotation, James wrote: "No, my dear fellow, with the publication
of my report on Mrs. Piper's Hodgson Control, and with that of an article to appear
in the American Magazine next fall my *active* connexion with psychical research ceases.
It is too *zeitraubend* and *umständlich,* and requires quicker perceptive faculties and
more memory for details than I am possessed of, to lead to anything, so I take a back
seat."

on fols. 51–52 are found deleted on fol. 52 verso. Part II's final ink foliation is [1] 2–16 16½ 17–26 29–30 32–47 [47½] 48–54 59–86 88–93 117–123 136–141 141½ 142–144 145a 145b 146 149 153–154 155–156 (joint numbered) 157 160–161 161½ 162–166 166½ 167–181. The gaps in the text represented by the missing leaves are discussed below. The first nine pages of Part II are written on the backs of discarded leaves from Part I. Thereafter, fols. 12, 16, 22, 23, 33, 53, 149, 161½ are written or typed on the backs of false starts discarded from Part II. The texts of these deleted versos are transcribed in the apparatus under the heading *Deleted Versos*.

The manuscript is a mixture of James's holograph, his own typing, and inserted sections of typescript of sittings by other hands. There is reason to believe that, on the balance, James's own typescripts are usually fair copies that revise earlier holograph drafts. The first four pages of Part I, for example, are typed by James in a ribbon copy on standard typewriter paper 11 x 8½″ watermarked *Dixie Bond*. The title 'Preliminary report on Mrs. Piper's Hodgson-control.' (triple underlined) is written in James's hand above double-spaced typing which changes to his usual triple-space with fol. 2. Unnumbered fol. 4ᵛ of Part II on the same paper contains deleted holograph text that begins in mid-sentence but is broken off about two-thirds down the page. The start of the text seems related in part to the hypothetical explanations for Mrs. Piper's knowledge contained in items 3 and 5 of the list of seven given by James in typed 255.21 and 255.25–27; but in the deleted draft these precede a list of three proposed theories, of which the first—*telepathy*—is complete and the second—*access to some cosmic reservoir*—is scarcely begun before James stopped.[25] Obviously, this deleted text represents material related to the opening pages in a different form from the preserved revision and in James's hand instead of typing.

Further revision of the early pages is documented by a considerable amount of holograph rejected draft text. The typing of Part I stops halfway down on fol. 4 with 'Meanwhile we can leave its meaning very indeterminate,' (255.13–14), text which James then completed by hand to the foot of the page before deleting it and typing another version starting on fol. 5. Two points are of interest here. First, the Dixie Bond paper of the first four leaves (and of the discarded draft on fol. 4 of Part II) changes on retyped fol. 5 to a paper watermarked *L. C. Smith & Bros. Typewriter Co USA*. Second, holograph draft text continuing the deleted handwritten text on the lower half of fol. 4 is continued on the deleted verso (numbered 5) of Part II fol. 1, corresponding roughly to 255.25–37, and on the verso (numbered 6) of fol. 2, corresponding to 255.37–256.11 but

---

25 It is worthy of note that the two explanations given in the draft constitute what James called the 'supernatural' or 'mystical', whereas the five that he later inserted before them he called the 'natural'. In the draft it is odd that the 'cosmic reservoir' theory is numbered 7 (as in the final version) instead of 2. Possibly the perception that the other items would need to be added led James to break off his writing.

with the reference to the various items keyed to the earlier order. This text is not directly continued, but on deleted fol. 7^v (numbered 8) the general continuity remains with text starting on 256.23 despite the loss of two intervening pages. But instead of continuing the general discussion before taking up the messages in detail (as in 256.36–39), the rejected draft text on fol. 7^v continues for four lines on fol. 3^v (numbered 9) before breaking off just at the point where the first appearance of the R. H. Control is about to be described, corresponding to 257.32.

Unnumbered deleted fol. 5^v of Part II seems to represent a different layer of composition. Its text begins a discussion of the fact that the Hodgson case is a poor one for the establishment of veridical facts presumably unknown to the medium, as in the final text at 256.26–27. This draft is continued on deleted unnumbered fol. 8^v, then on deleted unnumbered fol. 9^v (taking up material found at 256.39–257.16), to end on deleted unnumbered fol. 6^v with material like that in 257.16–31. The text breaks off in mid-sentence and represents the last of the draft for the early pages of Part I that was fortunately preserved by the thrifty reuse of discarded pages from Part I in writing the start of Part II. The paper on which these drafts were written presents a problem. Part I had started with Dixie Bond up to the point where on fol. 4 the typing gave way to holograph that was subsequently continued in the drafts. As remarked, a very early stretch of text that seems to precede the typing of Part I fols. 1–4 is found also on Dixie Bond as fol. 4^v of Part II. However, the two drafts numbered 5–6 which continued the deleted autograph addition on fol. 4 switch to a paper watermarked *L. L. Brown*. When the draft leaves resume after a break with fol. 7^v (numbered 8), the paper is still L. L. Brown as it is in the continuation on fol. 3^v, broken off after only a few lines. The last block of rejected early and unnumbered text that begins on Part II fol. 5^v (256.26–27) starts on Dixie Bond paper and continues on this paper on fols. 8^v and 9^v to its conclusion on fol. 6^v (approximately 257.16). The intrusion of the L. L. Brown paper is odd, especially given the reappearance after a break of the early Dixie Bond paper on fols. 5^v, 8^v, 9^v and 6^v of Part II. Given the fact that these last four leaves are unnumbered, it is possible that they may represent original autograph composition up to a point before typing began of the handwritten material beginning Part I initially. Yet it is a distinct anomaly that the L. L. Brown paper does not appear again in Part I and is used again only toward the end of Part II. After the introduction in Part I of the L. C. Smith paper on fol. 5, it and the Dixie Bond paper are mixed, agreeing more or less with the nature of the material and possibly its occasional revision.

Typed text on Smith paper, beginning with fol. 5 at 255.14–15, goes on to fol. 9, which is numbered 9 over an original 8. Whether this was an inadvertent error or a sign of revision is not wholly clear. Folio 9 starts with 'For many years past he had seen her three times' (257.16–17), which repeats the words deleted at the foot of fol. 8. Very likely some disruption is evidenced here. The typing of fol. 9 ends about three-quarters down on the page, and beginning with the paragraph 'The spirit Hodgsons' at 257.32 James switched to handwritten text, continued for six lines on fol. 10 ('who . . . been writing, when' 257.35–38) which paraphrases the deleted start of typed fol. 11. This fol. 11 starts a previously typed block describing Hodgson's first appearance at a sitting with Miss Pope. The paper changes to Dixie Bond and the foliation 11 is written after deleted ink 2. This block of text from 'suddenly' (written-in) at 258.1 to 'leave you now' (259.26) continues the revised numbering as 12 over 3 and then 13 before deleted 4. Folio 14 (259.27–32) is handwritten in eight lines on Smith paper and, possibly with some condensation of James's original typed transcript of the notes for the séance, seems to introduce another block of James's typed notes of a sitting. Here Dixie paper is used and the pages are headed in pencil 'Pope'. The final foliation 15 is written to the right of an ink 15 over a 14 which in turn is written over pencil 6. This block describes Hodgson's second appearance (260.1–262.4) and consists of three of James's typed leaves, fol. 15 (as described), 16 over pencil 7 headed 'Pope', a replacement three-line handwritten fol. 17 on Smith paper, and fol. 18 (over pencil 9) headed 'Pope', the top half deleted.[26] It is clear that handwritten fol. 17 is a later abbreviated substitute for a removed 'Pope' fol. 17 over pencil 8, the end of the deleted material being marked by the crossed-out upper half of fol. 18. The two typed blocks of fols. 11–14 and 15–18 share the Dixie paper (except for the replacement holograph Smith leaves) and seem originally to have been numbered as a sequence, the first Hodgson sitting in ink as 2–4 (plus lost 5 replaced by holograph fol. 14) and the second sitting in pencil as 6–7, holograph fol. 17, and 9.

The sitting for January 23, 1906 (fols. 19–20) at 262.5–263.16 is typed on a thinner kind of Dixie paper, not every leaf of which is watermarked. In a blank space in the lower fifth of fol. 20, James wrote and then deleted a comment about Hodgson as a swimmer. The continuation has been lost and apparently has been replaced by handwritten fol. 21 on Smith paper (263.17–24). Folio 22 starts a block of typing describing another sitting, that of the Ring Incident (263.25–268.16), ending with a white space in the lower quarter of fol. 30. The paper is Dixie Bond (the normal thicker kind) but the copy is a carbon which has been numbered in the upper right corner 1–9. This numbering (3 over 2) has been touched up in ink on fols. 5–6 but seems to have been made in the ribbon copy so that the numbers are part of the carbon. Moreover, a few of the handwritten alterations were also made in the ribbon copy while the carbon paper was still present between the two sheets, thus revealing themselves as current changes. On the verso of fol. 28 in pencil is the arithmetical calculation of 75 multiplied by 6 to give a result of 450. Folio 30 ends the carbon typing with a bottom white space indicating a break.

[26] Folio 16 is backed by its mirror-image carbon, the carbon paper having been inserted the wrong way.

The next sitting concerns the so-called 'Nigger-Talk Case'[27] (268.17–269.42, 270.24–35), which occupies fols. 31–34 of Dixie paper, the typing ending about halfway down on fol. 34. The introduction (268.10–16) has been tinkered with. What would have been the first typed line has been cut off and the rest of the typed page of Dixie paper (which ends, oddly, at 268.21 with a quarter-page white space) has been pasted on a sheet of Smith paper and a substitute beginning at the head of the Smith paper has been written, 'The next incident I will cite is one which at a certain' (268.10). Since the original foliation has been replaced, on this Smith paper the 31 is in ink without alteration. However, two other numerical series start with fol. 32, which is to the right of deleted ink 11, as 33 is to the left of deleted 12, and 34 (the 3 possibly altered from 1) to the right of deleted 13. The leaves are also foliated 2–4 in the upper right corner, only the 2 being deleted. This corner numbering refers to the sitting itself, of course, but the deleted centered 11–13 continue the corner number 9 of fol. 30, allowing for the removal of a 10 in the revision by paste-on fol. 31. Thus the Ring Incident and the Nigger-Talk Case were once numbered consecutively in order.

The sittings centered on the Huldah-Episode (270.1–275.35) reveal considerable autograph alteration of the original typing, perhaps dictated by James's desire to conceal the names of the participants. The preceding fol. 34 had ended about halfway down the page in line with James's custom of having typed the sittings separately so that they could be moved about within the narrative as required. The Huldah-Episode starts with typed fol. 35, a carbon on Dixie paper like the Ring-Episode, and proceeds to fol. 47, the leaves numbered 1–12 in the corner. The progress is not smooth, however. All is normal for the first three leaves 35–37 (1–3), but fols. 38–39 were at first numbered 5 and 6, which has been altered to 4 and 5. Since fol. 40, corner-numbered deleted 6, begins handwritten copy with a change to Smith paper, a temptation exists to associate the alteration of the sitting numeration with some sort of revision, but the typed copy on fols. 38–39 (4–5 over 5–6) is continuous with fol. 37. However, since fol. 38 (272.3–22) shifts from a carbon to the ribbon copy and may have been folded for enclosure in an envelope, it may be that the error in the corner numbering was inadvertent and that the numbering was applied, in pencil and in ink, after the typing of the episode had been completed. Certainly, the continuity of the corner numbering with 6 on fol. 40 when at 273.2 ('unlikely, in view') the copy shifts from typing to autograph and the paper from Dixie to Smith shows that a later substitution has been made for the original typescript. This substitute extends through 274.21 'W. J. Did you make anyone your confidant?' at the foot of fol. 44 (deleted corner number 9). However, in this handwritten sequence fol. 41 (corner 6½) is a substitute (273.8–13 'revelation . . . says:—') for a deletion at the foot

---

[27] The original title was 'THE NIGGER MINSTREL CASE' but by hand James changed 'MINSTREL' to 'TALK'. The typescript for this sitting of February 27, 1906, is preserved in the archives of the Society for Psychical Research, New York.

of fol. 40(6). That typed fol. 45(10), still a ribbon copy on Smith paper, continues without a break the numbering in the right corner indicates that this numeration was added after the episode's typing had been completed in its final mixed form but before it had been intercalated in the whole sequential manuscript.

The Huldah-Episode narrative in typed form had begun with a sitting on May 2, 1906 (270.2), a carbon on Dixie paper, unfolded, but then in the middle of a sitting, at 272.3 (although after the quotation of a letter from 'Ella Densmore' and the beginning of James's analysis of the possible naturalistic explanations), the copy shifts to ribbon. The paper is still Dixie. But then—in mid-sentence 'seemed, however, highly | unlikely'—fol. 40(6) (273.2) [*printed text*: seems | unlikely] the copy changes to James's handwriting on Smith paper. The typing with ribbon but on Smith paper resumes on fol. 45(10) at 274.22 with what had been the formal start of a new sitting on October 24 (altered from 29) which, however, is now integrated with the conclusion of the autograph copy on fol. 44 by the deletion of its heading, 'SITTING OF OCTOBER "(TWENTY *fourth [*aft. del.* 'NINTH'] | W. J. ASKS ABOUT Huldah": Did you make anyone your confidant?' James's opening question (274.21), deleted from the top of fol. 45, is then squeezed in at the foot of fol. 44. Not only the deleted heading of what had been an independent report of a new sitting, but also the typing on Smith instead of Dixie paper, indicates that despite the corner numbering there had originally been a break at fol. 45.

The typing on Smith paper that started with fol. 45 proceeds on fol. 46 (11 altered from 10) with four deleted typed lines that continue the three deleted bottom lines on fol. 45(10), these four lines plus an ink commentary note, followed by two typed lines revised in ink. Nevertheless, these deleted lines 275.4–10 on fols. 45–46 are found complete in print though not in the typescript (TMs) made from the manuscript of Part I, for which see below.[28] After this two-line remnant of the typed text heading fol. 46—less than the upper third of the page—James then continued the narrative by hand. This fol. 46 is numbered in the corner as 11, altered from 10, followed on handwritten fol. 47 by 12 altered from 11. Although the misnumbering may have been inadvertent, a case might be made for the possibility that holograph pages 40(6)–44(9) have replaced typed material differently numbered, with some connection perhaps with the original misnumbering of fols. 38–39 as 5–6 corrected to 4–5. That fols. 46–47 are substitutes (275.7–276.1) is a possibility also; but the substitute nature of holograph fol. 48 (276.2–11 'The . . . cited the') is closer to a certainty. At the foot of fol. 47 the heading 'THE PECUNIARY MESSAGES.' had originally formed the normal ending of a sentence in the form 'the pecuniary *messages. [*ab. del.* 'cases.']', but James made this into a heading by altering 't' to 'T' and double underlining the phrase as well as centering it by an arrow. He then began in the last three lines some re-

[28] Also, the bracketed W.J. comment at 275.11–16, though present in the print, is wanting in MS, another sign of revision between MS and the published text.

marks about Hodgson's salary but deleted these as well as the continuing first two lines on the next page, fol. 48 (not numbered in the corner), before beginning with a revised opening such as is now found in the print at 276.2. However, this revised handwritten version ends three-quarters down on the page in mid-sentence with a part-line 'other things [', contain' *del.*] cited the'. This part-line is completed on typed fol. 49 (altered from 48), a Dixie Bond carbon, but this continuation comes only after the deletion of the first five and a half lines of typed text. Not only the altered folio number which had originally followed with 48 the manufactured heading at the foot of fol. 47 but also the nature of the deleted text (which explicitly names Mrs. Lyman as Hodgson's bene-factress, a fact concealed on fol. 48 by the vague '*an american [*ab. del.* 'a'] friend' [276.8]) suggests the strong probability that this typed fol. 49 (276.11–34 'story . . . come.') was the original start of a typed block of narrative about related sittings that has been heavily revised by substitute handwritten fols. 50–51, probably carrying over to the end of the episodes on fol. 52, about halfway down, and the start of the Part I conclusion (277.27), which ends Part I on fol. 56, still handwritten. That the handwritten sheets 50–52 were themselves rewritten is shown by the deleted start of a paragraph on fol. 52ᵛ, a draft for 'Few . . . explanations' (277.23–25), which in its final form constitutes not a separate paragraph but a part of continuous text starting toward the end of the last line on fol. 51 and proceeding normally at the head of fol. 52. (Folio 51 joins with the text on handwritten fol. 50 without any break.) The fact that the Smith paper begins for these final handwritten sheets after the Dixie paper of the typed carbon on fol. 49 is also suggestive of rewriting, since the order of use of these two papers appears to be firmly established, later revisions and interjections appearing exclusively on this Smith paper.

There is another interesting feature of these final pages of Part I. That James was anxious for the approval of the sitters involved in the various episodes, and was much concerned to preserve their privacy by altering the stenographic transcripts of sittings if necessary, is a fact backed by a considerable amount of evidence, including his sending to George Dorr proof of the Oldfarm episodes in which he was involved. In the course of this practice it would appear that James sent through the mails certain pages so that the subjects would have the opportunity to review his versions. Beginning with fol. 38 (272.3) and continuing to fol. 52 (277.34) most of the leaves (though apparently not all) seem to have been folded as for mailing, and on the verso of fol. 52 is the note 'Pray return these! | to W. J.' Similarly, on the verso of fol. 163 of Part II appears the note in pencil, 'Dear Annie — Is this all right to print? | WJ.', apparently addressed to Miss Anne Putnam and referring to the quotation from her sitting at 353.17–21, written exclusively on the recto of the leaf.

Part II was written independently of the Preliminary Report, or Part I, and specifically for publication, not for delivery. The first leaf has squeezed in by hand at the top the heading 'Final report on Mrs. Piper's

Hodgson-Control[1'], the 'M' of 'Mrs.' written over what was probably the foliation number '1'. This leaf seems to be a revision, rewritten, perhaps immediately, after the deletion of the first four lines of fol. 2, since its last words 'Prof. Hyslop [*comma del.*] and I' are repeated (deleted) below the deletion of antecedent text about Hyslop at the head of fol. 2. Part II was handwritten from fols. 1 through 32. The early leaves utilize the blank versos from the discarded draft for the early pages of Part I. Folios 1–3 and 7 are written on paper watermarked *L. L. Brown*, which does not appear again until Part II's fol. 170 where it continues to the end.[29] Folio 4 was inscribed on the back of a very early rejected Part I draft, unnumbered, on Dixie Bond paper. This fol. 4 consists of only three lines (279.32–33), which replace several sentences of deleted text and then revise the last line or two deleted at the foot of fol. 3 and the first line and a half of fol. 5. Since fol. 5 was numbered 5 over an original 4, but 6 and the rest are not altered, this change must have been made within a relatively brief interval after the inscription of fol. 5 (over 4), also on Dixie paper, the same paper being used for fols. 6 and 8–9, written on versos of Part I drafts.

Thereafter, with fol. 10 (281.29–39, 282.35–42) the *L. C. Smith* watermarked paper starts, which is to be the regular paper for Part II as far as fol. 169. Folio 12 (282.7–20) is numbered 12 over 13, probably an inadvertency. Its verso contains an unnumbered one-line undeleted false start 'the reports with careful attention to each detail,' which seems to have carried on 'and reading' (282.36) in footnote 6, the last words on fol. 10.

The handwritten text continues normally on the Smith paper but with much revision. For example, fol. 16 was written on the blank obverse of a six-line broken-off paragraph, foliated 21 in pencil, which originally followed present fol. 19 (over 20). The 'dramatic probabilities' which in this deletion are taken as a determining factor in one's belief first appears as the 'dramatic interpretation of the phenomenon' in fol. 10 at 281.30–31 but in another context. A closer connection comes on fol. 12(13)[30] at 282.9–15; but the real parallel is contained in a deleted passage heading fol. 16½. This leaf was originally numbered 15, then altered to 16, and finally ½ was added in pencil. The first word 'factors' of the upper deleted half continues the lower deleted few lines of fol. 14 ending 'as cooperating [*comma del.*]'. It follows that fols. 15–16 are additions, substituted for the deleted foot of fol. 14 and the deleted head of fol. 16½, to which must also be added as a substitute the part-page fol. 17 (284.7–14 'all, . . . dealings'). The original start of the first fol. 15 is now found

---

[29] The use of this L. L. Brown paper so early in Part I, even for revisions, is anomalous. The text of the drafts on its leaves is presumably to be distinguished in time from that on the backs of the normal Dixie Bond paper.

[30] The original number 13 probably has no significance here. James started to continue fol. 11 and wrote a line before rejecting it and, turning the page over, inscribed the present fol. 12. The slip in numbering may have occurred because of this incident, provided James numbered the page before continuing to fol. 13.

numbered and deleted on the verso of fol. 23, its text continuing that on fol. 14 above the last four deleted lines which initially had continued on what is now fol. 16½. Folios 18 and 19 are numbered over 19 and 20 respectively while fols. 20–21 continue normally. The revision of original fols. 15, 16, and 17 and the renumbering of fols. 16½, 18, and 19 must have occurred just after the composition of the original part-page 21 (which was deleted and became the verso of fol. 16). Folio 22 is written on the verso of original 17 and fol. 23 on the verso of original 15. Folios 24 and 25 continue normally.

On fol. 26 the handwriting breaks off two-thirds down the page (286.38–287.10 'calling . . . there?" '). The heading at 287.1 was originally part of the continuous text, and it would seem that the antecedent matter ended with 'those interviews.' (287.8), for the next sentence 'At . . . there?" ' surrounds a now deleted centered heading. Below this added sentence is the pencil notation 'copy June 5th, p. 7–8 & notes'. At this point there is a gap in the MS of fols. 27–28 and the text does not resume until 289.31 heading fol. 29. Fortunately, the typewritten transcript of the sitting is preserved in London in the files of the Society for Psychical Research. (A special Historical Collation in the apparatus provides the substantive variants in the sitting and its notes so that one can see what alterations James [and possibly George B. Dorr in proof] made for publication.) One interesting fact from the transcript, concealed in the final text, is that Mrs. James was present with Dorr at the sitting.

This is the first of several similar places in the MS where pages are missing after a note by James that such and such a sitting should be copied. One cannot overlook the possibility that this was a note to himself on occasions when he did not want to delay his momentum, but it is more reasonable to take these notes as directions to the typist. By having a typed transcript of certain parts of the sittings ready at hand to work over, James spared himself a considerable time in copying out the text himself. That invariably the MS is missing after such a note implies strongly that James merely skipped the numeration of a few folios before proceeding and that the copy is not present because it existed only in the typist's preparation of the lost typescript for the printer. It should be noted, however, that the amount of rearrangement that James needed to make in this sitting not only to condense the text but also to intercalate within brackets Dorr's notes that in the sitting transcript are separately typed at the end and in a quite different order, would be considerable and might well have required retyping after he had revised and reordered the original typed pages from the sitting's transcript that he had requested.

On fol. 30 after copying on fol. 29 and the upper part of 30 the brief extract from the sitting of June 20 (289.31–290.10) James in pencil directs 'Copy note 10, p. 31' and fol. 31 is omitted to take account of the typist's copying of 290.11–18 from a sitting also preserved in London. When the text resumes with the sitting of July 2, on fol. 32 (written in pencil over deleted ink 32 and pencil 33) James merely introduces the séance in three lines and writes as the fourth 'G B D.—Can you give me - - -', this being a direction to House to continue the text with 'any names' (290.22) on the next leaf fol. 33 below deleted lines at the head. This leaf 33 begins a sequence of James's own typed pages, fols. 33–39, which he made from the transcript for Dorr's sitting of July 2, now preserved in London, James's pages being typed on Dixie Bond paper somewhat thinner than the previous uses. In the numbering, 33, in pencil, is written to the left of what seems to be a tinkered-with pencil-deleted ink 2, which in turn appears to the left of a centered figure 27, the 2 deleted by a strong vertical ink stroke and the 7 possibly made into an ink 1. In the upper right corner is written in pencil, 'Dorr sitting p. 1', and below the centered foliation is the pencil note, 'Similar material to copy in sitting of June 5th.' to which in blacker pencil has been appended '(buck board etc.' The original typed beginning has been deleted in ink: 'AS SPECIMENS of particularly good sitting, I willgiv give almost in extenso one with Mr. george B. Dorr, & two with professor William Romaine Newbold, both intimate friends of Hodgson. | Mr. DORR'S SITTING.ˣ | July 2nd. 1906. G. B. D. alone. | D. loq. (what can you tell me about Old-farm? [*paren del.*] ['[Oldfarm was' *del.*] [The ['T' *ov.* 't'] name of the Dorr's place *at Bar Harbor, where R. H. had often paid visits.] [*penc. del.*] Can you give me'. The footnote marker in the deleted heading refers to an undeleted handwritten vertical footnote in the left margin: 'ˣSitter's remarks are in parenthesis; comments are in square brackets; everything else is uttered by ['the' *del.*] 'control.'' This footnote (which was not used in the prints for obvious reasons) reveals the early state of this typescript, certainly one of James's original working-over of the Hodgson papers before he began the actual writing of the article. Other similar Jamesian transcripts of sittings that occur later merely confirm this note-taking stage of preparation. On the back of fol. 33, the first leaf of the Dorr transcript, is the heading 'LIST OF SITTINGS SINCE R. H.'S DEATH.' but without entries. The leaf has been folded, but succeeding leaves of the typescript do not show evidence of this folding. The succeeding leaves of this typing are numbered 34–35 to the right of centered pencil deleted 28–29. In the left upper corner is pencil 'Dorr 2' and 'Dorr, 3'. The next two typed leaves (Dorr 4–5) are foliated in ink 36 and 37, the 6 over a zero and the 7 over a pencil 1. Folio 38 (Smith paper), in ink with the 8 altering the numbering from 32, is handwritten (293.26–34 'a good ... follows:—]'), substituting for missing Dorr leaves 6–8, for when on fol. 39 (pencil deleted 33) the typing resumes, the first four and a half lines of text are deleted. This leaf ends with seven deleted typed lines and the addition of the ink note at 294.11–14. Thereafter, handwritten fols. 40–42 on Smith paper introduce the Owl's Head Series (294.15–295.9), both fols. 40 and 41 being numbered in pencil to the right of a deleted pencil 40.

Folios 43–51 represent a second of James's typed transcripts of sittings in preparation for writing the Report. They are leaves on the ordinary Dixie Bond paper, separated only after fol. 47 by the handwritten footnote 9 on Smith paper, headed 'Footnote to p. 47'. At the head of fol. 43 are various deleted pencil notes, reading from left to right: 'Call this 'The Owl's Head Series.'' ', then 'Bancroft 1', and then 'More might be supplied from D:̣ Bayley's sitting of April 4.' The original typed heading is deleted: 'Miss Bancroft's sitting, Feb 19, 06'. Because the carbon paper for fol. 45 was put in the typewriter the wrong way, and so produces a mirror image on the verso, fol. 45 is the sole ribbon copy, the rest being carbons. Folios 43–45 were originally headed 'Bancroft 1–3' but on fol. 46, containing the start of the second sitting (297.24), the heading changes to 'Bancroft-Bayley' and the numeration continues regularly from 4 to 9, with some corrections since 7 (corrected) was inadvertently numbered 6 at first, and although 8 is correct, 9 is written to the right of deleted 8. No textual disruption but simple inadvertency seems to have caused the errors.

The typed account of the April 4 Bayley sitting (both April 3 and April 4 are preserved in London) ends with 'very subject.' at 302.30, followed by a deleted line. The account of the sitting itself is completed on handwritten Smith paper fol. 52, where it is followed by the start of Miss Bancroft's sitting of June 20, 1906 (302.33), also preserved in London. Folio 52 is a rewritten version of the deleted upper half of fol. 53 (numbered over 52), which is written on the verso of deleted 303.14–15, and which, oddly, is exactly repeated at the head of fol. 54 in three lines (all Smith paper) before breaking off without warning. Presumably 303.16–304.28 was transcribed by House from the sitting record. The handwriting on Smith paper resumes at 304.29 on fol. 59 (altered from 56ᵃ), which ends with the first sentence of Miss Bancroft's sitting of December 3, 1907 (305.5–6), followed by the pencil note 'copy.' (The sitting is not preserved in London.) The text resumes at 305.29 on fol. 60, which starts with deleted typed matter that originally ended Dr. Bayley's sitting of April 4, 1906, condensed by the start of handwritten fol. 52. Since fol. 60 was altered from 52 and was originally headed 'Bancroft-Bayley, 10 [*aft. del.* '9']' (on Dixie Bond paper), it is clear that Miss Bancroft's sitting of June 20, 1906, and of December 3, 1907, were interpolations. Below the deleted typed lines on fol. 60 is James's handwritten summary of the Owl's Head series, ending on fol. 61 (altered from 53) at 306.22.

Professor Newbold's sittings start with James's introduction on handwritten fol. 62 (altered from 61 over 60). Its heading is written above deleted lines that were originally intended to conclude the Owl's Head sittings but instead were started below the typing on fol. 60. Folios 59–61, thus, are afterthoughts, and it would appear that James had proposed to follow the end of the December 3 sitting (on lost fol. 59ᵇ) with a brief conclusion[31] before moving on by a transition to the Newbold sittings. Moreover, the first leaf of the Newbold sitting is numbered 63 in pencil after deleted 55 and so might have been originally intended to follow fol. 54 (303.14) or the end (missing in MS) of the Bancroft sitting of June 20,

---

31 One should note that 'associated' at 305.30 is interlined in the deleted sentence on fol. 62 but is integral in the sentence of fol. 60.

1906. Or else—perhaps more likely—it might be a lost page after what is now fol. 61 but was originally 53, perhaps a different version of the introduction to the Newbold series now found on fol. 62, altered from 61 over 60, and so later than the inscription of the preceding leaves numbered originally 52 (now 60) and 53 (now 61).

The first Newbold sitting consists of a professional typescript (not made on James's typewriter), a carbon copy on *Agawam Bond* paper (not used elsewhere in the Report) which is a copy of the transcript of the June 27, 1906, transcript preserved in London. It is foliated 63–73, written in pencil to substitute for deleted 55–65, with various alterations. For example, fol. 67 replaced 57 which has deleted 59 to its left and deleted 58 to its right. The number 59 is correct, but the next leaf fol. 68 (which might just possibly have originally been written as 66) has deleted 58. Folio 69 is a handwritten interpolation, perhaps originally numbered 67 (311.23–27), which revises the deleted typed foot of preceding fol. 68. The James leaf is on Smith paper. The regular typescript then continues on fol. 70(62) to finish on 73(65). Actually, the finish is on fol. 74(66) which contains only a typed Newbold note headed deleted 16. Originally placed in the text after 'if such were possible.' at 313.9, James's written instruction on fol. 74, 'Note on p. 73', refers to his pencil '[Copy note on next page.]' placed on fol. 73 after 'thought he would not live.' (313.28–29).[32] The typed Newbold pages, their series pagination in the right corner running regularly from [1] to 10 (the note 16 page being unnumbered) end on fol. 73, at the foot of which James wrote the brief introduction to the July 3 sitting (314.5). This sitting is found in the MS starting with James's own typing on fols. 75–77 (altered from 67–69), a carbon on Dixie Bond paper, but continuing with Newbold's transcript on a different typewriter, also a carbon copy, on Agawam Bond paper, for fols. 78–85 (altered from 70–77). The James typing runs from 314.6 to 316.16 and the Newbold from 316.17 through 321.22. James's three leaves

[32] This typed note 16 on Agawam Bond paper must have been part of a numbered series appended to the sitting by Newbold but not preserved in the London Society's transcript. For instance, a typed '(Note 1)' appears after 306.34 and '(2)' after 'predictions' at 307.4. Certain notes, or James's versions of them, are supplied within the text by handwritten additions. One example is the deletion of '(3)' following 'happiness and' (307.14) after James had moved it by a guideline to follow 'discontented.' at the end of the sentence and then extended the guideline so that the '(3)' would follow 'up).' at 307.16. He then added in the margin the text of 307.17–18, this followed originally by 'N.', which was then deleted, to be replaced by 'W.J.' which was then deleted and 'N.' restored. The guideline for this marginal note places it after 'discontented.' One can only speculate that initially James intended note 3 from the appended typed series to be copied here by House but changed his mind. The insertion of his own initials makes it uncertain whether the note he added reproduced the typed note 3 or not. Less uncertainty may attach to the handwritten addition at 307.21–25 which is added to take the place of typed notation '(4)'. However, not all insertions are related to the numbered notes, as instance 308.2 for which no note number is present. Oddly, note 16 does not have its reference number typed in the text; but that it was supposed to be in sequence, and was very likely the final note, is indicated by the previously typed reference for note (15) which occurs on fol. 70(62) preceding 'Hello' at 312.6.

have pencilled in the upper left corner 'Newbold, July 3.' and are num-
bered 1–3. The original foliation starting with 67 (later altered in pencil
to 75) would have continued the original 66 of note 16 on fol. 74 of the
June 27 sitting. At its head is deleted typed: 'The next specimen sitting
I choose is that of Professor Newbold of the ['u' *del.*] University of Pennsylvania, ['An' *del.*] an intimate friend of Hodgson's, on July 3rd, 1906.
['After a' *del.*] Mr. Dorr was also present. After a few words with Rector,
Hodgson *appears & says:— [*added aft. del. ink* 'says:' *replacing typed*
'appears:']'. The terms of this original opening indicate that when James
typed it he had had no intention of introducing (or was not aware of)
Newbold's sitting of June 27.

The transition to Newbold's typescript at fol. 78(70) required James
to add at the head in ink Hodgson's brief remark at 316.17–18. The typewriter and paper are identical with the Newbold transcript of the June
27 sitting. Typed numbering appears in the upper right corner, in similar
manner, starting with 5 on fol. 78(70) and ending with 11 on fol. 85(77),
this sequence broken only by unnumbered fol. 81(73). The odd leaf 81(73)
is headed in ink 'Print as a note to p. 72', which would be the original
numbering of fol. 80. The text is a Newbold note numbered 19, the early
part of which James had deleted when he made it into footnote 11. On
fol. 80(72) James in ink at first positioned the note '(19)' after 'case.)',
where it is actually found in the prints, but then deleted this and added
an asterisk after 'characteristic.)' at 318.14 with the direction, '[Print
page 73 in the form of a *note*]'. In Newbold's typescript '(19)' had been
typed preceding the line beginning 'While' (318.12) and a '20' before
the line beginning 'You' (318.15). James had originally in ink written
a footnote indicator '(20)' after 'always.' (318.15) but deleted it. The unnumbered fol. 81(73) continuing the typed Newbold note 19 ends with
a quarter or more of the page blank, with space to begin a note 20, but
none appears, just possibly because each note had been typed on a separate piece of paper. In the two preceding Newbold typed pages beginning
with fol. 78(70) no typed references to notes occur. It seems plausible to
conjecture, therefore, that although the two sittings of June 27 and July
3 are separately paged, the sequence of notes on unnumbered pages was
keyed to take in both typed sittings combined, and that Newbold notes
17 and 18 had been keyed on the four lost leaves for which the James
typing is a substitute. This sitting of July 3 (minus notes) is preserved
in London, as is the transcript for the sitting of June 27.

The double foliation persists for only one more leaf, the handwritten
86(78), James's summing-up of the Newbold sittings on Smith paper,
which ends with the words in a part-line, ' "The evidence' (322.2), followed by a gap in the foliation. The missing fol. 87 would seem to have
been left open deliberately in order to take account of Newbold's letter,
quoted in 322.2–8 and James's accompanying footnote 14, handed to the
typist to copy.

With fol. 88 (322.9) James began a series of handwritten pages on
Smith paper with current numbering. This series on Hyslop ends on

part-page fol. 93 at 323.30 after the introduction to James's own sittings, with 'R. H. enters, saying:—'. This last follows the identical words deleted on the same line and would appear to be a revision since after a space a new paragraph had begun as 'A sitting', now deleted. The typist House must have worked directly from James's notes, for the MS does not begin again until fol. 117 with James's summing-up starting at 338.9. Thereafter the handwritten text picks up again on Smith paper and continues without incident through fol. 123 (altered from the inadvertent error 133) and the part-line 'Do you remember' at its foot (340.14). Like the sittings with James, these with Miss Bergman (a pseudonym for Miss Mary Hillard) have not been preserved so far as is known.[33]

The Australian Recollections that begin on fol. 137 at 345.31 follow on the resumption of the MS at fol. 136 with James's comments on the 'Bergman' sittings (345.22–30). They are written-out complete on Smith paper, ending at 347.24 near the foot of fol. 141 after which comes the excerpted matter from various sittings starting at 347.25 also on Smith paper. On fol. 141 an asterisk is placed after 'world.' at 347.19 and the circled line is inserted, '*Insert Mrs. Piper's letter as a note'. This editorially numbered footnote 20 in the print was keyed, instead, to follow 'part' at 347.7. Its introductory lines are written as the only text on fol. 141½, headed 'Note', but the letter itself is not preserved in the manuscript and was doubtless copied direct by House. The text starting fol. 142 'Additional citations' (347.26–348.1) is placed below James's circled 'blank line' and is prefixed by a paragraph sign, neither of which is observed in the print, perhaps correctly.

Some disruption of the text occurs on fol. 144 (348.29–349.2 '12th. . . . W.J.]ˣ'): the number 144 is followed by a comma and then by deleted 145 as if the leaf had at one time been planned as two pages. So far as can be seen, the text is continuous, but it is clear from the spacing that footnote 21 starting at the foot of fol. 144 and continuing on 145ᵃ (written in ink over pencil 146) to end on part-page 145ᵇ, was an afterthought and that the original text ending 349.2 had continued with '[(2)' *del.*] Ask Margie' (349.19) to complete the page with 'Chocorua. W. J.]', the next page originally numbered 146 beginning 'In Hodgsons rooms' (349.26). But James altered the period after 'Chocorua' to a comma, deleted the 'W. J.' and the beginning of the bracketed comment, and then at the foot of fol. 144 and the head of renumbered 145ᵃ squeezed in the extra material that made the text into a footnote. Since 349.5–15 'You . . . M. M. J.' was typed by House from now missing copy, fol. 146 contains only its introduction at 349.3–4 and the deleted start of 349.5 which, in error, had been given the speech-heading 'W. J.' Again, 350.1–31 'I am . . . T. P.]²²' was also typed from a transcript; it is missing in the MS except for its introduction 349.16–17 on fol. 149, which is written on the

---

[33] Miss Hillard's sittings are referred to in a letter to her on December 7, 1908, for which see footnote 16 above. It may be that James abstracted these leaves to preserve her anonymity but more probably her notes were acceptable as copy and House typed directly, a gap being left in the MS foliation to take account of this material.

blank verso of a trial for the same material but also continues for a few lines with what was proposed as the start of quotation from the sitting, now found at 350.10–11. The text resumes with 351.1 on fol. 153. Textual disruption is present on fol. 154 which consists of a paste-on upper half attached to the original leaf.[34] This paste-on accommodates the undeleted text of what is clearly an addition somewhat squeezed in at the foot of fol. 153 and completed on the slip pasted at the head of fol. 154. Curiously, this item, numbered 7 in the manuscript, was not printed: possibly when reviewing House's typescript James decided that it was too personal or of little value for the Report. The item in MS reads:

(7) The R. H. control *expressed to [*ab. del.* 'showed on'] several *sitters [*ab. del.* 'occasions'] solicitude about certain *facts, [*comma insrtd.*] ['(?)' *del.*] *—if they were facts, [*insrtd.*]|[*fol.* 154] connected with his pecuniary relations with F. W. H. Myers. *Since, [*comma insrtd.*] however, [*intrl.*] these *facts [*ab. del.* 'relations'] may ['however' *del.*] have been, *and probably were [*ab. del.* 'ventilated'] communicated to the Imperator-group during Hodgson's life time, his *bringing [*ab. del.* 'repeating'] them *out [*intrl.*] now cannot count as evidential [*insrtd.* 'in' *del.*] of ['spirit ret' *del.*] the return of his spirit.

At 351.11 present printed item (7) in the MS had started in the space left by the paragraph indention filled by separately deleted 'thought-of' that had concluded the deleted sentence on the original leaf under the paste-over. The item was originally numbered (9) out in the left margin, but this was deleted and (8) was interlined. It would seem that James found himself rearranging and renumbering the items so that fol. 153 probably had ended almost at the foot with 'controls indiscriminately' (351.10), that original fols. 154–155 were discarded, and the next item (perhaps itself part of the shake-up and revision) was started on fol. 156, now numbered (8) in MS but (7) in the prints. Then the beginning of eventually discarded item (7) was squeezed in at the foot of fol. 153 and continued on the page numbered 154, which was a slip pasted over and extending to make a long leaf the original discarded leaf foliated 156. The text of this leaf runs-on normally at the head of the next leaf ('getting

[34] The paste-on is over the upper part of a discarded Smith-paper leaf foliated 156 in pencil and deleted by horizontal strokes. Originally it must have been the first leaf of Part II, for a false start appears intended either to begin Part II as at 279.21–22 or the second paragraph at 280.15. This starts with a paragraph 'Hodgson's friends were still | rather perplexed about the future of the | ['Americ' *del.*], and various plans were | thought-of'. Before breaking off James made two additions. In the first he interlined 'For weeks after' above a space even with the left margin and then after 'Hodgson's' he interlined 'death his' so that the trial read 'For weeks after Hodgson's death his friends were still rather perplexed about the future of the ['Americ' *del.*], and various plans were thought-of'. This leaf was then discarded. In a unique case of James using the recto of a discarded leaf instead of turning it over and writing on the verso, he much later used it to begin fol. 156. Underneath the interlineation 'For weeks after' he inserted 'The same sitter on Jan. 30th., |' but then interlined 'On' above 'on' to begin the sentence differently. He then seems to have inscribed 'had received' in the paragraph opening before 'Hodgson's' before abandoning the trial. This twice worked-on leaf was then used to hold the paste-on foliated in pencil 154.

an | endowment') at 351.21, which was originally foliated 157 but was then altered to the joint 155–156. This is a part-leaf, the text ending with several lines of white space.

The disruption in the numbering caused by the rearrangement and possible deletion of the items in this section continues on fol. 157, re-numbered from 153, a foliation that suggests that even present fol. 153, which starts item (6) may also be part of the revision. This leaf 157(153) ends halfway down with James's start for the typist 'Do you remember, etc.' which House, and the compositors, faithfully reproduced as well as the start of the missing material from 352.5 to 352.26. Item (9) (item 11 in the MS) begins with 352.27 at the head of fol. 160, altered from 158, the original 158 indicating that James had inadvertently not left a gap of two leaves to take account of the transcript that House typed in from a sitting which has not been preserved. The last few lines of fol. 160 re-lating to Professor Child's messages are deleted, with a fresh start made on what is probably a substitute leaf 161 (altered from 159), on Smith paper, a part leaf concluding the Child item (353.5–12). Folio 161½ is a short substitute leaf[35] starting excerpt (10), the same in both MS and print, down to the part-line 'R. H. Did you get my' (353.17). This re-vised text is written on the obverse of a discarded handwritten trial which reads, 'control. ['During the years' *del.*]', the paper being the thin Dixie Bond. This trial does not seem to link with any preserved earlier text on the thin Dixie Bond paper.

In error a Smith-paper leaf numbered 162 (unaltered) intervenes be-tween the broken-off text on fol. 161½ and its continuation fol. 163. This leaf 162 (which should be 163, as 163 should be 162) contains ex-cerpt (11) complete, altered from 10, which itself may have been altered from 11 (353.22–32). Folio 163 on Smith paper completes episode (10), started on 161½, with '['(3) [To Miss Putnam] Did you get my' *del.*] Christmas present?' (353.17–21). Its early excerpt number (3) at the original start, and the fact that the foliation 163 is written after deleted 145, indicate that originally this leaf was placed much earlier in the sequence of excerpts. It very well could have been placed after fol. 144 (numbered with a comma before deleted and possibly added 145) which in its present form ends episode (3) at 349.2 before beginning footnote 21 continued on 145[a] and 145[b]. Indeed, the abrupt start of the deleted first line of early numbered episode (3) on fol. 163(145) would make it very natural to continue the sitting of Mrs. James and Miss Putnam which now begins excerpt (3), the number squeezed in by interlineation, be-ginning on fol. 143 and carried on to fol. 144. More rearrangement of these numbered excerpts is certainly indicated. On the verso of fol. 163 James pencilled the note, 'Dear Annie— Is this all right to print? | W. J.',

---

[35] The slash between '1/2' is written over something that may be a letter (although James usually put these signs of supplementation in a superior position), but it is possible that actually James mended the slash over an initialed figure '1'. In the item number (10) the zero is rather elongated and may possibly have been written over a 1, making the item originally 11.

which may refer to the whole episode and not merely to the excerpt about Christmas contained on fol. 163(145). It is clear that Miss Putnam saw James's MS for her sitting(s) and approved before they were typed up by House.

With 354.1 starting fol. 164 James comes to the end of his much revised and rearranged series of excerpts from various sittings and embarks upon his final analysis of the events he has described. This shift is marked not only by the unaltered foliation numbers but also by the first use in Part II (added 161½ aside) of the thin Dixie Bond paper found in Part I. These pages run along without interruption except for footnote 24 which was inscribed on fol. 166½ on the same paper.[36]

What must be Mr. House's typescript of Part I, the carbon copy, has been preserved in the archives of the American Society for Psychical Research, New York City, in Box 3 (Historical), the file folder labeled 'Wm James on Hodgson control'. This TMs consists of 34 pages of L. C. Smith paper, the first four triple-spaced but with double-spacing from p. 5 on. The typescript was done with considerable faithfulness from the revised leaves of James's MS, using the James typewriter with which James himself had typed various pages of MS.[37] James worked over this TMs, inserting directions for blank lines, adding brackets for interpolated comments, guidelines for run-on lines, and a certain amount of textual revision.

That this TMs was copied directly from James's MS is indicated by the various faulty readings that may be put down to misinterpretation of James's handwriting, such as 'intricate' at 256.8, a misreading of MS 'intimate'. However, the clearest cases are represented by the faithful TMs copying at 258.11 of the MS typo 'assemts' and the mistake at 274.20 in which the typist misread the smudged colon after 'ask' as an exclamation point, which it strongly resembles.

Even though certain, the question of transmission is not without its

---

36 Initially this footnote had been keyed to follow 'knew it?' (354.28), with the circled direction 'x note on p. 166.' On fol. 166 the note is rekeyed to its present position at 354.31 and the marginal circled note 'x note on next page' directs the typist to fol. 166 1/2. The Dixie Bond paper ends on fol. 169 in mid-sentence ('complicate | the') at 356.4 and then shifts to the L. L. Brown paper which completes the Report without incident. No significance can be attached to this change of paper. The Report ends on fol. 181 subscribed 'William James [*double underlined*] | Cambridge [*comma del. by paren*] (Mass.), U. S. of A. | Jan 15. 09'.

Of the various sittings reported by James only the original transcripts for January 23, April 3, April 4, May 2, May 14, May 29, June 5, June 20, June 27, July 2, July 3, and July 4, all in 1906, have been preserved in the files of the Society for Psychical Research in London, and the sitting for February 27, 1906, in the archives of the American Society in New York, in Box 3, under Hyslop's Biographical Materials II, these offering, of course, the opportunity to analyze the various alterations that James made in the material and its presentation. Names for initials or pseudonyms found in these transcripts have been furnished in the Textual Notes keyed to the list of Emendations. Professor Skrupskelis' commentary Notes should also be consulted.

37 The most obvious identification is a break in the left limb of the lower-case 'v' and a tendency of the rondure of the lower-case 'p' to ink very lightly.

problems, nevertheless. Various typing mistakes, not all of which might be anticipated, include the omission of the italic underline in MS *'my'* (262.3) and of the single quotation marks about 'Huldah' (271.2), or some misinterpretations of James's revisions in the MS such as the omission of 'a' at 254.23 or of 'suddenly' at 258.1, or the very real error of misinterpretation that made MS 'A "B" and an "L"' read '"A", "B" and an "L"' at 258.25 (see Textual Notes). House, the typist, sometimes ignores guidelines transposing material to another position, as at 260.32–33 (see Textual Note). No great eventual harm is done by such errors even when passed on to the printed texts, since MS is present to demonstrate the TMs error and the correct reading.[38] More troublesome are a few occasions when a question arises about the state of MS when it was copied by House. For example, at 274.14–17 MS originally read 'that both he and Newbold would *erelong [insrtd.]* be made matrimonially happy, but that whereas the prophecy was being verified in *N's [ab. del.* 'the [*illeg. del.]* one'] case, it had been falsified in *his own, [ab. del.* 'the *other, [comma ov. period]* ['by' *del.]*']'. This is the MS text as typed verbatim and passed on to the prints, but in MS a further Jamesian alteration had been made in a somewhat lighter ink that disguised Newbold by interlining 'another friend' above deleted 'Newbold' and also interlining 'the one' before deleted interlined 'N.' It seems difficult to believe that the typist would have ignored these two clear alterations in favor of the deleted originals. One has therefore the choice of conjecturing that James altered the lost intermediate typescript back to his original text (thus restoring Newbold's name to the passage) so that the prints read as in the deleted version, or else that for some reason he made the change in MS after the TMs had been typed. In this case James allowed the TMs version to stand, but in another he changed TMs to agree with the alteration in the MS. At 273.11 in the MS James wrote in his own hand, 'The sitting of Prof. Newbold's to which I allude was held on Jan 27th. 1906.' At a later time he deleted 'of Prof. Newbold's', by error including 'to' in the deleting stroke, and interlined 'held by Prof Newbold' after undeleted 'held'. Nevertheless TMs has the original text typed, which James altered by deleting 'of Prof. Newboldt' ('Newboldt' typed in error for 'Newbold's') and interlining 'by Prof. *W. R. [intrl.]* Newbold' after '1906' (the original period after the date being changed to a comma). Here it is possible to reconstruct how House might have misunderstood the intention. The interlineation 'held by Prof Newbold' happens to fall in the MS directly beneath deleted 'of Prof. Newbold's to' |, and the guideline by which James intended to direct the interlineation 'held by Prof Newbold' to be placed after 'held' (in error) has an upward curl that might be mistaken as applying to the deletion. It is just possible that typing in haste House did not think through the MS alteration and so took it that the deletion was not to be observed. Of course,

---

[38] However, some distortion in the printed texts was caused by these, and especially by another error in the TMs, for which see the Emendations list and Textual Note for 254.5.

it is also possible that this is another alteration made in the MS after the typing stage.[39] At 262.19–21 it is odd to find the same interlineation 'R. H.'s chief association with W. J. jr had been when fishing or swimming in Chocorua Lake' in MS also made by hand, with a few small variants, in TMs. Whether the typist missed it, or James had an afterthought which he transferred from MS to TMs is uncertain. The only typed interlineation in TMs ('discussion of the control's suggestibility' at 269.16–17) agrees with a hand interlineation in MS. Whether House caught himself overlooking the interlineation and repaired the mistake, or whether James saw to it that a change he made in MS was transferred to TMs cannot be known. Equally odd in its own way is the hand deletion of 'extraordinarily' in TMs at 254.22, but then its restoration in the prints.

This TMs was marked by James with a number of ink revisions in the wording. It was also marked for copying either by printing or retyping with marginal directions for spaces between sections, brackets for commentary within dialogue, some directions for paragraphing and for the insetting of text, as well (with one significant exception) with double underlining of sitters' names typed in lower case with a capital. That it was also prepared for oral delivery may be suggested by at least two alterations made by hand in TMs. For example, at 256.35–36 TMs had followed MS in 'for which my various readers will make their sundry kinds of allowance', but in ink James altered TMs 'readers' to 'hearers'. At 268.2 TMs had also followed the MS word 'Readers', but here James changed TMs in ink to the neutral 'People'. The inference one may draw is definitely that James intended a copy of TMs to be read at the January 28, 1909, general meeting of the Society for Psychical Research in London; but the markings for format are ambiguous in that they would serve equally well if James at the time had proposed to use this TMs for the American printer or else for a further retyping in company with the typing of Part II.[40]

---

[39] It would be pure speculation that from time to time in sending portions of his Report to different persons for criticism and approval of the account of sittings, James had in hand no copy of TMs at the moment and had to send leaves from the MS instead. In looking them over before passing them, he could have been unable to resist making minor changes. Nevertheless, although here and there in Part II marks of folding in some MS leaves show that they were mailed, and there are other signs of early dissemination of the MS, such as the note to Miss Anne Putnam on fol. 163ᵛ, yet no physical evidence is present in Part I leaves to show that they were sent through the mail or otherwise shown for approval. It is possible, then, that these few MS alterations that do not appear in TMs are all typist errors, difficult as it is to account for such variants as take place at 262.19–21, 274.14–17, and even 273.11. Whatever the circumstances, it is evident that no TMs variant from the MS can be authoritative except for those readings that James inserted by hand.

[40] It is possible, of course, but unlikely that the preserved ribbon copy was the one read by Piddington in London on January 28, 1909, and then returned to James. But if so, it could not have arrived in Cambridge before James sent printer's copy to the Society in London on February 1. Since TMs was finished on December 19, 1908, no difficulty existed in getting a copy to England for the January 28 reading, but the return is another matter.

Preserved at Harvard with the MS is a carbon typescript, paged 10, making use of the James typewriter and of the same L. C. Smith paper as TMs and containing the correct text for p. 10 (259.14–260.7 'I . . . my') whereas the TMs leaf completes the sentence on the leaf with 'promise to shake you up?', which begins, also, the text at the start of p. 11. The separate leaf, which we may call TMs^a, thus fits precisely between pp. 9 and 11, whereas the New York TMs leaf, which we may call TMs^b, overlaps. All other leaves of TMs are numbered with a typed centered figure, but TMs^b as preserved in this typescript has no typed number and instead is paged in ink in the upper right corner with the figure 10. TMs^a, the separate leaf, has the typed numbering 10 in the usual place. TMs^b contains only one James ink marking, the notation '–R.' after 259.27, which was typed like MS without the necessary speech-prefix for Rector. Moreover, the other speech-prefixes on this page are not double underlined in ink as they are elsewhere in this area of TMs (save in fol. 9). On the other hand, James has double underlined the prefixes on TMs^a and in ink has inserted in the margin the direction for a blank line after 259.30. In addition, the two prefixes for Rector missing in MS and in TMs are correctly typed at 259.27 and 259.30 and of course are ink double underlined along with the other prefixes. The TMs^a separate leaf was in the direct line of transmission to the prints, whereas the TMs^b p. 10 was not. The TMs^a spelling 'practicing' (259.14) appears both in E and in A, whereas MS and TMs^b read 'practising'. The prints contain the two prefixes for Rector found in TMs^a but not TMs^b. More important, the MS-TMs^b 'AM' at 260.1 (whether or not an error) is repeated in both prints as 'am' from its TMs^a form. At 259.28 and 259.30 both prints copy the three TMs^a ellipsis dots instead of the conventional four found in TMs^b (MS has three at 259.28 but four at 259.30). Since the usage is entirely conventional there may be no significance to E and A copying the four ellipsis dots after 'to-day' at 260.4 found in TMs^a and MS instead of the irregular six in TMs^b. In E and A, as in TMs^a the narrative 'A . . . on:—', is enclosed in parentheses (MS ink square brackets) at 260.5–6 whereas no typed parentheses or brackets appear in TMs^b and none are marked.

The fact that the TMs^a leaf is numbered by the typewriter and joins with p. 11 textually, whereas TMs^b is irregular in both respects suggests that TMs^a is the originally typed leaf and served as the copy for the later transmission of the text to the prints. That TMs^b was typed directly from MS is demonstrable by its agreement with various features including the two important matters of 'AM' and the lack of prefixes for Rector.[41] That TMs^a was not typed from TMs^b but also goes back directly to MS as copy is indicated by one small but significant piece of

---

[41] These two prefixes are missing at 259.27 and 259.30 in a handwritten substitute fol. 14 in MS, whereas the prefix is correctly found just before at 259.16 in James's typed fol. 13(4). In adding the prefixes at 259.27 and 259.30 the typist was obviously following the sense of his copy (the earlier prefix having fallen on the same p. 10) whereas in TMs^b he was transcribing MS mechanically.

evidence. After the statement 'I AM Hodgson' MS and TMs[a] both add only two ellipsis dots, anomalously, whereas TMs[a] has the conventional three, in this case shared by the prints. Moreover, the omission at the foot of p. 10 of the improperly typed-in extra words of TMs[b] shows that the typist of TMs[a] was typing continuous copy and went correctly from the text at the foot of p. 10 to that at the head of p. 11, whereas the typist of TMs[b] seems to have known only the MS and thought it wise to tuck in the closing words of Hodgson's speech when he reached the foot of his page in case they were required.

External evidence points to no certain conclusion as to the cause for the retyping and the preservation of the retyped leaf in TMs. Such as it is, the evidence suggests the possibility that in some manner the original TMs[a] (and its carbon copy) had been temporarily mislaid[42] and that the substitute now found as TMs[b] in the complete Part I typescript was typed to replace it, using MS as its copy. If this is so, the retyping of TMs[b] would need to have been done subsequent to the use of TMs in the transmissional link with the prints and thus, presumably, to provide a complete set of pages. The case may prove to be more complicated when the full transmission of the text is studied, but for the moment the above may do as a tentative working hypothesis.[43]

From James's diary we know that Mr. House began to type Part I on December 18, 1908, and finished it the next day. This typescript must be TMs as we have it in the carbon copy. Since the copy had to be sent to England in time to be read on January 28, the ribbon must have been mailed immediately once James had looked it over and marked it for revised wording, but no diary or other record is preserved of the date of mailing or of the state of the copy. James began work on Part II, shortly, on December 21, presumably after mailing Part I. The diary entries indicate that he worked steadily, the dates December 22, 25, and 28 being recorded. On January 9, 1909, while James was still writing, House came to start the typescript intended for publication.[44] James completed the Report on January 15 and House, who must have been close behind, completed his typing on January 18. After revising this now lost typescript, James mailed it to England on February 1 and on February 3 disposed of the Piper documents.

---

42 Since—it will be argued—the transmission was not direct but through an intermediate typescript, the possibility might be thought to exist that this TMs[a] is for some reason the only surviving page of such an intermediary. But the coincidence with retyped TMs[b] p. 10 suggests something abnormal, and the exact fit between pp. 9 and 11 of TMs, which could be achieved only if an intermediary retyped its copy page for page (triple as well as double spaced), makes such a hypothesis difficult to credit.

43 That this TMs was preserved after James had cleared his desk of the Piper papers suggests that he presented it to the American Society. Earlier he may have circulated the typed copy instead of proofs for criticism among interested persons.

44 The odd phrase in the January 9 entry, 'Mr. House, type copyist' (he is usually 'typewriter') may or may not suggest that Part I was the first to be retyped. We cannot know the order.

The typescript of Part II that was made by House in January 1909 must have served as printer's copy for the English *Proceedings*. James's corrections and revisions in this copy can be identified by reference to the variants from the MS listed in the Historical Collation where agreement between E and A as against MS must—as a working hypothesis—be taken to represent authorial handwritten alterations made in the copy between January 15 and February 1.[45]

On the evidence of an extra typed leaf preserved with the MS we may catch a glimpse of House's typescript and of the kind of revision that James performed in copy. This leaf (TMs^c) is an oddity with some inexplicable features. It consists of a page of ribbon-copy typescript made up by pasting together cut-outs from two different typed pages comprising the text for 358.23–29, 359.1–14 'activity . . . only' attached together on a blank half-sheet of typewriter paper. The foundation sheet is numbered 107 in ink by James in the upper right corner. The paste-ons begin after a white space of about a quarter of the leaf, each measuring 3¼", the typing from James's typewriter. In the left margin of the white space is a 56 written in pencil above a sweeping line, probably not in James's hand. The upper paste-on begins with a part-line, the first third having been scissored off, so that the line starts with 'activity'. It is curious that 'activity' begins MS fol. 178, although final 'only' occurs within the eighth line of text on fol. 179. The typescript, as joined, reproduces the reworked state of the MS without a substantive variant of any sort, but makes three mistakes in spelling and punctuation, caused by misreading of James's handwriting and alterations. James has worked over the typescript text, making six substantive changes, adding one comma and removing another, altering a capital after a colon-dash to lower case, and changing six sets of single quotation marks to double. The paper of the two paste-ons and of the piece to which the upper is attached is thin and without watermark but it could perhaps be the thin Daisy Bond paper which occasionally is found without watermark. (The watermark of course might have appeared on the part of the leaves cut off.)

The ink foliation 107 on the blank piece could not be that of the original typewritten leaf of which the upper paste-on would comprise the last ten lines, for the upper piece is attached to the lower by its being pasted over the normal upper margin of the lower, which is paged with a typed 106. The pagination 107, therefore, must apply to the position of this made-up leaf after revision, and not to the original.[46] (The pur-

---

[45] Account must be taken, of course, of possible typist error not corrected by James and so perpetuated in the prints. Error of this sort means any typist departure from copy, compounded by similar compositorial departures. Not all such departures can be identified as non-authorial when found in a revised edition (which is substantially what E is as compared with the basic MS copy) unless they are obvious misprints or misreadings. Variants in the substantives are, of course, more readily evaluated for authority than those in certain forms of the accidentals like the punctuation, since accidentals are more susceptible of alteration by typist or compositor than substantives.

[46] The typed 106 pagination for the start of the lower section indicates that Part II would necessarily have been paged in a different series from Part I, like the MS.

pose of the non-Jamesian notation is obscure.[47]) Two points are worth noting. First, the reconstructed leaf is almost at the end of Part II so that perhaps no more than two leaves would have completed the typescript. Some revision of the ending that required retyping might seem to be indicated. Second, in the prints just such a revision is found in a seventy-one word addition not present in MS (359.14–20 'It tallies . . . contributions.'). Only the two words 'imperfectly aroused.' that end the sentence after the last word 'only' typed on the made-up leaf intervene before the start of this addition, which ends before the paragraph beginning 'It is enough' (359.21). Thus an added leaf, or a substitute rather, could have been contrived by pasting the new typed text of 359.14–20 above the detached typed paragraph 'It is enough' on another page of blank paper. There are problems in such a hypothesis, of course. On the preserved made-up leaf the last word 'only' is typed to end a part-line with about two-fifths of the line left blank. Moreover, since this typing was originally paged 106, it is clear that House's p. 106 was less than half a page of typescript before typing was broken off with 'only'. Whether or not James had used the final words of the sentence 'imperfectly aroused.' as a key or cue prefixed to his manuscript of the added passage in order to place it properly in the text, it would seem that p. 106 was typed as a part-page to be inserted before this other made-up leaf in order to join preceding text with it. It is, of course, a part of this preceding text that forms the upper section of the pasted-together leaf. However baffling is the removal of text in this section before 'activity' so that this word coincided with the first word of fol. 178 of the MS, the hypothesis that this upper piece was in its turn (seemingly after the expansion by added 359.14–20) sected in order to fit with preceding revised text has some evidence in its favor. Shortly before the lost start at the head of the page of this remaining piece, James added footnote 26 (358.33–40) to the typescript, which had not been present in the MS and so had to be inserted in the typescript after the page on which it was to appear had been typed. Hence if instead of having this footnote typed by itself on a supplementary page, James took the opportunity—being so close to the end of the typescript—to have the final pages retyped so that they would contain his text revisions already made in the typescript as well as the handwritten additions that must be typed, then he might well have provided copy for the retyping that consisted of just such pasted-together pages combined with his new manuscript as we see preserved in the made-up and renumbered fol. 107 (TMs^c). That this leaf has survived and was eventually inserted when the MS was mounted and bound indicates beyond any question that it could not have been the printer's copy and so must have been, instead, the copy for a retyping.

Despite the fact that the prints (and thus the retyped page) contain the handwritten alterations that James made in this p. 107, he must have worked over the retyped text further by making seven more revisions,

47 It is perhaps pure coincidence that 56 would approximate the number of words of typescript cut off at the head of the leaf before 'activity'.

as attested by the agreement of E and A in readings variant from those in the final text of the preserved leaf, plus the correction of the typo of 'redivious' in TMs^c (359.8).[48] Even in proof James continued his tinkering with this section of text by reworking the sentence 358.24–25 'The bodies . . . universe' in two different ways in E and in A; in addition, in E he extended the italics of *'rest'* (359.2) to include the remainder of the phrase.[49]

The evidence, both external in the diary and in the preserved discarded fol. 107, as well as internal throughout the text, demonstrates that a typescript was made from MS for Part II, this typescript being further revised between its completion on January 18 and the mailing of copy to England on February 1, 1909.[50] The question then arises whether TMs, the preserved typescript of Part I, was also retyped for the printer. The weight of the textual evidence, combined with the most obvious interpretation of what external evidence we have, indicates the high probability—if not the necessity for the action—that TMs Part I was retyped specifically for printing and that this typescript—like that for Part II—was further revised before mailing to England.

That a typescript for Part I was required for Piddington to read in London on January 28 (James had thought it would be January 23) accounts satisfactorily for the manufacture of the preserved TMs on December 18–19, 1908. We may take it with some confidence that Part I was in the mail before James began to write Part II on December 21, 1908; it follows that revision could not have been extensive in so brief an interval. Probabilities favor the hypothesis that this lost ribbon copy contained no more and perhaps some fewer alterations than those found in the preserved carbon.[51] What we cannot know is whether at this early

---

[48] Someone other than James has circled the offending mistyped syllable in pencil and added a question mark in the margin. Two punctuation changes in E and A may also be James's, as one may assume in the absence of evidence, although both are conventional and thus subject to interference by the typist or compositor.

[49] Another variant, the unique omission of 'and' in A at 358.27, may be a proof-alteration as well, but the failure to alter the preceding comma to a semicolon as would be required by the omission of 'and' casts some doubt on the authority, and in this edition it has been rejected as a probable compositorial error in A. The semicolon in the edited text is an emendation from MS: TMs^a has a comma, which is reproduced in both prints.

[50] The entry in the diary for February 1 should have more authority than the remark in a letter to T. S. Perry dated January 29, "I have just got off my report on the Hodgson control" (*Letters*, II, 319). In a letter to James H. Hyslop of January 20, James writes that he proposes to "mail the copy to England in a couple of days" (preserved in the archives of the Society for Psychical Research, New York, first published in *William James on Psychical Research*, ed. Gardner Murphy and Robert O. Ballou [New York: Viking, 1960], p. 114). This casual remark, of course, does not take account of the extra time he must have needed to make the numerous revisions in the typescript.

[51] James was not in the habit of taking the time and trouble to transfer alterations from one document to another (see the discussion in the textual introduction to *Some Problems of Philosophy*, WORKS). On the other hand, there was every reason to bring

date, before Part II was written, James had any firm idea of what would constitute printer's copy for Part I. If he hoped that the copy read in London would also serve for printing, he was soon disillusioned by the amount of revision required in House's transcript of Part II, finished on January 18, 1909, after James had completed the MS on January 15.

Both in Part I and Part II a very large number of substantive variants exist between the agreement of E and A and the preserved basic copy of TMs or of MS respectively. These variants are too numerous in substantives (and in accidentals sometimes too casual) to have resulted from similar alterations made in English and American proof.[52] Moreover, the actual proof-alterations may be identified in the relatively numerous unique variants in E when A agrees with TMs or MS, or, correspondingly, in the fewer unique variants in A when E and TMs or MS agree. The joint differences in E and A, therefore, must be referred to copy. In the fortunately preserved typed fol. 107 from Part II we see what James's ink alterations in the initial typescript were like, and in the joint variants of E and A in this same text we recognize the further equally extensive alterations that James must have made in the retyped copy, as well as one example of separate and varying proof-correction in each print.

We are now thrown back upon speculation as to why James ordered a retyping of Part I since the alterations he had made in the preserved copy by no means unfit it for the printer. As remarked above, the verbal and accidental alterations that he made may have been more numerous than those marked in the ribbon copy sent to London for reading. It follows that at the moment when the retyping was ordered, James was relatively satisfied with the Part I text, even though he subsequently made almost as many revisions in it as he did, comparatively, in Part II typed directly from MS. It is possible that for a time he felt that the Part I TMs would do as printer's copy for the American *Proceedings*, but—if so—he then faced the problem of copy for England since the paper read in London was beyond his reach for revision. The markings for blank lines and for the positioning of material, and even the ink changes of typewriter parentheses to square brackets, are all matched in the typed

---

his retained carbon of Part I into conformity with that sent abroad: on December 20 the exigencies of further revision may not yet have forced upon his attention a final decision about printer's copy and thus it might have seemed useful to correct his remaining copy in case it was needed for Hyslop's American *Proceedings*, say, or for more revision. The two changes in TMs to adapt the audience from readers to hearers suggests a transfer to TMs from the copy altered for London delivery.

52 James corrected English proof on March 1–2 (returned on March 3), March 5 (returned by March 10 after Dorr corrections), and April 13. The first American proof arrived May 8 with another batch recorded on May 11. That the joint variants in E and A originated in identical proof-alterations (James having kept a marked copy of his English proofs in order to deal with the American) is not only improbable, given his working habits, but is controverted by the evidence that both English and American prints underwent a separate round of unique correction which overlays the readings of joint variation from known copy. No mention of revises occurs in the diary, nor was there reasonable time for the E proof-corrections to have been made in revises after the return of the originals.

portions of MS and hence are as applicable as instructions for retyping as for printing. It is at least a reasonable working hypothesis that at the time James was revising the typescript of Part II he felt that a similar ribbon and carbon copy was necessary for Part I, that this was made from the preserved copy of TMs, and that it too was revised like the typescript for Part II before being sent to London on February 1, 1909.[53]

The basic printer's copy for the Report, then, was a now lost typescript of both parts that in general faithfully reproduced the TMs and MS copy[54] but was considerably worked over by James with revisory handwritten changes before being sent to the printer. This was the copy from which the copy-text English *Proceedings* was set. The copy for the American *Proceedings* now comes in question. Under ordinary circumstances one would expect this copy to have been the carbon of the copy mailed to England, with or without further alterations, depending in some small part upon the date at which printer's copy was sent to the American editor, James Hyslop, and the degree of care that James might have been expected to bestow on what it is clear he considered to be the less important publication. Evidence does not seem to be preserved to indicate whether from the start of his assignment in mid-1906 James had contemplated joint publication or whether his eyes had been fixed exclusively on England. However, in a letter of December 7, 1908, to Miss Mary Hillard (see footnote 16 above), written just about the time that he was starting the actual composition, he mentions his Report as "to be pub^{d} simultaneously by Hyslop and at London"; thus in the writing and in all subsequent arrangements he was conscious of double publication and would have needed to think in these terms. On January 20, 1909, two days after House had finished the typing, James wrote to Hyslop: "Gottlob, I've finished my Hyslop report, which I expect to fill nearly 100 pages of the English *Proceedings*, rather less perhaps of yours. I shall mail the copy to England in a couple of days, but should like to keep the copy destined for you a little while longer. I mailed a 'preliminary' report some weeks ago, to be read in London on the 23rd [actually January 28], but not pub. till after the February *Proceedings* are out, which would make it May, I suppose [actually June]. Miss Johnson expects that you will not publish ere she does, so I trust you will not. I wish they didn't delay so—I like to see a thing quick" (*William James on Psychical Research*, p. 114).

---

[53] That is, unless, as suggested above as a possibility, it was more convenient for House to start retyping Part I while James continued to write the latter part of Part II. However, if so, it may be a trifle odd that the two parts were separately paged (as seems to have been the case) whereas this would have been a necessity had Part I followed Part II.

[54] In the preserved page 107 from the original form of the typescript, no substantive changes from copy occur, and the only accidental differences are the misreadings 'ₐpsychometrically' ', 'vibrate,' and 'redivious' for 'redivivus'. In TMs the few substantive variants from the MS copy are likely to be found when House was dealing with James's interlineations and other alterations; on the whole the accidentals are relatively faithful.

At this time the copy destined for Hyslop was presumably the carbon of House's complete typescript of both parts. But also at this time it is probable that James had not finished his revision of this typescript in the ribbon copy to be sent to England, for it was not mailed until February 1. The reasons why James was not prepared to offer Hyslop his copy at the same time as the mailing to London are subject only to speculation. James's caution to Hyslop against prior publication may have had something to do with the deliberate delay since James did not altogether trust Hyslop's discretion and he may have seen no reason (the English publication being delayed, as he thought) why he should risk earlier American publication by the immediate dispatch of copy. Another problem may have been on his mind, however. Unless in a most uncharacteristic manner James had had ribbon and carbon spread before him as he read over the copy for London and so revised both sets of pages simultaneously, it is likely that in the main he revised only the copy for England as he rushed to get it in the mails[55] and thus that the carbon was in general in an unrevised state as compared with the worked-over English copy. James may have wanted to delay letting Hyslop have this copy until he had had a chance to revise it in some part, even though independently, and it is possible that he did so.

On the other hand, the textual evidence works against a hypothesis that the American *Proceedings* version was set from the carbon of the English typescript, whether or not revised. For the moment we may pass over the unique readings in E as against the agreement of A and of MS, and similar readings in A set against the agreement of E and MS. These are manifestly separate proof corrections, made independently and without reference to each other. What is significant, as illustrated by the listing in the Historical Collation in the present edition, is the very considerable amount of agreement between E and A, both in substantives and in accidentals, in their variant readings from the MS or TMs copy. In the substantives, the amount and the kind approximate the revision seen marked in the preserved typescript p. 107, with further revision in the lost retyped page that appears also in both prints. That this revision in the prints goes back to the annotation of House's typescript after it had been completed seems incontrovertible, and at first sight it would be a natural assumption that similarity of copy produced this similarity of revised readings. As remarked, however, the hypothesis that Hyslop was sent a marked carbon of the typescript depends completely upon the further hypothesis that James had taken the trouble to mark both copies with his hand revisions in the brief interval before he mailed the typescript to England. The improbability of this assumption may remain a

---

[55] Not much time elapsed between House's completion of the typescript on January 18 and the mailing on February 1 (or a day or two earlier), and in this time James also was writing his "Confidences of a Psychical Researcher" for the *American Mazazine* as well as revising the typescript. The labor of transferring his revisions to the American carbon might have seemed to him excessive and even unnecessary in this hectic period.

matter of opinion, and it can scarcely qualify as bibliographical evidence. It must be admitted that so far as the substantives are concerned, this hypothesis of similarly marked-up ribbon and carbon would produce the results observed in both prints.

However, the general agreement of the two prints in their accidentals variation from TMs and MS is another matter. It is true that if this agreement resulted from common readings in typescript and carbon, whether or not revisions, the same conditions would hold for accidentals as for substantives. The question is, whether the conditions are indeed the same. From James's revision of TMs as well as of p. 107 in the later typescript we know that he did concern himself with certain accidentals in his marking of the copy. But the accidentals variation between the two prints and the copy extends beyond what can reasonably be regarded as James's revisions and would need to be identified (if marked ribbon and carbon were the respective printers' copies) as typescript readings in which House had departed from his copy and which were not altered by James to restore the copy readings. The question thus reverts to the evidence we have about House's fidelity to the accidentals of his copy. In p. 107 he was nearly exact in following copy, but some variation may be detected in TMs although not of a very significant sort. In no sense can it be asserted that in TMs House attempted to repunctuate James's text. In a few places for consistency he supplied hyphens where James had inconsistently omitted them;[56] he makes such formal corrections as substituting a comma for James's period in MS '30th.' (276.17); he does omit the single quotes about 'Huldah' at 271.2 in a James interlineation; and at 253.14 he omitted the MS hyphen in 'spirit- | return', possibly because it occurred at the end of a line in MS. The one real revision, one might say, he makes is the necessary removal of MS comma in 'strength,' at 257.35 where it was syntactically incorrect and obscured the sense. Given this conservatism, the much more numerous punctuation changes in which E and A join against MS and TMs cannot be put down exclusively to unauthoritative changes in House's retyping but instead must contain as well a mixture of James's own alterations in the lost typescript and compositorial styling, especially in connection with such punctuation as a subordinate clause or a long phrase beginning a sentence and the like, as well as a certain amount of formal tidying up. It is worth mentioning that just such characteristics mark some of the changes that the printer made in the preserved proofs for "A Case of Automatism" (1896), and that Miss Alice Johnson, who was editing the *Proceedings*, completed the process by marking up her copy of the proofs with some frequency to make the light TMs copy punctuation heavier and more formal.

But if we accept the almost inevitable hypothesis that compositorial and editorial styling of the accidentals must have occurred in some part, we are faced with a difficult paradox. The number of cases of unique ac-

[56] See the TMs hyphen added without MS support after 'boat' (265.18), a necessary addition.

cidentals variation in either E or A, which would be the sign either of individual compositorial styling or of James's different proof-corrections, is remarkably small: the commonest and almost invariable departures from known copy involve the agreement of E and of A. Especially in Part II where joint accidentals agreement in variation from copy is found oftener in E and A than in Part I (James having in some part corrected the accidentals of the TMs Part I copy), coincidental compositorial variation could be only a very small factor. The conclusion is that the E–A agreement must go back to copy. Yet if this copy for both were the ribbon and carbon of the lost typescript, the amount of variation goes beyond that observed in House's relatively faithful typing and beyond that reasonably attributable, in addition, to James's alterations in proof: the frequent substantive agreement against the MS in E and in A would require the hypothesis that James carefully marked both copies with his alterations, in accidentals as in substantives, with a scrupulous attention to detail that is far from characteristic. There is an X-quantity in this textual situation which the hypothesis of common copy will not explain.

As a particularly significant example in Part I we may survey the treatment of a formal punctuational device, the colon-dash used to introduce an inset quotation from a sitting. MS and TMs agree in the simple colon without dash five times where E and A follow.[57] In four cases the MS–TMs agreement in the colon plus dash is followed by E and A.[58] In one case (261.19) a MS–TMs agreement in the simple colon produces a colon-dash in E and in A (this being the one instance when E–A disagree with the TMs copy by adding the dash).[59] Finally, twelve different times E–A jointly print only the colon when MS–TMs agree in the colon-dash.[60] This last statistic suggests the tendency found in E–A to remove the dash from the colon-dash combination. Adding the six cases where E–A followed TMs in omitting the dash (including 273.28) we have the use of the colon alone eighteen times, of which twelve are contrary to the TMs colon-dash, versus only five appearances in E–A of the colon-dash, in

---

[57] These occur at 259.3, 259.32, 263.38 (MS and TMs have a semicolon by mistake), 264.29, and 268.19.

[58] These occur at 259.5, 261.8, 261.13, and 262.17. In one additional instance at 273.28 TMs follows MS in a colon-dash but James deleted the dash in TMs, and E–A print the simple colon, following copy.

[59] One other divergence has no significance for the present study. At 274.20 MS had the simple colon but it was somewhat blurred and was misread in TMs as an exclamation mark. This error was followed from copy by A but was altered in E to the proper colon (the exclamation being singularly inappropriate). According to the theory for textual transmission advanced below, this divergence between E and A (the single instance in this study) would have been created when James corrected the exclamation to a colon in the E proof but overlooked it in the proof for A.

[60] These occur at 255.18, 262.7, 264.17, 265.33 (MS has two periods by mistake for the colon), 266.37, 270.3, 271.14, 271.28 (MS has a semicolon by mistake), 273.13, 276.18, 276.36, and 277.30. In three of these examples the dash has been added to the colon in MS and so was faithfully transmitted to TMs. To this list might be added the case at 270.15 where TMs follows MS in the colon-dash but in E and A only the dash appears.

which four follow TMs and one adds a dash missing in TMs. The twelve E–A changes against TMs in omitting the dash are, of course, the most significant. The question then arises, given the working hypothesis that TMs was itself retyped to furnish copy for E–A, whether the differences in treatment observed between E–A and TMs derive from this lost typescript or are attributable to some other source. Since Mr. House made the conjectured retyping, his fidelity to copy in this single punctuational formula can be tested by observing the correlation of MS with the preserved TMs. In this respect it is absolute (omitting the case of misreading at 274.20). In no case does House add or subtract a dash from whatever form he found in the MS. The 12 cases of E–A colon versus TMs colon-dash, then, can scarcely be attributed to House. If they originated in copy, they would need to have been James's ink alterations in the lost typescript. But as against the only case in which James deleted a dash in the colon-dash combination in TMs (at 273.28 where MS had the dash), one may set 271.8 (see HC entry 271.8–9) where he added a dash to a TMs colon. His lack of attention to consistency in this formula as exhibited in his revision of TMs does not suggest that he suddenly altered his practice when working over the lost general typescript and removed dashes that had been characteristic of his original composition in MS.

This evidence indicates that there is no basis for attributing the dropping of the dash in E–A to their independent and scrupulous adherence to the vagaries of their printers' copy; and, indeed, their absolute agreement in the inconsistency of this formula would require a fidelity to a typescript (whether or not marked up) that would be extraordinary in two groups of compositors accustomed to a certain amount of restyling in such formal matters that was characteristic of a printing-house. Some other explanation for this anomaly must be sought that will also help to explain the high degree of joint fidelity in the prints to other accidentals as well as to the numerous substantives that link the prints against MS, or MS and TMs when the latter is present.

The one piece of external evidence that we have is James's letter of January 20, 1909, to Hyslop, the editor of the American *Proceedings*, stating that he proposed to delay for the time being the copy of his Report 'destined' for Hyslop. It has been mentioned that at this time James was very likely concerned in the main that Hyslop observe the prohibition against publication prior to the appearance of the English *Proceedings* and hence took a step that would effectively reduce the time available to Hyslop's printers to set the type. This letter was written, one must repeat, only five days after James had completed the MS and two days after House had finished the typescript that was to be sent to England on February 1. At the time of the letter, then, James had scarcely had time to embark on very much of the considerable revision that he made in House's typescript. We do not know when he ultimately released printer's copy to Hyslop, but we do know that the first batch of English proof arrived on March 1, one month to the day after it had been dispatched, with more following on March 5, and what seems to have been the final lot of English proof on April 13. If Hyslop's printers were not able to provide proof before the diary entry on May 8, it is unlikely that James released the copy until about mid-April, a point that would coincide with what was probably the arrival of the last of the English proof which he noted in his diary as correcting on April 13. At this point it would be clear to James that all danger of prior American publication was past but that Hyslop now required copy if the planned simultaneous publication was to take effect.[61] One may conjecture, then, that Hyslop received his copy about April 15.

The important question now arises, finally, about the exact nature of this copy. If these conjectures are even approximately accurate, in mid-April James would have had available the carbon of House's typescript but in a completely unrevised state, or at best but partially revised. He would also have had in hand an extra copy of the complete English proof which had been set with all of the numerous revisions he had made in the ribbon typescript before mailing it to England. The English proof, itself further heavily revised, would by that time have been returned, starting in early March. James would have retained a spare set of these proofs, but that they would have contained all (or any) of the alterations he had marked in the master set is doubtful, and indeed on the evidence of the numerous unique readings in the English print that can be assigned to nothing other than his proof-correction, it is obvious that the extra set in his possession had not been brought into conformity with the master set before those galleys had been mailed to London.

Thus when the time came to send Hyslop his copy James had the choice of following his original plan and furnishing House's carbon typescript, which we must suppose lacked the major part if not all of the revisions James had made by hand in the ribbon typescript for England, or sending the extra set of English proof which contained these revisions and thus was in the superior state of elaboration save for the further alterations that James had made in the proof copy returned to London. It is the working hypothesis for the present edition—backed by the textual evidence—that it was indeed the uncorrected set of English proof that became the printer's copy for the American *Proceedings*. The joint readings in E and A that vary from MS, thus, can be identified largely as handwritten alterations made in the typescript before mailing, just as we see in the preserved p. 107 of a discarded leaf. The unique readings in E and in A which vary from the agreement of the other print with MS must be taken to represent alterations made in the respective proofs, the changes in A being made, of course, without reference to or, mostly,

[61] In fact, the American *Proceedings* appear to have been delayed in issue, the June date on the first page not agreeing with the July date on the cover, or with James's receipt of the news of publication from reading the July newspaper account of his Report as noted in his letter of July 14 to Bowditch. Whether before binding with the July date Hyslop had delayed June publication through some information about the proposed English date, or because James's late delivery of copy held back planned June publication is not known.

memory of alterations previously marked in the English set. It is possible that some few of these unique A readings represent James's annotation of the extra proof before sending it to Hyslop. No need exists for this assumption except that James could have looked over these proofs before sending them in and, for some reason, might have changed the format for the transcripts of the sittings. In the MS, initials of the sitters have either been added or were initially written before the different sitters' speeches with Hodgson, whereas Hodgson's discourse is usually differentiated as being without initials or any formal sign of speaker. This is the format of TMs, of course, and of E. On the other hand, in the American *Proceedings* the sitters' initials are removed and their speeches are distinguished by being enclosed in parentheses whereas Hodgson's are not. This is the more common form found in the transcripts of sittings, although some use the identifying initials. In fact, we cannot be sure that the change in format was not the result of Hyslop's editing to make the American version of the Report more conventional in form. Hyslop did add several footnotes and so worked over the proof-copy in his capacity as editor. Whether he made textual changes as well is not to be established. The change in the format is perhaps more believable as coming from him than from James, since James's motives would be obscure for taking the trouble to alter the American presentation in this manner.[62] If we take it that the extra set of the original English proofs (without transfer of the markings) served as printer's copy for the American *Proceedings*, the problem posed by the E–A agreement in many substantives variant from MS and in many accidentals—both meaningful and mechanical—is solved, and especially the singular problem of the rise in the two prints of the use of the simple colon instead of the colon-dash. The considerable removal of the dash in Part I (where we have the added evidence of TMs) is explicable as the stylistic preference of one or more of the English compositors passed on to the American. That the coincidence is so exact is, in fact, not surprising when one considers that in general compositors are more faithful in setting from already styled printed copy than from authorial typescripts. In most respects the setting of A follows the details of E in a respectful manner appropriate for a reproduction of already typeset copy and closer than one would expect from printers in two different countries each working from a copy of a typescript.

The Editorial Problem

The most serious editorial problem—the selection of the copy-text and then its treatment—could not be addressed until the transmission of the text in the preserved and in the hypothetically reconstructed lost docu-

---

62 The suppression of the initials did nothing to conceal the identities of the sitters, for whenever their initials appear they had been named in the introductory identification of the sitting. One may guess that the convention of parentheses developed as a device to speed the notetaking during a sitting. If the owners of the typed transcripts wished they could add the initials to identify the exact sitters' speeches, or they could leave the transcript as it was.

ments had been settled in accordance with a logical analysis of the evidence. If E and A had radiated independently from a typescript and its carbon, the variants in each would in theory have had equal authority and the choice of copy-text might have depended upon some arbitrary estimate of general faithfulness to the lost copy balanced against the possibility that such variants might, in theory, represent James's proof-corrections differing in each. However, the conclusion that A was set from a copy of unrevised E proof clarifies the problem of copy-text while somewhat complicating certain questions of textual authority. That is, textual variants between E and A can be taken as authoritative proof-corrections in E when A agrees with MS since A shows what the uncorrected E reading must have been. On the other hand, such variants in A when E agrees with MS cannot to the same degree authenticate the A reading since A is a terminal edition and can vary from E by printer's error as well as by James's independent proof-correction. Moreover, if the E and A texts had radiated from a common original, any reading in which they both agreed would be automatically authenticated as the reading of their lost copy and E–A variation from MS could then be evaluated as the result either of James's alterations in House's typescript or of House's straying from copy not corrected by James. As it is, however, concurrence of A with an E variant from MS is textually meaningless since A is merely a relatively faithful copy of E and hence the question of the authority of the joint E–A departures from MS rests entirely on an evaluation of the initial E reading.

All evidence indicates that the copy-text E, the English *Proceedings*, is the most carefully revised and fully proofread document in the chain of transmission. The MS is not to be ignored in questions of accidentals, particularly, but its substantives have undergone two stages of revision, in the lost typescript and again in proof. Thus as a general proposition the E text bears James's imprimatur as in all but one respect the representation of his final intentions. Only the independent proof-correction of A in a few readings can modify E's general authority. This E copy-text requires a certain amount of emendation, however, chiefly in respect to correction, the A proof-alterations being the only possible source for later authoritative revision. The copy-text, then, is emended in Part I by reference to the substantives of MS according to four situations involving TMs as a transmitter: (1) when James failed to adjust the text for reading instead of for delivery;[63] (2) when for some reason an MS word was lost in the typing of TMs;[64] (3) when an idiomatic form of a word characteristic of James has been transcribed conventionally;[65] and (4) when

---

[63] At 256.35 'readers' is drawn from MS when 'hearers' got into the textual transmission through an ink alteration of original 'readers' in TMs. At 268.2 under similar circumstances MS 'Readers' became 'People'.

[64] At 258.1 TMs seems to have skipped the MS interlineation of 'suddenly', with the result that the word was lost in all subsequent documents. At 260.32–33 TMs, followed by E, A, failed to reposition a clause as marked by a guideline in MS.

[65] At 275.2 James's own typed 'farther' became 'further' in TMs and its successors.

TMs misread the MS and became the source for a transmitted error.[66] In Part II where TMs is not present and the lost typescript copy for E was made directly from MS and then revised, substantives from MS on a few occasions emend the E copy-text (1) when the typist misread or sophisticated the MS reading;[67] or when the typist for some reason missed an MS hand alteration.[68]

More often, the characteristic or more consistent accidentals of MS are restored in Parts I and II either from observed change in TMs or hypothesized change in the lost typescript, or else by conjecture that they originated in the printer's shop. (In TMs, of course, any difference from MS not the result of James's hand alteration must be considered to be unauthoritative even when it has been 'confirmed,' so called, by retention in E–A after proofreading.[69]) Accidentals differences in E from MS are by the general law of copy-text taken to represent authority unless contrary evidence or inference is present. The strongest possible evidence in favor of an E variant derived from James's proofreading of E would occur when MS and A agree against E. In such cases the A reading would be taken to have followed the early E proof as faithfully transmitted from MS through the lost typescript. In other cases independent accidentals variation from MS in both E and A call for especial scrutiny to evaluate the possibility that the A variant represents James's proof-correction of that document in respect to an E reading that he disliked.

However, especially with joint E–A variation from MS it is only natural to assume that although many of the differences resulted from James's marking of the lost typescript, some will have originated with the E compositor(s) and with Miss Johnson, the editor.[70] With relatively neutral variants few or no grounds may exist to identify these two classes and so to deal with them systematically from a position of strength. Editorially it is necessary to sweep these together as the forms to be repro-

---

[66] At 279.5 TMs misread MS 'logical' as 'topical'. James caught this error but to repair it interlined 'tech' above deleted 'top'. Here we have a case of divided authority. The correction 'technical' makes sense and carries the authority of James's own pen. On the other hand, it is unlikely that James would have altered correctly typed 'logical' to 'technical'; hence in such a situation an editor is justified in reverting to the original authority of MS which James had forgotten (and did not consult) when he made the change of 'topical' to 'technical'.

[67] As, for example, at 307.23 where MS 'spiritistic' improperly becomes 'spiritualistic' in E–A, or at 338.24 when 'spiritual' was wrongly substituted for MS 'spiritist', or at 317.27 where MS 'new' was misread and appears in E–A as 'now'.

[68] For example, at 282.39 MS altered 'in them' to 'there' but 'in them' appears to have been typed and so was passed on to E–A. In such cases the chance exists, of course, that James changed his mind and restored the original reading by hand in the typescript.

[69] A necessary correction of an MS fault made by House in the typing must needs be adopted although in the strictest sense of the word it is unauthoritative. These are usually readings that an editor would correct on his own responsibility regardless of the copy.

[70] A few very likely originated with House, the typist, although the evidence of Part I TMs suggests that he was a generally faithful transcriber of the accidentals of his MS copy.

duced in an edited text according to the general rule of copy-text authority. Nonetheless, in various specific cases of Jamesian idiosyncrasy desirable to retain, the superior authority of the MS has been preferred to E as the assumed conventionalizing agent.[71]

Two particular accidentals conventions in E are restored to their usual MS form by a combination of reference to MS and of independent editorial emendation when MS is inconsistent. The first concerns James's distinction between single and double quotation marks. In this respect the MS is characteristic of James's other works in holograph in ordinarily distinguishing speech or quotation placed in double quotation marks and isolated words or phrases set off by single marks for emphasis or as an indication of special usage. In TMs House was usually faithful to the inconsistencies of James's MS, as in his reproduction of double quotation marks about 'Hodgson' and 'Rector' at 255.7–8 and 'spirit' at 255.11 and 13; yet he respected James's single marks, as about 'Telepathy' at 255.28 and about 'natural', 'supernatural', and 'mystical' at 255.33–34.[72] The English *Proceedings* text uses double quotation marks consistently throughout. Whether this was the usual compositorial styling or whether the E compositor(s) found only double marks in the lost typescript is uncertain. Ordinarily there would be no hesitation in attributing the alteration to the printer, given the evidence for House's following of copy. But—very curiously—in the preserved pasted-together page 107 of the original typescript James in ink altered six sets of typed single quotes about special terms to double. This deliberate alteration of his usual system suggests the possibility that throughout the whole of the typescript copy James had made the same changes. His reasons for abandoning his usual practice are obscure, but it is possible that (contrary to his custom elsewhere) he may have thought that it was simpler to adopt the conventional double quotes for publication purposes. Even though an editor may wonder whether James in fact took the considerable trouble to alter his typescript throughout in this manner, the changes in this discarded page may well give him pause as to James's final intentions. Nevertheless, the evidence of MS (and of similar manuscripts) is too strong to abandon lightly on what is, after all, only partial evidence; hence in the present text the manuscript system has been adopted in order to preserve a definite Jamesian characteristic.

The second accidentals convention to be restored and normalized is the use of a dash after a colon introducing inset matter of sitters' dialogue. The detailed statistics for the variation in E–A from TMs, already pro-

---

[71] An example is 'dialog' at 268.19. On the other hand, certain of James's simplified spellings, such as 'thru' and 'thoro', and lower-cased adjectives such as 'english' are not consistent in his manuscripts, and the E standard spelling has been allowed to stand.

[72] In MS James typed 'natural' with single quotes but he added the single quotes to the two other words by hand. After a start with double quotes it would seem that at 255.28 James reverted to his usual pattern: his use of single marks is repeatedly confirmed not only in holograph sections but added by hand, frequently, in his typed sections.

vided, suggest strongly that in Part I the 12 removals of the dash in E were compositorial styling. Despite his inconsistency, what James's own preferences were in this manuscript is sufficiently indicated by his use in Part I of the colon-dash combination fourteen times versus his use of the colon alone in only six instances.[73] Stronger grounds are furnished in Part II where MS contains twenty-one examples of the colon-dash versus only four of the simple colon. One of these, at 300.18 was added by hand when no punctuation appeared in James's original typed copy. Of these twenty-one cases, E–A follow the dash only once (348.29), this in an internal use which did not introduce inset matter. In two cases of an E–A colon the MS is wanting (332.35, 342.34), and in one case (348.34) the bridge words do not appear in MS. Given these figures, especially for Part II, it grows increasingly unlikely that James removed all of these dashes in proof or that he deleted them in House's copy.[74] Since regularization of such small matters in the accidentals is editorially desirable, dashes have been supplied, chiefly from MS but also as editorial emendations when MS itself failed to add the dash.

The TMs of Part I has no independent authority in its originally typed text since this derived directly from the preserved MS. However, the revisions that James made by hand in ink in TMs acquire authority as representing his later intentions. With only a few exceptions these were passed on to E through the lost intermediate typescript and so are adopted as part of the copy-text. Whether by inadvertence or for some other cause a handful of James's revisions seem not to have been transcribed in the intermediate typescript and so do not appear in E. If one grants that the odds do not favor James reverting in his working-over of the lost typescript or in the E proof to the original MS–TMs reading, these hand alterations in TMs contain an authority that must be preserved by emendation of the copy-text. One of the most interesting of these unique TMs alterations is James's change in ink of original typed 'heard' to the more precise 'had a letter' (271.22). Also, at 277.25 James's ink-interlined 'certain' was not passed on to E.[75]

Whether or not the textual hypothesis be accepted that the American *Proceedings* text derives from the original state of the E proof before James revised it, two postulates must be adopted. First, when A follows MS (or TMs) but E substantively diverges, the unique E verbal reading must ordinarily be retained when it is not an assumed compositorial

[73] At 261.19 where E, A have a colon-dash but TMs only a colon, it seems reasonably clear that James added the dash in the typescript made from TMs. Also worth noting is the addition of a dash in ink to a typed colon without dash at 255.18.

[74] It is interesting to observe the complete agreement of A in this formula with its copy, the E proof. This is not only a sign of compositorial fidelity to printed copy but also some indication, perhaps, that A approved of E's general styling of the colon alone in such situations.

[75] Other examples may be cited, such as the change from TMs 'Hand' to 'The hand' (258.11), the non-observance of a blank line marked by James at 268.9+, and the omission in E of 'below' added by hand at 258.29. This last is not the sort of deletion that one would expect James to make in later copy.

error since it will then represent an authoritative change that James made in the E proof. Second, a unique A substantive reading where E agrees with MS will ordinarily represent James's alteration of the American proof in all cases when the A variant does not appear to be an error. In the first case the copy-text authority of E is confirmed; in the second, the copy-text must be emended from A in order to include James's chronologically final intentions. As recorded in his diary, James read the two proofs at different times: the English proof between March 1 and April 13, but the American proofs only from May 8. The relatively few proof changes in A as compared with E attest to James's failure to mark a second set of proofs to bring them into conformity with those he had returned to England.[76] Abundant evidence is preserved that James was congenitally unable to reread copy or work over proofs without incorporating stylistic improvements that appealed to him. It is no surprise, then, that A contains a certain number of variants from the copy-text E that must be adopted as final intentions, even though they were made without reference to the proof-alterations marked for E.

The doctrine of final intention meets difficulty only when there is a chance that James's autograph revisions in proof were misread or that in his haste he was not correctly following the original line of his thought and so wrote-in an inappropriate alteration. Such a case seems to occur in footnote 3 at 262.38 when the addition of 'influenced' in A seems authentic but the alteration a little above from E 'coherent' to A 'correct' seems inapposite and a probable error. However, most A substantive variants appear to be authoritative. At 256.28 the change in A from MS-E 'poor' to 'bad' is explicable as an avoidance of the weak repetition of 'poor' from 256.27. The plural 's' added to the singular 'content' at 257.2 and to 'record' at 257.19 seem to be of a piece as confirming each other and they may be marginally preferable. The addition of 'for' at 258.1 might be thought to be sophistication were it not for the omission of 'very' in the next line.[77] Contiguity, as well as content, reinforces A 'stir each other up' at 356.15 for MS, E 'reinforce each other' and then of 'inert' for 'comparatively inert' shortly at 356.16 and 'effects' for 'activity' then at 356.19.

[76] It is speculation, of course, that since the Report had been written for the English Society, the influence and prestige of which was considerably greater than the reorganized American group under Hyslop, James was less concerned to see that all of the latest refinements that he had introduced into the English proofs were repeated in the American copy. In fact, we have no evidence as to the date at which he decided to substitute the early form of the English proofs (which would contain the numerous revisions he had made in the typescript) for the unrevised carbon of the typescript as printer's copy for Hyslop. This selection of the proofs was at least a considerable improvement over what was probably his original plan to reserve the typescript carbon for Hyslop.

[77] One could be suspicious of the omission of 'very' in the same line as the insertion of 'for' as a printer's device for justifying the line without running over were it not that such hanky-panky is usually reserved for economical alteration made in plates. Since the line in question ends a paragraph, a run-over caused by the insertion of 'for' would have posed no problem in galley-proof.

The doctrine of final intention may present problems when the same unsatisfactory reading in MS is altered differently in E and in A. For example, at 358.24–26 MS reads, with weak repetition, 'The bodies (including of course the brains) of Hodgson's friends who came as sitters are of course parts of the material universe which carry effects of his acts', which seems to have been the unaltered reading of the underlying typescript also. In the E proof James let the first 'of course' stand and altered the second to 'naturally'; but in A he reversed the order and allowing 'of course parts of' to stand he altered 'of course the brains' to ', naturally, the brains'. Since the proof of A was corrected later than the proof for E, chronology would suggest that the A reading should be adopted as James's final intention. But, textually, chronology has no bearing on the present question, for it is clear that the A proof-revision was made without specific memory of, and certainly without reference to, the E proofs and their changes. Under such circumstances an editor has little choice but to evaluate each variant and to adopt what seems to him to be critically the superior revision. If a choice seems arbitrary, as in the special case of 358.24–26, it may be thought wiser to give the preference to E as a general policy, it being the document that was most carefully and thoroughly revised.

Ordinarily, agreement of E or of A with MS in case of variance decides which is the true revision, but there are sections in which A and E disagree where MS is wanting and it is in these areas that editorial discretion must needs operate. In these circumstances the principle of 'radical revision'[78] may be helpful, as in the A variant 'me, she' for E 'me. She' at 347.34. In this case A seems to preserve Mrs. Piper's less than impeccable syntax (presumably copied in the typescript from her own letter) whereas E appears to be James's own smoothing-out in the proof-reading. Surface correctness should no doubt yield in this case to authenticity. Nevertheless, various of the unique A readings must be viewed with caution when no special reason seems to exist for their presence. On some few occasions the evidence suggests that they are more likely to represent A errors instead of James's alterations in proof. For example, at 308.11 the italic '*wish*' in MS is found in roman in A; but reference to the transcript of the sitting that James used shows that the word was underlined there. Under these circumstances it may seem more likely that the A compositor neglected to follow the italic than that James substituted roman in proof. Another example occurs at 315.9 where in the phrase 'gave me' in MS, E one sees that A omitted 'me'. This might be thought to represent a Jamesian tinkering with the style in the A proof (as it still may), but when one sees that the transcript of the sitting on which James's 'me' is based also has the 'me', the odds seem to favor an inadvertent omission in error by the A compositor.

The American *Proceedings* were edited by James Hyslop, who had taken a close interest in the sittings and had himself held various séances

[78] For a discussion of 'radical revision', with examples, see the textual introduction to *Some Problems of Philosophy*, WORKS, pp. 265–266.

with Mrs. Piper. It was only natural, therefore, that he should add a few explanatory or supplementary footnotes, signed, to James's text. Although not present in E, of course, these have nevertheless been incorporated in the present eclectic text since presumably James approved them in the A proof. A reasonable doubt may persist about the change of format in A by which the initials used as speech-prefixes for the sitters as in E are removed and sitters are distinguished from Hodgson only by the enclosure of their speeches in parentheses. Whether Hyslop or James was responsible for this difference is not to be determined. It has been remarked above that the A format more closely resembles the usual form of transcripts of sittings, and this may have had something to do with its adoption in A. It is perhaps not pertinent to the A format that James's early intention, as shown in the MS, agreed with the A formula but during the course of writing out the MS he changed his mind and adopted the initialed prefixes. At any rate, this particular difference between A (and also MS) and E is not recorded in the list of variants in the Historical Collation, where a full account would have overburdened the apparatus to no significant textual benefit.

38. THE CONFIDENCES OF A "PSYCHICAL RESEARCHER" (1909).

Copy-text: (P⁴) "The Confidences of a 'Psychical Researcher,' " *American Magazine*, 68 (October 1909), 580–589 (McD 1909:7).

Under the title of the article in the *American Magazine* came the editorial description: 'In which the author, after twenty-five years of "dabbling" in "Psychics," states his conclusions, goes on record, and describes the field wherein he thinks the greatest scientific conquests of the coming generation will be achieved. | By WILLIAM JAMES | Author of "The Powers of Men," etc. | Illustrated with Crayon Portraits by William Oberhardt'. The portraits are of James himself (legend: 'For thirty-five years Professor of Philosophy at Harvard College. One of the greatest living psychologists'); Giovanni Schiaparelli (legend: 'The Italian astronomer who discovered the so-called "canals" in Mars, and who is a well-known psychical researcher'); Eusapia Paladino (legend: 'The Neapolitan Medium, under observation for twenty years, who has convinced Schiaparelli and Lombroso of her genuineness, and who cheats in a bare-faced manner whenever she gets an opportunity'); Cesare Lombroso (legend: 'The famous criminologist who originated the theory that there is a definite criminal type, the born criminal, that may be distinguished from other men by physical stigmata. He is Paladino's most distinguished convert'); Mrs. Piper (legend: 'One of the most notable living mediums. Her control, "Rector," is a most impressive personage, who discerns in an extraordinary degree his sitter's inner needs, and is capable of giving elevated counsel to fastidious and critical minds'); James Hervey Hyslop (legend: 'Professor of Logic and Ethics at Columbia University, an ardent psychologist who believes that there is a well-defined "will to communicate" evinced by the spirit world'); and Richard Hodgson (legend:

'Secretary and Treasurer of the American Branch of the Society for Psychical Research up to the time of his death in 1905. Many of Mr. Hodgson's associates in psychical research assert that since his death, intelligent and characteristic communications have been received from him through various mediums'). Ten editorially inserted descriptive section headings are scattered through the text. These are recorded in the list of Emendations.

After finishing the manuscript of his Piper-Hodgson Report on January 15, 1909, and starting to work over the typed copy which he received on January 18, James began the "Confidences" on Sunday, January 24, 1909, according to his diary note: "Began article on psychics for american magazine." On the same day he wrote to his brother Henry: "Shall start this morning an article on Spiritism for the American Magazine— it will be queer if after all these years I have *nothing* to say!" (#2957). To Thomas Sergeant Perry James wrote on January 29 about the Piper-Hodgson Report and added, "I am also now engaged in writing a popular article, 'the avowals of a psychical researcher,'[79] for the 'American Magazine,' in which I simply state without argument my own convictions, and put myself on record. I think that public opinion is just now taking a step forward in these matters—*vide* the Eusapian boom! and possibly both these *Schriften* of mine will add their influence" (*Letters*, II, 320). On Sunday, January 31, the diary noted briefly, "I finish Article *on [*ab. del.* 'of'] psychics for American Mag." The next day, Monday, February 1, James wrote in his diary that he had mailed the Hodgson-Piper Report to Miss Johnson (of the English Society for Psychical Research) "& article to Phillip's", the editor of the *American Magazine*. Finally, on July 14, 1909, in answer to Henry Pickering Bowditch James wrote: "No, my dear fellow, with the publication of my report on Mrs. Piper's Hodgson Control, and with that of an article to appear in the American Magazine next fall my *active* connexion with psychical research ceases" (#812).

The original holograph manuscript of the "Confidences" is preserved in the Houghton Library as MS Am 1092.9 (4545). It consists of forty leaves (now mounted) of wove typewriter paper $10\frac{1}{2} \times 8''$ watermarked L. L. Brown. Discarded trials are found on the versos of fols. 19, 21, 23, and 33, their contents transcribed in the apparatus following the list of Alterations. The manuscript itself is heavily revised in ink, much of this alteration coming during the course of composition, with a few final touches given to the revisions in pencil. The leaves are numbered, centered (fol. 6 is foliated in the upper right corner), except for the first as follows: [1] 2–13 14,15 (joint numbering) 16–36 37ᵃ 37ᵇ 38–40. The unique placement of the number for fol. 6 (363.7-22 'of . . . harder') appears to have no significance since the text seems regular in every respect

---

[79] James seems to have had trouble finding a satisfactory title. His manuscript shows that originally he titled it 'The State of Mind of one "psychical researcher"', which he then altered to 'One "psychical researcher" at the Confessional' before adopting the final form.

with what precedes and follows. The number for fol. 9 (364.8–23 'tures,— . . . at') is written over an original 8, but the misnumbering is inadvertent, for, again, no signs of textual disruption appear.

However, two parts of the manuscript show rewriting and revision. The first begins with nine deleted lines at the foot of fol. 12 (see Alterations entry 365.19). Condensation and rewriting of four lost leaves, except for a discarded trial for part of this area now found on the verso of fol. 21, is indicated by the paraphrase of the deleted matter now found on fol. 14,15 (joint) and the fact that fol. 16 contains only four lines before joining the text on fol. 17. The evidence suggests, then, that the revision started on fol. 13 (365.20–33 'Fraud . . . yielding to'), continued on fol. 14,15 (365.33–366.7 'suggestion . . . divide') and ended on fol. 16 (366.7–10 'opinion . . . writes,'), its final words, ' "I regret," he writes, " ' requiring the deletion on fol. 17 of the first two words of the paragraph starting the page, 'I regret' and the insertion of double quotation marks before the following 'that'. It would seem that the foliation 15 was added, after a comma to 14 when the condensation of the text left only four lines on fol. 16 to join with already written fol. 17.

The revision that creates a fol. 37^b after 37^a is relatively simple. Heavily revised six lines at the foot of 37^a were deleted (see Alterations entry 374.2–8) and then simply rewritten on inserted fol. 37^b (the superior ^{a} being added to the preceding original 37) to join with the last undeleted text on 37^a and the start of fol. 38. This rewritten text comprises 374.2–8 'to work . . . conclusion'.

Since the manuscript was mailed to the editor of the *American Magazine* on February 1, 1909, the day after it was completed, it seems clear that the magazine set up the article direct from the manuscript and that there was insufficient time for a typescript to be made, even if James had contemplated the expense. The hasty composition (the whole being finished in a week, with doubtless some of the time also devoted to final revision of the typescript of the Piper-Hodgson Report) is manifested not only by the heavy alteration of the manuscript pages, slightly more than James usually revised but also by the almost unexampled amount of rewriting that he must have performed in proof. The entries in the Historical Collation witness more than the usual number of second thoughts, including the addition of a paragraph (374.35–375.2 'What . . . world?') just before the end.

Under the title "Final Impressions of a Psychical Researcher" the essay was reprinted in the posthumous collection *Memories and Studies* (1911), edited by Henry James, Jr. The substantive differences are recorded in the Historical Collation but none appears to be the result of authoritative revision.

Although the manuscript is extant and complete, the very particular care that James gave to the magazine proofs and the number of substantive alterations that he made (which presumably also included a number of accidentals alterations) make the selection of the magazine print the natural copy-text. On the other hand, little doubt can exist that either the printer or the magazine editor (and perhaps the typist if it chanced that the editor ordered a typescript of this difficult manuscript to be made in his office) not only styled James's characteristic spellings and use of lower case for adjectives of nationality but also materially increased the amount of parenthetical punctuation beyond that customary for James. Thus the manuscript has been called on at various occasions to restore Jamesian authority to certain accidentals variants in the copy-text print that are taken not to represent James's proof-alterations but instead editorial interference. In some few cases Jamesian spellings found in the manuscript have been allowed to stand in their normalized copy-text form. Thus spellings like 'tho', 'altho', and 'thru' have been given their conventional form on the simple ground that they are not consistent in themselves within this manuscript and are as likely to be spelled 'though', 'although', and 'through'. However, with consistently characteristic spellings like 'connexion' and 'honour' the copy-text has been emended to James's preferences in the manuscript. James often used a preterite in 't' as in his manuscript 'Lookt' at 369.30 and 'publisht' at 370.31. These are the only examples of the two words in the manuscript and hence James's consistency cannot be tested. Various other similarly pronounced words received the conventional -ed ending in the manuscript, and hence inconsistency and resulting normalization might be argued. On the other hand, although the evidence is not wholly on one side, James's letters do indicate that on the whole 'lookt' and 'publisht' were his ordinary forms. For this reason they have been admitted as characteristic emendations from the manuscript.

39. A Possible Case of Projections of the Double (1909).

Copy-text: (P[43]) "A Possible Case of Projections of the Double," *Journal of the American Society for Psychical Research*, 2 (April 1909), 253–254 (McD 1909:11).

Emendations

Every editorial change from the copy-text is recorded for the substantives, and every change in the accidentals as well save for such silent typographical adjustments as are remarked in A Note on the Editorial Method. The reading to the left of the bracket, the lemma, represents the form chosen in the present edition, usually as an emendation of the copy-text. (A prefixed superior [1] or [2] indicates which of any two identical words in the same line is intended.) The sigil immediately following the bracket is the identifying symbol for the earliest source of the emendation, followed by the sigla of any later agreeing documents or by a plus sign should all succeeding documents agree with the earliest source. Readings in parentheses after sigla indicate a difference in the form of the source from that of the emended reading to the left of the bracket. A semicolon follows the last of the sigla for emending sources. To the right of this semicolon appear the rejected readings of the copy-text and of any other recorded documents, followed by their sigla; a plus sign is used after a sigil when all later documents agree with its reading. A number of the essays in this volume were reprinted in *Memories and Studies* (M&S), edited by Henry James, Jr. (1911), and in *Collected Essays and Reviews* (CER), edited by R. B. Perry (1920); however, M&S and CER are not noted in the list of Emendations except when they are emending agents or rejected substantives. When an emendation needs to be made that is not drawn from any authoritative document, the editor's own alteration marked as H (Harvard) is used. The word *stet* after the bracket calls special attention to the retention of a copy-text reading. It may be employed to key a Textual Note, as marked by an asterisk before the page-line number. In a quotation it may indicate that James's version (differing from the source in some respect) has been retained in the edited text. It may also be used in rare instances to indicate that a possibly questionable or unusual reading has been retained in the text. When the phrase *et seq.* occurs, all subsequent readings within the essay are to be taken as agreeing with the particular feature of the reading being recorded (save for singulars and plurals and inessential typographical variation, as between roman and italic), unless specifically noted to the contrary by notation within the entry itself, or by the use of *stet* within the apparatus. Readings grouped together with multiple page-line references may also be concerned with only the particular feature being recorded and not with inessential types of variation.

For convenience, certain shorthand symbols familiar in textual notation are employed. A wavy dash ($\sim$) represents the same word that appears before the bracket and is used exclusively in recording punctuation or other accidental variants. An inferior caret ($_\wedge$) indicates the absence of a punctuation

Emendations

mark (or of a footnote superscript) when a difference in the punctuation constitutes the variant being recorded, or is part of the variant. A vertical stroke (|) represents a line ending, sometimes recorded as bearing on the cause of an error or fault. A hand symbol (☞) before a page-line reference draws attention to the parenthetical listing of additional lines where the forms of emendation are identical. The mark § indicates that an MS variant is included wholly or in part in an alteration in the manuscript, the description of which has been removed to the Emendations list from the list of Alterations in the Manuscripts. The double dagger (‡) indicates that the variant in the MS is part of a larger alteration not easily transferable to the Emendations, the details of which can be found in the Alterations in the Manuscripts. Quotations within the text are identified in Professor Skrupskelis' Notes. The sigil WJ/followed by the appropriate symbol (as WJ/P34) indicates James's autograph revisions, usually found in his file sets or private copies of journal articles, and in books, proofs, or clippings.

1. Review of *Planchette*, by Epes Sargent (1869)

The copy-text is BDA, "Planchette," *Boston Daily Advertiser*, March 10, 1869 (McDermott 1869:1).

4.14 trance] H; tranee BDA (*error*)

2. Circulars of the American Society for Psychical Research (1884–1906)

a. Organization (1884)

The copy-text is P31, "Circular No. 1: Issued by the Council," *Proceedings of the American Society for Psychical Research*, 1 (July 1885), 2–4 (McD [1885:6]).

6.26 Hollond] H; Holland P31 (*error*)   6.27 Noel] H; Noël P31

d. Circular Requesting Financial Support (1892)

The copy-text is RPJ, "Psychical Research," *Religio-Philosophical Journal*, n.s. 2 (May 7, 1892), 793 (McD [1892:12]).

11.12 spurious] H; spursious RPJ   11.39 6] H; 5 RPJ (*error*)
       (*error*)   12.13 to] H; to | to RPJ (*error*)

5. Letter on Professor Newcomb's Address before the American Society for Psychical Research (1886)

The copy-text is P36, "Professor Newcomb's Address before the American Society for Psychical Research," *Science*, 7 (February 5, 1886), 123 (McD [1886:7]).

20.5 -transference] H; -transferrence   20.5-7 'the . . . blindfold.'] H; *db. qts.*
      P36 (*error*)   P36

Emendations

7. Review of *Phantasms of the Living*, by Edmund Gurney et al. (1887)

The copy-text is P³⁶, "Phantasms of the Living," *Science*, 9 (January 7, 1887), 18–20 (McD 1887:1).

24.15 *Living*] H; living P³⁶
25.34 mythopoetic] H; mythopoietic
    P³⁶ (*error*)

27.6,8 -transference] H; -transferrence
    P³⁶ (*error*)

9. Review of "The Second Report on Experimental Psychology," by Charles Sedgwick Minot (1889)

The copy-text is P³¹, "Note to the Foregoing Report," *Proceedings of the American Society for Psychical Research*, 1 (March 1889), 317–319 (McD 1889:2). Reference is made to P³², "Third Report on Thought-Transference," *Proceedings of the Society for Psychical Research* (English), 1 (July 1883), 165.

34.26–27 inevitably . . . noticed] P³²;
    have been inevitably noticed P³¹
34.29 B. . . . S.] *stet* P³¹; Blackburn . . .
    Smith P³²
34.32 hesitating] P³²; hesitant P³¹

34.40 ²over] *stet* P³¹; which enveloped
    P³²
35.10 signalling] *stet* P³¹; such signal-
    ling Minot
35.12 Smith] *stet* P³¹; Smith in the
    reproduction of drawings Minot

10. Notes on Automatic Writing (1889)

The copy-text is P³¹, "Notes on Automatic Writing," *Proceedings of the American Society for Psychical Research*, 1 (March 1889), 548–564 (McD 1889:3).

38.40 -247] H; -249 P³¹
39.30 write.] H; ~ ∧ P³¹ (*error*)

40.27 -Hypnotic] H; *l.c.* P³¹
42.33 Triginta] H; Tringinta P³¹

11. The Census of Hallucinations (1889–1897)

b. Letter on Publicity for the Census (1890)

The copy-text is P³, "To the Editor of the American Journal of Psychology," *American Journal of Psychology*, 3 (April 1890), 292 (McD 1890:6). Two emendations are drawn from P⁸, *Boston Medical and Surgical Journal*, 122 (May 15, 1890), 484–485.

59.8 responsible] P⁸; reponsible P³
    (*error*)

59.12 committee] P⁸; commitee P³
    (*error*)

e. Review of Ueber die Trugwahrnehmung, by Edmund Parish (1895)

The copy-text is P³⁴, *Psychological Review*, 2 (January 1895), 65–67 (McD 1895:1).

64.18 ordinary] H; ordininary P³⁴
    (*error*)

64.30 delirium] H; delirum P³⁴ (*error*)
64.38 114] H; ii P³⁴ (*error*)

Emendations

f. Review of the "Report on the Census of Hallucinations" (1895)

The copy-text is P[34], *Psychological Review*, 2 (January 1895), 69–75 (McD 1895:3). Reference is made to P[32], the English report published in the *Proceedings of the Society for Psychical Research*, 10 (August 1894), 25–422.

66.38 for] H; of P[34]
67.26 have] *stet* P[34]; have then P[32]

68.26 seem] H; seems P[34]

h. Final American Report: Letter to Henry Sidgwick (1896)

The copy-text is ALS, James's holograph letter to Henry Sidgwick (H. 25 in the archives of the Society for Psychical Research) (McD [1897:15]). Reference is made to TMs, the carbon typescript of the same letter (bMS Am 1092.9 [3761]) and to Congr., the letter as partially reported in *Dritter Internationaler Congress für Psychologie in München*, 4 (1897), 392–394. The autograph alteration in TMs is designated as WJ/TMs.

74.2 Mass.] TMs,Congr.; ∼ ∧ ALS
74.6;76.12,14 and] TMs; & ALS
74.8 to . . . own∧] WJ/TMs (*tr. by guideline which deletes orig. comma aft. 'own'); aft. 'coincidence,' ALS
74.13 number] TMs,Congr.; No. ALS
74.20 and] TMs,Congr.; & ALS
74.30–31 hallucinations] TMs,Congr.; halls. ALS
74.32 of] TMs,Congr.; of of ALS (*error*)

75.3 *Proceedings*] TMs; *rom.* ALS; Proceedings (S. P. R.) Congr.
75.17 suppose] Congr.; Suppose ALS (*error*); TMs
75.24 they] Congr.; They ALS (*error*); TMs
76.2 scientific."] H; ∼ ∧" ALS (*error*)
76.14 2Miss∧] TMs; ∼ . ALS (*error*)
76.15 1have] TMs; has ALS
76.17 yours,] TMs; ∼ ∧ ALS
76.18 Wm.] TMs; ∼ ∧ ALS

i. Review of Zur Kritik des telepathischen Beweismaterials *and* Hallucinations and Illusions, *by Edmund Parish (1897)*

The copy-text is P[34], *Psychological Review*, 4 (November 1897), 657–658 (McD 1897:10). The notation WJ/P[34] indicates two handwritten corrections in James's private *Psychological Review* file.

77.28 affect] H; effect P[34] (*error*)
78.21 answerers] WJ/P[34]; answers P[34] (*error*)

78.22 answerer] WJ/P[34]; answer P[34] (*error*)

---

12. A Record of Observations of Certain Phenomena of Trance (1890)

The copy-text is P[32], "A Record of Observations of Certain Phenomena of Trance," *Proceedings of the Society for Psychical Research*, 6 (December 1890), 651–659 (McD 1890:3). Reference is made to RPJ, *Religio-Philosophical Journal*, n.s. 1 (January 17, 1891), 535–536.

88.4 raræ] H; raræ P[32], RPJ (*error*)

---

13. What Psychical Research Has Accomplished (1892)

The copy-text is P[10], "What Psychical Research Has Accomplished," *Forum*, 13 (August 1892), 727–742 (McD 1892:1). Reference is made to WB, *The Will to Believe*; for the details of the relationship, see The Text of *Essays in Psychical Research*. The note (*em.*) indicates emendation of the first printing of WB by the present editor to the form shown in the lemma.

90.8   Stainton$_\Lambda$] WB; Stanton- P10 (*error*)
90.25   a] H; *à* P10; WB (*em.*)
94.16   Relph's] H; Ralph's P10 (*error*)
94.23   II$_\Lambda$] H; I. P10 (*error*)
97.21   subconscious] WB; sub-conscious P10

98.13   itself] *stet* P10,WB; *om.* Myers
98.16   2in] Myers; *om.* P10;WB (*em.*)
104.16 extra-] H; ~ [*space*] | P10 (*error*)
104.22 "Étude ... fixes,"] H; "*Études sur un Cas d'Aboulie et d'Idées Fixes*," P10
104.25 *Salpêtrière*] H; *Salpétrière* P10

14. REVIEW OF *Science and a Future Life*, BY FREDERIC W. H. MYERS (1893)

The copy-text is P25, *Nation*, 57 (September 7, 1893), 176–177 (McD 1893:13).

107.2   Macmillan] H; Macmilman P25 (*error*)
108.31 as yet recognised] *stet* P25 (recognized); yet realised Myers
108.35–36   , many ... elsewhere,] *stet* P25; (~ ... ~) Myers
108.38–39   the departed] *stet* P25; men departed Myers

109.3   phenomena] *stet* P25; phenomena briefly noticed above Myers
109.7   bulk] *stet* P25; vast bulk Myers
109.24 repeat] *stet* P25; repeat the experiments Myers
110.3   30–36] H; 32, 35 P25

15. LETTER TO THE EDITOR OF *Mind* ON WARD'S REVIEW OF *Briefer Course* (1893)

The copy-text is P24, "To the Editor of *Mind*," *Mind*, n.s. 2 (January 1893), 144 (McD 1893:14).

111.4   are "a] H; "are a P24
111.10 scientists] *stet* P24; 'scientists'—a

name ugly enough for anything—Ward

17. TWO REVIEWS OF *Apparitions and Thought-Transference*, BY FRANK PODMORE (1895)

a. The copy-text is P34, *Psychological Review*, 2 (January 1895), 67–69 (McD 1895:2).

115.1   *Thought-*] H; ~ $_\Lambda$ P34
115.2–3   Science] H; Scientific P34

116.12 chance-] H; ~ $_\Lambda$ P34

18. TELEPATHY (1895)

The copy-text is J, *Johnson's Universal Cyclopædia* (New York: A. J. Johnson, D. Appleton, 1895), 8, 45–47 (McD 1895:16).

120.1   encouragement] H; encouragment J (*error*)
123.25 Schmoll] H; Schmall J (*error*)

123.25 Schrenck-] H; Schrenk- J
125.11 Dariex] H; Daniex J (*error*)
125.11 Tolosa$_\Lambda$] H; ~ , J (*error*)

Emendations

The copy-text is TMs, James's autograph revised typescript. Reference is made to P[32], "Address by the President," *Proceedings of the Society for Psychical Research*, 12 (June 1896), 2–10 (McD 1896:1) and to P[36], "Address of the President before the Society for Psychical Research," *Science*, n.s. 3 (June 19, 1896), 881–888. The sigil TMs(u) denotes the copy as it was originally typed; TMs(c) identifies James's alterations. Intermediate stages between Tms(u) and TMs(c) are indicated as TMs(u,c) or two stages of revision before the final text was reached as TMs(u,c,c). All alterations are recorded in the Emendations list and are to be taken as made in ink unless otherwise stated.

127.0   Address . . . Research] P[36] (Research*); The President's Address._∧ (*om. fn.*) TMs; ADDRESS BY THE PRESIDENT, _∧ | PROFESSOR WILLIAM JAMES. (*om. fn.*) P[32]

127.6   no disputed] TMs(c); neither TMs(u)

127.6   or] TMs(c); nor TMs(u)

127.7   all . . . it.] TMs(c); so forth. TMs(u)

127.7   steps_∧] TMs(c); ~ , TMs(u)

*127.10   pointing] P[36]; pointing now TMs,P[32]

127.11   no chance . . . leave] TMs(c); no way except by leaving TMs(u); nothing except to leave TMs(u,c)

127.13   ocean] TMs(c); water TMs(u)

127.13   not unaware] TMs(c); well aware TMs(u)

128.6   dozen . . . more] TMs(c); eleven years TMs(u)

128.9   *coup de grâce*] P[32,36]; coup de grace TMs

128.9   months] P[32,36]; years TMs

128.11   minds_∧] TMs(c); ~ , TMs(u)

128.11–12   *et seq. Proceedings*] P[32,36]; *rom.* TMs

128.18   gaps.] P[32,36]; ~ ' . TMs (*error*)

128.22   consistently] TMs(c); consistent | TMs(u)

*128.27   rigorously] P[32,36]; vigorously TMs

128.28   own,] TMs(c); ~ _∧ TMs(u)

128.30   *anybody*,] TMs(c); anybody_∧ TMs(u)

128.31   very] TMs(c); *om.* TMs(u)

128.40   rigor] TMs(c); vigor TMs(u)

129.2+   *et seq. space*] P[32]; *no space* TMs,P[36]

129.3   ¶ If] TMs(c); If (*no ¶*) TMs(u)

129.9   in.] P[32,36]; ~ , TMs (*error*)

129.9   Professor] P[32,36]; Prof. TMs

129.10   called] TMs(c); *om.* TMs(u)

129.11   causes] TMs(c); causes of the phenomenon TMs(u)

129.17   all—] P[32,36]; ~ , TMs

129.18   out] TMs(c); out when TMs(u)

129.18–19   below which] P[32,36]; but below that TMs

129.19   no . . . occur.] TMs(c); no conflagration whatever. TMs(u,c); there is no conflagration. TMs(u)

129.19   whether] P[32,36]; *om.* TMs

129.27   mind,] TMs(c); ~ _∧ TMs(u)

129.27   fail] TMs(c); well fail TMs(u)

129.27   convince] TMs(c); convince as it now stands TMs(u)

129.29   But . . . lacking] TMs(c); Or without TMs(u)

129.29–30   we . . . that] TMs(c); *om.* TMs(u)

129.30   are] TMs(c); may be TMs(u)

129.31   all] TMs(c); any TMs(u)

129.35   regards,] TMs(c); *typed aft. del.* typed 'respects_∧' TMs(u)

129.36   we can] TMs(c); I think we may TMs(u)

129.37   intelligent and] P[32,36]; *om.* TMs

129.37–38   work—I . . . advisedly—] P[32,36]; work, TMs

129.38   Report] P[32,36]; *l.c.* TMs

129.39   the . . . report,] P[32,36]; its conclusion_∧ TMs

130.2   ¹that] TMs(c); *om.* TMs(u)

130.2   still] P[32,36]; *om.* TMs

130.5–6   true, . . . unlikely,] P[32]; P[36] (seems); true; TMs

544

130.7 So neither] P32,36; Neither TMs

130.7 then] TMs(c); *typed aft. del. typed* 'alone,' TMs(u)

130.8 is . . . that] TMs(c) ('neccessary' *in error*); need TMs(u); is it neccessary TMs(u,c)

*130.8–9 definitely convinced] P36; convinced definitively TMs(u); definitively convinced TMs(c),P32

130.10 'Miss X∧'] H; ∧ ~ ~ ∧∧ TMs; "~ ~ ." P32; ' ~ ~ .' P36

130.12 one),] TMs(c); ~)∧ TMs(u)

130.23 ears. The] P32,36; ~ ; the TMs

130.24 usual] TMs(c); ordinary TMs(u)

130.27 facts] TMs(c); cases TMs(u)

130.28 holds] P36; still holds TMs,P32

130.31–32 so . . . Nature] TMs(c); the universal course of nature TMs(u)

130.32 altogether] TMs(c); *om.* TMs(u)

130.35 (as . . . do)] P32,36; *om.* TMs(u); , ~ . . . ~ , TMs(c)

130.35–36 great induction] TMs(c); psychological induction TMs(u); natural law TMs(u,c)

130.36 of psychology] P32,36; *om.* TMs

130.37 and other senses] P32,36; *om.* TMs

131.4 formed] TMs(c); found TMs(u)

131.7 strong,] TMs(c); ~ ∧ TMs(u)

131.9 proof] P32,36; evidence TMs

131.10 consistency;] P32,36; consistence, TMs(u); ~ , TMs(c)

131.11 speak. So] P32,36; ~ ; so TMs

131.12 lot;] P32,36; ~ , TMs

131.12 , as . . . see, ['that' *del.*]] TMs(c); *om.* TMs(u)

131.14 through] TMs(c); through the TMs(u)

131.15 sense] TMs(c); *typed aft. del. typed* 'the senses.' TMs(u)

131.16 for] TMs(c); if TMs(u)

131.16 to] TMs(c); *om.* TMs(u)

131.21 so- . . . 'rigorously scientific'] P36; scientific TMs(u); ~ - . . . " ~ ~ " TMs(c),P32

131.21 disbeliever,] TMs(c); ~ ∧ TMs(u)

131.23 *has*] TMs(c); has TMs(u)

131.29 prove] TMs(c); prove that TMs(u)

131.31 which] TMs(c); that TMs(u)

131.34 an explanatory] TMs(c); a TMs(u)

131.34–35 admitting] TMs(c); *om.* TMs(u)

131.35 such knowledge] TMs(c); it TMs(u)

131.37 rigorously] TMs(c); so-called rigorously TMs(u)

131.38 mind,] TMs(c); ~ ∧ TMs(u)

131.39 2be] TMs(c); were TMs(u)

131.40 may] TMs(c); might TMs(u)

131.40 collectively . . . weight.] TMs(c) (*typed in proper space*); collectively carry *rigorously [typed ov.* 'heavy weight'] scientific mind *may [ov. illeg.*]' TMs(u) (*typed between lines*)

132.1 ∧ in truth∧] TMs(c); *om.* TMs(u); , ~ ~ , P32,36

132.1 easily] TMs(c); easily TMs(u); conceivably TMs(u,c)

*132.1 over reach] TMs(c); overreach TMs(u),P32,36

132.7 review] TMs(c); views TMs(u)

132.7 question] TMs(c); matter TMs(u)

132.8 matters] TMs(c); the matter TMs(u)

132.8 them;] TMs(c); it, TMs(u); ~ , P32,36

132.11 the Paladino-] TMs(c); Eusapia Paladino∧ TMs(u)

132.14 Eusapia Paladino] TMs(c); The Eusapia episode TMs(u)

132.19 hastily] TMs(c); too hastily TMs(u)

*132.19 'the Island∧'] *stet* TMs; " ~ island," P32; ' ~ ~ ,' P36

132.20 the] TMs(c); when the TMs(u)

132.23 Whatever . . . documents] P36; Few documents TMs(u); Few documents, whatever their upshot TMs(u,c); Few documents, (whatever were the upshot of such a study, TMs(u,c,c); Whatever were . . . documents TMs(c),P32

132.29 feet∧] P32,36; ~), TMs

132.30 on] TMs(c); in TMs(u)

132.30 credit-] P32; ~ ∧ TMs,P36

132.34 Myers'] TMs(c); Myers's TMs(u)

132.34 these subjects] P32,36; this subject TMs

133.1–2 we . . . see] TMs(c) (*typed normally at head of page*); we begin to see TMs(u) (*written in ink at foot of shortened preceding page and then del.*)

133.2 begin] TMs(c); began TMs(u)

133.3 rudest] TMs(c); sadest TMs(u)

133.4 apparition,] TMs(c); ~ ∧ TMs(u)

133.4 Myers'] TMs(c); Myer's TMs(u)

133.16 way] TMs(c); temper TMs(u)

133.19 impossible"; yet] H; ~ ." Yet TMs; ~ ;" yet P32,36

133.22 at] P32,36; to TMs

133.22–23 (reading . . . subject)] P32,36; , ~ . . . ~ , TMs

133.24 cases] P32,36; cases at least TMs

133.24 Phelps-] P32; ~ ∧ TMs,P36

133.24 Andover,] TMs(c); ~ ∧ TMs(u)

133.25 *McClure's Magazine*] P32,36; Mc Clure's magazine TMs

133.26 Nevius's] TMs(c); Nevis's TMs(u)

133.27 ∧*Amherst Mystery*∧] H; "Amherst Mystery" TMs; " ~ ~ " P32; ' ~ ~ ' P36

133.28 Scotia∧] P36; ~ ; TMs; ~, P32

133.28 (New York, 1888);] P32,36; *om.* TMs

133.29 Mass.,] H; ~ .∧ TMs; *om.* P32,36

*133.29–30 recorded . . . 129);] P32,36; *om.* TMs

133.30 XXII,] H; ~ ., P32,36

133.30 Sharpe's] TMs(c); Sharp's TMs(u)

133.33–34 *Annales . . . Psychiques*] P32,36; *Revue Psychique* TMs

133.34 (p. 86)] P32,36; *om.* TMs

133.35 , near Hull,] P32,36; ∧ ~ ~ ∧ TMs

133.35 *Proceedings*,] P32,36; Proceedings∧ TMs

133.35 Vol. . . . pp.] P32,36; ~ ∧ . . . ~ ∧ TMs

133.37 by many persons] P32,36; *om.* TMs

134.1 touched the ground] P32,36; *om.* TMs

134.6 itself] P32,36; *om.* TMs

134.6 freak] P32,36; possible freak TMs

134.9 'disturbance'] P36; *om.* TMs; " ~ " P32

134.14 (if . . . any)] P32,36; , ~ . . . ~ , TMs

134.15 out; whilst] P32,36; ~ . Whilst TMs(u); ~ , ~ TMs(c)

134.15 will get] P32,36; get TMs(u); gets TMs(c)

134.16 that] TMs(c); which TMs(u)

134.25 Nature] TMs(c); *typed aft. del. typed* 'natural life' TMs(u)

134.28 rationalism,] TMs(c); ~ ∧ TMs(u)

134.34 mechanical] P36; mechanical one TMs; mechanical view P32

134.35 view] P32,36; one TMs

134.37 rationalism,] P32,36; ~ ∧ TMs

134.38 insubstantial illusion] TMs(c); unsubstantial appearance TMs(u); unsubstantial *appearance* TMs(u,c)

135.2 heart∧] P32,36; ~ , TMs

135.5 *untruth*] P32,36; untruth TMs

135.8 in fact] P36; *om.* TMs,P32

135.8 unchecked] TMs(c); philosophic TMs(u)

135.10 sufficient] TMs(c); general TMs(u)

135.10 -theory;] P32;P36(∧ ~); - ~ , TMs

135.16 *Journals*] P32,36; *rom.* TMs

135.20 training] TMs(c); *om.* TMs(u)

135.22 beside] TMs(c),P32; besides TMs(u),P36

135.23 perennially] TMs(c), P32,36; perenially TMs(u)

135.23–25 *facts . . . be;*] P36; *facts;* TMs; ~ . . . ~ , P32

135.26 —at . . . easy—] TMs(c),P32; , ~ . . . ~ , TMs(u),P36

135.26 much] P32,36; *om.* TMs

135.27 a] TMs(c); *om.* TMs(u)

135.31 , discontinuous∧] P36; *om.* TMs; , ~ , P32

135.32–33 seems to be] P32,36; is TMs

135.35 *may*] TMs(c); may TMs(u)

135.35 find∧ . . . find∧] P32; ~ , . . . ~ , TMs(u),P36; ~ , . . . ~ ∧ TMs(c)

136.1 both] P32,36; *om.* TMs

136.2–3 either . . . or] TMs(c); *om.* TMs(u)

136.15 Universe] P32,36; *l.c.* TMs

136.18 century] P32,36; *cap.* TMs

*136.21 Mill's∧] P36; *om.* TMs; ~ , P32

136.22 innocent] P32,36; *naive* TMs

136.25 the . . . latter] P32,36; our progeny TMs(u); their progeny TMs(u,c); their grandchildren TMs(c)

136.30–32 The . . . from] P32,36; Nothing in the spirit and principles of Science need hinder its TMs

136.32 successfully] TMs(c); *om.* TMs(u)

136.34 encounter, . . . have,] P32,36; and concretely experience TMs

136.35–36 thinking,] TMs(c); ∼ ∧ TMs(u)

136.37 one of the] TMs(c); as TMs(u)

136.37 elements] TMs(c); element TMs(u)

136.38 And this] P32,36; The TMs(u); And the TMs(c)

136.38 ∧ on Science's part∧] P32; *om.* TMs; , ∼ ∼ ∼ , P36

136.39 this] P32,36; the TMs

136.39–40 in . . . our world] P32,36; this TMs

137.3 own] TMs(c); *om.* TMs(u)

137.4 it] P32,36; it TMs

137.7 If] TMs(c); If∧ however∧ TMs(u); If, however, TMs(u,c); But if TMs(u,c,c)

137.9 'perspectiveless,'] P36; " ∼ , " TMs,P32

137.9 purpose;] P32,36; ∼ , TMs

137.10 definite] P32,36; definitive TMs

20. PSYCHICAL RESEARCH (1896)

The copy-text is P34, "Psychical Research," *Psychological Review*, 3 (November 1896), 649–652 (McD 1896:3). Reference is made to ALS, James's holograph letter to Henry Sidgwick (H. 25 in the archives of the Society for Psychical Research), to TMs, the carbon typescript of the same letter (bMS Am 1092.9 [3761]), and to Congr., the letter as partially reported in *Dritter Internationaler Congress für Psychologie in München*, 4 (1897), 392–394. TMs and Congr. have been collated for substantives only.

139.2 them] *stet* P34; them all Cattell

139.27 sea-] H; ∼ ∧ P34

140.30 them] ALS,TMs,Congr.; *om.* P34 (*error*)

140.33 numbers] ALS,TMs,Congr.; number P34 (*error*)

21. A CASE OF PSYCHIC AUTOMATISM (1896)

The copy-text is TMs, the typescript drawn up under James's supervision and containing corrections and revisions in his hand, found at the Society for Psychical Research. Reference is made to Pf, a set of galley proofs marked by Alice Johnson (AJ), and to P32, "A Case of Psychic Automatism, Including 'Speaking with Tongues,'" *Proceedings of the Society for Psychical Research*, 12 (December 1896), 277–297 (McD 1896:4). The sigil TMs(u) denotes the copy as originally typed; TMs(c) indentifies James's ink alterations (but occasionally those by Alice Johnson [AJ] or by an unknown hand designated as [printing hand]). The sigil Pf(u) denotes the original reading in the galley proofs; Pf(c) identifies Alice Johnson's alterations. All alterations (except corrected typographical errors) in TMs are to be found in the Emendations list.

143.0.2 Tongues,"] TMs(c) (∼ ."); ∼ ·∧ TMs(u)

143.0.3 by . . . Baron] TMs(c) (By) (AJ); *om.* TMs(u)

143.0.4 Professor] Pf(c)+; *om.* TMs,Pf(u)

143.1 '70s] H; '70-s TMs; seventies Pf+

143.8–9 volubility∧ . . . expression∧] TMs(c); ∼ , . . . ∼ , TMs(u)

143.13　St.] Pf+; Saint TMs

*143.13–14　which . . . from] P32; in which . . . been an adept, if we may believe TMs,Pf

143.18　all] TMs(c); *om.* TMs(u)

144.1　published; a] TMs(c); ∼ . A TMs(u)

*144.2　Evangel] Pf(c) (['Saint' *del.*] Evangel [AJ]); P32; Saint Evangel TMs(u); Aunt Serena TMs(c),Pf(u)

144.3–145.1　witness;[1] and correspondence] TMs(c) (Correspondence); ∼ . [¶] Correspondence TMs(u)

144.5　"*November* 26*th*, 1894.] TMs(c) (AJ) (Nov. 26th∧); *typed as subscription but del.* TMs(u)

144.7　Baron].] H; ∼ .] TMs+

144.16　'Hymn to Egypt,'] Pf+; " ∼ ∼ ∼ ," TMs

144.18　Some (*no* ¶)] TMs(c); ¶ TMs(u)

144.21–22　(Signed) . . . follows:] TMs(c) (AJ) (follows:—); *om.* TMs(u)

144.22　follows:∧] H; ∼ :– TMs(c)+

144.23　*April*] TMs(c) (*rom.*); Chicago, April TMs(u)

144.24　DEAR . . . JAMES] Pf+; dear Prof. Janes TMs (*error*)

144.24　. . . Mr.] TMs(c)+; [¶] Your kind letter came promptly to hand. It would have given me pleasure had I been able to answer you in detail sooner, but my time has been very fully occupied with the Greenacre work in New York and in this city, so that this is really the first quiet time in which I could take up the matter. [¶] Mr. TMs(u)

144.24,38;145.35,40　[Le Baron]] TMs(c); ∧Waters∧ TMs(u)

144.24　[our camp]] TMs(c); Eliot TMs(u)

144.25　—— ——] TMs(c) (*ab. del.* '—— Journal'); Boston Traveler TMs(u)

144.25　[our]] TMs(c); the Greenacre TMs(u)

144.25　been] TMs(c); been a student of Occultism abroad, and TMs(u)

144.27　[Shelter Island]] TMs(c); Greenacre TMs(u)

144.34　psychologized] Pf+ (psychologised); psycologized TMs (*error*)

144.37　and . . . over] TMs(c) *del. but restored*

144.44　journeys] TMs(c); journeys necessitated by his position on the newspaper TMs(u)

145.5　Baron,] TMs(c); ∼ ∧ TMs(u)

145.5　39] TMs(c); [39] TMs(u)

145.6　February] TMs(c) (∼ .); Feb. TMs(u)

145.11　vocal∧] TMs(c); ∼ - | TMs(u)

145.14　slow,] TMs(c); ∼ ∧ TMs(u)

145.17　analogous] TMs(c); similar TMs(u)

145.20　Rommany] TMs(c); Romanny TMs(u)

145.23　finally] TMs(c); at last TMs(u)

145.39　write.] TMs(c); write. [¶] May I ask you to consider this communication a personal one? I appreciate very much your kind interest in the subject, and your efforts to solve these perplexing but interesting problems. TMs(u)

145.42　upon.] TMs(c); upon. [¶] Our work at Greenacre last year was in every way helpful and successful, and we plan to continue it the coming Summer. May I ask if you are to be near home during July or August, and if so, if you would not be willing to come and give us an informal talk upon psychology? I would not ask you to prepare any lecture, but rather to speak to us in an informal way of experiences which you have had both here and abroad. [¶] Hoping that it may be possible for us to have you with us, I remain, TMs(u)

145.43　—— — ——.] TMs(c) (*insrtd. for del.* '[Saint Evangel]'); Sarah J. Farmer | Eliot, Maine. TMs(u) (*fancy script*)

146.2　rare∧] TMs(c); ∼ , TMs(u)

146.5–6　identification, . . . disguised;] Pf(c)+; ∼ ; . . . ∼ , TMs,Pf(u)

146.7　be] TMs(c); be all TMs(u)

146.7　, and] TMs(c); ∧ with TMs(u)

146.8   are correct] TMs(c) ('are' *ov.* 'all' *or* 'and'); *om.* TMs(u)

[*begin* Le Baron]

146.18 *et seq.*   Evangel] P³²; Saint Evangel TMs(u); Aunt Serena TMs(c) (AJ),Pf

*146.19   a . . . re-incarnation,] Pf(c)+; and TMs(u); a believer in re-incarnation, and a medium TMs(c), Pf(u)

146.23   ¹of] TMs(c); *om.* TMs(u)

*146.24   the hope] TMs(c) (printing hand); *om.* TMs(u)

146.31   tree] TMs(c) (printing hand); *om.* TMs(u)

146.40   force] TMs(c); psycho-automatic force TMs(u)

147.4–5   Oh . . . . Mutterings . . . . One (*no* ¶)] TMs(c); ¶ *each* TMs(u)

147.9   experience_∧] TMs(c); ∼ , TMs(u)

147.11   for] TMs(c) (printing hand); *om.* TMs(u)

147.14   desired] TMs(c) (possibly printing hand); they desire TMs(u)

147.15   James_∧] Pf+; ∼, TMs

☛147.19   Evangel] P³²; the Saint Evangel TMs(u); Aunt Serena TMs(c), Pf (*also* 147.28,31,37;148.11)

147.25   lips,] TMs(c); ∼ _∧ TMs(u)

147.28–29   He . . . . The . . . . In (*no* ¶)] TMs(c); ¶ *each* TMs(u)

147.28   lay] TMs(c); laid TMs(u)

147.39   nerves,] TMs(c); ∼ _∧ TMs(u)

148.3   Evangel] P³²; the [*insrtd. by* printing hand] Saint Evangel TMs(u); Aunt Serena TMs(c),Pf

*148.4   man.²] Pf(c)+; ∼ ._∧ (*om. fn.*) TMs,Pf(u)

148.11   occasion,] TMs(c); ∼ _∧ TMs(u)

148.18   light_∧] Pf+; ∼ , TMs

148.22   considered] TMs(c); considered by her TMs(u)

148.23   She had been] TMs(c); She believed the ring to have been her property during a former incarnation as an Egyptian Vestal Virgin. The ring was to be restored to her—by occult means when the *sublimation [*alt. fr.* 'sublimization'] of her soul was completed, and she had finally realized the purpose of her

incarnations. This time had come. St. Evangel was perfected. She believed herself now born into the world as a mystic fully equipped to assist the people of the earth up to a plane of consciousness, as serene, pure, elevated, peaceful and wonderful, as her own. Her mother's spiritualistic revelations to her constantly confirmed her as to her mission in life. [¶] As to the ring, St. Evangel was TMs(u)

148.24;160.39   this] TMs(c); the TMs(u)

148.24   talisman,] TMs(c); ∼ _∧ TMs(u)

148.25   gem] TMs(c); occult gem TMs(u)

148.25   Egypt,] TMs(c); ∼ _∧ TMs(u)

148.26   certain . . . gentleman] TMs(c) (american); merchant of Lowell, Mass., TMs(u)

148.27   Orient] Pf+; *l.c.* TMs

148.29   genuineness] TMs(c); authenticity and genuineness TMs(u)

148.29   spirit] TMs(c); holy spirit TMs(u)

148.32   work] TMs(c); holy work TMs(u)

148.33   sceptic] TMs(c); skeptic TMs(u)

149.10   automatism] TMs(c); spontaneity TMs(u)

149.13   from] TMs(c) (printing hand); *om.* TMs(u)

149.19   or_∧] Pf+; ∼ , TMs

149.29   message] TMs(c); messages TMs(u)

149.29   to] TMs(c) (printing hand); *om.* TMs(u)

149.30   Riverhead, . . . 6th_∧ and 8th,] Pf+; ∼ _∧ . . . 6, & ∼ _∧ TMs

149.38   September] Pf+; Sept. TMs

150.2   One] Pf+; one TMs

150.4–10   (in . . . me.] TMs(c) (typed cancel slip); the deific modes of address of civilization vary in the ratio that the consciousness of a people insert their own concrete value into such modes, I did not deem it impossible for the ['psycho-' *del.*] automatism to assume a deific rhetorical style. TMs(u) (*orig. typing del.*)

150.31 style] TMs(c); communicating *style* TMs(u)

150.34 deific object] TMs(c); *ital.* TMs(u)

150.35 style] TMs(c); *ital.* TMs(u)

150.37–38 to . . . . On] TMs(c) ('there' *aft. del.* 'til I had'); I would interest the citizens in the journal I was representing and "write up" the town. On TMs(u)

151.1 night,] Pf+; $\sim$ $_\wedge$ TMs

151.2 brotherhood";–] TMs(c); $\sim$" $_{\wedge\wedge}$ TMs(u)

151.24 my] TMs(c); the TMs(u)

151.28 form . . . style] TMs(c); style . . . form TMs(u)

*152.3 ¶ From] Pf(c)+; Among other things, this arose from the principle common to poodle and philosopher, that startling phenomena are interpreted by us as having a personal bearing, when we are distinctly told by any intelligence—we believe in— that they have. From TMs,Pf(u)

152.5 mystic$_\wedge$] TMs(c),Pf(c),P32; mystico- TMs(u); mystic- Pf(u)

152.8 withdrew] TMs(c); abandoned TMs(u)

152.17 -itself';] Pf+ (- $\sim$ "); - $\sim$;' TMs

152.24 ONE TWO THREE] TMs(c); One Two Three TMs(u)

152.31;154.33 seventy-] Pf+; $\sim$ $_\wedge$ TMs

153.8 whom] TMs(c); *om.* TMs(u)

153.15 later,] TMs(c); $\sim$ $_\wedge$ TMs(u)

153.17 princely-] Pf(u); $\sim$ $_\wedge$ TMs,Pf(c),P32

153.19 knew] TMs(c); knew the TMs(u)

153.19 Evangel] P32; ['the' *del.*] Saint Evangel TMs;Pf(u); Aunt Serena Pf(c)

154.2 -automatism$_\wedge$] TMs(c); - $\sim$, TMs(u)

154.7–29 The . . . love!] TMs(c); *each sentence a separate* ¶ TMs(u)

154.7 darkness,] Pf+; $\sim$ $_\wedge$ TMs

154.27 him] TMs(c) (printing hand); the [*illeg.*] TMs(u)

154.31 automatic-] TMs(c); mystico- TMs(u)

154.34–38 I . . . word!] TMs(c); *each sentence a separate* ¶ TMs(u)

154.40 any] TMs(c); a TMs(u)

155.4 which$_\wedge$ is] TMs(c); $\sim$, as TMs(u)

155.12 thee,] TMs(c); $\sim$ $_\wedge$ TMs(u)

155.16–17 phenomenon] TMs(c); phenomena TMs(u)

155.17 *dédoublement*] TMs(c); *doublement* TMs(u)

155.24 wilful] TMs(c); ordinary wilful TMs(u)

155.34 -automatism,] TMs(c); - $\sim$ $_\wedge$ TMs(u)

156.2 -mystic] TMs(c); -mystico TMs(u)

156.5 automatism] TMs(c); psycho-automatism TMs(u)

156.30 I] TMs(c); *om.* TMs(u)

156.30 construed] TMs(c); construed it TMs(u)

157.37 they] TMs(c); [*illeg. word del.*] they TMs(u)

157.40 Greeting: I] TMs(c); $\sim$: | [¶] I TMs(u)

158.2 sentences] TMs(c); sentence TMs(u)

158.4 were] TMs(c); was TMs(u)

158.6 *cæteris*] TMs(c),Pf(c),P32; *cæterus* TMs(u),Pf(u)

158.7 and . . . again$_\wedge$] Pf(c)+ (here, again,); since it constantly operated on the principle, which as I said before, is common to poodle and philosopher, to interpret startling and unusual phenomena as having some probable personal bearing. Hence, again$_\wedge$ TMs,Pf(u)

158.13 Monday . . . 1st,] Pf+; $\sim$ $_\wedge$ Oct. $\sim$ $_\wedge$ TMs

158.14 for] TMs(c); to 'write up' TMs(u)

158.16 interpretations] Pf+; interpretat|tions TMs (*error*)

◀158.17 The . . . tongue. Te] TMs(c); *The unknown tongue. [heading]* [¶] Te TMs(u) (*similar* 158.21,25,27,29,32,34;159.5,12,18,24, 30,36;160.3,10,12,14,21)

160.24 love of] TMs(c); love is of TMs(u)

160.24 Love-] Pf+; $\sim$ $_\wedge$ TMs

160.27 great] TMs(c) (printing hand); *om.* TMs(u)

160.29 In the] TMs(c) (AJ?); To TMs(u)

160.29 subsequently to] TMs(c); to subsequently TMs(u)

160.30 theories,] TMs(c); authoritative dogmas or theories‸ TMs(u)

☞160.32 *First Theory.* The] TMs(c); *First Authoritative Dogma or Theory [heading] [¶] The* TMs(u) (*similar* 160.35,38;161.5,7,12,16,19,26)

161.12 foregoing‸] H; ~ , TMs+

161.15 source,] TMs (c); ~ ‸ TMs(u)

162.13–14 translation:‸] H; ~ :— TMs+

162.23 mano.] Pf+; ~ ‸ TMs

162.36 'worked up'] H; " ~ ~ " TMs+

163.1 very] TMs(c); very very TMs(u)

163.1 cent‸] TMs(c); ~ . TMs(u)

163.4 angora;] H; ~ , TMs+

163.7 bono] Pf(c)+; bono, bobo TMs,Pf(u)

163.29 visited] TMs(c); visited and sketched TMs(u)

163.35 -Aryan] Pf+; *l.c.* TMs

163.36 cyclopædia] H; cyclo.*[pedia] [*typed intrl.*] TMs; cyclopœdia Pf(u); Cyclopœdia Pf(c)+

163.37 -Aryan] TMs(c); - ryan TMs(u)

163.38 mystic‸] TMs(c); mystico- TMs(u)

164.4 part.] Pf(c)+; part. | Le Baron TMs,Pf(u)

[*end Le Baron*]

22. Telepathy: Controversy with Titchener on Lehmann and Hansen (1896–1899)

a. Review of "Ueber unwillkürliches Flüstern," by F. C. C. Hansen and Alfred Lehmann (1896)

The copy-text is P[34], *Psychological Review*, 3 (January 1896), 98–99 (McD 1896:6).

167.5 Lehmann] H; Lehman P[34] (*error*)

167.6 –530.] H; ~ , P[34] (*error*)

b. Review of "Involuntary Whispering Considered in Relation to Thought-Transference," by Henry Sidgwick (1897)

The copy-text is P[34], *Psychological Review*, 4 (November 1897), 654–655 (McD 1897:8).

169.8 hypnotized] H; hynotized P[34] (*error*)

169.27 -transference] H; -tranference P[34] (*error*)

c. Letter: Lehmann and Hansen on the Telepathic Problem (1898)

The copy-text is P[36], "Lehmann and Hansen 'on the Telepathic Problem,' " *Science*, n.s. 8 (December 30, 1898), 956 (McD 1898:4). Reference is made to P[44], "Messrs. Hansen and Lehmann on the Telepathic Problem," *Journal of the Society for Psychical Research*, 9 (October 1899), 113–120 (McD 1899:6).

170.17 Lehmann] P[44]; Lehman P[36] (*error*)

d. Letter: Lehmann and Hansen on Telepathy (1899)

The copy-text is P[36], "Messrs. Lehmann and Hansen on Telepathy," *Science*, n.s. 9 (May 5, 1899), 654–655 (McD 1899:4a). Reference is made to P[44],

"Messrs. Hansen and Lehmann on the Telepathic Problem," *Journal of the Society for Psychical Research*, 9 (October 1899), 113–120 (McD 1899:6).

171.19 Messrs. . . . H.] *stet* P36;   telepathic 'problem' (*Philos. Studien*,
  Lehmann and Hansen upon the   1895, XI., 471) Titchener

e. Letter: Telepathy Once More, No. I (1899)

The copy-text is P36, "Telepathy Once More," *Science*, n.s. 9 (May 26, 1899), 752–753 (McD 1899:4b). Reference is made to P44, "Messrs. Hansen and Lehmann on the Telepathic Problem," *Journal of the Society for Psychical Research*, 9 (October 1899), 113–120 (McD 1899:6).

172.24 12th] P44; 10th P36 (*error*)

25. LETTER ON MRS. PIPER, THE MEDIUM (1898)

The copy-text is P36, "Mrs. Piper, 'the Medium,'" *Science*, 7 (May 6, 1898), 640–641 (McD 1898:2).

185.4 unto] Cattell; into P36   185.5 but] Cattell; and P36

26. REVIEW OF "A FURTHER RECORD OF OBSERVATIONS OF CERTAIN PHENOMENA
OF TRANCE," BY RICHARD HODGSON (1898)

The copy-text is P34, *Psychological Review*, 5 (July 1898), 420–424 (McD 1898:7).

188.18 'full-] H; ∧ ~ - P34 (*error*)

27. FREDERIC MYERS'S SERVICE TO PSYCHOLOGY (1901)

The copy-text is P32, "Frederic Myers's Service to Psychology," *Proceedings of the Society for Psychical Research*, 17 (May 1901), 13–23 (McD 1901:1). Reference is made to P29, "Frederic Myers's Service to Psychology," *Popular Science Monthly*, 59 (August 1901), 380–389 and to the reprint in M&S, "Frederic Myers' Services to Psychology," *Memories and Studies*, edited by Henry James, Jr., pp. 143–170 (McD 1911:2), which have been collated for substantives only.

195.13,39 Myers's] P29; Myers' P32   198.10–11 Obsessive] P29, M&S;
                                           Obssessive P32 (*error*)

28. REVIEW OF *Human Personality and Its Survival of Bodily Death*,
BY FREDERIC W. H. MYERS (1903)

The copy-text is P32, *Proceedings of the Society for Psychical Research*, 18 (June 1903), 22–33 (McD 1903:3).

208.8 etc.∧ . . . phenomena),] H; ~ .,   213.8 -generalised] H; -generalized P32
  . . . ~)∧ P32   213.34–37 It . . . involved] *stet* P32;
213.3 stepping-] H; ~ ∧ | P32   *all ital.* Myers

213.37 involved] Myers; used P³²
213.39 path of externalisation] *stet*
P³²; *ital.* Myers

214.3 morbid] *stet* P³²; *ital.* Myers

29. Telepathy Once More, No. II (1903)

The copy-text is P²⁵, "Telepathy Once More," the publication under Correspondence in the *Nation*, 76 (April 23, 1903), 330 (McD [1903:13]).

217.9 *a*] H; *à* P²⁵

217.21–22 "Observations . . .
-Transference,"] H; ₍ ~ . . . ₍ ~, ₍
P²⁵

34. A Case of Clairvoyance (1907)

The copy-text is P³¹, "A Case of Clairvoyance," *Proceedings of the American Society for Psychical Research*, 1 (January 1907), 221–236 (McD 1907:10).

235.1–2 'George . . . logs.'] H; *db.*
qts. P³¹ (*error*) (*similar*
235.6,8,8–10,11–12;243.4)
235.4 "Mr.] H; ₍ ~ P³¹ (*error*)

235.11–13 "The . . . body."] H; ₍ ~
. . . ~ ·₍ P³¹ (*error*)
237.18 Mascoma] H; Muscoma P³¹
(*error*)
242.12 *bottom?*"] H; ~ ?₍ P³¹ (*error*)

37. Report on Mrs. Piper's Hodgson-Control (1909)

The copy-text is E, "Report on Mrs. Piper's Hodgson-Control," *Proceedings of the Society for Psychical Research*, 23 (June 1909), 2–121 (McD 1909:6). Reference is made to MS (or MS[T]), a combination manuscript and typescript found in the James Collection (bMS Am 1092.9 [4544]), to TMs (and TMsᵇ), the carbon typescript of Part I, found in the archives of the American Society for Psychical Research, and to TMsᵃ and TMsᶜ, typescripts found with MS at Harvard. (For details, see The Text of "Report on Mrs. Piper's Hodgson-Control.") Reference is also made to A, "Report on Mrs. Piper's Hodgson-Control," *Proceedings of the American Society for Psychical Research*, 3 (July 1909), 470–589 and, for substantives only, to CER, *Collected Essays and Reviews*, edited by R. B. Perry, pp. 484–490 (McD 1920:2). The note (sitting) refers to the original transcripts of the sittings preserved in the archives of the Society for Psychical Research and the American Society for Psychical Research.

253.1–2 Summary . . . *Introduction*]
A (I. Introduction.); *om.* MS,TMs,E
*§253.9 'control'] MS(T) (*db. qts. alt.*
to sg. qts.); ₍ ~ ₍ TMs+
253.12 *primâ facie*] MS(T); prima facie
TMs; *prima facie* E,A
§253.13 'spirit'] MS(T) (*db. qts. alt.*
to sg. qts.); ₍ ~ ₍ TMs+
253.14 spirit-] MS(T); ~ ₍ TMs+

*§253.15 69] *stet* E; 75 [*penc. ab. del.*
ink 'ooo'] MS(T);TMs,A
*§254.5 Until . . . 1906,] MS(T)
(*added*); *om.* TMs+
254.11–12 'Control' . . . 'Rector.'] H;
no qts. MS(T),TMs; *db. qts.* E,A
254.15 favored] MS(T),TMs,A;
favoured E
*§254.23 a] MS(T) (*alt. fr.* 'an almost');
om. TMs+

*§255.7–8 'Hodgson' . . . 'Rector,'] H;
  db. qts. [*added*] MS(T)+

*255.18 follows:—] MS(T) (*dash added
  end of line*);TMs; ~ :∧ E,A

256.2 *et seq. Part* I H.-] H; ~ ·∧
  MS(T)+ (*except* 263.37)

§256.16 exists:] MS(T) (*colon alt. fr.
  period*);TMs; ~ . E,A

*256.28 bad] A; poor MS(T),TMs,E

*§256.35 readers] MS(T); hearers
  [*alt. fr.* 'readers'] TMs+

257.2 contents] A; content
  MS(T),TMs,E

257.8 Everyone] MS(T),TMs; Every
  one E,A

257.16 him—] MS(T),TMs; ~ ,— E,A

*257.19 records] A; record
  MS(T),TMs,E

257.26 of] A; *om.* MS(T),TMs,E

257.26 advantage] A; advantage of
  MS(T),TMs,E

*§258.1 suddenly] MS(T) (*insrtd.*);
  om. TMs+

258.1 for] A; *om.* MS(T),TMs,E

258.2 an] A; a very MS(T),TMs,E

258.6 HODGSON] MS(T); Hodgson
  TMs+

§258.11 The hand] TMs ('The' *insrtd*;
  'h' *of* 'hand' *ov.* 'H'); Hand
  MS(T),E,A

§258.24 "A 1 l"] MS(T) (*ab. del.*
  ' "All" [*db. qts. added but del. in
  error*]'); "All" [*db. qts. added*] TMs+

*258.25 A . . . "L"] MS(T); "A", "B"
  and an "L" TMs; "A," "B" and "L"
  E,A

§258.28 (For (*no* ¶)] TMs (*orig.* ¶ *but
  run-on by guideline*); ¶ MS(T)
  (*doubtful*);E,A

§258.29 below] TMs (*intrl.*); *om.*
  MS(T),E,A

259.3 follows:—] H; ~ :∧ MS(T)+
  (*similar* 259.32 [TMsa–b];
  264.29;265.22;268.19)

259.11 That] MS(T); *l.c.* TMs+

*259.13 Than . . . divine.] *stet*
  MS(T)+

259.14 practising] MS(T),TMsb;
  practicing TMsa,E,A

259.30 did. . . .] MS,TMsb,A; ~ ∧ . . .
  TMsa,E

*260.1 AM] MS(T), TMsb; am
  TMsa,E,A

*§260.24 Miss D——] MS(T) ('D.'
  intrl.); Miss D TMs+

260.28 probably] A; *om.* E

260.31 ah.] H; ~ , MS(T) (*error*); ~ ,
  (which written words indicate
  laughter.) TMs;E,A (laughter).)

§260.32 ah,"] MS(T) (*sg. qt.; comma
  added*); ~ ∧' TMs; ~ ∧" E,A

*260.32–33 which . . . laughter).]
  MS(T) (~ .]); *found aft.* 'ah.'
  [260.31] TMs+

262.6–7 lifelike] MS(T); life-|like
  TMs; life-like E,A

262.15 everything.] H; ~ ∧ | MS(T)+

*262.24 Q] *stet* MS(T)+

*262.29 G.D.] *stet* MS(T)+

262.37 endeavored] A; endeavoured E

262.38 influenced] A; *om.* E

263.4 mind. . . .] MS(T); ~.∧ TMs+

263.4 *absolutely*] MS(T); *rom.* TMs+

§263.6 George] TMs; George *[Dorr]
  [*intrl.*] MS(T);E,A

*263.22 singly,] MS; simply, TMs,E;
  simply∧ A

263.26 birthday∧] MS(T); ~, TMs+

*§263.36 B∧] MS(T) (*period del. when
  'L.' added*); ~, TMs+

263.38 wrote:—] H; ~ ; MS(T),TMs
  (*error*); ~ :∧ E,A

264.16 24th∧] MS(T); ~, TMs+

264.28 29th∧] MS(T); ~, TMs+

267.24–25;268.25 someone]
  MS(T),TMs; some one E,A

*§268.2 Readers] MS(T); People
  [*ab. del.* 'Readers'] TMs+

§268.5 incidents∧ . . . one∧] MS(T)
  (*commas carbon del.*); ~ , . . . ~,
  TMs+

268.9+ space] TMs (*marked* 'blank
  line');A; *no space* MS(T) (*new page*);E

268.10 recite] A; cite MS(T),TMs,E

268.19 dialog] MS(T),TMs; dialogue
  E,A

*268.20 return] *stet* MS(T)+

*269.27 up] *stet* MS(T),E,A

269.29 spirit.5 | 5It . . . promise."] A;
  ~ ·∧ (*om. fn.*) MS(T),TMs,E

269.41;310.27,37 connexion] H;
  connection A

270.2 1906] H; 1905 MS(T)+

270.5 *et seq. Part* I anyone] MS(T),TMs; any one E,A

*271.2 Huldah] *stet* MS(T)+

271.15 Ella.] MS (T),TMs; ～ ? E,A

§271.22 wife_∧] TMs (*comma del.*); ～ , [*comma insrtd.*] MS(T);E,A

*§271.22 had a letter] TMs (*ab. del.* 'heard'); heard MS(T),E,A

*273.6–7 Hodgson . . . disappointment,] *stet* MS+

§273.12 W.R.] TMs (*intrl.*); *om.* MS,E,A

273.27 Yes. Good] MS; ～ , ～ TMs,E; ～, good A

274.6 Myers . . . J.] TMs; Myers. MS; Myers. See below. E,A

274.14 prophecied] MS,TMs; prophesied E,A

*§274.14–16 Newbold . . . N.'s] *stet* E,A; *another friend [*ab. del.* 'Newbold'] . . . *the one [*intrl. bef. del.* 'N.'s [*ab. del.* 'the ['one' *del.*] one']'] MS; *another friend [*ab. del.* 'Newbold'] . . . *the other [*ab. del.* 'N.'s'] TMs

§274.15 erelong] MS (*insrtd.*); TMs; ere long E,A

§274.20 ask:–] H; ～_∧∧ [*colon del.*] MS; ～!_∧ TMs (*misreading of del. in* MS);A; ～:_∧ E

275.2 farther] MS(T); further TMs+

275.32+ *space*] H; *no space* MS+

275.35 them_∧∧] MS; ～ ,– TMs+

§276.11 banter, and_∧ . . . things_∧] MS (*comma aft.* 'things' *del.*); ～ , ～ _∧ . . . ～ , TMs; ～ _∧ ～ , . . . ～ , E,A

*276.25 himself] *stet* MS(T)+

277.4 parent-] MS,TMs; ～ _∧ E,A

*277.22 those] *stet* E; others A

*§277.25 certain] TMs(*intrl.*); *om.* MS,E,A

*277.31 (1)] *stet* E,A; 1. MS,TMs

278.20 XIII_∧] MS,TMs; ～ . E,A

‡278.31 insensible] A; deaf MS,TMs,E

*§279.5 logical] MS; technical ['techn' *ab. del.* 'top'] TMs+

§279.11–12 SELECTIONS . . . *Introduction*] A (I. Introduction); *FINAL REPORT ON **MRS. ['M' *ov.* 'I'] PIPER's HODGSON-CONTROL [*db. underl.*] MS; *om.* E

*§282.39 there] MS (*alt. fr.* 'in them'); in them E,A

284.8 230] H; 130 MS+ (*error*)

284.22 usually] A; *om.* E

*285.2 insincerity.] *stet* MS+

285.24–25 fastidious–] MS; ～ ,– E,A

285.25 meter] MS,A; metre E

*285.31 T.P.] *stet* MS+

285.31 *a*] MS (*rom.*);A; *à* E

*286.15 our] MS; the E,A

286.20 firstrate] MS; First rate E,A

§286.21 etc.,–] MS [*dash intrl.*]; ～ .,_∧ E,A

286.34–35 leaving] A; after leaving MS,E

287.16 seems] A; is E

287.33 in] H (*sitting*); on E,A

287.36 his] A (+*sitting*); the E

288.1 anyone] H (*sitting*); any one E,A

288.8 *out*] H (*sitting*); out E,A

288.27 talk–] H (*sitting*); ～ ,– E,A

289.16 anyone] H; any one E,A (+*sitting*)

☛289.32 H.-] H; ～ ._∧ MS+ (*also* 303.1;323.26;352.33)

290.9 D., who . . . first] A; D._∧ at first cannot MS,E

*291.3 [R. . . . names.]] *stet* MS(T)+

291.32 tablecloth] MS(T); ～ - ～ E,A

292.22 place–] MS(T); ～ ,– E,A

293.22 canvass] MS(T); canvas E,A

293.22 shoulder,] MS(T); ～ _∧ E,A

*294.1 von G.] *stet* MS (T)+

294.2 psychical-] MS(T); ～ _∧ E,A

294.16 control] MS,A; *cap.* E

295.2 Margaret] A; *om.* MS,E

§295.13,23;297.6,7 Firstrate] MS(T) (*alt. fr.* '～ ～'); First rate E,A

296.14 schoolchildren] MS(T); school children E,A

*296.31 Yes.] *stet* E; ～ ? MS(T); *om.* A

298.8,11 someone] MS(T); some one E,A

§299.1 Head_∧] MS(T) (*comma del.*); ～ , E,A

299.7 this] MS(T); thus E,A

299.9 right_∧] MS(T); ～ , E,A

299.13 *her*] A; her MS(T),E

299.15 W.R.] A; *om.* MS(T),E

*§300.15 might] MS(T) (*ab. del.*
   'would seem'); *ital.* E,A
300.16 Idiosyncrasies] H;
   Idiosyncracies MS(T)+ (*error*)
300.25 fly!] MS(T); ~ ? E,A
301.7 is] A; was MS(T),E
301.16 quite!] MS(T); ~ . E,A
302.4 all . . ."] H; ~ . . .‸ MS(T)+
   (*error*)
302.13 thinking–"] H; ~ –‸ MS(T)+
   (*error*)
302.16 piece."]] H; ~‸") MS; ~"].
   A,E
§302.20 'piece';] A; ' ~,' [*sg. qts.*
   insrtd.] MS(T);E
302.21 *have*] A; *rom.* MS(T),E
303.25;325.16 someone] H; some one
   E,A
304.22 sing'] H; ~ ‸ E,A (*error*)
*305.16 parallel]A; long E
*306.31 Hallo] *stet* E,A; Hello MS(T)
307.2 Beach] MS(T), A; Beech E
   (*error*)
307.7 Firstrate] H; First rate MS(T)+
307.10 you!] MS(T); ~ . E,A
307.23 spiritistic] MS(T); spiritualistic
   E,A
308.1 Firstrate] A; First‸rate MS(T);
   ~ - ~ E
308.9 did:] MS(T); ~ ! E,A
*309.9–10 [A . . . N.]] *stet* MS(T)+
*309.18–19 [A . . . N.]] *stet* MS(T)+
*310.2–3 [Statements . . . N.]] *stet*
   MS(T)+
310.6 who] MS(T); Who E,A
310.15 him.[11]] A; ~ .‸ (*om. fn.*)
   MS(T),E
310.23 him,'] H; ~ ,‸ A
310.35 'San. . .'.] H; ' ~ . . .'‸ A
310.36 Krebs] H; Kreb's A (*error*)
311.7 devil!] MS(T); ~ ? E,A
*311.26 Not for anything!] *stet* MS+
§312.26 Now‸]H (sitting); No,
   [*comma insrtd.*] MS(T)+
*313.3–4 [The . . . N.]] *stet* MS(T)+
313.4 ago.] A; ~‸ MS(T),E
*§313.10–13 [I . . . N.]] *stet* E,A; [He
   never said anything of the kind.*–N.]
   [*intrl.*] MS(T)
314.8 greet] H (sitting); meet MS(T)+
314.8 Firstrate] MS(T); ~ - ~ E,A
314.20 'kadoodle'] *stet sg. qts.* MS(T)+

315.8 W. . . . do.] MS(T) (*parens*); om.
   E,A
315.19 interested?] MS(T); ~ . E,A
*315.23 ****] *stet* MS(T)+
*316.2 them] *stet* MS(T)+
*316.11–12 [A . . . omit.]] *stet* MS(T)+
*316.20 ¹You] *stet* MS(T)+
316.28 N.]] MS(T),A; ~]. E (*error*)
*317.3–5 [I . . . N.]] *stet* MS(T)+
317.27 new] MS(T) (sitting); now E,A
318.7 someone] A; some one MS(T),E
318.14 Firstrate] H; ~ ‸ ~ MS(T);
   ~ - ~ E,A
318.35 connexion] H; connection
   MS(T)+
319.3 Billy?[13]] A; ~ ?‸ (*om. fn.*)
   MS(T),E
*319.10–12 [A . . . N.]] *stet* MS(T)+
‡319.10 firstrate] H; ~ - ~ MS(T)+
*320.11 Mrs. F. . .] *stet* MS(T)+
322.24 ²a] MS,A; as E
322.37 *trying*] A; *rom.* MS,E
§323.1 over‸'] MS (*comma del.*); ~ ,"
   E,A
323.18 feeling] MS; feelings E,A
324.1 Firstrate] H; ~ ~ E,A
*325.15 C.B.] *stet* E,A
326.25–27 [For . . . Hyslop.]] A; *om.* E
326.32;328.34 Denver] A; —— E
327.9 hysteria?[18]] A; ~ .‸ (*om. fn.*) E
327.14 J.][19]] A; ~ .]‸ (*om. fn.*) E
☞331.13–14 passwords:–] H; ~ :‸
   E,A (*similar* 332.35;342.34;345.1–2;
   348.34;350.15)
332.5,6 B——g] A; B. E
☞332.18 anyone] H; any one E,A
   (*also* 335.25;338.1;342.22)
333.9 like——"] H; ~ ——‸ E,A
333.32–33 [Names . . . H.]] A; *om.* E
334.8,31;338.5 firstrate] H; ~ - ~ E,A
335.25 colour] H; color E,A
336.19 H.-] H; ~ .‸ E,A
336.19 Bela] H; Biela E,A
337.4 nigger-] H; ~ ‸ | E,A
337.14 someone] H; some one E,A
§338.11 see above,] A; *supra*‸ [*aft. del.*
   'p. 20'] MS; ~ ~ ‸ E
338.16 someone] MS; some one E,A
338.21 'leakage,'] H; " ~ , " MS;
   ‸ ~ ,‸ E,A
*338.24 spiritist] MS; spiritual E,A
338.24 no] A; but little MS,E

339.23   The Hodgson-control] A;
Hodgson MS,E

339.24   R.H.] A; he MS,E

*339.34   M. Bergman] *stet* E;
R. Bergman MS,A

340.7;351.11   said:—] H; ~ :ᴧ MS+

344.37   *a*] A; *à* E

345.28   'spirit-return,'] *stet* MS,E;
" ~ - ~ " A

346.26   *and*] MS; and E,A

347.31   Australiaᴧ] A; ~ , E

347.31   ²themᴧ] A; ~ , E

347.33   youᴧ] A; ~ , E

347.34   me, she] A; ~ . She E

347.38   any body] A; anybody E

347.38   else's,] A; ~ ; E

347.39   'Q.'] *stet* E; " ~." A

347.42   am,] A; ~ ᴧ E

348.19   anyone] H; any one MS+

‡349.18,‡24;‡356.9   *Primâ*] MS (*rom.*);
Prima E,A

350.31   P.]²³] A; ~ .]ᴧ (*om. fn.*) E

351.13   home,] MS; ~ ᴧ E,A

352.3   anyone] H; any | one MS; any
one E,A

*352.4   him?] H; Do you remember,
etc. MS+

353.16   stands:—] H; ~ :ᴧ MS+

*353.23   hand] MS; hands E,A

*§354.30   (May 14th, 1906).] *stet* E,A;
*[May 14th. 1906, p. 26]ᴧ [*ab. del.*
'[I can't recover this passage or I
would give the exact reference
[*period del.*]]. [*period del. in error*]']
MS

354.30   asked-] MS; ~ ᴧ E,A

356.9   *primâ*] MS (*rom.*); *prima* E,A

356.15   stir . . . up] A,CER; reinforce
each other MS,E

‡356.16   inert] A,CER; comparatively
inert MS,E

§356.19   effects] A,CER; activity [*alt. fr.*
'action'] MS;E

356.27   planchette-] MS; planchet-
E,A

357.17   *Primâ*] H; *Prima* MS+

357.21   an] MS,A,CER; a E

358.31   Moffatt] A,CER; Moffett MS,E
(*error*)

358.31   II;] H; ~.: E

*358.24–25   of course . . . naturally]
stet E; of course . . . of course
MS,TMsᶜ; , naturally, . . . of course
A,CER

358.27   stations;] MS; ~ , TMsᶜ,E,A

38. The Confidences of a "Psychical Researcher" (1909)

The copy-text is P⁴, "The Confidences of a 'Psychical Researcher,'" *American Magazine*, 68 (October 1909), 580–589 (McD 1909:7), with reference to MS, the holograph manuscript preserved in the James Collection at Houghton (bMS Am 1092.9 [4545]). Reference is also made to the reprint published in M&S, *Memories and Studies*, edited by Henry James, Jr., pp. 171–206 (McD 1911:2), which has been collated for substantives only.

☞361.7–8 *et seq. similar* 'psychic']
MS; " ~ " P⁴ (*except*
365.34;366.5,21;367.25;368.9[*both*],
29,33[*first*],36;369.2,20;371.18,31–32;
374.22)

361.21   decision.] MS,M&S; ~ . | *Can
We "Communicate With Spirits?"* P⁴

362.6   creator] H; *cap.* MS,P⁴

362.8   ᴧ although ghosts,] MS; , ~ ~ ᴧ
P⁴

362.13   observations,] MS; ~ ᴧ P⁴

362.19   creator] MS; *cap.* P⁴

§362.23   -centuriesᴧ] MS (*intrl.*); - ~ ,
P⁴

362.34   neapolitan] MS; *cap.* P⁴

362.38   Everyone] H; Every one MS,P⁴

363.2–4   psychiatristᴧ . . . physiologistᴧ
. . . researcherᴧ] MS; ~ , . . . ~ ,
. . . ~ , P⁴

363.3   Bottazzi] H; Botazzi MS, P⁴

§363.4–5   *The . . . Spiritualism*] H;
*'the **pysical ['y' *ov.* 's'] [*ab. del.*
'psychical'] phenomena of
Spiritualism'* MS; *db. qts.* (*rom.*) P⁴

557

363.9 health-] MS; ~ ∧ P4

363.14 phenomenon.] MS,M&S;
~ . | *Scientists Who Cheat* P4

§363.15 *Origin of Species*] H; Origin
['O' *ov*. 'o'] of Species MS; *db. qts.*
(*rom*.) P4

363.26 spook-] MS; ~ ∧ | P4

363.35 english] H; *cap*. MS,P4

363.36 that∧] MS; ~ , P4

§363.37 Tactically,] MS (*ab. del.*
'Officially,'); ~ ∧ P4

363.39;370.31 *Proceedings*] H; *rom*.
MS,P4

364.3 But∧] MS; ~ , P4

364.12 that∧] MS; ~ , P4

§364.13 'centre of gravity'] MS (*penc.
added*); ∧ ~ ~ ~ ∧ P4

364.13,16 centre] MS; center P4

364.13 immoveable] MS; immovable
P4

364.19-20 american] MS; *cap*. P4

364.21 it.] MS,M&S; ~ . | *A Confession
By Professor James* P4

364.23 Theatre] MS; Theater P4

364.24 heart,] MS; ~ ∧ | P4

§364.30 gone, and∧] MS ('and' *insrtd*.);
~ ∧ ~ , P4

364.37-38 prophecied] MS; prophesied
P4

365.10 truth∧] MS; ~ , P4

*§365.11 sense] *stet* P4; as- |
['conscience at' *del*.] surance MS

365.19 conclusion.] MS,M&S; ~ . | *A
Shallow State of Public Opinion* P4

☞ 365.34 -'researching'] H; -" ~ "
MS,P4 (*similar* 366.5;368.33[*first*];
369.20;371.31-32; 374.22)

*365.35 pretension,] MS; ~ ∧ P4

§365.37 spirit-] MS (*alt. fr.* 'spiritual');
~ ∧ P4

§366.9,39 *Life and Letters*.] H; Life
and *Letters ['L' *ov*. 'l']. MS; "Life
and Letters:" P4

366.12 ever] *stet* MS,P4; *om*. Huxley

366.13 myself,] Huxley; ~ ∧ MS,P4

366.14 the] Huxley,MS; these P4,M&S

366.17 provincial] *stet* MS,P4;
cathedral Huxley

366.21 truth of 'Spiritualism'] Huxley;
"Truth" of spiritualism" MS; 'Truth
of Spiritualism' P4

366.23 -sweeper∧] Huxley,MS; -~ , P4

366.24 *séance*] Huxley; *cap*. MS;
Seance P4

§366.29-30 imposture.—] MS (*dash
intrl*.); ~ . ∧ P4

§366.33 this] MS (*underl. del*.); This P4

366.35 conclusions!] MS,M&S; ~ ! |
*One Way of Interpreting Certain
Phenomena* P4

367.21 faculty∧] MS; ~ , P4

367.25 'Psychics'] H; ∧ ~ ∧ MS;
" ~ " P4

367.33 checked-] MS; ~ ∧ P4

368.8 dream-] MS; ~ ∧ | P4

§368.9 'ouija-board' . . . 'planchet,'] H;
∧ouija [*aft. del*. 'ouija [*ov. doubtful*
'wiya']']-board∧ . . . ∧ ~ , ∧ MS;
" ~ - ~ " . . . " ~ ," P4

368.25 -world.] MS,M&S; -~ . | *What
is "Pure Bosh?"* P4

§368.29 'revelation or imposture,'] H;
" ~ ~ ~ ~ [*comma del*.]" MS;
" ~ ~ ~ ," P4

368.32 offhand] MS; off-hand P4

368.34-35;374.20 connexion] MS;
connection P4

368.35-36 -photographs∧] MS; -~ , P4

368.36 'bosh'] MS; ∧ ~ ∧ P4

368.38 loathe] MS; loath P4

‡369.2 'bosh'] H; ∧ ~ ∧ MS; " ~ " P4

§369.5 fancy∧] MS (*comma del*.; *ab.
del*. 'imagination,'); ~ , P4

369.19 regular,] MS; ~ ∧ P4

369.30 Lookt] MS; Looked P4

370.3 succeed.] MS,M&S; ~ . | *The
Effect on Myers and Hodgson* P4

370.28 anyone] H; any one MS,P4

370.31 publisht] MS; published P4

370.32 nothing,] MS; ~ ∧ | P4

370.35 Someone] MS; Some one P4

371.3 honour] MS; honor P4

371.4 it.] MS,M&S; ~ . | *There is
"Something in" These Phenomena*
P4

371.15 ∧ of course∧] MS; , ~ ~ , P4

371.18 'raps∧'] H; " ~ , " MS;
" ~ ∧ " P4

371.28 someone] H; some one MS,P4

371.33 -stock∧] MS; -~ , P4

§371.35 type∧] MS (*bef. del*. ', from
the way in'); ~ , P4

372.3 us.] MS,M&S; ~ . | *Professor*
   James Goes on Record P4
*372.21 a] MS; *om.* P4,M&S
372.21 name_∧] MS; ~ , P4
372.33 namely—] MS; ~ , P4
372.38 truth,] MS; ~ ∧ P4
373.17 parasitically_∧] MS; ~ , P4

374.5–6 concluding.] MS,M&S; ~ . |
   Great Scientific Conquests of the
   Future P4
§374.21 philosophy_∧] MS (*comma*
   del.); ~ , P4
374.32 'spirits'] H; " ~ " P4
374.37 connexion] H; connection P4
375.3 Vast_∧] MS; ~ , P4

39. A Possible Case of Projections of the Double (1909)

The copy-text is P43, "A Possible Case of Projections of the Double," *Journal of the American Society for Psychical Research*, 2 (April 1909), 253–254 (McD 1909:11).

377.22 to._∧] H; ~ ." P43 (*error*)

Textual Notes

127.10   pointing]   Among the very few unique substantive readings in *Science* (P³⁶) that could be either errors or James's proof-alterations (see the textual introduction) is this first, the omission of 'now' after 'pointing'. The figure of the mousetrap and of the wires that easily push aside to admit the mouse but that bar his exit is clear enough and the mousetrap figure agrees with James's opening sentence. The only question is whether the omission of 'now' is authorial or a printer's error. If one wishes to be scrupulous one could point out that there is no concrete antecedent reference to the wires except in the general idea of a mousetrap so that James could have crossed out the 'now' for the sake of consistency. The case is really indeterminate, however, and its acceptance here as a legitimate emendation rests as much on the evidence for James's proofreading of P³⁶ and his making a handful of changes, whereas only one manifest substantive error occurs, as it does on the sense, which is relatively neutral.

128.27   rigorously]   The agreement of P³²,³⁶ in 'rigorously' as against TMs 'vigorously' indicates only compositorial error or a change in proof, presumably but not necessarily authoritative. However, James's ink correction at 128.46 of TMs 'vigor' to 'rigor' suggests that in both places the typist misread James's 'r' as a 'v', an easy mistake to make, and that James observed the error only the second time. See also 131.21, 37; 132.15 for James's use of 'rigor'.

130.8–9   definitely convinced]   That the TMs, P³² reading 'definitively convinced' was no error may be demonstrated by James's alteration in TMs of 'convinced definitively' to 'definitively convinced', and his passing the word in the P³² proof. Indeed, one would be tempted to pass off the P³⁶ unique reading 'definitely' here as a simple printer's error were it not that at 137.10 both P³²,³⁶ read 'definite' where TMs has 'definitive'. In turn this may be a printer's error in setting the proof that James failed to recognize; but it may also be an authoritative change which, if a true revision in proof, would serve to authenticate the P³⁶ unique reading at 130.8 as a legitimate and parallel proof-correction. Either reading makes sense but 'definitely' has perhaps the more common and accessible meaning.

132.1   over reach]   The word was typed as 'overreach' but James drew a vertical stroke between the two parts to separate them. It seems clear that the compositor ignored James's TMs marking and set the word as 'overreach', which appears thus in P³²,³⁶.

132.19 'the Island_∧'] In the *Journal of the Society for Psychical Research*, 6 (November 1894), 306ff., Sir Oliver Lodge reported on a series of tests of Eusapia Paladino in which he was assisted by F. W. H. Myers and Dr. J. Ochorowicz, the meetings taking place between July 21–27, 1894. On p. 346, the first appendix to Lodge's paper, we learn that the place was the île Roubaud, Gien, which is in the Mediterranean off Hyères. This is the island referred to by James, of course, but whether the reduction of the capital with which it had been typed that took place in P³² (but not in P³⁶) is an authoritative correction is difficult to decide. All one can say is that the reduction to lower case in P³² must have been made in the revises, since the proof from which P³⁶ was set quite obviously followed the TMs in its capitalization. A few other minor changes were made in the revises but none that can be definitely attributed to James. It follows that the odds seem to favor an unauthoritative alteration by Miss Johnson, the *Proceedings* editor. For what it is worth, F. W. H. Myers in a letter to James of September 11, 1895, uses the capital in remarking, "I cannot altogether abandon the *Island* phenomena" (bMS Am 1092.9 [419]).

133.29–30 recorded . . . 129);] In TMs the identification 'Mass.' appeared after 'Fitchburg,' beginning the line, but then the rest of the line was left blank by the typist, clearly to leave room for the reference to be added later. (Actually the reference was not added in TMs but only in proof.) Somehow, it would seem, the identifying 'Mass.', which one would suppose necessary for an English audience, got dropped in the proof-alteration. It is restored here from TMs.

136.21 Mill's_∧] This name was omitted from TMs and so must have been supplied in proof, whence it appears in P³²,³⁶. However, the proof must have had a following comma, as in P³². The lack of a comma in P³⁶ is not authoritative, therefore, but has been adopted because its styling agrees with James's usual omission of a comma before the 'and' of a series, even though in this case it cannot be authoritative. We cannot know, of course, what form the proof correction took, and so whether the comma was an editorial addition or not. See also 135.31 for a similar case.

143.13–14 which . . . from] This is a curious and blander reading which occurs only in P³² and so represents proof correction later than the preserved proofs and hence in the lost revises, where it joins a handful of changes in Le Baron's narrative made in these same revises in addition to the change throughout represented by that at 144.2 (see textual note below). It is odd that James would have changed his somewhat grudging 'been an adept, if we may believe' found in TMs and set in the first P³² proofs, but it is not beyond possibility that Miss Johnson, the editor of the *Proceedings*, may have written to him, as she did to Waters about some readings, pointing out that James's phrase in the proofs might create an unfortunate impression. That she would herself censor James's language on her own responsibility at the latest stage of the revises does not seem probable. We must assume that James communicated the change to her although we cannot know whether she suggested it.

144.2 Evangel] James's typescript (TMs) reads always, 'Saint Evangel' (with 'Saint' occasionally abbreviated to 'St.'), but he seems to have carried on a discussion with Waters about the name—no doubt as part of his wish to disguise her identity—and to have settled on Aunt Serena. This name was duly interlined by Miss Johnson in the TMs, but correspondence between her and Waters reveals that it was ultimately not thought to be satisfactory. Waters at first

seems to have favored returning to the original 'Saint Evangel', but Miss Johnson must have objected for in a note written at the top of a letter from Waters
of August 28, 1896 she wrote 'ansᵈ Sep. 17. I have provisionally put "Evangel"
in proof. will be time to change, if he disapproves.' Hence though 'Aunt Serena'
appears in all the proofs the revises were altered to 'Evangel'. Only in the proof
of James's introduction is 'Aunt Serena' deleted. At first, in the margin, Miss
Johnson substituted 'Saint Evangel', but at a later time deleted the 'Saint'. Apparently there were no further objections for on the back of an envelope sent
from Cambridge, Mass., on October 7, and presumably containing James's approval (the letter itself is not preserved) Miss Johnson wrote 'use name Evangel,
omitting Saint.'

146.19   a . . . re-incarnation,]   This is part of a James interlineation in
TMs, which continues 'and a medium', whereas Waters' typescript had read
simply 'of the loftiest type, and whose psycho-automatic 'control' was her dead
mother'. In Waters' letter of August 28, 1896, to Miss Johnson about various
points of correction, he asks: "From the 9ᵗʰ line of slip two please erase the
words 'and a medium' as they are not in 'copy.' We do not wish to add any
more comments to the paper." It is a natural assumption that Waters had seen
James's modified TMs before it was sent to England since James would ordinarily have wished Waters' approval for his changes; if so, he had not objected
at the time. Actually, he does not object to the earlier part of James's 'comment', which was also not in the copy (meaning the unannotated TMs) but
only to the statement that Evangel was a medium. In fact, James appears to
have misunderstood the situation by calling Evangel a medium and Waters
was being accurate in requesting the removal. For this reason, the latter part
of the James annotation is editorially rejected.

146.24   the hope]   This interlineation is made in TMs in blue ink (in
contrast with James's black) and in an unknown printing hand. Although the
facts cannot be determined in any demonstrable manner, it is extremely probable that this and other changes in TMs made in this hand represent Waters'
alterations of TMs when (as we must assume) he was sent it for approval. Miss
Johnson's proof changes are all made in script, as are James's, and James was
not accustomed to print changes in copy or in proof. Waters' script is very
difficult and he may have been conscious of the need for clarity when making
up copy for the printer. Since no other candidate for the changes made in this
hand suggests itself, it is a natural assumption that they are Waters' and hence
have been accepted on that basis. Not all repair obvious errors like the present;
that at 146.31, for instance, is concerned with idiom. For other annotations in
TMs in this hand, see 147.11, 147.14(?), 148.3, 149.13, 149.29, 154.27 and 160.27.

148.4   *man.*²]   Miss Johnson evidently queried this episode, for in his letter
to her of August 28, Waters wrote: "No. I did not know before hand that her
father was lame. I was informed so when seen limping." Miss Johnson thereupon added the footnote in proof.

152.3   ¶From]   The deletion of the preceding sentence in proof—'[¶]
Among other things, this arose from the principle common to poodle and
philosopher, that startling phenomena are interpreted by us as having a personal bearing, when we are distinctly told by any intelligence—we believe in—
that they have.'—was made in the proof (where it had been faithfully set from
TMs) by Miss Johnson. Also deleted in proof was a companion passage, at 158.7

after 'succeeded admirably,' which read in TMs 'since it constantly operated on the principle, which as I said before, is common to poodle and philosopher, to interpret startling and unusual phenomena as having some probable personal bearing.' The TMs then continued 'Hence, again arose the temptation to yield' but the gap forced Miss Johnson to delete 'Hence' as well and to substitute on her own authority the words 'and here' to link with the phrase 'succeeded admirably,' preceding the deletion. Only a slight doubt may remain about these deletions. Among the various instructions that Waters sent to Miss Johnson in his letter of August 28, 1896, in response to various of her questions, was the following: "Omit the *duplicated* expressions 'interpreting phenomena as having some personal bearing.' " The plural 'expressions' seems clear enough that Waters wanted both passages omitted despite the ambiguity of 'duplicated' here as an adjective. Moreover, the phrase he wants removed cannot be detached without the rest of the sentence in each case. Thus it would seem that Miss Johnson acted under warrant in both cases, and her invented bridge was necessary as well as innocuous enough.

253.9   'control']   In James's manuscript double quotation marks were originally typed but then James changed them to single by means of rather long vertical ink strokes. It would seem that the typist of TMs mistook these strokes for full deletion marks and so omitted the single ones that James desired. The same markings and the same results are found also in 'spirit' in 253.13.

253.15   69]   The discrepancy between the figure 69 in E, and the coincidence of 75 as inserted in MS(T) above 'ooo' and thence copied in TMs, to be reproduced in A, indicates that E represents an alteration and hence is the most authoritative document. The simplest explanation is that James had available seventy-five reports but in the end decided to utilize only sixty-nine. The MS(T) and TMs version reads 'I have undertaken to collate the various sittings, now 75 in number' which does not specify that the sittings were American. In A this was revised to 'I have undertaken to collate the various American sittings (75 in number as I write, the latest being that of January 1st, 1908)', which, like MS(T), does not state that the seventy-five were all actually used, but instead that they were available. The E version 'I have collated 69' is clearly after the fact.

254.5   Until . . . 1906,]   The typist's fault in TMs caused an important gap here in TMs, followed by the printed texts. In MS(T) 'Until the spring of 1906,' is interlined after the interlined ink footnote-reference asterisk and the whole is brought down by an arrowed guideline to precede 'I had myself'. However, in a space deliberately left blank below this typed line, James later added footnote 2 by hand between two horizontal lines. Because the arrowhead of the guideline crossed the top footnote horizontal line, the typist of TMs, confused by the interlineation after the asterisk, took it that the asterisk was the footnote asterisk, not its reference in the text, and so set the interlineation as the start of his footnote, as '*Until the Spring of 1906, chief among'. In the prints this wrong introductory phrase is removed from the footnote but is not restored to the text.

254.23   a]   The omission of this word in TMs and thence in E and A appears to be accidental. In MS(T) James had originally typed 'an almost marvellous' but later by a horizontal ink stroke deleted the 'n' of 'an' and 'almost'. The remnant 'a' of this deletion seems to have been overlooked by the typist of TMs.

255.7–8 'Hodgson' . . . 'Rector,'] Although in his own typescript James was inclined to use double quotation marks, in his autograph parts of the present manuscript he was generally consistent in his usual custom of employing single quotation marks for definition but double for actual quotations as of speech. The TMs generally follows MS, but E and A use double quotation marks almost invariably as a part of their housestyling. James's characteristic autograph practice has been editorially imposed on the copy-text E. But since the mass of emendation would completely overload the apparatus if each change were recorded, the alteration has been made silently except that single quotes in the copy-text have been specifically identified. It follows that when single quotes appear in this text, the reader is to take it that double quotes were present in E, but in the autograph portions of the document single quotation marks would very likely have appeared.

255.18 follows:—] In this place James added an ink dash to MS(T). In other texts James was not much inclined to add a dash after a colon (although often the printer supplied them for him as a normal feature of housestyling). But in this text both in the typed and autograph parts James was fairly liberal with dashes, either original or added, although far from consistent in either document. A few dashes escape into E and A, but each print is more likely than not to omit them, although almost certainly not by James's proof-correction. There seems to be no particular system to the presence or omission of these dashes in MS, or marked in TMs. Editorially, therefore, they have been supplied silently when present in either MS or TMs and are allowed to stand in E whether or not present in MS or TMs. A few have been supplied as absolute emendations, and then only before inset dialogue.

256.28 bad] When A departs substantively from E in cases where MS (and TMs when present) agrees with E, it would seem that the A reading represents an independent proof correction, as here, where one could suggest that James came to dislike the repetition of 'poor', which had originally been intended for emphasis. The explanation for the original repetition of 'poor' may doubtless be found in the discarded version on fol. 7^v of Part II, which reads 'I have come to the conclusion that it *is* a particularly poor one', the italic *is* (not repeated in later versions) requiring the repetition. The adoption of unique A readings is discussed in the textual discourse under "The Editorial Problem."

256.35 readers] MS(T) has 'readers' which was at first copied by TMs but then James altered TMs to 'hearers', a reading followed by E and A. This is the reverse of 254.3 where MS originally read 'readers' but was altered in ink to 'hearers', which is found in TMs (perhaps by a misreading of a not too clear alteration) as 'readers', again a reading followed by E and A. For publication James would of course want 'readers', whereas for the oral delivery of the paper he would require 'hearers'.

257.19 records] The unique plural in A would seem to result from a James proof-correction. It may possibly be significant that in MS(T) the singular 'record' ends a line at full length; hence, the typewriter margin not being adjustable by a release key, James may have overlooked adding an 's' by hand. In his own typed MS he frequently had to read over a page and add necessary letters to the incomplete full line. It is significant, however, that in the discarded trial version on fol. 6^v of Part II the plural is used, and—in another context—the plural is also found in the discarded trial on fol. 2ᵛ. See the transcripts of deleted versos following the alterations in the Alterations in the Manuscripts.

258.1 suddenly] This word inserted in MS(T) but omitted in TMs and the prints seems to have been overlooked in error by the TMs typist. There has been textual disruption here in MS(T) when typed matter at the head of fol. 11(2) was deleted (see Alterations 257.32–258.1) and a substitute written by hand in a blank space at the foot of fol. 9, continued for a few lines on hand-written fol. 10. The word 'suddenly' was inserted before the deleted beginning of a paragraph, and the typist seems to have taken it that deletion of 'suddenly' was also intended.

258.25 A . . . "L"] After preceding 'that?'' James first typed 'Another spirit then took control' but then he endeavored to alter this by typing over it ' "B" AND and an L followed, but no explanation.', the last two words being in the clear. This largely illegible sequence was then deleted in ink and James typed, after it, ' "B" and an "L" followed,' and at some later time interlined in ink an 'A' with a caret before ' "B" '. It is apparent that the typist of TMs mistook the intention, and so typed ' "A", "B" and an "L" followed,' a misreading that James did not correct in TMs, E, or A (where the 'an' is omitted: James's proofreading?). The context makes perfectly clear that when 'A l l' had been written, followed by a 'B', and the question was asked—what is that?—the hand rewrote the 'B' after 'A l l' and then followed it with an L. Confirmation of the correct reading may be procured not only in the retyping that was deleted but also at 263.36 where Rector writes 'Margaret. a l l B L.' The explanation that James promised in an ink addition to MS(T) occurs at 267.10.

259.13 Than . . . divine.] This reading is perfectly normal in MS(T). But, oddly, the typist of TMs left a blank between lines 11 and 12 so that line 12 is at the foot of the page and line 13 was never typed. James filled in the missing line in ink.

260.1 AM] The most authoritative document, which of course is MS(T), reads 'I AM Hodgson', followed by the retyped page of TMs. The original page 10 of TMs had lower-case 'am'. (See the textual discourse, pp. 516–517 for a discussion of this retyping.) One could speculate that MS(T) 'AM' was an error, corrected to 'am' in the original page of TMs, but reappearing in the retyped page, which was done directly from MS(T). At 259.4, for example, Hodgson introduced himself in capitals: 'RICHARD HODGSON I AM WELL HAPPY GLAD I CAME GOD BLESS POPE' and it could be conjectured that here at 260.1 James at first proposed to type his introduction similarly in capitals but then gave it up when he realized that there was too much text for such a procedure. This possibility makes for some uncertainty. However, it would seem that the reading 'AM' may be confirmed by a similar case (except for the use of italic instead of roman capitals) at 343.35 where Hodgson writes, 'I *am* Richard Hodgson. *I am he.*' before going on in roman. Thus it would seem that 'AM' could be an authentic example of emphasis and no error, that the retyped page is also correct, and that E (and A), which followed the erroneous original page 10 of TMs, needs emending.

260.24 Miss D——] In MS(T) James first typed 'Miss ——' either in error or by a dash to conceal any clue to the actual name, but then in ink interlined 'D.' The typist of TMs followed the interlineation but omitted the dash so that both E and A copy it in the anomaly 'Miss D.' despite James's typed 'Miss D——' at 260.27, followed by E and A.

260.32–33 which . . . laughter).] MS(T) was originally typed as 'Yes. Ah, ah, ah.' Later, in ink, James added, within brackets, 'These *written [*intrl.*] words indicate laughter.' Still later, he altered the period after 'ah' to a comma and interlined 'which' above deleted 'These'. Finally, he moved the whole bracketed phrase by a guideline to follow line 32 instead of line 31. The typist of TMs did not notice the guideline and so typed 'which . . . laughter.' in parentheses following the comma, in which misplacement he was copied by E and A. MS(T) was in error, of course, in not changing the comma back to a period after the transposition was marked.

262.24 Q] In the sitting record 'Q' is also the only identification. However, in the sitting with George Dorr on May 29, 1906, in the transcript Hodgson says of Q: 'Her original and whole complete name was Jessie Turner Dunn. I have guarded that name most sacredly all my life.' Miss Dunn was Hodgson's Australian cousin; obviously he had a special relationship with her.

262.29 G. D.] Here the transcript of the sitting reads 'George Derham'.

263.22 singly,] The typist of TMs misread James's handwriting in the MS as 'simply,' a reading that was transmitted in error to E and A, although presumably by editorial or compositorial intervention the comma was removed in A. This is one of several such misreadings that James did not catch in proof.

263.36 B$_\wedge$] In MS(T) James at first ended his typed line with 'B' and of course put a syntactical period after it. Later, in ink, he deleted this period and added 'L.' The typist of TMs mistook the deleting stroke for a comma after 'B' and so set it, to be followed in this error by both E and A.

268.2 Readers] The alteration of this MS(T) reading to 'People' made in ink in TMs appears to be part of James's revisions in TMs for oral delivery. Since the ultimate intent for the Report was publication, the MS(T) reading needs to be preserved. See the Textual Note to 256.35 above.

268.20 return] The typed report of this sitting of February 27, 1906, at 9:53 A.M., lists James H. Hyslop as sitter with 'Mrs. L., assisting.' The passage quoted in the present text occurs on p. 7 of the transcript and is transcribed from 268.20–27; 'return' in James's manuscript (typed) is 'come' in the transcript, an indication that James might alter ambiguous words for the benefit of his readers. The report is preserved in the Archives of the American Society for Psychical Research under Hyslop's Biographical Materials II, Box 3, file folder. On the verso of the first leaf is the non-Jamesian handwritten note: 'ASPR New York | In Box 2, File: ASPR miscellaneous has ['copy of' *del.*] letter from Piddington to Hyslop Feb 21, 1907 on nigger-talk incident. [¶] "I came across a passage where either the Myers control asks the living Hodgson, or the living Hodgson asks the Myers' control, if he remembers a conversation about 'nigger-talk' " [¶] Told WJ about this [*short rule*] Letter Piddington to Hyslop 6 Aug 1907 Box 2: File, Noted Personalities II says incident took place at sitting of Feb 13, 1901'.

269.27 up] In TMs this word is smudged as if an attempt had been made to wipe it out. But James elsewhere in TMs deleted only by a horizontal stroke, not present here. In TMs the word 'up' is typed over 'in' before the phrase 'in me'; the smudge may have something to do with this error. The evidence is not sufficient to account the deletion of 'up' (if present) as a James revision.

271.2   Huldah]   The young lady's name was Etta Dunham and she lived in New York. In MS(T) at 270.5 and 270.8 James typed 'New York' and 'N.Y.' but then deleted these by hand and interlined 'Chicago' over both. The transcript for the sitting reads for 270.10–13: 'After the name Dunham was given, I asked if letters would be signed with the surname or Christian name. The name Huldah was then given as the name.' At 271.3–4 the transcript reads, 'Is Huldah a sister of Catherine and Helen and Etta Dunham?' to which Hodgson replies: 'Etta is the one. Huldah we used to call her.' At 275.18–19 Hodgson gives the nationality and the title of 'Huldah's' husband but fails to give his name. In notes preserved for the lost sitting of June 3, 1906, George Dorr writes that 'though I have known Etta Dunham, now Marchesa di Viti de Mario, well for longer than R.H. could have done I had no idea of an intimacy. She was one of the group R.H. knew when staying with Dorr' at the seaside (Oldfarm). The name Huldah was new to Dorr and makes him doubt the correctness of the rest. On June 5 Hodgson was thoroughly confused about Huldah. The passage at 271.14–19 reads in the transcript: '(G.B.D. Hodgson, A. J. and I are alone with you here. Can you tell us anything more about Huldah Dunham. You said the other day that she was the same person as Etta Dunham. Were you clear in saying that?) | Did I say that? That was a mistake. She is a sister. | (Is there a Huldah? There were five sisters in that family, Etta and the others. Are you sure that she is one of those sisters?) | She *is* one of those five sisters, but not Etta. I *know* what I am talking about! I saw Huldah in *New York*.' The next line reads '[See extra sheet.]', which is missing.

271.22   had a letter]   This reading was interlined in ink in TMs above deleted 'heard', which is the reading of all the other documents. Why it did not get into the transmission to E and A is obscure (see the discussion of this transmission in the textual discourse), but nevertheless it represents James's revised intention.

273.6–7   Hodgson . . . disappointment,]   In the left margin of MS fol. 40 at this point is the following note in the hand of Dr. William Romaine Newbold: 'Not quite so. The I. group had not yet turned up. The only communicator *in re* this matter was S. P. It is my impression that H. *had* *talked [aft. del. illeg.]* the matter over at sittings *before* his disappointment. WRN'. Beginning with fol. 38 and continuing to fol. 52 (272.3–277.34) most, though not all, of the leaves seem to have been folded, as if for mailing. It would seem likely that James had mailed some of them to Dr. Newbold, who then wrote this marginal comment. Nonetheless, despite this note James did not alter his statement about Hodgson and the Imperator group.

274.14–16   Newbold . . . N.'s]   In the MS 'Newbold' is deleted and 'another friend' interlined, the same change being made in TMs, an anomaly that suggests that TMs had been typed before this change was made in MS. In MS 'N.'s' was originally interlined above deleted 'the ['one' *del.*] one' but this 'N.'s' was then deleted and 'the one' restored above it. In TMs 'N.'s' had also been typed but it was deleted and 'the other' interlined above it. It is possible that we have here an anomaly in the transmission, such as that remarked above in the Textual Note to 271.22; otherwise we must suppose that James in both proofs for E and A decided to retain his original identification and to abandon the attempt at disguising the recipient of the marriage prophecy.

276.25   himself]   The originally typed 'herself' in MS(T), altered in ink, reveals James's care to conceal the donor. In MS(T) at the head of fol. 49 a deleted passage reveals that she was Mrs. Lyman, whose name is typed at 276.18 in MS(T) but deleted and 'this friend' interlined. It is important that the record of this sitting, as well as others of Mrs. Lyman's, has not been preserved in the English Society's archives, since the name itself seems to be a pseudonym.

277.22   those]   Lacking the evidence of MS and TMs in this passage we have no documentary evidence whether E 'those' or A 'others' is the revised form, for one of the two must have been altered in proof. It may be thought that the copy-text 'those' is superior to 'others', which could be ambiguous in context as possibly including the controls.

277.25   certain]   The interlined addition of 'certain' in TMs, as a revision not found in MS, was not followed by E or A. It is possible that James made the change after type had been set, and possible, also, that he decided in proof to reject the change and so altered both sets. Possibly the compositor overlooked the interlineation. Although James's final intentions are not entirely clear, the qualification seems to be a useful one: see 'knock-down proof' at 277.33.

277.31   (1)]   In MS (fol. 52) items 1 and 2 are run-on in the text, the numbers are interlined, and two ¶ signs in the margin indicate the typography. Beginning with the next page (fol. 53) and item 3 the items are written out paragraphed and discrete.

279.5   logical]   The word 'logical' is present in MS twice in the present phrase (once in a revision of a deleted passage), but was misread by the typist and typed as 'topical' in TMs, where James spotted the error and by hand wrote 'techn' above deleted 'top'. In one sense this is a later reading than 'logical'; but since it is unlikely that James consulted MS it cannot be considered to be a revision of 'logical' but instead a word suggested as a suitable correction of a misprint. Under these circumstances it is the more conservative course to reject 'technical' (to which James might never have revised 'logical') and to return to the purer original intention of MS instead of adapting a patched-up assumed correction.

282.39   there]   No question exists that in MS James first wrote 'in them' and then deleted 'in' and altered 'them' to 'there'. However, the deletion of 'in' was light and not entirely clear and it is very possible that the typist of lost TMs followed the original reading. Although simultaneous alteration of E and A proof is not impossible, it is improbable; hence if in fact James did alter his mind and change a hypothetically typed 'there' back to 'in them', it would need to have been done in the typescript. But misreading is the easier conclusion.

285.2   insincerity.]   Run-on after 'insincerity.' in MS is a deleted passage on the lower half of fol. 19 (see Alterations), the last sentence of which (following the deletion) directly continues the idea of the sentence ending 'insincerity.' Indeed, the context suggests that this last sentence was written after the intervening deletion and was intended to follow 'insincerity.' (For this sentence, see the Historical Collation.) It is quite possible that the typist, seeing the massive deletion, overlooked the undeleted lines that succeeded it, especially since part of this is also deleted at the left in the final line and might be taken to continue the main excision. Nevertheless, the case is not certain enough to risk adding to the established text this sentence, which James may have removed in the lost typescript as repetitive and ineffective.

285.31   T.P.]   'Miss Pope' (Theodate Pope) in the unaltered MS.

286.15   our]   The MS reading appears to represent James's intention and the E–A reading (deriving from the lost typescript) is almost certainly the result of the typist's misunderstanding of James's faulty alterations. As a part of the original inscription James had first written 'characteristic in the Piper-trance of things' but he then, without deleting the 'the' in error, altered 'Piper-' to 'Mrs. Piper's'; finally he deleted the revised 'Mrs. Piper's trance' and interlined 'our medium's utterances,' above deleted 'of things'. Because of the final interlined revision, 'our' is undoubtedly what James wanted and the 'the' of E and A was picked up by the typist because James had omitted to delete it when he came to revise the phrase.

291.3   [R. . . . names.]]   MS(T) continues after 'names.': 'The first three names were given unhesitatingly & *were correct,[']' *del.] save that **Mary ['ary' *ab. del.* 'ay'] should have been ***May [*alt. fr.* 'Mary'].] [*insrtd. for del. typed* '& they were right. The sister whose name was not given was one whom we saw oftener than Gertrude, while Hodgson could hardly have seen much of Robert.']'. The transcript of the sitting reads: 'R.H. makes one or two ineffectual attempts at this, suggesting names which were not right, in a tentative way, and gives it up for the moment, asking me not to tell him but to let him think it over. The first three names given were given at once and quite positively, and they were right. That the one I asked for should not have been given with them is rather curious because next to the one whom he calls Mary but whom I think he used to hear spoken of as May, not as Mary, the one whose name he could not give was the one of whom he saw the most. While the brother, Robert, I do not think he could ever have seen much of though he recalls his name.'

294.1   von G.]   The name is von Gaertner in the sitting transcript and in unaltered MS(T).

296.31   Yes.]   After having typed periods after 'fishing' and 'Yes' in MS(T), James changed both to question marks. The question mark after 'Yes' appears as a period in E; in A the word is omitted completely. It is a temptation to believe that James's ink revision in MS was accurate and that the intent was to have Hodgson prompt Miss Bancroft to the answers he wanted. On the other hand, the simple affirmation 'Yes' (not a query) is a characteristic of the Hodgson speech as reported: cf. 300.20 but especially 305.9 'We got a little fire and I helped. Yes.' and 305.15 'I said you ought to get a——in case of fire——pail, yes.' Given these examples it would seem that James mistook the situation when he added the question mark in MS but that he corrected it in the proof of E. Why the word came to be omitted in A is a mystery, although one could guess that James, correcting A's proof, was at the time so uncertain about the situation that he cut the knot by simple omission.

300.15   might]   In view of James having interlined 'might' in roman, without underline, above deleted 'would seem to' in MS(T), the transition from some doubt to exceptional doubt (indicated by the italic of E and A) may seem extreme. There is perhaps a physical explanation for the italic setting. In MS(T) the horizontal deleting stroke is unusually high across 'would seem to' and could easily have been mistaken by the typist for an underline. Otherwise, we must suppose that James inserted the underline in the lost typescript.

305.16 parallel] In the absence here of MS it is a gamble whether E 'long' or A 'parallel' is a proof revision. Since one must guess, it might be thought that *parallel* is more precise in context; but the reverse may be true. Another proof-change took place a few lines below when in 305.21 we read in E 'Mrs. Austin' but in A 'Mrs. A———'. The direction of this change is also moot, since James could as easily be protecting the privacy of Mrs. Austin in A as revealing her identity in E. The present text reads 'Mrs. Austin' without attempting to decide priority since as a matter of policy it endeavors to be as precise about names as the evidence permits.

306.31 Hallo] Both the actual transcript of the June 27, 1906, sitting and the non-James typescript of this sitting read 'Hello', so that 'Hallo' must have been a Jamesian alteration in the lost typescript copy for E. Unless James was in fact consulting the actual papers of the sitting (not the typed transcript) and there found 'Hallo', it is hard to see the reason for the change unless he deliberately imitated Professor Newbold's pronunciation. One could dismiss this instance as an aberration except that at 314.7 (the transcript again reading 'Hello') James's own MS(T) types 'Hallo', which is thus reproduced in E, A. The change seems deliberate on James's part, therefore, and should be preserved.

309.9–10 [A . . . N.]] The passage is very brief and in the transcript of the sitting consists only of 'Do you remember what you said about your father?'. Newbold first read the word as 'ticket' and answered 'No, I do not', whereupon Hodgson emphasized '*Father*' and Newbold replied, 'Yes. I think I do.'

309.18–19 [A . . . N.]] In the transcript the passage reads: 'You said your father was straight—straight, but you could not understand why he did not return.'

310.2–3 [Statements . . . N.]] In the transcript the passage reads: '(Dick!) | Hello! | (Have you seen my father?) | Yes indeed, I have———I have indeed———I have indeed———indeed. I find him a first rate fellow. | (Yes.——— Can't read that!) | Very unlike yourself however. He is very much pleased with your situation now and remembers your helping him on some writing. | (Can't read that.) | Writing. Yes, yes, writing———yes. And he is talking about it always. | Is it that 'always'?) | He thought you were too positive but he excuses it now. | (Dick, write that again.) | He thought you too positive but he understands, now. | (Thank you, Dick. Yes, that's correct, I believe.)'.

311.26 Not for anything!] A difference develops here between the transcript and James's version. The transcript reads, '(No, Dick, I did not say that. Not for anything!)'. In the next line, indented, comes Newbold's note: '[I noticed this at the time as a seeming case of change made in statement owing to sitter's answer, the 'not for anything' coming after contradiction of statement had been made. G. P. D.]'. On fol. 68(58) James originally typed 'Not for anything!' as in the transcript, ending with a parenthesis that indicated the conclusion of Newbold's speech. But then in the line below he typed, indented, 'N.B. I think 'Not for anything' is communicator's remark. Mr. Dorr has two originals.' He then typed as a separate paragraph Dorr's bracketed note, itself condensed by alteration before deletion. At first James endeavored to repair the anomaly by a guideline, making 'Not for anything!' a separate line and deleting Dorr's note after 'answer.' and adding a bracket. But then he deleted the whole and recopied it for clarity on the next page (fol. 69) by hand.

313.3–4 [The . . . N.]] The transcript reads: '(Dick, you sent me a message from my father. Can you get from him what he said to me just before he passed out?)'.

313.10–13 [I . . . N.]] This note is not present in this place in MS(T), fol. 72(64), but in its place is typed '[He never said anything of the kind–N.]', the '–N.]' added in ink above the deleted original bracket after 'kind'. However, on fol. 73(65) after 'live.' at 313.29 James wrote in pencil, '[Copy note on next page.]', and on fol. 74(66), at the head of the page of *Agawam Bond* paper, appears only the present note, typed (but not on James's typewriter) and unsigned. James has deleted a preliminary '16.' (which would have been the number of the note to the sitting) and added enclosing brackets. The note is certainly a part of Newbold's typescript used by James; but somehow, presumably in the lost typescript made from James's copy, the original note '[He never said anything of the kind–N.]' was omitted and the present note (now signed) was substituted, whether in typescript or in proof, in its place.

315.23 ****] This appears in the sitting transcript as '—— ——'.

316.2 them] The sitting transcript reads 'him', but the context seems to justify James's alteration to 'them'.

316.11–12 [A . . . omit.]] In the sitting transcript this section reads: 'Do you remember, Billy, how deserted you were at one time? | (Yes, Dick.) | At the college– | (Yes, Dick.) | University.' See also Alterations entry *ad loc.*

316.20 ¹You] The abruptness of this transition from Newbold's 'Thank you.' to Hodgson's 'You certainly did.' repeats MS(T) but is explained by the transcript of the sitting: 'Thank you. I did tell you just that kind of thing.'

317.3–5 [I . . . N.]] This interpolation was made by hand in MS(T), but the omitted material referred to has not been typed. The comment may have been amplified by Newbold later: originally his initials appeared after 'others.' but then '*Important veridically*–['W. R.' *del.*] N.]' was added by James to his note. The transcript of the sitting provides the missing material as follows: 'Yes. You said your wife did not care for the work. I made her nervous and she had not been scientifically trained–scientifically–s c i e n tif to understand the importance of investigating it. | (Right.) | Therefore you were satisfied to let others do it.'

319.10–12 [A . . . N.]] The veridical statement appears in the sitting record as: 'You wrote and asked me what you would better do about *her* mother. She was not so [word not clear] as she had been represented but was all right towards you——towards you. | (By Jingo! that is straight as a duck, Dick.) [To G. B. D. This is all ten years old.] | I remember it well. Good boy(?) I was so impressed by all that you said I never forgot it. | (That's good, Dick. Very characteristic of what there was between us.) | You bet! I recall also that you said you would not be happy ['until' read without] (No!) until all was definitely settled—— | (Right.) | ——which was very soon after——very soon after.'

320.11 Mrs. F. . .] 'LaFarge . . . Farge.' was originally typed, as in the transcript, but James deleted it and substituted 'F. . . ?' followed by a deleted bracket.

325.15 C.B.] The MS is wanting between 323.31 and 338.8; moreover, the transcript of this sitting has not been preserved in the London Society's archives. As a result, no external evidence is available to identify 'C.B.' here, as well as 'H——t' at 325.18, 'Mrs. C.' at 325.22, 'Mrs. P.' at 328.17, 'Mrs. M.' at 328.25, 349.8, etc., 'B——g' at 332.5, Annie, Mary, Mamie at 333.31–32, the father and a young man at 339.7, and the possibly confidential matter noted at 339.3. However, see Professor Skrupskelis' Notes.

338.24 spiritist] The E,A reading 'spiritual' must be the typist's error for MS 'spiritist', which is the correct meaning. For the same error made previously, see Emendations entry 307.23.

339.34 M. Bergman] In the MS James first wrote 'Mary Hillard' (twice) and then deleted it, interlining 'R. Bergman' over the first and 'Bergman' over the second. In the E proof he was somewhat less cautious, and altered 'R.' to 'M.' The name cannot be confirmed from transcripts since the London Society preserves no transcripts of Hodgson sittings after October 23, 1906. See also 350.21, missing in MS and in transcript.

352.4 him?] This word ends a line followed by ellipsis dots (which may be deleted) interlined above similar deleted dots. Beginning a new paragraph on the next line James wrote 'Do you remember, etc.', which is quite certainly his cue for the typist to copy some special pages now lost, for the text skips here from 352.4 to 352.27. Not understanding the cue, the typist seems to have copied it automatically as if it continued Hodgson's speech, and the proof-reading of E and A (and of the typescript) did not catch the error. The line in the lost MS would have read, of course, as in E and A: 'Mrs. M.: Do you remember any other special pipe?'.

353.23 hand] In the holograph MS the final 's' is deleted but seems to have been mistaken by the typist as an intended plural. It is possible that James may have reversed his decision when he came to read over the typescript, but the ambiguity of the alteration in MS leads one to adopt the singular as James's final intention.

354.30 (May 14th, 1906).] In MS this is interlined above deleted '[I can't recover this passage or I would give the exact reference]', and the date is followed by 'p. 26', perhaps a reference to the file James had succeeded in unearthing.

358.24–25 of course . . . naturally] We seem to have here a double proof correction in E and in A made without reference to each other. MS and TMsᶜ read '(including of course the brains) . . . are of course parts', which presumably was the form of the lost typescript. The repetition of 'of course' seems to have caught James's attention in proof. In A he altered the first 'of course' to 'naturally' (enclosed in commas), and let stand the second 'of course'; in E he reversed the process, retaining the first 'of course' and altering the second to 'naturally'. Final intention cannot be determined here since it is probable that each change was made independently and perhaps with no distinct memory of the other. In these circumstances, the simplest course is to reproduce the revision as found in the copy-text E.

365.11 sense] Some slight uncertainty may exist about the authority of this reading versus MS 'assurance'. The MS here is not entirely clear, and a compositor might readily have been led to attempt a clarification by substituting the simple 'sense' for what he could have mistaken as the nonce word 'surance'. The next to the last line of fol. 11 ends 'automatically, *& [*intrl.*] my as- | ['conscience at' *del.*] surance of this'. It is not wholly certain whether James started to write 'assurance' but changed his mind and (without deleting 'as-' |) began the next line with 'conscience at' before deleting this and continuing with 'surance', although this procedure is perhaps more probable than that he added 'as-' to end the line above and then continued after deleted original 'conscience at' with 'surance' even though as written there was room for the 'as' before 'surance'. The circumstances being so obscure, and the reading perhaps seeming uncertain, a compositor could have overlooked the 'as-' or thought that it was intended for deletion along with the first words of the next line and so never connected 'as-' with the lone 'surance' that followed deleted 'conscience at'. Still, a possibility is not a probability and the superior sense of 'sense' can be defended as making James less culpably cocky.

365.35 pretension,] The comma in MS is present, but since 'pretension,' was interlined above deleted 'value' (with a comma), its comma appears rather low down and could easily have been overlooked by the compositor.

372.21 a] The 'a' is part of the interlineation 'a fictitious' but is so widely separated from 'fictitious' as to have been easily overlooked.

Historical Collation

This list comprises the variant readings that differ from the edited text in the authoritative documents noted for each essay. Included for their intrinsic interest are the substantive variants (less bibliographical additions and cross-references) in the collection of James's essays, *Memories and Studies* (M&S), edited by Henry James, Jr., (1911), and in *Collected Essays and Reviews* (CER), edited by R. B. Perry (1920), in which a number of the essays in this volume were reprinted. The reading to the left of the bracket is that of the present edition. The rejected variants in the noted documents follow in chronological order to the right of the bracket. Any collated texts not recorded are to be taken as agreeing with the edition-reading to the left of the bracket; only variation appears to the right. The noting of variant readings is complete for the substantives (and for the accidentals where manuscript is present). To save space, however, both substantive and accidental variants are omitted in the Historical Collation whenever the copy-text has been emended and thus when the details may be found recorded in the list of Emendations. Otherwise the noting of variant readings is complete for the substantives save for the special cases of the editorial references and other strictly editorial changes in M&S and CER, and save for the rejected readings of the sources for James's quotations, which are confined to the Emendations list. The rejected accidental variants in collated texts when manuscript is present are also complete except for trivial differences in the accidental bibliographical details of footnotes. James's occasional inscription in manuscript of more than the usual three or four dots indicating ellipsis (unless the manuscript is the copy-text and is emended, in which case the emendation may be found in the Emendations list) and such purely typographical matters as the use of an asterisk instead of a number for a footnote are not recorded. Manuscript ampersands and variant spacing (as sometimes appears in words like *is n't*) are also not recorded.

The headnote to the Emendations list may be consulted for general conventions of notation. One special feature appearing in the Historical Collation, as in the Emendations, is the use of *et seq*. When this phrase occurs, all subsequent readings within the essay are to be taken as agreeing with the particular feature of the reading being recorded (save for singulars and plurals and inessential typographical variation, as between roman and italic), unless specifically noted to the contrary by notation within the entry itself. Readings grouped together with multiple page-line references may also be concerned with only the particular feature being recorded and not with inessential types of variation. A plus sign signifies all collated texts later than the text identified by the

574

sigil. Other arbitrary symbols employed in the Historical Collation when a document other than the manuscript is the copy-text include the § and the ‡. As in the Emendations, the § mark indicates that the variant is included wholly or in part in an alteration in the manuscript, the description of which has been removed to the Historical Collation from the list of Alterations in the Manuscripts. The double dagger (‡) indicates that the variant in the MS is part of a larger alteration not easily transferable to the Historical Collation, the details of which can be found in the Alterations in the Manuscripts. When used together, the two symbols show that the variant occurs both in a unique alteration and as part of a larger alteration. To find the details of the larger alteration the reader should consult the Alterations in the Manuscripts. In those cases when another document agrees with a revised manuscript variant, a semicolon separates that document's sigil from the listing of MS; this emphasizes the agreement of the document(s) with the final reading of the MS.

Occasionally a variant reading between an article copy-text and MS occurs because James has made a simple error, as in putting a caret in the wrong position to indicate an interline, or in failing to omit a word or punctuation mark in an otherwise deleted passage, or in deleting a word or punctuation mark in error and not restoring it. Such mistakes, if linked to an alteration, are recorded as part of the entry for the passage in the Alterations list instead of in the Historical Collation.

For conventions of description in alterations see the headnote to the list of Alterations in the Manuscripts.

1. REVIEW OF *Planchette*, BY EPES SARGENT (1869)

The copy-text is BDA, "Planchette," *Boston Daily Advertiser*, March 10, 1869 (McDermott 1869:1), with reference to CER, *Collected Essays and Reviews*, edited by R. B. Perry, pp. 1–3 (McD 1920:2), which has been collated for substantives only.

2.18   no] in no CER

11. THE CENSUS OF HALLUCINATIONS (1889–1897)

h. Final American Report: Letter to Henry Sidgwick (1896)

The copy-text is ALS, James's holograph letter to Henry Sidgwick (H. 25 in the archives of the Society for Psychical Research) (McD [1897:15]), with reference to substantive variants contained in TMs, the carbon typescript of the same letter (bMS Am 1092.9 [3761]), and to Congr., the letter as partially reported in *Dritter Internationaler Congress für Psychologie in München*, 4 (1897), 392–394. The autograph alteration in TMs is designated as WJ/TMs.

74.5-9 I . . . so.] *om.* Congr.	74.37 so] *om.* TMs
74.11 to . . . -probability] *om.*	74.38 on] on | *on* TMs (*error*)
TMs,Congr.	75.13 these] them TMs
74.12 follows] follow TMs,Congr.	75.16-17 −19 . . . 90] *om.* TMs
(*error*)	75.18 of our] WJ/TMs; out of TMs
74.27 I] *om.* TMs,Congr.	75.18 12] *om.* TMs
74.31 friends] persons TMs,Congr.	75.19 still] shall still TMs,Congr.

75.24 Actually,] *om.* TMs
75.32 these] these 12 Congr.
76.1–17 Better . . . yours,] *om.* Congr.

76.1–2 if . . . scientific."] *om.* TMs
76.7 weeks and] *om.* TMs

12. A Record of Observations of Certain Phenomena of Trance (1890)

The copy-text is P³², "A Record of Observations of Certain Phenomena of Trance," *Proceedings of the Society for Psychical Research*, 6 (December 1890), 651–659 (McD 1890:3). Reference is made to RPJ, *Religio-Philosophical Journal*, n.s. 1 (January 17, 1891), and to P³¹, "Report of the Committee on Mediumistic Phenomena," *Proceedings of the American Society for Psychical Research*, 1 (July 1886), 102–106 (McD 1886:2).

80.11 Miss] Mrs. RPJ
80.33 of] *om.* RPJ
[*begin* P³¹]
81.25 myself.¹] ~ ·ₐ (*om. fn.*) P³¹
81.26 sitters] sisters RPJ (*error*)
82.13 ³of] *om.* RPJ
82.28 affect] effect RPJ (*error*)
82.39 medium–] *om.* P³¹
83.5–7 No . . . state.] She was twice tried with epistolary letters in the medium-trance,—once indicating the contents in a way rather surprising to the sitter; once failing. In her normal waking state she made one hundred and twenty-seven guesses at playing-cards looked at by me,— I sometimes touching her, sometimes

not. Suit right (first guess) thirty-eight times,—an excess of only six over the "probable" number of thirty-two,—obviously affording no distinct evidence of thought-transference. P³¹
[*end* P³¹]
83.13 Piper's] P.'s RPJ
84.28 have] *om.* RPJ
85.8 experiences with] experience of RPJ
85.19 more] *om.* RPJ
85.33 was asked] was asked | was asked RPJ (*error*)
85.39 revelations] revelation RPJ (*error*)
87.3 the] a RPJ
88.14 strong] wrong RPJ (*error*)

13. What Psychical Research Has Accomplished (1892)

The copy-text is P¹⁰, "What Psychical Research Has Accomplished," *Forum*, 13 (August 1892), 727–742 (McD 1892:1). Reference is made to WB, *The Will to Believe*; for the details of the relationship see The Text of *Essays in Psychical Research*. The note (*em.*) indicates emendation of the first printing of WB by the present editor to the form shown in the lemma.

89.1–7 If . . . science] The Society for Psychical Research has been one means of bringing science and the occult together in England and America; and believing that this Society fulfils a function which, though limited, is destined to be not unimportant in the organization of human knowledge WB
89.10 ²the] this WB
89.11 is] *om.* WB

89.13 Sidgwick,ₐ] ~ ,¹ | ¹Written in 1891. Since then, Mr. Balfour, the present writer, and Professor William Crookes have held the presidential office. WB
☞89.19 amongst] among WB(*em.*) (*also* 90.9,14,27;97.26)
90.9 Alfred Russel] A. R. WB
90.13 "Society . . . Research"] S. P. R., as I shall call it for convenience, WB
90.13 February,] *om.* WB

90.15   Henry] *om.* WB
90.26;103.34   whilst] while WB(*em.*)
90.26   completely . . . and] *om.* WB
90.30–31   (as . . . it)] *om.* WB
90.37   in . . . Society] *om.* WB
91.3,14   Society] S. P. R. WB
91.9   quite] *om.* WB
91.10   there] cited WB
91.11   uncritical] imperfect WB
91.11–12   the . . . presumption] at most
they lead to the opinion WB
91.13   in . . . quarter] upon that
quarter in one's mind WB
91.16–17   The . . . done.] *om.* WB
91.17   have] have in every reported
case WB
91.19   narrative] story WB
91.23   seven] *om.* WB
91.25   Society's] *om.* WB
91.26   empirical] *om.* WB
91.28   could . . . exist] lives WB
91.29   case of] *om.* WB
91.29   of a] *om.* WB
91.31   would] will WB
91.32–33   who . . . long] we shall
doubtless end WB
91.34   found . . . theory] theorize WB
91.35   Those . . . Society] Its sustainers,
therefore, WB
91.38   in . . . generation] at first WB
91.39–92.14   Three . . . -supporting]
om. WB
92.15   One] But one WB
92.32   extraordinary] rare WB
92.40   the] *om.* WB
93.3   is certainly] was, when it
appeared, WB
93.5   volume] volumes WB
93.6   F.W.H.] Frederic WB
93.9   Mr.] Dr. WB
☞ 93.15   "case"] ∧ ∼ ∧ WB (*similar*
101.11–12;102.16;104.3,4,6)
93.15–17   Other . . . Marillier.] *om.* WB
93.19   *Proceedings.*1] Proceedings.∧
(*om. fn.*) WB
93.26–27   This . . . performances.] *om.*
WB
93.28   conditions] conditions of the
earlier series WB
93.28   then] *om.* WB
93.31   reader.] reader. Many critics of

the S. P. R. seem out of all its labors
to have heard only of this case. But
there are experiments recorded with
upwards of thirty other subjects. WB
93.32   other . . . subjects] *om.* WB
94.4   these] these latter WB
94.8   people's] persons' WB
94.9–16   present . . . Edwards'] witnesses
of these WB
94.16   were] were in fact WB
94.17;96.25   phenomenon] phenomena
WB
94.20–22   refuse . . . be] demand, for
so revolutionary a belief, a more
overwhelming bulk of testimony
than has yet been WB
94.23–25   Volume . . . *Proceedings.*]
om. WB
94.28–29   , the . . . example] *om.* WB
94.29   Omitting] But omitting WB
94.31–32   , of . . . doubtful] *om.* WB
95.4   considered] excluded WB
95.5   by far] *om.* WB
95.13   prove] seem to prove WB
95.16–17   whose . . . methods] *om.* WB
95.22   psychology;] ∼ , and WB
95.30–31   based on hallucinations] due
to either torture or hallucination WB
96.3   some] over WB
96.4;102.17   people] persons WB
96.7   that] that in England WB
96.9   and] and that WB
96.9   14 per cent] a large number WB
96.10   real] *om.* WB
96.10–12   In . . . precise.] *om.* WB
96.13   this . . . frequency] the frequency
of these latter cases WB
96.15–23   My . . . basis.] Mr. and Mrs.
Sidgwick have worked out this
problem on the basis of the English
returns, seventeen thousand in
number, with a care and
thoroughness that leave nothing
to be desired. Their conclusion is
that the cases where the apparition of
a person is seen on the day of his
death are four hundred and forty
times too numerous to be ascribed to
chance. The reasoning employed to
calculate this number is simple
enough. If there be only a fortuitous

connection between the death of an individual and the occurrence of his apparition to some one at a distance, the death is no more likely to fall on the same day as the apparition than it is to occur on the same day with any other event in nature. But the chance-probability that any individual's death will fall on any given day marked in advance by some other event is just equal to the chance-probability that the individual will die at all on any specified day; and the national death-rate gives that probability as one in nineteen thousand. If, then, when the death of a person coincides with an apparition of the same person, the coincidence be merely fortuitous, it ought not to occur oftener than once in nineteen thousand cases. As a matter of fact, however, it does occur (according to the census) once in forty-three cases, a number (as aforesaid) four hundred and forty times too great. The American census, of some seven thousand answers, gives a remarkably similar result. Against this conclusion the only rational answer that I can see is that the data are still too few; that the net was not cast wide enough; and that we need, to get fair averages, far more than twenty-four thousand answers to the census question. This may, of course, be true, though it seems exceedingly unlikely; and in our own twenty-four thousand answers veridical cases may possibly have heaped themselves unduly. WB

96.24   experimental] *om.* WB
96.28–29   In . . . "control,"] *om.* WB
96.32   all] all of them WB
96.32   shows] showed WB
96.35   which] that WB
96.37   of] on WB
96.40   hardly] not WB
96.40–97.13   Although . . . mind.
    (*no* ¶)] [¶] Physical mediumship in

all its phases has fared hard in the Proceedings. The latest case reported on is that of the famous Eusapia Paladino, who being detected in fraud at Cambridge, after a brilliant career of success on the continent, has, according to the draconian rules of method which govern the Society, been ruled out from a further hearing. The case of Stainton Moses, on the other hand, concerning which Mr. Myers has brought out a mass of unpublished testimony, seems to escape from the universal condemnation, and appears to force upon us what Mr. Andrew Lang calls the choice between a moral and a physical miracle. [¶] In the case of Mrs. Piper, not a physical but a trance medium, we seem to have no choice offered at all. Mr. Hodgson and others have made prolonged study of this lady's trances, and are all convinced that supernormal powers of cognition are displayed therein. These are *primâ facie* due to 'spirit-control.' But the conditions are so complex that a dogmatic decision either for or against the spirit-hypothesis must as yet be postponed. WB
98.6–7   I . . . -consciousness."] one might designate as ultra-marginal consciousness.∧ WB
98.22–23   , beyond . . . were.] *om.* WB
98.24–25   or . . . have] *om.* WB
98.28–29   in . . . attempt] *om.* WB
98.31–33   No . . . done.] *om.* WB
99.1   supernatural[2]] ∼ ∧ (*om. fn.*) WB
99.6–11   Cases . . . series.] *om.* WB
100.35   All . . . less] We all, scientists and non-scientists, live WB
100.38–39   But . . . probable] As a matter of fact WB
101.3   facts] occurrences WB
101.5   facts shall] things may WB
101.9   finally] *om.* WB
101.15–16   ingenious friend] able colleague WB
101.16–17   and . . . jolt,] *om.* WB

101.22–24 our . . . capable] the invisible segments of our minds are susceptible WB

101.27 know] now know WB

101.29–30 *scientific.* [¶] Science] in good scientific form,–for science WB

101.31–102.14 Sensorial . . . truth.] *om.* WB

102.15 during . . . years] *om.* WB

102.16 some . . . hundred] hundreds of WB

102.19 In . . . phases∧] At its lowest, WB

102.20 in] at WB

102.20 don't] do not WB

102.28 Whatever] It may be the feeling that some physiological period has elapsed; but, whatever WB

102.32 on] upon WB

102.38 used] accustomed WB

102.39 awakens] wakes WB

103.13 This] This also WB

103.13 some long-eclipsed] forgotten WB

103.23 *e.g.*] for example WB

103.27–28 by . . . people] experiences of persons WB

103.29 Then] Then, too, WB

103.30–31 (as . . . acquainted)] *om.* WB

103.33 superior . . . intellectually] fairly high intellectual level WB

103.36 operation] mental operation WB

103.38 tactics] tactics, if you wish to get rid of mystery, WB

19. Address of the President before the Society for Psychical Research (1896)

The copy-text is TMs, James's autograph revised typescript. Reference is made to P32, "Address by the President," *Proceedings of the Society for Psychical Research*, 12 (June 1896), 2–10 (McD 1896:1) and to P36, "Address of the President before the Society for Psychical Research," *Science*, n.s. 3 (June 19, 1896), 881–888. This list comprises all the accidental and substantive variant readings in P32 and P36 that differ from the edited text. British spellings not favored by James have not been recorded as variants.

127.2 mouse-trap] mousetrap P36

127.2 wide] wide is P32

127.3 2the] The P36

127.6 Republic] *l.c.* P32,36

127.6 exist;–] ~ ; ∧ P36

127.8 life∧] ~ , P32,36

127.10–11 him; . . . chance∧] ~ , . . . ~ , P32,36

127.13–14 unaware∧ . . . it∧] ~ , . . . ~ , P32,36

128.4 must∧ . . . rule∧] ~ , . . . ~ , P32,36

128.13–14 ∧for . . . subjects∧] , ~ . . . ~ , P32,36

128.14 records∧] ~ , P36

128.15–16 coefficient] co-efficient P32

128.20 ∧for . . . part∧] , ~ . . . ~ , P32,36

128.24 -on;] - ~ , P32

128.26 past∧] ~ , P32

128.31 essence;] ~ , P32,36

128.37–38 credulity] creduilty P36

129.1 experts∧] ~ , P32,36

129.11 ∧ to some degree∧] , ~ . . . ~ , P32,36

129.14 chance-] ~ ∧ P32,36

129.22–23 heterogeneous, . . . faultless, . . . prolonged,] ~ ; . . . ~ ; . . . ~ ; P32,36

129.27 yet∧] ~ , P32,36

129.28 *et seq.* sceptic] skeptic P36

129.29 picture-] ~ ∧ P36

129.31 flank∧] ~ , P32,36

129.33 clairvoyance∧] ~ , P32,36

129.33 'test-mediumship.'] *db. qts.* P32

129.39 death-] ~ ∧ P36

130.4 Census-] ~ ∧ P36

130.5 ∧ of course∧] , ~ ~ , P32,36

20. Psychical Research (1896)

The copy-text is P34, "Psychical Research," *Psychological Review*, 3 (November 1896), 649–652 (McD 1896:3). Reference is made to ALS, James's holograph letter to Henry Sidgwick (H. 25 in the archives of the Society for Psychical Research), to TMs, the carbon typescript of the same letter (bMS Am 1092.9 [3761]), and to Congr., the letter as partially reported in *Dritter Internationaler Congress für Psychologie in München*, 4 (1897), 392–394. TMs and Congr. have been collated for substantives only.

140.22 yeses] yes-es ALS	141.16 these percipients] them
140.25 all (*no* ¶)] ¶ 1) all ALS;TMs	ALS,TMs,Congr.
(All);Congr. (1. All)	141.17 them] these ALS,Congr.
140.26 all (*no* ¶)] ¶ 2) all ALS;TMs	141.19 one] 1 ALS
(All);Congr. (2. All)	141.19 case.] case—19 +71 = 90;
140.28 *Of these*] rom. ALS	ALS;Congr. (case:)
140.32 have] I have ALS	141.20–21 all. Suppose] ~ ; suppose
140.32 figure] figure of	ALS
ALS,TMs,Congr.	141.21 veridicals.] ~ : ALS
140.33 numbers).] ~)∧ ALS	141.21 shall] *om.* ALS
140.34 ¶ "*Let*] *no* ¶ ALS	141.22 1/19000,] ~ ∧ ALS
140.34–35 hallucinations] halls. ALS	141.23 to be urged] *om.*
140.35 persons] friends ALS	ALS,TMs,Congr.
140.35 tenth] 10th ALS	141.23 are:] ~ ∧ ALS
140.37 induced . . . and] *om.*	141.24 of numbers] *ital.* ALS
ALS,TMs,Congr.	141.26–27 As . . . 1they] Actually, They
140.38 apparitions,] ~ ∧ ALS	ALS,Congr.; They TMs
141.2–3 if . . . 1day] he may so appear	141.30 furnish] furnished
ALS,Congr.; he may appear TMs	ALS, TMs,Congr.
141.3 *et seq.* 1/19000] 1/19,000 ALS	141.33 first-] ~ ∧ ALS
141.4 *on*] on | *on* TMs (*error*)	141.34 these] these 12 Congr.
141.7 sent] sent to the Proceedings	141.36 against] *ital.* ALS
ALS;TMs (*Proceedings*); sent to the	141.37 result,] ~ ∧ ALS
Proceedings (S. P. R.) Congr.	141.37 otherwise] *ital.* ALS
141.11 *E.g.,*] ~ ∧ ALS	141.38 surface∧] ~ - ALS
141.11–12 collective,] ~ ; ALS	141.40 assurance] dogmatic assurance
141.12 reciprocal,] ~ ; ALS	ALS,TMs,Congr.
141.12 1] one ALS	141.41 death∧] ~ - ALS
141.12 agent,] ~ ; ALS	141.41 , if not lies,] *om.*
141.13 premonitory∧] ~ ; ALS	ALS,TMs,Congr.
141.16 reason,] ~ ; ALS	141.42 Better . . . it.] *om.* Congr.
	141.42 lies∧] ~ , ALS

21. A CASE OF PSYCHIC AUTOMATISM (1896)

The copy-text is TMs, the typescript drawn up under James's supervision, with reference to Pf, a set of galley proofs, and to P³², "A Case of Psychic Automatism, Including 'Speaking with Tongues,'" *Proceedings of the Society for Psychical Research*, 12 (December 1896), 277–297 (McD 1896:4). The sigil Pf(u) denotes the original reading in the galley proofs; Pf(c) denotes the alterations made in the hand of Miss Alice Johnson. Typographical errors corrected have been omitted.

143.2 country,] ~ ∧ Pf(u)	144.1 lady∧] ~ , Pf(u)
143.15 her,] ~ ∧ Pf(u)	144.2 narrative∧] ~ , Pf(u)

☞144.4 letter:₍ₐ₎] ~ :— Pf+ (*similar*
144.6;150.25;151.6;152.31;153.21;
154.33;156.34;157.37;158.16)
144.8 found₍ₐ₎] ~ , Pf
144.9 uplift₍ₐ₎] ~ , Pf(c)+
144.14 himself₍ₐ₎] ~, Pf(c)+
144.16 them,] ~ ₍ₐ₎ Pf+
144.17 now₍ₐ₎] ~ , Pf+
144.18 tongues,] ~ ₍ₐ₎ Pf+
144.20 value.₍ₐ₎] ~ .— Pf+
144.24 James:—] ~ ,— Pf+
144.24 Summer] *l.c.* Pf+
144.36 Saint] St. Pf+
144.39 affected,] ~ ₍ₐ₎ | Pf(u)
144.40 alarmed,] ~ ₍ₐ₎ Pf+
144.45 speaks,] ~ ₍ₐ₎ Pf+
145.2 automatism₍ₐ₎] ~ , Pf+
145.6 February₍ₐ₎] ~ , Pf+
145.35 this:₍ₐ₎ That] ~ :— ~ Pf(u);
~ :₍ₐ₎ that Pf(c)+
145.41 sure:₍ₐ₎ That] ~ :— ~ Pf(u);
~ :₍ₐ₎ that Pf(c)+
145.42 upon:₍ₐ₎] ~ .— Pf+
146.1 last₍ₐ₎] ~ , Pf(c)+
146.3 Subject] *l.c.* Pf+
146.4 follows,] ~ ₍ₐ₎ Pf(c)+
[*begin* Le Baron]
146.14 Coast] *l.c.* Pf+
146.17 ₍ₐ₎Critique₍ₐ₎] " ~ " Pf+
146.20 *et seq. similar* 'control']
" ~ " Pf+
147.14 anyone] any one Pf(c)
147.38 *rapport*,] ~ ₍ₐ₎ Pf(c)+
148.15 back₍ₐ₎] ~ , Pf+
148.16 vapory] vapoury Pf(c)+
148.25 round₍ₐ₎about₍ₐ₎] ~ - ~ - Pf(u);
~ - ~ ₍ₐ₎ Pf(c); roundabout₍ₐ₎ P32
148.39 writes:₍ₐ₎] ~ :— Pf(c)
149.6 control₍ₐ₎] ~ , Pf+
149.20 principle₍ₐ₎] ~ , Pf(c)+
149.22 grave₍ₐ₎] ~ - Pf(c)+
149.25 ₍ₐ₎Zoroaster,₍ₐ₎] " ~, " Pf(u)
149.26 ₍ₐ₎Critique.₍ₐ₎] " ~ ." Pf+
149.36 Stowe₍ₐ₎] ~ , Pf+
150.4 opinion₍ₐ₎] ~ , Pf+
150.11 did;] ~ , Pf+
150.11 shewed] showed Pf+
150.13 Bolton₍ₐ₎] ~ , Pf+
150.23 graveyard] grave-yard Pf(c)+
150.26 people₍ₐ₎] ~ , Pf+

150.28 hast] has Pf+
150.28 Valleys] *l.c.* Pf+
150.29 heart₍ₐ₎] ~ , Pf+
151.1 12] 12th Pf+
151.4 English₍ₐ₎] ~ - Pf(c)+
151.8 Jumba₍ₐ₎] ~ , Pf+
151.9 Egyptians₍ₐ₎] ~ , Pf+
151.10 Rameses₍ₐ₎] ~ , Pf+
151.12 people₍ₐ₎] ~ , Pf+
151.13 end₍ₐ₎] ~ , Pf+
151.13 keeping₍ₐ₎] ~ , Pf+
151.15 ¹Lord₍ₐ₎] ~ , Pf+
151.29 an] a Pf(c)+
151.36 night!] ~ . Pf+
152.4 re-incarnating] ~ ₍ₐ₎ ~ Pf(u)
152.5 ₍ₐ₎however₍ₐ₎] , ~ , Pf+
152.6 *fide*₍ₐ₎] ~ , Pf(c)+
152.7 common-sense] commonsense
Pf(u); ~ - ~ Pf(c); ~ ₍ₐ₎ ~ P32
152.9 -automatism₍ₐ₎] - ~ , Pf(c)+
152.9 nature, ... sublime,] ~ ₍ₐ₎ ... ~ ₍ₐ₎
Pf(c)+
152.22 17] 17th Pf+
152.24 ONE TWO THREE] *ONE,
TWO, THREE* Pf(c); *one, two, three*
P32
152.25;153.5 123₍ₐ₎] ~ , Pf+
152.32–36 glory₍ₐ₎ ... light₍ₐ₎ ... peace₍ₐ₎
... joy₍ₐ₎ ... exalted₍ₐ₎] *each word foll.
by a comma* Pf+
152.37 18] 18th Pf+
152.37 transportation₍ₐ₎] ~ , Pf+
153.1 was,] ~ : Pf(c)+
153.1 can] Can Pf+
153.1 I,] ~ ₍ₐ₎ P32
153.4–5 -surrender, ... -abandonment,
was] - ~ ₍ₐ₎ ... - ~ ₍ₐ₎ were Pf(c)+
153.11 princely-] ~ ₍ₐ₎ Pf(c)+
153.12 Great] *l.c.* Pf+
153.25–26 which₍ₐ₎ ... days₍ₐ₎]
~ , ... ~ , Pf+
153.27 anguish₍ₐ₎] ~ , Pf+
153.32–33 possible₍ₐ₎ ... environment₍ₐ₎]
~ , ... ~ , Pf+
153.36 etc.] *Etc.* Pf+
153.38 believed] believed that Pf+
154.2–3 assumption,] ~ ₍ₐ₎ Pf(c)+
154.8,14 love₍ₐ₎] ~ , Pf+
154.10 Day₍ₐ₎] ~ , Pf+
154.12 earth₍ₐ₎] ~ , Pf+

154.13 mother_∧] ∼ , Pf+
154.14 strength_∧] ∼ , Pf+
154.17 poor_∧] ∼ , Pf+
154.18 me_∧] ∼ , Pf+
154.19 ¹darkness_∧] ∼ , Pf+
154.20 terror_∧] ∼ , Pf+
154.20,21 man_∧] ∼ , Pf+
154.22 peace_∧] ∼ , Pf+
154.22 joy_∧] ∼ , Pf+
154.23 praise_∧] ∼ , Pf+
154.24 dark_∧] ∼ , Pf+
154.25 hope_∧] ∼ , Pf+
154.25 mourning_∧] ∼ , Pf+
154.26 pleasure_∧] ∼ , Pf+
154.27 steals_∧] ∼ , Pf+
154.27 has] hath Pf+
154.28 kills_∧] ∼ , Pf+
154.29 ¹world_∧] ∼ , Pf+
154.29 mine_∧] ∼ , Pf+
154.31 automatic-] ∼ ∧ Pf(c)+
154.38 word_∧] ∼ , Pf+
155.7 City_∧] ∼ , Pf(c)+
155.11 Day] day Pf+
155.16 evident,] ∼ ∧ Pf+
155.16 incipiency_∧] ∼ , Pf+
155.23 independent] independently P32
155.26 experience_∧] ∼ , Pf(c)+
155.29 on_∧] ∼ , Pf(c)+
155.31 *objectivity_∧*] ∼ , Pf(c)+
156.9 December_∧] ∼ , Pf+
156.13 , was,] ∧ ∼ ∧ Pf(c)+
156.14;158.5;161.40 worked_∧] ∼ - Pf+
156.20 ear,] ∼ ∧ Pf+
156.27 bed-room] bedroom Pf+
156.30 level_∧] ∼ - Pf(c)+
156.32 ∧at myself_∧] " ∼ ∼ " Pf(c)+
157.24,25,26,28 again_∧] ∼ , Pf+
157.26 flow_∧] ∼ , Pf+
157.27 beat_∧] ∼ , Pf+
157.28 young_∧] ∼ , Pf+
157.29 rest_∧] ∼ , Pf+
157.30 day_∧] ∼ , Pf+
157.37 assumed] seemed Pf(u)
158.4 but_∧] ∼ , Pf(c)
158.12 energy_∧] ∼ , Pf+

158.17 *unknown tongue._∧*] *Unknown Tongue.*– Pf+
158.21 *et seq. Translation._∧*] ∼ .– Pf+
158.25 *et seq. tongue._∧*] *Tongue.*– Pf+
158.34 Egypto._∧] ∼ .– Pf+
159.5 come.] ∼ ! Pf+
159.6 come_∧] ∼ , Pf+
159.6–7 darkness_∧] ∼ , Pf+
159.9 thee_∧] ∼ , Pf+
159.10 thine_∧] ∼ , Pf+
159.12 interlute] intelute Pf+
159.13 tinkalong] tinka ong P32
160.30 theories,] ∼ ∧ Pf+
160.32 *et seq. Theory._∧*] ∼ .– Pf+
161.5 foregoing_∧] ∼ , Pf(c)+
161.7 foregoing_∧] ∼ , Pf+
161.38 means_∧] ∼ , Pf+
162.1 prose_∧] ∼ , Pf+
162.2 *voce_∧*] ∼ , Pf(c)+
162.3 down_∧] ∼ , Pf+
162.5 'poems'] " ∼ " Pf(u); ∧ ∼ ∧ Pf(c)+
162.13 -automatism_∧] - ∼ , Pf(c)+
162.24 ¹looking_∧] ∼ , Pf+
162.24 daylight;] ∼ . Pf+
162.25 dark:] ∼ ; Pf+
162.30 spreading;] ∼ , Pf+
162.31 byways] ∼ - ∼ Pf+
162.31 spread:] ∼ ; Pf+
162.35 ∧ however_∧] ∼ , Pf+
162.38 October_∧] ∼ , Pf+
162.39;163.32 April_∧] ∼ , Pf+
163.28 any one] anyone Pf(u)
163.31 at,] ∼ ∧ Pf(c)+
163.36 ∧cyclopædia . . . India_∧] ∧cyclopœdia . . . ∼_∧ Pf(u); "Cyclopœdia . . . ∼" Pf(c)+
163.38 mystic_∧] mystic- Pf(u)
164.1 *rapport_∧*] ∼ , Pf(c)+
164.2 praise-worthy] praiseworthy Pf+
164.4 *negation_∧*] ∼ , P32
[*end* Le Baron]

26. Review of "A Further Record of Observations of Certain Phenomena of Trance," by Richard Hodgson (1898)

The copy-text is P[34], *Psychological Review*, 5 (July 1898), 420–424 (McD 1898:7), with reference to CER, *Collected Essays and Reviews*, edited by R. B. Perry, pp. 438–441 (McD 1920:2), which has been collated for substantives only.

191.17 a] *om.* CER

27. Frederic Myers's Service to Psychology (1901)

The copy-text is P[32], "Frederic Myers's Service to Psychology," *Proceedings of the Society for Psychical Research*, 17 (May 1901), 13–23 (McD 1901:1), with reference to the reprint published in M&S, *Memories and Studies*, edited by Henry James, Jr., pp. 143–170 (McD 1911:2), which has been collated for substantives only.

192.0 Service] SERVICES M&S   199.31 soon] sooner M&S

37. Report on Mrs. Piper's Hodgson-Control (1909)

The copy-text is E, "Report on Mrs. Piper's Hodgson-Control," *Proceedings of the Society for Psychical Research*, 23 (June 1909), 2–121 (McD 1909:6). Reference is made to MS (or MS[T]), a combination manuscript and typescript found in the James Collection (bMS Am 1092.9 [4544]), to TMs (and TMs[b]), the carbon typescript of Part I, found in the archives of the American Society for Psychical Research, and to TMs[a] and TMs[c], typescripts found with MS at Harvard. (For details, see The Text of "Report on Mrs. Piper's Hodgson-Control.") Reference is also made to A, "Report on Mrs. Piper's Hodgson-Control," *Proceedings of the American Society for Psychical Research*, 3 (July 1909), 470–589 and, for substantives only, to CER, *Collected Essays and Reviews*, edited by R. B. Perry, pp. 484–490 (McD 1920:2). Where MS is missing, substantive variants found in S, the original transcripts of the sittings preserved in the archives of the Society for Psychical Research and the American Society for Psychical Research, are included for their intrinsic interest.

Not recorded as variants are obvious typographical errors in MS(T) and TMs, space variants and the differentiating of speakers in areas of dialogue, dashes after speakers' initials in areas of dialogue, missing periods following titles (as Mr. and Mrs.) in TMs, and periods after dates in MS (or MS[T]) except when they substitute for commas.

The # symbol, unique to this essay, indicates that the variant in TMs is part of a larger alteration not easily transferable to the Historical Collation.

[*begin* MS(T),TMs,A]

253.0 Report] PRELIMINARY REPORT MS(T),TMs

253.0 Control$_\wedge$] ~ [1] | [1]This report is published simultaneously in the English *Proceedings*. I have merely substituted *parentheses* enclosing what the sitters say for initials used in the English Report. As in the English Report, Notes in brackets are distributed throughout the detailed records. Initials connected with Notes indicate the person who made them, usually the sitter. A

253.1,18–21 Part I[1] | [1]This . . . conjunction.] *om.* MS(T),TMs

253.11 thoroughly] thoroly MS(T),TMs

§253.15–16 collated . . . 1908)] undertaken to collate the various sittings, now *75 [*penc. ab. del. ink* 'ooo'] in number, MS(T);TMs; undertaken to collate the various American sittings (75 in number as I write, the latest being that of January 1st, 1908) A

253.16–254.1 (his . . . records)] *om.* MS(T),TMs,A

254.1 remarks] prefatory remarks MS(T),TMs,A

§254.1–2 phenomenon] Piper-*phenomenon [*alt. fr.* 'phenomena'] MS(T);TMs,A

§254.2 a good] to be *a needed [*ab. del.* 'the best'] MS(T);TMs,A

254.2 follows] is to follow MS(T),TMs,A

§254.3 readers] hearers [*alt. fr.* 'reader'] MS(T)

§254.6–7 had . . . years,] for *some [*insrtd. for del.* 'eigh'] nine ['or ten' *del.*] years *had hardly seen her, [*intrl. w. caret ov. comma*] MS(T);TMs

254.8 the typed records] typed reports MS(T),TMs

254.14 Imperator-] ~ ₍ MS(T),TMs

254.15 dream-] ~ ₍ TMs

254.18 rôles] roles TMs,A

§254.22 extraordinarily] *del.* TMs

254.23 marvellous] marvelous A

254.27 somewhat] somewhat toothless and MS(T),TMs

254.31 his] the MS(T)

254.38 Chief] Until the Spring of 1906, chief TMs

‡254.38 these] which MS(T),TMs

254.39 Sidgwick's] Sidwick's A (*error*)

‡254.40 *Life.*] Life; MS(T),TMs

255.7 The] Most of the MS(T)

§255.7 earliest] earlier [*intrl.*] MS(T)

255.8 but . . . name,] *om.* MS(T)

255.10–12 *Are . . . there?*] all rom. MS(T),TMs,A

255.11 '*spirit*'] "Spirit" MS(T),TMs; "spirit" A

§255.11 *was*] is MS(T); was [*ab. del.* 'is'] TMs;A

255.12 We . . . upon (*no* ¶)] [¶] Results can be reached only by eliminating other causes as improbable. In case they were all eliminated, the residual cause left on our hands would throw some light on MS(T)

255.12 yet] *om.* TMs

255.13 We] Meanwhile we MS(T)

255.13–14 the . . . word] its meaning MS(T)

255.14 provisionally] *om.* MS(T),TMs

255.15 to begin with] *om.* MS(T),TMs

255.15+ *space*] no space MS(T),TMs

255.19 *et seq. this series* (1)] 1. MS(T),TMs

‡255.22 H.,] ~ .₍ MS(T),TMs

255.36 at all] *om.* MS(T),TMs,A

256.8 intimate] intricate TMs,A

§256.15–16 at . . . Piper's,] at one of Mrs. Piper's *trances, [*comma insrtd. for del. closing paren*] MS(T)

256.18 Add,] ~ ₍ MS(T),TMs

256.28 an exceptionally] a particularly MS(T)

256.31 shown;] ~ , MS(T),TMs

§256.39 alive)₍] ~), [*paren ov. period; comma added*] MS(T)

257.12 place,] ~ ₍ MS(T)

257.26 *New York Herald*] rom. MS(T),TMs

257.31+ *space*] no space MS (T),TMs; [*space*] 2. Earlier Communications. A [*end* MS(T); *begin* MS]

‡257.32 spirit-Hodgson's] ~ ₍ Hodgsons MS

257.35 'strength₍'] ' ~ ,' MS

257.37 appearances,] ~ ₍ MS

257.37 Theodate] *om.* MS,TMs,A

257.38 28th,] ~ . MS

257.38 ₍Rector₍] ' ~ ' MS,TMs; " ~ " A [*end* MS; *begin* MS(T)]

258.1 dropped] dropt MS(T),TMs

☞§258.4–6 [The . . . "HODGSON."]] ₍ ~ . . . "~" .₍ [*ink bkts. del.*] TMs (*similar* 258.8–9,11)

258.24 then] *om.* MS(T),TMs

258.25 "what . . . that?"] *sg. qts.*
MS(T),TMs

#§258.28–29 (For . . . -268.)] *parens
del.* TMs

258.29+ *space] no space* MS(T)

258.31 for . . . time] again MS(T),TMs
[*end* MS(T); *begin* MS]

259.27,30 (RECTOR.)] *om.* MS,TMsᵇ

§259.27 all.] ∼ ₐ TMsᵃ; ∼ .*–R.
[*added*] TMsᵇ

‡259.31 1906),] ∼)ₐ MS,TMsᵃ⁻ᵇ
[*end* MS; *begin* MS(T)]

§260.9 P[elham]] Pelham ['elham'
ab. del. period] MS(T)

260.9 up.'] ∼ ₐ ' MS(T)

§260.17–18 name, a . . . hand.] nameₐ
*the medium's hand grasps a ['hair'
del.] brush that had belonged to
Hodgson [intrl.]–* MS(T); nameₐ
the medium's hand grasped a brush
that had belonged to Hodgson. TMs;
name. A . . . hand. A

‡260.24 Referring] *l.c.* MS(T)

260.27 Miss] 'Q'–Miss MS(T),TMs

§260.27–29 [This . . . J.]] *[Q's
correct name given.] [added]*
MS(T);TMs (givenₐ)

261.3 ever.] ∼ ! MS(T),TMs,

§261.5 [Rector . . . closes.]]
ₐ ∼ . . . ∼. ₐ [*bkts. del.*] MS(T);TMs

§261.7 either,] ∼ ₐ [*comma del.*]
MS(T)

261.12 [Miss . . . assents.]] ₐ ∼ . . . ∼·ₐ
MS(T);TMs (asserts)

261.13 5th,] 5th. MS(T)
[*end* MS(T); *begin* MS]

261.17 D——.] D.——ₐ MS,TMs

261.18–19 [After . . . says:–]]
ₐ ∼ . . . ∼:ₐₐ MS,TMs

261.18–19 , Miss Bancroft,] ₐ Miss
B.ₐ MS; , Miss B.ₐ TMs,A
[*end* MS; *begin* MS(T)]

261.25 Bancroft.] B——ₐ MS(T),TMs

261.25,28–29 –W. J.] *om.* MS(T),TMs

262.3 *my*] my TMs

‡262.4 watch."] ∼ ·ₐ MS(T),TMs
(*error*)

§262.5 1906,] ∼ ₐ [*intrl.*] MS(T)

262.5 James, Jr.,] ∼ ₐ ∼ ·ₐ MS(T);
∼ , ∼ ·ₐ TMs; ∼ ₐ ∼ ., A

262.7 follows:–³] (∼ :ₐ ¹ A,E) ∼ :–ₐ
(*om. fn.*) MS(T),TMs

262.9 Well] *l.c.* MS(T),TMs

262.9 Laughs.] ∼ ₐ TMs

262.11,21 Don't] Dont MS(T)

262.17 [After . . . again:–]]
ₐ ∼ . . . ∼:–ₐ MS(T),TMs

262.17 in] *om.* MS(T),TMs

§262.19–21 [R. H.'s . . . Lake.]]
*[Hodgson's . . . ['my' del.] W. J.ₐ
jr.ₐ . . . swimming or fishing at
. . . Lake.] [intrl.]* MS(T); *ₐ R. H.'s
. . . W. J.ₐ jrₐₐ . . . Lake.ₐ [intrl.]*
TMs

262.22 much.] ∼ₐ MS(T),TMs

§262.24 [Q]? [Q]] ' ∼ ' . [*alt. fr.* 'Q.' ']
' ∼ [*period del.*]' MS(T); ' ∼ ' ?
' ∼ ' TMs

‡262.25 His] his MS(T)

262.29 brother-] ∼ₐ MS(T)

262.29–31 [The . . . J.]] *om.*
MS(T),TMs

262.29 Hodgson-] *om.* A

262.32 Men (*no* ¶)] ¶ MS(T)

262.34 records,] ∼ ₐ A

262.36 coherent] correct A

§263.5 ₐThere] . . . . . ∼ [*orig.* ¶ *but
ellipsis dots added for run-on*] MS(T)

263.6 through] thru MS(T),TMs

263.8 Correct.] ∼ ₐ TMs

§263.11 ₐThis] . . . . . . ∼ [*orig.* ¶
but ellipsis dots added for run-on]
MS(T)

‡263.14 (*twice*) J.,] ∼ ·ₐ MS(T)

‡263.14 ²Jr.,] jrₐₐ MS(T); ∼ ·ₐ TMs
[*end* MS(T); *begin* MS]

263.19 Within the . . . limited] In a
single hour MS,TMs; In the . . .
limited A

‡263.20 *verbatim*] rom. MS,TMs

263.24 begin] will begin MS,TMs,A

263.24 callₐₐ] ∼ ,– TMs
[*end* MS; *begin* MS(T)]

263.25 *The*] 3. The A

☛263.25 *The . . . Incident] all caps.*
MS(T),TMs; *upper and lower case*
A (*similar* 268.17;270.1;276.1)

‡263.31 spirit),] ∼ ₐ, MS(T)

§263.34 ₐMiss . . . ring.ₐ] (∼ [*paren
added*] . . . ∼ .) MS(T)

264.1 ring] ring ring MS(T),TMs

264.5 Can] Can | Can MS(T)
264.8 ‸Oh . . . right.‸] (∼ . . . ∼.) MS(T)
264.20 Greek.] ∼‸ MS(T),TMs
264.22,23 Greek] *l.c.* MS(T),TMs
264.30 been] *om.* MS(T)
265.3 ‸Did . . . you?‸] [∼ . . . ∼?] TMs
§265.6 understand. She] ∼ *– ['nd' and dash added end of line] she MS(T); ∼‸ she TMs
265.8 Then] *l.c.* MS(T)
265.9 myself] my | self MS(T); my self TMs
§265.10 That . . . ring?] *(∼ . . . ∼ ?) [*parens added and not del. in error*] MS(T)
265.10 but] But MS(T)
§265.12 yourself.] ∼ ‸ ['f' *added end of line but period om. in error*] MS(T)
265.18 boat-] ∼ ‸ MS(T)
265.19 day.] ∼‸ MS(T)
265.22 [After . . . continues:]] ‸ ∼ . . . ∼ : ‸ MS(T),TMs
266.7 follows].] ∼]‸ MS(T)
§266.17 may] may *immediately [*intrl.*] MS(T)
266.19–20 may . . . been] is quite characteristic of MS(T),TMs
266.23 of . . . -cunning] *om.* MS(T),TMs
266.25 , moreover,] ‸ ∼ ‸ MS(T),TMs
266.29 natural] most natural MS(T)
266.34–35 of the . . . locker,] *om.* MS(T),TMs
266.35 vaguely,] ∼ ‸ MS(T),TMs
266.35 erroneously,] ∼ ‸ A
266.39 that] *om.* MS(T)
267.1 -record] *om.* MS(T)
267.4 Pope, the sitter,] P., MS(T),TMs
267.4 telepathically perhaps] possibly MS(T)
267.5 an] a rather MS(T),TMs
267.5 unusual-] ∼ ‸ MS(T),TMs
267.6,17 Pope] P. MS(T),TMs
‡267.12 (*twice*) Bancroft] B. MS(T),TMs
267.36 its] his MS(T),TMs
267.37–38 and . . . sympathetically,] *om.* MS(T),TMs,A
267.38 is] is | is MS(T)

§267.39 hypothesis.] hypothesis. You apperceive *the message [*ab. del.* 'it'] sympathetically. MS(T);TMs;A (hypothesis—you)
267.40 then,] *om.* MS(T),A
267.41 natural] other MS(T),TMs
267.41 causes,] ∼ ‸ A
268.2 this] the MS(T)
§268.2 ring-] ∼ ‸ [*ink ov. carbon intrl.*] MS(T);TMs
§268.3 itself‸] ∼ , [*comma added end of line*] MS(T)
§268.12–13 ‸reality-coefficient,‸] ' ∼ - ∼ ,' MS(T),TMs (*sg. qts. added in both; comma added in* MS[T]; *comma alt. fr. semicolon in* TMs)
§268.13 Professor] Prof. MS(T),TMs
268.17 *The*] 4. The A
268.18 27th,] ∼ ‸ MS(T)
268.18 1906] 1896 MS(T),TMs
268.18 Hyslop,] ∼ ‸ MS(T),TMs
§268.24 -talk?] ‸ ∼ *? [*alt. fr. period*] MS(T);TMs
268.29 and] and a MS(T),TMs,A
268.31 later‸ . . . Cambridge,] ∼ , . . . ∼ ‸ A
269.1,23 Piper-] ∼ ‸ MS(T),TMs
§269.6 nigger-] *cap.* MS(T),TMs
269.15–16 subsequently] on June 4th & subsequently MS(T),TMs
§269.19–20 Hodgson . . . -control,] the Myers-control *also [*intrl.*] had ['also' *del.*] used the words 'nigger-talk,' MS(T);TMs,A
269.21 Piper's] P's MS(T),TMs,A
269.21 trance-] ∼ ‸ MS(T)
269.26 ¹the] *om.* MS(T),TMs
269.26 had,] ∼ ‸ A
269.30 Dr. Hodgson] R.H. MS(T),TMs,A
§269.32 -talk?"‸‸] ∼ ?" ['lk' *and qst. mk. ov. dash and db. qts. added end of line*] | *.— [*period and dash insrtd.*] MS(T)
263.33 13th,] ∼ ‸ MS(T)
270.1 *The*] 5. The A
§270.2 the voice-sitting] *that [*ov.* 'the'] ['sitting' *del.*] [*intrl.*] MS(T); *the sitting [*ab. del.* 'that'] TMs
270.3 present] the sitter MS(T)

270.4-6 Pid. . . . them.] *within db. qts.
and run-on aft.* 'said:−' [270.3] MS(T)

270.5 [pseudonym]] *om.* MS(T),TMs

§270.15 information−] ~ :− [*colon
alt. fr. period; dash intrl.*]
MS(T);TMs

§271.1 Piddington] P. [*intrl.*]
MS(T);TMs

271.2 also] *om.* MS(T),TMs

271.2 'Huldah'] ∧ ~ ∧ TMs

271.3-4 "Is . . . Ella [pseudonym]?"]
∧ ~ . . . Ella?∧ MS(T),TMs

271.6 ¶ [This] *no* ¶ MS(T)

§271.8-9 Densmore.] ¶ No] ~ .] . . .
No (*no* ¶) MS(T); ~ :∧−[*colon ov.
period and paren del.; sq. bkt. om. in
error; dash ov. ellipsis dots*] [¶] No
[*opp. circled* 'set in' *in mrgn.*] TMs

§271.13 William] Wm. ['m' *ov. period*]
MS(T);TMs

‡271.18 *was*] was MS(T)

271.21 ∧The] "The MS(T) (*error*)

§271.29-34 ∧Regarding . . . Ella.∧]
" ~ . . . ~ ." [*db. qts. added*]
MS(T);TMs

271.29 Mrs.] Miss TMs

‡272.1 veracious] veridical MS(T)

‡272.1-2 utterances] utterance MS(T)

‡272.2 here,] ~ ∧ MS(T)

‡§272.2 they] it [*insrtd.*] MS(T)

‡272.3 lucky flukes] a lucky fluke
MS(T)

272.3 explanations] explanations of
it MS(T)

§272.9 gossipy] gossippy [*intrl.*] MS(T)

272.10,16 although] altho MS(T),TMs

272.22 to] *om.* MS(T),TMs,A

272.32 Christian] *l.c.* MS(T),TMs,A

272.33 'Huldah'] 'Huldah's MS(T)
(*error*)

‡272.33 has] had MS(T),TMs

‡272.33 , moreover,] ∧ ~ ∧ MS(T),TMs

§272.37 , indeed,] ∧ ~ ∧ [*intrl.*]
MS(T);TMs

§272.39 and] ['or' *del.*] MS(T)

273.1 But] *om.* MS(T)

273.1 could] would MS(T)

§273.2 seems] seemed, [*comma
added*] *however, highly [*ab. del.* 'in
the highest *degree [added*]'] MS(T)

[*end* MS(T); *begin* MS]

273.2 unlikely,] ~ ∧ MS,TMs

273.8 which] that MS

§273.9 Mrs. Piper's] the MS; her [*ab.
del.* 'the'] TMs;A

§273.11-12 held . . . Newbold.] held
*held by Prof Newbold [*intrl.*] on
Jan 27th. 1906. MS

273.12 Hodgson-] ~ ∧ MS

273.14 lady] *lady* MS,TMs,A

§273.14,24 [Chicago]] ∧ ~ ∧ [*sq. bkts.
del.*] MS;TMs

§273.19 *Note* . . . N.−] *all rom.* MS
(*intrl.*);TMs

273.22 won't] wont MS

§273.28 [Mr. . . . interjects:−]] ∧ ~ .
[*sq. bkt. del.*] . . . ~ :−∧ MS

273.28-29 "Do . . . Hodgson?"]
" ~ . . . ~?∧ MS; ∧ ~ . . . ~?∧ TMs

‡273.30 Australian cousin] earlier
flame MS; australian cousin TMs

273.31 W.J.] *ital.* A

273.34 [*Chicago*]] ∧ ~ ∧ MS,TMs

274.4 she] She MS

274.5 apparently,] *om.* MS,TMs

274.6 See . . . J.] *om.* MS

‡274.20 October 24th,] Oct∧ 24th.
MS; Oct. ~, TMs

[*end* MS; *begin* MS(T)]

274.22 though] tho MS(T),TMs

275.1 corroborates. . . .] ~ .∧ MS(T);
TMs (corroberates)

§275.3 etc.]] ~ . ['W. J.' *del.*]]
* . . . . [*insrtd.*] MS(T); ~ .]∧
[*ellipsis dots del. insrtd.*] TMs

§275.4-10 Do . . . so.] *del.* MS(T)
(society); *om.* TMs

§275.11-16 [Mrs. . . . J.]] ['[Mrs. T's
address being unknown, the question
has not yet been asked. W. J.]' *del.
insrtd.*] MS(T); *om.* TMs

275.13 refused. He] ~ , he A

§275.17 W.J. Do] W.J. *then asks:−
[*ab. del. dash*] "Do [*db. qts. in error*]
MS(T);TMs (∧Do

275.18-19 [To . . . name.]] ∧ ~ . . . ~·∧
MS(T),TMs

[*end* MS(T); *begin* MS]

276.1 *The*] 6. The A

274.3 the Secretary's] R.H.'s MS; the
secretary's A

276.3-4 Hodgson] he MS

276.4 had, after . . . years,] ~ ∧
since . . . ~ ∧ MS

276.6,7 embarrassment] embarassment
MS,TMs

276.7 Myers's] Myer's TMs (*error*)

276.8;277.18 American] *l.c.* MS
[*end* MS; *begin* MS(T)]

276.18 30th,] ~ . MS(T)

276.20 praying.] ~ ? MS,A

276.28 sitter's] sitter's | sitters MS(T)
(*error*)

276.34+ *space*] [*end of page*] MS(T)
[*end* MS(T); *begin* MS]

277.2–3 (who . . . work)] ∧ ~ . . . ~ ,
MS; , ~ . . . ~ , TMs

277.2–3 the Secretary's] his MS

§277.10 donor] friend [*aft. del.* 'sitter']
MS;TMs

277.11 Hodgson] Hodg- | [*end of page*]
MS

277.16 Vice-President] *l.c.* MS,TMs

277.16 Society] *l.c.* MS,TMs

§277.21–22 situation, . . . secret.]
situation. [¶] ['Of course,' *del.*] If ['I'
ov. 'i'] ['Mrs. *Piper's ['* 's' *insrtd.*]
kno [*ab. del.* 'be ruled out']' *del.*]
knowledge on Mrs. Piper's part be
ruled out [', and spirit-return
disallowed, the' *del.*] we seem reduced
to *either a [*ab. del.* 'the']
supernatural alternative or to
chance-coincidence. MS;TMs (out,)

277.23 ¶ Few] *no* ¶ MS,TMs

§277.23–25 but . . . explanations] and
[*insrtd. for del.* 'but'] of the two
possible supernaturalist explanations,
spirit-return, or reading of the
sitter's mind, different critics will
make their choice according to their
prepossions. *Meanwhile, [*insrtd.*]
With *thought-transference [*ab. del.*
'mind-reading'] as *its at least [*ab.
del.* 'a'] possible ['le' *ab. del.* 'ility']
explanation, [*intrl.*] MS;TMs
(prepossessions *and* with)

277.26+ *space*] *no space* MS

277.31 *et seq.* (1)] 1. MS,TMs

277.35 compatible] *ital.* MS,TMs

277.39–278.3 ∧Hodgson . . .
messenger.∧] [~ . . . ~ .] MS

278.4 Hodgson-] ~ ∧ MS,TMs

278.4 taken by itself] *ital.* MS,TMs,A

278.15 will,] ~ ∧ MS,TMs

278.20 Volume] *l.c.* MS

278.20 *Proceedings*] rom. MS,TMs

278.20 sections] *cap.* MS,TMs

§278.27 have been] were [*ab. del.* 'are']
MS;TMs,A

278.28 still] *om.* MS

278.29 ended . . . ¹as] thought them
MS

278.29 real;] ~ , MS

278.30 there being] *om.* MS

278.31 able] masterly MS,TMs

§278.40 at last] now [*ab. del.* 'at last']
MS

279.2 well] *om.* MS

279.5 forceps,] ~ ∧ A

279.6–7 Quantity . . . material.] *om.*
MS,TMs

279.7 will probably] may A

279.8 the facts] got them MS,TMs
[*end* TMs]

279.11 PART II] *om.* MS

279.13 "Believe . . . -CONTROL.] *om.* MS

279.14 Richard] *om.* MS

279.17 Branch∧] ~ , MS

279.17 of our Society] *om.* MS

✒‡279.17–18 although] altho MS
(*also* ‡283.6;‡287.4;‡338.23;‡339.28;
354.4)

279.18 -presidents] -presidents of the
S. P. R. MS

279.19 Edmunds,] ~ ∧ MS

‡279.23 Last,] ~ ∧ MS

‡279.25 H.'s] H.s MS

279.26 , Jr.,] ∧ jr.∧ MS

279.28 Members . . . Associates] *each*
l.c. MS

§279.30 Dr.] Mr. ['M' *ov.* 'P'; *insrtd.*]
MS

279.32 ¶ Absent] *no* ¶ MS

279.34 ¶ Prof.] *no* ¶ MS

§279.35–36 Part . . . 1909.] At Miss
Johnson's invitation I *sent ['t' *ov.*
'd'] a preliminary instalment of this
report to be read at the ['meeting'
del.] S. P. R. meeting in London,
Jan 23rd. 1909. ['To that paper,
printed on the Proceedings XXIII,
p. I will refer ['the rea' *del.*] my
readers,' *del.*] not wishing to repeat

matter already published, MS (*entire fn. found immediately bel. title at beginning of Part* II *of text; fn. marked off and* 'Note' *written in mrgn.*)

279.36   28th,] 23rd. MS; 23rd, A

279.37   Part I] that former paper MS

280.5   felt] left A (*error*)

280.11   ¶ There] *no* ¶ MS

280.18   English] *l.c.* MS

280.18–19   Branch, and to] branch; to MS

§280.19   Piper-reports] * ~ ∧ ~ [*ab. del.* 'records'] MS

280.20   Society] *l.c.* MS,A

§280.22   out,] ~ ∧ [*comma del.*] MS

280.29   Medium] *l.c.* MS,A

‡280.31   either] whether MS

‡280.35   which] who MS

§280.36   Dorr] D. [*period insrtd. and* 'orr' *del.*] MS

280.36–37   Henry James, Jr.,] H. J. jr∧∧ MS

§280.37–38   property;] *property, and about **pecuniary [*insrtd. for del.* 'his'] rights connected with Myers's book; [*ab. del.* 'effects; with P., L.,'] MS;A

280.38   with Piddington] *om.* MS

280.38   Dorr] D. MS

§281.1   about mediums] *about the [*intrl.*] case of a 'young light' MS

§281.2   Dorr . . . Lyman] D.∧ J., *P., [*intrl.*] & L. MS

§281.2–3   whom . . . sittings;] inducing Newbold, Mr. Hale, *or **myself [*ab. is ink del. penc.* 'Hale'] [*comma del.*] to manage the sittings, [*ab. del.* 'to assume the secretaryship;'] MS

281.4   ¹etc.,] ~ ∧, MS

281.9   with] with with MS

281.17   co-operates] cooperates MS

281.19   you think] *om.* MS,A

281.19   your] your own MS,A

281.20   met] met, either MS,A

281.25–26   confusions∧] ~ , MS (*error*)

281.26   ∧conditions,∧] ' ~ , ' MS

‡281.28   of us also,] people MS

281.28   react] *react* MS

‡281.28   our] their MS

281.30   loom] *loom* MS,A

281.32   cold] ~ - MS (*error*)

281.32   -reading;] - ~ , MS,A

281.37   copious,] ~ ∧ [*comma del. in error*] MS

282.5   incidents,] ~ ∧ MS

282.6   it∧] ~ , MS

282.9   here;] ~ , MS

282.17   spirit-] ~ ∧ MS

282.23   evidence∧] ~ , MS

‡282.25   ∧rule of presumption∧] ' ~ ~ ~ ' MS

‡282.25   scientific] sci-|tific MS

282.29   should] must MS

282.40   opinion,] ~; MS

§283.2   'spirits'] ∧Spirits∧∧ ['S' *ov.* 's' *and not reduced in error; final* 's' *added bef. del. hyphen*] MS

‡283.9   possible] *ital.* MS

283.9   these Hodgson-] the MS,A

283.11   everywhere;] ~ , MS

§283.23   , in fact,] ∧ * ~ ~ [*ov.* 'be s']∧ MS

§283.28–31   Yet . . . purpose.] Yet the meaning which ['those parts' *del.*] the ['whole' *del.*] machine expresses, and without which the parts would not be there [*comma del.*] *at all, [*insrtd.*] is more than push and pull, for the whole thing is working out a human purpose. MS

283.30   *meaning . . . expresses*] all rom. A

283.34–35   , as it were,] ∧ * ~ ~ ~ ∧ MS

§283.35   the mechanical] *the only [*ab. del.* 'the lower mechanical'] MS

§283.35   'spirits'] ['alone' *del. insrtd.*] a [*intrl.*] 'spirit['s' *del.*]' *can ['imperfectly' *del.*] [*intrl.*] MS

‡283.36   their thought] his thought at all MS

283.37   , therefore,] ∧ ~ ∧ MS

‡283.38–39   *the . . . us.*] all rom. MS

‡284.4   *in any event*] rom. MS

284.6   spirit-] ~ ∧ MS,A

§284.7–8   'impossible'∧ (as . . . 130),] ' ~ 'ˣ [*opening sg. qt. insrtd.*] | ˣAs ['A' *ov.* 'a'] my colleague *Münsterberg ['rg' *ov.* 'g'] does, Psychology & Life, ['p.' *del.*] 190 [*but poss.* '130'] p. MS

284.7–8   Münsterberg] Munsterberg A

284.8　thus] *om.* MS

284.10　2I] *om.* MS,A

284.21–23　Nor . . . life.] *om.* MS

284.24　phenomenon,] $\sim$ ∧ MS

§284.29–30　words . . . unlikely.] word 'humbug' *acquires a character of unlikeliness. [*ab. del.* 'seems to me a weird one.'] MS;A ("humbug")

‡284.31　in . . . respects] otherwise MS

‡284.32　monkeying] fraudulent MS

284.38　quantitative] *om.* MS

§285.1　sincere∧] $\sim$, [*ab. del.* 'at least sincere,'] MS

285.1　at . . . brutal] *om.* MS

285.1　however∧] $\sim$, A (*error*)

285.1　wholly] *ital.* MS

§285.2　insincerity.] Does it ['in the end' *del. intrl.*] seem ['more' *del. intrl.*] likely that so big a part of human life *should be ['it' *del.*] composed of [*ab. del.* 'such express *should [*insrtd.*] ['unmixed' *del.*] be ruled by'] pure mendacity? MS

285.11　recalcitrant∧] $\sim$, MS

‡285.12　Medium] *l.c.* MS,A

285.17–18　himself;] $\sim$, MS

285.18+　space] *no space* MS

285.23　, moreover,] ∧ $\sim$ ∧ MS

285.23　excessive,] $\sim$ ∧ MS

285.28　'control'–some] ' $\sim$.' Some MS

285.31　a propos] *rom.* MS

285.32 *et seq. similar*　16,] $\sim$. MS

285.36　Similarly,] $\sim$ ∧ MS

285.36　ultra-] extra- MS

286.2　course,] $\sim$ ∧ MS

§286.5　, however,] ∧ however∧ [*intrl.*] MS

286.11　me."∧] $\sim$."ˣ | ˣSitting of March 13, p. 9½. MS,A

‡286.12　in . . . soon] or to be given MS

§286.17　trance-] trance∧ [*bef. del.* 'stock'] MS

286.22　stock-] $\sim$ ∧ MS

286.22　Mrs.] $\sim$ ∧ MS

286.25　to-day] today A

286.26　got into] *rom.* A

‡286.29　thus∧] from it MS; $\sim$, A

286.30　G.P.,] *G.P.*∧ A

286.31　copiously,] $\sim$; MS

286.32　in∧] $\sim$, MS

286.37　sitters,] $\sim$ ∧ MS

§286.38　calling the first] [*on. fol.* 25] calling ['ing' *added*; *aft. del.* 'I will'] the first | [*fol.* 26] *calling the first [*intrl.*] MS (*error*)

286.39　1906] $\sim$, note 9 MS;A (Note)

287.1　*The*] 2. The A

‡287.1,2,10　*Oldfarm*] OLD FARM MS

287.5　Dorr∧] $\sim$, MS

287.6　the latter's] her MS

287.9 *et seq. similar*　5th,] $\sim$. MS

287.9　H.-] $\sim$. ∧ MS

[MS *missing,* 287.11–289.30]

[*begin* S]

288.17,37　G.B.D.] *om.* A (*which encloses the line in parens*)

288.38　or off] or S

289.18　Mr. Dorr then] G.B.D. S

289.19　friend] friend of G.B.D.'s S

289.19　where R.H. outwalked] where each of them tried to out-walk the other and R.H. outlasted S

289.22　in] at any time in S

289.25　them] these S

[*end* S]

§289.31–32　Mr. Dorr] ['Mr.' *del.*] G.B.D. MS

289.33　root?] $\sim$. MS

§289.34　Miss B. (to . . . D.)] * $\sim$ $\sim$., ∧ $\sim$ . . . $\sim$. ∧ [*db. underl.*] MS; [To G.B.D.] A

289.34　*you*] you MS

290.2　"yes."] ' $\sim$.' MS

290.6　Mr.] Mr. George MS

[MS *missing,* 290.11–18]

290.12　œuvre] oeuvre A

290.19　spoken] *om.* MS

290.19–20　taking . . . himself,] *om.* MS

[*end* MS; *begin* MS(T)]

290.22 *et seq.*　G.B.D.] *om.* MS(T),A (*parens subst.*)

290.25　No] R. H.— No MS(T)

☛290.25　can't] cant MS(T) (*similar* 296.24;297.5;299.21;300.22;302.12,19, 28;315.10,15,26)

290.28　Minna and Gemma] *ital.* A

§290.29　trances, but . . . reply.] trances [*period and bkt. del.*] *—not un-pertinent as a reply.] [*added*] MS(T)

290.32　[repeated . . . emphatically]] ∧ $\sim$ . . . $\sim$ ∧ A

290.32 emphatically].] ～ .] MS(T)

§290.33 Gertrude₍ₐ₎] ～ — [*dash insrtd. bel. two del. asterisks*] MS(T)

290.33 Mary. They] ～ ₍ₐ₎ they MS

§290.34–35 [Correct . . . May.]] ['[May, not Mary was correct–W.J.]' *added and then del.*] MS(T)

§291.3 names.]] names. The first three names were given unhesitatingly & *were correct, [*comma added, bkt. del.*] save that *Mary ['ary' *ab. del.* 'ay'] should have been *May [*alt. fr.* 'Mary'].] [*insrtd. for del.* '& they were right. The sister whose name was not given was one whom we saw oftener than Gertrude, while Hodgson could hardly have seen much of Robert.'] MS(T)

291.4 lady] woman MS(T)

‡291.12–13 correctly].] ～ .] MS(T)

§291.13 her,] her, the one who married *a—— [*insrtd. for del.* 'an [Austrian.]'] MS(T)

291.13 , you] —— ～ MS(T)

291.18 with.] ～ —. MS(T)

‡291.18 animus.—] *animus.* ₍ₐ₎ MS(T)

291.18 W.J.] *om.* A

291.20 Harbor] *l.c.* MS(T)

☛‡291.21 correct.—] ～ .₍ₐ₎ MS(T) (*similar* 292.5,25;293.3–4,17;‡295.28; 296.22;‡299.15;301.2,14,24;‡302.21–22; ‡307.2;‡308.2,23;314.23;320.12;‡321.8, 16,‡22)

‡291.21 D.] G.B.D. MS(T)

§291.28–29 of . . . J.]] ['later. *W. J.] [*added*]' *del.*] *of my previous report. W. J.] [*intrl.*] MS

292.6–15 ₍ₐ₎G. . . . sittings."₍ₐ₎] [～. . . .～. "] MS(T)

292.6 endeavoring] again endeavoring MS(T)

292.6 Bar₍ₐ₎] ～ - MS(T)

292.7 again] *om.* MS(T)

292.8 when] when staying MS(T)

292.9 that,] ～ ₍ₐ₎ A

292.12 remember] think MS(T)

292.12 meant to send] sent MS(T)

§292.13 garden,] garden *₍ₐ₎— [*opening db. qts. del.*] I remember I once meant *to, [*comma added*] MS(T)

292.16 through] thru MS(T)

292.18 back-] ～ ₍ₐ₎ MS(T)

§292.19 ₍ₐ₎ through the woods₍ₐ₎] *, thru ～ ～ , [*commas added*] MS(T)

292.23 the] a MS(T)

§292.25;293.17 D.] *G.B.D. [*added*] MS(T)

292.26–28 ₍ₐ₎G. . . . name.₍ₐ₎] [～. . . .～ .] MS(T)

§292.30 boat. . . .] ～ , ₍ₐ₎ I remember of—should not say [' 'OF' *del.*] 'of' [*asterisk del.*]—I *remember*—oh I *know* perfectly well—it shows the automatic *running ['r' *ab. del.* 'c'] of the machine. MS(T)

292.30 I (*no* ¶)] ¶ MS(T)

292.33 together₍ₐ₎] ～ , MS(T)

292.35 up] up in MS(T) (*error*)

§293.1 her 'spirit'] the *M.-spirit [*ab. del.* ' 'Minna'-personality'] MS(T); ～ " ～ " A

293.1 trances,] ～ ₍ₐ₎ MS(T)

§293.4 D.] ['This was referred to in one of my own sittings a few weeks ago.' *del.*] G.B.D. MS(T)

293.13 be] me MS(T)

293.15 nor] or MS(T)

‡293.23 it,] ～ ₍ₐ₎ MS(T)

293.24 though] tho MS(T)

293.26 years] years now MS(T)

293.26 The] But the MS(T)

[*end* MS(T); *begin* MS]

293.31 now.—] ～ . ₍ₐ₎ MS

293.31 D.] G.B.D. MS

293.32–34 ₍ₐ₎After . . . follows:—₍ₐ₎] [～ . . . ～ :—] MS

293.32(*second*),33 about] *om.* MS,A

293.33 some] all MS

293.34 noticed] noticed by me MS

[*end* MS; *begin* MS(T)]

‡294.4 violin,] ～ ₍ₐ₎ MS(T)

294.4 von] Von MS(T)

294.5–6 That . . . improbable.—] *om.* MS(T)

§294.6 D.] *G.B. [*intrl.*] D. MS(T)

294.10 you] you—I have seen Shaler MS(T)

‡294.11 says] tells me MS(T)

‡294.14 Dorrs'] Dorr's MS(T)

‡294.14 Boston.—W.J.] Boston.—For the Shaler episode, see below, p. W.J.] MS(T); Boston. A

[*end* MS(T); *begin* MS]

294.16 H.-] ∼ ·ʌ A

294.20 *a priori*] *rom.* MS

294.20 others] *cap.* MS (*error*)

294.22 -return,] -∼ʌ MS

294.22–23 is . . . explanation] are . . . explanations MS,A

294.24 fewness] *ital.* MS,A

§294.32 say,'] say;' [*semicolon ov. period*] MS

‡294.33 fancy,] ∼ ʌ MS

294.37 imagine.ʌ] ∼ .— MS

295.1 *The*] 3. The A

295.3 Harbor,] ∼ ʌ MS

295.3–4 Maine, . . . been.] Maine. MS

295.5 Bancroft] B. MS

295.8–9 Mr. . . . present,] *om.* MS

[*end* MS; *begin* MS(T)]

295.10 I] R. H.— I MS(T)

☞295.14 you.] ∼ ʌ MS(T) (*similar* 296.12;298.2[*second*];301.21;309.7,23, 25;310.3;311.16;312.25,34;313.4,6 [*second*];314.25;315.8,11;316.25; 317.9;319.30–31)

295.15 *must*] *rom.* MS(T),A

295.20–21 [The . . . script.]] *om.* MS(T)

295.22 subject,] ∼ ʌ MS(T)

‡295.27 however,] ∼ ʌ MS(T)

295.31 ¹Do] do MS(T)

[*end* MS(T); *begin* MS]

295.33 Here . . . reprinted,] *om.* MS

295.33 and remarks] in the writing, and all parts of the record which are MS

295.35 printed.—] ∼ ·ʌ MS

[*end* MS; *begin* MS(T)]

296.2–7 [Accurate . . . B.]] *found bel.* 'fire.' [296.8] *in* MS(T)

296.6 piazzaʌ] ∼ , MS(T)

296.7 B.] ∼ ʌ MS(T)

§296.20 pp. . . . 355] page ['s' *del.*] [*space*] MS(T)

296.26 , being] ʌ was MS(T)

‡296.26 'hat,' . . . asks:—] 'hat.' MS(T)

§297.7 Bayley] Baley [*penc. insrtd. in mrgn. for del.* 'Bayley [*ink ov. typed* 'Baley']'] MS(T)

§297.8 you? Jsp.] ∼ , [*comma added*] Jsp['(?)' *del.*]? [*qst. mk. added*] MS(T)

297.9 'him?'] ʌ∼ ?ʌ MS(T)

297.22 land,] ∼ ʌ MS(T)

§297.23 See . . . J.] *See **my preliminary report, [*ab. del.* 'above,'] p. ooo. [*added*] MS(T)

297.25 "How is Nellie?"] 'how ∼ ∼ ?' MS(T)

297.26 , presumably . . . Piper,] *om.* MS(T)

297.28 death,] ∼ ʌ MS(T)

298.13;302.1 Yes,] ∼ ʌ MS(T)

§298.22 See . . . J.] *See preliminary report p. ooo. W. J. [*added aft.* '5th.'] MS(T)

298.24 connexion] connection A

[*end* MS(T); *begin* MS]

298.25 *A propos*] *rom.* MS

298.25 Bancroft's] B.'s MS

§298.26 which . . . Piper,] with *Mrs. M., [*ab. del.* 'another person *(Oct. 17th. 1906), [*intrl.*] who was slightly acquainted with Miss B,'] [*in mrgn.* 'Mr. M.' *del.*] MS

298.28 himʌ] ∼ , MS

☞298.30 Bancroft] B. MS (*also* 302.32,33;303.2,3;304.35)

298.36 -lights,] - ∼ ʌ MS

[*end* MS; *begin* MS(T)]

299.1 Bancroft's] B's MS(T)

299.3 confusion,] ∼ʌ MS(T)

299.4 Bayley's] B's MS(T)

299.5 Hodgson-] ∼ ʌ MS(T)

‡§299.15 B.] W. [*ov.* 'a'] D. B. MS(T)

299.19 wanted] wanted first MS(T)

‡§299.22 correct.—W.J.]] ∼ʌʌ ['WJ' *del.*]*] [*bkt. undel. in error*] Compare preliminary report p. ooo WJ]. MS(T)

299.27 ¶ No] no ¶ MS(T)

‡299.28 , Dick,] ʌ ∼ ʌ MS(T)

299.29 ¶ [R.H.] no ¶ MS(T)

299.29 deep-] ∼ ʌ MS(T)

299.30–31 supposition] suspicion A

299.32 *et seq.* B.] W. D. B. MS(T)

300.10 *ALL.* . . .] ∼ ʌʌ MS(T)

300.19 to-day] today MS(T)

300.23;301.4;302.24 Bayley] B. MS(T)

300.30 ¹this] that MS(T)

§300.32–33 [Miss . . . fly'."]] *in error insrtd. aft. del. closing bkt. aft.* 'B.' *at* 300.27 MS(T)

‡300.32 [Miss] ∧ ~ MS(T)

‡300.32 "I] ∧ ~ MS(T)

‡300.32 'peacemaker'] ∧ ~ ∧ MS(T)

‡§300.33 I] *illeg. letter del.* MS(T)

‡300.33 'shoo fly'."] ∧ ~ ~ ∧ · ∧ MS(T)

301.1–2 handed to the medium] *om.* MS(T)

301.2 but] & MS(T)

301.3 cigar] *ital.* MS(T),A

301.10 ball-] Ball- MS(T)

301.17–18 ∧Next . . . . Then:–∧] [~ . . . . ~ :–] MS(T)

‡301.20 Report] *l.c.* MS(T)

301.20 *Proceedings*] Proceedings LVII MS(T)

301.20 ∧Vol. . . . 65.—] (vol∧ . . . 65)∧ MS(T)

301.27 [Blavatsky]] *om.* MS(T)

301.28 [Correct . . . J.]] *om.* MS(T); [~ . . . knowledge.] A

‡302.5,8 also] *om.* MS(T)

302.7 tricks] trick MS(T),A

§302.16 place?] *qst. mk. del. in error* MS(T)

302.16 Possibly] *l.c.* MS(T),A

302.21 however,] *om.* MS(T),A

§302.21 2heard] *think I heard [ab. del.* 'associate'] MS(T),A

302.24 watch.] ~ . [Correct.–W. D. B.] MS(T)

302.25 [Miss (*no* ¶)] ¶ A

302.26 accepting] *om.* MS(T)

[*end* MS(T); *begin* MS]

302.31 sincerity."∧] ~ ."– MS,A

302.32 'light.']] '~.'∧ MS (*error*)

302.33 1906,] ~∧ MS

302.34 this,] ~ ∧ MS

302.35 to her sitting] *om.* MS

§303.1–2 The control] He [*insrtd. for del.* 'He'] MS,A

303.8 me.] ~ ∧ MS (*error*)

303.11–12 [Miss B. (*no* ¶)] ¶ A

[MS *missing,* 303.16–304.28]

304.23 you] *om.* A

304.24 me?"] ~ " ; A

§304.29 had] has [*intrl.*] had MS

304.29 sittings, on Dec. . . . 1907] sittings, (Dec. . . . 1907) MS

304.31 wall-] ~ ∧ MS

304.31–32 of yellow colour,] yellow; MS

304.32 colour] color A

304.32 -house,] - ~ ; MS

304.32 etc.,] ~ .; MS

304.34 ¶ He] *no* ¶ MS

304.34 very] rather MS

305.2 3rd] 4 MS

[MS *missing,* 305.7–28]

305.21 Austin] A—— A

‡305.30 not incoherent] very coherent MS

305.33 them∧] ~ , MS

306.4 Billy,] ~∧ MS

‡306.5 items,] ~ ∧ MS

‡306.9 repetitions∧] ~ , MS

306.11 ¶ Dr.] *no* ¶ MS

306.11 his] the MS

306.16 name,] ~ ∧ MS

306.16 2knew] *om.* MS

306.23 *Professor*] 4. Professor A

306.24 ∧*i.e.*] –i. e. MS

§306.26 had] has [*ab. del. insrtd.* 'has'] had MS

306.26 written] *om.* MS

[*end* MS; *begin non*-WJ MS(T)]

306.31 Hallo] Hello MS(T)

‡307.1 splendid] glorious MS(T)

‡307.2 July,] ~ ∧ MS(T)

‡§307.2;308.23 N.] *W. R. N. [added]* MS(T)

§307.4 predictions∧ which] predictions—— ['(2)' *del.*] | (Indeed you did!) | ——which MS(T)

307.7 that.] ~! MS(T)

307.8 up] [up] MS(T)

307.12 *I . . . you*] *each rom.* MS(T)

‡307.25 you."] ~ . ∧ MS(T)

307.28 1as] *om.* MS(T)

308.1 Firstrate!] ~. MS(T)

308.6 ago?] ~ . MS(T)

308.11 *wish*] wish A

308.16–17 which . . . omits.–N.] *om.* MS(T),A

§308.18 [Correct.]∧ until] ['(7)' *del.*] [Correct. *W. R. N. [added]*] | ['(I don't get that.)' *del.*] | ——until MS(T)

308.22 and] ——and——MS(T)

308.22 We] 8 We MS(T)

§309.6 them] them. ['10' *del.*] (9)
  [*added*] MS(T)

‡309.9 veridical] correct MS(T)

309.17 Dick;] ~ : MS(T)

§309.18 ∧A . . . me∧∧ ∧which]
  *"~ . . . ~," [*db. qts. and comma
  added*] *Dᴿ Newbold writes, [*intrl.*]
  "which [*db. qts. added*] MS(T)

§309.19 thought, . . . N.]] ~ ; I do not
  recall making it to H *who went on
  to say:"–[*intrl.*] MS(T)

309.24 H.'s] H∧'s MS(T)

309.24 June,] ~ ∧ MS(T)

309.25;310.3 –N.] *om.* MS(T)

309.26 Good,] ~ ∧ MS(T)

§309.26 And (*no¶*)] ¶ And [*ab. is del.*
  '11.'] MS(T)

309.28 Boston,] ~ ∧ MS(T)

310.2 are here] in portion MS(T)

310.3 evidentially] *om.* MS(T)

310.3 significant.–] ~ ∧∧ MS(T)

310.7 do——] do——a possible case
  MS(T)

‡310.12 ∧Some] –~ MS(T)

‡310.12 had] had [*intrl.*] MS(T)

310.15 And] (Banker? No, go on.) | and
  MS(T)

310.19 a] a——saw a MS(T)

310.20 yes.] ~ ! MS(T)

311.4 [name . . . here]] ∧—— ——∧
  MS(T)

§311.15 ∧was∧] [~] [*intrl.*] MS(T)

311.16 remember no] do not remember
  any MS(T)

§311.22 up.] ~ ∧ (14) MS(T)
  [*end* MS(T); *begin* MS]

311.24 Deanship] *l.c.* MS
  [*end* MS; *begin non*-WJ MS(T)]

311.29 You (*no ¶*)] ¶ MS(T)

312.3 your] your—— I recall your
  MS(T)

312.4 next] then MS(T)

312.6 Hello] 15. Hello MS(T)

312.14 ¹No] no MS(T)

312.15 No!] No! NO! MS(T)

312.22 drinking——] drinking——
  drinking—— MS(T)

312.22 ²Yes,] ~ ∧ MS(T)

312.24 cigarette,] ~ ∧ MS(T),A

312.30 the very] the last time, the
  very MS(T)

§312.32 "Life"] ' ~ ' [*sg. qts. insrtd.
  bef. del. intrl.* '[weekly paper]'] MS(T)

‡312.32 –Some] ∧ ~ MS(T)

312.34 [Word (*no ¶)*)] ¶ MS(T)

313.2 ¹I . . . clear.] *run-on aft.* 'writing.'
  A (*error*)

313.4 –N.] *om.* MS(T)

313.15 But] Yes. But MS(T)

313.18 body?] ~. MS(T)

313.19 "Come . . . alive."]
  ∧ ~ . . . ~——∧ MS(T)

§313.21 "I . . . me."] ∧ ~ . . . ~ · ∧
  [Incorrect.–N.] [added] MS(T)

313.27 so,] ~ ∧ MS(T)

313.29 live.] *foll. by penc.* '[Copy
  note on next page.]'; *next page (fol.
  74(66) is headed in penc.* 'Note on
  p. 73'; *below is typed* '['16.' *del.*] [I
  saw the person here referred to not
  long before his death. He made no
  reference of any kind to the future
  life. Such a promise as is here
  ascribed to him is quite incongruous
  with all I ever knew of him–I do
  not believe the thought would have
  occurred to him.]' MS(T)

313.30 now] *om.* MS(T)

313.30 R.H.] they MS(T)

313.33 Now,] ~ ∧ MS(T)
  [*end non-*WJ MS(T)]

314.9 Dick!] ~. MS(T)

§314.18 "I tried] ∧I ['tr' | *del.*] MS(T)

314.21 –As] ∧~ MS(T)

314.22–23 in . . . sitting] *om.* MS(T)

315.9 me] *om.* A

315.10 No,] ~ ∧ MS(T)

§315.12 hypnotism,] ~ ∧ [*intrl.*] MS(T)

315.17–20 [Hyslop . . . . Do . . . .
  [Possibly] *each begins new line* MS(T)

☛315.22 N.] W. R. N. MS(T)
  (*also* 320.12;321.7,16)

315.33 Yes,] [After some difficulty:]
  (Yes, MS(T)

316.4 [The] *new line* MS(T)

316.5 had] *om.* MS(T)

316.11 here∧] *om.* MS(T); ~ , A
  [*non-*WJ MS(T)]

316.29 Yes,] ~ ∧ MS(T)

317.1 Billy.] ~ . [What W.R.N.
  here said was lost.] MS(T)

317.4 others.–] ~ · ∧ MS(T)

317.6 Dick,] ∼ ; MS(T)

317.9 [Refers] *run-on* MS(T)

317.9 next] *om.* MS(T)

317.10 You] [Hand bangs on table.] |
You MS(T)

317.12 Dick,] ∼ ₐ MS(T)

§317.18 expressions and] ∼ .
['Understand?' *del.*] And MS(T)

317.18 why] Why MS(T)

317.25 that therefore] , therefore,
MS(T)

§318.9 man] men [*alt. fr.* 'man'] MS(T)

§318.11 case.¹²] ∼ ·ₐ MS(T) (*fn.
indicator insrtd. aft.* 'characteristic'
[318.14] *w. autograph note:* '[Print
page 73 in the form of a note]');
bef. del. insrtd. '(19)'

‡318.16 *had*] had MS(T)

†318.16 -sided!] - ∼ . MS(T)

318.16 ₐDo] —— ∼ MS(T)

318.26 mentioned,] ∼ ₐ MS(T),A

318.29 manifestations,"] ∼ ₐ"
MS(T),A

318.30 so-] ∼ ₐ MS(T)

318.30 phenomena,"] ∼ ₐ" MS(T)

318.37 answer:] ∼ ; MS(T)

§318.38 —N.] ['N.' *del.*] MS(T)

‡319.12 —N.] ₐW.R.N. MS(T)

§319.17 shore?] ∼ ? ['22' *del. insrtd.*]
*[He told me then of two
['mediumistic' *del.*] women, but I
forget their names.—N.] [*insrtd.*]
MS(T)

319.30 up,] ∼ ₐ MS(T)

320.1 won't] Oh won't MS(T)

320.2 am,] ∼ ₐ MS(T)

320.7 lady] *lady* MS(T)

320.9 'Huldah'-] " ∼ " ₐ A

‡320.10 Part . . . this] preliminary
MS(T)

‡320.10 See pp. 270–275] See
Proceedings, 000 p. 000 MS(T)

320.12 recall . . . no] do recall this now
but not MS(T)

320.21 friend?] ∼ₐ MS(T)

§320.23 astronomer? . . .] ∼ ? | *(Oh
yes.) [*tr. by guideline fr. two lines
bel.*] | [This happened in 1895. H.
was interested in the inhabitants of
Mars [*closing bkt. del.*] *W.R.N.]
[*added*] | [Something said [*comma

del.] *by W.R.N., [*intrl.*] not
recorded] | Of course I do. MS(T)

320.27 [This . . . N.]] *om.* MS(T)

321.4 last week] *om.* MS(T)

321.7 sitting] first sitting MS(T)

‡321.8 P.ₐ] P., MS(T)

§321.10 careful.] ∼ . *[Correct. [*ab.
del.* 'Ditto'] W. J. MS(T)

321.13 [I . . . J.]] *om.* MS(T)

321.17 However,] ∼ ₐ MS(T)

321.20 , possibly . . . Piper] *om.* MS(T)

[*end* MS(T); *begin* MS]

321.25 are . . . and] *om.* MS

§321.26 others] others that ['I' *del.*]
have been held since Hodgson's death
MS

321.26 who] that MS

321.27 Piper's] Pipers MS

321.28–29 (compare . . . above)] *om.*
MS

321.32–33 two of the] the two MS

321.33 printed,] ∼ ₐ MS,A

322.1 resultant] result and A (*error*)

322.1 words:] ∼ . MS,A

[MS *missing*, 322.2–8, *plus fn.* 14]

322.11 them,] ∼ ₐ A

§322.16 ₐ namely₍ₐ₎] , *∼ , [*intrl.*] MS

§322.19 ¶ Dr.] (*no* ¶) Dr. [*aft. del.*
'The sittings I am reporting on'] MS

§322.20 coercive] *coercive*['ly evident'
del.] MS

‡322.21 alternatives—] ∼ ,— MS

322.23 Hodgson,ₐ] ∼ ,— MS

322.30;323.10 Hyslop's] Hyslops MS

322.33 pp. 6–49] 1899 A

322.38 trances] tranec MS

322.39–40 (*Proceedings* . . .–38.)] *om.*
MS,A

323.2 Hyslop] H. MS

323.8 'cheese'] ₐ ∼ ₐ MS

323.12 etc.,] ∼ ₐ, MS

‡323.12 this] all this MS,A

323.14 was,] ∼ ₐ MS

323.21 *W.J.'s*] 5. William James' A

323.25 *verbatim*] rom. MS

323.27 voice-] *om.* MS

323.28 (May . . . 1906)] *om.* MS

323.29 tedious] insipid MS

[MS *missing*, 323.31–338.8]

323.31;324.26 is——] ∼ . . . . A

324.8 [R. (*no* ¶)] ¶ A

325.10   [Hodgson (*no* ¶)] ¶ A
326.3   H.,] ~ .ₐ A
326.11–12   ²that . . . been] of an MS.
reply to Osler A
327.23   Mrs. J.] *om.* A
328.30   A.M.R.] *om.* A
329.20   myself] *om.* A
330.20   W.J.] *om.* A
331.8   clothing?] ~ , A
332.8   Doctor] *l.c.* A
332.30   , you know,] ₐ ~ ~ ₐ A
332.33   pp. 263–268] *om.* A
333.20   is,] ~ ₐ A
333.32   names.] ~ ! A
334.12   not. You] not, but you A
335.14   rooms?] ~ . A
335.26   [Not . . . J.]] *om.* A
335.35   had seen] knew of A
336.19   12thₐ] 12, A
337.30   cleverly] clearly A
§338.13   'pitfall,'] ' ~ ₐ' [*comma del.*]
MS
338.22   positively] *om.* MS
§338.22   was] was *even [*intrl.*] MS
338.23   at all] *om.* MS
338.29   *Mind*] Mind MS
338.29   to] *om.* MS
338.30   Neither . . . anything] He could
remember nothing MS
338.31   Psychical Research] P. R. MS
338.32   mentioned] gave MS
338.32   dress-] ~ ₐ MS
338.33   boots,ₐ] ~ , A
338.35   Paris,] ~ ₐ MS,A
§338.37   "God . . . her."] ' ~ . . . ~ ' :
[*dash del.*] MS
338.38   lead . . . identification] name
no lady in particular MS
339.7   (known . . . life)] [~ . . . ~] MS
339.8   made . . . himself] ['ma' *del.*]
taken his own life MS
339.10   ₐthe father'sₐ] [~ ~] MS
339.11   though] tho' MS
339.11   gloves,] ~ ₐ MS
‡339.12–13   suggested to me] prompted
MS
§339.25   group,] group, [*ab. del.*
'circle,'] especially at *their ['ir'
added] Adirondack *'camp' [*ab. del.*
'['Camp' *del.*] settlement'] MS
339.26–27   , but . . . 353),] *om.* MS

339.27   poor;] *om.* A (*error*)
339.28   ¹was] *om.* MS
339.29   sitter's] sitters' A
§339.31   latter] *del.* MS; *om.* A
§339.31–32   There . . . omit.] The
only *item in it [*ab. del.* 'dis str
veridical thing'] that *seemed
['decisive' *del.*] supernormal ['on that
occasion' *del.*] [*ab. del.* 'was
striking in it, and possibly evidential,
*in it, [*intrl.*]'] was Hodgson's
reminding *Dʳ P. [*ab. del.* 'the
sitter'] of his feeling *during life
[*intrl.*] towards a certain common
friend and saying: "it has changed—
I do not think her selfish now."
This related to *confidential [*intrl.*]
talks which Dʳ P. *distinctly [*intrl.*]
remembered, and could be explained,
*apart from accidental coincidence,
[*intrl.*] only by *Mrs. P. [*intrl.*]
tapping his mind, or by R. *H.'s[' 's'
del. and restored] ['['being there'
del.] ['memory' *del.*] still being alive'
del.] memories [*insrtd.*] still being
operative [*comma del.*] behind the
scenes. MS
339.32+   space] no space MS; [*space*] 6.
Miss Bergman's Sittings. A
‡339.34   M.] R. MS,A
339.37   December 31st, 1907,] *om.* MS
340.1   them] *om.* MS
§340.1   sitting, . . . 1908,] sittingₐ ['was'
del.] MS
340.4   spirit-] ~ ₐ MS,A
340.4–5   (names . . . -evidential)]
[~ . . . -~] MS
340.5   trance-] ~ ₐ MS
340.7   Bergman] H. MS
§340.12   Correct,] ~ ,— [*comma
doubtful; dash ov. period*] MS
‡§340.12   M.B.] ['M.' *del.*] R.B. MS;A
340.13   while] change of control MS
340.13   reappears,] ~ ; MS
[MS *missing*, 340.14–345.21]
340.22;344.20   M.B.] R.B. A
341.28   several] *om.* A
342.1   sitting,] ~ ₐ A
343.5–6   [Already . . . awake.]] *found
aft.* 'work.' [343.9] A
344.16   time,] ~ ₐ A

597

344.25   mind,] ∼ ∧ A
345.22   thus] *om.* MS
§345.23   hotels] Hotels ['at which they stayed' *del.*] MS
‡345.23   stayed,] ∼ ∧ MS
345.31   *Australian*] 7. Australian A
345.32   messages,] ∼∧ MS
345.32   affection∧] ∼ , MS
‡345.36   what follows is] that follow are MS
345.37–38   "Do . . . Cooper?"] *sg. qts.* MS
346.1   etc.∧ Compare] ∼ ∧—Compare MS; ∼ .—compare A
346.2;347.14   *Proceedings*] rom. MS
346.2   Vol. VIII] vol, viii MS
346.6   *Melbourne*] June 4th.— *Melbourne* MS
§346.7   town,] Town, [*comma insrtd. bef. del.* '&'] MS
‡346.10   Robertson] *ital.* MS
346.10   recalled.] ∼ ; MS
346.12   *where*] rom. A (*error*)
346.12   *play.*] ∼ ∧ MS
346.13   *Rebecca.*] ∼ ∧ MS
§346.14   *-yard.* [False?]] - ∼ ∧ *[false?] [*penc. added*] MS
§346.19–20   *et seq. similar through* 346.37   light. [Not remembered.]∧] ∼ ∧ [not ∼ ∧]. MS (*except at* 347.28) (*periods del. at* 346.19,20,21[*second*], 24,34,37)
346.22   *Hydes*'] Hyde's MS
346.23   Name] name MS
346.24,33   Not] not MS
346.26   *fly-the-garter*] ∼ ∧ ∼ ∧ ∼ MS,A
346.27   *Roberts*] (?) *Roberts* MS,A
346.27   from Miss Hodgson] *om.* MS
346.30   Wrong] *l.c.* MS
346.31   False] *l.c.* MS
§346.32–33   "Let . . . themselves."] ∧let . . . *themselves∧∧ [*period del.*] MS
‡346.34,36   Possibly] *l.c.* MS
346.38   one about] *om.* MS
346.39   Bergman] Hillard MS
346.40   p. 344] p. [*space*] MS
347.1   whole] *om.* MS
347.6   mind . . . sitters∧] sitter's mind, MS
347.7   normal] (probably) normal MS
347.7   part21] *fn.* 21 *attached to*

'world.' *at* 347.19 *in* MS
347.8   probably] *om.* MS
347.11–12   fictitious] such MS
347.13;349.26   Hodgson's] Hodgsons MS
347.13   1888] –8 MS
347.14   Vol.] *om.* MS,A
347.14   pp. 60–67] 60ff. MS; 60 pp. A (*error*)
347.15   'Enid,'] 'Rebecca,' 'Enid,' MS
347.15   'Ellen,'] ' ∼ ∧ ' MS (*error*)
347.16   'Q.'] ∧Q.∧ *in full* MS
347.16–17   (Hodgson . . . 60)] [∼ . . . ∼] MS
347.16   Phinuit] Phinnuit MS
347.17   —see *loc. cit.*,] [*loc.* [*bkt. in error*] *cit.*∧ MS
347.17   in full,] *om.* MS
347.17   inadvertently,] ∼ ∧ MS
347.19–21   The . . . eliminated.] *om.* MS
347.21   , however,] *om.* A
347.24   so . . . that] possible, so MS
347.24+   *space*] *no space* A
347.26   Additional] *begins line marked* ' ¶ ' *with circled* 'blank line' MS
§347.27   for] ['to' *del.*] asking ['ing' *insrtd.*] *her to [*ab. del.* 'if she could ['g' *del.*] inform me'] give me MS
347.27   H.'s Australian] any of R. H.'s australian MS
347.27   Here is] I print MS
347.29–42   "Boston . . . PIPER."] MS *missing*
347.39   'Q.'] " ∼ ." A
347.41   "I] ∧ ∼ A
347.42   PIPER."] ∼ . ∧ A (*error*)
348.2   *verbatim*] rom. MS
348.4   scientific' mind∧] ∼ ∧ ∼ ' MS;A (*db. qts. as in* E)
348.5   category,] category, of MS
348.11   probabilities.] ∼ . [*space*] | 8. Conclusion. A
‡348.13   cite] bring up MS
348.13   additional evidential] *om.* MS
§348.13   points] points that ['seem to have evidential significance, and' *del.*] had no place in the sittings from which my quotations came MS
‡348.14   order] logical order MS
348.15–16   was . . . and] *om.* MS

§348.17 , some . . . quotation.] *similar
to [*ab. del.* 'other [*intrl.*] than'] that
addrest to Dr Putnam about a certain
lady's 'selfishness,' and of the same
['ten' *del.*] nature. Naturally *they
[*alt. fr.* 'these [*alt. fr.* 'they']'] wont
bear citation. MS

‡348.18 thought] tho't MS

348.20–23 A . . . sitter.] *om.* MS

348.25 records] sittings MS,A

§348.28 belongs] belong['s' *del. and
not restored in error*] MS

348.29 Mrs. J.] A.H.J. MS

§348.31 [Mrs. J's sister]] ['[her sister]'
del.] MS

348.32 ∧when] " ∼ MS (*error*)

348.33–34 threateningly," . . . came]
threateningly" MS

348.37 ¶ [I] *guideline marks* MS ¶
for run-on

348.37 fist-shaking] *om.* MS

349.1 -law's] -laws MS

349.3 written] *om.* MS

§349.3 1907] '07 [*aft. del.* '06'] MS
[MS *missing*, 349.5–15]

349.13 ill,] ∼ ∧ A

349.15 M.M.J.] Margaret J. A

349.17 H.,] ∼ ·∧ MS

‡349.18,‡24 *facie*] facie MS

349.19,29 R.H.] *om.* MS

349.23 ∧ as visitors∧] , ∼ ∼ , MS

349.23 therefore] *om.* MS

349.27 Jan.] ∼ ∧ MS

349.33 though] tho MS
[MS *missing*, 350.1–36]

350.25 -Hodgson,] - ∼ ∧ A

351.3 piazzas] piazza's MS

351.4 as] *om.* MS,A

351.5–10 [R. . . . indiscriminately.]]
∧∼ . . . . ∼ ·∧ MS

351.6 Pope's] P.'s MS

351.7 another] another one MS

§351.11 ¶ (7) On] (*no* ¶) (7) The R. H.
control *expressed to [ab. del.*
'showed on'] several *sitters [ab. del.*
'occasions'] solicitude about certain
*facts, [*comma insrtd. bef. del.*
'(?)'] *—if they were facts, [*insrtd.*]
[*begin paste-on*] connected with his
pecuniary relations with F. W. H.
Myers. *Since, [*comma insrtd.*]

however, [*intrl.*] these *facts [*ab. del.*
'relations'] may ['however' *del.*]
have *been, [*comma insrtd.*] *and
probably were, [*ab. del.* 'ventilated']
communicated to the
Imperator-group during Hodgson's
life time, his *bringing [*ab. del.*
'repeating'] them *out [*intrl.*] now
cannot count as evidential [*illeg. del.*]
of ['spirit ret' *del.*] the return of
his spirit. [*end paste-on*] ['thought-of'
del.] (8) [*insrtd. for del. insrtd.*
'(9)'] On MS

351.11 1906,] '06∧ MS

351.12–13 ∧Do . . . work?∧] *within db.
qts. and run-on after* 'said:—'
[351.11] MS

351.12 in] *om.* MS

351.19 no—] ∼ : MS

351.19 remember!] ∼ ? A

351.20–25 ¶ ∧Mrs. . . . survival.∧]
(*no* ¶) [∼ . . . . ∼ .] MS

351.21 American] *om.* MS

§351.21 operations∧] ∼ , [*ab. del.*
'work,'] MS

351.23 naturally] *om.* MS

351.26 (8)] (9) MS

351.26 sitter,] ∼ ∧ MS

§351.26 occasion∧ . . . 1906),] ∼ ,
*(March 5th. 1906∧ [*intrl.*] MS

351.34 *me*] me MS,A

§351.34 etc.] ∼ ∧ [*intrl.*] MS

351.34 Mrs. M.]∧] M.] . . . . MS
[MS *missing*, 352.5–26]

352.27 (9)] (11) MS

352.27 Harvard∧] ∼ - MS

352.29 Professor] *om.* MS,A

§352.30–32 (for . . . did)] , *for
[*ab. del. dash*] . . . did, ['yet no'
del.]— MS

§352.33 him] Prof. [*intrl.*] Child MS;A

‡353.1 assuredly] surely MS,A

‡§353.1 C.] *F.J.C. [*ab. del.* 'these
friends'] MS

353.1–2 ²had . . . spirit,] *om.* MS

‡353.5 through] thru MS

353.6 1906] '06 MS

353.10 body.∧] ∼ .—— MS

353.11 *i.e.*∧] i.e., MS

353.12 —W.J.] *om.* MS

353.15 out.] ∼ — MS

353.18   P.]] ~ .]. MS
353.20   addressed] adressed MS
353.22   Mrs. M.,] The same sitter∧ MS
353.22   30th,] ~ . ∧ MS
‡354.2   be,] ~ ∧ MS
354.2–3   On . . . supernormal.] om. MS
354.4   much like] like much MS,A
‡354.7   the . . . general] it MS
354.7   to be] as MS; to be as A
354.13   would] could MS
354.13   , if printed,] om. MS
354.14–15   , by . . . records,] om. MS
§354.16   unintelligibility,] ~ , ['an'
del.] unverifiability, and *even
[intrl.] positive misstatement, MS
354.22   The . . . bulk] om. MS
‡354.22–23   'Passwords,'] ∧ ~ , ∧ MS
354.25   Latin] l.c. MS
354.26   e.g.] e.g. MS
354.26   "Nebus . . . fecrum"] sg. qts. MS
354.28   weak] om. MS
354.31   given,] ~ ∧ MS
354.31   ¹etc.] ~ ∧ MS
‡354.34   instance,] ~ ∧ MS
354.37   namely,] ~ ∧ | MS
354.38   He] he MS
355.3   Nevertheless,] ~ ∧ MS
355.4   records,] ~ ∧ MS
355.7   the will] that MS
355.8   Piper's] Pipers MS
355.9   , etc.,] ∧ ~ . ∧ MS
355.11   it∧] ~ , MS (error)
355.12   different—] ~ , MS
355.13   bring] get MS
355.13–14   Dramatically,] ~∧ MS
‡355.14   'bosh'] ∧ ~ ∧ MS
§355.17   so] del. MS
355.17–19   approximate . . . more.]
approximate? MS
§355.19   ('Zeivorn,'] (' ~ ∧ ' [paren ov.
bracket] MS
§355.20   example, . . . 329] example∧
*(above∧ [paren in error] p∧ [space].
MS
355.22   control] control quite suddenly
MS
355.22   quite suddenly] om. MS
355.23   way∧] ~ , MS,A
355.29   sitters∧] ~ , MS
355.29   the] om. MS (error)
355.31   recall,'] ~ ∧' MS

§355.33   with . . . firmness] equally
[ab. del. 'as'] firmly MS
§355.37   stored,] ~ ∧ [comma del.] MS
§355.39–356.1   minds . . . it] telepathic
*factors in it [ab. del. 'features of
it'] MS
356.3–4   by . . . itself] om. MS
§356.5   Extraneous 'wills' ['The
[alt. fr. 'These'] field [intrl.] may be'
del.] A [ov. 'a'] 'will MS; Extraneous
"Wills" A
356.7   kinds of will] wills MS
356.9   , in . . . instance,] om. MS
356.9   facie] rom. MS
§356.11–12   ²the . . . found] that *the
spirit [insrtd.] *has found [ab. del.
'it *finds [ov. 'found']'] MS
§356.17   might] might *even [intrl.]
MS
356.24   to;] ~ , MS
356.24   and,] ~ ∧ MS
356.25   -telling] -making MS
356.28   Personally,] ~ ∧ MS
356.29   crucial proof] ital. MS
‡356.30   alone,] ~ ∧ MS
356.37   In] in MS
357.4   'daimons,'] ∧demons,∧ MS
§357.7   arising] actively [intrl.] arising
MS
§357.9   in . . . thereof] there [intrl.]
MS
357.9–13   ∧The . . . rest.∧] bkts. MS
357.11   potential∧] ~ , MS
357.15   a priori] rom. MS
357.15   other spiritual beings] inferior
spirits MS
357.16   co-operate] co operate MS
§357.18–19   other . . . on an] inferior
spirits ['show themselves' del. ab. del.
'seem to be present on an'] ['pretend
to appear on an' del. intrl.]
*profess on an [insrtd.] MS
§357.19   scale] scale *to appear [intrl.]
MS
‡357.20   Myers] Myer's MS (error)
‡357.20   Automatisms] poss. l.c. MS
‡357.21   'enlightenment'] ' ~ ∧ MS
(error)
‡357.23   tradition∧ . . . experience∧]
~ , . . . ~ , MS

357.25–26 (not . . . -theory)] *om.*
MS,A,CER

§357.26–27 certain. One] certain—
[*dash ov. period*] [*del.* 'Only
'scientific' ignorance can be blind to
the ['fact.' *del.*] probability of such
a change.'] one MS

357.27 'scientific' indeed,] *'streng
wissenschaftlich' [*insrtd. for del.*
' 'scientific' '] MS

357.29 somnambulistic or automatic]
om. MS

357.29 participated in and] *om.* MS

357.30 a different] an inferior MS

357.31 probable] *om.* MS

‡357.32 *personate*] rom. MS

‡§357.34 alone, . . . lower] alone.
*Lower [*insrtd. for del.* 'Lower']
spirits MS

§357.35 ones may] *spirits may
[*ab. del.* 'ones produce the mo'] MS

‡357.35–36 some . . . more] the
otherwise MS

357.36+ *space*] no space MS,A

357.38 ask] consider MS

358.1 intervals‸] ~ , MS

‡358.1 become] be MS

‡358.1 as] in MS

‡358.2 spirit-] ~ ‸ MS

§358.4 for] ['for' *del.*] to MS

358.5 *Zend-Avesta*25] rom. MS;
fn. indicator aft. 'elsewhere'
MS,A,CER

358.7 co-ordinated] co ordinated MS

‡358.9–10 *traced . . . universe*] all
rom. MS

358.11 mainly] *om.* MS

358.13 actions] action MS (*poss.*
'actions')

358.16 it.26] ~ ·‸ (*om. fn.*) MS

358.23 the potentiality of] *om.* MS

[*begin* TMs^c]

358.23 systematic activity] activity
systematically MS,TMs^c

§358.25 come] came MS; come ['o'
ov. 'a'] TMs^c

§358.26 some . . . traces] effects MS;
some . . . *traces [*ab. del.* 'effects']
TMs^c

358.26 ancient] *om.* MS,TMs^c

358.26 function] act MS, TMs^c

358.27 and] *om.* A,CER

§358.28–29 'psychometrically,']
' ~ ‸' MS; " ~ ," [*comma and
opening db. qts. insrtd.; closing db.
qts. alt. fr. sg. qts.*] TMs^c

358.29 by . . . is] *through his body,
and as what [*ab. del.* 'as ['a m' *del.*]
what'] came in the trance-jargon
to be MS; TMs^c *corr. by* WJ
to agree with E,A (*except* '‸ *in* . . .
-jargon‸' TMs^c)

[*end* TMs^c]

§358.31 II;] ~ , in which a *more
popular account of [*ab. del.* 'sketch
of'] Fechner's theory of immortality
is given. MS;A,CER

358.31–32 and . . . IV.] *om.* MS

358.31 and] And A

358.37 Händel‸] ~ , A

[*begin* TMs^c]

☞359.1 'influence'] db. qts. alt. fr.
sg. qts. TMs^c (*similar* 359.7,12
[*twice*])

359.2–3 of . . . traces] all rom.
MS,TMs^c,A

359.5 human] *om.* MS,TMs^c

359.6–7 in the cosmos] *om.* MS,TMs^c

359.8 redivivus] redivious TMs^c (*error*)

359.9–10 the reality of] *om.* MS,TMs^c

359.10 this scheme] this ['general'
del.] ['scheme of' *del.*] Fechner's
*scheme [*ab. del.* 'theory'] MS;TMs^c
(*del.* 'Fechner's')

359.10–11 phenomena] facts MS,TMs^c

§359.13 ‸system‸] ' ~ ' MS;
" ~ " TMs^c [*alt. fr. sg. qts.*];A

[*end* TMs^c]

359.14–20 It . . . contributions.] *om.*
MS

359.18 off;] ~ , A

359.19 shown the way] drawn in
A,CER

359.19 up,] ~ ‸ A

359.20+ *space*] no space MS,A

359.21 which] which the mind of MS

§359.23 his] one's [*ab. del.* 'the'] MS

‡359.23 His] The MS

§359.23–24 ever it be] it *ever be
[*ab. del.* 'is'] MS;A

§359.25 his] *del.* MS

§359.25 in him.] *in one. [*ab. del.* 'in him.'] MS

‡359.25–26 *I . . . there*] all rom. MS

‡359.27 doubting,] ~ ∧ MS

§359.30 Hodgson's] *the old [*intrl.*] Hodgson's MS

359.31 mere] inferior MS

§359.31 I remain] *I have to remain [*ab. del.* 'I [*undel. in error*] ['am' *del.*] remain'] MS

359.31 uncertain∧] ~ , MS

§359.32 await] must [*intrl.*] wait for MS

§359.32 point clearly] clearly [*ab. del.* 'clearly'] point MS

359.33+ *space*] no space MS,A

359.35 having] my having considered it my duty MS; my having A

§359.35 itself] *the discussion [*ab. del.* 'myself'] MS; myself A

359.36 alone] by itself MS,A

§359.36–37 The . . . ¹is] *Its content is [*ab. del.* 'In itself, it is'] MS

359.37;360.4 Piper-] ~ ∧ MS

360.3 body] systematic body MS

360.3 Piper-] *om.* MS

360.5 give] have given MS

360.6 its] its (and my) MS

§360.6–7 ¹friends . . . mine] friends. | WILLIAM JAMES | Cambridge *(Mass.) [*parens ov. commas*], U. S. of A. | Jan 15. 09 MS

360.8 assertion,] ~ ∧ MS

360.8 Hyslop's] Hyslops MS

38. THE CONFIDENCES OF A "PSYCHICAL RESEARCHER" (1909)

The copy-text is P⁴, "The Confidences of a 'Psychical Researcher,' " *American Magazine*, 68 (October 1909), 580–589 (McD 1909:7). Reference is made to MS, the holograph manuscript preserved in the James Collection at Houghton (bMS Am 1092.9 [4545]) and to the reprint published in M&S, *Memories and Studies*, edited by Henry James, Jr., pp. 171–206 (McD 1911:2), which has been collated for substantives only.

361.0 The Confidences] Final Impressions M&S

§361.10 at—] at *at all— [*intrl.*] MS

§361.10 established] founded MS

361.11 Psychical Research] *l.c.* MS

361.22 twenty-] ~ ∧ MS

‡362.1 acquaintance] personal acquaintance MS

362.2 though] tho MS

362.9 messages from spirits] spirit-returns MS

§362.14 worthless, . . . that] worthless. [*ab. del.* 'erroneous.'] Yet MS

‡362.15 aught] anything MS

§362.17 upon; so] ~ , [*comma ov. period*] So [*unreduced in error*] MS

362.30–31 (or . . . production);] , ~ . . . ~ ∧; MS

362.34 twenty] 20 MS

§362.35 Schiaparelli, the astronomer,] ~ ∧ *the [*aft. del.* 'L'] ~ ∧ MS

§362.39 opportunity. The] opportunity[', but all' *del.*] —the MS

363.1 account. Yet] ~ —yet MS

§363.1 credit∧] credit, [*ab. del.* 'stock'; *comma in error*] MS

363.4 Carrington,] ~ ∧ MS

363.8 becomes] ever becomes MS

363.8 also] *om.* MS

§363.10–11 Florence . . . medium),] *Florence Cook, [*intrl.*] MS

‡363.17 half-] ~ ∧ MS

§363.21 solider] solider [*ab. del.* 'ampler'] & stronger MS

363.23 Oken∧ and Lamarck∧] ~ , & ~ , MS

§363.24 Darwin] Darwin *['giving' *del.*] only [*ab. del.* 'only doing their work'] MS

‡363.25 only] *om.* MS

363.36 matter] mere matter MS

363.38 much;] ~ , MS

§363.39   row] array [*aft. del.*
'imposing'] MS

§363.39–40   to . . . intention] *the
['desire' *del.*] intention [*ab. del.* 'to
[*del. in error*] willingness'] MS

364.3   as a] in point of MS

364.3   S. P. R.'s] S. P. R. MS

364.4   truth_∧] ∼ , MS

§364.8   lectures–] ∼ ,– [*dash intrl.*] MS

364.9   well-known] perverse MS

364.14   wobble,] ∼ ∧ MS

364.15   *I*] I MS

364.16   *drive a nail*] *rom.* MS

364.20   rabbit'–] ∼ ,' MS

364.27   while] as MS

364.30   although] altho MS

364.37   colleague] collegue MS

364.38   ¹the] that the MS

‡364.38   failing;] ∼ , MS

§365.2   this;] this, [*alt. fr.* 'the'; *comma
added bef. del.* 'essential truth,'] MS

§365.2–3   and . . . specimen] *& one
[*ab. del.* 'the'] excentric ['['action'
del.] failure of ['an' *del.*]' *del.*]
specimen's [' 's' *intrl.*] misconduct
[*intrl.*] MS

365.3   of his words] *om.* MS

365.5   former] *om.* MS

§365.6   Harvard] Harvard, [*comma
added bef. del.* 'University,'] the
Reverend James Walker MS

365.11   automatically;] ∼ , MS

365.15   won't] don't MS

365.17   everything] every thing MS

365.23   of mediums] *om.* MS

§365.25   has . . . being] is *unluckily
[*ab. del.* 'a kind of reality ['fated'
del.] unhappily'] MS

365.27   , 'Rector,'] ∧ ' ∼ ∧ ' MS

§365.28   who discerns] discerning [*aft.
del.* 'capable of the'] MS

365.29   his] of his MS

365.29   needs,] ∼ ∧ MS

365.29   is] *om.* MS

365.31   humbug_∧] ∼ , MS

365.31   —such . . . least–] *om.* MS

365.32   nonplussed by] helpless
before MS

§365.34   Now the] ['To' *del.*] The ['T'
ov. 't'] ['non-expert mind' *del.*] MS

§365.34   looks upon such] *conceives
of [*ab. del.* 'the phenomenon taken']
the MS

365.35   simply] *om.* MS

‡365.35   -pretension] -pretensions
MS (*doubtful*)

§365.36   may] may *otherwise [*ab. del.*
'really'] MS

365.36   below the surface] *om.* MS

365.38   frauds] fraud MS

365.40   public opinion] the public
mind MS

366.5   beforehand] by 'Science' MS

366.7   entirely] *om.* MS

366.8   them!] ∼ . MS

366.8   expression] statement MS

366.9   occurs] is given MS

366.9   Huxley's] Huxleys MS

366.10   ¶ "I] no ¶ MS

§366.25   two] the [*intrl.*] two MS

366.26   namely] *om.* MS

366.27   by.] ∼ : MS

366.29   exists anyhow;] exists, MS

§366.34   dingy twaddle] not [*ab. del.*
'un'] romantic MS

366.37   phenomena_∧] ∼ , MS

366.38–367.1   enough . . . spiritual]
om. MS

366.39   240.] ∼ ∧ MS

§367.7   that a] of [*bef. del.* 'the
[*ab. del.* 'a']'] MS

‡367.7   may abide] abiding MS

‡367.8   has] had MS

367.9   or objective] *om.* MS

§367.12   apparitions] apparitions of
the dying [*comma del.*] MS

§367.12   ¹the] *del.* MS

367.12   ²the] *om.* MS

367.13–14   this . . . Gurney's] Gurney's
telepathic theory MS

367.16   mixed] general MS

367.17   phenomena;] ∼ , MS

367.19   still] *om.* MS

367.19   all,] ∼ ? MS

367.25   which_∧] ∼ , fortunately, MS

367.26   only] *om.* MS

§367.27   anything] any *thing
[*ab. del.* 'other'] MS

367.28   repellent_∧] ∼ , MS

§367.30 *penicillium glaucum*]
penicillium *glaucum [*intrl.*] MS

367.30 *bacterium termo*] rom. MS

367.32 work] dabble MS

367.38 phenomena] phenomenon MS

‡367.38–39 *there . . . displayed*] all
rom. MS

368.2 own] *om.* MS

368.2 thus] *om.* MS

§368.4–5 spirits_∧ . . . tapped] ∼ ,
[*comma undel. in error*] *be tapped
[*penc. insrtd.*] MS

368.6–7 would be] are MS

368.7 originally] *om.* MS

368.12 automatist] medium MS

368.12 his or] *om.* MS

368.14 *will to personate*] desire to
personate MS

§368.16 beings, stray] beings_∧ [*ab. del.*
'parts of *it, [*comma del. in error*]']
stray [*intrl.*] MS

368.17–18 being . . . ¹it] knowing it
any more MS

368.18 is . . . of] knows MS

368.22 for us] *om.* MS

368.23 questions] both MS

§368.27 consider,] ∼ _∧ ['& discuss,'
del.] MS

‡368.29 *naïve*] naive MS

368.31 phenomena are . . . their]
phenomenon is . . . its MS

368.39–369.1 in Nature] *om.* MS

369.2 laws;] ∼ , MS

369.8 animals_∧] ∼ , MS

369.8 plants,] ∼ _∧ MS

‡369.9–10 far-off] faroff MS

369.12 of that time] *om.* MS

§369.13 regular performance]
permanence ['be' *del.*] and order MS

§369.15 history] *the history [*ab. del.*
'time'] MS

‡369.17 wandered] or wandered MS

369.17 else] *om.* MS

369.20 now] *om.* MS

369.22,22–23 ought to] would MS

§369.24 should] would [*ab. del.*
'had never'] MS

369.24 enough in themselves] in
themselves enough MS

369.32 wayward and] *om.* MS

§369.34–35 seem like] are [*ab. del.*
'seem a'] MS

370.1 bates] baits MS

370.4 often] so often MS

370.4 ²say,] ∼ _∧ MS

§370.4 not] not *wholly [*intrl.*] MS

370.5 reason),] ∼)_∧ MS

370.11 anywhere] any where MS

‡370.24 handsome,] ∼ _∧ MS

370.25 Both] *om.* MS

§370.25 kept] both ['grew handsomer
both' *del.*] kept MS

370.28 seek_∧] ∼ , MS

370.30 science] *doubtful cap.* MS

370.30 evidence;] ∼ , MS

370.32 though] tho MS

370.36 twenty-five] 25 MS

370.36 Psychics] *l.c.* MS

371.6 -return,] - ∼ _∧ MS

§371.12 phenomena] phenomenon
['on' *ov.* 'a'] MS

371.18 objects moving] moving objects
MS

371.20 tying] typing MS

§371.21 exclusively_∧] ∼ , [*comma ov.
poss. period*] MS

371.21 for him] *om.* MS

§371.30 yourself,] now_∧ [*ab. del.*
'try'] MS

371.31 kind] form MS

371.38;372.15 although] altho MS

372.2 wish] wish that MS

§372.3 to . . . us.] *to be double.
[*ab. del.* 'mine.'] MS

372.21 ouija-] ∼ _∧ MS

‡372.28–29 *I . . . commonness*] all rom.
MS

372.30 *the presence*] rom. MS

372.31 of] of MS

‡373.4 own] get at MS

373.12 faculties] facuties MS (*error*)

§373.13 *other consciousness*] _∧other_∧
[*sg. qts. del.*] consciousness MS

373.13 of some sort] *om.* MS

§373.17 air,] ∼ _∧ [*comma del. in error
bef. del.* 'so to speak,'] MS

‡373.18 human minds] a human mind
MS

‡373.19 sleeping] *om.* MS

‡373.21–22 opportunities]
opportunity MS

373.24   little] so little MS

‡373.28-29   *for . . . anyhow*] all rom.
MS

§373.29   *phenomenon*] ['whole' *del.*]
phenomena ['a' *ov.* 'on'] MS

373.30   Messrs.] ～ ∧ MS

‡373.32-34   ∧I . . . messengers.∧]
[～ . . . ～ .] MS

373.35   deceive] decieve MS (*error*)

373.36   (possibly?)] [possibly?] [*insrtd.*
for del. '*[opening paren del.*]
possibly, and as a concession to
appearances [*closing paren del.*] [*ab.*
del. '['(or not able)' *del.*] (according
to)']'] MS

373.39   Who] *l.c.* MS

374.1   in them] *om.* MS

374.3   convinced] *om.* MS

§374.15   builds] forms [*alt. fr. poss.*
'fas'] MS

374.18   environment,] ～ ; MS

§374.25-26   , or . . . do,] *(～ . . . ～)
[*parens ov. commas*] MS

‡374.28   scientific] *doubtful cap.* MS

374.30   mother-] ～ ∧ MS

374.31   in it] therein MS

374.31-32   Are . . . there?] *om.* MS

374.33   these then] they MS

374.33   ²How] *l.c.* MS

374.35-375.2   What . . . world?] *om.* MS

375.3   ¶ Vast] no ¶ MS

375.5   mediumistic] personal MS

‡375.7   stirred] moved MS

‡375.8   yet,] ～ ∧ MS (*error*)

375.10   is] is chiefly MS

375.12   *Kühn . . . Lohn!*] all rom. MS

375.12   *Mühen*] mühen MS

375.12   *Lohn!*∧] Lohn!" MS (*error*)

Alterations in the Manuscripts

All alterations made during the course of writing and of revision are recorded here except for strengthened letters to clarify a reading, a very few mendings over illegible letters, and false starts for the same word. The medium is the black ink of the original inscription unless otherwise specified. It is certain that many of the alterations were made *currente calamo* and others as part of one or more reviews. The two are ordinarily so indistinguishable in the intensity of ink or in the kind of pen, however, as not to yield to systematic recording by categories on the physical evidence. In the description of the alterations, when no record of position is given the inference should be that the change was made in the line of the text and during the course of the original writing. *Deleted* or *deletion* is given the abbreviation *del.*; *over* (*ov.*) means inscribed over the letters of the original without interlining; *altered from* (*alt. fr.*) indicates the changing of letters in a word in order to form a new word, as in 'she' *alt. fr.* 'they'; *above* (*ab.*) always describes an independent interlineation. When an addition is a simple interlineation, either with or without a caret, the description *intrl.* is used; when an interlineation is a substitute for one or more deleted words, the formula reads, instead, *ab. del.* 'xyz'. The word *inserted* (*insrtd.*) ordinarily refers to marginal additions or to squeezed-in letters, syllables, and words that also cannot properly be called interlines but are of the same nature. When reference is made to one or the other of two identical words in the same line of the present edition, some preceding or following word or punctuation mark is added for identification, or else the designated word is identified with a superscript [1] or [2] according as it is the first or second occurrence in the line. A superscript is also used to indicate which of more than one identical letter in the same word is referred to. A vertical stroke | signifies a line ending.

In order to ease the difficulty of reading quoted revised material of some length and complexity, the following convention is adopted. The quoted text will ordinarily be the final version in the manuscript, whereas the processes of revision are described within square brackets. To specify what words in the text are being affected by the description within square brackets, an asterisk is placed before the first word to which the description in brackets applies; thus it is to be taken that all following words before the square brackets are a part of the described material. For example, at 68.2 in *Some Problems of Philosophy* (WORKS) James altered 'one' to 'One' when he deleted four succeeding sentences. In the first sentence, which he subsequently may have independently deleted, he wrote 'We may mean' and then interlined 'for instance', following

606

it with 'that' and a false start 'it is our' which he deleted. For the false start he substituted 'we treat the whole of it', deleted that, and wrote above it 'the whole of it can be taken', ending the sentence with 'as one topic of discourse.' He began the second sentence with 'We do this by the' which he deleted. He started again with 'Whenever we use the word 'universe' we' in which he wrote 'W' over 'w' in 'Whenever', interlined 'take it thus,' above deleted 'do this,', interlined 'for', continued with 'we mean that no item of reality shall', wrote 'escape' above deleted 'be left out', wrote 'from what' and inserted 'our word covers;' in the margin for deleted 'we point to,' which he inscribed above deleted 'is signified,'. He carried on beyond the semicolon with 'but this unity of abstract reference, altho it has been made much of by', crossed out 'some rationalists,' above which he wrote 'idealistic writers,' and ended with 'is insignificant in the extreme.' In the third sentence James wrote 'It carries no', altered 'other' to 'further', continued with 'sort of connection with it, and would apply as well to', interlined 'any' above deleted 'an utter', and ended with 'chaos as to our actual world.' The final sentence reads 'Both would be *knowable-together* in the same barren way.' with 'the' written over 'this'. In formulaic terms the alteration entry is transcribed as 68.2 One] ('O' *ov.* 'o'); *bef. del.* '[*del.* 'We may mean *for instance [*intrl.*] that *the whole of it can be taken [*ab. del.* '['it is our' *del.*] we treat the whole of it'] as one topic of discourse. We do this by the'] Whenever ['W' *ov.* 'w'] we use the word 'universe' we *take it thus, [*ab. del.* 'do this,'] for [*intrl.*] we mean that no item of reality shall *escape [*ab. del.* 'be left out'] from what *our word covers; [*insrtd. for del.* '*we point to, [*ab. del.* 'is signified,']'] but this unity of abstract reference, altho it has been made much of by *idealistic writers, [*ab. del.* 'some rationalists,'] is insignificant in the extreme. It carries no *further [*alt. fr.* 'other'] sort of connection with it, and would apply as well to *any [*ab. del.* 'an utter'] chaos as to our actual world. Both would be *knowable-together* in *the [*alt. fr.* 'this'] same barren way.'

In formulaic transcriptions double asterisks can also be used to set off subsidiary alterations occurring between the single asterisk and the bracketed description that applies to this single asterisk, as, for example, 'In all these modes of union *some parts **of the world [*intrl.*] prove [*ab. del.* 'several aspects seem'] to be conjoined'. Inferior brackets clarify subsidiary bracketed descriptions within or before the main bracketed entry with or without the use of asterisks according to circumstances. The full details of this system may be found in F. Bowers, "Transcription of Manuscripts: The Record of Variants," *Studies in Bibliography*, 29 (1976), 212–264.

The lemmata (the readings to the left of the bracket) are ordinarily drawn from the present edition and represent the agreement of book and manuscript. Occasionally, however, a lemma, drawn from the present edition, may vary from the manuscript reading. When such cases occur, and in order to permit condensed entries, a single dagger prefixed to the page-line reference warns the user to refer to the Historical Collation (or in some few instances of emended readings to the Emendations list since emendations are not repeated in the Historical Collation) for the exact manuscript reading. For example, in this volume, at 284.31–32 the edition-text reads 'preposterous monkeying self annexed' whereas the manuscript reading is 'preposterous fraudulent self annexed'. The daggered entry in the Alterations, †284.31–32 preposterous . . . annexed] *ab. del.* 'purely humbugging *possible self [*insrtd.*] addition', saves space by referring the reader to the Historical Collation for the variant manuscript reading, ‡284.32 monkeying] fraudulent MS (the double dagger in turn signaling the reader that the manuscript reading is part of an alteration found in the list of Alterations).

On the contrary, twin daggers warn the user that the lemma is not the reading of the present edition but instead is that of the manuscript. This convention is employed only when the two readings are so similar that a reader following the edition-text in the Alterations list will be able to identify with certainty the reading that is intended, without recourse to the Historical Collation (or Emendations list). A simple substantive example comes at 367.8 where the manuscript reads 'had been given.', but the edition-text has 'has been given.' The alteration is noted as ††367.8 had been given.] *intrl.*; the variant ‡367.8 has] had MS (again the double dagger cross-referencing to the Alterations entry) may be found in the Historical Collation should the reader wish to consult that part of the apparatus. A simple example of an accidental difference occurs at 369.9–10 where the manuscript's 'faroff' is hyphenated in the present edition. The entry in the Alterations reads ††369.9–10 faroff antiquity] *ab. del.* 'time'; the variant in the Historical Collation is noted as ‡369.9–10 far-off] faroff MS.

There are two instances, however, in which a twin-daggered variant cannot be found in the Historical Collation (or Emendations). If James has made an obvious error in the course of an alteration in the manuscript, the error may be cited in the Alterations entry and if so, is not repeated in the Historical Collation. Second, when the manuscript reading used in the lemma corresponds to a variant in the edition-text that has been silently emended or is not recorded in the Historical Collation (as indicated in A Note on the Editorial Method and in the headnote to the Historical Collation), twin daggers refer to no other section of the apparatus but merely draw attention to the easily construed variant between text and manuscript.

Whenever practicable, alterations in the manuscript that also comprise textual variants complete in themselves appear in the Historical Collation or in the Emendations list instead of in the list of Alterations. For the details of these entries, see the headnotes to those two sections.

The use of three dots to the right of the bracket almost invariably indicates ellipsis rather than the existence of dots in the manuscript. This is the only violation of the bibliographical rule that material within single quotes is cited exactly as it appears in the original document. In order to avoid confusion with the asterisks used in formulaic description, James's footnote markers, which are frequently asterisks, are invariably indicated by a superior 'ˣ'.

Deleted versos that do not apparently relate to revisions in the main body of the Alterations list or that are revisions of continuous deleted material already set out therein are transcribed in a separate section following the list of Alterations for each manuscript.

11. THE CENSUS OF HALLUCINATIONS (1889–1897)

h. Final American Report: Letter to Henry Sidgwick (1896)

74.7   order] *bef. del.* 'that'

74.10   ratio] *aft. del.* 'improbability figure is'

74.11   from . . . figure.] ('f' *of* 'from' *ov. period*); *insrtd.*

74.14   105¹] *final* '1' *ov.* '3'

74.17   Only] *intrl.*

74.17   subjects] *aft. del.* 'cases'

74.24   occurred . . . ¹of] *ab. del.* 'coincided with'

74.27   I] *insrtd., mended*
74.31   really] *intrl.*
74.33   due] *aft. del.* 'that'
74.37   so] *intrl.*
75.4   but] *aft. del.* 'th'
75.5   insignificant‸] *comma del.*
75.6   an] *ab. del.* 'the'
75.10   veridical,] *comma ov. period*
75.11   occultism] 't' *intrl.*
75.12   19] '9' *ov. doubtful* '7'
75.13   these] *alt. fr.* 'them'

75.16–17   —19 . . . 90;] *intrl. ab. del. period*
75.24   Actually,] *intrl.*
75.35   result‸] *comma del.*
75.36   similarly)] *paren ov. period*
75.36   ratio] *aft. del. db. underl.* 'ratio'
76.1   it,] *comma ov. period*
76.1–2   if . . . scientific."] *insrtd.*
76.7   weeks and] *intrl.*
76.14   especially] ¹'e' *ov.* 'E'
76.15   put] *bef. del.* 'in'

37. REPORT ON MRS. PIPER'S HODGSON-CONTROL (1909)

a. Alterations in MS and MS(T)

All alterations are in ink and in James's hand. In the manuscript portions, all alterations are recorded. Not listed as alterations in the typed portions are: underlining, added hyphens, corrected typographical errors and the addition of sitters' names. Additions at the ends of lines are recorded only where punctuation is involved or when more than one word could have been formed.

[*begin* MS(T)]
253.3   suddenly upon] *intrl.*
253.9   her] *ab. del.* 'things'
253.9   she] *alt. fr.* 'they'
253.10   yet] *intrl.*
253.11   difficulties] *aft. del.* 'mundane'
253.11–12   ‸on this side‸] *intrl.; sg. qts. del.*
253.12   *primâ facie*] *intrl.*
254.3   my] *ab. del.* 'the'
254.3   are] *ab. del.* 'is'
††254.5   mediumship.ˣ] 'x' *added*
254.6   myself] *bef. del.* '*hardly seen Mrs. P and [*insrtd. for del.* 'been absent from Mrs. P's s']'
254.6   Mrs. Piper and] *intrl. for del.* 'her [*ab. del.* 'Mrs. P.']'
254.7   most] *ab. del.* '*the last five [*ab. del.* 'several'] years'
254.8   informed] *ab. del.* '*au courant*'
254.10   had] *ab. del.* 'did'
254.10   asked] 'ed' *intrl.*
254.10–11   to be observed.] *added ov. period*
254.12   personage] *aft. del.* 'benignant and clerical'
254.13   ²of] *insrtd.*
254.14   is] *ab. del.* 'was'
254.14   have] *intrl.*

254.15   -creations] *hyphen insrtd.;* 'creations' *ab. del.* 'personalities'
254.16   trance,] *comma added end of line*
254.17   personalities] 'ies' *ov.* 'y'; *aft. del.* 'consistent & typical types of'
254.18   rôles] *circumflex added; aft. del.* 'typical'
254.19   which] *ab. del.* 'that'
254.20   Rector's] ' 's' *intrl.*
254.21   creature] *ab. del.* 'personality'
254.21   sort,] *comma added*
254.22   the] *ab. del.* 'an'
254.24   sitters] *final* 's' *added*
254.24   addresses,] *comma added*
254.24   troubles] 's' *added*
254.25   them] *ab. del.* 'it'
254.25   you] *ab. del.* 'each one'
254.25   were] *aft. del.* '*were devoted [*ab. del.* 'knew no other, as if he']'
254.26   most devoted] *ab. del.* 'oldest & *wisest ['wis' *ab. del.* 'old']'
254.26   your] *ov.* 'his'; *intrl.*
254.26   appears] *ab. del.* 'seem'
254.26–27   and . . . writing,] *ab. del.* ', & in the voice sittings'
254.29   desiring] *bef. del.* 'only'
254.31   wisdom,] 'm,' *added end of line*

254.34 greatly] *ab. del.* 'immeasurably'

254.35 As . . . it] *ab. del.* 'It'; *opp. mrgn.* '¶'

254.35 this] *ov.* 'the'

†254.38–40 Chief . . . *Life.*] *insrtd. in ink in planned space*

254.39 Mrs.] *aft. del.* 'Hyslop's in vol'

254.39 long] *intrl.*

255.1 that] *bef. del.* ', as I conce | the matter,'

255.1 she] *bef. del.* 'then'

255.2–3 inserted— . . . will—] *dashes ab. del. commas*

255.3 at any rate] *intrl.*

255.6 most] *insrtd.*

255.6 comes from] *ab. del.* 'is communicated by'

††255.11 something] *aft. del.* 'anys'

255.14 indeterminate,] *bef. del. continuation in ink* 'the *vague [intrl.] popular *notion of what a 'spirit' is [*ab. del.* 'view'] is enough. *Sources other than R. H.'s surviving spirit [*ab. del.* '['The ['other' *del.*]' *del.*] Causes ['C' *ov.* 'c']'] for the veridical communications from the Hodgson-Control may be enumerated as follows: [¶] 1. Indications unwarily furnished by *the [*intrl.*] sitter['s' *del.*]. [¶] 2. Lucky chance-hits. [¶] [*del.* '3. Communications *made by R. H [*intrl.*] during *his [*ab. del.* 'R. H.'s'] life time *and [*intrl.*] stored up in Mrs. Piper's memory, either *sub ['b' *ov.* 'p'] or supraliminally. [¶] 4. *Comm ['C' *ov.* 'P']'] [¶] 3. Information received *during R. H.'s life-time [*ab. del.* 'from the living R. H.'] by the waking Mrs. P., and stored up (either sub- or supra- liminally) in her memory. [¶] 4. Information received from the living R. H.'

††255.20 2. Common gossip.] '2' *ov.* '4'; *tr. by guideline fr. aft.* 'sitters.' | [255.21] *and circled mrgn.* 'tr.'

††255.22–24 4. Information . . . memory.] '4' *ov.* '2'; *tr. by guideline*

255.22 from] *ab. del.* 'during'

255.22 during his] *ab. del.* ''s *aft.* 'H.'

255.22 lifetime,] *comma added*

255.25 , or others,] *commas added*

255.25–26 sittings,] 'ngs,' *added end of line*

255.29 an] *ab. del.* 'some'

255.30 reservoir,] *comma added*

255.33(*second*);256.3 the] 'he' *added end of line*

255.34 'supernatural' or 'mystical.'] *sg. qts. added*

255.37 time for] *ab. del.* 'the turn of'

255.38 and] *ab. del.* '& of'

256.2–3 , for . . . part,] *commas added*

256.5 in principle] *intrl.*

256.6 4] *ov.* '2'

256.6 3] *ab. del.* 'I'

256.7 2] *ov.* '4'

256.8 either] *intrl.*

256.8 trivial . . . intimate] *intrl.*

256.11 , for . . . least,] *commas added*

256.13 now] *intrl.*

256.13 voluminous] *bef. del.* 'by this time'

256.14 , so] *comma insrtd. for del. opening paren*

256.15 1of] 'f' *added end of line*

256.19 source,] *comma added*

256.25 test] *bef. del.* 'Mrs Piper'

256.27 for that purpose.] *ab. del. period*

256.31 for his successes] *intrl.*

256.32 available] *bef. del.* 'in explanation of his successes'

256.32 2the] *intrl.*

256.32 spirits] *aft. del.* 'returning'

256.32–33 who . . . Piper.] ('w' *of* 'who' *ov. period*); *added*

256.35 will] *ab. del.* 'must'

256.36 But before] 'But' *insrtd.*; 'b' *ov.* 'B'

256.36 detail,] *bef. del.* ', let me say'

256.37–38 instanced_∧ (conversations] *paren insrtd. aft. del. comma*

256.38 between] *aft. del.* 'with th'; *bef. del.* 'the liv'

256.39 is in order.] *intrl.*

257.2 trance] *aft. del.* 'waking'

257.6 simulating] *ab. del.* 'substantiating'

257.10 order,] *comma added*

257.16–17 For . . . times] *at top of fol.
9 aft. del. foot of fol. 8* 'For many
years past he had seen her three times'

257.27 R.H.] *ab. del.* 'He'

257.29 among] *aft. del.* 'of'

[*end MS(T); begin MS*]

†257.32–258.1 The . . . suddenly]
subst. on fols. 9–11 for del. typed
'[*fol.* 11] [¶] The first appearance of
Hodgson was at a sitting which Miss
Theodate Pope had with Mrs. Piper
eight days after *H.'s [*insrtd. for del.*
'his'] death. I transcribe Miss Pope's
record:– [¶] [After some writing
from Rector]'

††257.32 The spirit] *insrtd.; opp.
mrgn.* '¶'

257.32 manifestation] *ab. del.*
'appearance'

257.33 dramatically] *aft. del. intrl.* 'so'

257.33 so] *ab. del.* 'life-'

257.34 him] *intrl.*

257.34 the] *ab. del.* 'his'

257.34 of] *intrl. bef. del.* 'upon
[*ab. del.* 'in']'

257.34 those] *alt. fr.* 'these'

257.34 days] *ab. del.* 'appearances'

257.34 gradually] *aft. del.* 'th'

257.36 a . . . these] *ab. del.* 'quoting
these'

257.36 earliest] *alt. fr.* 'earlier'

257.37 of . . . at] *ab. del.* 'almost *in
extenso,* beginning with'

[*end MS; begin MS(T)*]

258.6 broken.] *bef. del.* '(see Fig. I).';
foll. in line bel. by del. circled ink
'figure 1'

258.6 It . . . "HODGSON."] *tr. by
guideline fr. separate para. to
continuing aft.* 'broken.'; 'run in'
circled in mrgn.

258.6 "HODGSON."] *db. qts. and
period added; bef. del.* 'as in Figure
2.'; *foll. in line bel. by del. circled ink*
'figure 2'

258.8 "I am"] *db. qts. added*

258.9 order] *bef. del.* '(see Fig. 3)';
foll. in line bel. by del. circled ink
'figure 3'

258.19 it,] 't,' *added end of line*

258.24 "B"] *db. qts. added*

258.24 Miss P.] *ab. del.* 'I'

258.25 A] *ab. ink del. typed* '*"B"
AND and an L followed, but no
explanation. [*typed ov.* 'Another
spirit then took control']'

††258.25–26 ₐThe . . . later.]] *added*

†258.28–29 (For . . . 268.)] ('sequel to'
ab. del. 'rest of'; 'this' *alt. fr.* 'the');
*added (but w. sq. bkts.) aft. the foll.
del. typed text, w. ink* 'don't copy'
in mrgn. 'Miss Pope's contemporary
note on the ring-reference is as
follows [*period del.*] *:– [*insrtd. for
del.* '(fo | the rest of the *ring-[*intrl.*]
episode see pp.)'] [¶] "Several
inquiries have recently been made
to me as one of Dr. Hodgson's
intended ['executors,' *del.*]
administrators, with regard to a
ring given him this *fall, ['f' *ov.*
'F'] & which he showed me & spoke
of a few weeks ago. He did not have
this ring on, apparently, when he
died, & so far it has not turned up, nor
have I been able to get any
information concerning it. I have
said nothing to Mrs Piper herself,
nor to the control in my own last
sitting regarding this, & it is
improbable, tho not *impossible,
[*comma added*] that she should
have had knowledge of the matter
in her waking state. It is to this ring
that the context would seem to refer,
tho there is of course no actual
evidence of it." '

258.30 Miss₍ₐ₎] *period del.*

††258.30 (, ['Jan. 2nd.,' *del.*] five . . .
later),] *parens ov. commas; commas
added, but first comma not del. in
error*

258.31–259.1 , and . . . hand] ('the'
ov. 'a'; 'of' *aft. del.* 'that'); *insrtd. for
del.* '[on fol. 12] as follows: ['I'
del.]–[*fol.* 13] [¶] [Hand *first
[*intrl.*]'

259.1 cramped] 'ed' *ov.* 's'

259.1 dropped] 'ped' *ab.* 's [*undel. in
error*]' *and del. comma*

259.2 broke] 'oke' *ab. del.* 'eaks'

259.2 ¹the] *insrtd.*

††259.2–3 ['then' *del.*] wrote as
follows:] *insrtd. aft. del.* ', [*comma
undel. in error*] rocking from side to
side, *writes:—] [*dash added*]'

259.4 HODGSON₍ₐ₎] *period del.*

††259.5 [Then . . . wrote:—₍ₐ₎ (*closing
bkt. om. in error*); *added*

259.11 shine,] *comma added*

259.12 skies] *bef. del.* 'than these are'
[*end* MS(T); *begin* MS]

†259.31–32 At . . . follows:—] *subst. on
fol. 14 for del. typed* '[*fol.* 15] At
Miss Pope's *next [*ab. del.* 'second']
sitting *but one [*intrl.*] (Jan. 8th
'06) Hodgson appeared again,
writing at first with diffulty, as
follows:—'
[*end* MS; *begin* MS(T)]

260.3 must] 'ust' *added end of line*

260.4 to-day. . . .] *ellipsis dots added*

260.5 presently] *intrl.*

260.6 as an 'influence,'] *ab. del.* 'at
this point,'

260.6 on:—)] *bel. is ink del. typed line*
'(*Rector, are you writing for him?
[*typed ov.* 'I am now registering for
him'])'

260.7–8 | ber my promise] *orig. the
typing read* | 'ber my promise to
shake you up?' *but then James
inadvertently typed ov.* 'promise . . .
up?' *what should have been the
next line* '(I asked G. P. to shake me
up' *at which point he typed aft. a
double space* 'my promise to shake
you up*? [*added end of line*]' *(the
'my' inadvertently repeating the
word at the start of the line) and
then ink del. the entire typed ov. line
up to* 'promise'

260.9 once] *intrl.*

260.9 Geo.] 'eo' *insrtd.*

††260.9 up] *as an afterthought James
typed in empty space at right and
then ink del.* '[Miss P.' *del.*] [I once
at a sitting had challenged G.P.
to make me *directly [*intrl.*] aware
of his presence. He responded by
saying he would 'shake me up'. Was
R. H. recaling this? *T.P.] [*added*]'.
The subsequent typing takes account

*of this insertion, which must,
therefore, have been made before
line* 12 *was typed.*

260.13 it.] *bef. del.* '*[He had often
said this. T.P.] [*orig. tr. by guideline
to aft.* 'did.' [260.14]]'

260.14 remember—indeed] *dash ov.
period;* 'i' *ov.* 'I'

260.22 Yes] *aft. del.* 'I was'

††260.24–25 [referring . . . sitting.]]
added aft. del. '(['Q' *del.*] 'Q')?'

†260.32–33 which . . . laughter).]
('which' *ab. del.* 'These'; 'written'
intrl.); *added but w. sq. bkts.; tr. by
guideline fr. aft.* 'ah.' [260.31]

††261.1 haven't₍ₐ₎] *bef. del.* '[*period
del. and not restored in error*]—
[*meaning the lines to Miss D——see
sitting of Jan 2nd *(P——, above)
[*parens ov. commas*] in which *a
[*intrl.*] poem purporting to be
written by R. H. is ['written.' *del.*]
given] [*added*]'

261.2 life,] *comma added*

261.5 the] *intrl.*

††261.6 16th. & 17th.,] *both* 'th.' *and
comma intrl.*

261.7 without] *insrtd. for del.*
'neither in matter nor in manner
was there'

261.7 evidential₍ₐ₎] *period del.*

261.7 matter—] *dash ab. del. comma*

††261.12 ₍ₐ₎Miss Pope assents.₍ₐ₎ (*no
sq. bkts.*); *added aft. del.* '(yes.)';
opp. mrgn. '¶' ; *bel. is ink del. typed*
'*Who wrote it? [*ov. typed* '(How
[*three illeg. letters*] here']'
[*end* MS(T); *begin* MS]

††261.18 ₍ₐ₎After] *opp. mrgn.* '¶'

261.18 his] *ab. del.* 'a'
[*end* MS; *begin* MS(T)]

261.20 Give] *aft. penc. del. at head of
page* '[¶] (I have just met her, is'nt
she nice?) [¶] *Lovely.* I should say so.
No one here knows anything about
this. I dont believe anyone could
know this. [¶] [I may have had a
letter written by R.H. from Owl's
head., but cannot remember. I never
heard of Miss Bancroft till I met
her three days ago. She then told me

that R.H. had visited her in the
summer, & probably said Owl's Head,
tho my question shows that the
name was not consciously in my
mind when R.H. mentioned it. Miss
Bancroft writes to me of 'owl's
eyes' as follows:—"At Owl's Head
we had two owls as andirons, & when
the fire was burning the eyes of
those owls were frequentky spoken
of by Mr. Hodgson who admired
them very much." *T. P.] [*added*]'

261.23   sense] *intrl.*

††261.25   [Correct.]] *added aft. period insrtd. for del. period*

††261.28   [Correct.]] *ab. del. added* '[Absolutely accurate.—M. B., [*dash del.*] W.J.]'

261.31   message,] *comma added end of line*

††262.3–4   had . . . watch.]] *added at foot of page*

262.5   Wm.] 'm.' *ov. period*

262.6   sitting] *aft. del. intrl.* 'voi'

262.6   used . . . gave] *ab. del.* 'spoke more copiously than he had yet done, *giving ['ing' ab. del. 'e']'

262.7   The record] *insrtd. for del.* 'Unfortunately there was no stenographer by, so the record is incomplete. It'

262.9   Laughs.] *period added*

262.10   [Laughs.]] *intrl.*

262.16   Myers. . . . rest.] *typed aft. ink del.* '*After an interval R.H. comes again [*inadvertently* typed *ov.* 'Myers. I must rest.']'

262.17   he] *ab. del.* 'R.H.'

262.19   take] *bef. del.* 'to'

262.22   it!] *exclm. mk. added end of line*

262.22   [He . . . so.]] *intrl.*

262.24   Rebecca,] *comma added*

††262.25   [his sister.]] *insrtd.*

262.32   tennis?] *bef. del.* 'Oh what good times we had fishing! Believe, Billy,' *then underdotted for retention and 'stet' written in mrgn. but then 'stet' del. and passage del. again*

263.2,9   [James]] *intrl.*

263.2   [Dorr]] *intrl.*

263.3   'private'] *sg. qts. added*

263.4   mind. . . .] *ellipsis dots intrl. for del.* 'So far as Miss E. is concerned, I should much prefer that she left things in George's hands.'

263.4–5   George . . . faith.] *first del., then underdotted for retention and* 'stet' *written in mrgn.; foll. by del.* 'No one could so adequately fill his place.'

263.7   them] 'm' *added end of line*

263.7   to the sitters.] *intrl.*

263.8   [Correct.]] *intrl.*

263.9–10   [They . . . Piper.]] ('a fact' *ab. del. dash); insrtd. aft. del.* '[In reply to questions, R.R. [*i.e.* H.] then gave much advice as to who might best be qualified to take his place as manager of sittings. He sent additional messages to his family in Australia, & ended in this wise [*period del.*] :—]'

263.13   better] *intrl.*

263.14   art?] '?' *added end of line*

†263.14–15   [W.J. . . . painting.]] *intrl.*

263.15   had,] *comma added*

263.16   God.] *bel. is del. insrtd.* '[¶] The question of privacy in certain records had been already noted ['at a' *del.*] between Rector and Mr. Dorr at a sitting January 1st. The cipher notes were *duly [*insrtd.*] found. Hodgson was a famous swimmer. When' [*end of page*]

[*end MS(T); begin MS*]

263.17   first] *bef. del.* 'manner of'

263.20   hardly] *intrl.*

263.20   quote] *bef. del.* 'al-|[*undel. in error*]most nothing from *the [*del. in error*]'

††263.20   verbatim, for they] *ab. del.* ', which'

263.21   to] 't' *ov.* 'c'

263.21   best] *ab. del.* 'most'

263.23   alternatives] *aft. del.* 'naturalistic or spiritistic'

[*end MS; begin MS(T)*]

263.26   a . . . call] *intrl.*

263.29   himself,] 'If,' *added end of line*

263.31;265.15   R.H.] *ov.* 'r.h.'

†263.31–32 appearance . . . control]
'appearance' *alt. fr.* 'reappearance'
and closing paren added end of line;
orig. paren del. when '['as a control'
del.] as . . . spirit [*paren om. in*
error] . . . control' *intrl.*

263.32 had] *intrl.*

263.32 Pope,] 'ope,' *ab. del. period and*
undel. comma

263.33–34 "He . . . means?"] *db. qts.*
alt. fr. sg. qts.

263.33 under|] *penc. ab. typed*
'under [*ov. typed* 'Miss P.']'

263.36 a] *insrtd.*

263.36 L.] *ov. added doubtful* 'I';
bel. are two del. lines '(what is that?) |
Rector——B L [No further
explanation]'

263.37 Miss] *aft. del.* 'the same'

263.37 Pope] *intrl.*

263.37 again] *intrl.*

264.1–2 [Mrs. . . . Margaret.]] *insrtd.*

264.17 wrote:—] *added aft. del.* 'said:'

264.18 fiftieth] *ab. del.* '50th ['th'
undel. in error]'

264.19 me,] *comma added*

264.27 it.] *added end of line*

264.28 The] *ab. del.* 'T'

264.29 wrote:] *aft. del.* 'said'

265.1–2 I . . . you.] *insrtd.*

265.8 possible] 'e' *ov.* 'y'

265.8 2a] *ab. del.* 'an engraved'

265.11 test] *bef. del.* '-q'

265.13 Pope] 'ope' *ab. del. period*

265.15 inquires of] *ab. del.* 'asks'

265.16 then] *insrtd.*

265.16–17 "Did . . . club?"] *db. qts.*
added

265.19 on] *ab. del.* 'od'

265.21 finger.] 'er.' *added end of line*

265.22 words] *ab. del.* 'questions'

265.23 club,] 'b,' *added end of line*

265.32 16th,] *comma added; bef. del.*
'R.H.'

265.32 found,] *insrtd.*

††265.33 the R.H. control] *ab. del.* 'he'

266.1 ∧I] *db. qt. added and del.*

266.3 2he] *intrl.*

266.4 lives,] *comma added*

266.4 house] *intrl.*

266.9 this] 'is' *added end of line*

266.11 waistcoat,] *comma added*

266.13 had] 'ad' *added end of line*

266.15 easily] *aft. del.* 'most'

266.17 suspected] *ab. del.* 'guessed
['['a' *del.*] twice at' *del. intrl.*]'

266.18 The] *aft. del.* 'The explanation
of the first refe-' [*end of page*]

266.18 misleading] *ab. del.* 'false'

266.19 'Margaret'] *sg. qts. added*

266.20 to cover] *intrl.*

266.21 description] *aft. carbon del.*
'vague'

266.22 of the] *intrl.*

266.22 to] *aft. carbon del.* 'whom'

266.22 possession] *aft. carbon del.* 'all'

266.24 but little] *ab. del.* 'un'

266.25 very . . . very] *each intrl.*

266.27 state,] *comma added*

266.28 automatic] 'c' *ov.* 'sm'

266.28 machinery] *intrl.*

266.29 that] *insrtd. for del.* 'the'

266.30 and] *insrtd.* ('&')

266.31 'on his mind'] *sg. qts. added*

266.31 her,] *comma added*

266.33 2of] *intrl.*

266.35 quite] *ab. del.* 'positively'

266.35 erroneously,] *comma added*

266.38 "No] *db. qts. added*

267.1 me] *ab. del.* 'it'

267.5 lately worn] *carbon intrl.*

267.5 which] *carbon ab. del.* 'which
she had but recently see| him wear,
& that'

267.7 that] *bef. carbon del.* 'wh' |

267.7 was] *aft. del.* 'did not'

267.10 word . . . and the] *intrl.*

267.10–11 which . . . sitting] *intrl.*

††267.12 Margaret B. and] *ab. carbon
del.* 'B. &'

267.12 that] *intrl.*

267.14 dislike] *aft. carbon del.* 'desi'

267.15 mentioned] *ab. is carbon del.
intrl.* 'n-'

††267.18–19 "there . . . it."] *db. qts. alt.
fr. sg. qts.*

267.19–20 Then . . . Lyman,] ('Then
I myself' *in carbon*); *ab. carbon del.*
'On january24 I'

267.24 tends] 's' *added*

267.25 H.] *carbon ab. del.* 'the man'

267.26 remark] *carbon intrl.*

267.28 strong] 'ong' *added end of line*; 'ong' *del. at beg. of next line*

267.30 involved; but knowing] *semicolon alt. fr. period*; 'but' *ink ov. carbon intrl.; carbon* 'k' *ov.* 'K'

267.34 haunts us] *carbon ab. del.* 'recurs'

267.37 -automatism,] *comma insrtd.*

267.40 since] *ink ov. carbon intrl.*

267.41 is] *carbon ab. del.* 'is'

267.42 continue] *aft. carbon del.* 'explain things by'

268.5 hardly] *bef. carbon del.* 'any'

268.8 natural,] *carbon comma added*

268.8–9 and finally] *carbon ab. del.* 'then'

268.9 probable] *ab. del.* 'sympathetic'

†268.10 The . . . at] *ink added*

268.10 a certain] *intrl. bef. del. intrl.* 'a'

†268.13 as . . . it,] *intrl.*

268.13 absent] *aft. del.* 'am'

268.15 nigger-] 'n' *ov.* 'N'

268.16 talk] *insrtd. for del.* 'minstrel'

††268.17 -TALK] *ab. del.* 'MINSTREL'

268.31 records] *aft. del.* 'the'

268.32 sittings] *aft. del.* 'the'

268.33 failed] *aft. del.* 'absolutely'

268.35 had . . . had] *ab. del.* 'used to have'

269.2 these] *aft. del.* 'that'; 'ese' *ab. del.* 'y'

269.2 words] *ab. del.* 'message'

269.3 ¹had] *intrl.*

269.3 namely] *intrl.*

††269.3 , more that once,] *commas added*; 'that' *error for* 'than'

269.4 change] *aft. del.* 'turn'

269.5 |rator-group] *added end of line*

269.5 completely] *intrl.*

†269.6 'talking . . . -minstrels.'] *sg. qts. added*

269.8 associations] *final* 's' *added*

269.12–13 of his survival.] *ab. del.* '-message also.'

269.13 the] *ab. del.* 'sb'

269.16–17 anything . . . set |] ('['the' *del.*] discussion . . . suggestibility' *orig. intrl. w. guideline aft.* 'phrase,' [269.18], *but then that guideline del.*

and new guideline joined to 'anything . . . set-'); *ab. del.* 'the set-' |

269.17 memory] *insrtd. for del.* 'mind'

269.20 so . . . expression] *ab. del.* 'which'

269.20 be] *aft. del.* 'therefore'

269.21 Such] *insrtd. for del.* 'Such'

269.25 extraordinarily] *intrl.*

269.26 had, . . . lately,] *commas added*

269.27 wish] *ab. del.* 'desire'

269.27 in me] *intrl.*

269.29 own] *intrl.*

270.2 During] *aft. del.* '[¶ This has already been partly touched upon in* ['th full repor| of' *del.*] Mr. Dorr's sitting *reported above. [ab. del. period]*'

††270.5 Chicago.] *ab. del.* 'New York.'; *bef. del. intrl.* '[substituted name of place.]'

††270.7 J.G.P.—] *alt. fr.* 'Pid.' *and dash intrl.*

270.8 Chicago.] *ab. del.* 'N. Y.'

270.8 them] 'em' *added end of line*

270.9 world.] *bef. del.* '[Two Pp. of original Ms. written here ar| retained BY by Piddington, who writes as follows concerning them:'

††270.10–13 [ₐThe . . . signed."]] *db. qts. del.; closing db. qts. undel. in error; opp. mrgn.* '¶'

270.10 name] *final* 's' *del.*

270.10 'Densmore'] *sg. qts. added; bef. del.* '*[substitute for the name written] [intrl.] & [undel. in error]* Huldah *were then written. [ab. del.* 'appeared.'] *After the name* Densmore'

270.10–11 then . . . Piddington] ('M' *of* 'Mr.' *ov.* 'P'); *ab. del.* 'given, I'

270.12;272.26 'Huldah'] *sg. qts. added*

270.14 14] *ab. del.* '29'

270.14 Piddington] 'iddington' *ab. del. period*

270.14 R.H.] *intrl.*

270.16–17 "Can . . . lately?"] *orig. marked for new paragraph w. sq. bkt. bef.* 'Can' *and* '¶' *in mrgn., but then sq. bkt. del.* ('¶' *undel. in error*) *and db. qts. insrtd.; closing db. qts. added*

270.22 correspondence?] *qst. mk. alt. fr. period*

271.2 'Huldah'] *ink ov. carbon intrl.*

271.4 Jenny] *aft. carbon del.* 'of [*carbon ab. del.* 'a']'

271.6 This . . . spoken.] *ink ov. carbon intrl.*

271.6 followed] 'ed' *added end of line*

271.6–7 (not . . . notes)] *ink ov. carbon parens added*

271.13 James] 'ames' *ab. del. period*

††271.13 Mr∧] *intrl.*

271.14–16 "Can . . . that?"] *carbon db. qts. added*

271.14–15 Densmore?] *carbon qst. mk. ov. period*

271.16 clear] *carbon* 'ear' *added end of line* ('r' *touched up in ink*)

††271.18 [She was Ella.]] *intrl.*

271.19 Chicago] *ab. del.* 'New York'

††271.20 me."] *ov. period; db. qts. in error*

271.22 already] *intrl.*

271.22 called] *aft. del.* 'who is'

271.24 she] *intrl.*

271.25 corresponded,] *comma ov. period*

271.25–26 ¹or . . . Huldah.] *intrl.*

271.26 her,] *comma added*

271.31 Mr. H.] *ab. del.* 'he'

†271.31 him, and] *comma ov. period;* '&' *intrl.*

271.32 which . . . kept.] *ab. del. period*

271.33 have] *intrl.*

271.34 , Hannah,] *commas added*

271.34 [She . . . family.]] *insrtd.*

†272.1–3 In . . . flukes.] ('I' *of* 'In' *ov.* 'i'; 'i' *of* 'it' *ov.* 'I'; 'pervades' *bef. del.* 'it.'); *alt. by guidelines and* 'tr' *in mrgn. fr.* 'It seems improbable that Hodgson's veridical utterance here should merely have been a lucky fluke in spite of the confusion that pervades it.'

272.3 Two] *insrtd. for del.* 'We have as'

272.3–4 offer . . . immediately.] *ab. del.* 'are possible.'

††272.5 (I)] *aft. vert. stroke for new paragraph and* '¶' *in mrgn.*

272.6 explanation] *intrl.*

272.7 as] *ab. del.* '(2)' *typed by mistake ov.* 'as'

272.9 to] *ab. del.* 'as far as'

272.12 love] *bef. del.* 'recently,'

272.16 suggested] *ab. del.* 'thought of'

272.19 expansiveness] *bef. del.* 'I have ever known,'

272.20 say,] *comma added*

272.22 himself] *bef. del.* 'in ordinary conversation'

272.22 Piper.] *period added bef. del. intrl.* 'herself.'

272.24 him.] 'm.' *added end of line*

272.25 nevertheless] *intrl.*

272.25 that] *ab. del.* 'how many'

272.25 were] *bef. del.* 'wholly'

272.31–32 the false . . . and a] *ab. del.* 'the name Huldah &'

272.32 real] *intrl.*

272.32–33 name. The . . . -called] ('the ['t' *ov.* 'T']' *aft. del.* 'and [*ov. doubtful* 'in']'); *period ab. del. comma;* 'The . . . -called' *ab. del.* 'so it seemed to me an fit to be regarded as an excellent test communication'

†272.33 has . . . moreover,] ('me moreover' *added later w. diff. pen*); *ab. del.* 'sister *told [*ov.* 'tells [*ab. del.* 'has ['s' *ab. del.* 'd'] told']'] me'

272.34 thought that] *ab. del.* 'thinks [*alt. fr. faint* 'thought [*ab. del.* 'thought']'] her sister had told'

272.34–35 knew . . . R.H.'s] *ab. del.* 'of [*undel. in error*] the fact R.H.*'s [*undel. in error*]'

272.35 himself] *intrl.*

272.35 told] *intrl.*

272.36 an] *aft. del.* 'to me'

272.39 'Huldah's'] *sg. qts. and* 's' *added*

273.2 real] *intrl. bef. del. intrl.* 'full' [*end MS(T); begin MS*]

273.3 have] *bef. del.* 'however'

273.4–5 contain, but] *comma ov. period;* 'but' *ab. del.* 'That they do contain something that would establish a naturalistic explanation'

273.5 fortunately] 'f' *ov.* 'F'

273.5 Piper] *final* ''s' *del.*

273.6 decease] *ab. del.* 'death'

273.8   reasonable] *ab. del.* 'rational'
273.8   ²the] *insrtd. for del.* 'whatever'
and bef. del. 'revelation [*ab. del.*
'facts'] regarding his relations to
Miss Densmore that so surprised
Mr. Dorr & myself ['when *Mrs. Piper
[*ab. del.* 'her sittings'] brought them
out' *del. intrl.*] were implanted in
the trance-memory at that time.
['The sitt' *del.*] [¶] The sitting in
question was one which Prof.
Newbold held on June 27th. 1906
The Hodgson-control suddenly
['asks:' *del.*] says:—'
273.9   thus] *intrl.*
273.10   previous] *aft. del.* 'his [*ab. del.*
'Mrs.']'
273.11   sitting] *bef. del.* 'of Prof.
Newbold's *to [*del. in error*]'
273.13   says] *aft. del.* 'asks'
273.19   Such a lady] *insrtd. for del.*
'That Miss D.'
273.25   ∧Densmore∧?] *sq. bkts. del.*
†273.30–31   of . . . J.]] *intrl.*
274.4   ¹and] *intrl.*
††274.5–6   [Correct . . . Myers.]]
insrtd. for del. '[Miss D's sister *thinks*
that R. H. told Myers.]'
274.12   letter] *ab. del.* 'private letter
to himself from Hodgso'
274.13   1895] *aft. del.* 'June'
274.14   Piper] *aft. del.* 'controls'
274.16–17   his own,] *ab. del.* 'the other,
by'
††274.19–20   own, Oct∧ 24th. 1906.]
comma ov. period; 'Oct . . . 1906.'
intrl.
274.21   W.J.] *bef. del. db. qts.*
[*end MS; begin MS(T)*]
274.22   No] *aft. del. at head of page*
'SITTING OF OCTOBER
"(TWENTY *fourth [*added aft. del.*
'NINTH']. | W. J. ASKS ABOUT
Huldah": Did you make anyone your
confidant? | R.H.—'
274.30   correctly] *intrl.*
274.31   matter,] *comma ov. period*
275.2   probably] *intrl.*
275.6   No,] *comma added*
275.7   Blair . . .] 'lair' *del.; dots intrl.*
ab. del. comma

275.8   Blair Thaw] 'lair' *and* 'haw' *del.*
275.9   Thaw] 'haw' *del.*
275.17   Huldah's] *ab. del.* 'her'
275.18   To which] *intrl.*
275.18   replies by] *intrl. for del. intrl.*
'then'
275.18   giving] *alt. fr.* 'gives'
275.18   country] *ab. del.* 'right'
275.18   correctly,] *intrl.*
[*end MS(T); begin MS*]
275.21   have no] *ab. del.* 'be without'
275.22   assurance] *ab. del.* 'proof'
275.23   at . . . blush] *ab. del.* 'on their
face'
275.25   indeed] *ab. del.* 'certainly'
275.28   this] *bef. del.* 'also'
275.28   as a] *insrtd.*
275.28   too.] *aft. del.* 'too.'
275.30   the] *final* 'y' *del.*
275.30–31   record . . . plausibly]
('plausibly' *aft. del.* 'easily'); *ab. del.*
'*lends ['s' *added*] itself [*ov.*
'them-'] [*tr. by guideline to aft.*
'explanation,'] | self'
275.31   explanation,] *bef. del.* 'as easily
as they do in this instance,'
275.31   we] *bef. del.* 'must conclude
against the spiritist interpretation.'
275.33   to] *bef. del. doubtful* 'thes'
275.35   financial] *ab. del.* 'pecuniary'
††276.1   THE PECUNIARY MESSAGES.]
('T' *ov.* 't'; 'MESSAGES.' *ab. del.*
'cases.'); *orig. run-on as text but then
db. underl. and moved by arrow to
center for heading*
276.2   The] *aft. del.* '[¶] Hodgson's
salary as secretary of the Branch *was*
always small, and as the American
Branch had never fully paid
expenses and to guard his
independence better, he had been
reluctant after the first years, to'
276.3   very] *intrl.*
276.5   the] *aft. del.* 'the'
276.5   been] *bef. del.* 'severe'
276.6   last] 'l' *ov.* 'v'
††276.8   an american] *ab. del.* 'a'
276.8   divining] *aft. del.* '['divin' *del.*]
in Ame' |
276.11   cited] *aft. del.* 'contain'
[*end MS; begin MS(T)*]

276.11 story] *aft. del. at head of page* '[¶] The Mrs *Lyman, [*comma added*] whose gift of a ring was in R.H.'s pocket a | the time of his death, had been the means some years before, ['when Hodgson was in temporary pecunaiary straigts, of sending him as' *del.*] of extricating him from a temporary pecuniary embarrassment. He wrote a bantering ['at the time' *del.*] letter to her in reply, incidentally telling in it *the [*ab. del.* 'a']'

276.12 overheard] 'over' *intrl.; bef. del.* 'praying aloud for god'

276.13 to] *aft. del.* 'fo'

276.13 The] *ov.* 'He'

276.13 atheist] *intrl.*

276.14 bread] *intrl.*

276.16–17 "Well . . . it."] *db. qts. added*

276.18 this friend's] *alt. fr.* 'Mrs Lyman's'

276.22 ¹it] *aft. del.* 'the'

276.23–24 . . . . About . . . speaking.] *insrtd.*

276.25 The sitter] *ab. del.* 'Mrs Lyman'

276.25 himself] 'im' *ab. del.* 'er'

276.27 Others] *ab. del.* 'Readers'

276.27 either] *intrl.*

276.27 favor] *bef. del.* 'the same view,'

276.28 of it,] *ab. del. comma*

276.28 ¹or] *bef. del.* 'will'

276.28 ²it] *intrl.*

276.28 treat it as] *ab. del.* 'will consider the episode to have been'

276.30 morally certain] *ab. del.* 'quite sure'

276.31 and of] *ab. del.* 'of incid nt [*illeg.*]'

276.32 me] *underl. added*

276.32 , as anyone,] *commas added* [*end* MS(T); *begin* MS]

276.35 Of the] 'Of' *added*; 'the' *ov. doubtful* 'One'

276.35 message] *bef. del.* 'was this:—'

276.35 written] *intrl.*

276.35 record] *bef. del.* 'of the sitting'

276.35 exists,] *bef. del.* 'so I quote it from the ver'

276.36 acquainted] *aft. del.* 'certified'

276.36 which] *ov.* 'To'

276.36 ran as follows:—] *intrl. aft. del. intrl.* 'was this'

277.1 To] *added aft. circled mrgn.* '¶'

277.3 R.] *aft. del.* 'the'

277.4 parent-] *ab. del.* 'English'

277.5 pay] *ab. del.* 'give'

277.5 into] 'in' *insrtd.*

277.6 deficit] *aft. del.* 'the yearly'; *bef. del.* '[' , in Hodgson's nominal salary' *del.*] ['provided' *del.*] in the salary'

277.6 should] *ab. del.* 'might'

277.8 sitting] *bef. del.* 'of th'

277.9 'spirit' of R.H.] *intrl.*

277.11 may] *bef. del.* 'always'

277.12 aid‸] *comma del.*

277.14 acquainted] *aft. del.* 'aware'

277.15 is] *bef. del.* 'in the highest degree'

277.15 donor's name] *ab. del.* 'secret'

277.16 had] 'd' *ov.* 's'

277.17 accounts] *aft. del.* 'a pecu'

277.17 known] *ab. del.* '['supposed until I heard' *del.*] ['been allowed by Mr. Dorr to' *del.*] supposed ['d' *added*]'

277.17 deficit] *bef. del.* 'was [*ab. del.* 'had been'] made up by several *persons who believed in the value of [*ab. del.* 'by several american friends of ['the' *del.*]'] Hodgson's work, and Mr. Dorr had never'

277.19 ‸I] *db. qts. del.*

277.19–20 understand] *ab. del.* 'conceive'

277.20 Mrs.] *aft. del. doubtful* 'na'

277.29 will] *aft. del.* 'are'

277.30 as follows:—] *intrl.*

††277.31–33 1. . . . 2.] *each intrl.; each opp. circled mrgn.* '¶'

277.31 an exceptionally] *ab. del.* 'a very'

277.32 ²to] *insrtd. for del.* 'for other'

277.33 presents] *bef. del.* 'are compatible'

277.35 well] *intrl.*

277.36 Piper] *aft. del.* ' 'subliminal' [*alt. fr. doubtful* 'sub lie'] Mrs.'

277.36 -organism] *intrl.*

277.37 curtain,] *ab. del.* 'veil,'

277.38 disturbingly] *ab. del.*
'pervertingly'
277.39 spirit-] *intrl.*
278.1 distant] *intrl.*
278.1–2 who . . . intercourse] ('carry'
aft. del. 'try to'; 'their' *intrl.*; 'social'
aft. del. 'intercourse'); *ab. del.* 'trying
to correspond with each other'
278.5 the best] *ab. del.* 'the utmost'
278.7 belong] *insrtd.*
278.8 is] 'i' *ov.* 'a'
278.9 total] *intrl.*
278.9 exists] *final* 's' *ov.* 'ence'
278.11 lavish] *ab. del.* 'generous'
278.12 | liminal] *ab. del.* '-conscious'
278.12 there] *insrtd. for del.* 'it'
278.13 which] *bef. del.* 'probably'
278.13 can only] *intrl.*
278.13 mean] *final* 's' *del.*
278.14 parts] *insrtd. for del.* 'elements'
278.14 Piper-] *intrl.*
278.14 really] *intrl.*
278.15 personal] *intrl.*
278.15 connected] *aft. del.* 'continuing
['those' *del.*] the lives of ['person'
del.] persons who'
278.17 decisively] 'sively' *ab. del.*
'dedly'
278.17 then] *aft. del. doubtful* 'ob'
278.18 as] *aft. del.* 'in the light of'
278.18 at least] *intrl.*
278.19 own] *bef. del.* 'masterly'
278.19 Piper] *aft. del.* 'pi'
278.20 in] *insrtd.*
278.21 where,] *ab. del.* 'in which,'
278.21 mass] *aft. del. insrtd.*
'unwieldy'
278.23 anywhere] *intrl.*
278.23 so] *ab. del.* 'a more'
278.23 a] *intrl.*
278.24 and] *bef. del.* '&'
278.24 his] *ab. del.* '['the conc' *del.*]
those'
278.24 conclusions‸] *comma del.*
278.25 denials . . . paper] ('s' *in*
'denials' *added*; 'present' *aft. del.*
'paper'); *ab. del.* '['negative verdict'
del.] denial that proof is yet
furnished of his own return,'
278.26 ¹the] *ab. del.* '[*doubtful*
'known' *del.*] short-sighted'

278.26 the narrowness] ('ness' *added
to* 'narrow'); *ab. del.* '['too' *del.*]
my ['narrow' *del.*] ['small' *del.*]
confinement [alt. fr. 'confining'
and bef. del. 'myself'] to so **narrow
[*undel.*] [*intrl.*] an amount'
278.26 my] *intrl.*
278.26 material,] *bef. del.* 'being used,'
278.26 R.H.'s] *ab. del.* 'his'
278.27 has been] 'has' *ov.* 'is'; 'been'
insrtd.
278.27 all the time,] *intrl.*
278.28 believe] *ab. del.* '['have' *del.*]
think'
278.28 'Imperator-] *aft. del.* 'creato'
278.30 general] *ab. del.* 'general'
278.30 real] *bef. del.* 'personal'
††278.31 cannot be deaf] *ab. del.* 'am
inclined to ['bow to' *del.*] ['recognize
Hodgson's superior expertness'
del.] bow'
278.32 or . . . feel] *ab. del.* 'and to
recognize'
278.32 which] *ab. del.* 'of'
278.33 gave] *ov.* 'gives'
278.33 in . . . field.] *period added and
moved by guideline fr. aft.*
'experience'
278.34 our] *ab. del.* 'a'
278.35 these] *bef. del.* 'extraordinarily
complex'
278.35 tend] *ab. del.* 'substantiate'
278.35 to corroborate] *ab. del.* 'the'
278.36 hypothesis] ¹'h' *ov.* 's'
278.36 production] *alt. fr.* 'causation'
278.37 ²to] *intrl.*
278.38 this limited] *ab. del.* '['these'
del.] a very'
278.38 report.] *period added bef. del.*
'based [*intrl.*] on such a limited
material as this.'
278.38 facts] *ab. del.* 'phenomena'
††278.39 &] *intrl.*
278.39 as yet] *intrl.*
278.39 ²the] *bef. del.* | 'th'
278.40 them.] *alt. fr.* 'their' *and period
added bef. del.* 'mass. [*period
ov. comma*]'
278.40 But] 'B' *ov.* 'b'
278.40 has] *aft. del.* 'of them'
279.1 of ours] *intrl.*

279.1 surely] *bef. del.* 'have to'

279.1-2 one day] *intrl.*

279.2 discoveries] *ab. del.* 'ones'

279.3 make. I consequently] *ab. del.* 'collect. I dis-' |

279.3 disbelieve] 'dis' *added*

279.3 being too] *ab. del.* 'applying'

279.3-4 with our] *intrl.*

279.4 of] *ab. del.* 'to'

279.4 in our squeezing] *ab. del.* '['to' *del.*] applying ['our' *del.*] logical forceps to'

279.5 material] *aft. del.* 'mes'

279.5-6 too . . . stage.] *intrl.*

279.6 need] *bef. del.* 'most'

279.9-10 We . . . game.] *added*

279.14 seemed] *aft. del.* 'felt and'

279.14 and felt] *intrl.*

279.15 death] *aft. del.* 'sudden'

279.17 practically] *intrl.*

††279.17-18 and altho] *ab. del.* 'his only expert coadjutor being'

279.18 Hyslop$_\wedge$] *comma del.*

279.18 and I] *on fol.* 1 *bef. del.* '[*fol.* 2] Hyslop was at the time of Hodgsons taking off, anxiously engaged in the arduous enterprise of founding a purely American Society. Hyslop and I were vice-presi' |

279.18 minute] *bef. del.* 'practical'

279.19 details] *aft. del.* 'the'

279.20 the . . . was] *ab. del.* 'was in charge.'

279.21 about] *ab. del.* 'with'

279.21-22 Branch? . . . records? . . . property?—] *qst. mks. ov. commas; dash ab. del.* 'was the qu'

279.23 problems] *ab. del.* 'questions'

279.23 solution] *alt. fr.* 'decision'

†279.23-24 Last . . . future.] *intrl.*

†279.25 The . . . property] *(circled* '¶ *and* 'The' *insrtd.); ab. del.* 'The ['latter' *del.*] last question'

279.26 Messrs.] *ab. del.* 'Messrs. George B.'

279.27 his] *ab. del.* 'Hodgson's'

279.27 left] *aft. del.* 'die'

279.27 great] *ab. del.* 'other'

279.29 other] *ab. del.* 'two larger'

279.29 to] *bef. del.* 'the decision of'

279.30 I] *bef. del.* ', being vice-presidents of the S. P. R.,'

279.31 official] *insrtd. for del.* 'nominal [*ab. del.* 'authority to decide any']'

279.31 authority.] *period added bef. del.* 'to decide in case of disagreement. ['I mention these' *del.*] These peculiarities in the general situation ['were taken acco' *del.*] must be mentioned here, for ['they' *del.*] the trance-utterances *refer to [*ab. del.* 'take account of'] them, and *they must be to a certain extent taken into account [*comma del.*] in [*ab. del.* 'they are relevant to'] our interpretation of the latter. ['we must take account of them.' *del.*] [¶] In the group of persons actively interested in *the [*ab. del.* 'the'] practical['ly' *del.*] decisions ['sions' *ab. del.* 'ding']—I myself *was [*ab. del.* 'being'] absent in California for [*end fol.* 3; *begin fol.* 5 [*ov.* '4']] about 5 months—certain differences of opinion naturally developed.'

279.32 Absent] 'A' *ov.* 'a'; *aft. del.* 'I was'

279.32 I] *ab. del.* 'and'

279.33 at] *aft. del. illeg. letter;* 't' *ov.* 's'

279.34 expended] *ab. del.* 'spent'

280.1 wished,] *comma added*

280.1 if possible,] *intrl.*

280.2 was] *bef. del.* 'engaged in'

280.2 whose] *alt. fr.* 'who'; *bef. del.* 'had been 'sitters' '

280.3 that] *ab. del.* 'private property in'

280.6 England.] *period aft. del. comma*

280.6 protested] *aft. del.* 'refused'

280.8 There] *aft. del.* 'In'

280.8 to] *bef. del.* 'take charge of'

280.9 sittings] *aft. del. insrtd.* 'future'

280.10 her . . . arisen] *ab. del.* 'their [*alt. fr.* 'them' *and undel. in error*] *conduct of these **had [*intrl.*] arisen [*ab. del.* 'had developed']'

280.11 strain$_\wedge$] *comma del.*

280.15 fair minds and] *ab. del.* '['the' *del.*] great['est' *del.*]'

280.16 got] *ab. del.* 'was decided'

280.19 practically] *insrtd. for del.* 'alone [*ab. del.* 'practically']'

280.20 should] *aft. del.* 'w'

280.20 possession of] *insrtd.*

280.20 records] *aft. del.* 'records'

280.21 workable] *aft. del.* 'a'

280.21 arrangements] 's' *added*

280.21 Piper[' 's' *del.*]] *bef. del.* 'sittings'

280.21–22 the . . . short,] *ab. del.* 'and everything'

280.23–24 for . . . part] *intrl.*

280.24 been] *bef. del.* 'personally'

280.25 all this period] *ab. del.* '['th' *del.*] what for brevity this *quandary [enclosing sg. qts. del.*]-period, *as [*intrl.*] I shall call it, [*tr. by guideline fr. aft.* 'brevity']'

280.26 'controls'] *aft. del.* 'trance'

280.26 ¹of] *bef. del.* 'all'

280.26 main] *intrl.*

280.26 perplexity] *insrtd. for del.* 'quandary. [*insrtd. for del.* 'perplexity. [*ab. del.* 'the situation.']']'

280.27 There] 'Th' *ov.* 'In'

280.27 at] *ab. del.* '['during this' *del.*] of information during'

280.27 epoch] *ab. del.* 'time'

280.27 that] *bef. del.* 'nothi'

280.29 Whether] *aft. del.* 'Mrs. [*end of fol. 6*]'

280.31 could] *bef. del.* 'easily'

280.31 her] *ab. del.* 'ordinary'

280.31 imagination,] *comma ov. period*

††280.31–32 whether waking . . . . The] *ab. del.* 'The'

280.33 feeling] *ab. del.* 'sense'

280.33 that₍₎] *comma del.*

280.33 the . . . -personality] *ab. del.* 'whoever'

280.34 talked] 'ed' *ov.* 'ing'; *aft. del.* 'were'

280.34 whether . . . Hodgson,] *ab. del.* 'it'

††280.35 who understood . . . situation.] *ab. del.* '*with a sense of [*ab. del.* 'that had a practical hold of'] ['the quand' *del.*] the *puzzling [*intrl.*] practical quandary.'

280.35 appropriately] *ab. del.* 'intelligently'

280.36 certain] *ab. del.* 'the private'

280.36 not . . . public;] *ab. del.* 'which were private property,'

280.37 books] *aft. del.* 'effe'

280.38 Hyslop's] *bef. del.* 'concern of mind, with Hyslop about'

280.39 his . . . and] *intrl. for del.* 'a [*ab. del.* 'some']'

281.4 the] *aft. del.* 'so that'

281.4–5 outcome being] *ab. del.* 'result was'

281.5 or her problems] *ab. del.* 'interests'

281.5–6 discriminatingly perceived] ('perceived' *in penc.*); *ab. del.* 'wisely [*intrl.*] being ['intelligently' *del.*] . followed. [*period insrtd. bef. del.* 'and that he had been talking with wisely ['understood and' *del.*] participated in *and unders [*intrl.*]']'

281.8 during the sittings] *intrl.*

281.9 remote,] *comma insrtd. bef. del. dash*

281.11 difference] 'diffe-' | *bef. del.* | 'rence it makes to'

281.11 Piper-] *aft. del.* 'sitti'

281.12 playing an active] *penc. ab. del.* 'taking'

281.13 One] *ab. del.* 'The sitter'

281.13 in . . . far] ('usually' *penc. insrtd.*); *ab. del.* 'has by far the'

281.14 sense,] *comma added bef. del.* 'of'

281.16 required . . . us,] ('bring *the [*ink ov. penc.*] reality' *and* 'home to us,' *in penc.*); *ab. del.* 'what give us the sense of its ['rel' *del.*] reality,'

281.17 -talk] *intrl.*

††281.18 &] *intrl.*

281.18 when] *bef. del.* 'in turn'

281.21 banter,] *comma alt. fr. semicolon*

281.21 thankfully . . . to] *ab. del.* 'received'

281.22 believe] *final* 'd' *del.*

281.23 something . . . a] *ab. del.* 'a sincere'

281.24   phenomenon.] *insrtd. for del.*
'reality. ['The other factor shares your
own' *del.*] Your own *warmth,
[*ov. illeg.*]'

281.24   talk] *ab. del.* 'process'

281.24   warmed ['up' *del.*]] *ab. del.*
'pervaded'

281.25   and] *ab. del.* 'reality, and so'

281.25   reality] *ab. del.* 'rich colour'

281.25   ['life;' *del.*] part . . . its]
ab. del. 'contribution, and the'

281.26   and] *aft. del.* 'misstatements,';
bef. del. 'other'

281.26   ¹you] *ab. del.* 'are'

281.26   charge] *final* 'd' *del.*

281.26   the imperfect] *intrl. for del.*
'*the obstructive [*ab. del.* 'the
account of the']'

281.27   genuineness] 'ness' *added;*
bef. del. 'pres'

281.27   communicating] 'ing' *ov.* 'or'

†281.27–28   spirit . . . sitters,]
('people' *insrtd. for del.* 'of us';
'when sitters,' *in penc.*); *ab. del.*
period and 'Your activity as a sitter
inevitably awakens *more ['m' *ov.* 'a']
and you inevitably'

†281.28   prick . . . to] ('their' *insrtd.*
for del. 'our [*alt. fr.* 'your'] ey
[*doubtful*]'); *ab. del.* 'as ['a' *del.*]
sitters, ['s,' *added ov. comma*] upon'

281.29   communication.] *period alt.*
fr. comma bef. del. 'for you emphasize
these, ['and in your memory' *del.*]
and in *our [*alt. fr.* 'your'] memory
these ['are dram' *del.*] remain
dramatically more emphatic [*period*
del.] than the other parts. [*period*
insrtd. for del. comma and 'and
furnish'] [¶] *They *loom* **more
[*intrl.*] dramatically, and give
[*insrtd.*] the key to our
interpretation.'

281.31   But a] *ab. del.* 'Most *sitters
[*ab. del.* 'persons'], I fancy, find that
*their [*ab. del.* 'a'] sitting shrinks in
value on a cold reading of the record,
and to readers who played no active
part in the conversation the record
may seem altogether thin and

insignificant ['A recor' *del.*] A
[*insrtd.*]'

281.31   thus] *intrl.*

281.31–32   important] *aft. del.* 'very'

281.33   thin and] *intrl.*

281.35   which] *bef. del.* 'one of
Mrs Piper's most frequent sitters
gave me.'

281.36   Piper's] *bef. del.* 'earliest and'

281.36   assiduous clients.] *ab. del.*
'frequent [*doubtful* 'eve' *del. intrl.*]
sitters, and'

281.36   Her] 'H' *ov.* 'h'

281.36–37   conversations with] *ab. del.*
'communications from'

281.37   spirit-control] *ab. del.* 'control'

281.37   ['an' *del.*] fluent and] *intrl.*

281.37   veridical,] *bef. del.*
'comforting,'

281.38   and elevating,] *ab. del. comma*

281.38   manuscript_∧] *comma del.*

281.39   , she thought,] *commas added*

281.39   was] *ab. del.* 'had been'

282.1–3   Somewhat . . . reader.] *ab. del.*
'The difference in reality-feeling in
the two cases is due to the presence
during the sitting of activity-factors
absent during the reading.'

282.1   Somewhat similar] *insrtd. for*
del. 'Similar'

282.1   fluctuations] *bef. del.* 'in his'

282.1   the] *intrl.*

282.2   records] *insrtd. for del.* 'sittings
awaken'

282.3   reader.] *bef. del.* 'of their
records.'

282.3   this] *bef. del. intrl.* 'Hodgson'

282.3   of sittings] *ab. del.* 'of sittings'

282.4–5   be . . . logic.] ('logic. [*period*
ov. comma]' *bef. del.* 'by'); *ab. del.*
'hang on'

282.5   Certain] 'C' *ov.* 'c'

282.5–6   I . . . for] *ab. del.* 'making for
one or other'

282.6   way. But] *period bef. del.*
comma; 'B' *ov.* 'b'

282.7   it] *ab. del.* 'I went over'

282.7   goes] 'es' *added*

282.9   by] *bef. del.* 'on'

282.11   another] *alt. fr.* 'any'

282.12 illogical] *insrtd. for del.*
'irresponsible [*ab. del.*
'unaccountable']'

282.14 more] *intrl.*

282.14 signify,] *bef. del.* 'be [*ab. del.*
'mean and'] laboring ['ing' *insrtd.*] to
express,'

282.14 well] *ab. del.* 'be- | ['be' *del.*] a
spiritist like Hodgson.'

282.15 to] *bef. del.* 'the'

282.17 by] *alt. fr.* 'but'

282.18 Hodgson-] *aft. del.* 'material'

282.19 reversed] *aft. del.* 'ref'

282.20 phenomena] *ab. del.*
'experience'

282.21 the proof] *ab. del.* '['one is still'
del.] the evidence'

282.22 whether] *bef. del.* 'this is to be
charged to'

282.22 or] *insrtd. for del.* 'or to'

282.23 be [*ov.* 'is'] . . . this,] *ab. del.*
'others'

282.24 be] *insrtd.*

282.24 decided] *final* 'd' *ov. period*

282.25 The] *ab. del.* 'A good'

†282.25 of . . . is] *ab. del.* 'of [*ov.* 'is']'

282.28 one] *ab. del.* 'cause'

282.28 usual] *ab. del.* 'more *probable
[*ab. del.* 'usual']'

282.28 more] *aft. del.* 'the'

282.28–29 probable, and] *insrtd. for
del.* 'usual [*ab. del.* 'likely, and']'

282.29–30 when . . . is] *ab. del.* 'under
stress of sheer necessity when others
are'

282.30 Fraud] 'r' *ov.* 'o'

282.30–31 a . . . and common,]
('agency' *ov. doubtful* 'failing');
ab. del. '*both a [*ab. del.* 'a'] known
agent and *a [*ab. del.* 'is'] common
[*period del.*] one,'

282.31 cynics] *ab. del.* 'is often'

282.32 suppose;] *final* 'd' *del.*;
semicolon ov. period

282.32 'personation'] 'p' *ov.* 'P'; *aft.
del.* 'Sub-conscious'

282.32 is] *ov.* 'in'

282.32 common] *aft. del.* 'a'; *bef. del.*
'factor'

282.33 our] *intrl.*

282.33 operations;] *semicolon ov.
period*

282.33 'telepathy'] 't' *ov.* 'T'

282.33–283.1 fairly established] *ab. del.*
'to be made out'

282.34 from it] *intrl.*

282.34 too] *bef. del.* 'pri'

282.34 ethical] *aft. del.* 'simply'

282.35 Never] *aft. del.* 'Not havi'

282.36 readers] *aft. del.* 'any'; 's'
added

282.37 communications] *ab. del.* 'work
an'

282.37 their] 'ir' *added; bef. del.*
'author of the manuscript had foun'

282.38 vital] *ab. del.* 'animal'

282.38 what] *aft. del.* 'the'

282.38 well] *intrl.*

282.39 this] *penc. ab. del.* 'my'

282.40 contrast] *ab. del.* 'difference'

††282.40 view,] *comma in error;
ab. del.* 'feeling'

283.1 fact,] *ab. del.* 'vera causa,'

283.1 questionable;] *insrtd. for del.*
'a question;'

283.1–2 accidental . . . rarely;] ('occur,
however' *ab. del.* 'are real, even if';
semicolon ov. period aft. 'rarely');
intrl.

†283.2–3 of . . . indeed] *ab. del.*
'['return is unknown elsewhere than
in the very phenomena under
investigation.' *del.*] and [*opening
sg. qt. del.*] parasitic *'elementals,'
[*comma added*] *altho [*ov.* 'the'] they
[*ab. del.* 'are']'

283.3 seem . . . so] ('to' *bef. del.*
'exist'; 'ves' *of* 'themselves' *ov.*
'so'); *ab. del.* 'indeed, but, as'

283.4 concrete] *intrl.*

283.4–5 nowhere ['unless' *del.*] except]
ab. del. 'it exists only'

283.5 Our] *ab. del.* 'The'

283.6 of presumption] *intrl.*

283.6 should] 'sh' *ov.* 'w'

283.6 deny . . . to] ('deny' *insrtd. for
del.* 'rule out'); *intrl.*

283.8 lucky] *aft. del.* 'acciden'

283.9 remains] *insrtd. for del.* 'were
[*ab. del.* 'is']'

†283.9 possible.] *period added bef. del.*
', [*comma alt. fr. semicolon*] *and
taking* *these [*ab. del.* 'each'] *details
[*'s' added*] [*'in such succession' del.*]
piecemeal'
283.11 practically] *intrl.*
283.11 as] *intrl.*
283.12 mere] *ab. del.* 'cold'
283.12 presumption,] *comma ov.
period*
283.12–13 ²the . . . good.] ('the
conclusion' *ab. del.* 'holds [*insrtd. for
del.* 'the logical conclusion is']';
'holds good.' *ab. del. comma*); *tr. by
guideline fr. bef.* 'as long'
283.14–15 is bound to] *ab. del.* 'may'
283.15 leave] *final* 's' *added and then
del.*
283.15 a] *aft. del.* 'there comes'
283.16 us;] *bef. del.* '*and so far as
**its [*doubtful*] records go, ['spirits'
del.] spirits have a finger in the pie,
here [*ab. del.* 'and after all there
may [''be' *del.*] spirits;'] for the same
phenomena which the other
principles explain *so well, [*insrtd.*]
are fully compatible with *our
conceiving [*intrl.*] them as
cooperating,'
283.16 there . . . bare] *ab. del.* 'the'
283.16 that] *ab. del.* '*at least
[*intrl.*] in'
283.16–17 before . . . be] *ab. del.* 'we
are considering is that it *may be
[*undel. in error*]'
283.17 such] *intrl.*
283.17 at . . . us] *ab. del.* 'that
immediately concerns us here,'
283.18 possibility] *aft. del.* 'treatmen'
283.18 'spirits'] *apostrophe bef. final*
's' *del.*
283.18 really] *ab. del.* 'return.'
283.19 compatible] *underl. del.*
283.20 explicable] *ab. del.* 'well'
283.20 be] *bef. del.* 'explained [*ab. del.*
'explicable']'
283.20 Spirits] *alt. fr.* 'The 'spirits''
283.21 harnessing] *ab. del.* 'using'
283.23 their wishes.] *ab. del.* 'at all.ˣ'
foll. by del. fn. line and del. 'ˣI mean
by this that'

†283.23–36 The . . . imperfectly.]
*orig. fn., but then fn. lines and
instructions del. and fn. run-on as
text by guideline and circled* 'no
break' *in mrgn.*
283.23 The] 'T' *ov.* 't'
283.23 be] *insrtd.*
283.23 a] *ab. del.* 'the'
283.24 wishes what] *ab. del.*
'intention as the'
283.25 aims.] *ab. del.* 'intention.'
283.25 A ['man' *del.*] spectator,]
ab. del. 'If we'
283.25 confining] 'ing' *ov.* 'e'
283.25 his] *ab. del.* 'our'
283.26 ²and] *intrl. aft. del.* '*we and
[*ab. del.* 'we']'
283.26 finding] 'ing' *added*
283.27 may] *aft. del.* 'and'
283.27 be . . . to] *intrl.*
283.27–28 the . . . of] *ab. del.* 'to it'
283.31–32 of the machine] *intrl.*
283.32 all this] *intrl.*
283.33 personation,] *aft. del.* 'fraud,';
bef. del. 'telepathy,'
283.34 using . . . may] *ab. del.* 'etc may'
283.36 her living] *ab. del.* '['a [*ab. del.*
'the'] medium's organism express
their higher' *del.*] *a living person's
[*ab. del.* 'a living']'
†283.36 their . . . imperfectly.] *insrtd.
for del.* '*his thought['s' *del.*],
however imperfectly. [*ab. del.* 'their
higher intention.'; *bel. is del. fn. line
and del. circled* 'Note continued'
in mrgn.]'
283.37 As] *opp. in mrgn. is del. circled*
'Text'
283.37 rule] *final* 's' *del.*
283.37 presumption] *aft. del.* 'method'
283.38 that] *intrl.*
†283.39 question] *bef. del.* 'resolves
itself into ['dramatic probabi' *del.*]
['a balancing of' *del.*] that of the pro'
†283.39 as to] *intrl.*
†283.39 the] *ab. del.* 'an'
†283.39 case] *bef. del.* 'really'
283.40 probabilities] 'ies' *ov.* 'y'
283.40 and] *insrtd. for del.* 'or [*ab. del.*
'and']'
283.40 improbabilities.] 'ies.' *ov.* 'y.'

284.1 who∧ ... decision∧] *commas del.*
284.3 his] *aft. del.* 'his the'
284.3–4 The explanation] *insrtd. at foot of fol.* 16 *bef. del.* '[*fol.* 16½] factors. Between the two possibilities there seems as yet no test that is crucial. *But as [*ab. del.* 'As'] soon as we *['apart from' *del. intrl.*] **drop our [*ab. del.* 'abandon ['many' *del.*]'] routine ***rules of [*ab. del.* 'and'] method, [*orig. tr. by guideline to aft.* 'truth,' *in line bel., but then guideline del.*] and [*insrtd. for del.* 'and'] ask for *straight [*ab. del.* '['truth' *del.*] naked'] truth, ['however reached, *we [*insrtd. for del.* 'we'] see' *del.*] that the whole question *is one [*ab. del.* '['is one of' *del.*] turns upon degrees'] of probability, and that *the sense of what is **probable ['e' *ov.* 'y'], in every human [*ab. del.* 'in every human'] being without exception who makes a decision in ['such a' *del.*] cases [*final* 's' *added*] *like this [*intrl.*] instead of suspending his judgment, ['the sense of what is probable' *del.*] depends on the forms of dramatic imagination of which *our [*ab. del.* 'the'] mind is ['capable' *del.*] antecedently capable. The *explanation [*intrl.*] has in'
†284.4 has *in*] *insrtd.*
†284.4 *event*] *ab. del.* 'case'
284.5 are] *aft. del.* 'all'
284.5 all of them] *intrl.*
284.6 imagination] *ab. del.* 'mind'
284.6 ['seriously' *del.*] conceiving] *ab. del.* 'even seriously entertaining'
284.7 at] *bef. del.* 'all^x ['as the *imagination [*ab. del.* 'mind'] is of those 'scientific' philosophers' *del.*] *you will [*ab. del.* 'who'] proclaim it *dram[*ab. del.* 'dog']matically proclaim it *simply [*intrl.*] 'impossible' [*comma del.*] *schlechthin, [*intrl.*] beforehand,^x *and [*ab. del.* 'you are'] rule['d' *del.*] yourself [*intrl.*] out *beforehand [*intrl.*] from ['all' *del.*] ['serious' *del.*]

[*fn. line*] ^xE.g. Münsterberg, Psychology & Life [*fn. line*] ['discussion of' *del.*] competency to discuss the *phenomena, ['a' *ov.* 'on'] ['seriously.' *del.*]—for the world may *perfectly well [*intrl.*] harbor ['these mundanely' *del.*] such unusual agents.'
284.7 just] *ab. del.* 'simply'
284.7 it] *bef. del. intrl.* ' 'scientifically'
284.9 alternative] *ab. del.* 'phenomenon'
284.10 spirit-agency,] *aft. del.* 'the'; *bef. del.* 'as a dramatic hypothesis,'
284.14 each of] *intrl.*
284.14 them∧] *comma del.*
284.14–15 not ... more,] ('not' *aft. del.* 'and'; 'mixing' *intrl.*); *ab. del.* 'and mixing them so little,'
284.15 profusely,] *intrl.*
284.15 quite] *intrl.*
284.17 one] *aft. del.* 'the'
284.18 skill] *ab. del.* 'freedom'
284.18 suppose] *bef. del.* 'that'
284.19 once] *aft. del.* 'ha'
284.19 have had] *ab. del.* 'be possessed that it must pretend by'
284.19–20 suggested to it] *intrl.*
284.20 must] *underl. del.*
284.20 sitters,] *bef. del.* 'its expertne'
284.20 fair] *intrl.*
284.21 virtuosity] *ab. del.* 'expertness'
284.21 surprise] *aft. del.* '*very greatly [*ab. del.* 'particularly']'
284.24 details] *aft. del.* 'particular'
††284.24 to ... phenomenon∧] ('whole' *bef. del.* 'kind'); *ab. del.* 'of the machinery *here [*del. intrl.*] to the idea of ['the' *del.*] its total process'
284.26 know] *ab. del.* 'believe to exist'
284.27 record] *ab. del.* 'history'
284.27 notion] *aft. del. intrl.* 'bai'
284.28 experience] *aft. del. intrl.* 'human'
284.29 absolutely nothing] *ab. del.* '['not h' *del.*] no idea'
284.30 that] *insrtd. for del.* 'of'
†284.30–31 men ... have] ('men ... *enough∧ [*comma om. in error*]' *insrtd. for del.* 'human beings must'); *ab. del.* 'of us having'

†284.31–32 preposterous . . . annexed]
ab. del. 'purely humbugging
*possible self [*insrtd.*] addition'

284.32 their personality] *ab. del.* 'our
consciousness'

284.33 that] *bef. del.* 'I turn to'

††284.33–34 immediately . . .
appearace [*error*].] *alt. fr.*
'immediately looks more probable.'
alt. fr. 'takes on an increment of
probability.' *alt. fr.* 'with an increase
of hospitality.'

284.34 indeed] *ab. del.* 'at any rate'

284.35 complications] *ab. del.*
'obstructions'

284.35 at] *aft. del.* 'they'

284.35 least‸] *comma del.*

284.36 are . . . some] *ab. del.* 'have
a finger in the pie [*comma del.*]
there is *some['thing' *del.*] [*underl.
del.*]'

284.36 is] *intrl.*

284.36 a whole] *ab. del.* 'that *sphere
[*ab. del.* 'part'] of the universe'

284.37 run by] *intrl.*

284.37 pure] *final* 'ly' *del.*

284.37 deception.] *insrtd. for del.*
'mendacious. [*ab. del.* 'crazy. [*period
insrtd. bef. del.* 'and irrational.']']'

284.38 phenomenon] *bef. del.* 'of
mediumship'

284.39 world] *ab. del.* 'universe'

284.40 whose] 's' *ov.* 'l'

284.40 vaster] *ab. del.* 'larger'

285.1 feature] *bef. del.* 'alone'

285.2 insincerity.] *bef. del.* '*This is
essentially what **I ['have' *del. intrl.*]
call *a [*insrtd.*] feeling of dramatic
probability [*insrtd.*] [¶] I have to
confess, therefore, to *an ['n' *added*]
inward [*ab. del.* 'certain'] vacillation,
in my thought, according as I *have
[*intrl.*] attended ['ed' *added*] to the
single items of *these ['se' *added*]
records ['s' *added*] and followed the
*safe [*intrl.*] methodical *rule
[*ab. del.* 'canon'] of the logic of
probability, never taking a rarer
explanation where there is a
commoner one, or according as I
have *turned to [*ab. del.* 'thought of']

the ['wh' *del.*] phenomenon in its
totality, and sought for the idea
that might be animating it.'

285.3 If] *aft. del.* '[¶] Having ['H'
ov. 'P'] exhibited my own *sl ['l'
doubtful]'

285.3 yield] *final* 'ing' *del.*

285.3 find] *aft. del.* 'then'

285.5 all] *intrl.*

285.5 lower] *ab. del.* 'other'

285.7 at] *aft. del.* 'to'

285.8 familiarity,] *ab. del.*
'acquaintance, ['with it,' *del.*]'

285.8 ¹which] *aft. del.* 'to into';
bef. del. 'to'

285.8 shares] *aft. del.* 'has shared'

285.8 most] *bef. del.* 'sitters'

285.10 the] *ab. del.* 'Hodgson s'

285.10 spirit] *final* 's' *del.*

285.10 of R.H.] *insrtd.*

285.10 talking to me] *ab. del.* 'and
others ['moul' *del.*] ['using' *del.*]
talking'

285.11 forcing] *ab. del.* 'moulding'

285.11–12 or . . . consilient[' ,' *del.*]]
intrl.

††285.12 in the medium] *intrl.*

285.12 his] *ab. del.* 'their'

285.13 dimly.] *aft. del.*
'approximately.'

285.15 give.] *bef. del.* 'The reader will
make allowance for it in *what is to
[*ab. del.* 'my treatment of the
matters that'] follow.'

285.16 and] *bef. del.* 'it will show
throughout my narrative.'

285.18 arrange the material.] *ab. del.*
'['sugg' *del.*] cull the data for him.
As probably the best way to begin, I
will give a couple of specimens,
almost in extenso, of particularly
good sittings.'

285.19 ²to] *ab. del.* 'by'

285.19 begin] *final* 'ning' *del.*

285.21 great] *ab. del.* 'immense'

285.21 spirits.] *period added bef. del.*
', and by an almost diseased appetite
for poetry [*comma del.*]'

285.22 chaff] *aft. del.* 'and'

285.22 and repartee,] *ab. del.* 'and'

285.23 excessive] *intrl.*

285.24 poetry.] *period added bef. del.*
'that might almost be called diseased,
in as much as it seemed to be for the'

285.25 he] *aft. del.* 'his'

285.25 sonorous] *insrtd.*

285.26 quality and sentiment] *ab. del.*
'thought clothed in them'

285.28 my] *ab. del.* 'the'

285.28 report.] *bef. del.* 'Quotations
*of chaff have a silly sound, [*ab. del.*
'would sound silly,'] but the slang
and chaffing seemed as a rule very
natural to the sitters.'

285.30 of . . . -control] *intrl.*

285.31 T.P.] *ab. del.* 'Miss Pope'

285.32 bantering] *aft. del.* 'chaff'

285.36 Dr.] 'D' *ov.* 'd'

285.37 H.:∧] *dash aft. colon del.*

285.37 were] *bef. del.* 'often'

286.4 For] *ab. del.* 'appropriately for'

††286.4 The control . . . sitters] *moved
by guideline fr. start of sentence
w. caret of guideline ov. orig. period
aft.* 'conversations'; 'The' *not reduced
in error*

286.4 chose] *ab. del.* 'selected'

286.5 well] *ab. del.* 'One lady with
whom he had'

286.6 very] *intrl.*

†286.12–13 The . . . what] ('or to be
given' *insrtd.*); *ab. del.* 'Specimens
of what'

286.13 manner.] *period added bef. del.*
'will appear'

286.15 manifested the] *ab. del.* 'began
to show the characteristic'

286.15–16 our . . . utterances,] *ab. del.*
'the [*undel. in error*] Mrs. [*intrl.*]
Piper's [*alt. fr.* 'Piper.'] trance of
things'

286.16 stereotyped.] *period added bef.
del.* 'automatically. *R. [*doubtful*]
P.'s appearance have in late years
degenerated into a hasty'

286.18 then] *intrl.*

286.18–19 acquired] *ab. del.* '['began
to' *del.*] fell into'

286.20 Delighted] 'D' *ov.* 'd'; *aft. del.*
'I'm g'

286.20 firstrate?] *bef. del.* ' " etc.'

††286.21 at last∧ "] (*comma aft.* 'last'
del. in error); *intrl.*

286.21 This] 'T' *ov.* 't'; *aft. del.*
'Recognizing'

286.22 habitual use] *ab. del.* 'tendency
*in Mrs Piper [*intrl.*] to ['st' *del.*]
form a [' 'stock' at' *del.*] set'

††286.22 by Mrs∧ Piper] *intrl.*

286.22 be] *aft. del.* 'forget'

286.23 significance] *final* 's' *and period
del.; aft. del.* 'phenomenon's'

286.23 of her mediumship.] *intrl.*

286.24 in it,] *intrl.*

286.24 whatever . . . be] *insrtd. for del.*
'be essential'

286.25 to-day] *ab. del.* 'now'

286.26 have] *bef. del. intrl.*
'originally'

286.26 at] *ab. del.* 'in'

286.26 former] *intrl.*

286.27 Supernormal] 'S' *ov.* 's';
aft. del. 'There certainly *is*'; *bef. del.*
'receptivity; [*ab. del.* 'information;']
and I believe that the matter of its'

286.27 receptivity] *bef. del.* 'is
certainly involved in the'

286.28 total phenomenon,] *ab. del.*
'results,'

286.28 that] *bef. del.* 'the'

††286.29 that . . . came from it] *ab. del.*
'it gives *out to us, [*intrl.*]'

286.30 at] *aft. del.* 'was'

286.31 but . . . has] *ab. del.* 'later
[*alt. fr.* 'lately'] he has'

286.32 shadow] *ab. del.* 'ghost'

286.32–33 quickly out] *ab. del.* 'out'

286.33 an] 'n' *added*

286.33 almost . . . of] *ab. del.*
'stereotyped'

286.33–34 may . . . first,] *insrtd. for del.*
'was' *ab. del.* 'he is,'

286.34 at last] *ab. del.* 'now'

286.36 now] *ab. del.* 'next'

286.38 affairs,] *comma ov. period*

286.38 these] *bef. del.* 'the'

†287.1 The . . . Series.] *triple underl.*;
'O' *ov.* 'B'; *hyphen aft.* 'Old' *del. and
words joined; marked as* ¶

287.2 Oldfarm] *text orig. run-on but
marked for* ¶

287.2 George B.] *intrl.*

287.2 place] *aft. del.* 'country'

287.3 Maine,] *comma ov. period*

287.3 where . . . guest.] ('often'
aft. del. 'made'; 'been . . . guest.'
insrtd. for del. 'made visits during the
summer.'); *intrl.*

††287.5 and altho] *ab. del.* 'tho'

287.5 ²had] *ab. del.* 'hav'

287.5 as well] *insrtd. for del.* 'both'

287.6 as] *ab. del.* 'and'

287.7 small] *bef. del.* 'details'

287.9 1906,] *insrtd.*

287.9 asks] 's' *ov.* 'ed'

[MS *missing*, 287.11–289.30]

289.31 Miss Bancroft's] *ab. del.* '['of'
del.] ['with Miss' *del.*] ['of Mrs' *del.*]
another person'

289.32 R.] *ov.* 'ar'

289.32 suddenly] *aft. del.* 'as'; *bef. del.*
'asks:—'

289.33 Celle] 'elle' *ab. del.* 'elle'
foll. by two del. hyphens

290.10 appends] *penc. ab. del.* 'writes'

[MS *missing*, 290.11–18; *begin* MS(T)
at 290.22]

290.22 any] *aft. del.* '[¶ AS
SPECIMENS of particularly good
sitting, I willgiv give almost in
extenso one with Mr. george B. Dorr,
& two with professor William
Romaine Newbold, both intimate
friends of Hodgson. | [*centered*]
MR. DORR'S SITTING.ˣ [*ink fn.
indicator*] | [*in mrgn. undel. ink fn.*
'ˣSitter's remarks are in parenthesis;
comments are in square brackets;
everything else is uttered by ['the'
del.] 'controls.' '] | [*centered underl.*]
July 2nd. 1906. G. B. D. alone. | [¶]
D. loq. (what can you tell me about
Oldfarm? [*closing paren del.*]
['[Oldfarm was' *del.*] [The ['T' *ov.* 't']
name of the Dorr's place *at Bar
Harbor, where R. H. had often
paid visits.] [*penc. del.*] Can you
give me'

290.28 medium in] *ab. del.* 'Controls,
through'

290.32 Minturns] 'inturns' *del. but
restored by underdotting and mrgn.
circled* 'stet'

291.1 us—] *dash ov. two del. asterisks*

291.4 can't] *apostrophe insrtd.*

††291.5 find?)] 'd?)' *added end of line*

291.6 Densmore.] *added aft. del.*
'Blank.'

291.10 difficult] *intrl.*

††291.12 a——— . . . correctly.]] ('ality'
of 'nationality' *intrl.*); *insrtd. in
mrgn. w. guideline for del.* 'an
[Austrian!] *[substitute for name
[*intrl.*]'

291.17 up—] *dash ov. two del. asterisks*

†291.18 [Correct . . . J.]] *added*

††291.19 (Was] *aft. del.* '(Did you
want to marry her?)'

††291.21 [Correct. *G.B.D. [*intrl.*]]]
added

††291.26 any.)] 'y.)' *added end of line*

291.28 [This] *ab. del.* '[I will treat of
the entire'

291.28 is treated] *intrl.*

291.30 ¹I] *in mrgn. is* '¶'

291.32 [My] *aft. del.* '[This is
excellent.'

291.35 The custom is] *ov.* 'It is'

291.35 not] *bef. del.* 'a'

291.35 enough] *bef. del.* 'custom'

292.1 nor] *bef. del.* 'i'

292.2 it] *bef. del.* 'either'

292.3 which] *aft. del.* '& freshness of
impression'

292.5 ['G.B.' *del.*] D.]] *added*

292.6 to extract] *intrl.*

292.9 gave] *aft. del.* 'in searching for
it he'

292.9 "It] *aft. del.* 'This seemed
to me also good, for he would not
have been likely to mention Miller
in talking to anyone of his visits
to Bar Harbor, for he saw but little
of him, tho his name was familiar
enough. He did not call him the
gardner, however, but simply gave
his name as one that came back
in connexion with the place.
Later note:'

292.10 possible,"] *comma and db.
qts. added*

292.10 Mr. Dorr writes,] *intrl.*

292.10 "that] *db. qts. added*

††292.15 sittings."]] *db. qts. and bkt.*

added bef. del. '['—this would
however not have' *del.*] this however
would not have been the case in
regard to the pansies & other facts
recalled by R. H.]'

292.18 [A] *aft. del.* '[This also is
excellent.'

292.24 spoken] *bef. del.* 'of'

292.30 fishing—] *dash ov. two del.
asterisks*

292.31 it,] *comma added*

292.32,35 M.] *ab. del.* 'Minna'

292.33 retire—] *dash aft. two del.
asterisks*

292.34 would be] *ab. del.* 'too is good,'

292.35 She] *bef. del.* ', who was an
Italian on her mother's side,'

292.36–37 person . . . whom] *insrtd.
for del. intrl.* 'woman'

293.1 possibly] *intrl.*

293.1 this incident] *ab. del.* 'it'

293.2 M.] 'inna' *del.*

293.3 —certainly not] *ab. del.* 'or'

293.3 , either] *insrtd. for del.* 'in
trance'

293.9 it] *alt. fr.* 'I t'

293.13 R.H.'s] *insrtd. for del.* '[¶ ['I
have recollection of R. H.'s going
fishing with John Rich, who was our
boatman, among other things.'
del.] [R. H. was fond of fishing &
I was not; & he went off with Rich in
that way occasionally [*comma del.*]—
but rarely, for we generally walked
& did things on shore. His'

293.13 good,] *ab. del.* 'excellent,'

293.15 with] *bef. del.* 'ot'

293.15 or] *bef. del.* 'with'

293.15 happened,—] *dash added*

††293.22–23 and . . . it$_\wedge$] *insrtd.*

293.35 Do] *aft. del.* 'for them to do so?
Can you tell me anything about that?)
[¶] We are on the border-line, as it
were. [¶] (Physically speaking, do
you mean?) [¶] No, no, the etherial
veil that separates the ['two' *del.*]
worlds is what we term the
bordrer-line.'

293.37 I] *aft. del.* 'ai'

293.37 him] *typed line bel. del.* 'play
*This describes [*typed ov.* 'his

violin.'] A little gentleman—I
remember him very well.'

294.1 G.,] 'aertner' *del.; period and
comma added*

294.3 faculty.] *bef. del.* 'We did
some things at Dr. Weir Mitchell's
house, & Mitchell said afterwards that
v. G. was the only person who had
given him an impression of their
reality of such phenomena.'

††294.4 the violin$_\wedge$] *intrl.*

294.4 G.] 'aertner' *del.; period added*

294.8 I] *ov.* 'he'

294.8 him] *alt. fr.* 'me'

†294.11–14 [Prof. . . . J.]] *insrtd. aft.
del.* 'He has been talking about
Miss Fetting, his niece. If he can give
his wife any message—he is anxious
his wife should know he is not
totally annihilated. Ask her from him
if she remembers a conversation
they had together about this life, &
how ['the more' *del.*] he said the
more he tho't of it the more
perplexed he *became, [*comma
added*] & that he began to feel that
perhaps death ends all.'

294.12 in] *ab. del.* 'with'

[*end MS(T); begin MS*]

294.15 whole] *ab. del.* 'sum total'

294.15 matter] *aft. del.* 'Old farm'

294.15 Oldfarm] *aft. del.* 'Hodgson's'

294.16 which] *bef. del.* 'has'

294.17 and] *aft. del.* 'but'; *bef. del.*
'there are'

294.18 mistakes$_\wedge$] *comma del.*

294.18 of fact,] *intrl.*

294.18 it] *aft. del.* 'the'

294.19 Piper$_\wedge$] *comma del.*

294.20 Some] *aft. del.* '['Either
chance-coin' *del.*] Chance-'

294.20 indeed] *intrl.*

294.20 likely] *intrl.*

††294.20 priori;] *semicolon insrtd. bef.
del.* 'likely [*semicolon del.*];'

294.21 chance-] *aft. del.* 'lucky'

294.24 of] 'f' *ov.* 'n'

294.26 if] *insrtd.*

294.27 2the] *ab. del.* 'our'

294.31 it] *ab. del.* 'us'

294.32 genial] *ab. del.* 'genial'

294.32 ₄what . . . say,'] *del. sg. qt. bef.*
'what'; *sg. qt. added aft. del. db.*
qts. aft. 'say'

294.32 and it] *ab. del.* 'It'

††294.33 I fancy₄] *intrl.*

294.35 facts] *aft. del.* 'appropriate'

294.38 ¶ I] *guideline runs-on ¶* 'I'

294.38 call] *bef. del.* 'the'

295.4 very] *aft. del.* 'made gre'

295.6 been] *bef. del.* 'a former'

295.6 Piper's] *bef. del.* '['and good'
del.] good'

[*end MS; begin* MS(T)]

295.10 I am] *bel. del.* 'Miss Bancroft'
sitting, Feb. 19, 06'

295.18 chance?] *bef. del.* 'Do you
remember what I said about'

295.26 subconsciousness₄] *comma del.*

295.26 other] *aft. del.* 'in some'

†295.27–28 Rector . . . J.]] *insrtd.*

295.31 were?] 'e?' *added end of line*

[*end* MS(T); *begin* MS]

295.33 omit] *bef. del.* 'those parts
of the recor'

295.34 not . . . with] *ab. del.*
'irrelevant to'

295.34 recollections.] *aft. del.* 'Owl's
Head'

295.35 is] *insrtd. for del.* 'I'

[*end* MS; *begin* MS(T)]

296.4 happy.] *intrl.*

296.4 'lights'] *sg. qts. added*

296.6 had] *intrl.*

296.6 spoken] 'n' *added*

296.7,15 —M.B.] *added*

296.9 there] *intrl.*

296.14 ¹of] *bef. del.* 'Miss B's'

296.20 For] *aft. del.* '[Miss B. was
unacquainted with the Putnams,
at whose camp ['in the' *del.*] at Keene
Heights R. H. had spent part of
his summer vacation *for many
[*ab. del.* 'one'] years ['s' *added*].'

296.20 this] 'is' *ov.* 'e'

296.22 W.J.] *added*

††296.26 wrongly . . . 'hat.'] *insrtd.*
for del. 'read aloud as 'hats' '

296.29 clearly.] *in line bel.* WJ *first
typed* 'Do you remember fishing?'
then typed ov. it 'I am trying to recall
about that hat.)' *and then del. line*

297.8 Owls.] *bef. del.* '. . . R.'

297.16 between] *aft. del.* 'about'

297.24 sitting,] *comma ov. period;*
bef. del. 'The name of *'Mama
[*sg. qt. added*] Fuss' was mentioned,'

297.25 ²is] *ab. del.* 'being'

297.29 'psychic'] *aft. del.* 'Pschic P'

297.29 had] *intrl.*

298.5 o'clock] WJ *in the next line
typed and then del.* '[¶ *I saw you.
[*in error ov.* 'Crristmas morning.'] I
heard you speak to me'

298.12 [Nellie . . . B.]] *added*

298.16–17 [Correct.—M.B.]] *insrtd.
for del.* '[When I felt the presence, I
reached over & turned on the
electric light. [*asterisk del.*]—M.B.]'

††298.20 this₄] *period insrtd. and not
del. in error, foll. by del. but
underdotted to preserve* 'unless . . .
Pope's *reception of a [*ab. del.*
'reference to'] message to me'

298.21 in] *ab. del.* 'from [*insrtd. for
del.* 'in']'

298.22 —M.B.]] *bef. ink added fn.
indicator and circled penc.* 'copy
footnote on next page'

298.24 Dr.] *aft. del.* 'The'

298.24 Bayley,] *comma added*

298.24 to] *ab. del.* 'OF'

298.24 reference] *aft. del.* 'it was
question at'

[*end* MS(T); *begin* MS]

298.25 at] *aft. del.* 'R.H.'

298.25–26 on . . . 1906,] *intrl.*

298.27 Mrs. M.] *insrtd. bef. del.*
'Sitter'

298.28 [the . . . of] *intrl. ab. del. bkt.;
orig.* 'but' *had been enclosed in bkts.
and in error the bkt. aft.* 'but' *was
retained instead of being added aft.*
'of' *in the intrl.*

298.30 The] *aft. del.* 'Margaret B.
remarks on this that she was
awakened'

298.30 immediately] *intrl.*

298.30 Miss] *intrl.*

298.30–31 with . . . acquainted,] *intrl.*

298.31 of] *intrl.*

298.33 sleep,] *bef. del.* '. . . sat up in
bed so attentive that I s'

298.38 . . .] *intrl.*

[*end* MS; *begin* MS(T)]

299.1 Head] *bef. del.* ', had two sittings in April'

299.1 sitting,] *comma added*

299.2 which] *bef. del.* 'R. H. reproduced very'

299.4 handwriting; and] '; and' *insrtd. for del.* '&'

299.6 went,] *intrl.*

299.6 passage] *ab. del.* 'item'

††299.8 R.H.—Get] *ab. del.* '*I received the [*typed in error ov.* 'R.H.']'

299.10 sent] *ab. del.* 'mailed'

299.11 They] 'T' *ov.* 't'; *aft. del.* 'Dying on the 20th of December'

299.11 mailed] *ab. del.* 'sent'

299.11 death_∧] *period del.*

299.11–14 on . . . friends.]] *insrtd.*

†299.15 [My . . . B.]] ('My friend' *ab. del.* 'Meaning'; *closing bkt. insrtd. bef. del.* 'friend of Dr. Bayley as well as of R.H. W.J.]'); *insrtd.*

299.18 how] *aft. del.* 'I'

299.21 it.] *intrl.*

†299.21–22 [Proves . . . J.]] *insrtd.*

299.23 Also . . . chil|] *del. but underdotted for retention*

299.25–26 [W. . . . children.]] ('him' *intrl.*); *insrtd.*

††299.29 (Why . . . will] (*aft. circled* '¶' *and vert. stroke*); *ab. del. typing error overlay*

299.32 'fishing'] *sg. qts. added*

300.3–4 water? . . . ducking?] *qst. mks. alt. fr. periods*

300.15 Laugh?] *aft. del.* 'T'

300.15 distinct] *ab. del.* 'clear'

300.25 words] *intrl.*

301.7 [This . . . B.]] *insrtd.*

301.10 Well, H.,] *insrtd. bef.* 'Neither [*not reduced in error*]'

†301.20 [Compare . . . J.]] *added*

301.28 tricks?] 'ks?' *added end of line*

††301.30 summer?)] '?)' *added end of line*

302.3 Wopsey] *bef. del. qst. mk.*

302.5–6 [Known . . . J.]] *insrtd. aft.* 'tired.'

302.8 [Known . . . J.]] *insrtd. aft.* 'trick?'

302.14 [Known . . . J.]] *added in penc.*; 'W.J.' *in ink aft. ink del. penc.* 'see letter'

302.20 'place,'] *sg. qts. insrtd.*

302.20 my . . . ¹that] *intrl.*

302.21 'piece,'] *sg. qts. insrtd.*

302.21 from] *ab. del.* 'with'

302.22 W.J.] *added*

302.26 consulted] *ab. del.* 'went to'

302.27 things] *bef. del.* 'to me'

302.27 sensitiveness;] 'ness;' *ab. del. final* 'e'; *bef. del.* 'nature;'

302.30 subject.] *bef. del.* 'I told him Dr. Bayley never seemed to think I was absolutely true, &c.'

[*end* MS(T); *begin* MS]

302.34 M.,] *comma aft. del. comma*

††302.34–35 had taken a] *ab. del.* 'took in'

302.35 remained] *ab. del.* 'was'

303.1 R.H.] *intrl.*

303.1 its] 's' *ov. period*

303.1 disposition.] *intrl.*

303.3 to . . . later] ('a' *ov.* 'in'); *ab. del.* 'of June, 20th.'

303.6 Yes,] *comma aft. del. start of exclm. mk.*

†303.8 me.] *starting line bel. is del.* '[*on fol.* 52] [¶] There is help coming to you to enlarge the house [*fol.* 53] . . . . He said he would certainly convince D⨪ Bayley of my sincerity." —['I have already informed' *del.*] The ['T' *ov.* 't'] reader ['that M' *del.*] knows already that Miss B. is a "light." [¶] On ['Dec 2nd. 1907' *del.*] June 20th. 1906, Miss Bancroft had her 3rd sitting. R. H. appears and quickly says to Miss B.:— [¶] R. H.—Get my cross? [¶] M. B.— (Yes: thank you very much.) [H., when he gave me the cross, *had [*intrl.*] requested me not to mention the fact of the gift—M. B.]'

303.12 sittings] *aft. del.* 'previous'

303.13 in] *bef. del.* 'Febr'

[MS *missing*, 303.16–304.28]

304.29 2nd] *ov.* '3rd'

††304.32–33 ; none . . . known.] ('none'

ab. del. 'None'; 'in a way' *ab. del.*
'likely'); *intrl.*

304.34   of a] *bef. del.* 'personal trouble'

304.34–35   affair . . . other] *ab. del.*
'matter, ['that had' *del.*] concerning'

[MS *missing*, 305.7–28]

305.29   So] *aft. del.* MS(T) '. . . . He
said he would certainly convince
D.ͬ [*intrl.*] Bayley of my sincerity."]
It touches me deeply that he should
have remembered his promise.] It
was like a voice from the dead."
['I have already said' *del.*] The
reader has already seen that Margaret
is a 'light'. [¶] What advice have you
to give to Margaret [*begin* MS]
[¶] The reader knows already that
M. B. is a 'light.' '

†305.29–30   So . . . facts.] '¶' *in mrgn.*;
ab. del. '[¶] In reviewing the Owl's
Head record one sees that few'

305.31   Few of the] *intrl.*

305.31–32   on . . . that] *ab. del.* 'that'

305.32   tastes and habits] *ab. del.*
'habits, as his late hours, love of
swimming, *fishing, [*intrl.*] smoking
etc,'

305.33   might] *bef. del.* 'easily'

305.33   some] *ab. del.* 'many'

305.33–306.1   (swimming . . . example)]
intrl.

306.1   abstract] *intrl.*

306.2   now] *intrl.*

306.2   also] *intrl.*

306.3   for] *bef. del.* 'Mrs.'

306.3   such] *ab. del.* 'the rest, the
names, other'

306.3   as] *intrl.*

306.3   Nellie] 'N' *ov.* 'n'

306.4   with] *bef. del.* 'Newbold, etc.'

306.5   'fire-buckets,'] *ab. del.* 'last two
items,'

306.5   'sincerity,'] *aft. del.* '&'

††306.5   & other items*ᴧ*] *intrl.*

306.6   either] *intrl.*

306.7   condensed] *ab. del.* 'abridged'

306.8   some] *insrtd.*

306.9   Head] 'H' *ov.* 'h'

†306.9–10   some . . . script.] ('some . . .
all' *intrl.*; 'slowness in deciphering'
ab. del. 'D.*ͬ Bayley's inability to read';

period insrtd. aft. 'script' *and bef.
del.* 'and some'); *tr. by guideline
fr. aft.* 'leaving out'

306.12   to] *aft. del.* 'on'

306.13–17   I . . . Newbold.] *insrtd.*

306.17   reader] *bef. del.* 'loses much in'

306.19   subtleties] *aft. del.* 'impossible'

306.20   over] *aft. del.* 'of'

306.23   *Professor . . . Sittings.*] *triple
underl.; insrtd. for del.* '[¶] So much
for the Owls' Head series of
conversations, which, the reader will
doubtless think, *follow [*ab. del.*
'run along'] a very coherent thread
of *associated [*intrl.*] facts.'

306.24   The] *opp. mrgn.* '¶'

306.24   Wm.] 'm' *insrtd.*

306.25   next] *ab. del.* 'this'

306.25   this] *bef. del.* 'friend in'

306.26   sittings,] *comma insrtd. bef. del.*
'since R. H.'s death,'

306.28   June] *aft. del.* 'the'

[*end* MS; *begin non*-WJ MS(T)]

††306.30   (R.H.)] *aft. del.* 'Sitting with
Mrs. Piper. | June 27th, 1906. | [*to
left*] W. R. Newbold | George B.
Dorr | [*to right*] Time. 10.10 A.M. |
*Prof. Newbold's Sittings. [WJ
*autograph, centered and triple
underl.*] | Hail! | We greet you with
joy and peace + R. We are glad
to greet you, friend of earth. |
(W. R. N. Yes, I am glad to be here.) |
We have called for you often and
have seen you many times. Peace and
blessings go to you. We shall soon
bring a friend who desires to greet
you here. | (I shall be delighted to
see him here.) | Hail, friend! [To
G. B. D.] We are glad to have your
help.'

306.34   together—] *bef. del.* '(Note 1)'

†307.1–2   [Our . . . N.]] ('afternoon'
aft. del. 'July'; 'of July 1905'
intrl.); *insrtd. aft. del.* '[Word 'waves'
written four times as it was not
decipherable at first.]'

307.4   me.] *bef. del.* '(2)'

307.6   my work.] *aft. del.* 'my work—'

307.10   Dick] *aft. del.* '(Good for you,'

307.14 and] *bef. del.* '(3) [*tr. by
guideline to aft.* 'discontented.']'

†307.17–18 [This . . . N.]] ('N.' *aft. del.*
'WJ [*aft. del.* 'N']'); *insrtd.*

307.20 ²not!] *bef. del. insrtd.* '[I can
not find it in the letters. N.]'

307.21 boss] *bef. del.* 'things on———
Boss——BOSS——*(4) [*undel.
in error*]'

†307.21–25 [R. . . . N.]] *insrtd.*

307.30 wish.] *bef. del.* '———what I
wish.'

307.31 happiness.] *bef. del.* '(6)'

†308.2 [I . . . letters.]] *insrtd.*

308.4 Well,] *comma added*

308.4 dear] *aft. del.* 'dear,'

308.7 difficulties?] *bef. del.* '(5) Very
true *[Correct. W.R.N.] [added]'

††308.13 (You were!)] *insrtd. ab. del.
typed line* '[Apparently read as "Do
you remember"] (Yes I do, Dick.'

308.22 waited] *aft. del.* | '(I can't
read that now, Dick.) | ———waited
until the boat returned———'

308.25 music.] *bef. del.* | '[Sequence
of events confused here.]'

309.1 cigar.] *bef. del.* ') [He never
failed to ask me to have a cigar.]'

309.2 think] *bef. del.* '———recall'

309.4 cooked?] *bef. del.* '10 P. A.'

309.8 remember.] *bef. del. long dash*

309.9 [A] *ab. del.* 'In'; *aft. del.* '———'

309.9 ¹is] *intrl.*

†309.9 here . . . veridical] *intrl.*

309.10 private] *intrl.*

309.10;311.16 —N.] *added*

309.11 Billy,] *comma ov. period;
bef. del.* 'Slowly. I loose——loose
[sic] much you say'

309.14 received.] *bef. del.*
'———received (10.)'

309.18 was next] *ab. del.* 'is'

309.21 Do] *aft. penc. del.* '[¶] Yes';
tr. by penc. guideline to foll.
'listener.'

310.1 Yes,] *ab. del.* 'Well, I should
say so.'

310.1 you] 'y' *ov.* 'Y'

310.3 whole,] *comma insrtd.*

310.4 clergyman——] *bef. del.* '12.'

310.9 of,] *comma insrtd.*

310.11 written] *aft. del.* 'which follows'

†310.12–14 Some . . . N.] *insrtd.*

311.3 trances] *bef. del.* '———induced
———induced———'

311.5 recall his] *joined by guideline;*
'recall' *bef. del.* '——— | (Can't read
that.) | recall———'

311.5 on] *bef. del.* '———on ideas on'

311.15 ⁴she] *insrtd. aft. del.* '———sure
———she———'

311.17 but] *intrl.*

311.17 me, . . . can,] *commas insrtd.*

311.23 that.] *bef. del.* '*(No, Dick,
I did not say that.) [*undel. in error*]
Not for anything!) ['N. B. I think
'Not for anything' is communicator's
remark. Mr. Dorr has two originals.'
del.] [I [*tr. by guideline to aft.*
'anything!)' *w. circled* 'no break' *and*
'¶' *in mrgn.*] noticed this at the
time as *Seeming ['S' *ov.* 's'] case of
change made in statement owing to
sitter's *answer. [*period aft. del.
comma*]] the 'not for anything'
coming after contradiction of
statement had been made. G. B. D.] |
Do you remember our talk about
hypnotism?'

[*end non-*WJ *MS(T); begin *MS]

311.23 my] *bef. del.* 'head'

[*end *MS; *begin non-*WJ *MS(T)]

311.28 hypnotism.] *bef. del.* 'I don't
recall talking to H. but *have often
talked about **it, [*comma ov. period*]
[*undel. in error*] *and probably to
H., among others.—N.] [*ab. del.*
'& said I would not do it save for good
reason.']'

311.29 students.] *bef. del.* | '(Try that
last again) | S t u d e n t s. | No, I can't
read that.) [Not read at sitting but
perfectly distinct. | Students.] |
(I don't catch that, Dick.)'

311.29 mind] *aft. del.* 'mind on [word
'mind' difficult to read] mind———
mind———'

311.31 said,] *comma insrtd.*

312.3 very clearly.] *aft. del.* | '[W. R. N.
trys to read word aloud.] |
(Psychological? Psychology?) |
teaching———yes———'

††312.4 goes ⌃out⌃] *ab. del.* 'steps'

312.4 rest,] *comma insrtd. bef. del.*
'and G. B. D. asks R. about
arrangement for coming meeting.]'

312.4 but . . . a] *ab. del.* 'R. H. back
after'

312.4–5 of Rector] *intrl.*

312.10 boat,] *comma insrtd.*

312.13 eat.] *bef. del.* '[We did not *do
this [*intrl.*]*–N.] [*added*]'

312.16 get] *bef. del.* 'weighed——
weight——'

312.20 remember,] *comma added*

312.23 me,] *comma insrtd.*

312.24 cigar,] *comma insrtd. bef. del.*
'——cigar——smoke cigar'

312.24 also] *bef. del.* '——get it?'

312.24 pipe——] *bef. del.* 'Get it?'

312.25 –N.] *added*

††312.32 ⌃Some . . . N.]] *added bef. del.*
| '(Can't read that?) | to——to
read——read——to read——read.
| (I can't read that; let me read it
over.) | Yes kindly. Beach
S T A N D N D   Bech——
beach——Where——yes——'

312.35 You] *aft. del.* '(Note) | See 2) |
to let——boat————'

313.3 now] *intrl.*

313.4 definitely named] *intrl.*

313.6 –N.] *intrl.*

313.7 had] *ab. del.* 'would'

313.7 it.] *ab. del.* | '(Wait a minute,
Dick!) | would better keep out of it!'

313.14 He] *aft. del.* 'Yes!'; *bel. del.* |
'W.R.N. repeats.)' |

313.14 different.] *bef. del.* |
'(Differently? Try that again!) |
Differently——differently | (Is that
different?)'

313.20 No] *aft. del.* | '(Repeats. (Try
to give that better.) | —— if you are
alive' |

†313.21 me."] *bel. is typed and ink
del.* '[I did not.]'; *on line bel. typed
and ink del.* '(Did I say that to him,
Dick?)'

313.22 that's] 't' *ov.* 'T'; *aft. del.*
'can't read that.'

313.23 clearer.] *period insrtd. bef. del.*
'and give it again.)'

313.25 [Incorrect.–N.]] *added aft. del.*
'[I did not]'

313.28 often] *bef. del.* '(16)'

313.31 better] 'tter' *ab. del.* 'st'

314.3 letters. I] *sep. lines joined by
guideline skipping del.* | '(I think the
light is getting weak.)'

314.4 figment! Goodbye!] *sep. lines
joined by guideline*

314.4 R.H.] *aft. del.* '(And you too.)';
bef. del. | 'We cease now and
may the blessings of God be on you. |
[*ink cross*] Farwell. (R.)'

314.5 The . . . follows:–]
('Hodgson . . . the' *intrl.*); *ink
added at bottom of fol.* 73 *bef. del*
WJ *typed text at head of fol.* 75 '[¶
The next specimen sitting I choose
is that of Professor Newbold of the
University of Pennsylvania, ['An'
del.] an intimate friend of Hodgson's,
on July 3rd, 1906. ['After a' *del.*]
Mr. Dorr was also present. After
a few words with Rector, Hodgson
appears: *['says:' *del.*] appears, &
says:– [*added in ink*]'

314.8 Firstrate?] 'te?' *added end of line*
[*end non-*WJ MS(T); *begin* MS(T)]

314.9 am,] *comma insrtd.*

314.11 ¹you] *intrl.*

314.11 left] *aft. del.* 'met yo'

314.21 it."] *period and db. qts. insrtd.
for del. comma bef. del.* 'but gave
some other words that wre were in
the same line." The reference
to Mr Judah has thus no evidential
significance'

314.21 this] *aft. del.* 'all'

314.21–22 attempt] *intrl.*

314.28 minute.] 'ute.' *ab. del.* 'ute.
I shall be clearer in a minute.'

314.32 not] *intrl.*

315.1 just] *aft. del.* '&'

315.2 good.] *bel. are del. lines* | 'I
have . . . | (Dick, write that again.)'

315.20 1899] ²'9' *added end of line*

316.5 N.] *aft. del.* 'W.R.'

316.6 Is] *insrtd.*

††316.6 This] 'T' *not reduced in error;
bef. del.* 'is'

††316.11–12 . . . ? [a [*l.c. in error*] . . .

omit.]] *ab. del.* ', how deserted
you were at one time? at the College,
the *University? [*qst. mk. ov.
period*]'

316.14   I] *aft. del. insrtd.* 'University.'
[*end* MS(T); *begin non-*WJ MS(T)]

†316.17–18   And . . . delight.] (*period
aft.* 'all' *om. in error*); *intrl.*

316.20–21   material] *aft. del.* 'material
way [Word not understood and
repeated.] In a'

316.24   it] *ab. del.* 'you'

316.26   You] *tr. w. guideline to aft.*
'delight.' *skipping del.* '[W.R.N. To
himself] (I think I see what it means!
We are both very demonstrative–)
| (I don't recall this, yet it is
characteristic of the way H. used
to talk of his work.'

316.27   for] *bef. del.* '——even——
even for'

316.28   [I . . . N.]] *added*

††316.32   Would] *tr. w. guideline
skipping del.* '[Reading] (Is that
right?)'

317.1   Oh . . . Billy.] *bel. del.* | '(First
rate.) [This reply must be wrong.
*or something omitted from the
record. W. R. N. [*intrl.*] | *You
laughed and said you were **. . .
[*undel.*] [*and* 'Oh . . . Billy' *tr. w.
guideline bel.* 'lost.'] [*not found
in text; see* HC 317.1]'; *guideline
leading to aft.* 'wonderfully.'
not del. in error]'

317.1–2   wonderfully.] *bef. del.* 'See 18.'

317.3–5   [I . . . N.]] ('Important
veridically.–' *aft. del.* 'W.R.N.]';
'N.' *aft. del.* 'W.R.'); *insrtd.*

317.10   made,] *comma ov. period*

317.11   blind,] *bef. del.* '—— [I did]
| (No, Dick.) | – '

317.14   Hodgson,] *comma insrtd.*

317.18   You . . . about] *bel. del.* | '(Now
let me read this to you 'I am' and
then there is a word I can't read.) |
Drawing. Correct!'; *bef. del.* '——
laughed about'

††317.18   the *ungramatical [*error*]]
bef. del. '—— | (No, I can't read

that,) | Ungratmatical——
gratmatical'

317.19   grammar?] *qst. mk. ov. period*

317.21   explanation] *bef. del.* '——
went into——about it'

317.21   to the] *bef. del.* '——
attributed——'

317.22   but] *bef. del.* '——were rather
amused——but'

317.28   And] *tr. w. guideline skipping
del.* | '[W.R.N. reads and hand
pounds assent.] ' |

317.35   random,] *comma insrtd.*

318.2   than] *bel. del.* | '(Last word I
can't read.) | modus operandi'

318.6   choose] *aft. del.* 'choose such
methods——would'

318.9   of,] *comma insrtd.*

318.10   manifestations,] *comma insrtd.
bef. del.* '——manifestations'

318.12   While] *aft. del.* '(19)'

318.13   and] *aft. del.* '(I drifted away
a little there, Billy)'

318.15   You] *aft. del.* '20'

††318.15–16   [R.H.'s . . . one-['(20)'
del. insrtd.]sided.–N.]] *intrl.*

318.26   When] *note is headed on fol.*
81(73), *circled,* 'Print as note to p. 72',
*bel. which is del. typed start of
orig. text:* '19. Two objections to
the spiritistic theory are here ascribed
to me—the frequent use of bad
grammar and the choice of "such
methods" of communication. The
first I often urged, but not with much
force. [¶] H. explained it by the
difficulty of using the machine and
the explanation I admitted to be
plausible.' *foll. by undel. intrl.* 'Note
by W.R.N.–' *and then text,* 'When'

318.26   methods] *alt. fr.* 'means'

318.28   it,] *comma insrtd.*

319.7   Go] *aft. del.* '[I can't recall this.]'

319.9   saying‸] *comma del.*

†319.10–12   [A . . . N.]] ('W.R.N.]'
del. aft. 'here.'; *final* 's' *of* 'matters'
del.); *insrtd. aft. circled* '¶'

††319.13   (By . . . ago.)] *insrtd. bel. del.*
| '(What is after 'things.') 21 |
Perplexed you.' |

319.14–15   clearly written.] 'ly written.'
insrtd.
319.16   No] *aft. del.* '22'
319.17   shore?] *bef. del.* '*22
[He told me then of two
['mediumistic' *del.*] women, but I
forget their names.—N.] [*added*]'
319.18   did,] *comma insrtd.*
319.20   Do] *bel. del.* | '[W.R.N. to
himself. I do remember it!]' |
319.27   up—] *bef. del.* 'shake—'
319.29   [I] *aft. del.* '[See note 4.'
319.31   —N.]] *added aft. del. bkt.*
320.3   yours] *bef. del.* '——no worse
than yours——'
320.5   ²forget] *intrl. within bkts.*
320.6   memories] *bef. del.* '('those'
repeated several times.)'
320.6   recall] *aft. del.* 'recall——'
320.7   [Chicago]] *ab. del.* 'New York'
†320.9–10   [Here . . . J.]] *insrtd.*
320.11   Do] *bel. del.* | 'Yes. [*undel.*] |
[['Note' *del.*] That Miss D. was
frequently mentioned at sittings in
1895 & H. was told he would marry
her. I was present when these
statements were made, if my memory
serves me.[']' *del.*] *['W. R.' *del.*]—
[*intrl.*] N.] [*added*] | Tell me *more,
[*comma insrtd.*] so *I* won't tell
you!) | And my position regarding
her. | (I wasn't sure it was in *Chicago
[*ab. del.* 'New York'].) | Do you
remember ['——Dunham' *del.*]
*——Densmore? [*added*] | (Was it
Jessie ['Dunham?)' *del.*] *Densmore?)
[*added*] | Yes. Good. | *Mr. Dorr,
who was present, interjects:—"Do
[*ab. del. but underdotted* '(G. B. D.
Do'] you mean the name was *Jessie*
*Densmore [*ab. del.* 'Dunham']
Hodgson?) | [*del.* '[To W. J. J.
Suppose you will not publish this
name. Use your own judgment as to
the reference to be made to the
incident.] | No, no, no, no!'] *No,
no, no, no.' [*added*] | ['(Can you speak
before Mr. Dorr? I think he knows
everything, does he not?) | Only
fire away! Fire away!' *del.*] | (Dick,
you told me years ago about a lady

you were interested in but I have
forgotten her name and where she
lived.) | She lived in *Chicago.
[*insrtd. for del.* 'New York.'] | (Dick,
it comes back to me as, as a
cloud——) | She was a Miss
*Densmore [*ab. del.* 'Dunham;'] I
loved her dearly. | (You used to tell
me about her years ago.) | Yes.
And she afterwards married. Yes, I
told you and you are the only man I
ever told. [Miss *D's sister [*ab. del.*
'Helen Dunham'] says that R. H.
told Myers. *W. J.] [*added*] | (I'm
not sure you told me her name.) |
Yes, I did. | (The name is the least
likely thing for me to remember.)'
320.11   F. . . ?] *bef. del. bkt.; added
aft. del.* 'LaFarge . . . Farge.'
††320.12   ∧W.R.N.]] *added*
320.15   Dick,] *bel. del.* | '(What is
the married name of Miss *Densmore.
[*ab. del.* 'Dunham?']) | Heaven
knows! It has gone from me and I
shall soon go myself.' |
320.17   aunts.] *bef. del.* '——uncles.'
320.18   also.] *bef. del.* '——also.'
320.18   am.] *bef. del.* 'Do not make me
worse than I am W. O R S E Worse.'
320.27   indeed,] *bef. del.* 'I do indeed,'
320.29–31   [R.H.'s . . . J.]] *added*
320.33   This] 'T' *ov.* 't'; *aft. del.*
'Of course I do well;'
†321.3–4   talk . . . N.]] *added aft.
del. bkt.*
321.5   talking—] *bef. del.* 'and then
he—'
321.6   at] *intrl.*
321.7   my . . . ¹with] *insrtd. for del.*
'talk to'
††321.8   , a . . . J.]] ('a week' *ab. del.*
'on the'; 'previous.' *period insrtd. bef.
del.* 'day.—'); *ab. del.* 'W. J. (June
27th)]'
321.10   Yes] *bel. del.* | '[But not this]' |
321.10   careful.] *bef. added* 'Correct.
[*ab. del.* 'Ditto']'
321.12   was,] *comma insrtd.*
321.14   so.] *bef. del.* 'And'
†321.16   [I . . . N.]] *typed intrl. except
'W.R.N.' added*

321.20   —N.]] *dash ab. del. added*
'W.R.'; *added aft. del. bkt.*
††321.22   Adieu.ᴧ R.H.] *added*
[*end non-*WJ MS(T); *begin* MS]
321.23   much] *aft. del.* 'better s'
321.25   quotedᴧ] *comma del.*
321.25   contain] *bef. del.* 'on the
whole'
321.26   perhaps,] *intrl.*
321.26   If] *bef. del.* 'Mrs. Piper's
['sublim' *del.*] subconscious self
were'
321.27   be] *ab. del.* 'were'
321.29–30   accumulating] *bef. del.*
'appropriate'
321.30   in . . . items,] *intrl. aft. del.
comma*
321.30   getting] *aft. del.* 'going'
321.31   right personal] *intrl.*
321.31   Not many] *ab. del.* 'Few'
321.31   certainly] *aft. del.* 'postively w'
321.32   and . . . were] *ab. del.* 'tho not
all ['were' *del.*] are'
[MS *missing,* 322.2–8, *plus fn.* 14]
322.9(*twice*),25;323.16   Dr.] *ab. del.*
'Prof.'
322.10   which] *aft. del.* 'but'
322.10   numberᴧ] *comma del.*
322.11   he] *ab. del.* 'Hyslop'
322.13–14   largely . . . Piper,] *intrl.
aft. insrtd. comma*
322.14   spiritist] 'ist' *intrl.*
322.14–15   of . . . it] ('such' *ab. del.*
'her'); *ab. del.* ', and that the
Hodgson control's communications
confirmed rather than shook his
belief. [', [*comma insrtd.*] holding
it' *del.*]'
322.15   similar] *aft. del.* 'very'
322.15   2to] *intrl.*
322.15   Hodgson] *bef. del.* 'himself'
322.15   led,] *comma insrtd. bef. del.*
'to adopt, and'
322.16   communicating,] 'ting,'
added end of line bef. del. | 'ting,'
322.16–17   2the . . . themselves]
tr. w. guideline fr. aft. 'that' [322.16]
322.17   dreamy] *aft. del.* 'sort of'
322.17   and] *intrl.*
322.20   contain] *final* 'ed' *del.; aft. del.*
'have'

†322.20–21   as . . . doubt] ('field of'
insrtd.); *ab. del.* 'and I doubt'
322.22   make] *aft. del.* 'cla'
322.22   any] *intrl.*
322.22   such] *bef. del.* 'a'
322.22   them—] *dash ab. del. comma*
322.22–23   lend . . . that] ('lend'
alt. fr. 'lent'; 'easily' *aft. del.* 'most');
ab. del. '['followed an extremely
natural course of' *del.*] were *very
[*ab. del.* 'most'] congruous with
['the' *del.*] a surviving'
322.23   in . . . amnesic] *ab. del.*
'somewhat amnesic'
322.23–24   state, was] ('was' *ov.* 'is');
ab. del. '['Hodgson' *del. intrl.*],
[*comma insrtd.*] —being ['was' *del.*
intrl.*]'
322.24   such a] *ab. del.* '['Hodgson'
del.] a surviving'
322.25   have] *intrl.*
322.25   followed] 'ed' *added*
††322.27   these matters:] *ab. del.* '['the
way of belief' *del.*] this field of
research:'
322.39   in spots,] *intrl. aft. del. intrl.*
'here and there,'
322.39   the minds] *insrtd. for del.*
'those'
323.1   and] *aft. del.* ', reminded'
323.4   messages] *final* 's' *added; aft. del.*
'a [*undel. in error*] recent'
323.5   was] *ab. del.* 'had'
323.5   receiving] 'ing' *ab. del.* 'ed';
bef. del. 'from a'
323.5   mediumᴧ] *comma del.; aft. del.*
'['pr' *del.*] ['some' *del.*] anot'
323.5–6   other . . . especially] *intrl.*
323.7   in] *ab. del.* 'in'
323.7   sent] *alt. fr.* 'seem'
323.8   recalled] *aft. del.* 'asked'
323.8   certain] *bef. del.* 'lunch with'
323.8   of] *intrl.*
323.9   Hyslop] *ab. del.* 'the sitter'
323.9   partaken] *bef. del.* 'together'
323.9   occasionᴧ] *semicolon del.*
323.9   together;] *bef. del.* 'etc., etc.—
all this indeed in a very scanty way,
but with such naturalness of tone and
language, and ['such' *del.*] following
such characteristic lines of'

323.10   practical] *ab. del.* 'plans and'
323.11   expressed] 'ed' *ov.* 'ions';
aft. del. '['showed' *del.*] gave most
appropriate'
323.11   his] *ab. del.* 'of'
††323.12   most of all] *ab. del.* 'all'
323.12   an exceedingly] *ab. del.*
'a very'
323.13   tone] *aft. del.* 'language, as'
323.16–17   *Apperceptionsmasse*] '*A*'
ov. '*a*'
323.17   find] *insrtd. for del.* 'to be
equally con'
323.19   all] *aft. del.* 'the whole
phenomen'
323.21   *W.J.'s Sitting.*] *triple underl;*
insrtd. w. no space ab. and bel.
323.22   sort of thing] *intrl.*
323.22–23   and . . . reading,] ('makes'
aft. del. 'is so insipid'); *intrl.*
323.23–24   of . . . full.] *ab. del.*
'sittings *in extenso*, as it were.'
323.25   on] *aft. del.* 'to base'
323.26   so] *aft. del.* 'withal,'
323.26   as] *aft. del.* 'one more sitting'
323.26   a] *insrtd. for del.* '*[*'a good'
del.] a fair [*ab. del.* 'another']'
323.26   the] *insrtd.*
323.26   control's] *aft. del.* 'average
[*tr. by guideline to foll.* 'control's']
avera'
323.26–27   utterances . . . of] *ab. del.*
['a couple of s' *del.*] the only'
††323.30   R.H. . . . saying:—ᴀ] *aft. del.*
'R. H. enters, saying:—'; *bel. is del.*
'[¶] A Sitting'
[MS *missing,* 323.31–338.8]
338.9   somewhat diluted sitting,] *intrl.*
338.10   it] *bef. del.* 'all'
338.10   to me] *intrl.*
338.11   The] 'T' *ov.* 'I'
338.12   seems to survive] *intrl.*
338.12   else's.] *bef. del.* '(['It' *del.*]
Could ['C' *ov.* 'c'] it [*insrtd.*] hardly
could have got to Mrs. Piper's
knowledge & come up after so many
years?)'
338.12   hoping for] *ab. del.* 'expecting'
338.13   namely,] *insrtd.*
338.14   was] *aft. del.* 'to'

338.14   Either] *intrl.*
338.14   tapping] 't' *ov.* 'T'
338.15   would . . . it,] *ab. del.* 'seem,
to ['most reasonable be if possible
explanations, ['to' *del.*]' *del.*] be the
most reasonable ones to choose
between,'
338.16   were] *ab. del.* 'be'
338.16   assume] *aft. del.* 'invoke'
338.17   was now] *ab. del.* 'had'
338.18   reproducing] 'ing' *ov.* 'ed'
338.18   it.] *period insrtd. bef. del.*
'now.'
338.19   probability] *aft. del.* 'pos'
338.19   differ] *final* 's' *del.*
338.19   the] *alt. fr.* 'his'
338.19–20   line of his] *insrtd.*
338.20   experiences.] *ab. del.* 'education
in this field.'
338.20–21   possibilities] *ab. del.*
'amount'
338.21   trace,] *ab. del.* 'account for'
338.21   whole] *intrl.*
338.21   be] *aft. del.* 'even'
338.22   that] *bef. del.* '['it' *del.*] Pi'
††338.23   supernormal.] *betw.* 'u' *and*
'p' *is a del. letter, possibly a* 'b';
period aft. del. comma
338.23   The] *aft. del.* 'the'
338.24   me] *bef. del.* 'not to force
one to it at all.'
338.27   later.] *period insrtd. aft.
comma; bef. del.* 'and from wh'
338.27   same matters,] *insrtd. for del.*
'trend in the first,' *ab. del.* 'same
ground,'
338.28   vainly] *intrl.*
338.29   give . . . of] *intrl.*
338.29   Brown] *final* 'e' *del.*
338.30   there.] *ab. del. comma and
added period undel. in error*
338.31   about] *ab. del.* 'of'
338.31   the American] *aft. del.* 'the
[*undel. in error*] state [*ab. del.*
'affairs'] of [*undel. in error*]'
338.33   boots] *bef. del.* 'at that time,
but these were'
338.33   questioned] 'ed' *added poss. ov.*
's'
338.35   ²whom] 'm' *added*

338.35 we] *intrl.*

338.36 identify] 'y' *ov.* 'ied'; *aft. del.* 'be i-'

338.36 He] *intrl.*

338.36 insisted] ¹'i' *ov.* 'I'

338.36 a certain] *ab. del.* 'an unnamed'

338.39 The] *run-on but marked for* ¶ *in mrgn.*

339.1 incident.] *period alt. fr. colon*

339.2 elicit . . . a] *ab. del.* 'see whether any'

339.2 from] *aft. del.* 'would possible'

339.4 naturally] *intrl.*

339.5 when] *ab. del.* '['which was unknown to the living Hodgson' *del.*] ['any' *del.*] R. [*ov.* 'H'] H.'

339.5–6 with . . . startling] *ab. del.* 'very suddenly and in a sudden'

339.6 his] *intrl.*

339.6 serious] *aft. del.* 'very'

339.11 another] *ab. del.* 'a wrong'

339.11 by the gloves] *tr. by guideline fr. aft.* 'suicide,'

339.12 tone] *bef. del.* 'that'

††339.12–13 prompted the notion . . . influence] ('prompted' *insrtd. for del.* 'aroused'; 'shedding' *aft. del.* 'was'); *ab. del.* 'suggested some supernormal influence from the object'

339.14 'psychometric.'] *period insrtd. bef. del.* 'in spe'

339.14–15 about the suicide] *intrl.*

339.15 veridical;] *semicolon aft. del. comma*

339.15 ²the] *ab. del.* 'such'

339.15–16 in the case,] *intrl.*

339.17 After] *bef. del.* 'a'

339.17 seems] *final* 's' *added; aft. del.* 'might'

339.18 hardly worth while] *ab. del.* 'well *to [del. in error]*'

339.18 full] *intrl.*

339.19 phenomenon.] *period aft. del. comma*

††339.19 Were . . . a appropriate] 'Were . . . so,' *ab. del.* 'and'; 'a' *intrl. orig. bef.* 'good' *and not alt. to* 'an' *in error when* 'appropriate' *insrtd. for del.* 'good'

339.19 ²the] *ov.* 'this'

339.20 that] *aft. del.* 'either'

339.20 of] *bef. del.* 'Dr. J. J. Putnam or of his sister,'

339.21 good] *insrtd. for del.* 'naturally good' *ab. del.* 'much better'

339.21 naturally,] *ab. del.* 'than others, auto'

339.22 also,] *bef. del.* 'the'

339.23 free.] *bef. del.* 'Dʳ and Mrs Putnam were among Hodgson's most intim'

339.24 talk] *aft. del.* 'sit, with him'

339.24 had been] *ab. del.* 'was'

339.26 might] *bef. del.* 'natur'

339.26 expected.] *period insrtd. bef. del.* 'a priori beforehand. The'

339.28 good,] *comma ov. period*

††339.28–29 altho . . . sitter's] *ab. del.* 'I will not copy the records, however, for the reader's imagination can supply.'

339.29 difficulty] 'd' *ov.* 'D'

339.31 this] *alt. fr.* 'the'

339.33 end] *ab. del.* 'close'

††339.34 R. Bergman [pseudonym].] *ab. del.* 'Mary Hillard's.'

339.34 ²Bergman] *ab. del.* 'Hillard had had'

339.36 her] *aft. del.* 'all'

339.37 At] *aft. del.* '['At th' *del.*] Her first'

339.37 visit,] *aft. del.* '['sitting' *del.*] session'; *bef. del.* 'of'

340.1 At] *intrl.*

340.1 ¹the] 't' *ov.* 'T'

340.5 made] *aft. del.* 'an'

340.6 cemetery] 'c' *ov.* 's'

†340.12 'Hotel . . . B.]] *added aft. del. bkt.*

[MS *missing,* 340.14–345.21]

345.22 displayed] *intrl.*

345.22 conversations] *bef. del.* '*the two ladies at the [*ab. del.* 'with Miss Hillard and Miss Pope']'

††345.23 where . . . stayed∧] *intrl.*

345.24 is] *ab. del.* 'seems most'

345.25 such] *aft. del.* 'such a mass of trivial detail should'

345.25 unimportant] *ab. del.* 'an'

345.25 conversations] *final* 's' *added*

345.25–26 by . . . H.] *ab. del.* 'in any
*detail [*ab. del.* 'natural manner']'

345.26 with] *ab. del.* 'in'

345.27 sitters;] *ab. del.* 'company,'

345.27 plausible] *bef. del.* 'alternative
*explanation [*intrl.*] *lies between
[*ab. del.* 'is'] mind-reading on the
medium's part, or spirit-return'

345.28 Either] *aft. del.* 'I now pass to'

345.28 spells] *ab. del.* 'means'

345.28 telepathic ₄reading₄]
'telepathic' *ab. del.* ' 'mind-'; *opening
sg. qt. insrtd. and del. bef.* 'reading
[*sg. qt. del.*]'

345.33 sister] *aft. del.* 'sitter'

345.35 which] *aft. del.* 'Miss'

345.35 duly] *intrl.*

†345.35–36 replies . . . based.] *insrtd.*

345.36 of these messages] *intrl.*

345.36 general] *ab. del.* 'trivial'

345.37–38 reading . . . Cooper?")]
ab. del. 'early morning rides on
horseback when attending the
University?')'

345.38 had] *bef. del.* 'already'

346.1 Hyde,'] *intrl.*

346.3 awoke] *aft. del.* 'were not
remembered'

346.3 no] *bef. del.* 'recognition'

346.4 There] 're' *ov.* 'y'; *aft. del.* 'On
the whole they were disappointing.
Miss Hodgson writes: "To my mind
there is nothing striking in any
of the statements." '

346.4 many] *aft. del.* 'long'

346.5 significant ones] *ab. del.*
'important points'

346.5 time-] *ab. del.* 'date-'

346.6 *Melbourne;*] *bef. del.* 'bush in
yard with red'

346.6 *Street;*] *bef. del.* dash

346.6–7 [Correct,] *comma added aft.
del. bkt.*

346.7 and] *aft. del.* 'bush'

346.7 Miss H.] *bef. del. bkt.*

346.8 Had] *ab. del.* '] Query: *[Could
[*bkt. undel. in error;* 'C' *ov.* 'c']'

346.8 ever] *ab. del.* 'ever have'

346.8 Latrobe . . . bush] *ab. del.* 'these
facts'

346.8 Piper?] *qst. mk. insrtd. for del.
qst. mk. and closing bkt.*

346.9 —of . . . Melbourne.]] *added aft.
del. bkt.*

346.10 *et seq. similar through* 346.14
₄Charley . . . University.₄] *sg. qts. del.*

††346.10 (or *Robertson*)] *parens ov.
bkts.; aft. del.* 'o'

346.11 There . . . school.]] *added
aft. del. bkt.*

346.15 H.,] *comma insrtd.*

346.15 ten . . . sat] *ab. del.* 'used to sit'

346.19 *et seq. similar through* 346.29
₄Sister . . . light.₄] *sg. qts. del.*

346.24 *raised*] 'd' *added; aft. del.*
'we used to'

346.24–25 particularly recalled] *ab.
del.* 'recognized as true'

††346.26 brother]₄] *comma om. in
error bef. del.* 'and'

346.29 *losses*] *bef. del.* '—mother *had
better business head. [*ab. del.* 'could
manage better']'

346.30 ₄*Description*] *sg. qt. del.*

††346.34 possibly,] *comma insrtd.
bef. del.* 'correct'

††346.36 possibly true] *ab. del.* 'not
recalled'

346.39 The] *aft. del.* 'R.'; *bef. del.*
'control's'

347.1 collection of] *intrl.*

347.2 She] 'S' *ov.* 'T'

347.3 three] *aft. del.* 'two or three'

347.3 test-] *intrl.*

347.5–6 responsibly] *intrl.*

347.6 tapping] *ab. del.* 'telepathy
from'

347.7 must] *ab. del.* 'have to'

347.8 excluded₄] *comma del.*

347.8 as explanations.] *ab. del.* 'so that
['we' *del.*]'

347.8 If] 'I' *ov.* 'i'

347.8–9 interpretation were] *ab. del.*
'explanation be'

347.11 be] *ab. del.* 'do the ['work' *del.*]'

347.11 chiefly] 'ly' *added*

347.11 relied upon.] *ab. del.* 'work.'

347.14 used] *ab. del.* '['repro-' | *del.*]
utilized'

347.15 'Eric,'] *insrtd.*

347.15 added] *aft. del.* 'given'

347.15   three] *aft. del.* 'full'
347.16   apparently] *ab. del.* 'only given'
347.16   first] *aft. del.* 'chris'
347.18   Hodgson] 's' *intrl.*
347.18   insisting] *aft. del.* 'afterwards'
347.18   at . . . time] *intrl.*
347.19   revealed] *bef. del. period and*
   del. insrtd. 'It rem on'
††347.19   to . . . world.ˣ] *insrtd.; bel. is*
   circled 'ˣInsert Mrs. Piper's letter
   as a note'
347.22   this] *alt. fr.* 'the'; *bef. del.* 'sitt'
347.25   time] 't' *ov.* 's'
347.25   has] *bef. del.* 'an'
347.27   wrote] *ab. del.* 'have written'
[MS *missing*, 347.29–42]
348.2   reports,] *ab. del.* 'sittings,'
348.2   , it is true,] *intrl.*
348.4   generally;] *intrl.*
348.4–5   rejoice to find] *intrl. bef. del.*
   'feel' *ab. del.* 'feel'
348.5   its] *bef. del.* 'foregone conclusion
   of 'bosh!' [*comma del.*] strengthened
   thereby'
348.5   explanatory] *ab. del.* 'solving'
348.5   'Bosh,'] *comma insrtd. aft. del.*
   exclm. mk.
348.6   of the records] *intrl.*
348.6   hold] *aft. del.* 'either [*intrl.*]
   have to'
348.7   in] *aft. del.* 'in solution, or'
348.7   if] *aft. del.* 'else,'
348.7   inclines] 's' *added; aft. del.*
   '['incline' *del.*] should'
348.8   be] *aft. del.* 'probably'
348.8   an] *aft. del.* 'of a'
348.9   balance of] *ab. del.* 'scientific
   [*intrl.*] balance of'
348.9   ᴧpresumptionsᴧ] *sg. qts. del.*
348.10   because] *ab. del.* 'the dramatic
   probability of'
348.10   has come to] *intrl.*
348.10   seem] *final* 's' *del.; bef. del.*
   'to him'
348.10   unpermissible] *ab. del.* 'such
   unnatural'
348.11   natural] *intrl.*
348.11   probabilities.] *period insrtd.*
   bef. del. 'which nature includes.'
348.12   of my own] *intrl.*
348.12   Nature's] 'N' *ov.* 'n'

††348.13   up a few] ('a few' *aft. del.*
   'one or two'); *ab. del.* 'together a few
   scattered'
†348.13–14   ²I . . . occur.] *insrtd.*
348.15   several] *aft. del.* 'there were'
348.16   supernormal.] *period alt. fr.*
   comma
348.16   These were] ('s' *of* 'These' *ov.*
   'r'; 'were' *bef. del.* 'other'); *ab. del.*
   'certain'
348.17   remarks] *aft. del.* 'personal'
348.18   could] 'c' *ov.* 'w'
††348.18   tho't of] *ab. del.* 'invented'
348.19   Another] *alt. fr.* 'others';
   aft. del. '['Another' *del.*] Two'
348.19   I think,] *intrl. aft. insrtd.*
   comma
348.24   (2) Again, there] *insrtd. with*
   ¶ *sign; aft. del.* 'Again, [*intrl.*] there
   ['t' *ov.* 'T']'
348.28   (3)] *intrl., with mrgn.* ¶ *sign*
   foll. by del. '(3.)'
348.28   incident] *final* 's' *del.; aft. del.*
   intrl. 'two' *aft. del. insrtd.* 'three'
348.28–29   and Miss Putnam's] *intrl.*
††348.29   A.H.J.] *aft. vert. stroke and*
   del. intrl. '(1)'
348.33   fist] *aft. del.* 'han'
348.36   it.] *bef. del.* '[A.'
348.38   over] *ab. del.* 'at'
348.38   taken] *aft. del.* 'departed for'
349.1   angry] *ab. del.* 'hot'
349.4   came:–] *ab. del. line* 'W. J.
   You seem to think ['etc' *del.*]'
[MS *missing*, 349.5–15]
349.17   at] *ov.* 'in'
†349.18   *Primâ* . . . evidential:–]
   insrtd. bef. del. '(2)', *showing fn.*
   was afterthought
349.21   This] *ab. del.* '['This' *del.*]
   Correct! it'
349.21   as . . . remember,] *intrl. aft.*
   insrtd. comma
349.21   Chocorua,] *comma ov. period;*
   bef. del. 'W. J.]'
349.21–23   but . . . 'leaky.'] *insrtd.*
349.22   on . . . when] *ab. del.* 'when'
349.23   as] *aft. del.* 'together'
†349.24–25   Another . . . enough:–]
   insrtd.
349.26   In] *insrtd.*

††349.26 Hodgson s] 's' *without apostrophe added*

349.26 rooms] *ab. del.* 'left'

349.26 was] *ov.* 'in'

349.26 found, in] *intrl.*

349.27 mentioned] *bef. del. colon dash*

349.33 has] *aft. del.* 'did'

349.34 I . . . cipher] *ab. del.* 'If Mrs. Piper knew of the cipher, or if ['a remark' *del.*] a question about ['of' *del.*] it'

349.34 here] *intrl.*

349.35 has] 's' *ov.* 'd'

349.35-36 If . . . remarkable] *aft. period insrtd. for del. comma; ab. del.* 'there would be nothing unusual'

349.36 record] *ab. del.* 'note taker'

††349.36 &] *ab. del.* 'but the *notes ['s' added; '-taker' del.*], of [*insrtd.*] one of my sons, *who was in attendance for the purpose of taking [*ab. del.* 'was'] ['could follow very fast. On the face of the record' *del.*] them, were *unusually complete. [*ab. del.* 'very full indeed.'] Our [*ov.* 'Any'] verdict has under the circumstances to be doubtful, [*comma ov. period*] for the evidence is leak'

349.37 2the] *intrl.*

349.37 is now] *ab. del.* 'are'

[MS *missing*, 350.1–31]

351.4 true,] *bef. del.* 'at the time,'

351.5 like] *aft. del.* 'either'; *bef. del.* 'telepathy' *alt. fr.* 'telepathic'

351.5 R.H.'s saying] *insrtd. for del.* 'It'

351.6 (April 16th)] *intrl.*

351.20 2had] *aft. del.* 'had dreams of'

351.20 dreams] *ab. del.* 'vague projects'

351.20 extending] *ov.* 'enlarging'

351.23 this] *alt. fr.* 'the'

351.23 veridical] *intrl.*

351.23 by] *aft. del.* 'of a'

351.24 private] *intrl.*

351.24 as] *aft. del.* 'to the effect,'

††351.33 ones?)] *on line bel. are del. ellipsis dots*

351.34 [The] *orig.* ¶ *but tr. w. guideline and circled* 'run in.'

352.2 [I . . . M.]] *insrtd.*

††352.3 to.)] *bef. del.* '[. . . .'

352.4 him?] *bef. four ellipsis dots partly del. ab. del. dots*

[MS *missing*, 352.5–26]

352.27 own] *intrl.*

352.28 Child.] *period ov. comma; bef. del.* 'and one of the nearest was N. S. Shaler'

352.29 met] *ab. del.* 'known'

352.29 Child.] *period insrtd. bef. del.* ', and I doubt whether he had ever ['known' *del.*] spoken to Shaler.'

352.29 looks] *ab. del.* 'seems'

352.29 like] *aft. del.* 'characteristic of'

352.31 existence] *ab. del.* 'fact'

352.32 to me] *intrl.*

352.33 should have been] *ab. del.* 'and Shaler were both'

†353.1 I . . . Piper,] *intrl.*

353.2 and if] *insrtd. for del.* 'if [*insrtd. for del.* 'If']'

353.3 him . . . living] ('to' *bef. del.* 'F. J. C.'); *ab. del.* 'these friends to'

353.3 R.H.] *bef. del.* 'intra vitam' *ab. del.* 'during his life'

353.4 evidential.] *bef. del.* '['Certainly' *del.*] I *had surely [*intrl.*] never ['had' *del.*] mentioned them to Mrs. Piper. 'Child's' message'

353.5 message] *aft. del.* 'Child'

††353.5 thru R.H.] *intrl.*

††353.10 He says . . . .] *intrl. ab. del. ellipsis dots*

353.11 2the] *insrtd. for del.* '['the' *del.*] Lizzie, the name by which Mrs. Child's familiar'

353.12 name] *bef. del. period and bkt.*

353.14 matters] *insrtd. for del.* 'things'

353.17 Christmas] *aft. del.* '(3) [To Miss Putnam [*period del.*] Did you get my C'

353.19 sent.] *period insrtd. bef. del.* 'without'

353.21 unenveloped.] *ab. del.* 'unenclosed.'

353.22 (11)] *ab. del.* '10' *ov.* '11'

353.22 volume] *ab. del.* 'manuscript ['m' *ov.* 'M'] book of poetry'

353.25 C——] *aft. del. long dash*

353.29 The] *aft. del.* '['Mrs.' *del.*] The copy h'

353.29 poems] *aft. del.* 'copies of'

353.30 ere] *aft. del.* 'during life'

353.30 had] *aft. del.* 'was now brought to the sitting'

353.31 and] *aft. del.* 'by'

354.1 These] 'T' *ov.* 't'; *aft. del.* 'Most of th' *ab. del.* 'On the whole'

354.1 incidents] *bef. del. comma and del. intrl.* 'so far as they are not'

354.1 deliberate] *ab. del.* 'supernormal'

††354.2 whoever . . . be$_\wedge$] ('ever' *of* 'whoever' *ov.* 'ere'); *intrl.*

††354.4–5 (altho . . . knowing)] *parens ov. commas*

354.5 all] *intrl.*

354.5–6 documents . . . report] *ab. del.* 'reports [*ab. del.* 'pages'] that have preceded'

†354.7 who . . . 'bosh.'] ('who' *bef. del.* 'call it'; 'pure' *insrtd. aft. del. insrtd.* 'purely'); *ab. del.* 'hostilely disposed.'

354.8 a . . . there] *ab. del.* '['even' *del. intrl.*] some of the *latter [*ab. del.* 'bosh-philosophers']'

354.10 behind] *ab. del.* 'at the bottom of'

354.10 Most of] *ab. del.* 'Meanwhile ['to' *del.*]'

354.10 remain] *ab. del.* 'are still'

354.11 would, however,] *ab. del.* 'may'

354.12 mass] *aft. del.* 'record'

354.12 given them] *intrl.*

354.14 discredit] *aft. del.* 'positively undermine anything'

354.15 mere . . . much] *ab. del.* 'hesitation,'

354.16 hesitation] *aft. del.* 'irrelevance,'

354.17 up] *intrl.*

354.17 false] *intrl.*

354.17 tracks,] *bef. del.* 'so much automatic mannerism'

354.18 false] *insrtd. for del.* 'vain'

354.18 ¹to] *aft. del.* 'of'

354.18 and . . . suggestion,] *intrl.*

354.20 lost] *aft. del.* 'greatly diluted *and [undel. in error]*'

354.20 total] *ab. del.* 'resultant'

†354.21–23 effect . . . example,] ('be' *ab. del.* 'suggest'; 'more . . . 'humbug.' '

insrtd. for del. '*more than a **vague [intrl.] suggestion of 'humbug.' [insrtd. for del.* 'but *'humbug.' [period insrtd. bef. del.* 'to the mind.']']'); *ab. del.* 'expression is not the same. Passwords, for example, ple'

354.25 prove] *aft. del.* 'be'

354.25 written] *aft. del.* 'given'

354.26 or . . . that] *ab. del.* 'if it can be read at all'

354.27 how] *aft. del.* 'it'

354.28 never] *aft. del.* 'd'

354.28 knew] *insrtd. for del.* 'heard'

354.28 it?$_\wedge$] *fn. indicator del.; bel. is del. circled* '$^{\times}$note on p. 166.'

354.28 talk] *aft. del.* 'cant'

354.29 as where] *ab. del. dash*

354.29 pretends] 's' *ov.* 'ing'; *aft. del.* 'somewhere'

354.29 no longer] *insrtd. for del.* 'doesn't'

354.30 knows] 's' *added*

354.30 'seven minutes'] *ab. del.* 'a week' '

354.30 mean] *final* 's' *del.*

354.31 mass] *ab. del. mended* 'mass'

354.32 in ['abstract,' *del.*] abridgement,] *ab. del.* 'by me,'

354.33–355.1 anyhow] *intrl.*

††354.34 For instance$_\wedge$] *intrl.*

354.34 on] 'o' *ov.* 'O'

354.35 six] *ab. del.* 'five'

354.35,36 five] *ab. del.* 'four'

354.36 were] *aft. del.* 'had'

354.37 those] *ab. del.* 'what was'

354.38 writes] *aft. del.* 'says'

355.5 all] *intrl.*

355.5 this] *alt. fr.* 'the'

355.5 material] *aft. del.* 'm'

355.5 tended to assume.] *insrtd. for del.* 'taken. [', and the' *del.*] On any hypothesis of the'

355.5 The] *insrtd.*

355.5–6 cause of the] *ab. del.* 'force ['involved ['ed' *ov.* 'ing'] in a' *del.*] responsible for'

355.6 communications] 'ions' *ov.* 'ing,'; *bef. del.* '[', it belongs for the most' *del.*] ['that force' *del.*] that cause is a will'

355.7 be it] *ab. del.* 'whether'

355.7 of lower . . . intelligences,] *intrl.*

355.8 and] *bef. del.* 'the 'bosh' material cannot be regarded as fulfilment, as plausibly as it can be regarded frustration by untoward'

355.8 rubbish] *ab. del.* 'bosh-material'

355.9 (certain] *ab. del.* 'for the purpose of gaining time, ('

355.9 hesitations, misspellings] *each final 's' insrtd.*

355.10 clue,] *comma aft. del. closing paren*

355.10 certain] *intrl.*

355.11 the major part] *ab. del.* 'most'

355.11 is] *intrl.*

355.11 suggestive] 'ive' *ov.* 's'

355.12 2will] *aft. del.* 'failed entirely'

355.13 which . . . through.] ('fails ['s' *ov.* 'ed']' *aft. del.* 'involuntary had lost the path'); *ab. del.* 'different, that had gone astray because of interferences and substitutions.'

†355.14 most . . . is] *ab. del.* 'this 'bosh' is far'

355.14 to me] *intrl.*

355.14 dreaminess] *bef. del.* 'of mind'

355.16 prefer . . . incorrect] ('prefer' *bef. del.* 'incorrect'); *ab. del.* 'plausibly plump in with false'

355.16 names] *bef. del.* 'that ['suggest the true' *del.*] ['true ones' *del.*] to true ones'

355.16 often,] *comma insrtd. bef. del. qst. mk.*

355.17 1to] *ab. del.* 'to'

355.19 so] *intrl.*

355.19 'passwords'] *bef. del.* 'and stick to them'

355.20 and . . . them?] *intrl.*

355.21 definite,] *ab. del.* 'that isn't reached'

355.23-24 let . . .2a] ('let pass' *bef. del.* 'let'); *ab. del.* 'the chance had to be jumped at of getting the'

355.24 message.] *period insrtd. bef. del.* 'through.'

355.25 a name which] *ab. del.* 'a *lad [ab. del.* 'boy'] whose ['se' *ov.* 'm']'

355.26 knew,] *alt. fr.* 'knows,'; *aft. del.* 'knos'

355.26 which popped] *ab. del.* 'whose ['se' *added*] ['had nothing to do with what was being talked of' *del.*] name['s' *del.*] comes'

355.26-27 to . . . when] *ab. del. period and* 'Again'

355.27 preceded or followed] *alt. fr.* 'precedes or follows'

355.30 final] *intrl.*

355.30 denial,] *del. intrl. dash ab. comma*

355.30 if] *bef. del.* 'it had [*illeg. letter*]'

355.30 covered] *aft. del.* 'corresponded to something'

355.30 erroneously,] *ab. del.* 'wrongly,'

355.31 distinct] *ab. del.* 'definite incident which ought to be'

355.31 which] *aft. del.* 'an incident,'

355.32 Piper-] *intrl.*

355.33 I fully] *insrtd. for del.* 'I have no doubt whatever, and I have just firmly'

355.33 and] *aft. del.* 'that'

355.34 ∧supernormal∧] *sg. qts. del.*

355.34 sources] *alt. fr.* 'resources'

355.35 1possibly∧] *comma del.*

355.35-36 human] *aft. del.* 'living'

355.36 the] *ab. del.* 'earths'

355.39 be] *bef. del.* 'pure'

355.39 the] *intrl. bef. del.* 'its' *ab. del.* 'the'

356.1 rôle∧∧] *period and fn. indicator del.*

356.2 fished out] *penc. ab. del.* 'chosen'

356.6 contribute . . . results] *ab. del.* 'be a factor'

††356.9 primâ facie] *ab. del.* 'most obvious'

356.10 the will] *ab. del.* 'that'

356.10 a] *aft. del.* 'the'

356.11 to suppose] *intrl.*

356.12 'the light,'] ' 'the' *sg. qt. added; sg. qt. del. bef.* 'light'

356.12 can make] *ab. del.* 'could send flashes and gleams of its own'

356.13 wishes] *final 's' ov.* 'd'

356.13 mix] *bef. del.* 'in'

356.14 rubbish of] *ab. del.* 'personating activities of'

356.16 even] *intrl.*

644

†356.16   would be inert] *ab. del.* 'were
a very faint ['tenden' *del.*] tendency'
356.16–17   it . . . activity] *ab. del.*
'stimulate [*ab. del.* 'reinforced']'
356.17   other will.] (*opening sg. qt. bef.*
'will' *del.*); *intrl. w. period insrtd.*
bef. del. '*to communicate,
[*closing sg. qt. del.*] in the **jenseits.
[*surrounding sg. qts. del.*] [*ab. del.*
'coadjutor on the *farther [*alt. fr.*
'other'] side.']'
356.19   when alone,] *ab. del.* 'alone a'
356.20   if] *bef. del.* 'the other be pre'
356.20   present,] *bef. del.* 'with a'
356.21   action] *aft. del.* 'the'
356.22   connect] *ab. del.* 'express'
356.23   elements in] *ab. del.* 'abstract
[*insrtd.*] possibilities of'
356.23   Its] *ab. del.* 'The'
356.23   are] *ab. del.* ', the non-rubbish
and the veridical stream are both'
356.24   by] *aft. del.* 'are not defined'
356.24   ¹the] *alt. fr.* 'their'
356.24–25   -making∧] *comma del.*
356.26   manifestation] *aft. del.*
'automatic'
356.27   silly] *intrl.*
356.27   best] *intrl.*
356.27   its] *aft. del.* 'a'
356.28   although] *aft. del.* 'altho I'
356.29   no] *bef. del.* 'proof is forth'
356.29   of the presence] *ab. del.* 'is
forthcoming'
356.30   Hodgson-] *aft. del.* 'R'
356.30   -control∧] *comma del.*
††356.30   taken alone and] *intrl.*
356.32   the] *aft. del.* '['the' *del.*] my
['whole' *del.*] dealing with the'
356.32   whole] *intrl.*
356.32   similar] *intrl.*
356.32–33   phenomena] *bef. penc. del.*
'(so far as I know them)'
356.34   it,] *bef. del.* 'by a plus b,'
356.37   The] *orig. run-on but then
marked for ¶ w. vert. line and
circled '¶' in mrgn.*
356.37   is] *bef. del.* 'such [*ab. del.* 'the']
'will to communicate' there?'
356.38   is actually] *ab. del.* 'is really
['concretely' *del.*]'
356.39   again] *bef. del.* 'we can make a

scheme of the diagram of various
possibilities.'
357.1   considered] *ab. del.* 'taken'
357.1   abstract] *ab. del.* 'schematic'
357.1   Thus the] *ab. del.* 'There may
be'
357.1–2   to communicate] *penc. intrl.*
357.2   either] *penc. intrl.*
357.3   entity] *bef. del.* 'pro
[*diacritical mark del.*] rê nata.'
††357.4   (demons] *paren ov. comma*
357.6   An improvised] *ab. del.* 'The
occasional'
357.6   a limited] ('a' *alt. fr.* 'an';
'limited' *aft. del.* 'active'); *ab. del.*
'an individualized'
357.8   when] *ab. del.* 'where'
357.8   systematized] *aft. del.* 'such';
bef. del. '& limited'
357.9–10   in that case] *ab. del.* 'here'
357.10   conceived . . . when] *ab. del.*
'symbolized [*insrtd. bel. is del.*
'happens'] by the *uncertain [*insrtd.*]
creation of'
††357.11–12   are . . . &] *ab. del.* 'which'
357.12   cause] *alt. fr.* 'causing'
357.13   of space] *ab. del.* 'of'
357.13   the seat] *insrtd.*
357.13   of] *ov.* 'at'
357.16   either] *intrl.*
357.16   at . . . time] *intrl.*
357.17   alternately produce] *ab. del.*
'share'
357.17   manifestations.] *period insrtd.*
bef. del. 'between them.'
357.19   historic] *aft. del.* 'vast'
†357.20–21   which . . . refusal] ('first'
ab. del. 'classed in'; 'The' *insrtd. ab.
period del. in error*); *ab. del.* 'under
study. The complete aversion'
††357.21 | ment to treat] *ab. del.*
| 'ment' from the consideration of
demon-'
357.21   as] *aft. del.* ', that ever'
357.22   be] *bef. del.* 'even'
357.22   even] *intrl.*
357.22–23   massive human] *ab. del.*
'great universal'
††357.23   based . . . experience,] *intrl.*
357.25   things scientific.] *ab. del.*
'shaping public opinion.'

357.25 the] *intrl.*
357.25 theory] *ab. del.* 'possession'
357.27 has] *ab. del.* 'would have'
357.28 But if the] *ab. del.* 'If possession ['by' *del.*] or obsession ['by' *del.*] in'
357.28 have] *aft. del.* 'interfere'
357.30–31 ever . . . a] *ab. del.* 'be [*ab. del.* 'were'] not only a conjectural theory, but an established'
357.31 then] *aft. del.* 'then'
357.31 not . . . called] ('not' *bef. del.* 'not'; 'have' *aft. del.* 'called'); *ab. del.* 'the will to personate, as ['what' *del. insrtd.*] well as'
357.32 communicate] *aft. del.* 'pers'
††357.32 but . . . personate] *insrtd.*
357.33 The] 'T' *ov.* 't'; *aft. del.* '['Not only she, but the 'spirits' ' *del.*] She [*insrtd.*] may *not [*intrl.*] be accountable, *all alone, [*intrl.*] for'
††357.33–34 may . . . alone.] *intrl. ab. del. period*
357.34–35 than hers] *intrl.*
††357.36 otherwise inexplicable] *ab. del.* 'more unaccountable'
357.36 in the stream.] *added aft. del. period*
357.37 plot] *ab. del.* 'scheme'
357.38 a . . . is] *ab. del.* 'spirit personality [', dormant in the intervals may become re animated, or a' *del.*] may conceivably *have [*ab. del.* 'have'] *feel a [*ab. del.* 'its'] will to communicate and *a [*ab. del.* 'its'] feel [*ab. del.* 'power'] to influence 'the light,' '
††358.1 may be consciously] *intrl.*
†358.1–2 as a . . . occurrence] *ab. del.* '['by' *del.*] under the ['conditions' *del.*] presence'
358.5 elsewhere_∧] *comma del.*
358.6 parallel, all] *comma ov. period*; 'all' *ab. del.* 'All'
358.6–7 being . . . him,] *ab. del.* 'are'
358.7 yours] *ab. del.* 'mine'
358.8 leave] *aft. del.* 'throw the physi'
358.8 traces] 's' *added; aft. del.* 'a'
358.9 ²the] *alt. fr.* 'these'
††358.9 traced] *intrl.*
††358.9 said] *ab. del.* 'material'

358.11 ¹your] *intrl. bef. del. intrl.* 'my'
358.11 ²your] *ab. del.* 'the'
358.12(*twice*),13 your] *ab. del.* 'my'
358.12 exist] *aft. del.* '['are in all' *del.*] all'
358.14 as] *aft. del.* 'in'
358.14 ¹the] *ab. del.* 'its'
358.14 effects,] *comma ov. period*
358.14 immediate . . . the] *ab. del.* 'the ['t' *ov.* 'T']'
358.15 being] *ab. del.* 'is'
358.15 different_∧] *comma del.*
358.16 of ours] *insrtd.*
358.16 just] *intrl.*
358.17 room] *aft. del.* 'dining'
358.17 simultaneously used] *ab. del.* '['tra' *del.*] used and traversed'
358.18 for] *aft. del.* 'which use it for'
358.19 ether] *ab. del.* 'air'
††358.19 to &] *intrl.*
358.20 mutually attuned] *intrl.*
358.21–22 emphasized] *insrtd.*
358.22 whenever] 'ever' *intrl.*
358.22 of] *aft. del.* 'to which'
358.23 a] *ab. del.* 'the'
358.23 in] *ab. del.* 'to'
358.23 such] *ab. del.* 'that'
358.24 bodies] *aft. del.* 'material'
358.24 friends] *aft. del.* 'sitters'
358.25 parts] *aft. del.* 'part'
358.26 which carry] *ab. del.* '['connect['ed' *del.*]' *del.*] embody['ing' *del.*]'
358.27 Hodgson] *bef. del.* 'himself'
358.28 was] *aft. del.* '['was inclined' *del.*] suggest'
358.28 the . . . acts] *ab. del.* 'the sitter's body *acts ['s' *ov.* 'ed']'
358.31 York,] *bef. del.* 'f'
359.1 attracting . . . and] *intrl.*
359.2 communications] 's' *added; aft. del.* 'kind of'
359.2 other side.] *ab. del.* 'material world.'
359.2 If,] *comma insrtd.*
359.2 now,] *intrl.*
359.3 were] *bef. del.* 'then'
359.4 its extent,] *ab. del.* 'the System,'
359.5 made] *bef. del.* 'to vitr'
359.5 all] *intrl.*
†359.5–6 by . . . medium,] *intrl.*

359.8 might] *ab. del.* 'would'

359.8 redivivus] *first* 'i' *ov.* 'e'

359.9 momentary] *intrl.*

359.9 fair] *intrl.*

359.12 the] *bef. del.* 'w'

359.13 1the] 't' *ov.* 'T'

359.14 then] *intrl.*

359.21 which] *aft. del.* 'between'; *bef. del.* 'one's'

359.22 between] *aft. del.* 'which'

359.23 decision] 'on' *ov.* 've'

†359.23 must . . . (if] ('always' *insrtd.*); *ab. del.* 'vote is cast, *if [ab. del.* 'where']'

359.24 sense] *aft. del.* 'sense of individuals' '

359.24 2the] *intrl. bef. del. intrl.* 'natur'

359.24 probabilities] 'ities' *aft. del.* 'ity'

359.25 has] *insrtd. for del.* 'may have'

†359.25-26 feel . . . external] *ab. del.*

'incline to believe *that [ab. del.* 'in'] a'

††359.26 were ['most' *del.*] probably there,] *ab. del.* 'is *there, [comma ov. period]* But ['B' *ov.* 'b'] I am re'

†359.27 I . . . consequence] *ab. del.* 'I doubt, in consequence of as a result'

359.29 with] *bef. del.* 'supernormal ['pow' *del.*]'

359.29 accounts] 's' *added; aft. del.* 'can'

359.29 for] *bef. del.* 'the'

359.29-30 results found.] *insrtd. for del.* 'phenomena.' *ab. del.* 'facts.'

359.30 if asked whether] *ab. del.* 'between assuming'

359.30 be] *aft. del.* 'to'

359.31 be] *intrl.*

359.31 -counterfeit] *final* 's' *del.*

359.34 been] *bef. del.* 'decidedly'

359.37 2is] *intrl.*

360.1 days] *aft. del.* 'old Phinuit'

b. *Alterations in TMs*

All alterations are in ink and in James's hand. Not listed as alterations are: James's square brackets placed about his interjections and parentheses changed to brackets in the records of sittings, typographical errors corrected either in the course of typing or by hand, the double underlining of names in the records of sittings. All other alterations appear on this list, even when repeated in the Emendations or Historical Collation. For reference, the MS readings have been listed.

254.22 extraordinarily] *del.* [MS(T): extraordinarily]

254.31 his] *ab. del.* 'the' [MS(T): the]

255.7 The earliest] ('T' *ov.* 't'; 'st' *ov.* 'r'); *aft. del.* 'Most of' [MS(T): Most of the earlier]

255.8 but . . . name,] *intrl.* [MS(T): *om.*]

††255.11 was] *ab. del.* 'is' [MS(T): is]

†255.12 We . . . upon] *ab. del.* '[¶] Results can be reached only by eliminating other causes as improbable. In case they were all eliminated, the residual cause left on our hands would throw some light on' [MS(T): [¶] Results can be reached only by eliminating other causes as improbable. In case they were

all eliminated, the residual cause left on our hands would throw some light on]

255.13 We] 'W' *ov.* 'w'; *aft. del.* 'Meanwhile,' [MS(T): Meanwhile‸ we]

255.13 the] *ov.* 'its' [MS(T): its]

255.14 of the word] *intrl.* [MS(T): *om.*]

255.15 2is] *intrl.* [MS(T): is]

††255.28 i.e.] *aft. del.* 'I' [MS(T): I i.e.]

256.15 any . . . of] *ab. del.* 'one of' [MS(T): one of]

256.16 Piper's,] *comma insrtd. bef. del.* 'trances,' [MS(T): Piper's trances,]

256.28 an exceptionally] *ab. del.* 'a particularly' [MS(T): a particularly]

††256.35 hearers] 'hear' *ab. del.* 'read' [MS(T): readers]

256.37-38 instanced] *bef. del.* '&'

(misreading) [MS(T): instanced
['c' *del.*]]

257.12 place,] *comma insrtd.* [MS(T):
$\sim_\Lambda$]

257.32 spirit-] *hyphen added*
[MS: $\sim_\Lambda$]

257.37 appearances,] *comma added*
[MS: $\sim_\Lambda$]

††258.4–6 $_\Lambda$The . . . "Hodgson".$_\Lambda$]
bkts. del. [MS(T):
[$\sim$ . . . "HODGSON."]]

††258.8–9 $_\Lambda$The . . . order.$_\Lambda$] *bkts. del.*
[MS(T): [$\sim$ . . . $\sim$.]]

258.11 The hand] 'The' *insrtd.*; 'h' *of*
'hand' *ov.* 'H' [MS(T): Hand]

††258.11 $_\Lambda$The . . . -pad.$_\Lambda$] *bkts. del.*
[MS(T): [Hand . . . - $\sim$.]]

††258.12 $_\Lambda$RECTOR.$_\Lambda$] *db. underl., then*
underl. del. and circled 'rom'
insrtd. in mrgn., then del. and circled
'sm. caps' *insrtd.* [MS(T): *Rector*]

††258.24 $_\Lambda$"All"] *opening paren del.*
and db. qts. added [MS(T): A   1 1
[*ab. del.* ' "All" ']]

258.25–26 [The . . . later.]] *orig. aft.*
'that?' ', *but tr. by guideline to aft.*
'explanation. [*paren del.*]' [MS(T):
correct position]

††258.28–29 $_\Lambda$For . . . pp. $_{\Lambda\Lambda}$] *enclosing*
parens del.; orig. ¶ *but moved by*
guideline to aft. 'appeared.' [MS(T):
[¶] [$\sim$ . . . pp. ooo$_\Lambda$] (¶ *doubtful*)]

258.29 below] *intrl.* [MS(T): *om.*]

258.29+ space] *no space but circled*
'blank line' *in mrgn.* [MS(T):
no space]

259.4 POPE] 1'P' *ab. del.* 'H' [MS(T):
POPE]

259.13 Than . . . divine.] *insrtd. in*
incorrect blank space ab. 'Tho . . .
skies' *and brought down to end of*
page by guideline [MS(T): *correct*
position]

259.27 (RECTOR.)] *om.* TMs^b *but to*
right of line '—R.' *insrtd.*; $_\Lambda$RECTOR$_\Lambda$
TMs^a [MS: *om.*]

259.30+ space] *no space* TMs^{a-b} *but*
'blank line' *in mrgn. in* TMs^a
[MS: *no space*]

261.5+ space] *no space but circled*
'blank line' *in mrgn.* [MS(T): *space*]

262.4+ space] *no space but* 'blank line'
in mrgn. [MS(T): *end of page*]

††262.19–21 $_\Lambda$R.H.'s . . . W.J. jr$_{\Lambda\Lambda}$ . . .
Lake.$_\Lambda$] *intrl.* [MS(T): *[Hodgson's . . .*
['my' *del.*] W.J. jr.$_\Lambda$ . . . Lake.]
[*intrl.*]]

262.32 Men] *orig.* ¶ *but connected to*
'tennis?' *by guideline and* 'run in'
circled in mrgn. [MS(T): [¶] Men]

263.6 George] *bef. del.* '[Dorr]'
[MS(T): George [Dorr]]

263.16+ space] *no space but* 'blank
line' *in mrgn.* [MS: *top of page*]

263.20 the] *intrl.* [MS: *del. in error*]

263.21 cull] 'u' *ab. del.* 'a' [MS: cull]

263.31 spirit), it] *alt. fr.* 'spirit). It'
[MS(T): spirit$_\Lambda$, it]

263.35 $_\Lambda$MISS . . . ring.$_\Lambda$] *parens del.*
[MS(T): *enclosing parens in error*]

264.1 Lyman's] *aft. del. added* '[Mrs'
[MS(T): Lyman's]

264.8 $_\Lambda$Oh . . . right.$_\Lambda$] *parens del.*
[MS(T): *enclosing parens in error*]

264.15+ space] *no space but* 'blank
line' *in mrgn.* [MS(T): *no space*]

265.8 Then] 'T' *ov.* 't' [MS(T): then]

266.17 may] *bef. del.* 'immediately'
[MS(T): may immediately]

266.29 natural] *aft. del.* 'most'
[MS(T): most natural]

266.39 that] *intrl.* [MS(T): *om.*]

267.1 trance-record.] *hyphen ov.*
period and 'record.' *intrl.* [MS(T):
trance.]

267.4 telepathically perhaps] *ab. del.*
'possibly' [MS(T): possibly]

267.40 then,] *intrl.* [MS(T): *om.*]

†268.2 Readers] 'People' *ab. del.*
'Readers' [MS(T): Readers]

268.2 this] *alt. fr.* 'the' [MS(T): the]

268.9+ space] *no space but* 'blank
line' *in mrgn.* [MS(T): *text ends bef.*
end of page]

††268.12–13 'reality-coefficient,']
sg. qts. added; comma alt. fr.
semicolon [MS(T): ' $\sim$ - $\sim$,']

268.22,25 HYSLOP.] *insrtd. for del.*
'J. H. H.' [MS(T): J. H. H.]

††270.2 the sitting] *ab. del.* 'that'
[MS(T): that]

270.3 present,] *ab. del.* 'the sitter,'
[MS(T): the sitter,]

270.7 P.] *intrl.* [MS(T): P.]

270.10–13 ∧The . . . signed.∧∧]
*enclosing parens and closing db. qts.
del.* [MS(T): *enclosing bkts.; closing
db. qts. undel. in error*]

270.10 [pseudonym]] *intrl.* [MS(T):
om.]

270.10 Mr.] *ab. del.* 'Rev.' [MS(T):
Mr.]

270.16 "Can] *db. qts. added* [MS(T):
db. qts. added]

271.6 ¶ [This] *run-on but* '¶' *in mrgn.*
[MS(T): *no* ¶]

††271.8–9 Densmore:∧–[¶] No] *colon
ov. period and paren del.; bkt. om.
in error; dash ov. ellipsis dots;* 'No'
marked to be set in; circled 'set
in' *in mrgn.* [MS(T): ~ .] . . . No
(*no* ¶)]

271.18 was] *underl. added* [MS(T):
was]

271.21 ∧The] *db. qts. del.* [MS(T):
"The]

271.22 wife∧] *comma del.* [MS(T):
wife,]

271.22 had a letter] *ab. del.* 'heard'
[MS(T): heard]

272.1 veracious] 'acious' *ab. del.* 'idical'
[MS(T): veridical]

272.1–2 utterances] 's' *added* [MS(T):
utterance]

272.2 they] *ab. del.* 'it' [MS(T): it]

272.3 lucky flukes] *aft. del.* 'a'; 's'
added [MS(T): a lucky fluke]

272.3 explanations] *bef. del.* 'of it'
[MS(T): explanations of it]

272.34 lips] *ov.* 'life' (*misreading*)
[MS(T): lips [*intrl.*]]

272.39 and] *intrl.* [MS(T): *om.*]

273.1 But] *intrl.* [MS(T): *om.*]

273.1 that] 't' *ov.* 'T' [MS(T): That]

273.1 could] 'c' *ab. del.* 'w' [MS(T):
would]

273.2 seems] 's' *ab. del.* 'ed'; *bef. del.*
'however rightly' [MS(T):
seemed, *however, highly [*intrl.*]]

273.8 which] *insrtd. for del.* 'that'
[MS: that]

††273.9 her] *insrtd. for del.* 'the'
[MS: the]

273.11 sitting] *bef. del.* 'of Prof.
Newboldt' [MS: sitting ['of Prof.
Newboldt's *to [*del. in error*]' *del.*]]

273.11 1906,] *comma ov. period*
[MS: 1906.]

273.12 by . . . Newbold.] *intrl.* ('W. R.'
additionally intrl.) [MS: by Prof
Newbold]

273.12 Hodgson-] *hyphen added*
[MS: Hodgson∧]

††273.28 interjects:∧] *dash del.* [MS:
interjects:—]

††273.30 australian cousin,] *insrtd.
for del.* 'earlier flame,' [MS: earlier
flame]

274.2 ¶ She] *run-on but marked for*
¶ *and in mrgn. circled* '¶, set in'
[MS: ¶ She]

274.6 —see below.—W.J.]] *added*
(*first dash ov. period*) [MS: *om.*]

274.11 Heaven] *in left mrgn. is
circled* 'R.H.' [MS: *om.*]

††274.14 another friend] *ab. del.*
'Newbold' [MS: Newbold]

††274.16 the other] *ab. del.* 'N's'
[MS: N's]

275.3 etc.]∧] *four ellipsis dots del.*
[MS(T): etc.] . . . .]

275.17 W.J.] *marked for* ¶ *with vertical
line and circled* '¶' *in mrgn.*
[MS(T): W.J.]

275.31 explanation] *bef. del.* 'itself'
(*misreading*) [MS: 'lends itself'
tr. w. guideline to aft. 'explanation,']

276.3 the Secretary's] 'the Secretary'
ab. del. 'R.H.' [MS: 'R.H.'s]

276.3–4 Hodgson] *ab. del.* 'he'
[MS: he]

276.4 had, . . . years,] *commas insrtd.*
[MS: *no commas*]

276.4 after] *ab. del.* 'since' [MS: since]

††276.21 SITTER:—] *insrtd.* [MS(T):
om.]

276.34+ space] *no space but* 'blank
line' *in mrgn.* [MS(T): *foot of page*]

277.2–3 the Secretary's] *ab. del.* 'his'
[MS: his]

277.25 certain] *intrl.* [MS: *om.*]

277.26+   space] *no space but* 'blank line' *in mrgn.* [MS: *no space*]

277.31   -return] 'turn' *ab. del.* 'lation' [MS: -return]

277.36   not only] *typed bef.* 'transmits' *but tr. w. guideline to aft.* 'assume' [MS: not only transmits]

277.39   conditions] 's' *intrl.* [MS: conditions]

278.13   (which . . . simplicity)] *parens insrtd.* [MS: *parens*]

278.21   where,] *comma added* [MS: where,]

278.22   spiritist] 'ist' *ab. del.* 'ual' [MS: spiritist]

278.28   still] *intrl.* [MS: *om.*]

278.29   ended . . . ¹as] *ab. del.* 'thought them' [MS: thought them]

278.30   there being] *insrtd.* [MS: *om.*]

278.34   repeat] 'eat' *ab. del.* 'ort' [MS: repeat]

278.40   at last] *ab. del.* 'now' [MS: now]

279.2   well] *insrtd.* [MS: *om.*]

††279.5   technical] 'techn' *ab. del.* 'top' (*misreading*) [MS: logical]

DELETED VERSOS FOR "REPORT ON MRS. PIPER'S HODGSON-CONTROL" MANUSCRIPT

Part I

[*del. fol.* 52ᵛ *(Part I): earlier form of fol. 52, corresponding to text 277.23–24*] 'or to chance coincidence. *[¶] Few persons will accept chance-coincidence **hence [*insrtd.*] [*intrl.*] ['The supernatural' *del.*] explanation offers *the [*intrl.*] two possibilities[', th' *del.*] of reading the sitter's mind, or spirit-intercourse

Pray return these!
to W.J.'

Part II

[*del. fols.* 1ᵛ *and* 2ᵛ *(Part II) (foliated 5 and 6): probable earlier form of fols. 5 and 6 in Part I, corresponding to text 255.25–256.11*] '[*fol.* 1ᵛ] ['by the' *del.*] during *his [*intrl.*] conversations with the Controls in *the [*ab. del.* 'her'] trances, and stored up ['b' *del.*] in the *trance-memory, [*ab. del.* 'memory of said Controls,'] but not in Mrs. P's waking memory.

5. Common gossip.

6. 'Telepathy'—i.e. tapping the sitter's mind, or the mind of some distant *living [*intrl.*] person, in an inexplicable way.

7 Access to some cosmic reservoir where *the [*ab. del.* 'mundane'] memory ['y' *ov.* 'ies'] *of all ['of' *del.*] mundan['c' *del.*]e facts is [*ab. del.* 'are pooled in ways'] kept, and grouped round personal centres of association.

['The first 5' *del.*] Let us call the first five explanations 'natural,' the last two 'supernatural.' It is obvious that *no [*ab. del.* 'neither'] supernatural explanation should be invoked so long as a natural one is *plausible. [*ab. del.* 'likely.'] *Only after the more [*ab. del.* 'When the'] natural explanations *have been [*ab. del.* 'are'] ruled out, *it [*ab. del.* 'then it is'] the turn [*fol.* 2ᵛ] of the telepathy-theory and the cosmic reservoir theory to *be [*intrl.*] compared ['them' *del.*] with the theory of R.H's surviving spirit.

The ['total' *del. intrl.*] amount of truthful information communicated by the R.H.-control to the various sitters is *very copious. [*ab. del.* 'in the aggregate very great.'] It *comes [*ab. del.* 'consists'] for the most part *in ['only' *del.*] his [*ab. del.* 'of'] reminding them of *events [*ab. del.* '['incidents' *del.*] experiences'] *(**usually [*ab. del.* 'mostly'] unimportant ones) [*parens ov.*

commas] ['in' *del. insrtd.*] which they ['had' *del.*] and the living R.H. had experienced together. Taking any one of these incidents singly, it is *never [*ab. del.* 'im'] possible to exclude ['I'exp' *del.*] natural' *del.*] explanations *number [*intrl.*] 2 and 3. *Number [*ab. del.* 'Explanation'] 5 is often excluded by the nature of the case. *A complete [*ab. del.* 'The'] record of the sitting ought generally to *decide about [*ab. del.* 'settle'] number 1. Number 4 ['is *sur [*doubtful*]' *del.*] would be easily settled if the *records ['s' *added*] of the *living [*insrtd.*] Hodgson's sittings with Mrs. Piper were complete and accessible. They are supposed (during the'

[*del. fol.* 4ᵛ: *poss. earlier form of fol. 5 in Part I, corresponding in part to text* 255.28–30] 'total mass ['of veridical communication from the R.H. control' *del.*] is explicable, ['by' *del.*] when conversations ['duri' *del.*] with Mrs. Piper's controls *during her trances [*intrl.*] are added *to making conversations. [*insrtd.*] much may be credited to these *two [*intrl.*] sources; but there is too much left over, as I think that the details of what follows will show, and for this residuum, supernormal *sources ['so' *ov.* 'ca'] of information must be resorted to.

Of such sources three may be enumerated.

1) 'Telepathy':—*i.e.* tapping the sitter's mind or the mind of some distant living person, in an inexplicable way.

7) Access to some cosmic reservoir where the'

[*del. fol.* 7ᵛ *(foliated 8): poss. earlier form of fol. 7 in Part I, corresponding to text* 256.23–36; *del. fol.* 3ᵛ *(foliated 9): poss. earlier form of material found on fol. 9 in Part I, corresponding to text* 257.32] '[*fol.* 7ᵛ] So far from *his [*ab. del.* 'the'] particular case ['of R.H.' *del.*] being an unusually good one *by which [*intrl.*] to test Mrs Piper ['by,' *del.*] and *to sift [*ab. del.* 'to test'] our various explanations *of **her [*intrl.*] veridical matter [*intrl.*] ['by' *del.*] it would *thus [*intrl.*] seem to be a particularly poor one. ['owing to so many explanations of the veridical matter being possible.' *del.*] I have come to the conclusion that it *is* a particularly poor one. His ['living' *del.*] familiarity with the difficulties here when alive has not made him *show [*intrl.*] any more *expertness ['ness' *insrtd.*] *as a spirit, [*intrl.*] than other communicators *have [*intrl.*] shown ['n' *added ov. comma*], and there are ['far' *del.*] more *ambiguous [*insrtd.*] loopholes, *and more [*ab. del.* 'in his case for'] naturalistic explanations *possible in his case [*intrl.*] than in ['most' *del.*] other cases.

So much for generalities, and so *much [*insrtd.*] for my own 'personal equation [*comma del.*]' *for which the **various [*intrl.*] readers will make their own kinds of allowance. [*ab. del.* 'which the reader ought to bear in mind throughout the following discussion.'] I now proceed to take up the messages in some detail, *but [*insrtd. for del.* 'and'] solely ['from the point of' *del.*] with reference [*fol.* 3ᵛ] to the question whether they ['really' *del.*] indicate ['the presence' *del.*] unmistakeably a surviving Richard Hodgson.

The R.H. Control's first appearance

The'

[*del. fol.* 5ᵛ: *poss. earlier form of fols. 6 and 7 in Part I, corresponding to text* 256.26–31,256.1–2; *del. fol.* 8ᵛ: *poss. earlier form of fols. 6 and 8 in Part I, corresponding to text* 256.10–17,256.38–257.1; *del. fol.* 9ᵛ: *poss. earlier form of fol. 8 in Part I, corresponding to text* 257.1–16; *del. fol.* 6ᵛ: *poss. earlier form of fol.*

9 *in Part* I, *corresponding to text* 257.16–31] '[*fol.* 5ᵛ] [¶] In point of fact it turns out to be a particularly poor case. Hodgson's expertness seems to leave him in the lurch, once on the other side; and the abundance of his dealings with Mrs. Piper, both in trance and out of it, during his lifetime, leave an unusually large ['scope for interpreting ['natural' *del.*] veridical messages purporting now to come from him, as re-editings of *impressions [*ab. del.* 'matter'] left by him in conversation upon the Piper-memory.' *del.*] loophole for a purely naturalistic interpretation of whatever communications, now purporting to come from him, may be veridical. They may conceivably all be traces of his previous conversations with Mrs. Piper or with her trance-controls.

The veridical information given by the Hodgson control or spirit is very copious indeed. There are other naturalistic explana-[*fol.* 8ᵛ]tions for all of Mrs Piper's veridical matter besides the one suggested. Some of it may be lucky chance-hits. Some may be due to indications unwarily furnished by sitters. Some may come from common gossip, once the sitters person['s' *del.*] is recognized. But *earlier [*ab. del.* 'previous'] conversations with the living Hodgson must be the great 'scientific' explanation of *his* veridical matter, as brought out in the recent trances.

As regards conversations with the Piper controls in trances at which R.H. was present, the records of trance['s' *del.*] for a dozen years past is supposed to be, *save for a few sitters [*intrl.*] complete. But some of it is in *Hodgsons [*intrl.*] cipher, and it is so unwieldy that to hunt *them [*ab. del.* 'it'] thru for any one ['previous' *del.*] fact now put forth by the R.H. control is practically out of the question within any reasonable time. Doubt will therefore always be possible.

As regards conversations with the waking Mrs. Piper, there is this to be said. Abstractly it sounds very plausible to suppose that R.H., [*fol.* 9ᵛ] (who [*paren insrtd.*] systematically imposed on himself the law of never mentioning the content of any trance in her *waking [*intrl.*] presence) [*paren ov. comma*] methodically adopted a plan of entertaining her on his visits by reciting ['som' *del.*] all the *little [*ab. del.* 'small'] happenings of his days, and that *this [*alt. fr.* 'these'] *chronicle of small beer, [*intrl.*] stored up in her memory, now comes out ['as recollections ['adapted to' *del.*] fitted to test ['his' *del.*] the identity of his spirit.' *del.*] for service as *a [*intrl.*] test [*enclosing sg. qts. and final* 's' *del.*] of his spirit-identity.

Concretely, however, this is not a highly probable hypothesis. Everyone who knew Hodgson agrees that he was little given to *anecdotal [*ab. del.* 'the'] small change ['of anecdote' *del.*], unless the incident were ['highly' *del.*] comic or otherwise expressive, and that his *souvenirs* *of fact [*intrl.*] were *usually [*ab. del.* 'all'] of a ['more' *del. intrl.*] broad and synthetic order. He had had 'a splendid time' at such a place, 'glorious' landscape, [*closing sg. qt. del.*] swim, or hill-climb, but no farther detail. Gifted with *great powers [*ab. del.* 'extraordinary'] of reserve by nature, he was professionally schooled to extraordinary secretiveness, and ['had' *del.*] a decidedly incommunicative habit in the way of personal gossip had become a second nature with him—especially towards Mrs. Piper. For [*fol.* 6ᵛ] many years past he had seen her three times weekly ['during the' *del.*] (except [*paren insrtd.*] during *the months of [*intrl.*] her summer *vacation) [*paren ov. comma*] and had had to transcribe the records afterwards. The work was time-consuming and he found it excessively fatiguing. He *had [*intrl.*] economized energy upon it by adopting for many years past a purely business ['towa' *del.*] tone with the medium, entering, starting the trance, and leaving when it was over, with as few *unnecessary [*intrl.*] words as possible. *Great [*ab. del.* 'Such'] *brusquerie* was among the excellent R.H.'s potentialities, and for a while the amount of it displayed towards Mrs P. led to a state of feeling on her part which a New York Herald reporter *once [*intrl.*] took advantage of to exploit publicly. He was remonstrated with, and behaved better afterwards. It may well be that *Mrs. P. had [*ab. del.* 'she'] heard this or that little incident, among those ['of' *del.*] to be discussed in the following report, from his living lips, but that any *large [*intrl.*] *mass* of these incidents ['came' *del.*] are to be traced to this origin I find ['it impossible' *del.*] incredible.

Neither do I believe that the'

[*del. fol.* 12^v: *orig. cont. of fol.* 10, *corresponding to text* 282.36–37] 'the reports with careful attention to each detail, I'

[*del. fol.* 16^v (*foliated* 21 *in pencil*): *orig. cont. of fol.* 19 (*ov.* 20), *similar to text* 282.6–15] '[¶] I know that no critic of mine, however scientific, if he really *believe* in his conclusion, whichever it be, *will be [*ab. del.* 'is'] in the end determined by anything else than this residual *balance in his mind of [*ab. del.* 'sense of'] the *dramatic probabilities*. I shall myself leave the problem'

[*del. fol.* 22^v (*foliated* 17): *earlier trial for fol.* 17, *corresponding to text* 284.10–14] 'I find in my own case that the dramatic probabilities alter as I take a narrower or a wider look at the phenomenon to be interpreted. Considering it in detail, the notion that Mrs. Piper's subconscious self should ['so ex' *del.*] keep her sitters apart as expertly as it does, remembering its past dealings ['with them' *del.*]'

[*del. fol.* 23^v (*foliated* 15): *earlier trial for fols.* 14–16, *corresponding to text* 283.16–21,37–38] 'and the question *always is; [*ab. del.* 'now is'] Is *this* *case [*intrl.*] likely to be an['d' *del.*] exception? If *the ['our' *del.*] case ['ca' *ov.* doubtful 'ex'] we are discussing be [*ab. del.* 'it is'] an exception, and 'spirits' really *can [*ab. del.* '['return' *del.*] should'] return, ['in this way,' *del.*] the record is fully *compatible* with their *being there, [*ab. del.* 'having a finger in it,'] and co operating with the other factors. As soon as we drop our routine rules of method, and ask for the truth straight,'

[*del. typed fol.* 33^v: *no parallel*] 'LIST OF SITTINGS SINCE R.H.'S DEATH.'

[*del. fol.* 53^v: *earlier form of fol.* 54, *corresponding to text* 303.14–15] '– . . . . . . There is more help coming to you to enlarge the house. . . . You remember you thought it necessary to have more room.'

[*del. fol.* 149^v (*foliated* 149): *earlier form of passage on fol.* 149, *corresponding to text* 349.16–17; *fol. missing for the passage which corresponds to text* 350.10–11] '*On Feb. 7. '06. [*insrtd. in penc.*] R.H. asked Miss Pope:|Do you remember a story I told you about my old friend Sidgwick? | Don't you remember how I imitated'

[*del. orig. fol.* 156 *found beneath paste-on fol.* 154 *and corresponding to text* 351.11 *and* 279.21–23] 'The same sitter *on [*ab. is* 'On' *and ab. this, brought down by a guideline is another* 'On'] Jan. 30th., | had received [*space*] *For weeks after [*intrl.*] Hodgson's *death his [*intrl.*] friends were still rather perplexed about the future of the [*illeg.*], and various plans were'

[*del. fol.* 161ᵛ *(unidentified): poss. false start for passage found on fol.* 160, *corresponding to text* 353.1] 'Control. ['During the years' *del.*]'

38. THE CONFIDENCES OF A "PSYCHICAL RESEARCHER"

†361.0 The . . . Researcher"] *triple underl.; orig.* 'The State of Mind of [*poss.* 'our' *del.*] one "psychical researcher" ' *alt. to* 'One "psychical researcher" at the Confessional.'; *bel. is* '*by William James [*triple underl.*]'

361.1 The late Professor] *intrl.*

361.1 Sidgwick] *bef. del.* ', the founder of the Society for Psychical Research,'

361.1 the rare] *ab. del.* '['his almost *del.*] *a certain rare [*ab. del.* 'the extraordinary']'

361.3 The liberal] *ab. del.* 'His'

361.3 which . . . work] ('work' *bef. del.* 'in harness'); *ab. del.* '['of general faith' *del.*] was united'

361.4 acted] *ab. del.* 'worked'

361.5 belief] *ab. del.* 'faith'

361.5 was] *aft. del.* 'could be presented.'

361.5–6 A . . . century] *ab. del.* 'Twenty-five years'

361.7,8 of] *insrtd.*

361.8 which] *bef. del.* 'the spiritists gulp'

361.9 scientifically trained] *ab. del.* 'competently ['critical' *del.*]'

361.9 mostly] *intrl.*

361.10 Professor Barrett,] *intrl.*

361.11–12 These men] *ab. del.* 'He'

361.12 if . . . treated] *ab. del.* 'by treating the reports'

361.13 objective] *aft. del.* 'that'

361.13 would] *ab. del.* 'ought to'

361.13 and] *bef. del.* 'that'

361.14 subject] *ab. del.* 'matter *could [*ab. del.* 'might'] be'

361.14 from] *bef. del.* 'the two'

361.14–15 dogmatizing] *ab. del.* 'dogmatic'

361.15 Sidgwick] *ab. del.* 'he'

361.16 the year] *aft. del.* '['nearly twenty' *del.*] in 1901'

361.17 at the outset] *ab. del.* 'twenty years earlier'

361.18 after] *aft. del.* 'he would be,'

361.18 years] *bef. del.* 'of research,'

361.18 he] *ov.* 'in'

361.18 would be in] *ab. del.* 'exactly'

361.18 identical] *intrl.*

361.19 balance] *bef. del.* 'about most of these phenomena especially'

361.20 impossible] *alt. fr.* 'inevitable'

361.20 that amount] *ab. del.* 'the sifting'

361.21 handling] *intrl.*

361.21 bring] *bef. del.* 'no final decision'

361.23 touch] *aft. del. doubtful* 'dou'

†362.1 have . . . numerous] *ab. del.* 'with the work of many psychical'

†362.2–3 (though . . . spent)] *parens ov. commas*

362.3 trying] 'tr' *ov. doubtful* 'en'

362.4 theoretically] *ab. del.* 'practically'

362.6 has eternally] *intrl.*

362.7 remain] *bef. del.* 'forever'

362.7 our] *intrl.*

††362.9 raps &] *intrl.*

362.9 are] *ab. del.* 'should be'

362.10 can] *ab. del.* 'could'

362.10 fully] *intrl.*

362.10 they] *bef. del.* 'should'

362.10 ²can] *intrl.*

362.11 full] *aft. del.* 'methodical [*ab. del.* 'definitive [*alt. fr.* 'definite']']'

362.12 that] *bef. del.* ', that [*illeg. del. intrl.*]'

362.13 possible] *aft. del.* 'err'

362.13 deception] *ab. del.* 'error'

362.14 lot of them] *ab. del.* 'thing'

362.14   comparatively] *ab. del.* 'very'
362.15   cases] *bef. del.* 'indeed'
††362.15   anything ['worse' *del.*] . . .
   than] *ab. del.* 'more than'
362.15   vague] *intrl.*
362.16   error] *ab. del.* 'deception'
362.17   bare] *ab. del.* 'mere'
362.17   build upon] 'build' *ab. del.*
   'establish her conclusions'; 'up'
   added to 'on'
362.18   —I . . . 'scientist'—] *intrl.*
362.19   hard] *final* 'ly' *del.*
362.19   believe] *final* 'r' *del.*
362.19   that] *aft. del.* 'in the'
362.20   put] *aft. del.* 'intended a vast'
362.20   any big] *ab. del.* 'an ['n' *added*]
   ['vast' *del.*]'
362.21   defy and mock] *ab. del.* 'irritate'
362.21   so] *ab. del.* 'and'
362.21   deeper] *ab. del.* 'real'
362.22   we] *aft. del.* 'sci'
362.22   our] *ab. del.* 'their'
362.23   we] *ab. del.* 'they'
362.23   expect to mark] *ab. del.* 'count'
362.23,24   by] *bef. del.* 'the'
362.23,24   -centuries] *intrl.*
362.24   or] *bef. del.* 'by the'
362.24   centuries] 'ies' *ov.* 'y'
362.25   my] *ab. del.* 'an'
362.25   that] *aft. del.* 'that I get'
362.26   taken] *ab. del.* 'made'
362.26   by] *ov.* 'in'
362.27   competent] *ab. del.* 'public'
362.27–28   (movements] *aft. del.* ',
   [*comma undel. in error*] tables mov'
362.28   lights,] *bef. del.* 'and'
362.29   etc.)] *insrtd.*
362.29   have] *alt. fr.* 'has'
362.29   regions] *ab. del.* 'departments
   of [del. in error]'
362.30   baffling] *bef. del. comma*
††362.30–31   certain & . . . has] *ab. del.*
   'immense has'
362.32   even] *intrl.*
362.32   of testimony] *intrl.*
362.33   towards] *bef. del.* 'the supernat'
362.37   men . . . have] ('men of'
   bef. del. '['esp' *del.*] enormous
   standing'); *ab. del.* 'scientific men
   have'

362.38   that she] *ab. del.* 'as to her
   barefaced [intrl.]'
362.38   cheats] 's' *ov.* 'ing'
362.38–39   in . . . manner] *ab. del.*
   'profusely &'
363.2   converts] *ab. del.* 'conquests'
363.2   eminent] *aft. del. doubtful* 'res'
363.3   Morselli,] *bef. del.* '['of' *del.*]
   and'
363.5   conquest] *alt. fr.* 'conversion'
363.6   If] *insrtd. for del.* 'If [*penc.
   del. ab. del.* 'When']'
363.6–7   prosecuting attorney] *insrtd.
   for del.* 'advocatus diaboli'
363.7   the . . . as] *ab. del.* 'all'
363.7   are concerned,] *intrl.*
363.8   around] *aft. del.* 'around'
363.9   Getting] *alt. fr.* 'gets'; *aft. del.*
   'If Eusapia'
363.9   Eusapia will then] ('a' *of*
   'Eusapia' *intrl. and* 'i' *ov.* 'a'; 'then'
   penc. added); *ab. del.* 'she will'
363.12   genuineness] *aft. del.* 'possible'
363.13   all . . . this] *ab. del.* '['that
   whole parti' *del.*] a'
363.14   ˄supernatural˄] *sg. qts. del.*;
   aft. del. 'phenomenon'
363.15   Not long] *ab. del.* '['Falsus in
   uno, falsus in omnibus' *del.*] ['When'
   del.] Shortly'
363.15–16   studying] *bef. del.* 'anatomy'
363.16   anatomist and man,] *intrl.*
363.17   yet] *aft. del.* 'but'
†363.17–18   so . . . views;] *ab. del.*
   'only a half-convert, as yet,'
363.19   the] 't' *ov.* 'S'; *aft. del.* 'the'
363.21   orthodox] *aft. penc. del.* 'that'
363.21   seeming] *alt. fr.* 'looking'
363.22   abolish,] *ab. del.* 'do [*ab. del.*
   'make'] away with,'
363.22   is] *ab. del.* 'much'
363.23   Chambers] *ab. del.* 'the Vestiges'
363.23–24   despatched and buried,]
   ('despatched' *ab. del.* 'killed');
   ab. del. 'refuted,'
363.24   making] *insrtd. for del.*
   '*greater prestige to [ab. del.*
   'triumphantly resuscitating their
   heresy.']'
363.24   very] *intrl.*

†363.25 seem . . . plausible.] *intrl. ab. del. period*

363.25–26 killed off] *ab. del.* '['refuted' *del.*] laughed at'

363.26 laid] *intrl. bef. del.* 'put [*ab. del.* 'buried']'

363.27 away underground] *intrl.*

363.28 offered] *aft. del.* 'before us in such'

363.30 the . . . of] ('expedients' *bef. del.* 'that'); *insrtd. for del.* 'that'

363.31 orthodoxy.] *period insrtd. bef. del.* 'can oppose to it.'

363.31 something] *aft. del.* 'a genuine realm of natural phenomena, and not a mere chapter'

363.36 think] *aft. del.* 'thing'

363.38 exceptional] *intrl.*

363.40 belief] *ab. del. comma*

364.1 investment] *bef. del.* 'of belief'

364.4 as . . . of] *ab. del.* 'in point of'

364.5 human] *bef. del.* ', man's character being mixed as it is,'

364.8 at] *ab. del.* 'in'

364.9 obey their] *penc. ab. del.* ' 'fail' as *they have a [ink and penc. del.*]'

364.9 towards] *intrl.*

364.9 failure] *penc. ab. ink del.* 'to do'

364.10 had . . . the] *ab. del.* 'inherited his'

364.11 of] *ab. del.* 'from'

364.12 however] *aft. del.* 'wha'

364.13 its] *penc. ab. del.* 'the'

364.20 , he said,] *insrtd.*

364.21 pretended to have] *ab. del.* 'pre- [*added; undel. in error*] | had (not!!)'

364.21 it.] *period insrtd. bef. del.* '(tho' he *pretended [ab. del.* 'seemed'] to). I ha'

364.22 To] '¶' *added in mrgn.*

364.23 once] *intrl.*

364.24 heart] *aft. del.* 'turtle's'

364.25 This] *alt. fr.* 'The'

364.25 heart,] *comma insrtd.*

364.25–26 which . . . turtle,] *intrl.*

364.26 a moving] *ab. del.* 'the'

364.26 shadow,] *final 's' del.; comma added*

364.27 greatly . . . upon] *ab. del.* 'of its movements on'

364.27 heart] *ab. del.* 'organ'

364.28 certain] *aft. del.* 'a'

364.28 nerves] 'er' *ab. del. illeg.;* 's' *added*

364.28 were] *ab. del.* 'was'

364.29 act . . . ways] ('certain' *aft. del.* 'in' *and bef. del.* 'way'); *ab. del.* 'stop beating, then recommence in a certain manner'

364.29 heart[' 's' *del.*]] *ab. del.* '['turtles's' *del.*] life'

364.31 final] *intrl.*

364.31 life's tether.] *ab. del.* 'activity.'

364.32 performance,] *comma added bef. del.* 'of my temporary protégé,'

364.33 suddenly] *intrl.*

364.33 like . . . military] ('military' *aft. del.* 'rare'); *ab. del.* 'as any general does, whose'

364.33 geniuses] 'es' *added*

364.33 who] *intrl.*

364.34 convert] *final* 's' *del.; bef. del.* 'an unexpected'

364.34 There] *aft. del.* 'With my forefinger'

364.36 I] *insrtd. for* 'I' *del. in error*

364.36 impulsively and automatically] *tr. by guideline fr. aft.* 'shadow,'

364.38 undergo.] *ab. del.* 'occasion. [*ab. del.* 'impart to it.']'

††364.38 kept . . . failing,] ('kept' *ab. del.* 'saved'); *ab. del.* 'rescued the situation from *ignominy ['y' ov.* 'ious'],'

364.39 not only] *intrl.*

364.39 my] *aft. del.* 'both'

364.39 a] *intrl.*

364.39 humiliation] *final* 's' *del.*

364.40 that] *bef. del.* 'for a m'

364.40 their] *aft. del.* 'unavoidably'

364.40 lot,] *ab. del.* 'portion,'

365.1 established in] *intrl. aft. del.* '*clinched in [ab. del.* 'confirmed']'

365.1 audience] *bef. del.* 'in'

365.1 true] *final* 'r' *del.*

365.5 a] *ab. del.* 'a [*insrtd. for del.* 'the late']'

365.5 venerated] 'ted' *ab. del.* 'ble'

365.6–7 been . . . ¹the] *ab. del.* 'given the'

365.7 and . . . lecturer.] *ab. del.* 'a very false impression'

365.7 It] *ab. del.* '—[*intrl.*] it'

365.8–9 even . . . think] *ab. del.* 'in retrospect I am not sure to-day'

365.9 acted] 'ed' *added; aft. del.* 'didn not'

365.10 correctly.] *ab. del.* 'rightly.'

††365.11 &] *intrl.*

365.11 was] *intrl.*

365.11 what] *insrtd. for del.* 'pre-' |

365.11 prevented] 'pre' *insrtd.*

365.12 the] *ab. del.* 'my *looser [doubtful] and'

365.12 and . . . my] *intrl.*

365.13 finger. To] *period insrtd. for del. comma bef. del.* 'and'; 'T' *ov.* 't'

365.13 memory] *insrtd. for del.* 'thought of'

365.14 critical] *aft. del.* 'moment'

365.16 On] *alt. fr.* 'In'

365.16 principles] *ab. del.* 'eyes'

365.17 ought to] *ab. del.* 'would'

365.17 ever] *intrl. bef. del.* 'now [*ab. del.* 'say or']'

365.17–18 ²everything . . . article,] *ab. del.* 'or say on any other'

365.19 conclusion.] *aft. del.* 'consequence.'; *bef. del.* 'to be drawn. [¶] Serious inquiry into occult phenomena is ['kept rare by the' *del.*] forced ['into the background' *del.*] by the prevalence in the foreground of two opposite sentimentalisms, *each [*ab. del.* 'both'] of which is its enemy. Your uncritical and *romantic-minded person, getting [*ab. del.* 'wonder-loving softhead, hearing'] spirit messages about *the [*intrl.*] happiness and flowers and lectures in the summer land, ['and finding them signed by the' *del.*] signed' |

365.20 Fraud,] *comma added*

365.20 conscious or unconscious,] *intrl.*

365.21 of spiritism,] *intrl. w. caret ov. comma*

365.21 false] *aft. del.* 'pers'

365.24 the] *ab. del.* 'if it is at any rate'

365.24–25 (if . . . be)] *parens ov. commas*

365.25 everywhere to] *insrtd. for del.* 'to'

365.26 seldom stops,] *ab. del.* 'is everywhere'

365.26 itself] *bef. del.* 'inextricably'

365.30 Yet] *aft. del.* 'J'

365.31 is] *ab. del.* 'impresses me as'

365.32 a] *intrl.*

365.34 non-] *aft. del.* 'non-expert mind'

365.35 phenomena] 'a' *ov.* 'on'

365.35 according to] *ab. del.* 'at'

†365.35–36 pretension . . . asking] *ab. del.* 'value not seeking'

365.37 revealers] *ab. del.* 'a [*intrl.*] spiritual ['ual' *added*] revelation['s' *del.*]'

365.38 being absolutely] *intrl.*

365.38 being absolute] *intrl.*

365.39 judged.] *ab. del.* 'taken.'

365.40 One] *aft. del.* 'The'

366.1 given,] *bef. del.* 'are satisfie'

366.4 revelation's] *intrl.*

366.4 contents,] *ab. del.* 'emptiness of the revelation,'

366.6 from] *bef. del.* 'such'

366.8 A] *alt. fr.* 'An'

366.8 good] *ab. del.* 'excellent'

366.10 "that] *db. qts. added aft. del.* '[on fol. 16 *opening db. qts. undel. in error*] [fol. 17] I regret'

366.12 have] *intrl.*

366.19 wisely] 'y' *ov.* 'l'

366.25 excellent] ¹'e' *ov.* 'H'

366.25 here] *intrl.*

366.26 whole-souled] *intrl.*

366.26 imposture] *ab. del.* 'fraud'

366.27 reasons] *bef. del. comma and del. intrl.* 'he think'

366.27 bar] *bef. del.* 'out'

366.27 out, for] *intrl. ab. comma undel. in error*

366.28 messages,] *comma insrtd.*

366.28 he thinks,] *intrl.*

366.28 for that;] *intrl.*

366.29 nothing but imposture] *ab. del.* 'fraud pure and simple'

366.30 point] *ab. del.* 'thing'

366.31 that] *bef. del.* 'their premise is identical with that'

366.31 are] *insrtd.*

366.31 using] *alt. fr.* 'use'

366.31   ²the . . . premise] ('major'
ov. 'and' and aft. del. 'logic'); ab. del.
'an identical ['premise' del.] major
premise,'

366.32   differing] 'ing' added

366.32,33   is:] colon added bef. del.
'that'

366.32   Any] 'A' ov. 'a'

366.34   this] underl. del.

366.37   these] alt. fr. 'this'; bef. del.
'whole department of'

366.37   far too] ab. del. 'indefinitely'

366.37   complex] bef. del. ', and that'

366.38   feelings . . . not] ab. del.
'*notions of the [insrtd. for del.
'*requirements about what is
sufficiently [aft. del. 'prejudices either
way about what *our ['o' ov. 'a']
pos']']'

366.38   romantic] bef. del. 'are quite
irrelevant'

367.1   causal factors] ab. del. 'elements'

367.2   traced] aft. del. 'unravelled,x
['x' intrl.]'

367.3   forms,] comma insrtd. bef. del.
'in which they appear,'

367.4   various] intrl.

367.4   resultants] final 's' added

367.6   sensory and motor,] intrl.

367.6   experimental] intrl.

††367.7   abiding . . . post-] ab. del.
'concerned in the phenomena of'

††367.8   had been given.] intrl.

367.8   Here we have] ab. del. 'These
are'

367.8–9   but are not] ab. del. 'Are
there any'

367.9   also] intrl.

367.11   a good] ab. del. 'an original'

367.13   harmonious] intrl.

367.14   will] aft. del. 'here'

367.14–15   of . . . it,] intrl.

367.17   ¹all] aft. del. 'most'

367.18–19   off— . . . many—] dashes
intrl.

367.19   forces] aft. del. 'remains'

367.19   Are] 'A' ov. 'a'

367.20   residual] intrl.

367.21   Richet's] aft. del. 'Richel'

367.21   term)] paren ov. comma

367.23   is] intrl.

367.23   simple] ab. del. '*['offhand'
del.] opposed [ab. del. 'opposite']'

367.24   leave . . . completely.] ab. del.
'show their incompetence.'

367.27   ²as] bef. del. intrl. 'in'

367.27   in] ab. del. 'department of'

367.27   Nature] 'N' ov. 'n'

367.28   reject] ab. del. 'condemn'

367.29   is] ab. del. 'woul [ov. 'is']'

367.29   rejecting bacteriology]
('bacteriology' aft. del.
'microbiology'); ab. del. 'condemning
bacteriology for its origin in the
study of fungi'

367.30   -dung] 'ung' ab. del. 'ung'

367.31   Scientific] alt. fr. 'Science';
bef. del. 'ought long ago to have
grown ashamed'

367.31   long] bef. del. 'learned'

367.31–32   ceased . . . ²of] insrtd. for
del. 'thrown dignity to the winds in'

367.32   ²the] alt. fr. 'their'

367.32   When] 'W' ov. doubtful 'T'

367.32   imposture] ab. del. 'fraud'

367.33   checked-off] ab. del. 'allowed
for'

367.33   chance] intrl. aft. del. 'the
[ab. del. 'accidental']'

367.35   noted . . . in] ab. del. 'taken
account of, when refinements of'

367.36   the] intrl.

367.36   of] ov. 'in'

367.36–37   bystanders] ab. del. 'those
present'

367.37   in,] insrtd. for del. '['out,'
del.] in,'

367.37–38   acquaintance] 'ance' ab. del.
'ed'

367.38   admit] aft. del. 'of mediumship
in its various grades'

367.38   in] aft. del. 'there'

†367.38   good . . . is] ab. del. 'an
unexplained'

368.1   used] ab. del. 'invented'

368.2   may be] ab. del. 'are'

368.4   telepathically,] intrl.

368.5   On] aft. del. 'This'

368.5   should] insrtd.

368.6   of a] ab. del. 'the'

368.6   They] ab. del. 'Her

performances—oftenest she is a woman—'

368.7 odd] 'o' *ov.* 'a'

368.8–9 [Most . . . we] ('M' *ov.* 'm'); *ab. del.* '['The 'control' which speaks through her motion' *del.*] Such a tendency seems to exist in everyone, who lets it come out by'

368.9 handle] 'e' *ov.* 'ing'

368.10 let . . . a] *ab. del.* 'an automatically writing'

368.10 ²a] *ab. del.* 'the'

368.11 and] *ov.* 'as'

368.12 her] *ab. del.* 'the'

368.13 building] *penc. ab. del.* 'making'

368.13 out] *aft. del.* 'plausible and building him up'

368.13–14 plausibly.] *penc. ab. del.* 'consistently.'

368.15 runs] *aft. del.* 'him'

368.15 involved in it] *ab. del.* 'part of the game'

368.16 she] *penc. ab. del.* 'the medium'

††368.17 & use] *intrl.*

368.18 own] *intrl.*

368.18 similarly] *intrl.*

368.20 This] 'T' *ov.* 'S'

368.20 type] *penc. alt. fr.* 'typical'

368.20 of] *penc. intrl.*

368.21 It] *bef. del.* 'seeks to do justice to all the factors'

368.23 about] *insrtd. for del.* 'as regards the constitution of the mediumistic trance-condition'

368.24 curious] *final* 'ly' *del.*

368.24 about] *penc. ab. del.* 'as regards'

368.25 about] *ab. del.* 'as regards'

368.25 an] 'n' *added*

368.25 existent] *intrl.*

368.26 do not] *intrl.*

368.26 this] *ab. del.* 'such ['s' *ov.* 'j'] a'

368.26 theory] *bef. del.* ', not'

368.26 show] *bef. del.* 'into'

368.27 complicated] *ab. del.* 'kinds of'

368.27 hypotheses] 2'e' *ov.* 'i'

368.28 looks at] *ab. del.* 'takes up'

368.28 facts . . . complexity] ('complexity' *aft. del.* 'in its'); *insrtd. for del.* 'phenomenon *concretely, [comma undel. in error]'*

368.29 back] 'b' *ov.* 'f'

††368.29 *naive* alternative] *ab. del.* 'silly scientific disjunction'

368.29–30 which is] *aft. del.* 'which in'; *bef. del.* '['all that the' *del.*] is'

368.30 ¹thought] *penc. ab. ink del.* 'thought'

368.30 ²thought] *aft. del.* 'can see.'

368.32 are] *bef. penc. del.* 'all'

368.32 little understood] *penc. ab. del.* 'obscurely *known [insrtd.]'*

368.32 judgments,] *comma insrtd. bef. del.* 'of sp'

368.33 the one as] *penc. ab. del.* 'equally'

368.33 as the other.] *penc. ab. del.* ', and shallow.'

368.34 we] *bef. del.* 'bring in this'

368.34 subject] *penc. ab. del.* 'case'

368.34–35 what connexion] *penc. intrl. aft. penc. del.* 'whether [*ab. ink del.* 'in connexion with it,']'

368.35 rappings] *ab. del.* 'table-tipping'

368.35 poltergeists,] *bef. del.* 'and'

368.36 may] *penc. intrl.*

368.36 with] *aft. penc. del.* 'any connexion'

368.37 your] *insrtd. for del.* 'the'

368.38 still . . . up.] *ab. del.* 'does nt give up.'

368.38 He] *bef. del.* 'collects and'

368.38 the] *ab. del.* 'more and more'

368.39 believes] *ab. del.* 'knows'

368.39 an] *bef. del.* 'explanatory category in'

369.1 , or . . . category] *comma added;* 'or . . . category' *intrl.*

369.2 in] *aft. del.* '*['either thing' *del.*] such a thing [*ab. del.* 'an ultimate element']'

††369.2 Every . . . ₐbosh\] ('Every' *bef. del.* 'Each'); *ab. del.* 'Bosh'

369.2 own] *ab. del.* 'definite'

369.3 patient] *final* 't' *ov.* 'ce'

369.3 study] *insrtd. for del.* 'writing'

369.3 bring] *ab. del.* 'put'

369.3 definitely to light.] *ab. del.* 'into our hands.'

369.5–6 imagine] *aft. del.* 'fancy'

369.6 readers] (*aft. del.* 'of my');

ab. del. 'minds of the stock-scientist type'

369.6 seriously adopt.] ('seriously' *bef. del.* 'earnestly'); *ab. del.* 'put up with.'

369.7 it] *bef. del.* 'to'

369.7 the] *insrtd. for del.* 'geology and'

369.7 rock] *final* 's' *del.; bef. del.* 'and'

369.8 ¹the] *ab. del.* 'and'

369.8 ²the] *intrl.*

369.8 stars,] *bef. del.* 'and'

††369.9–10 faroff antiquity] *ab. del.* 'time'

369.10 then] *intrl.*

369.10 things] *aft. del.* 'all'

369.11 out] *aft. del.* 'things'

369.11 the] 'e' *ov.* 'y'

††369.12 & habits] *intrl.*

369.12 the] *ab. del.* 'a'

369.12–13 rudiments] 's' *added*

369.13 of] *bef. del.* 'order and'

369.14 law and] *intrl.*

369.16 variations,] *comma added bef. del.* 'were'

369.16 being] *intrl.*

††369.16–17 disappeared from being, or] *ab. del.* '& connected,'

369.17 unrelated] *penc. intrl. aft. del. intrl.* 'disconnected'

369.17 or] *aft. del.* 'disconnected with the cosmos by any law, or'

369.18 so imperfectly] *intrl.*

369.18 of the world] *intrl.*

369.19 by] *bef. del.* 'lawless'

†369.20 'psychic'] *aft. del.* 'phys'

369.21 our] *ab. del.* '['our s' *del.*] the'

369.21 scientifically] *alt. fr.* ' 'scientific' '; *bef. del.* 'worl'

369.21 such a] *ab. del.* 'this p'

369.22 forever,] *comma alt. fr. period*

369.22 that] 't' *ov.* 'T'

369.23 intractable to] *intrl.*

369.23 intellectual] *final* 'ly' *del.*

369.23 methods,] *intrl. aft. del.* 'treatment [*ab. del.* 'unorganizable']'

369.24 be] *ab. del.* 'yet got'

369.25 would be] *ab. del.* 'are'

369.26 affect] *ab. del.* '['send [*illeg.*]' *del.*] touch'

369.27 momentary] *intrl.*

369.27 gleam] *aft. del.* 'meteoric'

369.28 followed up] *underl. del.*

369.28 Their] 'ir' *ov.* 're'

369.29 tangential] *aft. del.* '*external and [*insrtd. for del.* 'only [*ab. del.* 'merely']']'

369.30 make just] *ab. del.* ', seem exactly like'

369.31 impression.] *ab. del.* 'thing, capricious ['disturbances' *del.*] interruptions of the naturalistic order,'

369.31 ¹are] *ab. del.* 'seem'

369.33 disturbance,] *ab. del.* 'interruption,'

369.34 apparent] *intrl.*

369.34 purpose] *aft. del.* 'reason'

369.35 stray] *intrl. aft. del. intrl.* 'lost'

369.37 dogmatically] *intrl.*

369.37 save] *ab. del.* 'be'

369.37 labor,] *comma insrtd. bef. del.* 'saving,'

369.38 many] *bef. del.* 'of our'

370.2 some] *aft. del.* 'so r'

370.2 treatment] *ab. del.* 'analysis'

370.3 will] *aft. del.* 'can be made.'

370.4 good] *aft. del.* 'people'

370.4–5 (as . . . reason)] *parens ov. commas*

370.5 such] *ab. del.* 'occultism'

370.5 us] *ov.* 'one'; *ab. del.* 'the *mind [*ab. del.* 'intellect']'

370.6 jelly,] *bef. del.* 'breaks down the ['int' *del.*] faculty of'

370.6 disintegrates] 'r' *del. bef. final* 's'

370.6 liquefies] *ab. del.* 'weakens'

370.7 generally] *aft. del.* 'by profession'

370.9 research,] *comma ov. period*

370.9–10 and . . . spiritism.] *intrl.*

370.12 that] *ab. del.* 'the'

370.12 form] *aft. del. intrl.* 'a'

370.12 which] *ab. del.* 'and'

370.14 satisfied by] *insrtd. for del.* '*caught up in [*insrtd. for del.* '*['satisfied by' *del.*] appealed to by [*ab. del.* 'enlisted in']']'

370.15 also] *intrl.*

370.15 grew] *ab. del.* 'was *certainly [*ab. del.* 'surely']'

370.15 stronger] *bef. del.* 'and higher'

370.16 sentiment,] *ab. del.*

'aestheticism, a social success ['open
to social' *del.*]'

370.17 a] *aft. del.* 'th'

370.17 passionate, disdainful,] *ab. del.*
'he was ['conver' *del.*] ['made over'
del.] intolerant'

370.17 he was] *ab. del.* 'his [*alt. fr.* 'he']
character was wholly'

370.18 again] *ab. del.* 'in character'

370.19 learned] *aft. del.* 'scientifically'

370.19 in . . . circumspect,] *intrl.*

370.20 in sympathy,] ('in' *ov. comma*);
insrtd.

370.20 and] *aft. del.* 'and *critical
[*ab. del.* 'sympathetic,']'

370.22 by] *aft. del.* 'for him'

370.23 the] *intrl.*

370.23 gradually] *intrl.*

††370.24 shine . . . handsome['r'
del.]∧] *ab. del.* 'shine *and [*ab. del.*
'with'] 'handsome,' [*alt. fr.*
' 'handsomeness' ']'

370.24 one.] *period added bef. del.* ',
and'

370.25 Hodgson] *final* ' 's' *del.*

370.25 Myers] *bef. del.* ' 's faces'

370.25 ever] *intrl.*

370.25 handsomer∧] *period del.*

370.28 at all] *intrl.*

370.28 article] *aft. del.* 'short'

370.29 branch] *aft. del.* 'bran'

370.30 and] *aft. del.* 'and be'

370.31 for] *intrl.*

370.31 volumes] *aft. del. intrl.*
'stately row of'

370.31–32 count for nothing,] *ab. del.*
'are as naught,'

370.32 their] *bef. del. intrl.* 'happ'

370.35 my] *intrl.*

370.36 dabbling in] *ab. del.* 'contact
with'

370.37 shameful] *ab. del.* 'shameful
if no conclusions whatever of a
['form' *del.*] formulable character
had been engendered in my mind. I'

370.37 I] *intrl.*

370.38 a . . . had] *insrtd. for del.* 'the
result, and urged me to put myself on
paper. I had'

370.38–39 take . . . and] *intrl.*

370.39 such] *ab. del.* 'whatever'

370.39 convictions as] 'victions as'
ab. del. 'clusions'

371.1 me∧] *comma del.*

371.1 by] *ov.* 'but'

371.1 same] *ab. del.* 'same convictions'

371.1 ones.] *ab. del. period*

371.2 dooming] *insrtd. for del.*
'sending'

371.5 this] *ov.* 'the'

371.6 special] *ab. del.* 'general'

371.7 constantly] *insrtd.*

371.7 what] *aft. del.* 'the interpretation
of almost ev'

371.8 story,] *ab. del.* 'observation,'

371.8 error] *aft. del.* 'unknown'

371.8 are] *ab. del.* '['are usually beyond
our computation' *del.*] can'

371.9 fully knowable.] *ab. del.* 'be
*known. [*insrtd. for del.* 'considered.
[*ab. del.* 'controlled exhaustively.']']'

371.9 weak] *aft. del.* 'many'

371.9 strong] *aft. del.* 'a'

371.9 faggots] 's' *added*

371.9 when] *bef. del.* 'all'

371.10 stories] *bef. del.* 'mostly point
one way one gets a sense that one
is dealing with a type of real
phenomenon.'

371.10 sorts] *ab. del.* 'types,'

371.10–11 a . . . direction,] *ab. del.*
'one way,'

371.12 types] *ab. del.* 'kinds'

371.12 there] 're' *ov.* 'ir'

371.12 such real] *intrl.*

371.13 ignored by] *ab. del.* 'of which
ordi'

371.13 science,] *comma insrtd. bef. del.*
'so far takes no account,'

371.14 I] *ov.* 'h'; *bef. del.* 'hav'

371.14 fully] *intrl.*

371.14 of it.] *ab. del.* '['that there
are such phenomena' *del.*] ['¶
in mrgn.] I am convinced, first of all,
that ['the' *del.*] 'psychic' phenomena
(awful word!) form a field of
experience imposing by its vastness,
and that they are *much [*ab. del.*
'far'] frequenter than people suppose,'

371.14 get] *ab. del.* 'use coercive or'

371.14 proof] *final* 's' *del.*

371.16 liable to] *ab. del.* 'very'

371.16   err,] *alt. fr.* 'erring,'

371.16   the] *intrl.*

371.17   obey . . . of] *ab. del.* 'follow'

371.18   business] *ab. del.* 'field'

371.19   so] *bef. del.* 's'

371.20   the darkness,] *intrl.*

371.20–21   a sort of] *ab. del.* ' 'the [*insrtd. for del.* 'a']'

371.21   life] *intrl.*

371.21   and 'swindling'] *ab. del.* '['Fraud and' *del.*] *and a sort [*ab. del.* 'Deliberate fraud']'

371.23   majority] *ab. del.* 'number'

371.24   swindling should] *ab. del.* 'fraud has'

371.24   have] *intrl.*

371.24   some] *bef. del.* 'genuine nucleus'

371.24   originally] 'ly' *added*

371.25   genuine] *intrl.*

371.25   human] *aft. del.* 'the general history of'; *bef. del.* '['invention' *del.*] fraud [*start of* 'w']'

371.26,27 *(twice)* swindler] *ab. del.* 'impostor'

371.27   imitated] *bef. del.* 'reality'

††371.28   an absolutely,] *(comma in error);* *ab. del.* '['an' *del.*] a'

371.29–30   trick . . . it.] *orig.* 'trick, without any *previous [*intrl.*] basis ['s' *ov. poss.* 'c'], than you can create a new word at command— ['There is an *absolutely ['ly' *poss. added*] novelty, [*comma alt. fr. semicolon*]' *del.*] even in the world of humbugs. Let the' *alt. to* 'trick . . . word. [*period insrtd. bef. del.* 'at command—']' *alt. to* 'trick, [*comma undel. in error*] than you can create a new *word. without any previous basis ['without . . . basis' *tr. by guideline w. caret outside period in error*]*—You . . . it. [*insrtd.*]'

371.30   Try,] *insrtd. aft. del.* 'Let the'

371.30   reader,] *comma added*

371.31   invent] *bef. del.* 'a new'

371.31   physical] 'phy' *ab. del.* 'psych'

371.31   phenomenon‸] *db. qts. del.*

††371.31–32   spiritualism.''] *db. qts. added*

371.32   When] 'W' *ov.* 'I'

371.32–33   mentally . . . medium-]

ab. del. 'fumbling about the'

371.33   and] *aft. del.* 'reporting [*alt. fr.* 'réportage'] of mediums'

371.33   thinking] *ab. del.* 'asking'

371.33   improve some item.] *ab. del.* 'modify one.'

371.36   ²I] *bef. del.* 'therefore'

371.38   yet] *intrl.*

371.38–39   positive . . . something.] *ab. del.* 'idea of what is in them.'

371.39   becomes to] *intrl. aft. del.* '*is known as to [*ab. del.* 'remains to']'

371.39   simply a very] *ab. del.* 'a worthy, in fact an intensely'

371.39–372.1   problem for] *ab. del.* ', topic of'

372.1   investigation.] *period insrtd. bef. del.* ', and having as good a claim as any one to the privilege of being a fool'

372.2   opposite] *bef. del.* '['feelings of prob' *del.*] sense of pr''

372.3   feel the] *ab. del.* 'admit *the double [*ab. del.* 'his own']'

372.3   do,] *comma added*

372.4   Nature] 'N' *ov.* 'n'

372.5   his,] *alt. fr.* 'he'; *comma insrtd. bef. del.* 'does,'

372.5   pause] *ab. del.* 'do so'

372.5   realized] *bef. del.* 'the vastness'

372.5   vast] *bef. del.* 'f'

372.6   fraudulency] *alt. fr.* 'fraud is'

372.6   in consistency] *ab. del.* 'which'

372.6   her.] *ab. del.* 'nature.'

372.8   dishonest,] *comma ov. period*

372.8   and] *intrl.*

372.8   even] 'e' *ov.* 'E'; *bef. del.* 'on'

372.9   intellect,] *comma insrtd. bef. del.* 'of man'

372.9–10   few . . . categories,] *intrl. bef. del.* 'simple [*ab. del.* 'few categories of conception'] ways of thinking,'

372.11   penumbra] *aft. del.* 'borderland where'

372.11   in us all] *intrl.*

372.12   beliefs] 's' *added*

372.12   conduct,] *ab. del.* 'actions,'

372.12   where] *bef. del.* 'a scoundrel is not purely scoundrel'

372.13   to the depths] *ab. del. comma*

372.13 for] *ab. del.* 'to'

372.14 ago.] *period alt. fr. semicolon*

372.15 unhesitatingly] *alt. fr.*
'hesitation'; *aft. del.* 'had no'

372.15 thought of] *intrl. bef. del.*
'called [*ab. del.* 'in ['con' *del.*]
deeming']'

372.15 as deceit,] *insrtd. for del.*
'fraud,'

372.16 vague] *intrl. aft. del. intrl.*
'faint'

372.17 one . . . a] *ab. del.* 'an event'

372.18 vast . . . ¹is] *intrl.*

372.18 enigmatic.] *period insrtd. bef.
del.* 'as it is vast.'

372.19 something] *aft. del.* 'e'

372.19–20 encourages . . . ¹himself]
insrtd. for del. '*perpetrates
it [*ab. del.* 'does embark on it']'

372.20 ²himself] *aft. del.* 'in s'; *bef. del.*
'in some degree'

372.21 a fictitious] *ab. del.* 'the'

372.21 name] *bef. del.* 'of a ['de' *del.*]
'spirit.' '

372.22 messages] *aft. del.* 'the name'

372.22 Our] *aft. del.* 'We are a prey to
an'

372.23–24 make-believe,'] *ab. del.*
'deceive,'

372.24 external] *intrl.*

372.24 impelling us to] *ab. del.* 'of'

372.26 inexpert person] *ab. del.*
'common scientist'

372.26–27 commonness . . . of the]
ab. del. 'vastness *& generally [*intrl.*]
of the'

372.28 it] *aft. del.* 'of a'; *bef. del.* 'is'

372.28 be] *aft. del.* 'mer'

†372.28–29 *wish . . . record*] *ab. del.*
'stand'

†372.29 *commonness.*] *penc. ab. del.*
'vastness.'

372.30 wish to] *ab. del.* 'sha'

372.33 namely—] *dash aft. del. comma;
bef. del.* 'working ['in the' *del.*] over'

372.34 knowledge . . . abundant,]
ab. del. 'information is profuse,'

372.35 unconnected.] *aft. del.*
'incohesive.'

372.35 Really] *intrl.*

372.36 are] *insrtd. for del.* 'appear
to be'

372.37 less . . . regions] ('brilliant'
aft. del. 'well-developed'); *ab. del.*
'skirts and margins'

372.38 slight but odd] *intrl.*

372.39 this kind of] *penc. ab. del.*
'supernormal'

372.40–373.1 It . . . view.] *intrl.*

††373.1–2 & inferior] *intrl.*

373.2 to forge messages,] *ab. del.*
'which is a'

373.2 systematically] 'ally' *intrl.*

373.3 embedded . . . soul] ('the soul'
aft. del. 'soul o'); *ab. del.* 'part of
the psychology'

373.3 it] *aft. del.* 'it is weird to'

†373.4 then . . . this] *ab. del.* '['own'
del.] have possession of'

373.4 information] *aft. del.* ' 'items of'

373.4–5 on . . . hand] *intrl.*

373.6 phenomenon] *aft. del.*
'interpretation of the whole'

373.6 it . . . and] *intrl.*

373.6 ought we to] *insrtd.*

373.8 are] *bef. del.* 'absolutely'

373.9 upon] 'u' *ov.* 'o'

373.9 instinctive] *ab. del.* 'irresponsible
['unaided' *del. insrtd.*]'

373.10 My] 'M' *ov.* 'm'; *aft. del.*
'Prima facie'

373.10 tends] *aft. del. doubtful* 'wo'

373.11 picture] *aft. del.* 'apperceive
the thing'

373.12 slumbering . . . in] *ab. del.*
'a [*ab. del.* 'the'] more subconscious
*region [*ab. del.* 'parts ['s' *added*]'] of'

373.12 a] *ab. del.* 'an en'

373.14 the . . . lot] *ab. del.* 'our
[*ab. del.* 'the'] world a mass'

373.14–15 soul-stuff] *ab. del.* '['and'
del.] consciousness'

373.15 itself] *bef. del.* 'to become
concent'

373.16 permanent] *intrl.*

373.16 always] *penc. intrl.*

373.18 weak] *aft. del. intrl.* 'the'

373.18 spots . . . of] *ab. del.* 'moments
in'

††373.18–19 mind, . . . in] *ab. del.*
'being's life'

373.20 induce] *ab. del.* 'establish'

373.20 subconscious . . . the] *intrl.*

373.21 prolong] *ab. del.* 'perpetuate'

††373.21–22 social opportunity] *ab. del.* 'parasitic privilege'

373.23 stray] *intrl.*

373.24 by] *bef. del.* 'making such'

373.25 any . . . story.] ('important or significant' *insrtd. for del.* 'elaborate [*ab. del. intrl.* 'instructive']'); *ab. del.* 'coherence.'

373.26 view] *ab. del.* 'attitude [*ab. del.* 'view']'

373.27 takes,] *comma ov. period*

373.27 and . . . of] *ab. del.* 'It'

373.27 falling] 'ing' *ov.* 's'

373.28 views] *aft. del.* 'rival'

373.28 of others] *intrl.*

373.28 just as] *ab. del.* 'equally'

††373.29 actuated] *bef. del. intrl.* 'anyhow'

††373.29 will] *underl. del.; aft. del.* 'a'

††373.29 of] *ab. del.* 'of some kind in'

††373.29 sort anyhow,] *ab. del.* 'shape,'

373.31 through] *aft. del.* 'with inconf'

††373.32 [I] *aft. del.* 'H'

373.33 those] *ab. del.* 'what they would be'

373.33 of] *ov.* 'if'

373.33 who on] *ab. del.* 'on the oth'

373.34 should] *bef. del.* 'each'

373.34 only] *ab. del.* 'communicate'

373.34 to use] *tr. by guideline fr. aft.* 'have'

373.35 scientist,] *comma insrtd.*

373.35 for his part,] *intrl.*

373.38 Which] *bef. del.* 'will [*comma del.*] is'

373.38–39 inherently] *intrl.*

373.39 probable] 'e' *ov.* 'y'

373.39 with certainty? The] *ab. del.* '? The'

373.39 ²certainty] 'ty' *added; aft. del.* 'thing'

373.40 enormously] *ab. del.* 'immensely'

††374.1 includes such] *ab. del.* 'takes in the higher'

374.1 as] *aft. del.* ', such'

374.1–2 Swedenborg's] 'S' *ov.* 's'

374.2 and] *aft. del.* '*into account, [*ab. del.* 'and Andrew Jackson *Davis's [*apostrophe ab. del.* 'e']']'

374.2–8 to . . . conclusion] *subst. for. del.* '*work ['in' *del.*] the [*ab. del.* 'to co ordinate ['the' *del.*]'] 'physical phenomena' *in [*intrl.*] with them. That is why *personally I ['remain' *del.*] am [*ab. del.* 'I am still'] neither *a [*ab. del.* 'a'] 'spiritist' nor *an [*insrtd.*] unbeliever [*alt. fr.* 'a believer'] in 'elementals,' nor [*intrl.*] a [*ab. del.* 'a'] 'scientist,' but *still remain [*intrl.*] a psychical researcher *waiting for more facts before concluding. [*ab. del.* ', and patient waiter [*comma del.*] pure and simple.'] [¶] Out of ['all' *del.*] my experience, such as it is (and ['I' *del.*] it is limited enough) one fixed conclusion'

374.3 as yet] *intrl.*

374.4 in] *bef. del.* 'elementals or'

374.7 (and] *paren ov. comma*

374.8–9 we with] *insrtd.*

374.9 lives] *aft. del.* 'conscious [²'c' *ov.* 's'] lif'

374.9 sea] *ab. del.* 'Ocean'

374.10 maple . . . pine] ('pine' *aft. del.* 'beech'); *ab. del.* 'trees'

374.11 Conanicut . . . -horns.] *ab. del.* 'the islands *exchange the [*ab. del.* 'send the'] sounds *of fog horns [*ab. del.* 'of their surf'] across the water['s' *del.*].'

374.12 trees] *ab. del.* 'beech-tree and the maple-tree, as I have heard my colleague Josiah Royce say,'

374.12 commingle] 'com' *intrl.*

374.12–13 in the . . . underground,] *intrl. bef. del.* '*the earth's darkness [*ab. del.* 'below the surface,']'

374.13 and] *ab. del.* 'and Martha's'

374.13 also hang together] *ab. del.* 'communicate'

374.14 there] 're' *ov.* 'ir'

374.15 against] *ab. del.* 'in the midst of'

374.15 individuality] *ab. del.* 'personal isolation['s' *del.*]'

374.15 fences,] *intrl.*
374.16 several] *aft. del.* 'm'
374.16 as] *aft. del.* 'their roots'
374.16 -sea] *ab. del.* '-pool'
374.17 circumscribed] *ab. del.* 'told
off and fenced-in'
374.18 external] *penc. intrl.*
374.18 fence] *aft. del.* 'adaptation
suffers interruption'
374.19 beyond] *insrtd. for del.* 'beyon
[*ab. del.* 'the ['realer' *del.*] less
visible environment']'
374.19–20 otherwise . . . connexion.]
('unverifiable' *insrtd. for del.*
'unsuspected'); *ab. del.* 'presence of
the deeper unity which otherwise we
*never [*tr. fr. aft.* 'should'] should
suspect.'
374.21 philosophy$_\wedge$] *comma del.*
374.21 biology] *penc. ab. del.* 'science'
374.21–22 in . . . ways] *insrtd.*
374.22 such] *intrl.*
374.23 ²this . . . reservoir] ('this' *insrtd.
for del.* 'such a'); *ab. del.* 'this pool'
374.23 of] *bef. del.* 'cosmic'
374.24 to . . . upon] ('to' *aft. del.*
'of'; 'this bank upon' *insrtd. for del.*
'this pool from'); *ab. del.* 'upon'
374.25 in some way] *intrl.*
374.26 own] *ab. del.* 'inner'
374.27 inner] *ab. del.* 'own'
374.27 first] *intrl.*
374.27–28 formulated] *ab. del.* 'put
into this way'
374.28 ²by] *ov.* 'in'; *bef. del.* 'the'
††374.28–29 Scientific men hereafter.]
('tific' of 'Scientific' *ab. del.* 'ce';
'men' *bef. del.* 'of'); *ab. del.* 'of the
future.'
374.29 are] *ov.* 'is'
374.29 conditions] *ab. del.* 'principle'
374.29–30 or insulation] *insrtd.*

374.30 this] *alt. fr.* 'the'
374.30 active] *aft. del.* 'functionally'
374.31 functioning separately] *ab. del.*
'operating'
374.31 do] *bef. del.* 'our'
374.33 hierarchic] *intrl.*
374.33 orders] *bef. del.* 'of complexity'
374.34 And] *bef. del.* ', on occasion,'
374.34 with one another] *penc. ab. del.*
ink *insrtd.* '& complex'
375.3 difficult] *ab. del.* 'prolonged'
375.3 inquirer's . . . the] *ab. del.*
'prospect of inquiry. The'
375.4 just] *penc. intrl.*
375.5 facts] *intrl. aft. del.* 'phenomena
[*ab. del.* 'facts ['at' *del.*].']'
375.6 so] *intrl.*
375.6 But] *insrtd. bef.* 'When
[*unreduced in error*]'
375.6 was] *ab. del.* 'did'
††375.7 moved to . . . by] ('moved . . .
activities' *insrtd. for del.* 'inspired');
ab. del. 'take its start in'
375.8 rebellious] *ab. del.* '['ex' *del.*]
insignificant'
†375.8–9 Hardly . . . has] *ab. del.*
'As far as accurate looking at them
goes,'
375.9 ¹the] 't' *ov.* 'T'
375.9 of . . . called] *ab. del.* 'of ['these'
del.]'
375.9 begun] ('be' *penc. insrtd.*);
aft. del. '['data' *del.*] facts has *as
yet [*intrl.*] hardly be-' | ; *bef. del. intrl.*
'yet even'
375.10 following] *intrl.*
375.10 these] *alt. fr.* 'them'
375.10 facts,] *intrl.*
375.11 greatest] *alt. fr.* 'great'
375.11 scientific] *ab. del.* 'intellectual'
375.11 coming] *aft. del.* 'future'
375.11–12 generation] *final 's' del.*

<small>Deleted Versos for "The Confidences of a 'Psychical
Researcher' " Manuscript</small>

[*undel. fol.* 19ᵛ: *poss. orig. continuation of penultimate line* ('causation . . .
complex') *of fol.* 18 (*see Alterations entries* 366.37 *and* 366.38)] 'no such simple
*alternative ['ive' *ov.* 'ion'] ['sentence' *del.*] [*ab. del.* 'disjunction'] as either conscious fraud or revelation" is applicable to them in their totality. ['There' *del.*]'

[*del. fol.* 21ᵛ: *trial for revised fols.* 14,15 *(joint) and* 16, *corresponding to text* 366.1–9] 'by the spirits of his loved ones, ['takes them' *del.*] | ['and' *del.*] fails to be struck by their intellectual poverty *and takes them all for gospel. [*tr. by guideline fr. insrtd. bef.* '['and' *del.*] fails'] Your hard-headed critic sees nothing but the poverty, and uses the *same romantic [*ab. del.* 'same emotional'] premise to found his opposite conclusion. *The messages are anything but [*ab. del.* '*ir content is [*ab. del.* 'They are not']'] romantic, ['enough,' *del.*] so there can be no truth in them. In Huxley's *Life ['L' *ov.* 'l'] there is a letter which expresses admirably the ['state of mind' *del.*] romantic [*ab. del.* 'unscientific'] state of mind I mean'

[*del. fol.* 23ᵛ: *orig. continuation of fol.* 21; *trial for upper half of fol.* 22, *corresponding to text* 368.6–15] 'of *the typical [*ab. del.* 'a successful'] 'test-medium.' The ['whole *character* of the' *del.*] phenomenon ['here' *del. intrl.*] *she shows, if she be a woman, [*intrl.*] is due to a tendency to personate, found in *her [*insrtd. for del.* 'the medium's'] dream-life as it expresses itself in trance. This ['perf' *del.*] perverse subconscious tendency *actively [*intrl.*] runs the whole show, the medium's 'control' '

[*undel. fol.* 33ᵛ: *orig. continuation of del. text at foot of fol.* 30 *(see Alterations entry* 371.14)] '[*del.* 'if ['one takes' *del.*] account *be taken [*intrl.*] of *the [*intrl.*] incipient and'] highly developed *['and' *del.*] or abortive [*intrl.*] forms of them.'

Word-Division

The following is a list of compound words divided at the ends of lines in the copy-text, which could be read either as one word or as a hyphenated compound. These compounds were not confirmed in their forms as printed in the present edition because the copy-text did not derive either from a manuscript or some other earlier document at these points. In a sense, then, the hyphenation or the non-hyphenation of possible compounds in the present list is in the nature of editorial emendation. When the compounds were divided in the copy-text at the ends of lines but their probable form was evidenced in the source, this edition prints the reading of the source (unless emended by record), and no list is provided here.

38.10	non-hysteric	194.4	non-human
72.34	half-month	196.30	Post-hypnotic
85.10	non-intercourse	201.8	half-fitted
138.11	malobservation	213.3	stepping-stones
152.7	common-sense	252.4	to-day
163.2	non-Aryan	326.23	death-bed
170.18	well-meant	365.32	nonplussed
183.5;375.2	psycho-physical	368.8	dream-life
191.10	extra-marginal		

The following is a list of words divided at the ends of lines in the present edition but which represent authentic hyphenated compounds as found within the lines of the copy-text. Except for this list, all other hyphenations at the ends of lines in the present edition are the modern printer's and are not hyphenated forms in the copy-text.

25.16	coincidence-|cases	86.12;113.20;129.7,10;168.39;204.32	
35.19	diagram-|habit		thought-|transference
39.1	pin-|pricks	87.19	-in-|law's
42.9	hand-|writing	89.15	vice-|president
62.26	ghost-|seers	97.3	hyper-|normal
67.9	Yes-|cases	98.6	extra-|consciousness
75.4	death-|apparitions	98.23	mind-|cures
78.16	death-|visions	104.1	medium-|trance
83.15	time-|consuming	124.5	eighty-|one

130.4	Census-|question	219.5	sub-|conscious
131.29	white-|crow	221.20	hand-|movements
132.11	Paladino-|episode	222.15	every-|day
132.25	rat-|hole	232.9	to-|night
134.9	red-|handed	262.29	Hodgson-|family
140.1	fair-|minded	262.30	trance-|consciousness
140.9	chance-|coincidence	267.39	knock-|down
146.19	psycho-|automatic	268.2	ring-|episode
146.27	Gnostic-|Platonism	268.12	reality-|coefficient
147.37;152.8	psycho-|automatism	268.15	nigger-|talk
149.22,32	psycho-|spontaneity	272.36	spirit-|return
155.39	self-|surrender	277.39	spirit-|communication
160.23	word-|man	285.36	ultra-|vivacious
164.21	*word-|hearing*	338.32	dress-|suit
165.15	little-|known	349.1	slate-|writing
165.26	self-|hypnotisation	352.33	H.-|control
171.27	scientifically-|minded	354.30	asked-|for
171.31	quasi-|mathematical	356.24	rubbish-|making
176.12	quasi-|mathematics	357.25	devil-|theory
178.28	number-|habit	359.16	drainage-|opening
182.8	short-|range	361.22	twenty-|five
183.4	auto-|suggestion	366.32	spirit-|revelation
188.18	full-|strength	368.35	spirit-|photographs
188.28	trance-|states	369.7	rock-|strata
203.18	co-|ordinated	369.9	far-|off
204.40	after-|results	372.23	make-|believe
207.21	self-|suggestion	373.14	soul-|stuff
210.8	space-|invasions		

The following are actual or possible hyphenated compounds broken at the ends of lines in both the copy-text and the present edition.

17.16 diagram-|guessing (*i.e.,* diagram-guessing)

40.26 Post-|Hypnotic (*i.e.,* Post-Hypnotic)

44.7 wrapping-|paper (*i.e.,* wrapping-paper)

48.11 mirror-|writing (*i.e.,* mirror-writing)

54.30 post-|script (*i.e.,* postscript)

68.8 death-|rate (*i.e.,* death-rate)

69.6 chance-|coincidence (*i.e.,* chance-coincidence)

86.20 spirit-|return (*i.e.,* spirit-return)

91.17 cross-|examined (*i.e.,* cross-examined)

150.31;162.35 psycho-|automatism (*i.e.,* psycho-automatism)

168.39 *Thought-|Transference* (*i.e.,* *Thought-Transference*)

204.8 neuro-|pathologists (*i.e.,* neuro-pathologists)

208.32 starting-|point (*i.e.,* starting-point)

208.33 psycho-|physical (*i.e.,* psycho-physical)

264.28 Hodgson-|control (*i.e.,* Hodgson-control)

287.18 half-|real (*i.e.,* half-real)

354.10 'bosh'-|interpretation (*i.e.,* 'bosh'-interpretation)

Index

This index is a name and subject index for the text of *Essays in Psychical Research* and Appendixes I and IV. It is an index of names only for the "Notes," "A Note on the Editorial Method," "The Text of *Essays in Psychical Research*," and Appendixes II, III, and V. The Introduction by Professor McDermott is not indexed.

Index

Index

Index

Index